CRUISERS
of World War Two
An International Encyclopedia

BROCKHAMPTON PRESS
LONDON

Chester on 20 July 1943. (Courtesy Louis Parker)

CRUISERS
of World War Two
An International Encyclopedia

M. J. WHITLEY

Arms and Armour Press
A Cassell Imprint
Wellington House, 125/130 Strand, London WC2R 0BB

Reprinted 1996

British Library Cataloguing-in-Publication Data: a catalogue record for this
book is available from the British Library

This edition published 1999 by Brockhampton Press.
    a member of Hodder Headline PLC Group

ISBN 1 86019 8740

Designed and edited by DAG Publications Ltd. Designed by David Gibbons;
layout by Anthony A. Evans; edited by Philip Jarrett.

Jacket illustration: HMS *Sheffield* on Arctic patrol with *Duke of York* and
Jamaica; from a painting by John Hamilton, with the permission of Mrs Betty
Hamilton.
Printed at Oriental Press, Dubai, U.A.E.

Contents

Preface

This book is intended to be a companion volume to *Destroyers of World War Two*, and follows the same format. It sets out to record the details of all cruisers extant during the period 1939 to 1945 in the Allied, Axis and Neutral navies. Since the term 'cruiser' was sometimes a slightly loose one, the basic criteria for inclusion has been a displacement of over 4,500 tons, an armament of four or more guns of 5.5in calibre or over, and a speed of over 20kts. However, where a ship did not quite meet this definition but was important to the navy concerned, it has also been included. Some cruisers in the South American fleets fall into this category, for example. On the other hand, a couple of others which did meet the criteria have not been included because they were no longer employed as cruisers in the true sense by 1939. These were the two former Chinese ships *Ning Hai* and *Ping Hai*, which, although armed with six 5.5in guns and capable of over 20kts, were used only in the Coast Defence role by Japanese-controlled China and later by the Japanese themselves. Also excluded were the German Panzerschiffe which, although reclassified as Heavy Cruisers in 1940, were conceived as Capital Ships and properly should be considered in a volume on that topic.

The format includes a section on design which will in general be found more extensive than that in the destroyers volume, followed by a discussion on modifications to the design which were carried out in the 1939/45 period, together with a survey of the operational activities of each ship. For reasons of space, postwar modifications and service have not usually been included, but wherever possible some indication of service history before 1939 has been included. For similar reasons, it has been thought best to dispense with a separate introductory section to each naval power, and rely instead on a more general introduction at the beginning of the book.

Happily, in this volume it has been possible to provide much more authoritative data on the Soviet ships than has hitherto been the case, owing to political developments in the last few years. These unfortunately came just too late for the destroyers volume, much to the author's regret. I have to extend grateful thanks to Réne Greger, Marek Twardowski and Captain Huan for extensive assistance in the section on the Soviet Union.

Complete building dates have been provided for almost all ships, as well as details of the final disposals as far as is known. Inevitably there still remain gaps which need to be filled, and the author would be grateful for additional information, correction or comment in the future.

Source materials have intentionally been almost exclusively of a secondary but authoritative nature, and can be found listed on page 282. In addition, it is necessary to thank the many individuals and organisations without whose assistance this book would not have been possible:

Argentina: Captain G. J. Montenegro of the Estado Mayor General de la Armarda; Australia: Commander Bloomfield RAN, Mr J. Straczek and the staff of the Australian War Memorial; Brazil: Captain A. M. Cabral; Canada: Dr Carl A. Christie of the National Defence HQ and Mr K. Macpherson; Chile: Captain de Navio G. M. Watkins, Public Relations Officer Chilean Navy; France: Contre Adm. Kessler and the staff of the Service Historique de la Marine, M. Jean Guiglini, Captain C. Huan; Germany: Hans Knobloch and Reinhard Hoheisel; Great Britain: Paul Kemp and the Staff of the Imperial War Museum, R. G. Todd and D. Hodge of the Maritime Information Centre, G. Ransome; Italy: Cdr. G. Cucchiaro of the Italian Embassy in London and Dr A. Rastelli; Netherlands: Dr P. C. van Royen, Director of Naval History, Afdeling Maritieme Historia; Poland: Marek Twardowski; Soviet Union: Rene Greger, Marek Twardowski and Captain C. Huan; Spain: the staff of the Instituto de Historia y Cultura Naval; Sweden: Captain (R) Per Insulander and the Staff of the Militärhögskolan, Cdr. M. Ellis; United States of America: Louis Parker, and Marshall Skidmore (for much valued assistance with photographs and for the onerous task of reading the text of the USN section) and Bob Meade. If I have inadvertently omitted to mention anyone who has assisted me, I most sincerely apologise.

I should also like to acknowledge the advice and assistance given by my publishers and by David Gibbons and Tony Evans of DAG Publications. Any errors or omissions in the following pages are of course my own responsibility. Finally, I must thank my wife Rita for her patience and understanding during my many hours of absence in my den whilst working on this book.

Introduction

From Sail to Steam, 1850 to 1914

The cruiser can be considered the logical successor to the frigate of the age of sail. Both types of warship had similar tasks, i.e. to act as the eyes of the fleet and to patrol the ocean sea-lanes to protect mercantile trade. As the Industrial Revolution progressed, ships became first less dependant on, then finally independent of the vagaries of the wind, and an age of change came about in the world's sea powers. The traditional sail frigate disappeared and was not initially replaced as the powers struggled to adapt to the new technology of iron, steam, and then steel. Much of the effort went towards capital ship development, to the detriment of smaller ships such as frigates and their replacements. Consequently, the mid-nineteenth century saw a strange mixture of prototype and experimental battleships, many of them one-offs, as this new technology was incorporated into sea service. The state of technology did not yet allow the construction of fast, small vessels which could act as the eyes of the fleet. For the major seapower of the day, Great Britain, this new technology was a two-edged weapon, as it presented the possibility of lesser powers gaining a superiority over the Royal Navy by its means, rather than by numerical superiority, which had been the previous criteria. Despite these fears, however, the British Admiralty grasped the opportunities offered, often in the face of opposition from the more traditional seagoing officers. Thus, after a period of indecisiveness, the beginnings of the twentieth-century order of battle for naval powers could be discerned by the second half of the nineteenth century. At this time Britain still considered the main threat to come from France, but there remained a vast empire which had to be policed and its communications secured, which at that time meant ships on station. With such a large part of the world under its wing, and with no real major power opposition except possibly in European waters, Britain could carry out its police and trade protection duties economically and effectively using the successor to the sail frigate, the steam frigate. These ships, in which both old and new technology were combined, were well suited to distant foreign stations where resources for the repair of machinery were non-existent, but they could not effectively assume an ocean trade protection role because they were not fast enough to escape from superior ships. In the event of any major dispute arising in foreign waters, they were expected to suffice until heavier reinforcements could be sent out from Europe, from where, in any case, the enemy also had to come in that age. As far as Britain was concerned, therefore, numbers were important, given the area of the globe to be policed, and that, in turn, meant ships of none too great a size.

Sail, whilst requiring little or no logistical support, was uneconomical in weight and manpower, and by the 1880s had been almost abandoned by the major powers. The British Admiralty at this time re-evaluated the requirements for cruising ships, as they became known, altering hull form and power plant, and adopting steel construction and the screw propeller. A protective armoured deck was introduced in the *Comus* class of 1876, which had a 1½in deck above the machinery and magazine spaces. They retained the sail rig and were successful colonial cruisers, eleven being constructed between 1878 and 1881. Their speed was only a mediocre 13kts, however, and they could not act as fleet cruisers. For this task, speed was raised to 16½kts in the next class, which carried a heavier armament (ten, 6in), had better protection in that the armoured deck was raised and sloped at the sides, and were given greater endurance. They retained the sail rig, however, but this was eliminated in their successors, the *Mersey* class of 1883, by which time the recognisable features of the 2nd class cruiser had emerged. One of these, *Forth*, lasted until 1947 in subsidiary roles.

Cruiser development was given a boost from the 1880s by the involvement of the shipbuilder Elswick, on the Tyne, who developed a series of designs for foreign account, which were fast at 18kts, armed with guns as large as 10in and which had also dispensed with the sail rig. Known simply as the 'Elswick' cruisers, they were advanced for their day and were supplied to Argentina, Austria, Chile, China, Italy, Japan and the United States. Some of these, too, were to serve for many decades, as the section on Chile in this book reveals. Their story warrants a book in itself.

By the end of the 1890s, British cruisers of the 2nd (Protected) and 3rd classes, whose main role was trade protection and colonial police work, were joined by the 1st class cruiser and the armoured cruiser. The reconnaissance or scout role had not yet been assumed. The armoured cruiser led eventually to the battlecruiser, an essentially flawed concept in which protection was sacrificed for speed, which itself was intended to be their protection. This culminated in the ships being employed in the battle line, with fatal consequences, as at Jutland in 1916.

France was in disarray at this time as far as naval policy was concerned, and, despite her large empire, did not build many of the type of cruiser favoured by Britain, most being one-offs. However, in 1882 she began the construction of modern cruisers, and by 1887 had the ships of the *Forbin* class and their successors, which were fast at over 20kts and armed with 5.5in guns. They had a protective deck and were specifically intended for attacking mercantile trade routes, a role that had not gone unnoticed by Great Britain, whose suspicion of France had in all probability not been diminished by the new *Entente Cordiale*. The result was a ship designed to counter the predatory trade cruisers of France and, to some extent, of Imperial Russia too, as the latter country had also put into service some well armed cruisers, such as the *Pamiat Azova*, which was armed with two 8in and thirteen 6in guns, this pattern of armament, two or four heavy guns and a lighter battery, being the standard at this time. The new British cruisers, the *Orlando* class, were known as armoured cruisers because their protection was not limited to an armoured deck, but also incorporated vertical armour, in this case a 10in waterline belt. They were armed with two 9.2in and ten 6in guns, and had a displacement of 5,600 tons. Unfortunately, growth during construction increased their draught so much that the side armour was submerged and their usefulness reduced. In consequence, the Admiralty temporarily abandoned the type after seven ships had been built. They were one of the casualties of the Fisher reforms in 1904, when obsolete or ineffective ships were ruthlessly culled.

As the turn of the century approached, there were further advances in the design of both engines and boilers, as well as in ordnance. In the case of the latter, the most important development was the advent of the quick-firing (QF) gun, which used brass-cased charges and had a rapidly working breech mechanism which gave it a higher rate of fire. It was employed in calibres up to 4.7in in general.

In 1888 Britain laid down the first of a new type of 1st class Protected Cruiser, armed with two 9.2in guns and ten 6in QF guns, and introduced armoured casemates for the 6in guns. These ships, *Blake* and *Blenheim*, were intended for the trade protection role and served with success throughout the world. Although they had been relegated to Torpedoboat depot ships by the First World War, their design influenced future British and foreign designers for some time thereafter.

The rise of Imperial German naval power towards the end of the nineteenth century, and Germany's acquisition of colonies in Africa, the Far East and the Pacific, presented an ill-disguised threat to British Empire trade routes that was made more effective by the introduction of the first recognisable 'light' cruiser by Germany in the 1890s. This was *Gazelle*, commissioned in 1900, which displaced about 2,600 tons and was armed with a uniform battery of 4.1in guns. Ten ships were constructed in the period up to 1904, and they had obvious employment in either the fleet scouting or trade war roles. At this time Britain was still arming her cruisers with mixed batteries, usually of 6in and 12pdr (3in) calibres, of which the former had a slower rate of fire than the German 4.1in, while the latter was but an anti-torpedoboat destroyer (TBD) weapon. The German solution was both economic and practical, not least in the spotting of fall of shot.

From the turn of the century, cruiser development was essentially in the hands of the Royal and the Imperial German navies, as France was in a torpor and Imperial Russia lacked the industrial base to keep pace with advancing technology. In the Far East, Japan had learned much from her experiences in the Russo-Japanese war of 1904 and steadily built up her industrial base using western technology, but this did not bear fruit until the early 1920s. The only other industrial power, the USA, paid little attention to naval matters until after the Spanish-American war of 1898, but, even so, no great strides were made until after the US entry into the First World War, which brought it into contact with the Royal Navy. Again, it was to be the 1920s which saw the gradual build-up of US cruiser strength which culminated in the huge fleet of 1945. Neither of the remaining two former naval powers, Spain and the Netherlands, could contribute to the development of the cruiser because of the defeat of the former in the war with the USA and the lack of technology in the case of the latter.

Thus, in the period up to the First World War, Britain continued with four main lines of development, building 34 armoured cruisers generally armed with a mixture of 9.2in and 6in guns, although one class, *Monmouth*, had all 6in and one, *Devonshire*, had 7.5in instead of the 9.2in. These ships had both side and deck protection. Secondly, there were some 39 large protected cruisers built, given only deck protection and armed with a variety of outfits of 9.2in and 6in guns, culminating in the two ships of the *Powerful* class of 14,200 tons. In addition, nearly fifty smaller protected cruisers were built, many of which were assigned to remote foreign stations. This class of ship was one of the main casualties of the Fisher reforms, so their numbers had declined by 1914. Thirdly, the advent of the TBD brought the need for a ship capable of acting as a leader and support vessel for these fast but lightly armed ships. For this role the scout cruiser came into being, of which six relatively small classes had been built by 1913. Finally there was the trade protection/fleet role cruiser typified by the Town Class ships, beginning with the *Bristol* of 1911 and resulting in a series of classes which eventually totalled twenty ships. These ships adopted a uniform 6in armament, except for *Bristol* and two ships requisitioned from foreign account after 1914. By 1913, however, the likely operational demands of a war in the confined waters of the North Sea, with Imperial Germany as the enemy, resulted in a complete change of direction. The scout cruiser was developed into a larger but still relatively small cruiser for duties with the Grand Fleet, and all other types of cruiser were discontinued.

Germany, on the other hand, built only a small number of armoured cruisers, with 8.2in guns, culminating in the *Blücher* of 1909, which was almost a battlecruiser but not quite, and suffered a similar fate. Apart from a small group of protected cruisers, the German strength was in the ten classes of light cruisers armed with ten, and later twelve, 4.1in guns. There were 35 such ships built in the period leading up to 1914.

The First World War, 1914 to 1918

When the war broke out in August 1914, Britain had the largest cruiser force by far, with 34 armoured and 52 protected cruisers, of which barely 25 were under ten years old and most of the remainder were well obsolete. There were fifteen of the scouts, attached to the destroyer flotillas, and seventeen of the Town Class, which had been completed since 1910. This force was augmented by a couple of ships requisitioned from Greece, and a large new construction programme of small cruisers had been put in hand just before war was declared. Great Britain's main ally, France, had nineteen armoured cruisers and six protected cruisers, virtually none of which were under ten years old, and many dated back to the turn of the century. More importantly, there was no construction programme in hand at all as far as cruisers were concerned. Italy had a motley collection of scout and protected cruisers amounting to no more than thirteen in all, few of which could be considered effective ships. In the Baltic and Black Seas, Imperial Russia could call on six armoured cruisers, including the 10in-gunned *Rurik*, together with six old protected cruisers. In addition, quite an ambitious new light cruiser construction programme had been started in 1913. Finally, there was Japan, far removed from the main theatres of action but in possession of quite a respectable force of over twenty cruisers.

The Triple Alliance powers, Imperial Germany, Austria-Hungary and Turkey, were far stronger on the ground than they were at sea, but as a result of the efforts of the Kaiser and Admiral Tirpitz, Germany had built up a modern navy by 1914, having eight armoured, seventeen protected and twenty-five light cruisers, and a continuing construction programme. The light cruisers in particular were fast and well armed. The small fleet of Austria-Hungary, confined to the restricted waters of the Adriatic, was a respectable force which included two armoured cruisers and four modern light cruisers. Turkey, on the other hand, was of no consequence as far as naval power was concerned.

The initial hostile activities included ocean cruiser warfare as Great Britain and her allies hunted the German cruisers which had sailed from her colonies to attack Allied merchant shipping, the hunt for the German East Asiatic Squadron, and action in the North Sea, where the two main protagonists faced one another. By 1915 German cruisers had been driven from the oceans by a combination of superior force and lack of friendly bases, but not before some significant and famous actions had taken place. Admiral von Spee and the Asiatic Squadron of cruisers emerged as the victors in the Battle of Coronel, but were themselves annihilated at the Battle of the Falklands, where the battle cruiser acted in a decisive role for the one and only time before the folly of the concept proved itself at the Battle of Jutland in 1916. The remains of von Spee's force was then hunted down in the wastes of the Pacific. Apart from these actions, cruiser-versus-cruiser action was rare, most of the action being in the North Sea, when skirmishes between British and German cruiser and destroyer forces were the usual events. In the only major fleet action of the war, at Jutland in 1916, the Royal Navy lost three armoured cruisers while Germany lost one protected and three light cruisers. Most wartime losses were caused by submarine torpedoes and mines. During hostilities, Britain lost thirteen armoured, four protected, two scout, two Town and one light cruiser, most of the casualties being amongst the older ships. These would undoubtedly have been higher but for the fact that many of the elderly protected cruisers were employed on remote stations or reduced to subsidiary duties during the war. Five were sunk as blockships in 1918. Of the armoured cruiser losses, three fell victim to one submarine attack on 22 September 1914.

Germany lost eighteen ships, including six out of seven armoured cruisers and one protected cruiser (the rest were only employed in subsidiary duties by 1914). Of the smaller cruisers, three were lost at the Battle of Heligoland Bight on 22 August 1914, six on the oceans in the wake of the Falklands action, three at Jutland and three in other incidents, one of which was with Russian ships and one in the Mediterranean.

Britain's wartime programmes concentrated on the smaller cruiser for North Sea Fleet use, with a further 44 ships being completed or laid down during hostilities, many of which survived and appear in this volume. Germany likewise continued the cycle of light cruisers, completing twelve more ships, including two requisitioned from Russian account. Eight more were never completed.

By the end of the war Britain had begun to build ships armed with 7.5in guns for an ocean cruiser role, rather than the restricted North Sea 6in-gunned light cruiser. This new ship was to have an impor-

tant influence on international construction. Of the other powers, only Imperial Russia had a significant construction programme. However, two of her ten ships had been requisitioned by Germany, and the remaining eight were so severely delayed by Russia's dependence on foreign assistance, both for equipment and expertise, coupled with the inefficient state of her industry, that they were incomplete at the time of the Bolshevik Revolution in 1917. Some, however, were eventually completed after long delays, and appear in this volume. There was no construction of any significance by France, Italy, the USA or Japan during the war, and Turkey was not capable of indigenous construction. Austria-Hungary completed some light cruisers begun before the war, and planned others, but the war prevented any further progress.

Technical Progress Postwar

The First World War saw no great technical advances, both major powers concentrating their effort on refining prewar designs. Britain introduced the larger *Hawkins*, armed with 7.5in guns, by the end of the war. Turbine propulsion had been tried in the British *Amethyst* and German *Lübeck* of 1904, and was adopted in the *Boadiceas* and *Dresdens* of 1909. The USA installed turbines in the *Salem* and *Chester* of 1908, but built no further cruisers until after the First World War. Peru, suprisingly, had cruisers with turbines as early as 1908, but of foreign construction, while Japan had turbine-driven cruisers by 1912. Coal firing was gradually replaced by oil, Britain using liquid fuel in *Boadicea* (1909) and onwards. Germany, with her strategic limitations, did not adopt full oil-firing until the 1930s. Armaments changed little, broadside armaments persisting after the end of the First World War, as did casemates. The main change in armament was caused by the increased effectiveness of airpower, which resulted in a proportion of the guns being installed on high-angle (HA) mountings, although fire control in the HA role was non-existent. By the latter years of the war, too, cruisers had begun to ship their own aircraft for long-range scouting purposes, a facility that was to remain aboard US cruisers long after this role had been rendered redundant by the advent of radar almost a quarter of a century later.

After the end of the First World War, the main influence on cruiser design came from the various naval treaties of the 1920s and 1930s, which spawned the heavy and light cruiser designations and inadvertently standardised armaments at 8in and 6in guns respectively. Inevitably, there was a continuing rivalry between the naval powers and their hereditary enemies, Italy building against France, and Japan against the USA, for example. This was not always in the best interests of any of the powers concerned. As the thirties wore on, greater attention was paid to HA armament, but in general without the necessary advances in fire control. Heavier automatic and semi-automatic weapons appeared, with the Netherlands producing possibly the most advanced gun control systems for AA use. In the machinery field, diesel propulsion had no practical application for cruisers, and the major advance was in terms of increased boiler pressures for better economy. Germany took the lead in this respect, but her designs were faulty, and it was the USA which was to gain the most from this feature. Advances in electronics were swift during the years subsequent to 1939, and played a major role in war operations. This led to the abandonment of shipboard aircraft installations in most of the major navies, except suprisingly, the USN, which maintained this feature until well after the end of the Second World War.

The Second World War

During the Second World War the cruiser's duties were wide and varied. It was used in the classic trade protection role on the oceans, as a commerce destroyer on the high seas, as a scout for the fleet, in support of destroyers in coastal waters, and for shore bombardment. New roles acquired during hostilities included the provision of AA protection to carrier task forces in the Pacific and in supporting invasion forces. Cruiser-versus-cruiser action was more common, perhaps, than in the previous world war, as actions took place between British and Italian ships, as well as between US and Japanese vessels.

As in the First World War, British and French cruisers were patrolling the oceans in the trade-protection role from the opening of hostilities in September 1939. Germany, on the other hand, did not send her cruisers to sea as she had done in 1914 because she no longer possessed any overseas bases, apart from the one secret base in North Russia. Moreover, her existing light cruisers, built under the strict conditions of the Treaty of Versailles, were technically deficient and incapable of ocean employment. Instead, Germany sent the Panzerschiffe *Admiral Graf Spee* and *Deutschland* which, armed with 11in guns, were formidable opponents for cruisers. Nevertheless, it was cruisers armed with 8in and 6in guns which scored the first morale-boosting victory for the Allies off the River Plate in December 1939, when three British cruisers engaged *Admiral Graf Spee*. Later, Allied cruisers were employed to hunt the German heavy cruisers when they did eventually appear in the Atlantic, but otherwise they were employed to scour the seas for blockade-running German merchantmen attempting to return home after being caught overseas in 1939, and to escort valuable troop convoys. It was the Norwegian campaign of 1940 that first brought home the seriousness of the air threat, which was to be responsible for the major alterations applied to all classes of ship thereafter. These lessons were soon taken to heart both by the belligerents and by neutral nations, particularly the USA in the latter category, even if the wherewithal to make the necessary changes were lacking. The dangers associated with operating large ships with weak AA outfits in the absence of air superiority was demonstrated very clearly after the fall of France, when the Royal Navy, operating in confined waters and in close proximity to enemy air bases in the Mediterranean, encountered Italian and German bombers. The ships suffered severely at their hands in the waters off Crete and Greece in 1940/41.

At sea level, however, things were different. The Royal Italian Navy, tasked with covering the supply routes to North Africa, lacked the radar expertise and sea-air co-operation of the British, and suffered accordingly. British cruisers played a major role in the Malta Convoys and in the various actions with the Italian fleet on the rare occasions when it was brought to action. No French cruisers joined the British under the Free French movement, so for the moment they were not involved in action, except for one incident in the Far East.

The opening of the war in the Far East in December 1941 turned the Second World War into a worldwide conflict on a greater scale than the war of 1914/18. During that earlier conflict, although Japan had played a minor part in the hunt for the German East Asiatic Squadron in 1914, and had had a presence in the Mediterranean, her activities were limited. In 1941 it was different; Japan was the aggressor, aiming to gain control of vast areas of territory in the Pacific basin. In the Dutch East Indies Japanese cruisers clashed with British, Australian, Dutch and US cruisers in actions which left the Allies in retreat with heavy losses. Poor co-ordination, lack of prior co-operation and poor planning left the Allied navies toothless in the South-West Pacific at the beginning of 1942. As the war progressed, however, US industry geared up for total war, and although it took many, many months for the USN to absorb the lessons learned, Japan's navy was finally ground down by US sea- and air-power. In the intervening years, though, the vicious campaigns in the close waters of the Solomon Islands claimed many cruisers among their victims.

Meanwhile, in the North Atlantic and Arctic, British cruisers performed a difficult task in often appalling weather conditions, covering convoys to the USA and to North Russia against the real but rarely exercised threat from the Kriegsmarine battleships and cruisers based in Norway. Their opponents in this theatre, apart from the weather, were more usually U-boats and torpedo aircraft, with the occasional foray by German destroyers to contend with.

At the end of 1942 the Allies were strong enough to launch the landings in North Africa, when cruisers were extensively employed in shore bombardment for the first time. They also became engaged with Vichy French cruisers when the latter, fighting in a tight corner, suffered, particularly at the hands of US ships. In the meantime, Soviet cruisers had been heavily involved, particularly in the Black Sea, in supporting the Red Army ashore by means of their gunfire – the main role of the Soviet Navy. Off the Crimea and along the shores of the Black Sea from Romania to the Caucasus, they were used against the advancing Axis armies. A similar role was played by the Baltic fleet cruisers, albeit much more briefly, owing to the speed of the German advance. In fact, all of the Russian cruisers actions were in shore support, from 1941 to 1944.

The Mediterranean campaigns of 1943/44 saw British and US cruisers heavily involved in shore support, too, with the landings in Sicily and Italy, when airpower was the main opposition and the guided bomb was encountered for the first time. Italy having capitulated, there remained no naval opposition greater than a few destroyers operated by the remnant German naval forces in the Aegean and Adriatic.

For the opening of the second front, the invasion of France in June 1944, British, US, French, Canadian, Dutch and Polish cruisers were committed to support duties, and their gunfire was often locally decisive. Some of these ships then went south to the Mediterranean for the invasion of the south of France in August, and performed the same duties there.

Some time before this, however, the main thrust of the naval war as far as cruisers were concerned had moved to the Pacific, where an ever-increasing US cruiser force was extensively employed in the island-hopping campaign against the ever-decreasing power of the

Imperial Japanese Navy. The US cruisers were used as guardians for the fast Carrier Task Forces in the South and South-West Pacific, providing voluminous AA barrages against the growing threat from Kamikaze attacks. They were also used to support the hundreds of landing operations against the shrinking perimeter of the Japanese Greater Co-Prosperity Sphere. Losses of US cruisers virtually stopped after January 1943, only two being sunk thereafter, but the Imperial Japanese fleet, increasingly bereft of close air cover, suffered terribly at the hands of US submarines and aircraft. When Japan finally capitulated in 1945, only two cruisers remained afloat.

During the period of hostilities Great Britain lost 31 ships, including those in RAN and Allied service, but completed 29 new cruisers. Germany lost six ships and completed only one new ship. Italy lost fifteen ships and commissioned three new ones, while France lost ten cruisers but did not commission any new ships. The Soviet Union completed five cruisers but lost two, and the Netherlands lost two ships also. The USA completed 47 new cruisers and lost ten ships. Japan completed only five new ships but lost 41.

The losses can be analysed by cause in the table below. In addition, France lost seven ships scuttled at Toulon and one by accidental explosion. Italy lost a further three ships scuttled at the capitulation. Britain lost two ships expended as breakwaters, one in collision, and one by stranding. Germany lost a further ship to shore batteries.

By the end of the war the cruiser's scout role had been assumed by radar and air power, leaving the traditional trade protection task as arguably its main role. This, too, could also be performed by carrier-borne aircraft, and as time went by the place of the cruiser became less clear. Thus, after the Second World War, Britain's cruiser force swiftly declined, most of the US fleet was mothballed, and only the Soviet Union started a large new programme, which itself never reached full completion. The need for a gun-armed cruiser was seen to have disappeared until Korea and, later still, Vietnam, proved that a requirement still existed and was most economically fulfilled by a ship offshore with heavy guns. Cruisers would even have had a role in the Falklands in 1982, had they been available.

Cruiser losses by cause:

	Mine	Submarine	Aircraft	Surface action
Britain	1	8	10	8
USA		2	1	7
France			1	1
Soviet Union			2	
Italy		3	3	6
Japan		16	20	5
Germany		1	3	
Netherlands				2

Below: The German light cruiser *Köln* before the Second World War. (Drüppel)

Argentina

VEINTICINCO DE MAYO CLASS

Ship	Builder	Laid Down	Launched	Completed	Fate
Almirante Brown	OTO, La-Foce	12 Oct 27	28 Sep 29	18 Jul 31	Stricken 27 Jun 61
Veinticinco de Mayo	OTO, Livorno	29 Nov 27	11 Aug 29	11 Jul 31	Stricken 24 Mar 60

Displacement: 6,800 tons/6,908 tonnes (standard); 9,000 tons/ 9,144 tonnes (full load).

Length: 560ft 4in/170.8m (oa); 533ft 3in/162.5m (wl).

Beam: 58ft 6in/17.82m; Draught: 15ft 6in/4.66m (mean).

Machinery: 2-Shaft Parsons geared turbines, 6 Yarrow boilers.

Performance: 85,000shp=32 kts; Bunkerage: 2,300 tons oil fuel.

Range: 8,030nm at 14kts.

Protection: 1in deck; 2.75in sides; 2.33in conning tower; 2in turrets.

Guns: six 7.5in (190mm) (3x2); twelve 4in (102mm) DP (6x2); six 40mm (6x1).

Torpedoes: six 21in (2x3).

Aircraft: two; one catapult.

Complement: 780.

Design These two ships were the most important result of the 75 million Gold Peso naval programme authorised in 1926, which formulated the requirements of the Argentine Navy for the following ten years. The contract for the two cruisers (a third was authorised but not proceeded with) was won by the Italian Odero Terni Orlando company with a design reputedly based upon the Royal Italian Navy's new Washington Treaty heavy cruiser, *Trento*. This ship had herself only been laid down in February 1925, and was to be followed on the same slipway at Livorno by one of the Argentine vessels, *Veinticinco de Mayo*. Her sister was the last vessel to be built at the La Foce yard. In fact, there appears to be little resemblance between the two designs, as the Italian ship was longer, beamier and more heavily protected than the Argentine ship. There were also differences in armament, machinery and layout. Just about all that they had in common was that both conformed to contemporary Italian design practice in that they were fast, lightly built and weakly protected, although these features were partly the result of the Treaty constraints.

Under the agreements of the Washington Treaty, all ships with guns above 8in were classed as 'Heavy Cruisers', and the Argentine ships fell into that classification, being the first and in fact only examples in any South American Navy. Argentina acquired Heavy Cruisers before several of the more recognised naval powers, and her possession of these two ships gave her a leading position amongst the 'ABC' powers on the subcontinent.

The main armament, 190mm (7.5in)/52 calibre, was unusual, only the British *Hawkins* class (q.v.) having the same weapon calibre as designed. These were carried in twin turrets, with two forward, having 46° elevation. Maximum range was 27,300m. 150rpg was the ship's book oufit. Secondary armament consisted of six twin 102mm (4in) O-T guns disposed on the forecastle deck amidships. These guns had a maximum elevation of 80° in the AA role. A total of 3,000 rounds was allowed for. Twelve torpedoes were carried. As built, the aircraft installation consisted of a Gagnotto fixed catapult on the forecastle in accordance with current Italian designs, with a hangar for two aircraft below. The aircraft were initially Vought Corsair O2Us, then Grumman G5s, these being replaced by the Supermarine Walrus and, finally, the Grumman J2F.

Protection was limited to the centre section in the way of the vital areas, i.e. machinery spaces, magazines etc. The horizontal component comprised 25mm armour over these compartments. The vertical protection consisted of a side belt, 50mm thick, extending from 60cm below the waterline to the plane of the lower deck, with 25mm plating from the lower deck to the main deck.

Contrary to opinions expressed abroad, these two ships were held in high regard by the Argentines and were considered very successful.

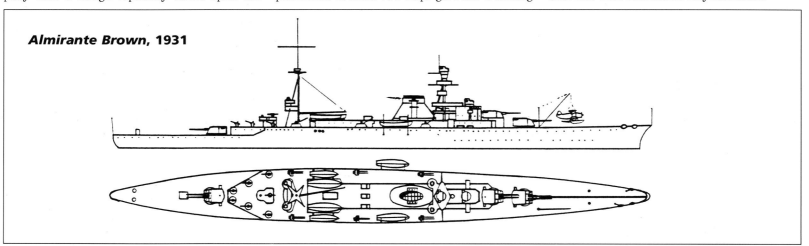

Almirante Brown, 1931

Above: *Veintecinco de Mayo*, seen here with catapult and Grumman J2F-6 Duck general utility amphibian floatplane. (USN)

Modifications Shortly after the vessels entered service, the mast arrangements were altered, the foremast being cut down and the main increased in height. The original hangar under the forecastle was converted for accommodation uses in 1937, and in 1939 a new trainable catapult of Rapier Ransome type was fitted on the modified superstructure between the funnels. A new-type crane was fitted in 1944, and, at the end of the 1940s, Type 268 radar was fitted. In June 1950 four twin 40mm supplanted the six Vickers/Terni 40mm, and in 1956 the 102mm guns were also landed and a further six twin 40mm fitted.

Service *Veinticinco de Mayo* was named after the date upon which the Spanish colonies in La Plata, the Argentine Confederation, revolted against the Spanish Crown and initiated the drive for independence. *Almirante Brown* commemorated the Irishman in command of the Argentine fleet in the War of Independence and in the conflict with Brazil 1826-1828.

The two ships were delivered to the navy on 5 July 1931 and sailed for Argentina from Genoa on 27 July 1931, reaching La Plata on 15 September and being incorporated into the Fleet the following day. Their careers mainly consisted of routine goodwill visits to other South American countries in the years preceding the Second World War, but *Veintecinco de Mayo* served in Spanish waters, arriving in Alicante on 22 August 1936 to look after Argentine nationals and interests, as well as many other refugees, during the Civil War then in progress. She returned home on 14 December 1936. Otherwise, their prewar service was in South American waters. *Almirante Brown* collided with and sank the destroyer *Corrientes* during exercises in bad weather on 3 October 1941, and was in turn rammed in the stern by the battleship *Rivadavia*, suffering considerable damage which necessitated three months' repair at Puerto Belgrano. Argentina being neutral during the Second World War, no active service was seen by the navy. Postwar, both ships participated in the 1947-48 Antarctic campaign and thereafter continued the usual peacetime routine, *Almirante Brown* making a goodwill cruise to New York in 1949. On 20 April 1950 a Bell helicopter made the first landing of such a machine on an Argentine ship when it alighted on *Almirante Brown*. In 1959 *25 De Mayo* was placed in reserve, and was offered for sale the following year, when her sister was also disarmed. Both were stricken on 31 July 1961. The two ships were sold for scrapping to the Italian Soc. Com. Trasimeno Spa. of Milan, and left together under tow for shipbreakers in Italy on 2 March 1962.

LA ARGENTINA CLASS

Ship	Builder	Laid Down	Launched	Completed	Fate
La Argentina	VA, Barrow	11 Jan 36	16 Mar 37	31 Jan 39	Discarded 1974

Displacement: 6,500 tons/6,604 tonnes 7,500 tons/7,620tonnes (standard); (full load).
Length: 540ft 10in/164.89m (oa); 509ft 9in/155.44m (pp).
Beam: 56ft 6in/17.22 m; Draught: 16ft 6in/5.03m (mean).
Machinery: 4-shaft Parsons geared turbines; 4 Yarrow boilers.
Performance: 54,000shp=30kts; Bunkerage: 1,484 tons oil fuel.

Range: 10,000nm at 12kts.
Protection: 2in deck; 3in sides; 3in conning tower; 2in turrets.
Guns: nine 6in (3x3); four 4in (4x1); eight 2pdr (8x1).
Torpedoes: six 21in (2x3).
Aircraft: One, one catapult.
Complement: 800, inc 60 cadets.

Design This cruiser, as unmistakably British in origin as *Veintecinco de Mayo* was Italian, appears to have been an amalgam of several contemporary designs being built by British yards in the late 1930s. Outwardly she was not dissimilar to *Arethusa* (q.v.), but she was larger and differed in many respects. Designed as a training ship to replace the elderly *Presidente Sarmiento*, which had been completed as early as 1899, she was probably ordered instead of the third *Veintecinco de Mayo* ship, but this may be speculation. Authorised under the Law of 29 September 1934, the contract this time, however, was won by a British yard and placed on 31 July 1935. It was worth a

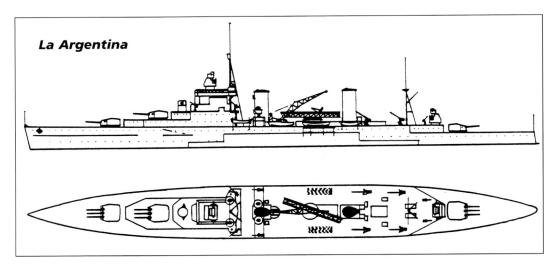

La Argentina

reputed 6 million Gold Pesos. To use a cruiser for training purposes was not a new idea; they were of an ideal size to accommodate a useful number of cadets and to carry a variety of extra equipment for the purpose, but the construction of a purpose-designed vessel of this type was uncommon. A precedent, in the form of the French *Jeanne d'Arc*, did exist, however, and it is perhaps surprising that the contract did not go to France. In comparison with the French ship, only 60 cadets could be accommodated, but the requirements of the Argentine navy were not as great.

The design, developed by Vickers, resulted in a very useful multipurpose cruiser, quite capable of normal cruiser duties in the event of hostilities, armed with no fewer than nine 6in guns, known as the Mk W, in triple turrets with 45° elevation and with each gun in a separate cradle, although all or pairs could be linked together. The heavy AA outfit comprised the standard British four 4in, the guns being 50cal Vickers Mk Ps with 90° elevation. Light AA originally comprised twelve 1in Vickers air-cooled MG in twin mountings, firing a 250g shell. A full torpedo armament and aircraft installation were also worked into the design. One Walrus amphibian was the normal complement.

The hull was of longitudinal construction, fabricated from D steel according to British practice, with a double bottom in the way of the machinery spaces. Compartmentation was such as to assure survival with three adjacent compartments flooded.

With her standard four-shaft cruiser geared turbine machinery installation developing 54,000shp, *La Argentina* was some 5kts faster than her French predecessor. Her trial results showed a maximum speed of 30.46kts on 7,590 tons with 54,500shp.

Although laid down in 1936 and launched the following year, this ship was delayed by the Royal Navy's rearmament programme, and it was not until early 1939 that she was accepted.

Modifications No significant modifications were made during the period of the war years. In October 1946 Type 268 radar was fitted. In 1949 the catapult and aircraft were removed and fire-control (Mk 8) and navigational radars were fitted. The 4in guns and the twin Vickers MG were replaced by 40mm AA, one twin 40/60 Bofors for each 4in and one single 40/60 for each twin Vickers, to a total of 14. Air warning radar SA3 was added in 1952.

Service The ship sailed from Gravesend on 12 February 1939 and arrived at La Plata on 2 March, being incorporated into the fleet on 12 April. She then began her career as a training ship, making several training cruises in the years 1939 and 1940. However, the Second World War prevented further cruises. From January 1941 *La Argentina* joined the Cruiser Division, but as a unit of a neutral nation she saw no active service. In 1946 she resumed her role as a training ship until 1951, when she rejoined the Cruiser Division. In 1960 her training career was resumed, and she made her final training cruise in 1972, visiting ports as far apart as New York, Copenhagen and Hamburg. *La Argentina* was stricken from the Navy List on 10 January 1974.

Below: *La Argentina* in 1950. (W&L)

Australia

BIRMINGHAM CLASS

Ship	Builder	Laid Down	Launched	Completed	Fate
Adelaide	Cockatoo Island Dky	20 Nov 17	27 Jul 18	4 Aug 22	Arrived to break up 1949

Displacement: 5,550 tons/5,639 tonnes (standard); 6,160 tons/6,258 tonnes (full load).

Length: 462ft 9in/141.1m (oa); 430ft/131.1m (pp).

Beam: 50ft/15.2m; Draught: 16 ft/4.9m (mean).

Machinery: 2 shaft geared turbines, 10 Yarrow boilers.

Performance: 23,500shp=24.3kts; Bunkerage: 1,420 tons oil fuel.

Range: n/k

Protection: 3in main belt; 1½in deck; 4in conning tower.

Guns: eight 6in (8x1); three 4in AA (3x1).

Torpedoes: removed.

Aircraft: nil.

Complement: 470.

Design The oldest cruiser design left in active service in the Royal and Dominion navies, although not the oldest ship still extant, *Adelaide* was the sole survivor of this class, which was a development of a design dating from 1908. While her sisters had been completed in 1914, *Adelaide* was not completed until 1922, by which time the design was quite obsolete. The *Birmingham* class was a near-repeat of the 1911 *Chatham* class, but with an additional 6in gun on the forecastle. The Australian ship was not laid down until some two years after her sisters, in an Australian yard, by which time the outbreak of war seriously affected her construction. Accorded a low priority and dependant upon much material and equipment supplied by Britain, Australia's largest locally-built warship took about 7½ years to complete. Much of the delay was due to the loss en route from Britain of important turbine forgings and other machinery parts which could not be obtained locally. This delay led to her being referred to as HMAS *Long-Delayed*. Subsequently, the desire to incorporate war experience into the ship led to further delays. She originally carried an armament of nine 6in BL Mk XII guns which fired 100lb shells, all in single PX III shielded mountings.

Modifications The ship was completely refitted in 1938-39, when the coal-fired boilers in the forward boiler room were removed, reducing the shp to 23,500, with a consequent reduction in speed to 24.3kts. The forward funnel was also removed.

One 6in gun was landed and the remaining forecastle gun was resited on the centreline. Three 4in AA guns in single mountings were added, an HA fire control director being fitted above the main battery director on the tripod foremast, while the 3in guns and the torpedo tubes were landed. (The 12pdr guns had been removed in 1937). This refit was completed in March 1939. Later, between May and July 1942, six 20mm singles were fitted while the ship was under refit at Garden Island. The radar 271 in its distinctive lantern was probably also fitted at this time, between the bridge and fore funnel. From June to September 1943 a further refit took place at Williamstown Dockyard, during which the 6in and 4in outfits were further reduced to seven 6in and two 4in. Actually, two 6in were removed from the waist and replaced by four depth-charge throwers, but one of the 6in was relocated to superfire over the after gun, displacing one 4in AA, which was landed. This retained a five-gun broadside. The older pattern heavy armoured gunshields were replaced by a lighter, bullet-proof type. She received radar 285 for the HACS on the foremast and US pattern SC radar at the foremast truck.

Service *Adelaide* commissioned as a training ship and spent her early service in Australian waters

Below: *Adelaide* in November 1939 with eight 6in guns. Note 4in HA aft. (Australian War Memorial, AWM)

Right: *Adelaide* in a later configuration, probably in 1942, now armed with seven 6in. She is fitted with both RN and USN radars. (AWM)

until April 1924, when she joined the Special Service Squadron (RN) for the world cruise of 1924. She eventually returned to Australia in April 1925. On 27 June 1928 the ship paid off into reserve at Sydney and remained in this condition for over ten years, until taken in hand for refit at Cockatoo Island in 1938. She recommissioned on 13 March 1939, but paid off again on 17 May to allow her crew to man the new *Perth*. She recommissioned for war service on 1 September 1939, and from December 1939 until January 1940 she was based at Fremantle. After a refit at Sydney from February to April, she saw service in the Pacific, escorting troop convoys, and in the New Hebrides in connection with conflicts between Free and Vichy France. From 1940 until May 1942 the ship was on the Australia station (she was present at Sydney at the time of the Japanese midget submarine attack), carrying out patrol duties. From July she was based at Freetown for duty in the Indian Ocean, where she sank the German blockade runner *Ramses* on 28 November 1942,

in company with the Dutch *Heemskerck*, while escorting convoy OW1. Her further service was without incident, and on 26 February 1945 she paid off at Sydney, only to recommission again on 19 May 1945 as a tender to the shore establish-

ment *Penguin*. After paying off for the last time on 13 May 1946, *Adelaide* was used as a night gunnery target in 1947 before being sold for disposal on 24 January 1949 and towed to Port Kembla between 1 and 2 April 1949 for breaking up.

COUNTY CLASS

Ship	Builder	Laid Down	Launched	Completed	Fate
Australia	John Brown, Clydebank	26 Aug 25	17 Mar 27	24 Apr 28	Sold for scrapping 25 Jan 55
Canberra	John Brown, Clydebank	9 Sep 25	31 May 27	10 Jul 28	Lost 9 Aug 42

Displacement 9,850 tons/10,007 tonnes (standard); 13,500 tons/13,716 tonnes (full load).
Length: 630ft/192.07m (oa); 590ft/179.87m (pp).
Beam: 68ft 3in/20.8m; Draught: 16ft 3in/4.95m (mean).
Machinery: 4-shaft Brown-Curtis geared turbines, 8 Admiralty 3-drum boilers.
Performance: 80,000shp=31.5 kts; Bunkerage: 3,300 tons oil fuel.
Range: 9,500nm at 12 kts.
Protection: 4½in on 1in machinery spaces; 1⅜ in deck; 4in box (magazines); 1in turrets.
Guns: eight 8in Mk VIII (4x2); four 4in Mk V (4x1); four 2pdr (4x1).
Torpedoes: eight 21in Mk VIII (2x4).
Aircraft: one with catapult.
Complement: 848 (war).

Design See County Class, Royal Navy. These two ships were ordered as part of a five-year naval development programme begun in 1924 and completed in 1929.

Modifications As completed, the Australian ships *Australia* and *Canberra* differed from their Royal Navy counterparts only in the type of torpedoes carried, the RAN selecting the Mk VII. A catapult and aircraft were fitted in *Australia* during 1935, and in *Canberra* during 1941. *Australia* underwent a major refit, having paid off on 24 April 1938, when a 4in armour belt was added to protect the machinery spaces and transmitting rooms. The single 4in were replaced by twins and mounted one deck lower. The trainable catapult was removed and replaced by an athwartships pattern, while the aircraft complement was increased to three. However, no box hangar was fitted. HACS fire control and two .5in machine-gun mountings were added. The latter were removed in 1942 and seven 20mm singles fitted, and the torpedo tubes were also removed after the ship was inclined. During the refits in 1944, tripod masts were fitted and the aircraft installations removed. Seven twin 20mm now replaced the sin-

gle mountings (March). In August the starboard crane was removed and sampson posts with 35ft derricks fitted. Then in February 1945 X turret (but not the barbette) and the port cranes were removed at Sydney during battle damage repair before she sailed for the UK and a major refit. During the UK refit, X barbette was removed and the radar suite modernised. Two Mk VI eight-barrel 2pdr mountings with RPC were added at the forward end of the after shelterdeck, two quadruple 40mm Bofors abreast B gun deck, one twin on X gun deck and two singles on the upperdeck amidships. This refit was finished off at Garden Island in 1946.

Canberra, on the other hand, merely had her 4in increased to eight, all in single mountings, two eight-barrel 2pdr added, and probably a few 20mm singles added before her loss in 1942.
Service *Australia* arrived in Sydney on 23 October 1928, and spent the next six years in Australian waters. However, on 10 December 1934 she sailed for England on exchange with HMS *Sussex*, and did not return to Sydney again until 11 August 1936. She was then employed in Australian/Pacific waters until 24 April, when she paid off into reserve for a major refit. After recommissioning on 28 August 1939, the ship was employed on ocean convoy duties between Australia, Capetown and Freetown until July 1940. Following duties in Norwegian waters, she partic-

ipated in the attack on Dakar in September 1940, where she shelled and damaged the contre-torpilleur *L'Audacieux* so badly that she had to be beached, but was later herself damaged by the cruisers *Georges Leygues* and *Montcalm*. The ship eventually returned to Australian waters in March 1941, carried out patrols in the Indian Ocean in 1941, and then, as flagship of the ANZAC squadron, moved to Noumea in February 1942. In April the ANZAC squadron became Task Force 44, and, in May, part of Task Force 17.

She saw action in the Coral Sea and at Guadalcanal, and from November 1943 to September 1944 she was involved in the bombardment of enemy-held islands in the South-West Pacific basin prior to Allied landings. On 21 October 1944 *Australia* was badly damaged by a kamikaze and put out of action until 5 January 1945, when she participated in the landings on Luzon island. Here she was again badly hit by further kamikaze attacks on 5, 6, 8, and 9 January, necessitating her return to Sydney with heavy casualties. Repairs

were partly carried out in Australia and finished in the UK, where she lay at the end of the war. *Australia* spent the last five years of her service as a training ship, and paid off for disposal on 31 August 1954. Sold for scrap on 25 January 1955, *Australia* left Sydney on 26 March in tow for the UK, where she was broken up by T. W. Ward at Barrow-in-Furness.

Canberra arrived in Fremantle on 25 January 1929 and remained in Australian waters, visiting New Zealand, Fiji and China in the years before the outbreak of war. The first nine months were spent patrolling home waters and the Tasman Sea; then, in July 1940, she moved into the Indian Ocean, searching for raiders, including the *Atlantis* and *Pinguin*. In 1941 the target was *Admiral Scheer*, again without success, but in March she and *Leander* intercepted and sank the German prize *Ketty Brovig* and the tanker *Coburg*. The second half of 1941 saw her escorting convoys between Australia, Singapore and Ceylon. This duty switched to the East Indies, New Guinea and the Malaya/Java theatre when the Pacific war broke out. *Canberra* was under refit at Sydney from 7 February until mid-May 1942, and was in Sydney harbour at the time of the Japanese midget submarine attack. From June

Below: *Australia* in 1943, with radars 271, 284 and SC. (IWM)

1942 she participated in sweeps in the Coral Sea as part of Task Force 44, with the USS *Chicago* and *Salt Lake City*, then supported the landings on Guadalcanal before being sunk off Savo Island, when the Southern Covering Force was surprised by a Japanese cruiser and destroyer force. After being reduced to a wreck by gunfire and torpedoes, she was finished off on the morning of 9 August by USS *Ellet*.

TRANSFERRED UNIT
Following the loss of *Canberra*, one of the RN's County class, *Shropshire*, was offered to the Royal Australian Navy in September 1942 and transferred on 25 June 1943. A unit of the *London* class, details of her design and modification before transfer will be found in that section. Before this ship was taken over, the .5in MG were landed, as were four single 20mm, and replaced by seven twin 20mm. The aircraft installation was also removed. In 1945 she had all 20mm removed and replaced by single 40/60 Bofors, and the torpedo tubes were deleted. The 40mm, fifteen in number, were disposed seven on the superstructure deck, six on the upper deck and one each on B and X turrets. By early 1946 the guns on the turret roofs had been landed, the remainder being six Mk IIIA, two Mk VII and one Mk IIIP.

Shropshire was operating as part of TF74 in the New Hebrides by November 1943, and then gave fire support to the landings on New Britain, Cape Gloucester and New Guinea over the next few months into the new year. As the year progressed and Allied forces advanced in the South-West Pacific, the ship saw action in the Admiralty Islands, off Hollandia and Aitape, and in May/

Left: *Canberra* pre-war. Note extra height to the funnels in comparison with the RN ships. (AWM)
Below: *Australia* in a very dark shade of grey, seen here with *Hobart*, probably in 1943. (AWM)

Above: *Shropshire* entering Sydney after her transfer to the RAN. (AWM)

July at Biak. September 1944 saw her in support of landings at Morotai before moving into Leyte Gulf in October. The Mindoro landings followed in December, then Lingayen Gulf, Subic Bay, Corregidor and Bataan in January 1945. Her final wartime operations were in support of amphibious landings once again, this time at Balikpapan in Borneo during June 1945, and then the ship proceeded to Japan and was present at the final surrender in August.

Postwar, *Shropshire* remained with the RAN and served in a training role until paid off in 1949. She was sold for scrapping in 1954, arriving at the Dalmuir yard of the shipbreakers Arnott Young on 20 January 1955.

SYDNEY CLASS

Ship	Builder	Laid Down	Launched	Completed	Fate
Sydney	Swan Hunter	8 Jul 33	22 Sep 34	24 Sep 35	Lost 19 Nov 41
Perth	HM Dky, Portsmouth	26 Jun 33	27 Jul 34	6 Jul 36	Lost 1 Mar 42
Hobart	HM Dky, Devonport	15 Aug 33	9 Oct 34	13 Jan 36	Scrapped 1962

Displacement: 6,830* tons/6,939* tonnes (standard); 8,850* tons/8,991* tonnes (full load).

Length: 562ft 3in/171.37m (oa); 522ft/159.10m (pp).

Beam: 56ft 8in/17.27m; Draught: 18ft 6in/5.64m (mean).

Machinery: 4-shaft Parsons geared turbines; 4 Admiralty 3-drum boilers.

Performance: 72,000shp=32½kts; Bunkerage: 1,606 tons oil fuel.

Range: 7,180nm at 12kts.

Protection: 3in on 1in main belt; 1-3½in box (magazines); 1in turrets.

Guns: eight 6in Mk XXIII (4x2); eight 4in Mk V (4x2); twelve .5in MG (3x4).

Torpedoes: eight 21in (2x4).

Aircraft: one with catapult.

Complement: 570.

* Figures refer to *Sydney*. *Perth* 6,980, *Hobart* 7,105 tons std: *Hobart* later 9,420 tons full load.

Design These three ships, generally described as 'Modified *Leanders*', were originally ordered by the Royal Navy, having been authorised under the 1931 and 1932 estimates as *Phaeton*, *Amphion* and *Apollo*. Their dimensions varied slightly from those of the original *Leanders*, and the outward appearance differed in that they had twin funnels, which allowed the aircraft installation to be fitted between the funnels. The reason behind this feature was the adoption of the unit machinery principle, following the example of the United States. This arrangement had already been approved for the *Arethusa* class in 1932, and it was also to be applied to future construction. Two new *Leanders* had been ordered in 1931, *Ajax* and *Amphion*, and the latter was apparently reordered in 1932 to the modified arrangement.

The main machinery power remained the same as the *Leander* at 72,000shp, but the number of boilers was reduced to four and the boiler rooms to two. This entailed an increase in the length of the machinery spaces and a consequent increase in the length of the armour belt, which absorbed much of the weight saved by the loss of two boilers. As the weight added was high up in the ship, beam had to be increased by 1ft 8in to retain stability. The resultant arrangements were extremely cramped.

Protection included a 4in belt (3in NC+1in D) over the machinery spaces, and a 1¼in D steel deck, with box protection to the magazines of 3½in NC sides and 2in NC crowns.

Welding was used extensively in their construction for economy in weight, and the ships came out under their designed displacement.

Main armament remained eight 6in guns, with the standard four 4in AA and multiple MGs. The heavy catapult could not at first be accommodated because there was insufficient space between the funnels, but eventually a further 6ft was found in the funnel spacing. There was much discussion on the question of the catapult, not least because of the requirements of the Royal Australian Navy, which had taken the ships over in the meantime and wished to operate the heavy Seagull amphibian.

Modifications As completed, the secondary armament comprised four 4in all in single mountings, but *Hobart* and *Perth* had theirs altered to four twin mountings before transfer. The 46ft fixed athwartships catapult was replaced by a 53ft trainable catapult and equipped to operate one Supermarine Seagull V amphibian, more familiarly known as the Walrus in the Fleet Air Arm. Thereafter, *Sydney* received little or no further additions except for a few 20mm singles, while *Perth* also received at least four 20mm, two on B and X turrets and two replacing the .5in MGs. For a short period she also carried a quadruple 2pdr amidships, fitted at Alexandria on 5 May 1941, but this was removed by July. She was also fitted with radar 271. *Hobart* initially received a few 20mm, and lost the catapult in June 1941. In October 1942, during repairs in Sydney that lasted from August 1943 until January 1945, the catapult structure was dismantled, tripod masts were fitted, the 4in guns repositioned, boat stowage altered and the radar fit updated. She now carried Types 281B (air warning), 277 (surface warning), 276 (surface and close air warning) and SG (surface warning). She also had Type 285 to the 4in, 282 for the 2pdr and 40mm, and 283 for the main armament. The close-range AA was altered to three twin 40mm Hazemeyer Mk IV and five single Mk III Bofors, together with two quadruple 2pdr Mk VII RP50 mountings on the boat deck. All four twin 20mm were landed, leaving only one single 20mm on the roof of X turret. The torpedo outfit was retained. 100 tonnes of ballast was

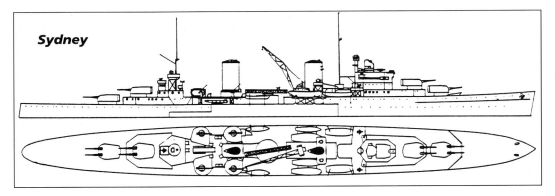

Sydney

removed, leaving 65 remaining (175 tons sic. of permanent ballast had been added at Morts Dock, Sydney, in May 1943 as a result of experiments with *Perth*). X turret was removed in June 1946, when a quadruple Bofors was scheduled to replace it. At this time the single 40mm outfit comprised one Mk IIIP Toadstool and one Mk VII, both on the after shelterdeck. Between 1953 and 1956, when it was cancelled, the ship underwent a major refit for use as a training ship.

Service *Hobart*'s service in the Royal Navy as HMS *Apollo* was initially on the America and West Indies Station during 1936/38. Then, on 28 September 1938, she was commissioned by the crew of *Albatros* (which had been transferred to the RN in part-payment for *Apollo*) earlier than intended because of the Munich crisis. She sailed for Australia towards the end of the year, and at the outbreak of the war was on patrol duties in the Bass Strait. By October she was in the East Indies, and thereafter escorted troop convoys across the Bay of Bengal and the Indian Ocean, finding herself at Aden when Italy entered the war. She supported the early campaign in the Red Sea, serving as the HQ for the evacuation of Berbera and finally bombarding the port on 19 August 1940. *Hobart* remained with the Red Sea Force until October, then went to Columbo for refit before returning to Australian waters, where she served on escort duties until the end of June 1941. In August she was transferred to the Mediterranean, and saw action there supporting the garrison at Tobruk. With the entry of Japan into the war, however, the ship was required in the east again, and sailed for Singapore, escorting troop convoy BM9A towards the end of the year. In Malaysian waters she was frequently subject to air attack as part of the Allied Combined Strike Force. She was heavily bombed while lying in Tandjong Priok oiling on 25 February 1942, but suffered only splinter damage which prevented refuelling being completed. As a result, *Hobart* missed the fatal Battle of the Java Sea on 27 February. Action in the Coral Sea with Task Forces 61 and 44 followed in May, and at Guadalcanal and Tulagi in the Solomon Islands in August. After a refit at Sydney in October, *Hobart* rejoined Task Force 44 on Coral Sea patrols. This formation was renumbered Task Force 74 in May 1943. In July 1943 TF74 was sent to the New Georgia to replace losses there, and on 20 July 1943 *Hobart* was badly damaged by torpedoes from the submarine *I11*. Escorted by *Warramunga* and *Arunta*, the cruiser reached Sydney for repairs on 26 August. Not until early 1945 was she serviceable again, when she rejoined TF74 to cover the landings at Tarakan, Borneo, in April and Balikpapan in July. She was present in Tokyo Bay for the surrender ceremony on 31 August 1945.

Postwar, *Hobart* remained in service, making three deployments to Japanese waters before returning to Sydney to pay off on 20 December 1947. Although she was earmarked for conversion to a training ship and a refit was started, changed requirements saw the work cancelled and the ship put up for disposal on 5 February 1960, after many years in reserve. On 22 February 1962 the cruiser was sold to Mitsui & Co (Aust. Pty.), and left Sydney in tow for the Miyachi shipyard, Osaka, Japan, on 3 March, arriving for breaking up on 2 April 1962.

Sydney, laid down as *Phaeton* for the Royal Navy but launched as an Australian ship, spent the early part of her career with the Mediterranean fleet and did not arrive in Australian waters until 2 August 1936. She remained in home waters until April 1940, when she escorted a Middle East-bound troop convoy (US2) to Columbo, where she arrived on 8 May. On 19 May she proceeded to the Mediterranean and joined the 7th Cruiser Squadron, bombarding Bardia on 21 June with an Anglo-French squadron. In June she assisted in the sinking of the destroyer *Espero* and picked up survivors, and in the following month covered

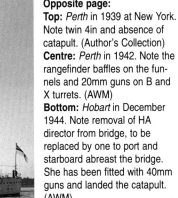

Left: *Sydney* in 1935. (W&L)

Opposite page:
Top: *Perth* in 1939 at New York. Note twin 4in and absence of catapult. (Author's Collection)
Centre: *Perth* in 1942. Note the rangefinder baffles on the funnels and 20mm guns on B and X turrets. (AWM)
Bottom: *Hobart* in December 1944. Note removal of HA director from bridge, to be replaced by one to port and starboard abreast the bridge. She has been fitted with 40mm guns and landed the catapult. (AWM)

Malta convoys and was present at the action off Calabria on the occasion of the engagement with the Italian Fleet on 9 July. In the same month she encountered two Italian cruisers, *Bartolomeo Colleoni* and *Giovanni delle Bande Nere*, northwest of Crete, shelling the former to a standstill, to be finished off by British destroyers. After operations in the eastern Mediterranean, Greece and the Adriatic, *Sydney* sailed for Australia from Alexandria on 11 January 1941, arriving home on 5 February. She now operated on Australian waters, occasionally in the Indian Ocean and around New Zealand until, on 19 November 1941, she fell in with the German raider *Kormoran* off Sharks Bay, Western Australia. For some unknown reason the Australian ship, although obviously suspicious, allowed the German ship too close, and in the close-quarters engagement was smothered in gunfire. Her own guns hit the raider so badly that she later sank, but the cruiser, on fire and badly damaged, steamed out of sight of the German survivors and was never seen again. There were no survivors.

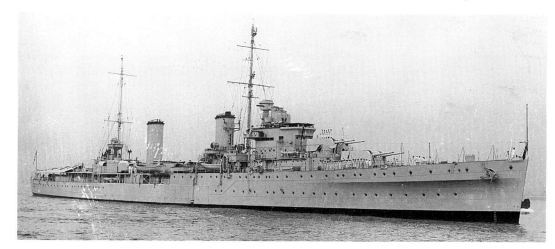

Perth was not acquired by the RAN until 29 June 1939, when she was manned by the crew of the paid-off *Adelaide*. Before this the ship had served as Flagship of the Africa Station at Capetown from 3 October 1936 until early October 1938, when she arrived in Portsmouth to pay off for refit. On completion of this, the ship, now Australian, visited New York for the World Fair in August 1939, intending to sail for Australia afterwards. However, on the outbreak of war *Perth* was ordered to the West Indies to protect the oil installations, and remained there until March 1940, apart from one brief sortie into the Pacific via the Panama Canal. On 31 March she secured at Garden Island, carried out a short refit, then escorted troop convoys bound for the Middle East. Between June and November 1940 the ship was Flagship, Australian Squadron. After escorting convoy US7 to Suez in December, *Perth* proceeded to Alexandria, where she joined the 7th Cruiser Squadron. She was damaged by near misses in Malta shortly after her arrival. She played a minor role during the Battle of Cape Matapan, and then supported operations in Greece, being damaged again by near misses on 22 May and hit by a bomb in a boiler room on 30 May. Following repairs, *Perth* participated in the operations against Vichy French Syria, but was relieved by *Hobart* on 15 July and sailed for Australia on 18 July. On her arrival, on 12 August, she went into the Cockatoo yard for a refit which lasted until 22 November 1941. She sailed for the Java theatre on 14 February 1942, and on 27/28 February took part in the battle of the Java Sea as a unit of the ABDA force. Only *Perth* and the US cruiser *Houston* survived this debacle, and they put into Tandjong Priok, from where they were ordered to Tjilatjap. Having sailed for the Sunda Strait, they were unfortunate enough to run into a Japanese landing operation in Banten Bay, Java. A confused night action then ensued with *Mikuma*, *Mogami* and destroyers until the Australian ship, having fired away most of her ammunition, was hit by four torpedoes in succession. She sank in the early hours of 1 March 1942.

Brazil

BAHIA CLASS

Ship	Builder	Laid Down	Launched	Completed	Fate
Bahia	Armstrong, Elswick	19 Aug 07	24 Apr 09	1910	Lost 4 Jul 45
Rio Grande do Sul	Armstrong, Elswick	30 Aug 07	20 Jan 09	1910	Stricken 1948

Displacement: 3,100 tons/3,150 tonnes (standard).
Length: 380ft/115.8m (pp).
Beam: 39ft/11.8m; Draught: 14ft 6in/4.4m (mean).
Machinery: 3-Shaft Brown-Curtis geared turbines, 6 Thornycroft boilers.
Performance: 18,000 shp=26½kts; Bunkerage: 640 tons oil fuel.
Range: 6,600nm at 10kts.
Protection: 7.5in deck; 3in conning tower.
Guns: ten 4.7in (10x1); four 3in (4x1); four 3pdr (6x1).
Torpedoes: four 21in (2x2).
Aircraft: nil.
Complement: 350.

Design These two Scout Cruisers were authorised as part of the 1904 Naval Programme, which, when it was completed some years later, transformed the Brazilian fleet into a modern navy. The contract for the ships was won by Elswick, then pre-eminent in cruiser design, the machinery being subcontracted to Vickers. Based upon contemporary British practice, the design was an updated and much-modified version of *Adventure*, which had been completed in 1905. It incorporated the new Parsons turbine machinery in a three-shaft arrangement, with 18,000shp giving a designed top speed of 26.5kts. The Royal Navy's *Boadicea*, building at the same time, was the first RN cruiser with turbines, *Adventure* having had reciprocating machinery. The new Brazilian ships proved very fast, *Bahia* reaching 27.02kts on 20,010shp and her sister 27.41kts, but coal firing would have made it difficult to maintain those speeds under service conditions. Armament comprised ten 4.7in (120mm) Elswick 50cal BL guns firing 45lb shells, in single shielded mountings.

These were disposed two abreast on the forecastle and quarterdeck and the remainder in the waist. Six 3pdr guns and two single 18in torpedo tubes completed the armament.

Modifications In 1925-26 both ships underwent major modernisation at the Companhia Nacional de Navegacao Costeira, Rio de Janiero, supervised by Messrs Thornycroft. In the course of this, new Brown-Curtis geared turbines replaced the former direct-drive type, and oil-fired Thornycroft boilers were fitted. The funnels were raised and director firing was installed. At the same time, the torpedo outfit was doubled and converted to 21in, and four 3in AA replaced part of the 3pdr outfit. This refit proved very successful, *Bahia* achieving 28.6kts on post-refit trials.

Modifications made during Brazil's participation in the Second World War are not known for certain, except for the installation of sonar and two DC throwers for 300lb DCs, plus, in all probability, the addition of a few 20mm guns.

Service In common with many ships of minor powers, these two vessels had long active careers. Both participated in Brazil's contribution to the First World War, seeing active service with the Brazilian squadron deployed off the north-west coast of Africa in 1917/18. They were again involved in hostilities after Brazil's declaration of war on the Axis on 22 August 1942. Their tasks were mainly of A/S and anti-blockade breaker patrol and escort nature, both participating in the convoy work associated with the transfer of the Brazilian Expeditionary Force to Italy from the summer of 1944. *Bahia*, serving in the main with the north-eastern naval forces, participated in the escorting of a total of 64 convoys between Recife, Salvador and Rio, while *Rio Grande do Sul* escorted 62. They participated in eleven and fifteen other operations respectively. These included work in the central South Atlantic between Dakar and Natal, acting as Air Sea Rescue patrols for US troop transport flights in 1945. While employed on such duties, *Bahia* exploded and sank with heavy loss of life. *Rio Grande do Sul* survived the war and was disposed of soon after.

Left: *Bahia* as rebuilt. (USN)

Opposite page: *Ontario* in June 1953. (Osbourne)

CANADA

TRANSFERRED UNITS

The British cruiser *Uganda*, which had been badly damaged off Salerno in 1943 (see page 126), was transferred to the RCN after being under repair at Charleston Navy Yard, South Carolina, for a year. She was commissioned as HMCS *Uganda* on 21 October 1944, and sailed for the UK the following month for further work. In January 1945 the ship sailed for the Pacific via the Suez Canal, to join the 4th Cruiser Squadron with the British Pacific Fleet. With the end of the war in Europe a manning problem arose, as Canada had no direct interest in a Pacific war, and many of her crew opted to return home rather than continue hostilities against Japan. Eventually matters were resolved and the ship became part of TF57 in the Okinawa area. By April 1945 *Uganda* was screening the carriers in raids on Formosa, and in March acted in a similar capacity during the raids on the Ryukyu Islands. In June she took part in the bombardment of Truk, shelling Dublon on the night of 14/15th. In July, as part of TF37, she screened the carriers in their final raids on the Japanese mainland, but was relieved by *Argonaut* on 27 July and sailed for Canada, arriving at Esquimalt on 10 August for refit.

Postwar the ship was used in a training role, being renamed *Quebec* on 14 January 1952. Paid off on 13 June 1956, *Quebec* was sold for scrapping and arrived at Osaka, Japan, on 6 February 1961 for breaking up.

Ontario was the former British cruiser *Minotaur* (see page 127), presented to the RCN before completion and renamed, being commissioned on 26 April 1945. She, too, sailed to join the 4th Cruiser Squadron in the Pacific Theatre, but was too late to see active service, although she was employed in the operations at Hong Kong, Manila and in Japan. She returned home for refit, arriving at Esquimalt on 27 November 1945. Like *Uganda*, she was used for training duties postwar until paid off on 15 October 1958. She arrived at Osaka for breaking up on 19 November 1960.

Chile

BLANCO ENCALADA CLASS

Ship	Builder	Laid Down	Launched	Completed	Fate
Blanco Encalada	Armstrongs, Elswick	Sept 92	9 Sept 93	Apr 94	Stricken 19 December 1945

Displacement: 3,435 tons/3,490 tonnes (standard); 4,480 tons/4,551 tonnes (full load).
Length: 398ft/130.57m (oa); 370ft/121.39m (pp).
Beam: 46ft 6in/15.25m; Draught: 19ft 6in/6.39m (mean).
Machinery: 2-shaft 4-cylinder vertical triple-expansion engines; 4 cylindrical boilers.
Performance: 14,500ihp=22.75kts; Bunkerage: 851 tons coal.
Range: 3,550nm at 9.5kts.
Protection: 4in deck; 6in gun shields.
Guns: two 8in, (2x1); ten 6in (10x1); five 3in (5x1).
Torpedoes: five 18in.
Aircraft: nil.
Complement: 427.

Design One of the famous Elswick cruisers built towards the end of the nineteenth century, this ship had been laid down by Armstrongs in 1992 as a speculative venture. She was a derivative of the contemporary Japanese Elswick cruiser *Yoshino* and, like her, was designed by Sir Philip Watts. In their day these cruisers had a high reputation, but by 1939 the few survivors were hopelessly outdated. The ship displaced 4,480 tons fully loaded, and was powered by twin-shaft four-cylinder vertical triple expansion (VTE) machinery. Curiously, Elswick retained the outdated cylindrical boiler, coal fired, for its cruisers, fitting four (150psi) in *Blanco Encalada*. At economical speed the coal consumption was 54 tons/24hr, but at maximum speed (22.7kts) this rose to 302 tons/24hr. The machinery was subcontracted to Humphrys Tennant & Co.

The protective scheme was limited to a 4in deck and a 6in conning tower. The hull was divided into fourteen watertight compartments.

The disposition of the armament was very much a throwback to the days of the ship of the line, most of the guns being on the broadside. Only the two heavy guns, Elswick model 8in 40cal, were centreline mounted, one each on the forecastle and quarterdeck. These were in shielded mounts, as were the Elswick 6in/40 guns, of which eight were carried, four on each beam. Two of these had some degree of bow or stern fire. There were also twelve 3pdr. Five 18in torpedo tubes were fitted, all above water, two on each beam and one in the bows.

Modifications Very little was done in the way of alterations during the whole of her 50 years' service, except for the removal of the 3pdr and replacement by 3in guns, plus the addition of one 2pdr and the probable deletion of the torpedo tubes.

Service As Chile was not involved in any real naval war during her career, *Blanco Encalada* saw no action. She arrived at Valparaiso on 26 January 1895. During her career she served as a training ship, as station ship in the Magellanes Squadron, and as a gunnery training ship. She underwent a major refit in 1920 and a short one in 1940, being finally stricken in 1945.

Below: Blanco Encalada as completed. (Courtesy Chilean Navy)

GENERAL O'HIGGINS CLASS

Ship	Builder	Laid Down	Launched	Completed	Fate
General O'Higgins	Armstrongs	Apr 96	17 May 97	Apr 98	Discarded 1954

Above: *General O'Higgins.* (Courtesy Chilean Navy)

Displacement: 7,796 tons/7,920 tonnes (standard); 8,475 tons/8,610 tonnes (full load).
Length: 446ft/146.32m (oa); 412ft/135.17m (pp).
Beam: 62ft 9in/22.88m; Draught: 22ft/7.21m (mean).
Machinery: 2-shaft triple-expansion, 30 Belville boilers.
Performance: 16,000ihp=20kts; Bunkerage: 1,253 tons coal.
Range: 4,580nm at 8kts.

Protection: 5 to 7in belt, 2in decks, 6in guns & casemates, 9in conning tower.
Guns: four 8in, (4x1); ten 6in (10x1); thirteen 3in (13x1).
Torpedoes: two 18in, submerged, one 18in a/w.
Aircraft: nil.
Complement: 500.

Design Another design by Sir Philip Watts, this ship, a protected cruiser of 7,700 tons, was ordered from Armstrongs in March 1896. Like the other two Chilean cruisers, she was equally dated and ineffective as a fighting unit by 1939, although the South American navies did not have a monopoly in this respect. The armoured deck extended the full length and beam of the ship, was 2in thick and was sloped at the sides. A 7ft-deep waterline belt 7in thick in the way of the machinery and magazines, reducing to 6in at the ends, extended 260ft amidships. Gun shields and casemates were protected by 6in to 7½in armour and the conning tower by 9in.

The main machinery, again constructed by Tennant's, remained a triple-expansion layout, but the boilers were now Belleville, 30 being required to provide the 16,500ihp for 20kts speed. Coal firing was also retained.

The hull was wood-sheathed and coppered.

The main armament comprised Armstrong 8in/40cal in single gunhouses, one each forward and aft, and another pair to port and starboard abreast the forward funnel. There were ten 6in/40, also of Armstrong manufacture; two in casemates abreast the bridge and eight aft, half in casemates and half in gunhouses directly above the casemates. Thirteen single 12pdr (3in) and four 2pdr pom-poms completed the artillery. There were three 18in torpedo tubes, two submerged on the beam and one in the stern.

Modifications Practically none, as far as is known.

Service *General O'Higgins* arrived in Chile in July 1898. In 1903 she was despatched to Panama during the confrontation between the USA and Colombia which led to the creation of the Panama Zone. Otherwise, she had an uneventful career, being given a major overhaul in 1928/29. For 24 years of her 35-year career she acted as headquarters ship, and was finally discarded only in 1954.

CHACABUCO CLASS

Ship	Builder	Laid Down	Launched	Completed	Fate
Chacabuco	Armstrong, Elswick	14 Aug 96	4 Jul 98	02	Stricken 15 Dec 1959

Displacement: 4,500 tons/4,572 tonnes (standard); 4,800 tons/4,877 tonnes (full load).
Length: 388ft 8in/127.51m (oa); 360ft 6in/118.27m (pp).
Beam: 44ft 6in/14.59m; Draught: 17ft 6in/5.74m (mean).
Machinery: 2-shaft vertical 4-cylinder triple-expansion engines; 8-cylindrical boilers.
Performance: 16,500ihp=24kts; Bunkerage: 985 tons coal.
Range: 7,200nm at 12kts.
Protection: 4½in max deck.
Guns: six 6in (6x1); ten 20mm (10x1).
Torpedoes: nil.

Aircraft: nil.
Complement: 400.

Design Another product of the Watts/Elswick combination, this small cruiser was also laid down as a speculation and later purchased in 1902 by Chile. She was a development of the Japanese *Takasago*, also built by Elswick, and followed the usual format of this type of cruiser. Machinery, subcontracted to Tennant, remained VTE with coal fired boilers, giving a speed of 24kts. She made 24¾kts on trial runs in December 1909.

The armour scheme included a 4½in deck over the vital areas, reducing to 1¾in at the ends. The 8in gun shields were 4½in, and those for the 6in guns 2½in.

The hull was divided into fourteen watertight compartments.

Her main armament as designed included two 8in/50 Armstrong guns in gunhouses forward and aft, and ten 4.7in in single shielded mountings, four of which were carried in casemates. There were also twelve 12pdr (3in), and five 18in fixed above-water torpedo tubes.

Modifications Between 1939 and 1941 the ship was refitted and modernised for service as a training ship. The 8in guns were landed, as were all 4.7in and 12pdr guns. The bridge was completely rebuilt, and the masts and rigging altered. Caps were added to both funnels. The armament was now six 6in, one each forward and aft, and two more shielded mountings on each beam. There were also four 3pdr in single mountings abreast the bridge. She is reported to have had ten 20mm added by 1945. The torpedo tubes were probably removed.

Service In 1911 *Chacabuco* was present at the Spithead Review for the Coronation of HM King George V. Otherwise, her routine was a normal peacetime one for her long career. From 1941 she was employed as a training ship until stricken at the end of 1959.

Below: *Chacabuco* as built. (MPL)
Bottom: *Chacabuco* after her 1941 refit. (USN)

France

DUGUAY-TROUIN CLASS

Ship	Builder	Laid Down	Launched	Completed*	Fate
Duguay-Trouin	Brest Navy Yard	4 Aug 22	14 Aug 23	2 Nov 26	Scrapped 29 Mar 52
Lamotte-Picquet	Lorient Navy Yard	17 Jan 23	21 Mar 24	5 Mar 27	Bombed and sunk 12 Jan 45
Primaguet	Brest Navy Yard	16 Aug 23	21 May 24	1 Apr 27	CTL 8 Nov 42

*Unless otherwise stated, all completion dates for French cruisers are 'Clôture d'Armament' as in *Destroyers of World War Two*.

Displacement: 7,249 tons/7,365 tonnes (standard); 9,350 tons/9,499 tonnes (full load).
Length: 595ft 9in/175.3m (oa); 575ft/175.3m (pp).
Beam: 56ft 6in/17.2m; Draught: 17ft/5.2m (mean).
Machinery: 4-shaft Parsons SR geared turbines; 8 Guyot boilers.
Performance: 100,000shp=33kts; Bunkerage: 1,500 tons oil fuel.
Range: 3,000nm at 15kts.
Protection: 20mm deck; 20mm magazine box citadel; 30mm turrets; 30mm conning tower.
Guns: eight 6.1in (4x2); four 75mm (4x1).
Torpedoes: twelve 21.7in (4x3).
Aircraft: two, one catapult.
Complement: 578.

Design The first postwar building programme was drawn up in June 1919, with the Italians in mind, but did not specify any number of light cruisers to be constructed. However, when the *Normandie* class battleships were cancelled, amongst the replacement ships envisaged were six 5,000-ton cruisers. By the end of 1919 the design of these cruisers had been thoroughly worked out. In broad terms, they were to carry eight 138.6mm (5.45in) guns in twin turrets at 30kts, were powered by a twin-shaft oil-fired installation, and had a displacement of 5,270 tons. Protection was minimal. This design was approved by the Finance Minister in 1920, although his implied criticism of it as 'dated' drew strenuous denials from the Navy, who pointed out that they used the 1912 Naval Bill only to support their case, and not that the design itself dated from that time. Nevertheless, doubts remained even within the Navy, and in February 1920 the Chief of the General Staff withdrew the design, whereupon discussions began all over again. Speed and size now began the inevitable upward spiral, while, in the meantime, several ex-enemy cruisers were put into service, which allowed examination of contemporary modern foreign design practice. It became apparent that the French design (Project 171) was indeed inferior, and in particular its main armament. After much discussion, a new calibre of 155mm was chosen, based on an army weapon.

By the end of 1920, having received copies of the plans of the US *Omaha* class, four layouts had been drafted with a hull based broadly on the US design, all armed with eight 155mm, four 75mm AA and twelve torpedo tubes, differing only in power and protection. Design 'C', with 34kts and no protection on a displacement of 7,890 tons, was selected in April 1921, and detailed design work began.

It was now referred to as the 8,000-ton cruiser. Protection was virtually nil, with only 30mm applied to the gunshields; barely splinter protection. It could be argued that this ship was merely an enlarged flotilla leader.

Internal subdivision was quite extensive, although the Engineer in Chief's objection to the lack of longitudinal subdivision in the boiler rooms was overruled. Full oil firing and single-reduction turbine machinery was adopted.

The 155mm (6.1in) M1920 gun was a BL type, with a screw breech, firing a 56.5kg shell with a two-part charge. It had a range of 26,100m at an elevation of 40°. Both guns were in separate cradles, with electro-hydraulic elevation and training. RPC was later fitted for training. This gun was employed only in this class, *Jean d'Arc*, and in single mountings in *Bearn*. The 75mm were of the M1922 pattern, firing a 12kg fixed round. Twelve torpedo tubes in four triple mountings, with a complete reload outfit, were worked into the design.

The construction of three units was finally approved on 18 April 1922, but considerable effort had to be expended in defending the design against various detractors who wished to 'improve' it. Change was successfully resisted, and the first two were ordered from the Brest Naval Yard on 14 April 1922 (*sic*). The order for the third was placed with Lorient Dockyard on 18 April.

Modifications All received a catapult on the quarterdeck after completion and carried two aircraft,

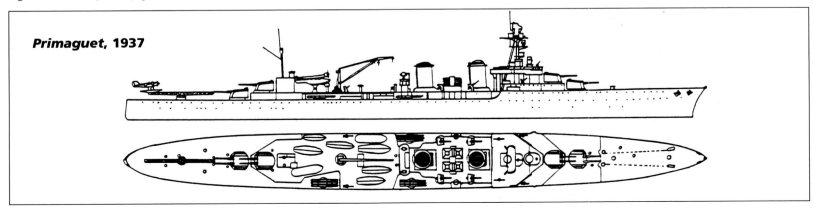
Primaguet, 1937

initially the Gourdou-Leseurre GL-812 and then the GL-832. The latter was replaced by the Loire-Nieuport 130 from the mid 1930s (except in *Lamotte-Piquet*), but only one could be accommodated. In 1942 *Primaguet* had the light AA increased by two 25mm and twenty 13.2mm MG, while *Duguay-Trouin* had her tubes removed on reactivation in 1943, receiving fifteen 20mm (15 x 1) and six 13.2mm (3 x 2). Her catapult and aircraft were also landed, whereas the other two retained theirs. In 1944 *Duguay-Trouin* was modified further, now having six 40mm (3 x 2) and twenty 20mm, all singles. Radar was also added. Postwar, the 155mm (6.1in) were replaced by guns from *Bearn*, her own having been worn out by bombardments off Indo-China. *Lamotte-Piquet* probably received little or no modification before her loss.

Service These ships proved most satisfactory in service, at least in peacetime and during their limited war service, when the thin skin was never called into account. On trials, all exceeded 33kts and were economical steamers as well as good seaboats. On the debit side, their high freeboard forward made them susceptible to winds and, as with all 'Mediterranean' designs, they were somewhat short-legged. Their armament proved satisfactory, except that the breech mechanism was slow in operation, leading to a reduction in the rate of fire.

Lamotte-Piquet served as a divisional flagship from completion until 1933, based initially at Brest with the 3rd Light division, part of the 2nd Squadron. In 1935 she was despatched to the Far East, where she was stationed at the outbreak of war. In the first instance her duties consisted mainly of patrols off the coast of Indo-China, in the China Sea and in the East Indies during 1939/40. However, increased tension along the borders with Siam, which began in November 1940, led to a naval force being despatched into the gulf of Siam the following year. *Lamotte-Piquet*, together with the sloops *Amiral Charnier*, *Dumont d'Urville*, *Marne* and *Tahure*, engaged a superior but anchored force of Siamese ships off the Koh Chang Archipelago on 17 January and sank the coast defence ship *Dhonburi* and two torpedoboats, severely damaging the remainder at no cost to the French forces. The French cruiser fired over 450 rounds and made two torpedo attacks during the engagement.

Thereafter, the activities of the Vichy French forces in the Far East were greatly curtailed, the cruiser making only a few local sorties, though these included a period in dock at Osaka, Japan, in September 1941. She was paid off to reserve at Saigon at the end of 1942, and then used as a training hulk, only to be sunk at her mooring by US carrier aircraft of TF38 on 12 January 1945.

Duguay-Trouin also joined the 2nd Squadron at Brest on completion. In 1929 she became flagship of the 3rd Light Division, part of the 1st Squadron in the Mediterranean. A long cruise to Indo-China was made in 1931, and then, between 1932 and 1935, she was flagship of the 2nd Squadron at Brest. At the end of 1936 *Duguay-Trouin* became a Gunnery Training ship, in which role she was still serving in June 1939, when she joined the 6th Cruiser Division. Early wartime service included Atlantic sweeps to intercept Axis merchantmen and raiders; the 5,889-ton *Halle* was one success, on 16 October 1939. At the beginning of May 1940 she was transferred to the Levant and based at Beiruit for operations in the Dodecanese and Adriatic, but as a result of the French collapse she joined Admiral Godfroy's Force X at Alexandria in July. She remained in a demilitarised state until she rejoined the Allied cause in July 1943, and was employed for the first six months of 1944 as a fast troop transport. Later, she participated in the landings in the south of France, and then undertook bombardment duties along the coast as far as Genoa until as late as April 1945. Postwar, *Duguay-Trouin* was transferred to Indo-China and served in that theatre, supporting the army operations against the Viet-Minh until 1952.

Primaguet began her service with a world cruise, leaving Brest on 20 April 1927 and returning on 20 December. For the next few years she spent several months each year on extended cruises. On 15 April 1932 she sailed for the Far East, where she remained until sailing for home for refit on 10 January 1936. After post-refit trials in September 1937, the ship

returned once more to the Far East, arriving in Saigon on 21 November. Relieved by *Suffren* at the outbreak of war, *Primaguet* carried out a couple of Atlantic patrols in 1939 and also escorted convoys. In March 1940 she was based in Oran and carried out a number of missions, including surveillance of the Canary Islands for Axis shipping. On 1 April 1940 she sailed for Fort de France in the West Indies, to replace *Jean d'Arc*, carrying out mercantile warfare duties en route. Five merchantmen of various nationalities were intercepted. After reaching Fort de France she operated in Dutch East Indies waters, searching some twenty ships in April. On 6 May 1940 *Primaguet* relieved HMS *Dundee* off Aruba and, when the Dutch surrender became known, the French cruiser landed forces to secure the oil installations. She returned to Dakar on 12 June 1940, and was present during the attack by the Royal Navy on 7/8 July. After the Armistice she was part of the naval forces in Morocco and participated in operations in support of African Vichy French territories when they were threatened by Free French activities. On 4 September the cruiser was ordered to Dakar to reinforce the forces there, and was then sent to escort an oiler in support of cruisers of the 4th Squadron (see *La Galissonnière* class) engaged in an operation to Libreville. In the Bight of Benin the French force was intercepted by the British cruisers *Cornwall* and *Dehli* when, as a result of negotiations, and, no doubt, a desire to avoid further

incidents like Dakar, *Primaguet* was ordered to turn back to Casablanca by Amiral Bourague, aboard *Georges Leygues*.

Primaguet remained at Casablanca, hampered by fuel shortages, until the Allied attack in November 1942. At this time she was under refit and not fully operational, but returned the US

gunfire, being hit herself three times by duds. The overwhelming superiority of US TF38 soon showed, and the French cruiser was heavily hit, suffering many casualties (45 dead and over 200 wounded). After burning throughout the night, the wreck was abandoned in the port and became a total loss.

DUQUESNE CLASS

Ship	Builder	Laid Down	Launched	Completed	Fate
Duquesne	Brest Navy Yard	30 Oct 24	17 Dec 25	6 Dec 28	Condemned 2 Jul 1955
Tourville	Lorient Navy Yard	4 Mar 25	24 Aug 26	1 Dec 28	Condemned 8 Mar 1962

Displacement: 10,000 tons/10,160 tonnes (standard); 12,200 tons/12,395 tonnes (full load).
Length: 626ft 9in/191m (oa); 607ft/185.0m (pp).
Beam: 62ft 3in/19.0m; Draught: 20ft 9in/6.32m (mean).
Machinery: 4-shaft Rateau-Bretagne SR geared turbines; 9 Guyot boilers.
Performance: 120,000shp=33¾kts; Bunkerage: 1,820tons oil fuel.

Range: 4,500nm at 15kts.
Protection: 30mm box citadel for magazines; 30mm deck, turrets & conning tower.
Guns: eight 8in (4x2); eight 75mm (8x1); eight 37mm (4x2); twelve 13.2mm MGs.
Torpedoes: twelve 21.7in (4x3).
Aircraft: two, one catapult.
Complement: 605.

Design France, as a major naval power, could not afford to ignore the advent of the 'Washington' 10,000-ton cruiser any more than could the other naval powers, irrespective of the need for such a design. In consequence, two such ships were authorised under the 1924 programme. In design and layout they appeared to be derived from the *Lamotte-Piquet* design, but this was hardly surprising, as there was no other modern French design on which to base the new ships. No 8in (203mm) gun existed in the French armoury, so one had to be designed, the 203mm/50 M1924, which fired a 134kg projectile. French naval architects soon found, like their contemporaries, that the Washington Treaty restrictions forced compromise in many areas of design. The French

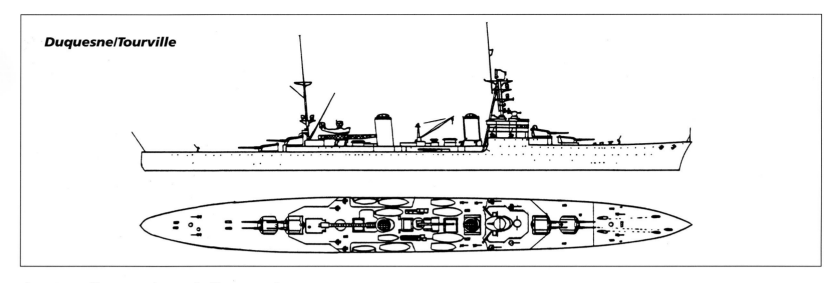

Duquesne/Tourville

chose to sacrifice protection, again like many of their rivals, to comply with the limits. The first light cruisers had but little protection, and these new ships were scarcely any better. Their armour amounted to about 3½ per cent of full load displacement, some 430 tons, being limited to a box citadel around the magazines and machinery, while the main deck was 30mm at the most.

The machinery installation, arranged on the unit principle, comprised nine Guyot boilers operating at a slightly higher pressure than those in *Lamotte-Piquet*, with a four-shaft Rateau-Bretagne single-reduction geared turbine arrangement producing 120,00shp for a maximum speed of 33¾kts. Both ships exceeded this on their trials.

The increased beam and length allowed the installation of double the 75mm outfit, but still as single mountings grouped amidships and around the after control position. They also received four of the new 37mm M1925-pattern single mountings at completion, these later being replaced by M1933 twins, together with the usual complement of 13.2mm MGs. This light AA was largely ineffective, as the 37mm was only semi-automatic, while the 13.2mm lacked stopping power, though the same could be said of many contemporary foreign designs. As with the previous ships, a heavy torpedo outfit was fitted, there being four triple mountings. The aircraft installation was moved forward to the after superstructure, where a catapult was fitted. The initial aircraft issued was the GL-812. This was superseded first by the GL-832 and then by the Loire-Nieuport 130 by the outbreak of war. Both ships were ordered from Naval yards, one each from Brest and Lorient, the orders being placed on 1 July 1924.

Modifications Little was done to these ships during their early years, and a 1935 proposal to convert

them into light carriers equipped for twelve to fourteen aircraft in view of their poor protection was abandoned for the construction of two true carriers (*Joffre* class). After their return to the Allied cause both were refitted; the aircraft installations and torpedo tubes were landed, the masting was altered, a distinctive cowl was added to the fore funnel and radar was installed. Light AA was increased to eight 40mm (2 x 4) on a platform in place of the main mast, and the original French pattern AA guns were supplanted by sixteen single 20mm, four each around the bridge, waist and quarterdeck.

Service *Duquesne* made her first appearance at the large naval review in Le Havre on 3 July 1928, following this with a cruise to Guadaloupe via

New York. The next year she made a seven-month cruise around Africa. From November 1929 she was flagship of the 1st Light Division as part of the 1st Squadron at Toulon. She made several more foreign cruises, including one, in October 1931, to the USA for the 150th anniversary of the Battle of Yorktown. From 1932 to 1938 the ship was based at Toulon with the 1st and 3rd Light Divisions, and then served with the Gunnery School until the outbreak of war. On 25 January 1940 she sailed for Dakar, where she remained until April as part of one of the Hunting Groups formed to find the German raiders then at sea. In May 1940 she sailed for Alexandria as flagship of the 2nd Cruiser Division of Force X, formed after the declaration

Left: *Tourville* in the 1920s. (MPL)
Above: *Duquesne* in December 1945, showing alterations made during her refit in the USA. (MB)

of war by Italy to reinforce British forces in the eastern Mediterranean. Their only operation before the fall of France was an abortive sortie into the Adriatic on 12/13 June. Immobilised until 24 June 1943, *Duquesne* then sailed around the Cape to Dakar, where she was based until April 1944. She was now (from December 1943) a unit of the 1st Cruiser Division engaged on anti-blockade runner duties in the Atlantic. In May 1944 *Duquesne* arrived on the Clyde and was used as a replenishment ship during Operation Neptune.

Thereafter she was attached to Group Lorraine of the French Naval Task force, formed in December 1944 for the purpose of bombarding the now isolated German-held 'fortress's' on the French Atlantic coast. By this time she was badly in need of refit, and spent from June to November 1945 under major refit in Brest. There followed a period on transport duties, including to Indo-China, where she participated in two campaigns, from January to November 1946 and December 1946 to August 1947, covering landings and bombarding shore positions. In August 1947 she was placed in Special reserve 'A' at Toulon, then transferred to Arzew in Algeria as a floating base ship for Amphibious Forces, where she remained until condemned for disposal on 2 July 1955.

Tourville sailed **for a world** cruise on 5 April 1929, returning to **Lorient** on 24 December. In 1930 she transferred to **Toulon** as a unit of the 1st Light Division, and in **1934** joined the 3rd Light Division. During the Spanish Civil War *Tourville* participated in the evacuation of refugees, and generally protected French interests between August 1936 and May 1937. At the beginning of January 1939 the ship began a major refit at Toulon, after which she joined the 2nd Cruiser Division at Toulon in August. She was engaged upon searching for Axis merchant ships in the Mediterranean, and made a cruise from Bizerte to Beiruit from 8 to 26 December, during which 32 ships were stopped. Another round trip from Toulon to Beiruit was made between 20 January and 7 February for the purpose of a large gold shipment. She joined Force X at Alexandria and operated with *Duquesne* until July, then remained demilitarised until 1943. Returning to service, she formed part of the 1st Cruiser Division at Dakar until sent to Bizerte for refit in June 1944, and then to Toulon in November, where, from December, she was used as a base ship for escort vessels.

Postwar she was despatched to Indo-China, arriving in Saigon on 16 January 1946 and serving in support of shore operations until her return to Toulon on 27 July 1946. A second tour followed between 8 October 1946 and 15 November 1947, and she arrived back in France on 11 December. This was the end of her active service. She was thereafter used as a pontoon and accommodation hulk at Brest until stricken on 28 April 1961, having been anchored at Lannion for 14 years. On 15 January 1963 *Tourville* was towed from Brest, bound for scrapping at Toulon La Ciotat.

SUFFREN CLASS

Ship	Builder	Laid Down	Launched	Completed	Fate
Suffren	Brest Navy Yard	17 Apr 26	3 May 27	1 Jan 30	Broken up 1974
Colbert	Brest Navy Yard	12 June 27	20 Apr 28	4 Mar 31	Scuttled at Toulon 27 Nov 42
Foch	Brest Navy Yard	21 Jun 28	24 Apr 29	15 Sep 31	Scuttled at Toulon 27 Nov 42
Dupleix	Brest Navy Yard	14 Nov 29	9 Oct 30	20 Jul 32	Scuttled at Toulon 27 Nov 42

Displacement: 10,000 tons/10,160 tonnes (standard); 12,780 tons/12,984 tonnes (full load).
Length: 636ft 6in/194.0m (oa); 607ft/185.0m (pp).
Beam: 63ft/19.10m; Draught: 20ft 9in/6.35m (mean).
Machinery: 3-shaft Rateau-Bretagne SR geared turbines; 9 Guyot boilers.
Performance: 90,000shp=31kts; Bunkerage: 1,800tons oil fuel.
Range: 4,500nm at 15 kts.
Protection: *Suffren*: 50mm main belt; 25mm U/deck & main deck; 30mm turrets; 30mm CT. Others: 54-60mm main belt; 22-25mm* U/deck & main deck; 30mm turrets; 30mm CT. *Dupleix* 30mm.
Guns: eight 8in (4x2); eight 3.5in (8x1) (*Dupleix* 4x2); *Suffren*: eight 75mm (8x1); eight 37mm (4x2); twelve 13.2mm MGs (4x3).
Torpedoes: six 21.7in (2x3).
Aircraft: three except *Suffren* two, two catapults.
Complement: 752 (war) except *Suffren*, 773.

Design The 1925 programme included provision for another 'Washington' or heavy cruiser, based on the *Tourville* design but sensibly incorporating increased protection at the expense of speed. Extra beam and a three-shaft machinery arrangement were noticeable variations from the *Tourville* design. The installed power was reduced by 25 per cent, but the weight saved allowed a 50mm armoured belt and a 25mm deck, the armour totalling 951 tons, twice that of *Tourville*, whilst the top speed was only reduced to 31kts. The 8in guns were of the same mark as those of the first French heavy cruisers, as were the secondary guns. The torpedo battery was reduced to two triple banks, but two catapults were fitted instead of the one, on the superstructure abaft the after funnel. The aircraft issued were Loire-Nieuport 130s, of which two could be accommodated. An order was placed with the Brest Naval Yard on 1 November 1925, and the

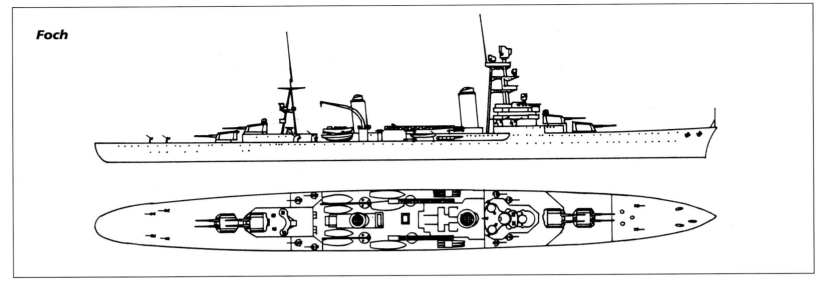

Foch

name *Suffren* allocated. A second ship was authorised under the 1926 programme (Law of 4 August 1926), and ordered from the same yard on 1 March 1927. However, while it was nominally a sister ship, the new unit, *Colbert*, differed in a number of ways and could properly be described as a half-sister. She was slightly shorter in length overall, and had reduced beam, partly as a result of a rearrangement of the armour. Her appearance differed from that of the first ship in that the catapults were now between the funnels, and a different pattern of crane was fitted. Three aircraft could now be accommodated. There were also other minor differences in rig details.

As far as the armament was concerned, the only change was the replacement of the 75mm AA by new M1926-pattern 90mm (3.54in) guns, still in single mountings.

Internally, economies in the weight of the machinery allowed the scale of protection to be increased to a total of 1,374 tons, of which the

vertical protection was brought inside the hull and increased to 54-60mm for the whole length of the machinery spaces, whilst the shell plating was reduced to 20mm (.79in). The side spaces abreast the after boiler room and along the engine rooms were filled with coal, which served as additional protection and as fuel for the auxiliary cruising boilers. Installed power was increased to 106,000shp for a maximum speed of 33kts.

In 1927 a third unit was authorised and ordered from Brest once more, with the name *Foch*. This ship differed again in detail, in that the coal-fired boilers were not fitted but the coal bunkers were retained as protection, while the auxiliary boiler room was converted to an oil bunker. Hull dimensions differed only marginally from those of *Colbert*, but again there were minor differences in rig.

Dupleix, the final unit of the class, differed yet again in that her protection was further augmented to a total of 1,553 tons, mainly due to an

increased main deck of 30mm (1.25in). Unlike the others, however, she shipped her 90mm in pattern M1930 twin mountings. Once again, the Brest Naval yard won the order, which was placed on 1 April 1929 under the programme for that year.

Modifications No major alterations were carried out before the war, nor for some time thereafter. *Suffren*, after her re-entry into active service in 1943, landed the aircraft fittings, torpedo tubes and main mast in exchange for two quadruple 40mm Bofors, which replaced the latter. Twenty 20mm singles were added, around the bridge, in the waist and on the quarterdeck. *Colbert* had her light AA augmented while in Vichy service in 1941/42, receiving six 37mm, (6 x 1), twenty 13.2mm (4 x 4, 2 x 2) and four 8mm (4 x 1). *Foch* and *Dupleix* received eight single 37mm and twenty 13.2mm, plus seven and three 8mm respectively.

Service *Suffren* entered service in 1929, having achieved an average speed of 32.5kts on trial with 100,089shp, then joined the 1st Light Division and served with the Mediterranean Squadron until 1939. However, in the spring of that year it had been decided to relieve *Primaguet* with *Suffren*, and as a result she sailed from Toulon on 21 June 1939 bound for Saigon, where she arrived on 23 July as flagship of the Indo-China squadron. On the outbreak of war she carried out patrols in the South China Sea and searched for German merchantmen off the Dutch East Indies. Then, at the end of November 1939, she arrived at Singapore to participate in the escorting of major

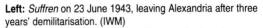

Left: *Suffren* on 23 June 1943, leaving Alexandria after three years' demilitarisation. (IWM)

Right: *Colbert* in February 1941. Note re-adoption of tricolour markings on the turrets. (MB)

Above: *Foch* prior to the war. (WZB)   Below: *Suffren* in January 1938. (MB)

Australian troopship convoys across the Indian Ocean, together with HMS *Kent*. These duties continued until the end of April 1940, and on 5 May *Suffren* sailed from Columbo to return to the eastern Mediterranean via Aden and Suez. On 18 May she arrived at Alexandria for service with Admiral Godfroy's squadron. There was time for only one raid into the Aegean after Italy's declaration of war and before the French armistice, between 11 and 13 June, but this was without result. A second operation for the purpose of bombarding the port of Bardia on 21 June in company with *Duguay-Trouin* and *Lorraine* was also completed. Then, as a result of the armistice, *Suffren* remained immobilised for the next three years until, in May 1943, Admiral Godfroy decided to rejoin the Allies. After circumnavigating Africa the cruiser arrived in Dakar on 3 September 1943, from where she immediately began search patrols into the south Atlantic for Axis blockade runners. This duty continued until 1944, the ship sailing as far afield as Recife in Brazil, and she then spent the remainder of the war under refit at Casablanca. Postwar, she carried out a number of transport and repatriation missions between Metropolitan France and Indo-China before an active tour of duty in Indo-China between 26 February 1946 and 21 March 1947, when she arrived back in Toulon. On 1 October 1947 the ship was placed in reserve and used as a pontoon base at Toulon.

Colbert joined the 1st Light Division in the Mediterranean on completion, where she spent the next few years in normal peacetime duties. A major refit was carried out at Lorient between 16 February 1935 and January 1936, after which she joined the International Patrol in Spanish waters during the Civil War. In September 1939 she was based at Oran, then returned to Toulon in January 1940, being placed under the orders of Admiral (Africa) on the 24th for patrol duties in connection with the search for *Admiral Hipper*. Returning to France in April, she remained based at Toulon until the declaration of war by Italy, when she participated in a raid into the Gulf of Genoa on 13 June, bombarding shore positions and in turn being attacked by Italian MTBs. After the armistice she began a major refit at Toulon on 1 August 1940 and was placed in care and maintenance until December. In January 1941 she joined the 1st Cruiser Division, but on 27 November 1942, on the entry of German forces into the unoccupied zone, she was sabotaged by her crew, the resultant fires burning for six days and breaking out again on 7 December, by which time the ship was a total loss. The burnt-out hulk was raised and scrapped in 1946/47.

Foch saw service in the protection of French interests during the troubles in Greece in March 1935, and thereafter served with the 1st Light

Division, the 3rd Light Division and finally with the 1st Cruiser Division of the 3rd Squadron, being based at Toulon by September 1939. In October she was detached to Oran to join the Franco-British hunting groups searching for German raiders in the Tropics, then carried out escort duties between Morocco and Bermuda until February, when she returned to Toulon for refit. After re-entering service, *Foch* participated in the bombardment of the Italian coast near Vado on 13/14 June, her last operation with the Allied forces. She remained in service with the Vichy French High Seas Force at Toulon until 4 October 1941, when she was reduced to care and maintenance. On 27 November 1942, following sabotage by her crew, *Foch* sank at her moorings. Refloated on 16 April 1943 by the Italians, she was then scrapped.

Dupleix served with the Mediterranean forces as part of the 1st Light Division from completion until the outbreak of war, undergoing a major refit in 1937. In 1939 she was detached to Dakar to

Above: *Dupleix* on 16 October 1940. Note twin 90mm. (MB)

hunt for German raiders and merchantmen in the south and central Atlantic, assisting in the capture of the 4,627-ton *Santa Fe* by contre-torpilleurs on 25 October. On her return to the Mediterranean she took part in the raid on Genoa in June 1940, and after the armistice remained at Toulon until she was scuttled on 27 November 1942. Although refloated on 3 July 1943, she was subsequently sunk again during an air raid in 1944.

JEANNE D'ARC CLASS

Ship	Builder	Laid Down	Launched	Completed	Fate
Jeanne d'Arc	A & C de St. Nazaire	31 Aug 28	14 Feb 30	14 Sep 31	Stricken 1965

Displacement: 6,496 tons/6,600 tonnes (standard); 8,950 tons/9,093 tonnes (full load).
Length: 557ft 9in/170.0m (oa); 525ft/160.0m (pp).
Beam: 58ft/17.7m; Draught: 21ft/6.4m (mean).
Machinery: 2-shaft Parsons SR geared turbines; 4 Penhoët boilers.
Performance: 32,500shp=25kts; Bunkerage: 1,400 tons oil fuel.
Range: 5,200nm at 11kts.
Protection: 20mm box citadel for magazines; 30mm CT.
Guns: eight 6.1in (4x2); four 75mm (4x1); four 37mm (2x2); twelve 13.2mm MGs (4x3).
Torpedoes: two 21.7in, (2x1).
Aircraft: two, no catapult.
Complement: 648 (war).

Design The 1926 programme, in addition to authorising *Colbert*, also sanctioned a new type of vessel for the French Navy, a cruiser which was specially fitted for the training role. A ship of cruiser size was ideal for such a purpose because of its ability to accommodate numbers of trainees, and obsolescent ships had been used in this manner previously. However, the construction of a new ship for the task was unusual. In the case of the French ship, she was given the full armament of a cruiser, eight 6.1in (155mm), in twin turrets as in *Duguay-Trouin*, and in fact was the only other cruiser to receive this model gun. A reduced torpedo outfit was incorporated, and the other main concession to

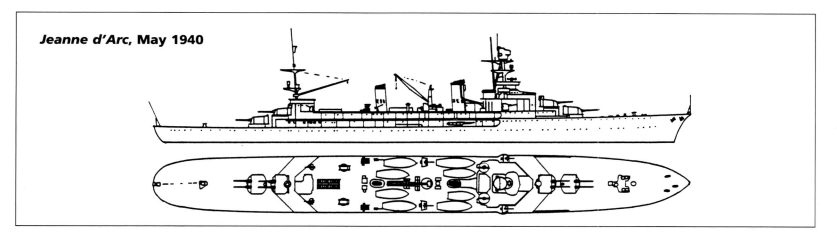

Jeanne d'Arc, May 1940

the space requirements of a large number men under instruction was the reduced machinery arrangement. A two-shaft geared turbine layout with only a four-boiler steam plant gave an installed shp of 32,500 for a maximum speed of 25kts.

In appearance the ship gave a liner-like impression, with the amidships structure built up by cabin accommodation, but otherwise the distinctive cruiser form was still evident. No protective scheme was included, save for some light plating in the way of the magazines. Two Loire-Nieuport 130 flying-boats could be accommodated, although the two catapults were finally deleted from the design and the aeroplanes handled by the cranes for take-off and alighting. The contract for the new ship was won by the Penhoët yard of

A & C de St Nazaire, the order being placed on 8 October 1928.

Modifications Few or no modifications were made until 1943, when the aircraft installations and torpedo tubes were landed, to be replaced by six 40mm (6 x 1) and twenty single 20mm. All of the original French light AA was removed at the same time, and the main mast was struck.

Service *Jeanne d'Arc* made her first cruise in the training role in 1931/32, when she visited Brazil and Argentina, rounded Cape Horn and returned to France by way of the Panama Canal, West Indies and Morocco. Later she also visited the Levant. The following year she made her first world cruise, followed by another in 1937/38, but her normal routine was to repeat

the 1931/32 itinerary. However, political events forced the curtailment of her eighth cruise, in 1939, which was to be the last before the war. Her initial duties were anti-blockade-runner patrols in the western Atlantic, then in May 1940 she and *Emile Bertin* were ordered to transport the French gold reserves, some 200 tons, to Halifax, Nova Scotia. On completion of this task she was ordered to Pointe-a-Pitre, in the French Antilles, where she remained until 1943. During this period *Jeanne d'Arc* escorted Atlantic convoys and patrolled the Caribbean. On 31 July 1943 she sailed from Fort de France

Below: *Jeanne d'Arc* on a cruise in the tropics, with awnings rigged. She is carrying a Loire 130 aircraft. (MPL)

en route for Philadelphia and refit, but this was subsequently cancelled and instead she sailed for Casablanca, where she arrived on 9 September. Moving into the Mediterranean once more, she was rearmed in Algiers by 300 specialists from the US repair ship *Vulcan* between the afternoon of 17 September and 3pm on 19 Sep-tember. Once rearmed she carried out transport missions to and from Ajaccio, Corsica, until her return to Casablanca on 20 January 1944 to start a refit. This was completed in May, when she returned to transport missions. During October 1944 to 15 March 1945 the ship was attached to the Flank Force and engaged upon the bom-bardment of German shore positions along the Ligurian coast.

Postwar, *Jeanne d'Arc* was refitted, resuming her peacetime role in July 1946. She subsequently made three more world cruises, in 1955/56, 1961/62 and 1962/63, before being stricken from the active list in 1965.

ALGÉRIE CLASS

Ship	Builder	Laid Down	Launched	Completed	Fate
Algérie	Brest Navy Yard	19 Mar 31	21 May 32	15 Sep 34	Scuttled at Toulon 27 Nov 42

Displacement: 10,000 tons/10,160 tonnes (standard); 13,461 tons/13,677 tonnes (full load).

Length: 610ft 9in/186.2m (oa); 590ft 9in/180m (pp).

Beam: 65ft 9in/20m; Draught: 20ft 3in/6.15m, (mean).

Machinery: 4-shaft Rateau-Bretagne SR geared turbines; 6 Indret boilers.

Performance: 84,000shp=31kts; Bunkerage: 2,935 tons oil fuel.

Range: 8,700nm at 15kts.

Protection: 110mm main belt; 80mm max main deck; 100mm turrets (face); 100mm CT.

Guns: eight 8in (4x2); twelve 3.9in (6x2); eight 37mm (4x2).

Torpedoes: six 21.7in (3x2).

Aircraft: three, one catapult.

Complement: 748.

Design In the year following that in which *Dupleix* was authorised, a seventh heavy cruiser was programmed which radically departed from the formula established for the earlier ships. Using the experience gained in the designing of ships to very tight treaty limits, the Technical Department was able to incorporate into the new design some significant advances, to produce perhaps one of the best Washington cruisers of any navy. The new ship reverted to quadruple-screw machinery, reintroduced exterior belt armour protection and abandoned the unit machinery principle in the interests of adopting a single funnel to conserve upper deck space. The hull was flush decked to enhance strength, and the familiar tripod foremast was dispensed with, endowing the ship with a unique silhouette.

In contrast to *Dupleix*, whose armour totalled 1,553 tons, this ship incorporated 1,720 tons in the hull and an additional 315 tons in the armament, a total of 2,035 tons. This included a side belt of 110mm (4.33in) between 3.75m and 4.45m high, a torpedo bulkhead of 40 to 60mm (1.57 to 2.36in), and an armoured deck of 80mm (3.14in) between the torpedo bulkheads and 30 to 40mm outside them. There was also an upper deck armour of 22mm (.86in) and three armoured transverse bulkheads of 70mm (2.75in). The turret faces and tops were 100mm, the sides and rear 70mm.

The main machinery comprised five Indret boilers working at a slightly increased pressure of 27kg/cm² and a Rateau-Bretagne geared turbine installation of 84,000shp. The machinery for the inner shafts was constructed by A. C. Bretagne, while that for the outer shafts was built by Indret. Trials proved particularly successful, 32.93kts being achieved on 93,230shp on 2 February 1934.

The usual eight 8in (203mm) guns in twin turrets were installed, but the secondary armament was increased to twelve 100mm (3.93in) Model M1930 in M1931 twin mounts. Light AA was made up of the standard 37mm M1925 in four single mountings and sixteen 13.2mm Hotchkiss in M1929 quadruple mountings. Provision was made for aircraft, but, unlike the previous class, this ship mounted only one catapult, abaft the funnel on the port side. No hangar was fitted, the two seaplanes being stowed on the spar deck and on the catapult. Initial equipment was the Gourdou-Leseurre 810, later supplanted by the 830 and finally by the larger Loire-Nieuport 130.

Yet again, the Brest Navy Yard won the order, the contract being placed in August 1930. The ship was laid down as *Algérie* on 19 March 1931. **Modifications** During a refit between January and March 1937, some alterations were made to the

Opposite page:

Top: *Algérie* in 1935, with GL 810 floatplanes. (MB)
Bottom: *Algérie* in August 1941, now with Loire 130 aircraft. (MB)

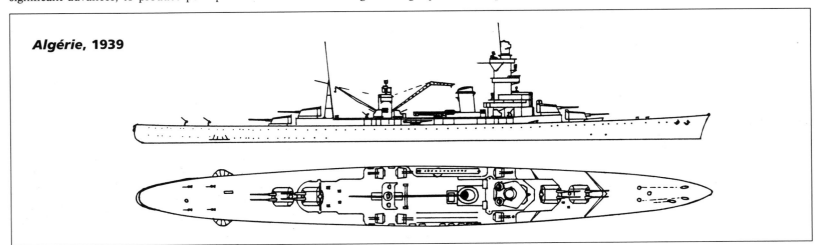

Algérie, 1939

Below: *Algérie* in her final state, August 1942. She appears to be equipped with some form of radar aerials either side of the range-finder clock on the foretop. (MB)

bridge, and the 5m rangefinder in the main director was replaced by one of 8m stereoscopic pattern. A year later the 37mm were regrouped on the quarterdeck and the quadruple 13.2mm at the after end of the boat deck were moved, one to the conning tower and the other to the after end of the quarterdeck.

Between November 1938 and the end of the year, C turret received an 8m stereo rangefinder in lieu of the 5m pattern, some modifications were made to the AA control position, and provision was made to take the larger Loire-Nieuport 130 aircraft. In the next refit, between December 1939 and the end of January 1940, the funnel cowl was altered and the 37mm was replaced by 37mm model M1937 twins. Four more 13.2mm (Browning) were added in the summer of 1941.

A major refit between May and August 1942 saw the main tripod mast removed and replaced by an AA superstructure on which were mounted two twin 37mm, two quadruple 13.2mm Hotchkiss and two single 13.2mm Browning. The remainder of the AA outfit was disposed as follows: two twin 37mm on the former admiral's bridge; two quadruple 13.2mm, one each port and starboard forward of P1 and S1 100mm guns; and one single 13.2mm abaft P3 and S3 100mm.

Service *Algérie* joined the 1st Squadron in the Mediterranean on commissioning as Flagship, forming the 1st Light Division with *Colbert* and *Dupleix*. She was, in fact, to serve as a flagship throughout her career. September 1939 saw *Algérie* as flagship of the 3rd Squadron, which comprised the 1st Cruiser Squadron (*Algérie*, *Dupleix*, *Foch* and *Duquesne*, *Tourville* and *Colbert*) and the 3rd Light Squadron (5th, 7th and 9th CT divisions). On 4 October a French squadron was formed for the purpose of hunting the German raiders in the Atlantic, comprising *Strasbourg*, *Algérie*, *Dupleix* and the British carrier *Hermes*, based at Dakar. This operated as Forces M and N, the duty lasting until 26 November for *Algérie*, which then arrived back in Toulon for a refit period. Her next task was to transport 1,179 cases of gold to Canada, together with *Bretagne* (1,820 cases), between 11 March and their return to France on 10 April 1940. After Italy's entry into the war, *Algérie* took part in the bombardment of Genoa on 13/14 June and then undertook a convoy cover operation on 17/18 June before the fall of France. She was included in the Vichy High Seas force from October 1940, which consisted of those ships remaining in active commissioned service, but the only sortie, other than exercises, was to escort *Provence* home after her escape from Oran in November 1940. *Algérie* was sabotaged by her crew on 27 November 1942, and burned for two days. On 18 March 1943 the wreck was refloated and subsequently broken up.

EMILE BERTIN CLASS

Ship	Builder	Laid Down	Launched	Completed	Fate
Emile Bertin	At & Ch St. Nazaire	18 Aug 31	9 May 33	28 Jan 35	Scrapped Oct 59

Displacement: 5,886 tons/5,980 tonnes (standard); 8,480 tons/8,615 tonnes (full load).

Length: 580ft 9in/177.0m (oa); 548ft/167.0m (pp).

Beam: 52ft 6in/16m; Draught: 21ft 9in/6.6m (mean).

Machinery: 4-shaft Parsons SR geared turbines; 6 Penhoët boilers.

Performance: 102,000shp=34kts; Bunkerage: 1,360 tons oil fuel.

Range: 3,600nm at 15kts.

Protection: 30mm box citadel to magazines; 20mm main deck; 20mm CT.

Guns: nine 6in (3x3); four 3.5in (1x2, 2x1); eight 37mm (4x2); eight 13.2mm MGs (4x2).

Torpedoes: six 21.7in (2x3).

Aircraft: two, one catapult.

Complement: 711.

Design At the same time as *Algérie* was authorised (Law of 12 January 1930), another cruiser was sanctioned, but this time as a minelayer, an improved *Pluton*, in fact. In contrast to that ship however, cruiser qualities were given greater emphasis in the new design and, as it turned out, the minelaying abilities, were never to be employed. Although frequently described as an improved *Pluton*, this ship appears to owe nothing to the earlier vessel, and seems to have been a completely new design. Classed as a light cruiser and armed with nine 6in, *Emile Bertin* introduced both a new model of gun and the triple turret into the French navy. The gun was the 152mm (actually 152.4mm) M1930, firing a 54.17kg (119lb) projectile with a range of 26,474m

(28,952yd). The turrets were electro-hydraulic with RPC, maximum elevation was 45°, and they proved very successful, unlike the DP version intended for the battleship *Richelieu*, which were too ambitious with their 90° elevation *and* loading. The secondary armament was all grouped aft around the after shelter deck, with the light AA on the forecastle abreast the bridge structure. In its designed role as a minelayer, 200 mines could be accommodated.

From the constructional point of view, the ship was very lightly built and, with a four-shaft 102,000shp (designed) machinery installation, exceedingly fast, recording a maximum speed of 39.66kts with 137,908shp on trials in inclement weather. According to some reports the ship well exceeded 40kts at times. However, continuous high-speed running in heavy weather under full service load conditions would certainly have been a different matter because of the light construc-

Below: *Emile Bertin* in August 1939. (MB)

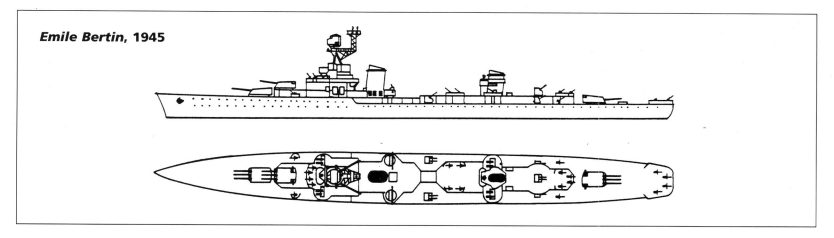

Emile Bertin, 1945

tion, as the need to strengthen the hull after entry into service (to permit salvo firing) illustrated.

The protective scheme was minimal, with a box citadel to the magazines of 30mm and a main deck of 25mm.

The order was placed with A & C de St Nazaire-Penhoët on 11 September 1931, the ship being named after the naval architect Emile Bertin.

Modifications During refit in the USA between August and December 1943, the AA outfit was modernised and augmented. Two twin 90mm were added on the main deck amidships, in lieu of the torpedo tubes, and the catapult and aircraft were removed. Four quadruple US-pattern 40mm were installed, two in the enlarged bridge wings port and starboard, and two on sponsons abreast the after funnel. Twenty single 20mm were added around the bridge, amidships, and on the extreme stern. All French-pattern light AA was landed. A lattice extension to the fore mast carried radar.

Service *Emile Bertin* assumed the role of Flagship of Admiral Commanding Contre-Torpilleur divisions, Light Divisions, Atlantic Squadron on her entry into service, but by the beginning of 1939 was serving in the Mediterranean at Toulon. When war broke out the ship was at Bizerte, and shortly thereafter was ordered to Beirut to embark a cargo in secret, which actually consisted of the gold reserves of the Bank of Poland. The cruiser arrived in the Lebanon on 23 September, loaded 57 tons of gold, and sailed for Toulon, where she arrived on 27 September. Following this exercise, *Emile Bertin* went into refit until January 1940. That month she participated in the surveillance operations carried out around the Canary Islands to ensure that no German forces were present, but by mid-February had proceeded to Brest for some dockyard work. At the beginning of April she was wearing the flag of Admiral Derrien, commanding Group Z, which comprised the cruiser *Montcalm* and the 2,400-tonne contre-torpilleurs *Tartu*, *Chevalier Paul*, *Maille Breze*, *Milan*, *Bison* and *Épervier*, as well as the 1,500-tonne *Brestois*, *Boulonnais* and *Foudroyant*. The group was under orders to support the Allied operations in Norway, and sailed for Scapa Flow on 6 April.

During these operations *Emile Bertin* was attacked by Junkers Ju 88s of II.KG 30 and damaged by bombs on 19 April. She returned to Brest for repair and remained there until 21 May, when she sailed for Halifax, Nova Scotia, in company with *Jeanne d'Arc*, carrying gold from the Bank of France, arriving on 1 June. After her return she carried out a second operation, sailing on 11 June, but after her arrival in Halifax the French Government asked for an armistice, and in consequence ship was ordered not to unload her cargo (some 254 tons). Instead, she was ordered to sail for Fort de France and await further orders, and successfully departed Halifax despite some belief that the Royal Navy would attempt to stop her. In Fort de France the gold was landed and the cruiser took part in preparations to defend the island from an expected British attack by the cruisers *Fiji* and *Dunedin*, which was called off only after an appeal through the President of the USA. For the next two years or so the ship remained at anchor off Fort de France, with only the occasional sea exercise until, on 16 May 1942, she was ordered by the Vichy authorities to be immobilised after pressure from the USA. She remained in this state until August 1943, when she sailed for Philadelphia for refit before rejoining the Allied cause. She did not return to Fort de France until 21 December, sailing a week later for Dakar. From February 1944 she operated in the Mediterranean and took part in the landings in the south of France, Operation Dragoon, giving gunfire support along the French riviera coastline until October. After a couple of missions to Lebanon in December, *Emile Bertin* went into refit at Toulon from 30 December until October 1945, and sailed for the Far East as flagship on re-entering service. She remained in Indo-China, engaged upon the reoccupation of the colony, until she sailed for home with *Tourville* on 2 July 1946. After a period of service as a gunnery training ship she was scrapped in the late 1950s.

PLUTON CLASS

Ship	Builder	Laid Down	Launched	Completed	Fate
Pluton	Lorient Navy Yard	16 Apr 28	10 Apr 29	1 Oct 31	Lost 13 Sep 39

Displacement: 4,773 tons/4,849 tonnes (standard); 6,500 tons/6,604 tonnes (full load).
Length: 500ft 3in/152.5m, (oa); 472ft 6in/144m (pp).
Beam: 51ft 3in/15.6m; Draught: 17ft/5.18m (mean).
Machinery: 2-shaft Bréguet SR geared turbines; 4 boilers.
Performance: 57,000shp=30kts; Bunkerage: 1,200 tons oil fuel.
Range: n/k.
Protection: nil.
Guns: four 5.5in (4x1); four 75mm (4x1); two 37mm (2x1); twelve 13.2mm MGs (4x3).
Mines: 290.
Torpedoes: nil.
Aircraft: not equipped.
Complement: 424.

Design Authorised under the 1925 programme, this ship was designed as a dedicated minelaying cruiser very much in the concept of the British *Adventure*, of which she was a slightly smaller version. Like her British contemporary, whilst classified as a cruiser she was given the firepower of a destroyer or contre-torpilleur and, although she was faster than *Adventure*, did not quite have the speed of a true cruiser. The machinery arrangement, a twin-screw geared turbine layout, developed 57,000shp for a designed maximum speed of 30kts. Her main armament was the standard 138.6mm (5.45in) M1927 pattern also fitted in the *Aigle* and *Cassard* classes of contre-torpilleurs. Up to 290 mines could be carried, accommodated on the spacious mine deck, where there were four separate mine tracks. No aircraft or torpedo fittings were included in the design. From the start this ship was intended to have a dual role, as she was also equipped as a troop trans-

port. However, in 1933 she was also designated for use as a gunnery training ship (to replace the worn out *Gueydon*) and fitted out for this role as well, despite strong objections from her current CO, who feared an adverse effect on the main role of minelaying. These fears were well founded, and may well have contributed to her tragic loss. Finally, it was decided in 1939 to refit her as a seagoing training ship for sub-lieutenants, in which role she was to start duty on 1 June 1940 with the new name of *La Tour d'Auvergne*. In the event, her loss occurred before either the change in role or change of name could be effected.

Modifications By 1936, shields had been fitted to the secondary guns, and she later had a modified crane fitted. Aerial supports were added to the after funnel, and a new, taller, director was fitted atop the bridge.

Service *Pluton* joined the Training Division of the 1st Squadron, based at Toulon, when she finally entered service in 1932. In 1933 she became a gunnery training ship, remaining in this duty until her loss. On 1 October 1938 she was incorporated into the Gunnery division of the Training Squadron, which had been formed on the dissolution of the Training division. When, in May 1939, it was decided to form an Atlantic Fleet from the 1st and 5th Squadrons, *Pluton* was attached to the 5th Squadron along with *Duguay-Trouin*, and the Training Squadron disbanded on 10 June 1939. Late in August the 6th Cruiser division (*Duguay-Trouin* and *Primaguet*) and the 7th (*Pluton* and *Jeanne d'Arc*) were combined, but the attachment of the latter two to the 5th Squadron was short-lived, as *Jeanne d'Arc* was despatched to the Antilles and *Pluton* was earmarked for a task in her designed role. Fears of the appearance of German Panzerschiffe off Africa as a result of increased political tension led to the despatch of the minelayer to Casablanca, the ship sailing on 2 September. Unfortunately, plans were altered on her arrival, and while armed mines were being disembarked on 13 September a huge explosion took place which destroyed the ship and caused many casualties.

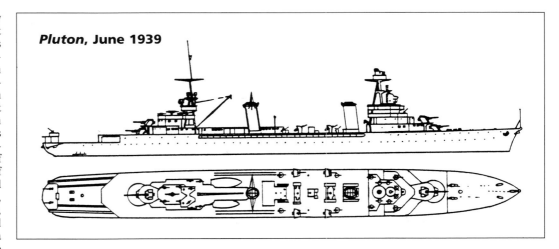

Pluton, June 1939

Below: *Pluton* in November 1938. (MB)

LA GALISSONNIÈRE CLASS

Ship	Builder	Laid Down	Launched	Completed	Fate
La Galissonnière	Brest Navy Yard	15 Dec 31	18 Nov 33	1 Apr 36	Scuttled at Toulon 27 Nov 42
Georges Leygues	At & Ch St. Nazaire	21 Sept 33	24 Mar 36	15 Nov 37	Scrapped Nov 1959
Gloire*	F & Ch Gironde	13 Nov 33	28 Sep 35	15 Nov 37	Scrapped Jan 1958
Jean de Vienne*	Lorient Navy Yard	20 Dec 31	31 Jul 35	10 Feb 37	Scuttled at Toulon 27 Nov 42
Marseillaise*	At & Ch de Loire	23 Oct 33	17 Jul 35	10 Oct 37	Scuttled at Toulon 27 Nov 42
Montcalm	F & Ch La Seyne	15 Nov 33	26 Oct 35	15 Nov 37	Hulked 1958

Displacement: 7,600 tons/7,721 tonnes (standard); 9,100 tons/9,245 tonnes (full load).
Length: 589ft/179.5m (oa); 564ft 3in/172.0m (pp).
Beam: 17ft 6in/17.48m; Draught: 17ft 6in/5.35m (mean).
Machinery: 2-shaft Parsons (*Rateau-Bretagne) SR geared turbines; 4 Indret boilers.

Performance: 84,000shp=31kts; Bunkerage:1,569 tons oil fuel.
Range: 7,000nm at 12kts.
Protection: 105mm main belt; 60mm end bulkheads; 38mm main deck; 100mm turrets; 95mm CT.
Guns: nine 6in (3x3); eight 3.5in (4x2); twelve 13.2mm MGs (4x3).
Torpedoes: four 21.7in (2x2).
Aircraft: four, one catapult.
Complement: 540.

Design The construction of two further light cruisers was authorised under the 1931 programme, an additional four being sanctioned the following year. The new design was considerably different to that of the first light cruisers constructed under the 1922 programme (*Duguay-Trouin*), and in general appearance at least owed more to *Emile Bertin*. Even so, there were major differences between the two designs. In particular, the protective scheme was more extensive, and returned to the concept of an external armour belt (105mm), closed off at the ends by transverse armoured bulkheads. In comparison to the minelaying cruiser, the main deck armour was

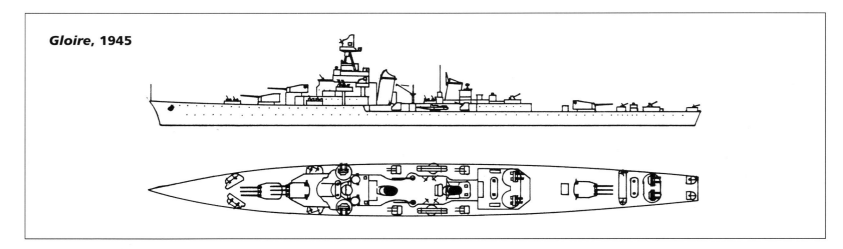

Gloire, 1945

also increased, but there had to be a compromise somewhere, and in this case it was speed; 31kts instead of 34kts. Nevertheless, designed maximum speeds were more theoretical than real. What counted was performance at sea under service conditions, and in this respect the *La Galissonnière* design gave good results. Three ships, *La Galissonnière*, *Georges Leygues* and *Montcalm*, received Parsons geared turbines, the remainder having Rateau-Bretagne machinery. Trial results were very favourable, *La Galissonnière* reaching 35.42kts with 90,000shp for 8hr, while *Marseillaise* made 34.98kts.

The main armament of nine 152mm (6in) in triple turrets was retained to become the future standard for French light cruiser design, with a single turret aft, its positioning dictated by the aircraft installation. For the first time, considerable attention had been given to the accommodation and servicing of the aircraft carried, which were four in number, and a large hangar was incorporated into the after superstructure under the main mast. This had two roller shutter doors opening on to the quarterdeck to allow the manoeuvring of aircraft out and on to the catapult, which was situated on top of the after turret. In consequence, this turret was positioned quite far aft on the spacious quarterdeck, with a good field of fire. Aircraft recovery was by means of a Hein mat deployed from an opening in the transom stern. It appears that the complement of four aircraft was seldom embarked,

except perhaps when the GL-832 was in service. When the Loire-Nieuport 130 was issued to ships the usual complement was two or three machines.

The secondary armament was doubled to eight 90mm M1926, all twin mountings on the main deck amidships, controlled by two directors on the bridge structure. However, the torpedo outfit was reduced to two twin mountings, sited between the 90mm guns. The usual complement of 37mm and 13.2mm light AA was included.

The contracts for the first two ships, named *La Galissonnière* and *Jean de Vienne*, were placed with the Naval yards at Brest and Lorient on 27 October 1931 and 12 November 1931 respectively. Both had been laid down before the turn of

the year. The four ships of the 1932 programme were ordered from private yards on 11 July 1933. Financial restraints and modifications seriously affected the progress of these ships during their construction, over five years elapsing before any entered service.

Modifications There were some detail differences between ships of the 1931 programme and those of the 1932 programme.

The fact that some of this class served with Vichy forces and some with the Allies led to two distinct levels of modification being carried out. *La Galissonnière, Jean de Vienne, Gloire* and *Georges Leygues* were given an additional 37mm, plus two 25mm (1 x 2) and two twin 13.2mm in 1941. The last two, plus *Montcalm*, received further modification while serving with the Allies, but *Marseillaise* appears not to have been modified. *Gloire* was refitted at New York in 1943, and *Montcalm* and *Georges Leygues* received their refits at Philadelphia between January and August 1943 and July and October 1943 respectively. In the course of these overhauls the catapult, hangar and aircraft installations and mainmast were landed, as was the complete French light AA outfit, but the torpedo tubes were retained. All of the boilers were retubed and the machinery overhauled. Six US-pattern 40mm quadruple Mk 2 mountings were fitted, two each on the bridge, after superstructure (in lieu of the hangar) and on the quarterdeck. Sixteen single 20mm in groups of four were added, on the forecastle, abreast the bridge on the forecastle deck, between the funnels and on the quarterdeck. Surface and air warning radars were added, and RPC was fitted to the 90mm gun mountings and their directors. Postwar, further refits were carried out which saw the reappearance of a pole mainmast to carry extra

Opposite page: *Marseillaise* in July 1941. (MB)
Below: *Georges Leygues*, also in July 1941. (MB)

radars and the removal of the tubes, except in *Georges Leygues*.

Service On completion, *La Galissonnière* joined the 2nd Light Division in the Mediterranean until further ships entered service, when, in October 1937, she formed the 3rd Cruiser Division at Toulon, together with *Jeanne de Vienne* and *Marseillaise*. On the outbreak of war she was at sea in the vicinity of Bizerte, and carried out patrol duties off the Tunisian coast until 18 November, when she started a major refit at Brest which lasted until 1 March 1940. The 3rd Cruiser Division was now part of the Toulon-based 4th Squadron. Apart from some patrol duties, however, the ship saw little action before the armistice intervened, and thereafter formed part of the Vichy High Seas Force at Toulon from January 1941, but remained in care and maintenance status until 15 April 1941. Between this date and 1 July she was disarmed, remaining in this state until her sabotage on 27 November 1942. The German forces allocated the ship to Italy after long and tedious negotiations, but did not allow the Italians to take title until December. Renamed *FR 12*, she was salvaged and refloated on 9 March 1943 with a view to being incorporated into the Royal Italian Navy, a rather short-sighted but probably politically inspired decision, given the chronic oil fuel shortage then being suffered by Italy. US bombers then damaged her in an air raid on 24 November 1943, but by this time Italy had also surrendered, although she did not restore the ship to France until May 1944. Unfortunately, during the attacks launched after the start of Operation Dragoon, *La Galissonnière* was bombed and sunk for a second time in a raid by B-25s of the 321st Bombardment Group, USAAF, on 18 August 1944. The hulk was raised and scrapped in 1952.

Jean de Vienne was a unit of the 3rd Cruiser Division, and had completed a major refit at Toulon when war was declared. She rejoined her Division at Bizerte, where the task of the 4th

Squadron was to secure the North African coast in the event of Italy entering the war. In November the cruiser division was tasked with the transport of gold from France to Halifax, Nova Scotia, arriving back in Toulon on 27 December. Until the entry of Italy into the war on 10 June 1940, her activities were limited, but subsequent fears of German pocket battleships forcing the Straits of Gibraltar led to a major sortie to protect the eastern approaches to the Straits, for which task the Royal Navy was short of ships. However, the only contact with the enemy was an attack by the Italian submarine *Dandolo* on *La Galissonnière*, but the two torpedoes missed. *Jean de Vienne* was at Algiers at the time of the French armistice, and covered the escape of *Strasbourg* and contre-torpilleurs from Mers-el-Kebir in July and escorted them to Toulon, where she remained. Placed in disarmed care and maintenance state, the ship did not resume active service until joining the High Seas Force in March 1941. With this force she participated in a number of exercises until, on 27 November 1942, she was scuttled by her crew at Toulon. Handed over to Italy and renamed *FR 11*, she was raised on 18 February 1943 and a refit began. This was not finished at time of the Italian surrender, and the vessel fell into German hands once more, only to be hit by incendiary bombs on 24 November 1943 and set on fire, gradually listing until she rested against the quayside. She was found in this state at the end of the war, and although a refit was briefly considered, the idea was abandoned and the ship was scrapped.

Marseillaise also joined the Mediterranean Squadron on entering service, and wore the flag of Contre-Amiral Decoux in 1938. In January 1939 she joined the 3rd Cruiser Division at Casablanca, and by August 1939 was attached to the 4th Naval Region. She was at Toulon on the declaration of war, wearing the flag of the Admiral Commanding 4th Squadron as part of Force Z. She participated in the transport of gold to Canada and in April 1940. As a result of the doubtful Italian attitude, French naval forces were regrouped, the 3rd Cruiser Division being sent to Bizerte as part of the Force de Raid. On 4 July 1940 she returned to Toulon, where, because of the British attack on Mers-el-Kebir, the Germans suspended the disarming of the French fleet. As a result the High Seas force was formed, of which *Marseillaise* was part. On 27 November 1942 the ship was sabotaged by her crew and set on fire, burning for twenty days. The burnt-out hulk was scrapped in 1946/47.

Gloire arrived in Brest, after completing trials, on 18 November 1937, then sailed for a cruise to Indo-China on 1 December, returning to Brest on 16 April 1938. After exercises and visits to the Atlantic and Channel ports, *Gloire* joined the 4th

Cruiser Division in January 1939, and made cruises to the UK and USA in the course of the year with her division. She was under refit between October and December, then sailed for Canada with *Dunkerque*, carrying gold and escorting a Canadian troop convoy on the return. Atlantic patrols as part of Admiral Gensoul's Force de Raid followed, and at the time of the armistice the ship was at Algiers, but returned to Toulon on 4th July, where the 4th Cruiser division formed part of the Independent Naval Force. When the success of the Free French forces in Chad and Cameroon became politically embarrassing, the Axis Naval Commission allowed the despatch of the 4th Cruiser Division to Dakar as Force Y, where they arrived on 14 September 1940. On 18 September the 4th Cruiser Division (*Gloire*, *Georges Leygues* and *Montcalm*) sailed for Libreville, but *Gloire* suffered machinery problems and turned back, being 'escorted' into Casablanca by the British cruisers *Australia* and *Cumberland*. Because of the problems with the *Primaguet* group (q.v.), the French squadron abandoned the task and returned to Dakar, but *Gloire* did not reach Dakar again until after the British attack. Between April and July she underwent a refit at Casablanca, and on 12 September participated in the rescue operations after *Laconia* had been sunk. After refit in the USA, *Gloire* operated from Dakar together with other French and Italian cruisers, searching for Axis blockade runners in the central and south Atlantic until 16 January 1944, when she moved into the Mediterranean. In February she supported the Allied landings at Anzio, bombarding enemy positions in the Bay of Gaete (firing 604 rounds) and transporting troops to Italy and Corsica. After refit at Algiers between 27 April and 17 June, she participated in the landing in the south of France in August, firing nearly 2,000 rounds in shore support between 15 and 28 August. This task continued along the French and Italian Rivieras until the end of the war, except for a special trip to the USA in December. Postwar, the cruiser made three deployments to Indo-China and was finally placed in reserve on 1 February 1955, being condemned for disposal on 2 January 1958.

Montcalm joined the 4th Cruiser Division at Brest on completion of trials, and immediately sailed on a long cruise with the division to Indo-China, arriving in Saigon in January 1938 and remaining there for two months. Back in France once more, she was part of the Atlantic Fleet, taking part in the usual peacetime routines, including a review for the King of England at Calais in July 1938 and representing her country at the International Fair in New York a year later. Part of the Force de Raid at the start of the war, she carried out Atlantic patrol and convoy escort duties, as well as a sweep for *Scharnhorst* and *Gneisenau*

after their sinking of *Rawalpindi*. She completed a major refit in April 1940, then sailed to relieve the damaged *Emile Bertin* as flagship of the French Scandinavian Force off Norway, where there were numerous engagements with the Luftwaffe. After her recall to the Force de Raid in May, *Montcalm* was based in North Africa until the events at Mers-el-Kebir, when she was ordered to Toulon. She sailed with her division on the sortie to Libreville described above, and, when it was aborted, put into Dakar, taking part in its defence on the occasion of the Anglo-Free French attack between 23 and 25 September 1940. The next couple of years saw only the occasional Atlantic patrol as part of Force Y, until she rejoined the Allied cause and sailed for the USA and refit on 30 January 1943, which lasted until August. Between September 1943 and March 1944 she was based at Dakar for anti-blockade-runner patrols, then sailed for the UK for Operation Neptune as part of Force C, off Omaha beach in June. After the Normandy landings she returned to the Mediterranean and covered the landings in Provence, Operation Anvil, and then the recapture of Toulon, Operation Dragoon, in August. Her final wartime duties were coastal bombard-

ments along the Riviera coastline until March 1945. Under refit at Chantiers de la Seyne from 22 May to the end of January 1946, the ship did not see service in Indo-China until she made one tour in 1955. She was placed in reserve on 1 May 1957 in Tunisia, but was towed to Toulon in 1959 to serve as an accommodation hulk for the submarine school, where she remained for ten years, having been degraded to special reserve B on 1 June 1961. Finally condemned on 31 December 1969, she was renamed *Q457* and turned over to the dockyard for disposal.

Georges Leygues, as a unit of the 4th Cruiser Division, formed part of the Force de Raid at the start of the war. Her first rounds fired in anger, however, were mistakenly targeted on the French submarine *Casabianca* during one of the early sorties. The Force de Raid sailed in response to several of the major German raiding cruises, but no contact was ever made with the enemy. When it was decided to reorganise the disposition of French forces to intimidate Italy in April 1940, the Atlantic Fleet was ordered to Oran on 24 April. Although alerted on the occasion of the British attack on Mers-el-Kebir, the 3rd and 4th Cruiser Divisions did not encounter the Royal Navy, and

Above: *Gloire* in April 1945, showing the alterations made during her refit in the USA. (MB)
Below: *Gloire* in 1943, the sole Allied vessel to sport this camouflage pattern. (IWM)

eventually put into Toulon. The next operation by the cruiser was the sortie to Libreville in September, after which she returned to Dakar and was present at the time of the attack on the port, when both she and *Montcalm* opened fire upon the bombarding British ships, obtaining two hits on the cruiser *Australia*. They successfully avoided Fleet Air Arm torpedo attacks themselves. *Georges Leygues* remained based at Dakar until ordered to transport gold bullion to Casablanca at the end of August 1941, where she remained until the end of November. On her return to Dakar the cruiser rejoined her division but saw little active service. After the Allied landings in North Africa an armistice was signed between Admiral Darlan and the Allies, but it was some time before any change in the status of the ships at Dakar took place. In fact, relations between the Free French and the ex-Vichy navies remained correct but cool. Early in 1943 she began Atlantic patrols from Dakar, and on 13 April intercepted the blockade runner *Portland*, which scuttled herself. On 24 June 1943 the ship sailed from Dakar, bound for refit in Philadelphia, and did not return to Oran until 23 November, resuming Atlantic patrols from Dakar. These continued into 1944, until her return to the Mediterranean in February, where she worked up for her next task, invasion duties. *Georges Leygues* sailed from Mers-el-Kebir with *Montcalm* on 14 April 1944 to work up with Royal Navy units in Scapa Flow before the operation, but the French cruisers were allocated to the Western (US) task force. They arrived off the beachhead on 6 June and remained on bombardment duties until 14 June, when they were ordered to Milford Haven. From this port they sailed south on 8 July, arriving in Taranto on 28 July. Both ships then joined the bombardment groups for the invasion of the south of France and the recapture of Toulon. The last few months of hostilities were spent bombarding positions along the coast between the French border and Genoa, with various transport missions as required, until the vessel arrived in Casablanca for a major refit which lasted until the end of January 1946.

DE GRASSE CLASS

Ship	Builder	Laid Down	Launched	Completed	Fate
De Grasse	Lorient Navy Yard	28 Aug 39	11 Sep 46	3 Sep 66	Broken up 1976
Chateaurenault	F & Ch La Seyne	not laid			
Guichen	F & Ch Gironde	not laid			

Displacement: 8,000 tons/8,128 tonnes (standard).
Length: 578ft 6in/176.3m (oa); 570ft 9in/174.0m (pp).
Beam: 59ft/18m.
Machinery: 2-shaft Rateau-Bretagne SR geared turbines; 4 Indret boilers.
Performance: 110,000shp=35kts: Bunkerage: n/k.
Range: n/k.
Protection: n/k.
Guns: nine 6in (3x3); six 3.5in (3x2); five 25mm (5x1); eight 13.2mm MGs.
Torpedoes: six 21.7in (2x3).
Aircraft: three or four, two catapults.
Complement: 580.

Design The 1937 programme authorised another light cruiser which was described as being a modified *La Galissonnière*. The order was placed with Lorient Naval Yard on 18 October 1938, the ship being named *De Grasse*. A second ship was authorised the following year, but although the vessel was to be allocated to F & C La Seyne, the actual order was never placed. She was to be named *Chateaurenault*. Finally, a third ship was authorised under the 1938bis programme, to be built by the F & C de la Gironde as *Guichen*, but again the order was not placed. *De Grasse* was laid down on 28 August 1939, but events dictated that little progress was made on her, and she remained in the early stages of construction throughout the war. She was not launched until September 1946, and was then suspended, being completed much later (1956) and to a much modified design.

Although described as modified *La Galissonnières*, visually these ships would have been considerably different because of their single-funnel layout, presumably as a result of a change in the internal machinery arrangements. The main machinery remained a two-shaft geared turbine installation, but the designed power was increased to 110,000shp for a maximum speed of 35kts. Armour protection was reportedly similar to that of the last class, and the main armament was identical. Some changes were made to the secondary armament, it being reduced by one twin mounting and regrouped at the after end of the superstructure, forward of the after turret. A second catapult was added, both being located amidships abaft the funnel, the turret roof mounting having been discarded, probably because of the problems of carrying heavy weights on the turret tops.

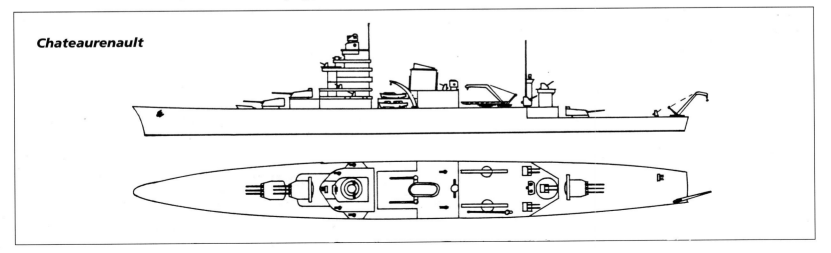

Chateaurenault

Germany

EMDEN CLASS

Ship	Builder	Laid Down	Launched	Completed	Fate
Emden	Marinewerft-Wilhelmshaven	8 Dec 21	7 Jan 25	15 Oct 25	Scuttled 3 May 45: Broken up 1947

Displacement: 5,600 tons/5,689 tonnes (standard); 6,990
  tons/7,102 tonnes (full load).
Length: 508ft 9in/155.1m (oa); 492ft 6in/150.1m (pp); 493ft
  6in/150.5m (wl).
Beam: 47ft/14.3m; Draught: 16ft 11in/5.15m (mean).
Machinery: 2-shaft Brown-Boverie SR geared turbines; 10
  Marine boilers.
Performance: 46,500shp=29.4kts; Bunkerage: 1,200 tons oil
  fuel.
Range: 5,300nm at 18kts.
Protection: 20 to 40mm deck; 50mm main belt; 100mm CT.
Guns: eight 5.9in (8x1); three 3.5in (3x1).
Torpedoes: four 21in (2x2).
Aircraft: nil.
Complement: 630.

Design Defeat in the First World War and the
subsequent Treaty of Versailles in 1919 left Germany with no effective fleet to speak of, save a
handful of pre-1914 ships. The aftermath of war,
political unrest and the economic problems
which afflicted the country in the early 1920s left
the new Reichsmarine with a pressing need to
replace aged ships, but without the finance or
political will to do so on any great scale. This situation was compounded by the run-down state
of the design departments of the Admiralty, and
of the dockyards themselves. Nevertheless, in
1921 the cruiser *Ariadne* would be 20 years old,
and could be replaced under the terms of the
Treaty of Versailles. Design work was therefore
begun on an *Ersatz Ariadne*, which of necessity
had to be based upon the experiences of the
1914-1918 period, as well as on the treaty limita-
tion of 6,000 tons maximum. The new ship was
designed, inevitably, to the maximum displacement allowable, with lines broadly based on the
Köln, the last design to see operational service,
albeit briefly. Shortages of materials, the occupation of the Ruhrland and the restrictions of the
Allied Control Commission all contributed to the
delays in completing this ship, but at the same
time forced the consideration and employment of
new construction techniques, including electric
welding.

Armed with eight 5.9in (15cm) SK/L45 guns,
the same as *Köln*, but with the forward pair superfiring instead of abreast, she nevertheless retained
beam guns in the waist, a feature abandoned in
most other navies by this time. Twin mountings
had been intended in the original design, but
these failed to materialise despite their being
ordered from Rheinmetall, again due to the occupation of the Rheinland. The forced adoption of

single mountings resulted in conflicting demands
for deck space, and the consequent deletion of
two twin banks of torpedo tubes. Mixed oil and
coal firing was adopted, there being originally six
oil- and four coal-fired boilers, with a twin-shaft
single reduction geared turbine machinery layout.

The protective scheme included a horizontal
deck 20 to 40mm thick with a 50mm belt.

In essence the ship was indeed a 'First War'
design, but her construction was robust and, had
the Kriegsmarine made use of her potential during
the later conflict, she might have emulated her
illustrious forebear on the world's oceans.
Modifications In 1926 the foremast was altered to
incorporate a heavier foretop with a longer-based
rangefinder. A major refit in 1933-34 saw the con-

Above: *Emden* as completed. (WZB)

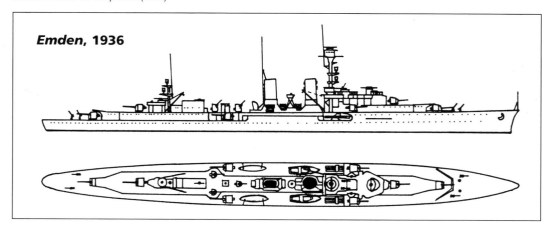

Emden, 1936

Above: *Emden* in the 1930s after refit. (WZB)
Right: *Emden* in 1940/41 (MB)

version to full oil firing, the mainmast greatly reduced in height, a new mast stepped abaft the after funnel and the fore funnel reduced in height by 2m, and in 1937-38 the form of the bow was modified. Plans to rearm her on the lines of the original twin turrets had come to naught again in 1929. During the war years some modifications were made, principally to the armament, the old-pattern L/45 15cm guns being replaced by newer Tbk C/36 weapons. She received a prototype 2cm Vierling in 1940, but was otherwise little altered until 1944, when the three 8.8cm flak were replaced by 10.5cm Sk C/32gE and the light flak was changed to two 4cm Flak 28 and two 3.7cm Sk C/30U, with twenty 2cm in twin LM44 mountings. Radar had also been fitted by 1942. However, it is unlikely that the final planned outfit of nine 3.7cm M42 was ever fitted.

Service After completion, *Emden* was extensively employed as a training cruiser, making nine long foreign cruises to all parts of the world. The first of these began on 14 November 1926, the ship returning home again in March 1928. One of her commanding officers in the interwar period was Arnauld de la Pierre, a famous First World War U-Boat captain. Another was the future chief of the U-boat arm and CinC, Karl Dönitz.

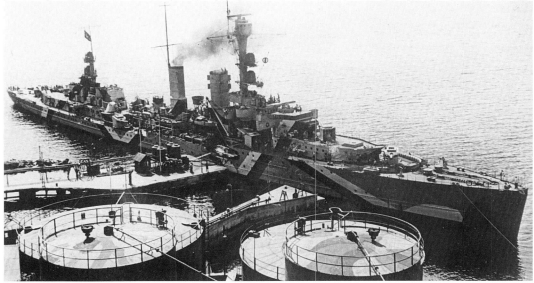

In the early days of the Second World War she was slightly damaged by a crashing British aircraft while at Wilhelmshaven. In April 1940 she participated in the invasion of Norway as part of Group 5, tasked with the occupation of Oslo, and in 1941 the invasion of Russia, when she bombarded shore batteries on the Sworbe and the Baltic islands. For most of the war, however, she was still employed as a training ship, with occasional forays on minelaying sorties. Then, in September 1944, she was ordered to the Skagerrak for operations with FdZ (Flag Officer, Destroyers), but ran heavily aground in Oslofjord on 9 December. As a result, Dönitz ordered her to repair at Königsberg, where she arrived on Christmas Day. Repairs were interrupted by the advance of the Soviet army, and she sailed from Königsberg once more on 23 January 1945. Guns were reshipped and the rest of the machinery repaired at Götenhafen before the ship sailed for the west on 2 February. Her refit was to have been finished at Kiel, but on 12 March she was hit by four incendiaries, which caused no damage below the armoured deck, and then, on 3 April, by a bomb which penetrated No.3 boiler room. Finally, on 13 April, *Emden* was hit again and near-missed when the ship was beached in Heikendorferbucht. Paid off on 26 April, when her crew were assigned to shore fighting, the ship was wrecked by explosives on 3 May, just before the capitulation.

Right: *Emden* in the winter of 1940/41. (Author's Collection)

KÖNIGSBERG CLASS

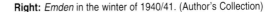

Ship	Builder	Laid Down	Launched	Completed	Fate
Königsberg	Marinewerft-Wilhelmshaven	14 Apr 26	26 Mar 27	17 Apr 29	Lost 10 Apr 40
Karlsruhe	Deutsche Werke, Kiel	27 Jul 26	20 Aug 27	6 Nov 29	Lost 10 Apr 40
Köln	Marinewerft-Wilhelmshaven	7 Aug 26	23 May 28	15 Jan 30	Lost 30 Mar 45

Displacement: 6,650 tons/6,756 tonnes (standard); 8,130 tons/8,260 tonnes (full load).
Length: 570ft 9in/174m (oa); 554ft 4in/169m (wl).
Beam: 50ft/15.3m; Draught: 18ft 4in/5.56m (mean).
Machinery: 2-shaft SR geared turbines; 2 MAN diesels; 6 Marine boilers.
Performance: 68,000shp=32.5kts; 1,800bhp=10kts; Bunkerage: 1,184+261 tons oil/diesel.
Range: 3,100nm at 13kts.
Protection: 40mm deck; 50-70mm main belt; 20-30mm turrets; 100mm CT.
Guns: nine 5.9in (3x3); six 3.5in (3x2); eight 3.7cm (4x2); four 2cm (4x1).
Torpedoes: twelve 21in (4x3).
Aircraft: two, one catapult.

Complement: 820.

Design Having made a start with *Emden*, the Design Office could look to the eventual replacement of the other aged cruisers, utilising the tonnage available to them, and in particular the benefit which arose from the definition of standard displacement resulting from the Washington Treaty of 1920, to which Germany was not a signatory, but of which they took advantage when it suited them. Specifically this meant that, in Washington Treaty terms, *Emden* displaced only 5,400 tons, some 600 tons less than allowed. Fortunately for Germany, the Allied Control Commission failed to appreciate the implications of the definition, and allowed the Reichsmarine to get away with the increase, which was exploited in the next designs.

Even with this windfall, it was still difficult for the constructors to design a ship of world standard given the displacement available. Compromise was necessary, and resulted in ships which could not be considered fit for their purpose, despite outward appearances. Triple turrets were adopted for the first time in German cruisers, to reduce the hull length, and electric welding was extensively employed to save weight. More seriously, the design calculations were based on somewhat dubious assumptions which resulted in inherent hull weakness, which compromised their fighting ability to such an extent that they were never really deployed in a front-line role. The main armament was a new 15cm gun designated Sk C/25, firing a 45.5kg shell and disposed in three triple turrets, unusually positioned one forward and two aft. This disposition should be looked at in the light of their designed role, scouting, when a chase action would be more probable than an attack. An unusual feature was the offset-

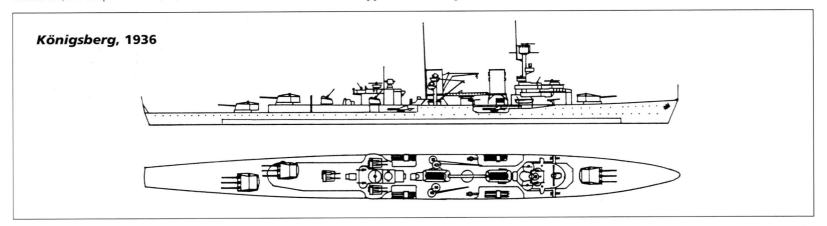

Königsberg, 1936

Above: *Königsberg* in the Solent in July 1935. (WL)

Below: *Köln* in the early 1930s. (Jak Showell)

The protective scheme included a 20mm armoured deck across the full beam of the ship, increased to 40mm over magazines, without the sloped edges, and a side belt of 50mm and side bulkhead of 10 to 15mm.

The first ship, '*Kreuzer B*', *Königsberg*, was ordered on 28 March 1925 and laid down in 1926, just as her successor was being discussed. At this time, April 1926, there was a move within the Reichsmarine for a heavier main armament. It was felt that *Kreuzer C*, (*Karlsruhe*) should be armed with 19cm guns in three twin turrets. Admiral Raeder agreed, but turrets would not be available until February 1929, and the ship was due for completion in autumn 1928. Furthermore, political considerations militated against the increase in calibre, and the question was to be reconsidered for Cruiser D, *Köln*. As a result, *Kreuzer C* was ordered on 21 May 1926 as a repeat of *Kreuzer B*. By December 1929 no progress had been made on the armament question, and the third ship, *Köln*, ordered on 25 October 1927, also received 15cm guns.

Modifications *Königsberg* completed initially without aircraft, 8.8cm guns, light flak and much equipment, while the initial torpedo outfit was for 50cm weapons. In the years up to the outbreak of the war the ships received their full equipment, including aircraft (initially the He 60 and later the Ar 196) and various modifications were made to their rig, as well as additions to the fire control

ting of the after turrets to port and starboard of the centre line, the reason for which is obscure. If it was intended to improve the ahead arcs, it was only marginal, and was not repeated in later designs. These ships were fitted for minelaying, but because of their structural and stability problems were restricted by the need to retain adequate ballast to compensate for the additional top-weight.

A diesel installation was considered for the machinery of these ships, but the state of the art at the time was inadequate, and in consequence

twin-shaft steam turbines were installed, with a cruising diesel on each which could be engaged by means of an hydraulic coupling. In practice this arrangement was found to be extremely wasteful of space.

Secondary armament was originally intended to be the new 8.8cm Sk C/25, but this proved unsatisfactory and the old 8.8cm L/45 single had to be fitted as an interim measure. No aircraft installation could be fitted on construction (this was prohibited by the Treaty of Versailles), but provision was made.

Above: *Königsberg* on a world training cruise in the 1930s. (Jak Showell)   **Below:** *Karlsruhe* after rebuilding, in 1939. (BA)

Below: *Karlsruhe* at Wilhelmshaven in November 1939. (Gröner)

system. *Köln* landed her aircraft and catapult in the summer of 1938 and never reshipped them. In view of their known weaknesses, plans were made for major rebuilding, but only *Karlsruhe* was taken in hand, in May 1938. On emerging from this refit her beam had been increased by about 1.4m, and an extra armoured shell plating had been added. Externally, her appearance had been altered by funnel caps and new masting. Other modifications to this class were minimal because of their early loss or employment in the training role. *Köln* landed the after tubes and two twin 3.7cm mountings when rated as a training ship in 1940. She received a radar set only in the summer of 1942, but was otherwise not altered until 1944, when refitted for active service. Four 4cm Flak in single mountings and sixteen 2cm in twin mountings were shipped, whilst two twin 3.7cm Sk C/30 were retained. In March 1945 she was to be fitted with two Fohn 7.3cm rocket launchers, but it is unlikely that these materialised.

Service Like *Emden*, these ships were employed for foreign training cruises in the interwar years, and were deployed to Spanish waters during the Civil War of 1936-39. Their activities as training ships for worldwide use were severely restricted following the discovery of inherent structural weakness while they were involved in the Civil War patrols. In September 1939 *Köln* was in the North Sea, carrying out two minelaying sorties in that month. She participated in the sweep to the Terschelling Bank in October, and towards the end of the following month undertook two mercantile warfare patrols in the Skagerrak, as well as supporting the destroyers returning from their minelaying sorties. *Königsberg* was working up in the Baltic, as was *Karlsruhe*. All three were committed to the invasion of Norway in April 1940, when *Königsberg* was sunk by Fleet Air Arm dive bombers at Bergen, and *Karlsruhe* by the submarine *Truant* off Kristiansund. After April 1940 *Köln* carried out a couple of minelaying tasks in the North Sea and Skagerrak in May and December until allocated for training duties. This task was briefly interrupted by the invasion of Russia, when the ship participated in the capture of the Baltic islands in October 1941, bombarding shore batteries on Ristna and Dago. After reverting to training duties once more, the ship remained in the Baltic until she was transferred to Norway for operational duty in July 1942. No suitable tasks could be found for the fragile ship, and her sojourn in northern waters was inactive throughout. She returned home on 8 February 1943, after the Barents Sea debacle. Paid off on 1 March 1943, *Köln* served as an accommodation ship at Kiel from June 1943 to February 1944, when she was towed to Königsberg for refit. She was recommissioned on 1 April 1944, but the refit was not finished until June, after which training duties followed. In

October 1944 *Köln* was ordered to the Skagerrak as flagship of FdZ (Flag Officer, Destroyers) for minelaying duties. Damage caused by bomb near-misses and her general poor condition resulted in her recall to Wilhelmshaven for refit in early 1945. In the course of this refit the ship was hit by bombs during a USAAF B-24 raid on 30 March, sinking to the bottom with her upper deck awash. On the night of 4-5 April preparations were made by her crew to destroy the ship, and she was paid off on the next day, her crew being drafted to the fortress defences. However, on the approach of the British army her turrets were manned again and, using makeshift ammunition supplies, she engaged the Allied forces until 3 May. The wreck was scrapped postwar.

Below: *Köln* on a wartime sortie in 1939/40. (BA)

LEIPZIG CLASS

Ship	Builder	Laid Down	Launched	Completed	Fate
Leipzig	Marinewerft-Wilhelmshaven	14 Apr 28	18 Oct 29	8 Oct 31	Scuttled 11 Jul 46

Displacement: 6,515 tons/6,619 tonnes (standard); 8,250 tons/8,382 tonnes (full load).

Length: 580ft 9in/177.1m (oa); 543ft 9in/165.8m (wl).

Beam: 53ft 3in/16.2m; Draught: 16ft/4.88m (mean).

Machinery: 2-shaft SR Parsons geared turbines; 1-shaft MAN diesel; 6 Marine boilers.

Performance: 60,000shp+12,400bhp=32kts; Bunkerage: 1,253+348 tons oil/diesel.

Range: 3,800nm at 15kts.

Protection: 20-25mm deck; 20-50mm main belt; 20-30mm turrets; CT 100mm.

Guns: nine 5.9in (3x3); six 3.5in (3x2); eight 3.7cm (4x2); four 2cm (4x1).

Torpedoes: twelve 21in (4x3).

Aircraft: two, one catapult.

Complement: 850.

Design Kreuzer E, later to be named *Leipzig*, was a modified K design, outwardly differing in having a single funnel. However, internally there was considerable difference, in particular in the machinery layout. Her displacement was slightly increased, with more beam, and electric welding even more extensively employed to save weight. The other difference was that the after turrets were placed on the centreline. In this design, more realistic parameters were adopted for the calculation of the longitudinal strength as compared with the K class, but even so the design could still not be considered robust.

Cruising turbines were not fitted. Instead, four MAN diesel motors were installed, driving a centreline shaft through Vulkan couplings, giving a cruising installation independent of the turbine machinery. When the centre shaft was not required the propeller could be feathered to reduce drag.

The protection scheme returned to the concept of an armoured carapace, with a rounded 25mm deck edge joining the 50mm side belt at its lower edge. This carapace extended to about 70 per cent of the waterline length. Wotan hart material was utilised for the first time for the armoured areas.

Main and secondary armament remained as in the Ks, so the new cruiser had no greater fighting strength. An order was placed with the Naval Yard at Wilhelmshaven on 25 October 1927, and the hull was laid down in April the following year.

Modifications In 1936 *Leipzig* was fitted with a catapult and aircraft handling crane, and the old-pattern 8.8cm guns were replaced initially by two of the new 8.8 Sk C/32 twin mountings, a third being added later. The new flak fire control system SL1 was also installed. The initial aircraft employed was the He 60. In 1939, during her last refit before the outbreak of war, the crane was replaced by a different type. When the problems of poor structural strength became evident, it was planned to take the ship in hand at the Howaldt yard for strengthening. This was to involve increasing the hull bulge so that displacement would increase by 120 tons, but draught was to remain at 5.68m. Calculations showed that steel work for the bulge and extra strengthening amounted to 210 tons and equipment additions to 60 tons, so that, with a reserve of 50 tons, the overall increase totalled 320 tons. This would increase draught by 10cm, but full stability and strength would be attained. Further plans to house the second aircraft in a splinterproof hangar were not possible owing to unacceptable weight. In the event, this work was not carried through because the outbreak of war occurred before yard capacity became available. Wartime alterations were limited in view of the damage sustained by the ship in 1939 and her subsequent

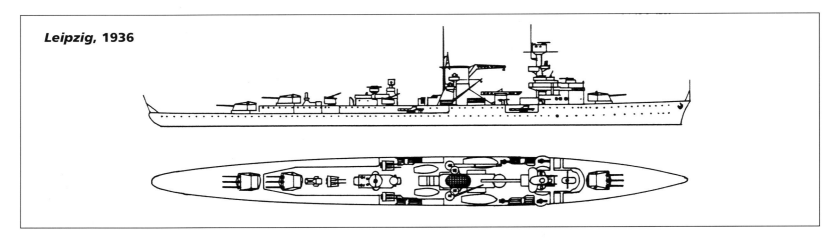

Leipzig, 1936

use as a training vessel, but she received two quadruple 2cm mountings. Her after tubes were allocated to *Scharnhorst/Gneisenau* in March 1941 and removed shortly afterwards, while the forward banks were allocated to *Admiral Hipper*. Not until 1944 was any real increase in flak planned, when her outfit was to be four 4cm Bofors, two twin 3.7cm mountings and a total of eight 2cm twin LM44 mountings. It is uncertain whether this outfit was ever fully installed, as she appears to have retained single 2cm to the end, but radar was fitted. Internally she possessed only

two boilers after her torpedoing in December 1939, and was never able to achieve more than about 23kts thereafter. The catapult and aircraft were also landed at this time.

Service *Leipzig* saw some active service during the Spanish Civil War from the summer of 1936, but suffered serious structural damage caused by heavy seas while on passage through the Bay of Biscay in the spring of 1937. This graphically demonstrated the weakness of the new cruisers, although *Leipzig* was by no means the worst. Only one major training cruise was undertaken by

this ship; to Tangier in the spring of 1939. After the outbreak of war she served initially in the North Sea on minelaying tasks, carrying out four sorties between 3 and 20 September 1939. After a period of mercantile warfare in the Skagerrak in November, she was then used to cover the destroyers returning home after minelaying off the east coast of England. During the course of one of these sorties, on 13 December 1939, she was severely damaged by torpedoes from the submarine *Salmon*, both forward boiler rooms being destroyed. This effectively finished her as a fight-

ing unit, and, apart from brief use for shore bombardment off the Sworbe in September 1941 during the invasion of Russia, she was used only for training duties. In the middle war years some consideration was given to restoring her full fighting capabilities, but it was estimated that the installation of four new boilers would require some seven months' work, and that the extensive recabling and rewiring, particularly of the fire control systems, needed another 16 months, before the boilers could be fitted. As this required vast amounts of scarce cabling and would occupy some 170 electricians for a year or so, the idea was abandoned. It is believed that new boilers were available for her before the end of the war, however. Further disaster struck in October 1944, when she was rammed by *Prinz Eugen*. She was then reclassified as a cadets' training hulk on 13 November. Her final actions were in support of the army as a floating battery at Götenhafen from April 1945, but she managed to escape to the west and was finally scuttled by the Allies, with gas ammunition aboard, off the Norwegian coast on 11 July 1946.

Opposite page: *Leipzig* in Kielfjord, 1939. Her catapult appears to be missing. (Gröner)
Above: *Leipzig* before the war. (WZB)
Right: *Leipzig* in the Baltic, 1941. (WZB)

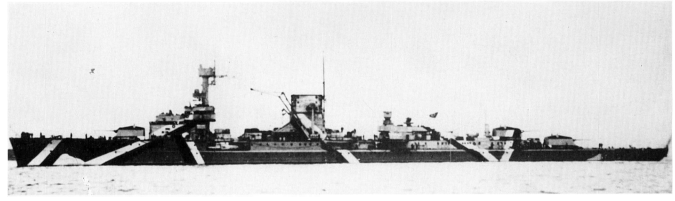

NÜRNBERG CLASS

Ship	Builder	Laid Down	Launched	Completed	Fate
Nürnberg	Deutsche Werke, Kiel	4 Nov 33	8 Dec 34	2 Nov 35	To USSR 5 Jan 46

Displacement: 6,980 tons/7,091 tonnes (standard); 8,971 tons/9,115 tonnes (full load).
Length: 593ft 9in/181m (oa); 557ft 6in/170m (wl).
Beam: 53ft 6in/16.4m; Draught: 16ft 6in/5m (mean).
Machinery: 2-shaft Krupp SR geared turbines; 1-shaft MAN diesel; 6 Marine boilers.
Performance: 66,000shp+12,400bhp=32kts; Bunkerage: 1,055+255 tons oil/diesel.
Range: 2,400nm at 13kts.
Protection: 20-25mm deck, 18-50mm main belt, 20-80mm turrets, 60mm CT.
Guns: nine 5.9in (3x3); eight 3.5in (4x2); eight 3.7cm (4x2); four 2cm (4x1).
Torpedoes: twelve 21in (4x3).
Aircraft: two, one catapult.
Complement: 896.

Design There was almost a 5½-year gap between the placing of the order for *Leipzig* and that for the next light cruiser, caused in the main by indecision as to the optimum gun calibre and displacement of future light cruisers. In the end, given the need for the design staffs to concentrate work on the 'Washington' heavy cruiser project, *Kreuzer F* was ordered on 16 March 1933 as almost a repeat *Leipzig*. She was the first large ship to be ordered under the National Socialist regime.

Internally, the ship differed a little from her predecessor in that the machinery spaces were slightly rearranged owing to the revised disposition of the 8.8cm guns, while the slight increase in displacement of some 100 tons allowed some extension of bunkerage and a selective increase in armour thickness. Externally, the most obvious differences were in the funnel and catapult positions, and in the bridge design.

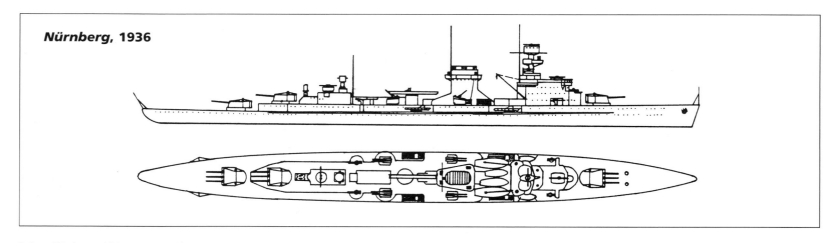

Nürnberg, 1936

Below: *Nürnberg* at Kiel in the 1930s. She still has the He 60 floatplane. (WZB)

The main armament remained the 15cm SK C/25 (6in) gun, with heavier armoured turrets, and the secondary armament was increased to eight 8.8cm guns in four twin mountings. This ship was the first to complete with its designed armament, including catapult and aircraft.

While the design of this ship was a considerable advance on earlier light cruisers, it still showed some weaknesses which necessitated restricting minimum fuel levels, with a consequent reduction in radius of action.

Modifications It had been intended to give this ship the same strengthening treatment as *Leipzig*, but this was never done either. The after tubes appear to have been landed before the ship went to Norway in June 1940. Other modifications to *Nürnberg* were limited to the removal of the aircraft installations during a refit at Kiel in February-August 1942, when they were replaced by a twin 3.7cm. In addition, two army-pattern 2cm quadruple mountings were added, the number of single 2cm was increased to five, and a radar set was added. She had the flak outfit further augmented in 1944, her final configuration including two 4cm (2 x 1); eight 3.7cm (4 x 2) and twenty-nine 2cm (2 x 4, 10 x 2 and 1 x 1). Shields were fit-ted to the 3.7cm and 2cm mountings. FuMo 25 and FuMo 63 were the radars carried at the war's end.

Service On commissioning, *Nürnberg* assumed the role of flagship for *Befehlshaber der Aufklarungsstreitkräfte* (Flag Officer Scouting Forces), and made her first foreign cruise in the spring of 1936. In August of that year she was deployed to Spanish waters on the outbreak of the Civil War, returning home on 8 December. She served again on this task between March and August 1937. On the outbreak of the Second World War she moved to the North Sea, where she participated in three of the minelaying sorties during the laying of the West Wall mine barrages in September, and escorted the destroyers returning from their minelaying sorties into British waters in November/December. She, too, was hit in the torpedo attack by *Salmon* on 13 December 1939, but her damage was not as serious as that to *Leipzig*. Nevertheless, repairs took until April 1940 to complete. *Nürnberg* sailed for Norway on 10 June 1940, and returned home with *Gneisenau* on 28 July without having seen any action. She spent the remainder of 1940 in the Baltic, and from 15 February 1941 was designated a training ship. On the invasion of Russia she formed part of the short-lived Baltenflotte in the Aaland Islands, then returned to training and exercises. After a major refit between January and August 1942, she was again deployed to northern waters, sailing on 11 November, but saw no action and was withdrawn to Germany once more in May 1943. Her remaining service was with the Training Squadron in Baltic waters until ordered to the Skagerrak at the end of 1944. Here she acted as Flagship for FdZ and as a minelayer when required, then sailed for Copenhagen at the end of January 1945, where she remained inactive until the surrender. While in that port she was subjected to an abortive attack by the Danish resistance, using a home-made model boat torpedo. She was briefly considered for use in the bombardment of the advancing Soviet armies along the Baltic coast, but her very low level of operational efficiency owing to employment as a cadet training ship, combined with the paralysing shortage of oil fuel, prevented this.

Postwar she was allocated to the Soviets as *Admiral Makarov*, and served in an active role until the 1950s, when she became a training ship. By the end of the 1950s she was stripped as a hulk, and she was scrapped in 1960.

Top right: *Nürnberg* off Trondheim in June 1940. Note the camouflage pattern and the absence of the after tubes. (BA)
Centre right: *Nürnberg* at Bogen Bay, Narvik, in 1943. (Gröner)
Right: *Nürnberg* in 1946 under the USSR flag, sailing for Russia. (IWM)

HIPPER/PRINZ EUGEN CLASS

Ship	Builder	Laid Down	Launched	Completed	Fate
Admiral Hipper	Blohm & Voss, Hamburg	6 Jul 35	6 Feb 37	29 Apr 39	Lost 9/10 Apr 45
Blücher	Deutsche Werke, Kiel	15 Aug 35	8 Jun 37	20 Sep 39	Lost 9 Apr 40
Prinz Eugen	Krupp, Germania	23 Apr 36	22 Aug 38	1 Aug 40	Expended in atomic bomb tests Jul 46
Seydlitz	Deschimag, Bremen	29 Dec 36	19 Jan 39	–	Scuttled at Königsberg 28/29 Jan 45
Lützow	Deschimag, Bremen	2 Aug 37	1 Jul 39	–	Sold to USSR Feb 40

Displacement: 14,247 tons/14,475 tonnes (standard); 18,208 tons/18,500 tonnes (full load).
Length: 675ft 4in/205.9m (oa); 636ft 9in/194.2m (wl).
Beam: 69ft 9in/21.3m; Draught: 19ft/5.83m (mean).
Machinery: 3-shaft SR Deschimag, (Blohm & Voss, *Admiral Hipper*) turbines; 12 Wagner (La Mont, *Admiral Hipper*) boilers.
Performance: 133,631shp=32.5kts; Bunkerage: 3,050 tons oil fuel.
Range: 6,500nm at 17kts.
Protection: 12-30mm upper deck; 20-50mm main deck;

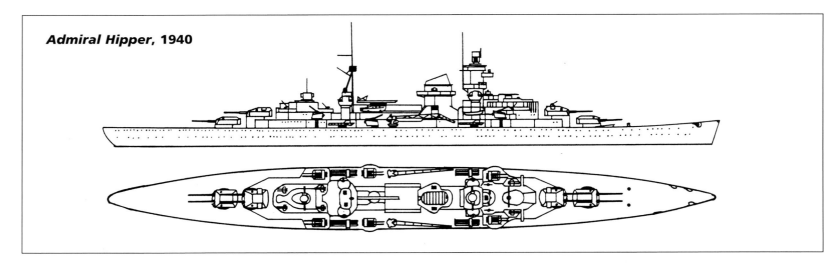

Admiral Hipper, 1940

70-80mm main belt; 70-105mm turrets; 50-150mm CT.
Guns: eight 8in (4x2); twelve 4.1in (6x2); twelve 3.7cm (6x2); eight 2cm (8x1).
Torpedoes: twelve 21in (4x3).
Aircraft: three, one catapult.
Complement: 1,600.

Prinz Eugen

Displacement: 14,271 tons/14,500 tonnes (standard); 18,700 tons/19,000 tonnes (full load).
Length: 681ft 3in/201.7m (oa); 654ft 4in/199.5m (wl).
Beam: 71ft 9in/21.9m; Draught: 20ft 9in/6.37m (mean).
Machinery as *Admiral Hipper* except La Mont/Brown Boverie boilers/turbines, *Prinz Eugen,* and Wagner/Deschimag boilers/turbines, other two.
Performance as *Admiral Hipper*; Bunkerage: 3,250 tons oil.
Range: 5,050nm at 15 kts.
Protection as *Admiral Hipper*.
Guns as *Admiral Hipper*.
Torpedoes as *Admiral Hipper*.

Aircraft as *Admiral Hipper*.
Complement: 1,600.

Design Germany began to consider designing heavy cruisers as early as the beginning of the 1930s, despite being forbidden to construct such vessels by the Treaty of Versailles. However, it was necessary to keep abreast of foreign developments, as it was almost certain that in any future war with the most likely antagonists, France and Great Britain, German warships would inevitably encounter such ships. Existing light cruisers available to the German Navy were far outclassed, so, in February 1934, there was a call for sketch designs based mainly on three requirements; a match for *Algérie,* faster than *Dunkerque,* and a radius of action suitable for Atlantic employment. Initially, the main armament was a choice between eight 20.3cm (8in) or twelve 15cm (6in), but Admiral Raeder soon opted for the heavier

calibre. This in turn forced a reconsideration of the desired design parameters, as the 8in armament needed an increase in dimensions. A compromise calibre of 19cm (7.48in) was not acceptable, so the design had to be enlarged progressively. The choice for the main propulsion was not easy either, given Germany's expertise in the field of diesels and the development of high-pressure steam boiler systems. Both were given consideration, as was turbo-electric machinery. By the summer of 1934 the main armament and machinery had been decided, high-pressure steam turbines being selected for the latter. At this time the weight distributions showed 2,140 tons for protection and 1,980 tons for machinery in a displacement of 10,700 tons. The vertical armour was 85mm (3.34in). Further conferences showed

Below: *Admiral Hipper* on trials in 1939. (Author's Collection)

Above: *Admiral Hipper* in 1940. (BA)

the design to be incapable of meeting all of the demands put upon it while remaining within the Treaty displacement, so the protective scheme was reduced. Germany was still not in a position to build a 'Heavy Cruiser' legally, but work continued in secret, an order for the two leading ships, *Admiral Hipper* and *Blücher*, being placed as early as 30 October 1934. The situation was resolved by Hitler's abrogation of the Treaty of Versailles on 16 March 1935.

Given Germany's somewhat cavalier attitude to the limitations of the Washington Treaty, to which she was not a signatory, the on-paper fighting strength of these ships was considerably in excess of that of their contemporaries.

A third ship, *Prinz Eugen*, was ordered on 16 November 1935, but she differed in many details from the first two. Two more ships, known initially as *Kreuzer K & L*, were eventually added to the programme, but they had a more tortuous

development path, having originally been planned as Class B ships armed with twelve 15cm (6in) guns in triple turrets. Political pressures, treaty considerations and international bargaining, however, led to their eventual construction as Class A ships on the grounds that the USSR had laid down the *Kirov* class (q.v.). Both ships were ordered on 18 July 1936 and launched as *Lützow* and *Seydlitz* respectively. They were to be of the same appearance as *Prinz Eugen*.

In addition to the now standard main armament of eight 8in guns, a heavy AA battery of twelve 10.5cm (4.1in) in stabilised twin mountings with a sophisticated stabilised HA fire control system was also carried. The last two ships were to ship their 10.5cm guns in the LC/37 twin mounting. The light AA outfit was heavier than foreign designs, but the gun itself, the 3.7cm SK C/30, was only semi-automatic. Twelve torpedo tubes, with ten reloads (twelve in the last three

ships), and an aircraft installation comprising a catapult and three floatplanes, rounded off the armament. *Admiral Hipper* and *Blücher* had single hangars, while the others had double hangars with the catapult placed differently.

As finalised, the protective scheme comprised a side belt of 70 to 80mm and an armoured deck of between 20mm and 30mm, with small areas of 40mm. In addition there was an armoured upper deck of 12 to 30mm. Barbette armour was 80mm.

On paper these ships were fast and powerful, but the reality was a little different, the adoption of the high-pressure steam system resulting in fragile and uneconomic machinery. *Prinz Eugen* was better than *Admiral Hipper* in this respect, while *Blücher* did not survive long enough to show her performance. The last two were never completed.

Modifications *Admiral Hipper* was modified between July and September 1939, when her bows were altered to a raked pattern and given more sheer, the navigating and Admiral's bridges were revised, and a prominent funnel cap was fitted. Radar FuMo 22 was fitted on the fore top rangefinder in January 1940. Two single 2cm in army-pattern mountings were fitted on the roofs of B and C turrets in April 1940, and remained aboard until her 1941 refit. By 1942 these had been supplanted by quadruple mountings, with a third replacing the forward searchlight and a fourth fitted to the forecastle. Radar FuMO 40 was now fitted to both the foretop and after rangefinders. When recommissioned in 1944 she had three tri-axial and two bi-axial 2cm quadruples, plus eight singles in addition to the original 3.7cm outfit. By later that year some augmentation had been carried out, and she had six 4cm Flak 28 in single mountings, twenty-eight 2cm (2 x 4, 8 x 2 and 4 x 1) and the 3.7cm reduced to four twin mountings. Her final authorised outfit, agreed in November 1944, was twenty 4cm, two bi-axial 2cm quadruples and seven LM44cm twin mountings. Quite how far this was achieved is unknown. Radar FuMo 25 was to have been included in this refit.

Blücher had her bows modified while under completion, receiving a more gracefully curved form than her sister, and a funnel cap was fitted during trials. Her bridge was also modified after commissioning, and FuMo 22 fitted to the cupola of the foretop rangefinder. No further modifications were made before her loss.

Prinz Eugen completed with the raked bow as *Blücher* and two radar sets, but without the

Above: *Admiral Hipper* in Norwegian waters, late 1942. (Author's Collection)

Below: *Seydlitz* fitting out at Deschimag in 1940/41. (BA)

Above: The incomplete *Lützow* in tow for the USSR, April 1940. (Gröner)

Below: Although sometimes captioned *Seydlitz*, this is almost certainly the former *Lützow* in Soviet hands postwar, probably whilst being dismantled. *Seydlitz* had been dismantled to upper deck level in 1942 and, furthermore, this ship's hull shows no sign of having sat on the bottom for any length of time. (Author's Collection)

spherical covers to the forward pair of flak directors. These were not fitted until 1941, at Brest. Four quadruple 2cm were added in December 1941, on the forecastle, B and C turrets and the quarterdeck. In January 1942 another was fitted in place of the forward searchlight, while those on the forecastle and quarterdeck were retained for her transfer to Norway. By 1943 the funnel searchlights had been replaced by quadruple 2cm and the single 2cm increased to eight. During the programme of major upgrading of flak outfits carried out from the autumn of 1944, she was to have

received six 4cm and twenty-eight 2cm (2 x 4, 10 x LM44 twins), four twin 3.7cm being retained. At the time of her collision with *Leipzig* this had at least been carried out in part, and at the surrender the ship was fitted with eighteen 4cm, six 2cm quadruples and four 2cm LM44 twins.

Service *Admiral Hipper's* first sortie was a strike against Allied convoy traffic to Scandinavia in February 1940, followed by the invasion of Norway, Operation Weser, in April that year. During the course of this task, the capture of Trondheim, she encountered and sank the destroyer *Glow-*

worm but received some damage herself. She returned to Wilhelmshaven for repairs which lasted until May. Her next sortie was Operation Juno, a strike against Allied forces in the Harstaad area to relieve pressure on the German army in Norway. In company with four destroyers, the ship sailed on 4 June to join *Scharnhorst* and *Gneisenau* for the sortie. This resulted in the sinking of the troopship *Orama*, the oiler *Oil Pioneer* and the trawler *Juniper*. Between 27 November and 27 December 1940 she made a raiding cruise into the Atlantic, but sank only one ship of 6,078 tons before putting into Brest. During this cruise she engaged a convoy escorted by the cruiser *Berwick*, hitting her four times and damaging a merchant ship. A second cruise from Brest between 1 and 14 February 1941 was more successful, with seven ships totalling 32,806 tons sunk. She returned to Germany for refit, arriving in Kiel on 28 March. After refit, *Admiral Hipper* sailed for Norway on 21 March 1942, participating in the abortive strike against PQ17, and in September laid a minefield off Novoya Zemelya, the only minelaying sortie by a German heavy cruiser. In December a strike was launched against convoy JW51B by *Admiral Hipper* and *Lützow* (the latter a panzerschiffe, *not* the cruiser of this class). In the ensuing debacle *Admiral Hipper* was so badly damaged by the British cruisers *Sheffield* and *Jamaica* that she was never to become fully operational again. Her forward boiler room was destroyed, and with much other damage she limped back to Kaafjord. The outcome of this action was the famous order from Adolph Hitler to scrap the capital ships. *Hipper* had completed temporary repairs by 24 January 1943, and sailed home for full dockyard repair, arriving in Kiel on 7 February. Ordered to Wilhelmshaven to repair, she paid off there on the 28th. Her repair, however, was cancelled as a result of the decree by the Führer, and the ship was towed instead to Pillau, where she arrived on 17 April. Late in 1943 it was decided to complete repair, and a construction party was appointed on 18 October. The ship did not recommission until 30 April 1944, and even then she was not fully operational, as No.3 boiler room remained out of action. She remained in the Training Squadron and saw no action, even in a bombardment role, until ordered to repair at Götenhafen from 1 January 1945. Transferred to Kiel as a result of the Russian advance, the ship was badly damaged by bombs on 3 May and was subsequently scuttled in Heinkendorferbucht, being broken up there *in situ* postwar.

Blücher had been badly delayed by the various modifications made to her and by the severe winter of 1939/40. She saw no operational service until the invasion of Norway in April 1940, and was damaged by gunfire and then sunk by shore-

Above: *Prinz Eugen* arrives at Brest after Rheinübung in 1941. (BA)
Left: *Prinz Eugen* de-ammunitions at Wilhelmshaven in 1945. (IWM)

Opposite page:
Top: *Blücher*, October 1939. (Gröner)
Right: *Blücher* in 1940. (BA)

based torpedoes from a battery on Kaaholm in Oslo Fjord on 9 April, with heavy loss of life.

Prinz Eugen was hit by bombs whilst fitting-out in July 1940, then touched off a magnetic mine while working up for the *Bismarck* sortie. During this sortie she scored some hits on *Prince of Wales* and reached Brest safely after the loss of the Flagship, having abandoned the intended raiding cruise because of machinery problems. While in Brest the ship was hit by a bomb on 2 July 1941, which caused severe internal damage. She remained trapped in Brest until February 1942, when Operation Cerberus, the 'Channel Dash', saw her return to Germany and almost immediate transfer to Norway. However, in the course of this move she was torpedoed and badly damaged by HM/SM *Trident* on 23 February, losing part of the stern. A makeshift repair was undertaken in Trondheim, and the ship was successfully brought home in May, arriving in Kiel on the 18th. Repairs took until the end of October,

Above: *Prinz Eugen* in 1943/44. (Gröner)

in support of the German army as part of the 2nd Task Force until she was surrendered at Copenhagen in May 1945. Allocated to the USA in 1946, *Prinz Eugen* was used as a target for the Bikini atomic bomb trials, finally foundering, due to the damage sustained, on 22 December 1946.

Lützow was sold to the USSR on 11 February 1940 as part of the pact between the USSR and Germany signed on 23 August 1939. She left Germany in tow for Leningrad on 15 April 1940. Her subsequent career will be found in the USSR section.

Seydlitz was also considered for sale to the USSR, but Hitler forbade it. Construction proceeded slowly, with periods when work was suspended, finally being stopped in June 1942 when the ship was almost complete. In 1943 Hitler ordered her to be completed as a carrier, and in consequence she was stripped to upper deck level and towed to Königsberg for further work, arriving there on 2 April 1944. Little more was done, and in December she was rated a hulk. When the Russians advanced she was inexpertly sabotaged on 29 January 1945 and abandoned to fall into Soviet hands. She was probably scrapped *in situ* postwar, but there is a report that an RAF PRU aircraft saw her on tow to Leningrad on 10 October 1946.

after which the cruiser was again ordered to Norway. After two unsuccessful attempts, however, her transfer north was cancelled at the end of February 1943. *Prinz Eugen* remained in the Baltic for the rest of the war, mostly employed as a training ship until mid-1944, when the situation on the Eastern Front became serious. For the remainder of the hostilities she bombarded shore positions

M CLASS

Ship	Builder	Laid Down	Launched	Completed	Fate
M	Deutsche Werke, Kiel	1 Nov 38	–		Broken up on slip 1942/43?
N	Marinewerft Wilhelmshaven	38*	–		Broken up on slip
O	Krupp, Germania	10 Mar 39*	–		Broken up on slip 1942/43
P	Krupp, Germania	Not laid			
Q	Schichau, Danzig	Not laid			
R	Deutsche Werke, Kiel	Not laid			

* see text

Displacement: 7,800 tons/7,925 tonnes (standard); 10,400 tons/10,566 tonnes (full load).
Length: 600ft 3in/183m (oa); 583ft 9in/178m (wl).
Beam: 55ft 9in/17m; Draught: 17ft 9in/5.42m (mean).
Machinery: 2-shaft SR Wagner turbines; 2-shaft MAN diesels; 4 Wagner boilers.
Performance: 100,000shp+16,500bhp=35.5kts; Bunkerage: 1,080+520 tons oil/diesel.
Range: 8,000nm at 19kts.
Protection: 20-35mm deck; 30-50mm main belt; 20-80mm turrets; 20-100mm CT.
Guns: eight 5.9in (4x2); four 3.5in (2x2); eight 3.7cm (4x2).
Torpedoes: eight 21in (2x4).
Aircraft: two, one catapult.
Complement: 920.

Design There was only one more attempt by the Kriegsmarine to produce a usable light cruiser for ocean deployment, and even this was to be frustrated by the premature start of the Second World War. As early as May 1936 there was issued a broad requirement for a light cruiser to be suitable for long-range commerce raiding on the oceans, in the manner of the First World War *Emden*. Unfortunately, interdepartmental bickering led to considerable delays and setbacks in the design process, such that the keel of the first ship was not to be laid until 1938.

The displacement as originally conceived was 8,000 tons, with four twin 15cm turrets and a speed of 35kts, for which some 100,000shp was necessary. Later, three twin or three triple turrets were considered because of the inability to achieve the desired speed and endurance, it being impossible to accommodate machinery of 100,000shp in a *Nürnberg*-size hull. Alternative designs based on enlarged destroyers and larger displacements were mooted, as was the use of diesels for main propulsion. It was not until November that some measure of agreement could be obtained between the interested parties; by this time the design was based upon a triple-shaft steam turbine layout for 36kts on 100,000shp, armed with the four twin 15cm turrets originally envisaged. Later the centre turbine was replaced by a diesel installation, and in January 1938 consideration was given to altering the main armament to 17cm (6.69in), but the weight penalty was not acceptable.

The protective scheme finally decided upon included a 50mm armoured deck, 35mm sloped edges and a vertical belt of 50mm. Above the side belt was a strake of 30mm armour to the upper deck, which was itself 20mm in the midships areas. Armour accounted for some 1,000 tons, 12.5 per cent of the type's displacement.

Main armament comprised the 15cm Sk C/28 as carried by *Bismarck*, but in lighter turrets. Elevation was 40°, and power elevation and training was provided. One point usually criticised in the design was the provision of only two twin 8.8cm guns as secondary and AA armament, but it should be recognised that, at the time of the design, the carrier-borne air threat had not been fully recognised, and that these ships were

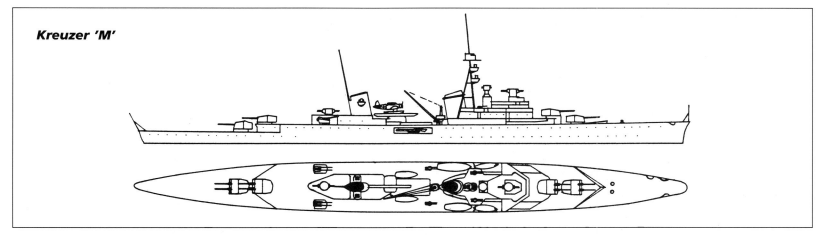

Kreuzer 'M'

intended for remote ocean employment, where their main antagonist was likely to be another cruiser.

Under the provisions of the grandiose Z Plan, up to twelve units (*M* to *X*) were to be constructed to enter service between 1942 and 1947, with the final target to be double this figure. From *Q* the design was to be modified, with increased protection, AA armament and radius of action. Unfortunately there was a shortage of suitable yards and slipways on which to build the new class, and much discussion took place in an attempt to accommodate the cruisers in the already over-extended capabilities of the German shipbuilding industry. The reality was that orders for four units were placed on 24 May 1938, with *Q* and *R* being

ordered on 8 August 1939. The first three had all been laid down by 10 July 1939, and the machinery for six units was ordered in 1938. The first two ships were to have boilers from Deschimag AG, turbines from Brown-Boverie and diesels from MAN. The second pair were to have boilers and turbines from Germania and MAN motors.

Ship *M* was laid on the slip vacated by *Graf Zeppelin*, *N* on No.1 slip at the Kriegsmarine Werft, and *O* on No.1 slip at DWK. Ship *P*, however, was not scheduled to lay down until 1942, three ships per year being the planned completion rate. It was recognised that, if war were to break out shortly after their commencement, their construction would have to be halted. So it proved, all six being cancelled on 19 September 1939.

However, the three laid down were not broken up immediately, and remained on the slip in a state of suspension until at least mid-June 1940, when the resumption of construction of *M*, *N* & *O* was being discussed. It was stated at that time that *M* could be immediately resumed, while the other two could not be restarted for three and five months respectively. The machinery for both *M* and *N* was almost complete. However, it was questioned at this time if *O* could be deleted from the future programme. Discussion on the subject of the *M* Class continued as late as March 1941, and the hulls themselves appear to have been left on the ways until the end of 1942 before they were dismantled. RAF PRU sorties were reporting *O* still on the slips in May 1942.

SPAHKREUZER

Ship	Builder	Laid Down	Launched	Completed	Fate
SP1	Krupp, Germania	30 Aug 41	-		Broken up on slip 1943
SP2	Krupp, Germania	not laid			
SP3	Krupp, Germania	not laid			

Displacement: 4,662 tons/4,736 tonnes (standard); 5,713 tons/5,804 tonnes (full load).
Length: 498ft 9in/152m (oa); 475ft 9in/145m (wl).
Beam: 48ft/14.6m; Draught: 15ft 3in/4.66m (mean).
Machinery: 2-shaft SR geared turbines; 1-shaft MAN diesel; 4 Bauer-Wagner boilers.
Performance: 77,500shp+14,500bhp=35.5kts; Bunkerage: 600 tons oil.
Range: 7,000nm at 17kts.
Protection: 10mm main deck; 18mm longitudinal bulkhead.
Guns: six 5.9in (3x2); two 3.5in (1x2); eight 3.7cm (4x2); eight 2cm (8x1).
Torpedoes: ten 21in (2x5).

Aircraft: nil.
Complement: 583.

Design The 'Super Destroyer' or Scout design which came up in discussions when the M Class was being considered was given further, separate attention, and emerged as a ship with armament superior to that of enemy destroyers and capable of out-running enemy cruisers; very much the concept of the 'Panzerschiffe'. The design progressed through several stages, being variously designated Spahkreuzer 38, 39 and 40, all of which were armed with six 15cm guns in three twin turrets, though they differed in the

layout of the weapons and machinery. It is debatable whether these ships were destroyers or cruisers; their armament was that of a destroyer, but they did have a very light protective armoured deck and a 50mm side belt. Despite the outbreak of war, the design work on these ships continued, perhaps another reason to consider them as destroyers, because at that time all construction of ships larger than destroyers, with five exceptions, was stopped. Orders were placed as late as 17 February 1941 with Germania, where they supplanted three destroyers on the programme (*Z40-42*), the ships being referred to as *SP1-SP3*. Orders for the main machinery of further units *SP4-6* were also placed that December. Only the first ship was laid down, on 30 August 1941, her existence being noted by RAF PRU flights by November. The whole programme was suspended on 23 March 1942, however, and no other was ship laid down. *SP1* remained on the slip until mid-1943, PRU reports noting that she had been completely dismantled by 31 July.

Great Britain

CALEDON CLASS

Ship	Builder	Laid Down	Launched	Completed	Fate
Caledon	Cammell Laird	17 Mar 16	25 Nov 16	6 Mar 17	Scrapped at Dover 1948
Calypso	Hawthorne Leslie	7 Feb 16	24 Jan 17	21 Jun 17	Lost 12 Jun 1940
Caradoc	Scotts	21 Feb16	23 Dec 16	15 Jun 17	Scrapped Briton Ferry 1946

Displacement: 4,180 tons/4,246 tonnes (standard); 4,950 tons/5,029 tonnes (full load).
Length: 449ft 10in/147.5m (oa); 425ft 4in/139.53m (pp).
Beam: 42ft 9in/14.02m; Draught: 14ft 3in/4.67m (mean).
Machinery: 2-shaft Parsons geared turbines; 6 Yarrow boilers.
Performance: 40,000shp=29kts; Bunkerage: 935 tons.
Range: 5,900nm at 10kts.
Protection: 3in sides (machinery spaces); 2¼in sides (magazines); 1in deck.
Guns: five 6in BL Mk XII (5x1); two 3in QF Mk I (2x1); two 2pdr (2x1).
Torpedoes: eight 21in (4x2).
Aircraft: nil.
Complement: 334

Design This class represented the fourth group of C class cruisers which were begun in the First World War as logical developments of the first light cruiser design, the *Arethusa* Class, and were designed for service in the North Sea. The design was a repeat of the earlier *Centaur* and *Concord*, except that it adopted twin-screw geared turbine machinery of a similar type to that fitted in the 1915 ship *Champion*. They were armed with five 6in guns, BL Mk XII on PXIII* mountings, a weapon introduced in the *Birmingham* of 1915, all centreline mounted. Four twin banks of 21in torpedo tubes replaced the underwater tubes of the earlier classes, giving them a heavier torpedo outfit than contemporary destroyers.

The machinery consisted of two boiler rooms forward, separated by the magazine arrangements for Q gun, abaft of which were the two engine rooms, the unit principle not yet having been adopted. All boilers were oil-fired.

The protective scheme was limited to 3in plating abreast the machinery spaces and 2in in the way of the magazines and fuel bunkers. Horizontal protection was given only to the steering gear, where it was 1in. A conning tower was still retained, but with only 3in armour, as opposed to the 6in of the first light cruisers.

Displacement increased over the earlier class as a result of the growth which had occurred since the C design had first been approved in 1913. Design displacement was 4,120 tons, with both length and beam increased.

Six repeat C class were authorised in 1915, of which four were immediately ordered, all having been laid down by April 1916. All four of this class completed for service in the First World War and, because of this, not all ran full trials, but *Cassandra* did so, reaching 29.1kts with 40,750shp on a displacement about 100 tons over designed figures. Although this ship survived the First World War, she was mined in an uncharted German minefield and sank off the island of Oesel in the Baltic on 5 December 1918, while on operations against the Bolsheviks.

Modifications In the main, only the modifications carried out in the immediate prewar or wartime periods will be considered for all following classes of British cruisers. No modifications of any note were made to this class before the Second World

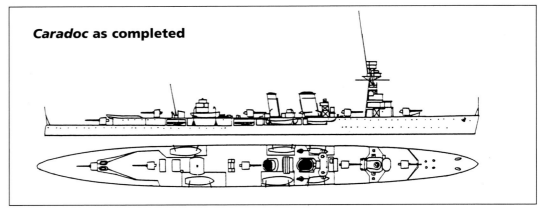

Caradoc as completed

Below: *Calypso* in July 1935. (W&L)

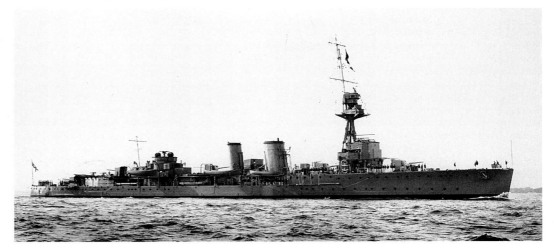

Above: *Caradoc* in May 1943. She has received only a couple of 20mm and is otherwise unaltered. (IWM)

War because, owing to their age, they had spent a good deal of the 1930s in reserve. *Caledon* may have had a few 20mm added in 1941, but it was not until 1942 that major changes were made, when, between September and December the following year, she was converted into an AA cruiser. All original guns and torpedo tubes were removed. In lieu she received three twin 4in, two twin Hazemeyer Bofors and six twin 20mm, with a full radar outfit. By April 1944 she was listed as having two further single 20mm. In September and October 1944 she received six single 40mm Bofors Mk III, which probably supplanted the twin 20mm and another 20mm single. However, in April 1945 the ship was disarmed. *Calypso*, as a relatively early war loss, received little attention

and no changes are listed for her. *Caradoc* had two single 2pdr and five single 20mm fitted at New York in 1941/42, and radar 271 and 290.

Service *Caledon* served with the Grand Fleet, 6th Light Cruiser Squadron, and later became Flagship, 1st LCS 1917/19, and saw action in the Heligoland Bight on 17 November 1917, when she was struck by a 12in shell. She then went to the Home and Atlantic Fleets during 1919-26, serving with the 2nd LCS. During this period she was detached to the Mediterranean (September 1922) and Baltic (January 1923). Paid off for refit on 17 August 1926, she subsequently joined the 3rd Cruiser Squadron in the Mediterranean on 5 September 1927. She reduced to reserve on 31 July 1931, until brought forward again in 1939 to join the 7th Cruiser Squadron, and was at Scapa Flow in August 1939. She was initially employed on the Northern Patrol until the summer of 1940 (joining the 12th Cruiser Squadron in October

1939), after which she was deployed to the Mediterranean, where she joined the 3rd Cruiser Squadron at Alexandria. Following convoy escort duties in the eastern Mediterranean, *Caledon* served in the Red Sea from August, during the campaign in British Somaliland, where she covered the evacuation of Berbera and bombarded shore positions. She remained in this theatre into 1941, having survived a brief plan to use her as a blockship at Tripoli in April/May. In 1941 she was under refit at Colombo between August and October for service with the Eastern Fleet, operating in the Indian Ocean in 1942. She returned to Chatham for conversion into an AA cruiser, which was carried out between 14 September 1942 and 7 December 1943, this being the last such C class conversion, and a somewhat leisurely process. After conversion she worked up with the Home Fleet, then served in the Mediterranean, defending convoys against Luftwaffe attacks from bases in the south of France. She was at the Dragoon landings in Provence in August 1944, then went to the eastern Mediterranean at the end of the year, where she operated in Greek waters. In 1945 she came home to be disarmed, and was placed in reserve by the end of the war in Europe. She was laid up in the Fal in 1946, then handed over to BISCO* for scrapping on 22 January 1948, arriving at the yard of Dover Industries, Dover, for breaking up, on 14 February 1948.

Calypso also served with the 6th LCS in the Grand Fleet 1917/1919, and was badly hit in the action in the Heligoland Bight on 17 November 1917. Deployed to the Baltic in 1918/19, she subsequently went to the 3rd Cruiser Squadron in the Mediterranean in March 1919, where she remained until returning home in 1932. The years before the Second World War were spent in the reserve fleet. At the outbreak of the war she was serving with the 7th Cruiser Squadron on Northern Patrol duty, and captured the blockade runners *Minden* on 24 September and

Konsul Hendrik Fisser on 22 November 1939. She was also deployed in the hunt for *Scharnhorst* and *Gneisenau* after their sinking of *Rawalpindi*. In 1940 she went to the eastern Mediterranean, based on Alexandria, and was torpedoed and sunk by the Italian submarine *Bagnolini* while on a sweep south-west of Crete on 12 June 1940.

Caradoc served with the 6th LCS in the Grand Fleet during 1917/19, including a period in the Baltic when the Soviet destroyers *Avtroil* and *Spartak* were captured. On 29 February 1919 she commissioned for the 3rd Cruiser Squadron in the Mediterranean until December 1926, when she sailed out to China. After returning home she paid off for refit on 15 September 1927, and on completion *Caradoc* went to the America and West Indies Station between October 1928 and February 1930. She paid off into reserve again in March 1930, then in July 1930 went out to China again (5th CS) until 1934. The years between 17 October 1934 and 1939 were spent in reserve. She was on the America and West Indies Station during

1939-42, transporting some £2 million in gold to Halifax, Nova Scotia, in October 1939 and intercepting the blockade runners *Emmy Friedrich* in the Yucatan Channel on 23 October 1939 and *Rhein* on 11 December 1940. After refit at New York between 28 October 1941 and 26 February 1942, *Caradoc* joined the Eastern Fleet until 1943, when she went to Durban in June for conversion into a gunnery training ship for the South African station. In 1944 the ship went to Colombo, where she served as a base ship until 1945, becoming Flagship, East Indies, in August 1945. After the war she returned to the UK and was handed over to BISCO on 5 April 1946, arriving at the Briton Ferry yard of T. W. Ward & Co for scrapping in May 1946.

After the war, all vessels for scrapping were handed over to the British Iron and Steel Corporation (BISCO), by whom they were allocated to a breaker's yard. They were not sold as such, but the proceeds from the scrapping operation were passed back to the Government, less agreed expenses and profit.

CERES CLASS

Ship	Builder	Laid Down	Launched	Completed	Fate
Cardiff	Fairfield	22 Jul 16	12 Apr 17	25 Jun 17	Scrapped at Troon, 1946
Ceres	John Brown	11 Jul 16	24 Mar 17	1 Jun 17	Scrapped at Blyth, 1946
Coventry	Swan Hunter	4 Aug 16	6 Jul 17	21 Feb 18	Lost 14 Sep 1942
Curacoa	Pembroke Dky	Jul 16	5 May 17	18 Feb 18	Lost 2 Oct 1942
Curlew	Vickers	21 Aug 16	5 Jul 17	14 Dec 17	Lost 26 May 1940

Displacement: 4,290 tons/4,358 tonnes (standard); 5,276 tons/5,360 tonnes (full load).

Length: 451ft 6in/137.6m (oa); 425ft/129.54m (pp).

Beam: 43ft 6in/13.28m; Draught: 14ft 3in/4.34m (mean).

Machinery: 2-shaft Brown-Curtis geared turbines; 6 Yarrow boilers.

Performance: 40,000shp= 29.5kts; Bunkerage: 935 tons (920 tons AA conversions).

Range: 5,900nm at 10kts (3,250nm at 12kts AA conversions).

Protection: 3in sides (machinery spaces); 2¼in sides (magazines); 1in deck.

Guns: five 6in BL Mk XII (5x1); two 3in QF Mk I (2x1); two 2pdr (2x1).

Torpedoes: eight 21in (4x2).

Coventry & Curlew: ten 4in Mk V (10x1); sixteen 2pdr, (2x8).

Torpedoes: nil.

Curacoa: eight 4in Mk XIX (4x2); four 2pdr (1x4).

Torpedoes: nil.

Aircraft: nil.

Complement: 334.

Design The five ships of this class comprised the two authorised in October 1915 and three more

approved early in 1916. They were all ordered in March-April 1916 as repeats of the earlier group, but design changes were made before they were laid down that were sufficient to make then a separate sub-group of the C class. In this class, No. 2 gun was resited ahead of the bridge so as to be superfiring on No. 1 gun, where it would benefit from much greater arcs of fire than previously. To this end, a shelter deck was added on the forecastle and, in consequence, the bridge had to be moved aft by some 46ft. This in turn necessitated considerable internal rearrangement of the compartments ahead of and including the forward boiler room. The increased height of No. 2 gun required a consequent increase in the height of the bridge structure, and, to maintain stability with the increased top-weight, beam was increased by 9in. The displacement rose to 4,190 tons (legend). Armament was the same as in the earlier class, except that the torpedo outfit was doubled to four banks of twin tubes, an alteration which was applied to the *Caledon* Class retrospectively, before completion.

The main machinery remained identical to that of the earlier class, as did protection, except that the conning tower was dispensed with in *Coventry* and *Curacoa* before completion. It was also removed from other ships of both classes in 1918/19.

Ceres achieved 29.1kts on 39,425shp with a displacement of 4,215 tons on trials in June 1917.

Modifications As noted above, the conning tower was removed at the end of the First World War. Two 2pdr single mountings were added in *Curlew*, *Coventry* and *Curacoa* in 1918, in *Ceres* in 1921/22 and in *Cardiff* in 1923/24. *Cardiff* was the only ship in the class to carry an aircraft for a period. Otherwise, interwar modifications were limited to minor structural alterations. However, the London Naval Treaty of 1930 implied the disposal of a number of cruisers, and in 1934 design work was started to convert these ships into AA cruisers, approval to convert all C class ships being given in the following year. *Coventry* and *Curlew* were selected as the prototypes and taken in hand in 1935/36. All original armament was landed and replaced by ten single 4in Mk V, one forward, six on the beam and three aft, together with two 8-barrel 2pdr Mk VI. Two HA control positions were fitted, and internal arrangements altered. All tubes were removed. The single 4in came from newer ships being rearmed with twin 4in, as there was a need to keep costs down. For the same reason, the after multiple 2pdr mounting had to be removed in 1938/39 to be fitted in other ships because of shortages. It was replaced by two of the useless quadruple .5in machine guns. Only one other ship of the class, *Curacoa*, received this conversion, and then not until the summer of 1939. Her conversion differed in that twin 4in Mk XlX were fitted in lieu of numbers 1, 3, 4 and 5 guns, a quadruple 2pdr Mk Vll in place of No.2 gun, and two quadruple .5in machine guns abreast the fore funnel. Two single 2pdr were also added. Again all of the torpedo outfit was removed.

During the war period *Cardiff* had received six 20mm singles and type 290 radar by April 1942, and had type 273 by late 1943. *Ceres* also had six 20mm singles by 1942, and by April 1944 had received radars 290 and 273. Between April and May 1944 the 3in and single 2pdrs were landed and replaced by eight 20mm singles. *Coventry* had five single 20mm added in May 1942. *Curacoa* had radars 282 and 285 fitted in 1941, and by September 1942 had also received type 273 and five single 20mm. *Curlew*, as an early war loss, had no modifications.

Service *Cardiff* completed in time to see service with the Grand Fleet during 1917/1919 as flag-

Above: *Cardiff.* (IWM) **Below:** The ill-fated *Curacoa* after her conversion to an AA cruiser. (Courtesy G. Ransome)

ship of the 6th LCS. She led the German High Seas Fleet into Scapa Flow in November 1918 after the Armistice, and served in the Baltic against Soviet Russian forces until 1919. She then went out to the Mediterranean for the 3rd Cruiser Squadron (Flag) until 1929. After refit in 1929/31 she served on the Africa Station as flagship, 6th Cruiser Squadron, until May 1933. *Cardiff* was in the reserve fleet between July 1933 and July 1938, when she recommissioned for the 5th Cruiser Squadron on the China Station. *Cardiff* left Hong Kong on 29 April 1939 to pay off into reserve until reactivated at the outbreak of war. As a unit of the 12th Cruiser Squadron she served with the Northern Patrol in 1939/40, then spent the remainder of the war as a gunnery training ship in the western approaches. She was handed over to BISCO for breaking up on 23 January 1946, and arrived at Arnott Young (Dalmuir) for scrapping on 18 March 1946.

Ceres joined the 6th LCS on completion, then went to the Mediterranean, 3rd Cruiser Squadron, from 1919 until 1927, which included a period in the Black Sea in 1920. After a refit in 1929/31 she reduced to reserve until recommissioned in May 1932 for the Mediterranean. She reduced to reserve again on 27 November 1932 and remained inactive until September 1939, when recommissioned for the Channel Force. In November she was with the 11th Cruiser Squadron on the Northern Patrol, but in the early part of 1940 she went out to the Far East, being at Singapore in April. She participated in the East African campaigns of 1940/41, assisting in the evacuation of Berbera, British Somaliland, in August 1940, and in February 1941 was involved in the blockade of Kismayu, Italian Somaliland, and also in the subsequent British offensive against the Italians in this theatre. *Ceres* remained in the East Indies and with the Eastern Fleet until October 1943,

when she went to the Mediterranean, then returned home to serve with the escort forces during the Normandy landings in June 1944. Later that year she reduced to reserve as an accommodation/base ship at Portsmouth, remaining in that status until the end of the war. *Ceres* was handed over for scrapping on 5 April 1946, and arrived at Hughes Bolkow, Blyth, for breaking up, on 12 July 1946.

Coventry served with the 5th LCS in the Harwich force from completion until 1919, including service in the Baltic and then as flagship of the 1st LCS in the Atlantic Fleet. In 1920/24 she was Commodore (D), then went to the Mediterranean in the same capacity during 1924/28. After a refit in 1928/30, the ship continued her Mediterranean service as Flag (D) until reducing to reserve on 1 October 1936. She subsequently served in the Mediterranean until 1938, when she returned to Portsmouth for conversion into an AA cruiser. In September 1939 *Coventry* was in the Mediterranean again, but served in Norway during the campaign there April/May 1940. In August she went to Gibraltar for the formation of Force H before being passed to the eastern Mediterranean. Based at Alexandria, she participated in attacks on Bengahzi and escorted Malta convoys during 1940, but on 13 December 1940 she was torpedoed and damaged by the Italian submarine *Neghelli*. In 1941 she covered the troop convoys to Greece, and their subsequent evacuation. Much of 1941 was again occupied by the attempts to run convoys to Malta, the evacuation of Crete (she rescued the survivors from *Calcutta*), and the Syrian Campaign. In 1942 she continued on the Malta convoys, but in September, while covering the disastrous Tobruk raid, she was badly damaged by aircraft and had to be scuttled by *Zulu*.

Curacoa also joined the Harwich Force at completion as Flagship, 5th LCS, then later

became flagship of the 1st LCS in the Atlantic Fleet. She went to the Baltic in April 1919, but on 13 May the ship was mined some 70 miles west of Reval whilst en route for Libau. She returned home for repairs, then served with the 2nd Light Cruiser Squadron as Flagship in the Atlantic fleet until 1928. After commissioning for the 3rd Cruiser Squadron on 4 September 1929, she served in the Mediterranean until 1932. *Curacoa* recommissioned for the gunnery school on 18 December 1933, until taken in hand in the summer of 1939 for conversion into an AA cruiser. This refit was completed in April 1940. She then participated in the Norwegian campaign and was badly damaged by aircraft on 24 April. Following repairs, she operated in the western approaches, escorting troop liner convoys. On 2 October 1942, off Bloody Foreland, north of Ireland, *Curacoa* was rammed and sunk by the liner *Queen Mary*, which she was escorting at the time.

Curlew joined the 5th LCS at Harwich on completion, and then, in 1919, the 1st LCS with the Atlantic Fleet, where she remained only a year before recommissioning for the 5th Cruiser Squadron on 27 April 1920 and going out to China. On 24 November 1922 she recommissioned for the 8th LCS on the America and West Indies Station, eventually returning home to reserve in 1927. She subsequently served with the 3rd Cruiser Squadron (November 1929 to August 1933), and with the 1st Cruiser Squadron until October 1936. After a period in reserve the ship was selected for one of the prototype conversions to an AA cruiser in 1935. She was in dockyard hands at the outbreak of war in 1939, then served with the Home Fleet until she was sunk by aircraft of *KG100* off Skaanland on 26 May 1940, during the Norwegian campaign.

CARLISLE CLASS

Ship	Builder	Laid Down	Launched	Completed	Fate
Cairo	Cammell Laird	28 Nov 17	19 Nov 18	14 Oct 19	Lost 12 Aug 1942
Calcutta	Vickers	18 Oct 17	9 Jul 18	21 Aug 19	Lost 1 Jun 1941
Capetown	Cammell Laird	23 Feb 18	28 Jun 19	10 Apr 22*	Scrapped at Preston 1948
Carlisle	Fairfield	2 Oct 17	9 Jul 18	16 Nov 18	CTL 9 Oct 1943
Colombo	Fairfield	8 Dec 17	18 Dec 18	18 Jun 19	Scrapped at Newport 1948

*Completed at Pembroke Dockyard.

Displacement: 4,200 tons/4,267 tonnes (standard); 5,300 tons/5,384 tonnes (full load).
Length: 451ft 6in/148.12m (oa); 425ft/129.58m (pp).
Beam: 43ft 6in/13.25m; Draught: 14ft 3in/4.34m (mean).
Machinery: 2-shaft Parsons (Brown Curtis in Columbo & Carlisle) geared turbines; 6 Yarrow boilers.
Performance: 40,000shp=29.5kts; Bunkerage: 935 tons.
Range: 5,900nm at 10kts.
Protection: 3in sides (machinery spaces); 2¼in sides (magazines); 1in deck.

Guns: five 6in BL Mk XII (5x1); two 3in QF Mk I (2x1); two 2pdr (2x1).
Torpedoes: eight 21in (4x2).
Cairo, Carlisle & Calcutta: eight 4in Mk XIX (4x2); four 2pdr, (1x4); eight .5in MGs (2x4).
Torpedoes: nil.
Aircraft: nil.
Complement: 334.

Design Ordered in July 1917, this class was laid down as repeat *Ceres* ships, but as a result of the pronounced wetness of the earlier C class cruisers the bows of this new class were altered after laying down, the stem being raised by 5ft, gradually reducing aft to meet the original deck line at No.1 gun. Because the original flare of the ship's side was not altered, the plating was continued up to the new deck by means of a knuckle. Otherwise there was no difference between these ships and the earlier classes.

Modifications *Carlisle* was completed with a hangar for an aircraft under the bridge, but this had been removed by 1920. *Cairo* and *Calcutta* were the second pair of C class ships to be taken in hand for conversion into AA cruisers, in 1938. They were rearmed with four twin 4in Mk XIX, one quadruple 2pdr Mk VII and two .5in multiple MGs, with all tubes landed. *Carlisle* was then taken in hand in the summer of 1939 after the completion of the first pair of this class. Her refit, which followed the pattern of the earlier ships, was not completed before the outbreak of war.

Cairo received little modification except for a number of single 20mm guns fitted in 1942. *Calcutta* similarly received little modification, owing to her early loss. Radar was never fitted. *Capetown*, on the other hand, never underwent conversion to an AA cruiser because of the outbreak of war and the shortage of dockyard resources. As an unconverted ship her additions were limited to six single 20mm and radar 290. Her outfit as late as April 1944 was two 3in, two 2pdr and six 20mm. *Carlisle* had two single 2pdr added by April 1941, and radar 281. A year later she had seven single 20mm fitted. After refit in

Below: *Colombo* as an AA cruiser with twin 4in guns. (Courtesy G. Ransome)

Calcutta, 1939

Above: *Carlisle* at Malta. (IWM)
Below: *Carlisle* later in the war. Note the additional HACS aft and the radars. (Courtesy G. Ransome)

Below: *Cairo* in 1940. Note the false bow waves. (IWM)

November 1942 the seven single 20mm were removed and five twin 20mm added, with radars 271, 282 and 285. By April 1944 this outfit had not altered, except that the 20mm were in twin power-worked mountings. *Colombo* did not begin her conversion into an AA cruiser until August 1942. This equipped her with three twin 4in Mk XlX, two twin Hazemeyer Bofors, six power-worked twin 20mm and two single, plus radars 281b, 272, 285 and 282. This remained unchanged in April 1944, but by the end of the war in Europe two twin 20mm had been removed and four single 40mm Bofors Mk III added.

Service None of this class was completed in time to see any war service in the First World War. *Cairo* went out to China for the 5th LCS in 1920, and remained on that station until recommissioning for the 4th LCS in the East Indies on 27 December 1921. She was stationed there until 1925, when she was temporarily detached to the China Station. Her next deployment was with the 8th Cruiser Squadron on the America and West Indies Station between 1927 and 1928. She then spent 1928 to 1930 in the Mediterranean as Flagship Rear Admiral (D). After a refit in 1931/32 she acted as Commodore (D) with the Home Fleet Flotillas until paid off on 25 November 1937. *Cairo* then underwent conversion to an AA cruiser at Chatham in 1938, which was completed in May 1939. In September of that year she was with the Channel Force, and by December was in the Humber. During the Norwegian campaign she was employed on escort duties and covered the landings. She rescued the survivors of *Effingham*. In 1941 she operated mostly in the North Atlantic before going to the Mediterranean in 1942. She served with Force H from Gibraltar, covering the Harpoon/Vigorous convoys and Operation Pinpoint in July 1942, when *Eagle* flew off fighters to Malta. During Operation Pedestal *Cairo* was torpedoed by the Italian submarine *Axum* on 12 August 1942, and her stern was blown off. The wreck had to be sunk by *Pathfinder* the next day.

Calcutta served on the America and West Indies Station with the 8th LCS from completion until ordered home to pay off in November 1927, her crew transferring to *Despatch*. On 18 September 1929 she recommissioned for the 6th Cruiser squadron (flag) on the Africa Station, paying off to reserve in 1931. The following years were spent in reserve or on subsidiary duties. In 1938 she was also taken in hand at Chatham for conversion to an AA cruiser, completing in July 1939. She served with the Humber Force from September 1939, then took part in the Norwegian campaign from April 1940 before assisting in Operation Dynamo in May. In June, while covering the evacuation of western France, she collided with the destroyer *Fraser* in the Gironde, and sank her. At the end of August *Calcutta* was transferred to Gibraltar with Force H and then served in the eastern Mediterranean, where she covered Malta convoys, and, with the 3rd Cruiser squadron, the attack on Benghazi in September. In 1941 she was involved in the transfer of troops to Greece and their subsequent evacuation, followed by the evacuation of Crete in May 1941. On 1 June 1941 the ship was attacked and sunk by aircraft of *II/LG1* about 100nm north of Alexandria.

Capetown also served on the America and West Indies Station from completion until 1929, when she reduced to reserve. On 17 July 1934 the ship recommissioned for the 5th Cruiser squadron on the China Station, where she spent a couple of commissions before returning home to reserve in August 1938. Her proposed conversion into an AA cruiser was cancelled at the outbreak of war. In September 1939 she was at Gibraltar with the North Atlantic Command, then went to the eastern Mediterranean with the 3rd Cruiser squadron, where she covered convoys in the Aegean. In 1941 *Capetown* went to the Indian Ocean for the British offensive against Italian Somaliland, where, on 6 April 1941, she was torpedoed by the MTB *MAS 213* and brought into Port Sudan under tow by *Parramatta* only with difficulty. She spent about a year under repair. In 1942/43 the ship was attached to the Eastern Fleet, but by 1944 had returned home. She was present at the Normandy Landings in June that year, but spent the remainder of the war as an accommodation

ship. On 5 April 1946 *Capetown* was handed over to BISCO for scrapping, and arrived at the Preston yard of T. W. Ward on 2 June 1946.

Carlisle joined the 5th LCS at Harwich on completion, then on 1 March 1919 recommissioned and went out to China with this Squadron until 1928. Under refit between 1928/29, she then served on the Africa Station with the 6th Cruiser Squadron until relieved by *Neptune* on 16 March 1937. On her return home she reduced to reserve. In the summer of 1939 she was converted into an AA ship, the work not being completed until after the outbreak of war. On her return to service she participated in the Norwegian campaign, during which she intercepted and sank the German troop transport *Nord Norge*. By August 1940 she was in the Red Sea, covering the evacuation of Berbera, then spent the remainder of her career in the Mediterranean, where she participated in the Greek and Crete campaigns, Malta convoy operations, the defence of Suez and the Sicily landings. By October 1943 she was operating in the Aegean, and on 9 October she was bombed and badly damaged while on a sortie in the Scarpanto Channel south of Piraeus with two destroyers. Towed into Alexandria by *Rockwood*, she was declared a constructional total loss and not repaired, remaining at Alexandria as a base ship for the rest of the war. She lasted as a hulk until 1948, and was finally broken up locally.

Colombo served on the China Station with the 5th LCS until recommissioned on 15 March

1922, then went to the East Indies with the 4th LCS until 1926. Then followed a period on the America and West Indies Station with the 8th Cruiser squadron until a refit was started in January 1930. After spending 1931/32 in the Mediterranean, *Colombo* sailed for the East Indies in July 1932 to relieve *Emerald*, remaining there until 1935. The years 1936 to 1939 were spent in reserve. She served with the 11th Cruiser squadron at the outbreak of war, based initially at Gibraltar, then carried out Northern Patrol duties, capturing the German *Henning Oldendorf* on 17 November 1939. In 1940/41 she served in the East Indies, where she participated in the blockade of Kismayu in Italian Somaliland in February 1941, and in the Madagascar operations of November. In 1942 she was attached to the Eastern Fleet before returning home for conversion to an AA cruiser between June 1942 and March 1943. On her return to service *Colombo* went to the Mediterranean, where she took part in the Sicily campaign and escorted convoys along the Algerian coast. By 1944 she was attached to the 31st Escort Group, and in August covered the landings in the south of France, Operation Dragoon. Her final operations were in the Aegean at the end of 1944, but she had reduced to reserve before the end of the war in Europe. *Colombo* was handed over to BISCO for scrapping on 22 January 1948, and arrived at Cashmore, Newport, for breaking up, on 13 May 1948.

D CLASS

Ship	Builder	Laid Down	Launched	Completed	Fate
Danae	Armstrongs	1 Dec 16	26 Jan 18	18 Jun 18	Scrapped at Barrow 1948
Dauntless	Palmers	3 Jan 17	10 Apr18	26 Nov 18	Scrapped at Inverkeithing 1946
Dragon	Scotts	24 Jan 17	29 Dec17	10 Aug 18	Sunk as breakwater 18 Jul 1944
Dehli	Armstrongs	29 Oct 17	23 Aug 18	31 May 19	Scrapped at Newport 1948
Dunedin	Armstrongs	5 Nov 17	19 Nov 18	13 Sep 19	Lost 24 November 1941
Durban	Scotts[1]	22 Jun 18	29 May 19	1 Nov 21	Sunk as breakwater 9 June 1944
Diomede	Vickers[2]	3 Jun 18	29 Apr 19	22 Oct 22	Scrapped at Dalmuir 1946
Despatch	Fairfield[3]	8 Jul 18	24 Sep 19	15 Jun 22	Scrapped at Troon 1946

Completed at [1] Devonport Dky; [2] Portsmouth Dky; [3] Chatham Dky.

Displacement: 4,850 tons/4,927 tonnes (standard); 6,030 tons/6,129 tonnes (full load).

Length: 471ft (first three); 472ft 6in (others)/143.5/144m (oa); 445ft/135.6m (pp).

Beam: 46ft (1st three), 46ft 6in/14.02/14.17m; Draught: 14ft 6in/4.42m (mean).

Machinery: 2-shaft Brown-Curtis geared turbines (*Dauntless* & *Diomede* Parsons); 6 Yarrow boilers.

Performance: 40,000shp=29kts; Bunkerage: 1,060 tons oil.

Range: 6,700nm at 10kts.

Protection: 3in sides (machinery spaces); 2¼in sides (magazines); 1in deck; 1in magazine box protection.

Guns: six 6in BL Mk XII (6x1 except *Diomede*, 1x2 & 4x1); three 4in Mk V (3x1); two 2pdr (2x1).

Torpedoes: twelve 21in (4x3).

Aircraft: nil.

Complement: 452.

Design Intelligence reports in early 1916 led the Admiralty to believe that Germany was constructing a new class of cruiser armed with 150mm (5.9in) guns, and that it was probable that they would ship ten or twelve guns, thus out-classing the *C* class. However, the German ships carried only two guns on the centreline; the remainder were on the beam, and therefore the effective broadside of these cruisers was not as heavy as might have appeared. The British were by this time abandoning the beam arrangement of guns for the more economical centreline arrangement, and it was therefore felt that, by increasing the firepower of the C design by one gun, the resultant ship would compare favourably with the new German ships without a large increase in displacement. This was done by the expedient of working in a deckhouse forward of the bridge, upon which a sixth 6in gun could be mounted, superfiring on No. 1 gun. To accommodate this alteration the fore end was lengthened by 20ft and the bridge moved 8ft aft. Similar alterations had to be made internally, especially regarding No. 1 boiler room. In fact, the internal arrangements required quite considerable alteration, because reduced-revolution machinery was to be installed at the same time to give greater propeller effi-

D Class

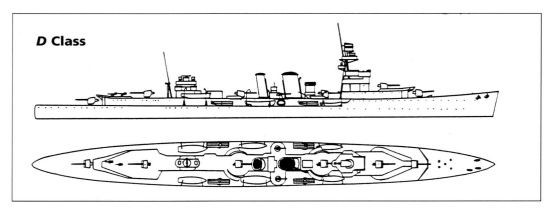

ciency and maintain a maximum speed of 29kts. This required heavier and longer machinery than in the previous class. The increased top weights owing to a higher bridge and the additional 6in gun necessitated the beam being increased by 2ft 9in over that of *Caledon*, and the displacement by some 430 tons. Protection was similar to that of the earlier ships, but the Battle of Jutland was fought while the design was still being worked on, and it was decided to include modifications as a result of several of the lessons learned. Among these were the fitting of an armoured box protection to the magazines and better protective plating to the gun shields. Other changes included the fitting of triple torpedo tubes in lieu of twin, and depth-charge throwers. Consequently the displacement grew to 5,635 tons (deep), at which a speed of just over 28kts was expected.

The main armament remained the 6in Mk XII on 30° mountings, but these were on CPXIV mountings. *Diomede*, however, was fitted with a prototype single 6in gun house Mk XVI in No.1 position, which had 40° elevation. This proved most satisfactory in service. This ship and *Despatch* also had 4in AA in lieu of the 3in in the earlier ships.

Three ships, *Danae*, *Dauntless* and *Dragon*, were ordered in September 1916, three repeats in July 1917 (*Dehli*, *Dunedin* and *Durban*), and six more in March 1918 (*Daedalus*, *Daring*, *Despatch*, *Diomede*, *Dryad* and *Desperate*). These last ships differed in having increased sheer forward, as in the *Carlisle* class, although only *Despatch* and *Diomede* were completed, the other four being cancelled in November 1918.

Modifications Two ships, *Dragon* and *Dauntless*, were completed with large hangars under the bridge structure which they retained into the 1920s, but the others, with the exception of *Danae* (which never carried aircraft), were fitted only with the standard flying-off platform forward of the after control position. Its intended replacement by a catapult never happened, and all aircraft fittings had been removed by the end of the

Below: *Durban*. (IWM)

1930s. Unlike the *C* class, the *D*s were never rearmed as AA cruisers before the war, despite a plan in 1936 to rearm them with four twin 4.5in Mk III UD mountings, HACS and a quadruple 2pdr. Pressure of other work prevented any such plan from materialising until 1941, when *Dehli* was rebuilt in the USA. Apart from this ship, modifications were limited, as they were mainly employed on distant stations for most of their careers.

Danae had two 2pdr added by 1939, and had received a quadruple 2pdr in lieu of the after 4in AA by 1942. By April 1943 she had one twin 4in added as well as a second quadruple 2pdr, four twin power-worked 20mm and radars 291 and 273. The single 2pdr were removed. This was still the same in April 1944, by which time the torpedo tubes had also been landed.

Dauntless received eight single 20mm and radars 291 and 273 early in 1942, plus two quadruple 2pdr by April 1943.

Dehli was refitted in the USA in 1941, and emerged with five single 5in 38cal Mk 30 US-pattern weapons, two Mk 37 directors, two quadruple 2pdr and eight single 20mm. All tubes were landed and she received a full radar outfit. In 1944 two single 20mm were replaced by two power-operated twin 20mm.

Despatch, which had two quadruple .5in MG mountings from 1939, received in addition, in 1942, eight single 20mm and radars 290 and 273, while retaining three 4in AA. April 1944 listings still show this armament, but at this time she was under refit and had all 6in removed to be replaced by sixteen single 40mm Mk III Bofors and two single 20mm.

Diomede, while in refit during 1942/43, landed the 6in gunhouse, which was replaced by a single shielded weapon, exchanged two single 2pdr for eight single 20mm and had radars 290 and 273 fitted. In 1943 two single 20mm were replaced by two twin 20mm.

Dragon had two quadruple 2pdr and eight single 20mm fitted by April 1943. By April 1944 one 6in, one 4in and four single 20mm had been landed, and the light AA was now five twin power-operated 20mm and four single with two 4in AA. All tubes were landed.

Dunedin had two quadruple .5in MGs added in 1939, instead of the 2pdr fitted in most other ships. She received radar 286m in 1940, but otherwise remained unaltered.

Durban received eight single 20mm in 1942, as well as radars 290 and 273. This, together with the standard pair of 2pdr guns, remained her outfit as late as April 1944.

Service *Danae* completed in time to see brief war service with the Harwich Force, 5th LCS, in 1918 to 1919 (including the Baltic campaign of 1919), before serving with the Atlantic Fleet during 1919-

24. In 1924/24 she was part of the Special Service Squadron for the Empire cruise, then went to the Mediterranean with the 1st Cruiser Squadron from September 1925 until 1929. After refit the ship served with the 8th Cruiser Squadron on the America and West Indies Station from August 1930 until 1935, when she was relieved by *Apollo* and paid off. She recommissioned on 25 August 1936 for the China Station, 5th Cruiser Squadron, returning home to pay off on 14 January 1938. Part of the 9th Cruiser Squadron at the outbreak of war in September 1939, she went out to China again in the same year. She formed part of the British Malaya Force in March 1940, and, when war with Japan broke out, operated from Singapore on escort duties as part of the China Force between Singapore, Sunda and Java. In February 1942 she took part in strikes from Batavia before departing from Sunda for Colombo on 28 February. Thereafter she served with the Eastern Fleet, 4th Cruiser Squadron, until 1944, undergoing major modernisation in the UK between 1 August 1942 and 7 July 1943. She returned home to participate in the Normandy landings as part of the Sword Beach bombardment force. On 4 October 1944 *Danae* was renamed *Conrad* when lent to the Polish Navy serving with the 10th Cruiser Squadron in the Home Fleet (see page 201). She was returned on 28 September 1946 and reverted to *Danae*. She was handed over to BISCO for scrapping on 22 January 1948, and arrived at the Barrow yard of T. W. Ward on 27 March that year for breaking up.

Dauntless went to the Baltic in 1919 from completion, and was then employed on detached service in the West Indies, followed by the Atlantic Fleet, 1st LCS, 1919-24. After the Empire cruise of 1923/24 she went to the Mediterranean for a couple of years with the 1st Cruiser Squadron, before recommissioning on 15 May 1938 for the 8th Cruiser Squadron on the America and West Indies Station in 1928. However, shortly after her arrival, she ran aground on the Thrum Cap shoal off Halifax, Nova Scotia, on 2 July 1928, and was badly damaged, the engine room and one boiler room being breached. Not until all guns, torpedo tubes and funnels, plus much other equipment, was removed could the ship be refloated on 12 July, towed off by *Despatch* and tugs. Repairs took until 1929, when the ship reduced to reserve. She was back on the America and West Indies Station in 1930, and in the South American Division in 1931/32. She relieved *Curlew* in the Mediterranean with the 3rd Cruiser Squadron in 1934, remaining there until 1935. She paid off to reserve again and remained out of service until 1939, when she recommissioned for the 9th Cruiser Squadron in the South Atlantic Command, where she was in September, but by December the squadron was on

the China Station. She formed part of the British Malaya force in March 1941, a collision with *Emerald* off Malacca on 15 June requiring repairs at Singapore until mid-August. She came home to refit at Portsmouth early in 1942, then served with the Eastern Fleet in 1942/43. Her remaining service was in the capacity of a training ship until 1945, reducing to reserve early that year. Handed over to BISCO for scrapping on 13 February 1946, she arrived at the Inverkeithing yard of T. W. Ward in April 1946 for breaking up.

Dehli served as flagship of the 1st LCS, Atlantic Fleet 1919, which included a deployment to the Baltic in 1919 as flagship of Admiral Cowan's squadron. She, too, participated in the Empire Cruise, then served in the Mediterranean after recommissioning on 18 November 1924 until 1926, when she joined the 1st Cruiser Squadron on the China Station until the end of 1928. She saw further service as Flagship of the 8th Cruiser Squadron on the American Station between December 1929 and 1932, when she joined the 3rd Cruiser Squadron in the Mediterranean. She returned home in March 1938 and reduced to reserve. Recommissioned for the 12th Cruiser Squadron at the outbreak of war, she served with the Home Fleet on Northern Patrol duties, intercepting the blockade runners *Rheingold* and *Mecklenburg* before the end of the year. In 1940 *Dehli* joined Force H at Gibraltar, participating in Operation Hurry in July, when naval aircraft attacked Sardinia. She then came under the command of C in C, South Atlantic, for operations against Vichy French forces in West Africa, including the Congo, Dakar, and the blockade of the Gabon coast in November. In 1941 she was selected for conversion into an AA cruiser and taken in hand at New York Navy Yard between 3 May and 31 December. This refit was finished off in Britain by the end of March 1942, when she joined the Home Fleet. In November she took part in the Torch landings in North Africa as part of the Centre task force, and was badly damaged by bombing on 20 November 1942, when her stern was blown off. After repairs she continued service in the Mediterranean, seeing action at the landings in Sicily in July 1943, at Salerno in September (collision with *Uganda*), and at Anzio in January 1944. By April 1944 she was covering convoys in the western Mediterranean, and in August supported the landings in the South of France, Operation Dragoon. Subsequently *Dehli* moved to the Adriatic, where, on 12 February 1945, she was damaged by explosive motorboats at Split. She was not repaired following this damage, but was patched up for her return home to reserve at Sheerness in April 1945. After use in ship target trials she was handed over for scrapping on 22 January 1948. The ship arrived at Cashmore's Newport yard to break up in April

1948, and was completely demolished by that October.

Despatch was towed to Chatham Dockyard for completion, and did not enter service until June 1922. On commissioning, she went out to the China Station, 5th LCS, until 1927, then served on the America and West Indies Station with the 8th Cruiser Squadron until the summer of 1931, when she reduced to reserve. After a refit which lasted until 1933, *Despatch* recommissioned on 3 February 1933 for the 3rd Cruiser Squadron and served in the Mediterranean until 24 November 1937, when she left Malta for home. She then spent the years up to the war in reserve and on training duties. She joined the 8th Cruiser Squadron on the America and West Indies Station on the outbreak of war. In the South Atlantic Command, *Despatch* captured the German merchantmen *Düsseldorf* off Chile in December 1939, *Troja* off Aruba in March 1940, and *Norderney* off the Amazon estuary with the AMC *Pretoria Castle* on 15 August 1941. She remained on this station until 1942, apart from a period with Force H in November 1940. In the spring of 1942 the ship was under refit in Britain, then went to the South Atlantic Command until 1943. By October that year she was back in Portsmouth, and was under refit there until May 1944, after which she was attached to the escort forces as headquarters ship for the invasion of Normandy in June 1944. By January 1945 she was in reserve as an accommodation ship. *Despatch* was handed over to BISCO for breaking up on 5 April

1946, and arrived for scrapping at Arnott Young, Troon, on 5 May 1946.

Diomede, like *Despatch*, was completed in a Royal dockyard, entering service in October 1922. After serving in China from 1922 to 1925 with the 5th LCS, the ship joined the New Zealand Squadron when recommissioned on 21 October 1925, where she remained, save for refit during 1929/30, until 1935. In that year, as a result of political crises, she served briefly on temporary detachment to the 4th Cruiser Squadron in the East Indies, and then paid off on 31 March 1936 on relief by *Achilles*, reverting to the RN. The late 1930s were spent in reserve or on trooping duties. September 1939 found her with the 7th Cruiser Squadron in the Home Fleet on Northern Patrol duties, after which she joined the 8th Cruiser Squadron, America and West Indies command in 1940-42, intercepting the blockade runner *Idarwald* off Tampico, Mexico, on 15 December 1940. She was in the South Atlantic Command and West Africa in 1942, but came home for refit and repair that year and was taken in hand at Rosyth between 22 July 1942 and 24 September 1943, when she was also converted into a training ship. She reduced to reserve in 1945, and was handed over to BISCO for breaking up on 5 April 1946, arriving at the Dalmuir yard of Arnott Young on 13 May 1946 for scrapping.

Dragon saw some brief war service with the 5th LCS in the Harwich Force until 1919, and was part of the Baltic Squadron that year, returning to Britain in January 1920. Between 1920 and 1925

the ship served in the Atlantic Fleet, 1st LCS, and she also participated in the Empire cruise. Following this, she was sent to the Mediterranean in February 1926 for the 1st Cruiser Squadron, where she remained until 1928, with a deployment to China in October 1926. She returned to Chatham on 19 December 1928 to pay off for refit. After refit, *Dragon* commissioned on 18 March 1930 for the America and West Indies Station before reducing to reserve on 16 July 1937. In September 1939 the ship was with the 7th Cruiser Squadron in the Home Fleet, then went to the Mediterranean, 3rd Cruiser Squadron, in March 1940. She also served in the South Atlantic Command, where she captured the Vichy French merchantman *Touareg* off the Congo in August 1940. During the Dakar operation of September 1940 she was attacked but missed by the French submarine *Persée*. By the end of the year she was employed on ocean patrols from St Helena when *Admiral Scheer* was at sea. In 1941 she went to the East Indies, and by December was at Singapore on escort duties, serving with the China Force from the beginning of 1942 until February. After carrying out strikes from Batavia at the end of February, *Dragon* sailed for Colombo on 28 February and joined the Eastern Feet, where she was attached to the Slow Division. After her return home she joined the 10th Cruiser Squadron with the Home Fleet, but paid off in December 1942. She was loaned to the Polish navy in January 1943 (name not changed), after which the ship took part in the Normandy Cam-

paign of June 1944 as a unit of Force B, in support of Sword Beach. However, in the early hours of 8 July the ship was irreparably damaged by Marder or Neger small battle units. She was declared a total loss on 11 July and scuttled as part of the invasion harbour defences. Further details of her service while Polish-manned are on page 200.

Dunedin joined the 1st Cruiser Squadron, Atlantic Fleet, in 1919, and then in May 1924 was loaned to the New Zealand Division, replacing *Chatham* until 1937, with a refit in 1931/32. After her relief by *Leander* on 29 March 1937 she returned to RN control to spend the years up the outbreak of war in reserve and training duties. In August 1939 the ship was with the 12th Cruiser Squadron in the Home Fleet and, in September, with the 11th Cruiser Squadron in the Orkneys and Shetlands Command. She spent the remainder of the year on the Northern Patrol, then went to the America and West Indies Station in 1940. This ship was another of the class to obtain a good score against enemy merchantmen in distant waters, both *Hannover* and *Heidelberg* falling victim to her in the Windward Passage in March 1940. She blockaded Vichy Martinique in June/July 1940. In December she formed part of the escort for convoy WS5a at the time of the attack by *Admiral Hipper*, but did not get into action. In 1941 she served in the South Atlantic. On 15 June 1941 she captured the German *Lothringen* in the central Atlantic, in the wake of

the *Bismarck* operation. This was followed, on 22 June, by the Vichy French *Ville de Rouen* off Natal, and then on 30 June she captured the *Ville de Tamative* east of the St Paul's rocks. *Dunedin* was earmarked in July as the second AA conversion following the prototype, *Dehli*, but this was never carried out because she was torpedoed and sunk by *U124* on 24 November 1941, while on lone patrol between Pernambuco and St Paul's rocks.

Durban was completed by Devonport Dockyard in 1921, then commissioned for the China Station, 5th LCS, where she remained until 1928. Between 1928 and 1930 the ship served on the America and West Indies Station, then commissioned for the South Atlantic Division on 1 July 1931. After relief by *York* in December 1933, she had a Mediterranean commission between

March 1934 and September 1936. In reserve until 1939, *Durban* joined the 9th Cruiser Squadron in the South Atlantic Command in September 1939, then went out to the East Indies in 1940 as part of the British Malaya Force. After Japan's entry into the war she operated in the Singapore theatre and as part of the China Force until February 1942. In the evacuation of Singapore she was damaged by bombs on 12 February, and withdrew to Colombo for temporary repairs later that month. Full repairs were carried out at New York in April, and further modifications were made in Portsmouth between June and August. Following the loss of the East Indies she joined the Eastern Fleet, where she served until 1943, then came home only to be paid off and scuttled as part of the Mulberry breakwaters off Normandy on 9 June 1944.

HAWKINS CLASS

Ship	Builder	Laid Down	Launched	Completed	Fate
Effingham	Portsmouth Dky	6 Apr 17	8 Jun 21	2 Jul 25	Lost 21 May 1940
Frobisher	Devonport Dky	2 Aug 16	20 Mar 20	20 Sep 24	scrapped at Newport 1949
Hawkins	Chatham Dky	3 June 16	1 Oct 17	23 Jul 19	Scrapped at Dalmuir 1947

Displacement: 9,860 tons/10,017 tonnes (standard); 12,800 tons/13,004 tonnes (full load).
Length: 605ft/184.4m (oa); 565ft/172.2m (pp).
Beam: 65ft/19.8m; Draught: 17ft 3in/5.25m (mean).
Machinery: 4-Shaft Brown Curtis (*Hawkins* Parsons) geared turbines: 12 (*Frobisher* 10, *Effingham*, 8) Yarrow boilers.
Performance: *Hawkins*, 55,000shp=29.5kts; *Effingham* & *Frobisher* 65,000shp=30.5kts.
Bunkerage: *Hawkins* 2,600 tons, *Frobisher* & *Effingham* 2,186 tons oil fuel.
Range: 5,400nm at 14kts.

Protection: 1½in to 3in main belt; 1 to 1½in decks; 3in conning tower; ½in to 1in magazines.
Guns: seven 7.5in BL Mk VI (7x1); four 4in Mk V (4x1); two 2pdr (2x1).
Torpedoes: six 21in (2uw & 4 aw).
Aircraft: nil.
Complement: 690.

Design These ships were designed as a counter to the German cruisers and AMCs which were at large during the 1914/15 period, and which caused disruption far beyond that which their

small numbers warranted. These raiders were armed with guns of up to 5.9in calibre, and in many cases had a good turn of speed. In June 1915 the British Admiralty started studies to produce a cruiser specifically intended to hunt down these raiders, powerful armament and useful speed being prime requirements. Initially, the request was for a *Birmingham* with heavier armament, better endurance and a higher speed of 30kts. The sketch designs showed a 9,000-ton ship with various combinations of armament, including 9.2in and 6in weapons. The 6in gun was considered too light for the intended task, while the 9.2in was cumbersome; consequently, a new gun of 7.5in calibre was adopted, developed from the Mk I gun used in the *Devonshire* class of 1904. This new gun, designated Mk VI, was a breech-loading, 46.5cal weapon firing a 200lb projectile with a maximum range of 21,110yd, (19,300m) at 30°.

The final design bore little resemblance to *Birmingham*. It was an altogether larger ship,

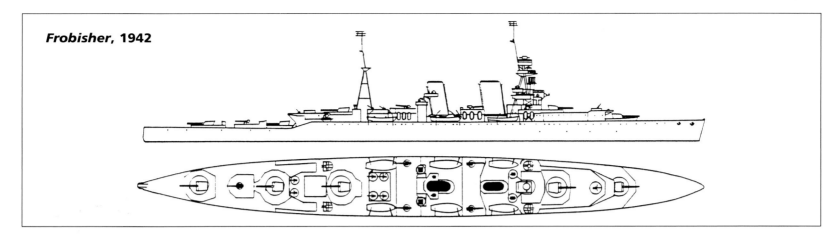

Frobisher, 1942

having more in common with *Furious*. Legend displacement was 9,750 tons. The main machinery was a 60,000shp quadruple-shaft, single-reduction-geared turbine arrangement, with the turbines in two spaces, the foremost unit driving the wing shafts. The steam plant was designed with detached employment in mind. Of the twelve boilers, the four in the after space were coal-burning (but with the addition of oil sprayers), because at that time oil fuel was not readily available in all areas of the world. The machinery was not arranged on the unit principle. In 1917 it was decided to increase the machinery output by forcing the oil-fired boilers, increasing the oil used in the coal-fired boilers and modifying the turbine blading, though these modifications could not be incorporated in the two leading ships, *Cavendish* and *Hawkins*, as they were too far advanced. This increased the designed power to 70,000shp. However, only *Raleigh* was completed to this design,

as the disappearance of the German raiders from the high seas by 1915 removed the urgency from the programme and construction was slowed down, *Effingham* not being laid down until the spring of 1917. By the time she and her sister, *Frobisher*, were under completion, the machinery had been revised once more. In these two ships the four coal-fired boilers were replaced by two oil-fired units, and the after boiler room was considerably reduced in size. The space thus gained was used to increase the bunker capacity to 2,150 tons. Installed power was now 65,00shp, giving a speed of 30.5kts.

The protective scheme included, for the first time, the concept of an armoured box around the magazines. Side protection of up to 3in abreast the machinery spaces extended to the upper deck and ran the full length of the hull, but tapered in thickness to 1½ in at the extremities. Additional protection was provided by the arrangement of

the coal bunkers. Horizontal protection was limited to a 1in maximum protective deck. Armour represented 8.3 per cent of the legend displacement. External bulges, 5ft deep, gave additional protection to the machinery spaces, and the internal subdivision was very thorough.

The main armament was disposed in single CP Mk V shielded mountings, two on the centreline forward with No.2 gun superfiring, two on the beam abreast the after funnel, and three on the centreline aft. Of these latter, No.5 gun superfired on No.6, which was on the quarterdeck, as was No.7, a considerable distance abaft of it. The wide spacing of the guns reduced the effects of blast in action. For secondary armament, the ship was given ten 3in Mk I in single mountings, of which

Below: *Effingham* as rebuilt just before the war. (Courtesy G. Ransome)

six were low-angle weapons and four were on HA mountings. During construction, two 2pdr AA were added and the original two 21in submerged torpedo tubes were augmented by two twin tubes above water banks.

Cavendish was rushed to completion before the end of the First World War, but as an aircraft carrier, and renamed *Vindictive*. Although reconverted into a cruiser in 1923-25, she was once again modified in 1937/38 to serve as a demilitarised training ship. As she never thereafter served in the cruiser role, she will not be discussed further here. Of the other ships, only *Hawkins* went afloat before the Armistice, while *Frobisher* and *Effingham* did not commission until the mid-1920s. These two ships completed with a slightly different armament, in that all 3in guns were suppressed and replaced by three 4in QF Mk IV.

Modifications In 1927 *Frobisher* was fitted with a catapult on the quarterdeck, together with a crane. This displaced one 4in gun, which was resited between the funnels with a fourth gun. *Hawkins* was refitted in 1929, when her coal-fired boilers were removed and the remaining oil-fired boilers modified to an output of 55,000shp for a maximum speed of 29.5kts. Bunker capacity was increased also. She received an additional 4in gun, which was sited between the funnels, as in *Frobisher*. One HACS director was also fitted.

In the mid-1920s there was a proposal to re-gun these ships with three twin 8in turrets, but this never progressed beyond planning. Then the London Naval Treaty of 1930 required their demilitarisation, following which, in 1932, *Frobisher* lost numbers 5 and 6 7.5in guns, as well as all but two 4in AA, to serve as a cadets training ship, while *Hawkins* and *Effingham* had all their 7.5in guns and the above-water tubes removed in 1937/38 before reducing to reserve. Before this had been done, however, there was already a proposal on the table for their conversion to 6in gun cruisers, and in fact the refit of *Effingham* had been approved. As the provisions of the London Treaty in this respect had by now lapsed, this conversion could proceed. Thus, in 1937/38, *Effingham* was taken in hand to receive nine 6in Mk XII (probably surplus C class guns after their conversion to AA cruisers), of which three were fitted in a tiered superfiring arrangement forward, two abeam amidships, and three in a widely separated tiered arrangement aft. Four 4in AA in single mountings and three quadruple .5in MGs were also added. She was fitted for, but not with, two multiple 2pdr mountings abreast the bridge at shelter deck level. Two HACS directors were provided for, but not fitted; one atop the rebuilt bridge and the second on the after superstructure. Provision was made for aircraft, but again the

Above: *Frobisher* in 1942. (WSS)

equipment was not fitted. Internally, she had the two after boilers and the after funnel removed, all uptakes being trunked into an enlarged single funnel. Finally, the submerged tubes were landed. This refit had in the main been completed by the summer of 1938, but it was not until the following year that the missing equipment was eventually fitted. By this time she had also received twin 4in AA in lieu of the singles. Both *Hawkins* and *Frobisher* were to be treated similarly, but the war intervened and, in the case of the former, her refit merely replaced the guns removed on demilitarisation.

Effingham in all probability received no further modification in view of her early loss. *Fro-*

bisher's refit was very leisurely, not being taken in hand until 5 January 1940. By completion, in March 1942, her armament consisted of five 7.5in (i.e. no wing guns), five single 4in AA, four quadruple 2pdr and seven single 20mm, together with radars 273, 281 and 285. In April 1944 this remained the same, but in May 1944 two eight-barrelled 2pdr replaced the four quadruple, and twelve 20mm singles were added.

Hawkins received four single 2pdr on her re-entry into service in January 1940, then in 1942 received two quadruple 2pdr and seven single 20mm as well as radars 273, 281 and 285. Two single 2pdr were landed. This remained her outfit until August 1944, when she received two eight-

Below: *Hawkins*. Note the different arrangement of the after searchlight platform. (WSS)

barrelled 2pdr in exchange for the four quadruples and an additional two single 20mm.

Service As noted earlier, *Vindictive* was converted into an aircraft carrier, while the fifth ship, *Raleigh*, was unfortunately wrecked in fog on Point Amour in the Straits of Belle Isle on 8 August 1922, while serving as flagship on the America and West Indies Station. She was declared a total loss after as much equipment as possible had been removed. The wreck was blown up by a party from *Calcutta* in July 1928.

Effingham served as flagship of the 4th Cruiser Squadron in the East Indies between 1925 and 1932. On her return home she was recommissioned on 20 September 1932 as flagship VA Reserve Fleet, and spent most of the prewar years in reserve status. She was a unit of the 12th Cruiser Squadron at the outbreak of war, and served in the Northern Patrol prior to escorting North Atlantic convoys before the end of 1939. She transported £2 million in gold to Halifax, Nova Scotia, in November. As one of the few ships of the Northern Patrol with good endurance, she was ordered into the Atlantic to join the hunting groups formed when it was suspected that German raiders were at sea; the precise task for which she had been designed 25 years earlier. She moved to the North Sea in April 1940 for the Norwegian campaign, and survived at attack by *U38*. She was employed in shelling enemy positions in and around Narvik until May, but while running reinforcements to Bodö she struck an isolated rock in the Narvik area on 18 May, becoming a total loss. The wreck was sunk by gunfire on 21 May. Although the rock was on the chart, it was obscured by the navigator's pencilled track, and the ship was dead on course!

Frobisher served in the Mediterranean as Flagship 1st Cruiser Squadron during 1924 to 1929, with a temporary detachment to the China Station in 1926. She then joined the 2nd Cruiser Squadron in the Atlantic Fleet in September 1929. She reduced to reserve in November 1930 until conversion to a cadets training ship in 1932, in which capacity she served until 1939. She was then laid up until entering refit on 5 January 1940, which extended until March 1942. She then joined the 4th Cruiser Squadron with the Eastern Fleet in the Indian Ocean until March 1944. After returning home, *Frobisher* took part in the landings in Normandy in June 1944 as part of Force D, off Sword Beach, but was damaged by a Dackel torpedo in August, after which she was employed as a cadets training ship. She was handed over to BISCO on 26 March 1949, and arrived at Cashmore's Newport yard to break up on 11 May.

Hawkins served as flagship, 5th LCS, on the China Station from 1919 until 12 November 1928, when she paid off at Chatham for refit. After

Above: *Frobisher* partly disarmed as a training ship in May 1945. (IWM)

recommissioning on 31 December 1929, the ship joined the 2nd Cruiser Squadron (flag) with the Atlantic Fleet, where she served until 5 May 1930, when she commissioned for the reserve. In September 1932 she became flagship, 4th Cruiser Squadron, in the East Indies, returning to reserve in April 1935. *Hawkins* became a cadets training ship in September 1938. She was rearming until January 1940. Thereafter she served with the South American Division, then moved to the Indian Ocean in 1941, participating in the raid on Mogadishu by Force K in February 1941 and capturing the Italian merchantman *Adria* off Kismayu on 12 February. After refit at Portsmouth between December 1941 and May 1942, the ship served with the Eastern Fleet until returning home in 1944. June 1944 saw her as part of the bombardment force off Utah Beach, after which she became a training ship again, reducing to reserve in 1945. *Hawkins* was allocated for ship target trials in 1947, and was subjected to bombing by RAF Lincoln bombers off Spithead in May, after which she was transferred to BISCO for scrapping on 26 August 1947 and subsequently broken up by Arnott Young at Dalmuir, where she arrived in December 1947.

E CLASS

Ship	Builder	Laid Down	Launched	Completed	Fate
Emerald	Armstrong[1]	23 Sep 18	19 May 20	15 Jan 26	Scrapped at Troon 1948
Enterprise	John Brown[2]	28 Jun 18	23 Dec 19	7 Apr 26	Scrapped at Newport 1946

[1] Completed at Chatham Dky: [2] Completed at Devonport Dky.

Displacement: 7,550 (Emerald), 7,580 (Enterprise)
 tons/7,670/7,701 tonnes (standard); 9,712 (Emerald)
 9,435 (Enterprise) tons/9,562/9,586 tonnes (full load).
Length: 570ft/173.7m (oa); 535ft/163m (pp).
Beam: 54ft 6in/16.61m; Draught: 16ft 3in/4.95m (mean).
Machinery: 4-shaft Brown-Curtis geared turbines; 8 Yarrow
 boilers.
Performance: 80,000shp=33kts; Bunkerage: 1,746 tons oil.
Range: 8,000nm at 15kts.
Protection: 3in sides (machinery spaces); 2¼in sides (maga-
 zines); 2in sides aft; 1in deck.
Guns: seven 6in BL Mk XII, (7x1, but Enterprise 1x2 & 5x1);
 three 4in Mk V (3x1); two 2pdr (2x1).
Torpedoes: twelve 21in (4x3).
Aircraft: one, one catapult.
Complement: 572.

Design Designed as a response to cruisers believed to be under construction by Germany in 1917, but which never materialised, these ships were to have a very high speed and carry one more 6in gun than the D class. To achieve the designed speed, a very fine hull and machinery of twice the power of the earlier cruisers was necessary. During the design work the dimensions and displacement naturally grew, both length and beam being increased to improve stability, layout and protection. While the protection remained essentially the same as earlier classes, it was found possible to give a 1in protective deck to the turbine spaces, partly as a result of which the armour represented 9.3 per cent of the legend displacement.

The machinery installation comprised two *Shakespeare*-class destroyer sets, each developing 40,000shp, which in turn necessitated a four-shaft arrangement. The eight boilers were paired in four spaces, with the forward engine room separating No.3 and No.4 boiler rooms to give a unit layout to the machinery. In Nos.1 and 4 boiler rooms the boilers were arranged fore and aft, and in the others, abreast.

As designed, these ships were to have seven 6in BL Mk XII in single CP XIV mountings, disposed two forward; two aft on the centreline, with Nos.2 and 6 guns superfiring; one on the centreline abaft the after funnel, where it had only limited arcs of fire; and the other pair on the beam at shelter deck level amidships. Two 4in AA Mk V and two 2pdr singles completed the gunnery department. Twelve 21in torpedo tubes in four triple banks were fitted on the main deck.

Contracts for three ships were placed in March 1918, but the end of the war caused the third ship, *Euphrates*, at Fairfield's, to be cancelled on 26 November 1918. A larger number of ships was impossible because of material and labour shortages. Work eventually proceeded on the other pair up until launch, after which they were towed to Royal Dockyards for completion. *Enterprise* went

Below: *Emerald* as built. (Author's collection)

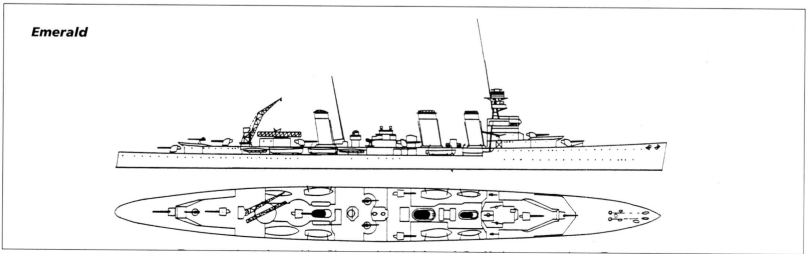

Emerald

to Devonport, and her sister to Chatham. Work continued fitfully, neither being completed until 1926. By this time the opportunity had been taken to modify their armament, only in detail as far as *Emerald* was concerned (she received three 4in in lieu of the intended two), though *Enterprise* was used as a trials ship for the new twin 6in Mk XVII. This was the prototype of the twin Mk XXII, and allowed 40° elevation. It was fitted in No.1 position and, as a result, the forward shelter deck was reduced in length. In addition she also received a prototype Director Control Tower fitted atop the bridge, and in consequence had a modified bridge and masting. She, too, received a third 4in gun, and both vessels were to be fitted with quadruple tubes, but these were not available at completion (they became available in 1928/29).

Modifications In the mid-1930s both ships were fitted with a catapult which replaced the outmoded flying-off platform and an HACS Mk I for the 4in guns, which was fitted amidships between the searchlight platform and the after funnel. The funnels were raised 5ft at this time. Later proposals to increase the AA outfit by the addition of twin 4in and multiple 2pdrs were thwarted by the outbreak of war. *Emerald* had received two quadruple .5 MGs before the war, then during refit between August 1942 and April 1943 she landed the after 6in, two 2pdr singles and the .5MGs to receive instead six power-operated twin 20mm, two quadruple 2pdr and radars 273, 281, 282 and 285. In April 1944 six 20mm singles were added and the catapult was removed.

Enterprise landed two 6in singles in 1941 and had one quadruple 2pdr fitted. She later had four

single 20mm fitted and then, in the course of a long refit between the end of December 1942 and October 1943, she lost the single 2pdr and 20mm weapons, receiving six twin power-operated mountings in lieu. The two 6in were reinstated and a second quadruple 2pdr fitted. She was fitted with radars 272, 281, 282, 284 and 285. In February she had an additional four single 20mm fitted and the catapult was removed.

Service *Emerald* went out to the East Indies, 4th Cruiser Squadron, on commissioning, finally returning home to pay off on 15 July 1933. After a refit at Chatham, the ship recommissioned for the East Indies again on 31 August 1934, which tour lasted until September 1937, on relief by *Liverpool*. On her return home she paid off to reserve. Recommissioned for war service, she joined the 12th Cruiser Squadron on Northern Patrol duties in September 1939. However, the appearance of German raiders in the Atlantic

resulted in her transfer to Halifax in October, to escort homeward-bound convoys, where she remained into 1940. Between October 1939 and August 1940 the ship carried £58 million in gold from Britain to Canada (her sister shipped another £10 million). In 1941 *Emerald* was transferred to the Indian Ocean, where she escorted troop convoys to the Middle East and stood by in the Persian Gulf during the operations in Iraq in April 1941. After Japan's entry into the war, in December 1941, *Emerald* joined the Eastern Fleet as part of the 'Fast Group', and in March 1942 was flagship. In August 1942 the ship returned home to refit at Portsmouth in August, and did not return to service until early April 1943. She rejoined the Eastern Fleet, 4th Cruiser Squadron, for escort duties, then returned home once more for the Invasion of Normandy, when she served with Force K in support of Gold Beach. By January 1945 *Emer-*

ald had joined the reserve fleet and, in 1947, was allocated for ship target trials. As a result of these trials the ship foundered in Kames Bay, Rothesay, on 24 October, and was not refloated until 9 June 1948, after which she was docked, examined, and then handed over to BISCO on 23 June 1948 for breaking up. She was scrapped at Arnott Young, Troon, where she arrived on 5 July 1948.

Enterprise served with the 4th Cruiser Squadron in the East Indies until 1934. After her return home she reduced to care and maintenance on 4 July 1934, followed by a major refit. She returned to the East Indies in January 1936, but was relieved by *Manchester* at the end of 1937 and came home. In 1938 she was employed to take crews to the China Station, returning home to pay off on 30 September 1938. *Enter-*

prise was also employed on Atlantic escort duties, with the Halifax Escort Force during 1939/40, before being transferred to the Home Fleet for the Norwegian Campaign. During April and May 1940 she supported the army ashore by bombardments in and around Narvik and, on 19 April, was attacked but missed by *U65*. After some repairs *Enterprise* joined the newly formed Force H in June 1940, participating in the action at Mers el Kebir in July. By the end of the year she was again on ocean patrol duties, this time in the hunt for *Thor* in the South Atlantic. At the turn of the year the appearance of *Admiral Scheer* in the Indian Ocean resulted in her transfer to that area to help in the hunt for the raider, but again without success. In 1942 *Enterprise* operated in the East Indies and Australian waters, escorting troop convoys, and then joined her sister in the

Eastern Fleet. At the end of 1942 she started a long refit in Britain which lasted until the end of October 1943, following which she joined the Home Fleet and was used to intercept Axis blockade runners arriving from the Far East, bound for the Bay of Biscay. In the course of one of these operations, in company with *Glasgow*, she fought in the action of 28 December 1943, when two German torpedo boats and a destroyer were sunk. Her next operation was Overlord, the Normandy landings, when she served as a unit of Force A, off Utah Beach. *Enterprise* joined the reserve fleet on 5 January 1945, but was used for trooping duties postwar, returning to the UK on 13 January 1946. She was handed over to BISCO for scrapping on 11 April 1946, arriving at Cashmore's yard at Newport on 21 April 1946 for breaking up.

KENT CLASS

Ship	Builder	Laid Down	Launched	Completed	Fate
Berwick	Fairfield	15 Sep 24	30 Mar 26	12 Jul 27	Scrapped at Blyth 1948
Cornwall	Devonport Dky	9 Oct 24	11 Mar 26	6 Dec 27	Lost 5 Apr 1942
Cumberland	VA (Barrow)	18 Oct 24	16 Mar 26	8 Dec 27	Scrapped at Newport 1959
Kent	Chatham Dky	15 Nov 24	16 Mar 26	25 Jun 28	Scrapped at Troon 1948
Suffolk	Portsmouth Dky	30 Jul 24	16 Feb 26	7 Feb 28	Scrapped at Newport 1948

Displacement: 10,900 approx tons/11,074 tonnes (standard); 14,900 tons/15,138 tonnes (full load).
Length: 630ft/192.02m (oa.); 590ft/179.8m (pp).
Beam: 68ft 5in/20.85m; Draught: 20ft 6in/6.24m (mean).
Machinery: 4-shaft Parsons (*Berwick* Brown-Curtis) geared turbines; 8 Admiralty 3-drum boilers.
Performance: 80,000shp=31½kts; Bunkerage: 3,200 tons oil.
Range: 9,350nm at 12kts.
Protection: 1in sides; 1in to 4⅜in magazine box protection; 1in turrets.

Guns: eight 8in BL Mk VIII (4x2); four 4in QF Mk V (4x1); four 2pdr (4x1).
Torpedoes: eight 21in (2x4).
Aircraft: one; one catapult.
Complement: 784.

Design This class was the result of political pressures rather than considered military requirements, being a direct result of the Washington Naval Treaty of 1922, which specified that cruis-

ers should not exceed 10,000 tons displacement, nor be armed with guns of a calibre greater than 8in (203mm). During the discussions, Britain had proposed that the upper displacement limit be set at 10,000 tons because of the existence of the new *Hawkins* class, which were the only modern trade route or ocean patrol cruisers available to the Royal Navy at that time. All the other cruisers were either obsolete or designed for the North Sea theatre, and no possibility of renouncing the *Hawkins* class could be countenanced. The choice of the 8in gun was similarly to Britain's advantage for the same reasons, i.e. the 7.5in in *Hawkins*, but it was believed that the USA at least was already considering such a calibre. It also quickly became apparent that the maximum limits would be at the same time the minimum limits, with all parties designing ships to the 10,000 ton/8in-gun configuration. For the Royal Navy the basic requirements were initially specified as eight 8in guns in twin turrets, a speed of

Suffolk

Above: *Suffolk* in April 1944.
(IWM)
Right: *Kent* towards the end
of 1942. (IWM)

33kts and a high freeboard for good seaworthiness. Single and triple turrets had also been studied, but were discarded for various reasons. Five initial design sketches were drawn up, but, like all the other signatories to the Treaty, Britain found that, to carry the desired armament at the speed required on 10,000 tons, there would be little or no allowance available for protection. The weight available for protection totalled only 820 tons according to initial estimates. This would have been insufficient to protect the vital areas, and it was suggested that only the magazines could be given armouring. To obtain better protection, speed was compromised from 33kts to 31kts and the machinery was reduced to 75,000shp from 100,000 shp, with a consequent weight saving which could be used to increase the general scheme of protection. This allowed 1in deck and 2in side armour to the machinery spaces, which was barely sufficient for protection against 6in gunfire but was better than nothing. Magazines and shell rooms had a box protection of 3in deck and bulkheads, with 4in sides to give protection from 8in shells at angles of descent of up to 40°. Later this scheme was modified, the weight gained for armour by the reduction in machinery power being spread more thinly over a wider area. Thus the side protection to the machinery spaces became 1in with a 1½in deck, the shell rooms only 1in sides and deck, plus some protective plating to the steering compartment. The weight now allocated to protection became 1,025 tons, or 10.25 per cent of the standard displacement. There was also a limited underwater bulge protection amidships. At the same time, the Engineer in

Chief reported that 80,000shp could be provided at no weight penalty, which, with an 8in reduction in beam combined with an increase of 2ft 3in in length, gave an extra ½kt.

The main machinery consisted of eight Admiralty three-drum boilers paired abreast in four boiler rooms and a four-shaft geared turbine arrangement, which was not on the unit principle.

The designed armament consisted of the new 8in BL Mk VIII in twin turrets Mk I, with 70° elevation and firing a 256lb (116kg) projectile. Maximum range was 30,650yd (28,030m) at 45°. This mounting was designed to have AA capacity, which the elevation gave but which the elevation and training controls did not. The mountings gave considerable trouble for a number of years after completion, although they had been rectified before the outbreak of war. The secondary armament was the standard 4in QF Mk V on single HA mountings, disposed two abreast on the superstructure deck amidships. Two multiple 2pdr mountings were specified, but were unavailable for some time after completion, so four single 2pdr Mk II were fitted as an interim measure. Four quadruple banks of tubes were fitted on the weather deck, and these were another cause of problems, as the ability of the torpedoes to withstand the impact on launch from such a height had not been considered. The question of aircraft was another area which exercised the minds of the Staff for some time, as there was insufficient margin for the weight of such equipment. In the end it was decided to design the ship to carry an aircraft and catapult, but not to mount these until completion, when the actual weight margin below

the 10,000-ton limit was known. Because of the great attention devoted to weight reduction by the use of high-tensile steel in the hull, the use of light alloys and other measures, it was found that a surplus weight of about 250 tons was available, despite the armament being overweight. This allowed the fitting of a catapult and aircraft (the initial aeroplane being the Fairey IIIF), extra boats for flagships, and increased ammunition stowage. It was not therefore necessary to reduce the main armament to six guns, as had at first been feared.

The Admiralty had worked on the assumption that 70 cruisers would be necessary to meet the strategic demands of the fleet, and initially proposed that 17 of the new cruisers be ordered, including eight in the 1924/25 programme. Political and financial considerations dictated otherwise, however, and only five were authorised (plus two for Australia, q.v.).

Modifications By 1932 all ships had received an HACS and a catapult, while *Cornwall*, *Kent* and *Berwick* were fitted with two quadruple .5in MGs by 1934. *Kent* had also received an extra two single 4in abreast the fore funnels in 1932/33.

In September 1934 an increase in the protective scheme was agreed which would comprise a) a 4½in armour belt abreast the machinery and magazine spaces, a similar thickness belt in the way of the dynamo space and TS as well as 4in

armour to the boiler room fans; **b)** the removal of the old aircraft equipment, to be replaced by a fixed, athwartships catapult and a hangar; and **c)** the replacement of the single 4in by 4in twins.

Cornwall and *Berwick* both received a major refit between July 1936 and December 1937 (*Cornwall*) and August 1937 to November 1938, when the extra armour was fitted, the single 4in were replaced by four twin 4in Mk XIX mountings, two eight-barrel 2pdr mountings replaced the quadruples and the forward director was replaced by a DCT. The bridge structure was modified and reduced in height, with 1in protection being fitted to the control positions. The quarterdeck was not cut down in these two ships.

When *Cumberland* and *Suffolk* underwent their major refits (*Cumberland* from February 1935 to July 1936, and her sister from August 1935 to October 1936), their modifications included the additional armour, catapult, hangar and extra 4in guns but *Cumberland* only received twin 4in in place of the after 4in singles, while *Suffolk* had four single shielded versions of the 4in Mk XIX added in lieu of the older guns. Both had two quadruple 2pdr fitted and two HACS. Torpedo tubes and single 2pdr were landed. Both had their quarterdecks cut down to save weight.

Kent was reconstructed between 1937 and July 1938, but as she had less available spare weight she was not given the athwartships catapult, merely a more powerful one which could take the Walrus aircraft that was now standard. This ship was not cut down aft.

During the war, *Cumberland* received five single 20mm and radars 281, 285 and 273 in the latter half of 1941, and in February 1943 had her .5 MGs and one single 20mm removed and replaced by five twin 20mm. By April 1944 her light AA comprised two quadruple 2pdr, five twin power-operated 20mm and four singles. Two further single 20mm were added before the end of the war. *Suffolk*, while under repair in 1940/41, landed two single 4in and received two twin 4in in lieu and four single 20mm, plus radars 279 and 285. In 1942 the .5in MGs and the radar 279 were removed, the ship receiving in exchange four single 20mm and radars 279 and 285. Her catapult and aircraft were removed in 1943, but the hangar was retained. Five single 20mm were exchanged for an equal number of 20mm. Three further single 20mm had been added by April 1944. *Cornwall* had few modifications, if any at all. *Kent* had six single 20mm fitted in 1941, together with radars 281, 284 and 285. Her aircraft arrangements were removed in 1942 and the quadruple .5 MGs as well, to be replaced by six single 20mm. In 1943 these were replaced by three twin 20mm, and by April 1944 her outfit

was two eight-barrel 2pdr, three twin power-operated 20mm and six singles. *Berwick* received radars 281, 284 and five single 20mm in 1941. In 1942 the aircraft fittings and the .5in MGs were removed and radar 273 and six single 20mm added. In the latter half of 1943 she received seven twin 20mm in exchange for the same number of singles. However, by April 1944 she is recorded as having only two single 20mm in addition to the twins.

Service *Berwick* went out to the China Station on completion, where she remained until a temporary detachment to the Mediterranean in 1936. After reconstruction in 1937/38, the ship served on the America and West Indies Station with the 8th Cruiser Squadron until 1939. From September that year she served on Ocean convoy escort duties, then formed part of Force F (with *York*) when hunting groups were formed to find the German raiders. She did not make contact with any raider, but intercepted the mercantile blockade runners *Wolfsburg* and *Uruguay* in the Denmark Straits during March 1940. In April she participated in the Norwegian Campaign, then later in the year was despatched to the Mediterranean, arriving at Gibraltar for Force H on 7 November. She participated in several operations in this theatre, including the action off Cape Spartivento, escorting the Taranto raid force, and

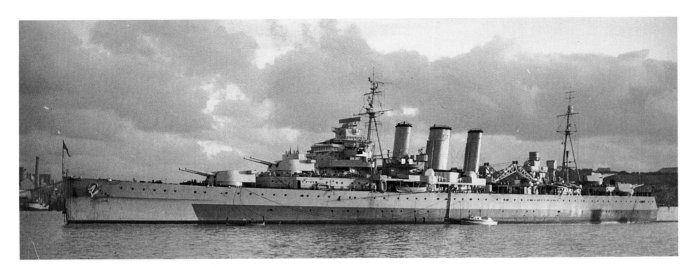

the transport of troops to Greece. On 24 November 1940 *Berwick*, *Formidable* and *Norfolk* were formed into Force K and despatched to Freetown to hunt for *Admiral Scheer*, but in the event *Berwick* never actually joined this group. She did, however, form part of the escort to convoy WS5a at the time of the attack on it by *Admiral Hipper* (q.v.) on 25 December, north-west of the Azores, when she was hit and damaged by the German cruiser. She returned to Britain for repairs, which were not finally completed until the end of June 1941, although the damage was not severe. She now joined the Home Fleet, taking part in operations against *Tirpitz* in February 1942. For the remainder of her wartime career *Berwick* served in the Arctic theatre, covering the Russian convoys, carrier raids on *Tirpitz* and, in 1944/45, carrier raids on the Norwegian coast. After the war she was allocated to BISCO for scrapping on 15 June 1948 and arrived at Hughes Bolkow, Blyth, on 12 July for breaking up.

Cornwall served on the China Station until 1936, then came home for reconstruction before joining the 2nd Cruiser Squadron in 1938. She went out to China again in 1939 as part of the 5th Cruiser Squadron, from where she moved to the Indian Ocean as part of Force I at Ceylon for anti-raider patrols, spending the remainder of the year in the hunt for *Admiral Graf Spee*. Later she moved to the South Atlantic Command, from where she was despatched to assist in the operations off Dakar in August 1940. The following month, in company with *Dehli*, she intercepted *Primaguet*'s group and forced it to put into Casablanca. Returning to the Indian Ocean, she intercepted and sank the raider *Pinguin* off the Seychelles on 8 May 1941. After Japan's entry into the war the cruiser escorted convoys across the Indian Ocean to the Sunda Straits until early 1942, before withdrawing to Colombo, Ceylon.

She formed part of the Fast Division of the Eastern Fleet. On 5 April she was caught at sea southwest of the Maldive Islands by Japanese naval aircraft and sunk by bombing.

Cumberland also served on the China Station until returning home early in 1935 for reconstruction. After completion of this work she returned to China until 1938, when she joined the 2nd Cruiser Squadron in 1939. At the outbreak of war the ship was in the South America division. During the hunt for *Admiral Graf Spee* she formed part of Force G off the west coast of South America in October 1939, and from then until the end of the year operated in the Falklands area and up to the Plate Estuary, where, on 5 December, while in company with *Ajax*, she intercepted the blockade runner *Ussukuma*. In June 1940 she provided ocean escort to the first WS Middle East troop convoys in the Atlantic. In July she was employed in operations to hunt for the raider *Thor* before moving to Freetown for Operation Menace. In the course of this operation, with the 1st Cruiser Squadron, she sank the Vichy-French munitions ship *Poitiers* on 16 September and received a hit herself during the action at Dakar. By December, however, she had returned to the western side of the South Atlantic, searching for raiders off the River Plate. In 1941 she joined the Home Fleet and served on Arctic convoy duties during 1942/44, then was sent to the Indian Ocean to join the Eastern Fleet in March 1944. Here she participated in the Sabang raid, carrier raids on Sumatra and the Nicobars, and the Leyte diversion. After the end of the war with Japan, *Cumberland* was involved in the reoccupation of the Netherlands East Indies. On her return home postwar she was eventually converted into a trials ship, and did not finally pay off until 1958. She arrived at Cashmore's, Newport, on 3 November 1958 for scrapping.

Kent served on the China Station with the 5th Cruiser Squadron from completion until 1939, her reconstruction being carried out in 1937/38. Her initial wartime duties were anti-raider patrols in the East Indies, before moving into the Indian Ocean to cover troop convoys in 1940. By the summer of that year she was in the Mediterranean with the 3rd Cruiser Squadron. After the bombardment of Bardia in August and an attack on Benghazi the following month, the ship was struck by a torpedo from an Italian aircraft on the night of 17/18 September, which hit near the stern. Full repairs were not completed until September 1941. From early 1942 she served in the Home Fleet on Arctic convoy duties, and in 1944 covered the carrier raids against the Norwegian coast. However, *Kent* was paid off in January 1945, remaining in reserve until allocated for ship target trials. She was allocated to BISCO on 22 January 1948, and arrived at Troon on 31 January to be broken up by West of Scotland Shipbreakers.

Suffolk, like her sisters, served on the China Station, save for reconstruction, until the outbreak of the war. She came home in 1939 and then patrolled the Denmark Straits in October 1939. In April 1940 she participated in the Norwegian Campaign, where, after a bombardment of the seaplane base at Stavanger, she was bombed on 17 April and so badly damaged that she was fortunate to survive. Repairs took until February 1941. Thereafter she served with the Home Fleet in Arctic waters until the end of 1942, then underwent a refit between December 1942 and April 1943. On completion of this the ship was ordered to the Eastern Fleet, operating in the Indian Ocean until the end of the war. *Suffolk* was allocated to Bisco on 25 March 1948 and was scrapped at Cashmore's, Newport, where she arrived on 24 June 1948.

LONDON CLASS

Ship	Builder	Laid Down	Launched	Completed	Fate
Devonshire	Devonport Dky	16 Mar 26	22 Oct 27	18 Mar 29	Scrapped at Newport 1954
London	Portsmouth Dky	23 Feb 26	14 Sep 27	31 Jan 29	Scrapped at Barrow 1950
Shropshire	Beardmore	24 Feb 27	5 Jul 28	12 Sep 29	Scrapped at Dalmuir 1955
Sussex	Hawthorne Leslie	1 Feb 27	22 Feb 28	19 Mar 29	Scrapped at Dalmuir 1955

Displacement: 9,850 tons/10,007 tonnes (standard); 13,315 tons/13,528 tonnes (full load).
Length: 632ft 8in/192.8m (oa); 595ft/181.35m (pp).
Beam: 66ft/20.12m; Draught: 20ft 9in/6.32m (mean).
Machinery: 4-shaft Parsons geared turbines; 8 Admiralty 3-drum boilers.
Performance: 80,000shp=32.3kts; Bunkerage: 3,190 tons oil.
Range: 9,120nm at 12kts.
Protection: as *Kent* Class but were not fitted with bulges.
Guns: as *Kent* class.
Torpedoes: as *Kent* class.
Aircraft: one; one catapult.
Complement: 784.

Design For the 1925/26 programme, the Admiralty wished to include further cruisers of the Washington type, based on the *Kent* but with several improvements. The main area considered in need of attention was the protective scheme, and to this end two separate schemes were considered. The first omitted the external bulge of *Kent*, which, by alteration of the hull lines, also increased the speed by about ¾kt. Protection to the 4in and warhead magazine was deleted, but armouring was provided for the TS and steering gear. Enough weight was left to allow aircraft fitment to be designed in. The second scheme proposed the omission of protection to the machinery, steering and 8in shell rooms, but had protection to the TS, exchange and lower steering position. Aircraft but no torpedo tubes were allowed for, and the resultant saving in weight was put to increasing the installed shp from 80,000 to 110,000 for a maximum speed of 34kts in standard condition. Neither scheme fully met requirements, and a compromise was reached. The omission of the bulge necessitated a revision of the hull lines and a consequent increase in length, with a slight reduction in beam. Internal layout was a little more spacious, and the bridge and funnels were moved further aft. The armament remained essentially the same as that of *Kent*. The two ships built in the Royal Dockyards, *Devonshire* and *London*, had their machinery manufactured at private yards, Vickers Armstrongs (Tyne) and Fairfield respectively.

Modifications From 1936 there were several schemes to modernise and improve this class, which included the replacement of the machinery, improvement of the protective scheme and rebuilding the superstructure. The machinery scheme was abandoned, but it was intended to proceed with the rebuilding of the bridge on the lines of the *Fiji*s and to increase the waterline armour to 3½in NC, (*vide* 4½ in *Kent*). War prevented all but *London* being taken in hand for major reconstruction. All ships received HACS Mk 1 on the roof of the after control in 1929/30, a catapult in 1931/32 and, in 1936/7, four additional 4in HA single mounts. Two .5in MG quadruple mountings were fitted abreast the foremast, and both *Sussex* and *Shropshire* received an additional HACS on the bridge. *London* was

Below: *Shropshire* in the 1930s. (See Australia for wartime appearance.) (Perkins)

Above: *Devonshire*. (WSS)   **Below:** *Sussex* before the war. (Author's collection)

and July 1945 she lost eight single 20mm for an additional four twin 20mm and four single 40mm Bofors Mk III.

Shropshire received two eight-barrelled 2pdrs early in 1941, and by the end of that year had exchanged her single 4in for four twin mountings, and had seven single 20mm fitted as well as radars 273, 281, 282 and 285. An additional three single 20mm had been installed by the end of 1942. After the refit between November 1942 and June 1943 which preceded her commissioning in the Royal Australian Navy, her outfit comprised two eight-barrelled 2pdr, seven power-operated twin 20mm and four singles. The aircraft fittings (except for the crane), .5in MGs and four single 20mm were removed. Two additional 20mm singles had been fitted by April 1944. Early in 1945 *Shropshire* received eleven 40mm Bofors single Mk III and landed six single and five twin 20mm. Radar 277 was fitted. The torpedo tubes and DC chutes were also removed. The Bofors outfit had been increased to fifteen by May 1945; seven on the superstructure deck, six on the upper deck and one each on B and X turrets, but in February 1946 this complement had been reduced to nine, four Mk IIIa on B gun deck, two Mk VII on the 4in gun deck, one Mk IIIp abaft the funnel and two Mk IIIa on the upper deck aft.

Sussex was fitted with two UP equipments in 1940. These and her .5 MGs were removed during repairs 1940/42, when her single 4in were replaced by four twins, two eight-barrelled 2pdrs were fitted and ten single 20mm added. Radars 273, 281, 282 and 285 were fitted. By December 1943 her single 20mm outfit was listed as 22 in number and her aircraft equipment had been removed. In a major refit from June 1944, X turret, the torpedo tubes and fifteen 20mm were landed to be replaced by four eight-barrelled 2pdr and four twin 20mm. Her radar fit was also updated.

Service *Devonshire*, like all of her sisters, joined the 1st Cruiser Squadron in the Mediterranean Fleet after completion, remaining there until 1939, except for a commission on the China Station between 1932 and 1933. After the outbreak of war she joined the Home Fleet, participating in the Norwegian campaign. In August 1940 she was part of the force tasked with the attack on Dakar, Operation Menace. During this abortive attack she shelled ships and batteries in and around the port. When the attack was abandoned she was employed in operations against Vichy French territories on the coast of equatorial Africa, blockading the Cameroons and Gabon. January 1941 saw the ship in the South Atlantic in the hunt for the raider *Kormoran*. She returned home to refit between February and May 1941, then joined the Home Fleet for operations off northern Norway and Russia until September. After transfer to the Eastern Fleet later in 1941, *Devonshire* was in

taken in hand at Chatham for major reconstruction in March 1939, which extended until February 1941. In the course of this work she received a 3½in waterline armour belt, a new bridge structure and hangars, a fixed catapult athwartships, four twin 4in Mk XIX, two eight-barrelled 2pdr mountings and new directors. This was accompanied by an increase in weight which severely strained the hull, making the ship almost a failure and requiring much subsequent work to improve matters, culminating in another five-month refit between December 1942 and May 1943.

During the war, *Devonshire* was given two eight-barrelled 2pdr and radar 281 early in 1941 and two single 20mm in September of that year. Between January and March 1942 she was fitted with four more 20mm singles and radar 273. By the end of 1942 the single 4in had been supplanted by four twin 4in Mk XIX and the number of 20mm singles increased to eight. The following year the ship landed the .5in MGs and six single

20mm, receiving in lieu two four-barrelled 2pdr and twelve twin 20mm. By April 1944 her light AA had been amended to six four-barrelled 2pdr, seven power-operated 20mm twin and twelve single 20mm; X turret and the aircraft installations were removed. She was now fitted with radars 281a, 282, 283 and 285. Postwar, her armament was reduced to two 8in and four 4in after conversion to a training ship.

London emerged from reconstruction armed with two eight-barrelled 2pdr and two quadruple .5in MGs, but at the end of 1941 lost the latter for eight single 20mm. Radar 273 was also fitted. In a refit between the end of December 1942 and May 1943 the aircraft equipment was removed (but the hangar was retained) and a further seven single 20mm added. Then, in another refit at the end of 1943, she received four twin 20mm but had three singles removed. By April 1944 her outfit is listed as four power-operated twin 20mm and sixteen single 20mm as well as the 2pdr. Between April

Above: *London* as rebuilt. (Admiralty via G. Ransome)
Right: *Devonshire* in 1940. (Courtesy G. Ransome)

command of the force which captured a complete Indo-China-bound Vichy French convoy east of the Cape of Good Hope on 2 November. A further success was the interception of the German raider *Atlantis* north of Ascension Island on 22 November. She was under refit at Norfolk, Virginia, between January and March 1942, then returned to the Indian Ocean, where she participated in the capture of Madagascar in April 1942. She remained in the Eastern Fleet until early 1943, covering Anzac troop convoys from Suez to Australia, then returned home to refit between May 1943 and March 1944. The rest of her war service was with the Home Fleet, covering the carrier raids against the Norwegian coast until 1945. Postwar, she was converted to a training ship in 1947 and served in that role until sold for scrapping on 16 June 1954, She arrived at Cashmore, Newport, on 12 December for breaking up.

London served with the 1st Cruiser Squadron until taken in hand for reconstruction in March 1939. On completion of this, in February 1941, she was deployed to the Atlantic in the hunt for *Bismarck* and, in the subsequent mopping-up operations with the destroyer *Brilliant*, intercepted the supply tankers *Esso Hamburg* and *Esso Colon* on 4 June, and, on the next day, the tanker *Egerland*. Finally, on 21 June, she intercepted the supply ship *Babitonga*, all in the central Atlantic. However, it was apparent that the extra weights added during reconstruction had greatly overstrained the hull, and the Atlantic

operations caused much damage to the hull. As a result she had to be docked again for repairs between October 1941 and January 1942. Thereafter, suprisingly, she was sent to the rough waters of the Arctic, where she operated on Russian convoy cover until November. This duty exposed more problems, and the ship had to be docked yet again between December 1942 and May 1943 for repairs. On her return to service she was sent out to the Eastern Fleet, with whom she operated until the end of the war. She sailed from Hong Kong in June 1949 and was laid up in the river Fal

until handed over to BISCO on 3 January 1950 and scrapped at T. W. Ward, Barrow, where she arrived on 25 January 1950.

Sussex went out to Australia from the Mediterranean in 1934, remaining there until 1936, after which she returned to the Mediterranean. In 1939 she formed Group H with *Shropshire* in the South Atlantic during the search for *Admiral Graf Spee*. On 2 December she intercepted the blockade runner *Watussi*. She then returned to the Home Fleet and took part in the Norwegian Campaign, then went into refit at Glasgow, where she was hit by bombs on 17/18 September 1940. These caused serious fires, gutting the after end, and she settled on the bottom with a heavy list. She did not return to service until August 1942. Subsequently she served in the Atlantic, where, on 20 February 1943, while searching for Axis blockade runners south-west of Cape Finisterre, she intercepted *Hohenfriedburg* and at the same time was narrowly missed by a salvo from *U264*. Thereafter she served in the Eastern Fleet and, after the end of the war with Japan, covered operations in the Dutch East Indies before returning home. Paid off in 1949, *Sussex* was handed over to BISCO on 3 January 1950, and arrived at Arnott Young's yard in Dalmuir on 23 February for breaking up.

Shropshire served with the Mediterranean Fleet until the outbreak of war, seeing service in the Abyssinian war and the Spanish Civil War, in which she played a leading part in the evacuation of refugees from Barcelona between August and September 1936. In September 1939 the ship was ordered to the South Atlantic for trade protection duties, forming part of Force H. On 9 December 1939 she intercepted the blockade runner *Adolf Leonhardt* between the Cape and St Helena. These patrols ended early in 1940 and the ship returned to Britain for refit before proceeding to the Indian Ocean, where she was employed on convoy cover duties between Capetown-Durban-Mombassa and Aden. In 1941 *Shropshire* participated in the campaign against Italian Somaliland,

bombarding both Mogadishu and Kismayu during the advance of the South African army from Kenya to Abyssinia, and sinking the Italian vessel *Pensilvania* off Mogadishu on 13 February. The ship remained in the South Atlantic, undergoing a refit at Simonstown between March and June 1941, then came home in October 1941 for a further major refit at Chatham between October 1941 and February 1942 before returning to the South Atlantic. On 8 September 1942 her transfer to the Royal Australian Navy was announced, as a replacement for HMAS *Canberra*. She was recalled from the South Atlantic and paid off at Chatham in December 1942 to refit for Australian service. Her subsequent career is detailed in the Australian section.

NORFOLK CLASS

Ship	Builder	Laid Down	Launched	Completed	Fate
Dorsetshire	Portsmouth Dky	21 Sep 27	29 Jan 29	30 Sep 30	Lost 5 Apr 1942
Norfolk	Fairfield	8 Jul 27	12 Dec 28	30 Apr 30	Scrapped at Newport 1950

Displacement: 9,975(*D*) 9,925(*N*) tons/10,083/10,134 tonnes (standard); 13,425/14,600 tons/13,639/14,833 tonnes (full load).
Length: 632ft 8in/192.83m (oa); 595ft/181.35m (pp).
Beam: 66ft/20.12m; Draught: 20ft 11in/6.37m (mean).
Machinery: 4-shaft Parsons geared turbines; 8 Admiralty 3-drum boilers.
Performance: 80,000shp=32.3kts Bunkerage: 3,190 tons oil.
Range: 12,500nm at 12kts.
Protection as *London* except for small details.
Guns as *Kent*.
Torpedoes as *Kent*.
Aircraft: one; one catapult.
Complement: 784.

Design The 1926 programme included three heavy cruisers, of which one was to be a smaller type (see *York*). The other pair were intended to be repeats of the *London*. However, it was decided to ship the new Mk II 8in twin turret to save weight and, at the same time, increase the protection to the magazines. The weight saved in the Mk II turret was to be used to extend the armouring to the shell rooms, but in fact the new turret proved considerably heavier than the Mk I, so savings had to be made elsewhere. The shell rooms were given 4in sides and 3in crowns. According to the legend design in October 1926, the total weight of armour and

protective plating was 1,060 tons, compared to 960 tons for *London*. Otherwise there was little difference between these ships and their predecessors. Two ships were ordered, one from HM Dockyard Portsmouth, the machinery for this vessel being ordered from Cammell Laird. It had been intended to order further ships in following years, but the class A cruiser included in the 1927/28 programme was to be of a better protected design than *Dorsetshire*. Considerable discussion then ensued on the subject of this ship and its protection, which is outside this narrative. Suffice it to say that in February 1929 it was approved to order two ships to a new design, with side armour of 5½in max. in thickness and a horizontal protection of 2¼in with 5¾in sides and 3⅜in to the magazines. Orders were to be placed on 15 May 1929 and the ships were to be named *Northumberland* and *Surrey*. Both were to be built in Royal dockyards, Portsmouth and Devonport respectively. Unfortunately, the advent of a Labour

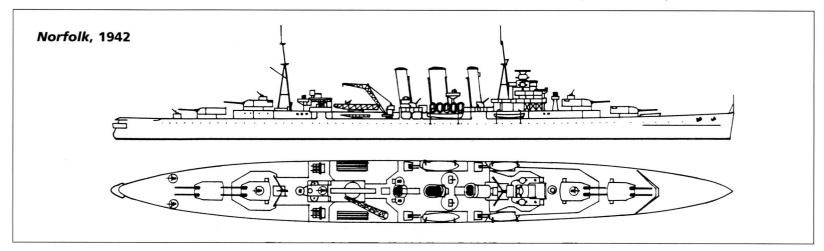

Norfolk, 1942

Above: *Norfolk* in China Station colours, November 1937. (Perkins)

Government in 1929 resulted in their suspension on 23 August 1929, before their keels had been laid, and on 14 January 1930 both were cancelled as an economy measure and a gesture of disarmament for the London Naval Conference of that year.

Modifications In 1931 they were fitted with a catapult and one HACS on the roof of the after control, and in 1933 two quadruple .5in MGs were added on platforms just forward of the second funnel. During refits in 1936/37 the AA outfit was modernised, the single 4in being supplanted by twins and two eight-barrelled 2pdrs being fitted abreast the after control position. A new catapult was fitted and a second HACS was added. The bridge was also enlarged.

During the war *Dorsetshire* received only nine single 20mm before her loss. *Norfolk*, on the other hand, received two UP mountings in the early summer of 1940, which were removed in a refit between July and September 1941. At this time she also lost the .5in MGs but received six single 20mm in lieu, as well as radars 273, 281, 284 and 285. A further three single 20mm were added in October 1942, when radar 273 was also installed. The aircraft installations were removed and a further nine single 20mm added in 1943.

However, the 20mm outfit was quoted as being fifteen singles in April 1944. A major refit was carried out in 1944, when X turret, two eight-barrelled 2pdr, two single 20mm and part of the radar outfit was landed, to be replaced by eleven twin power-operated 20mm and six quadruple 2pdr mountings. The 20mm singles were reduced to ten. The radar fit was modernised at the same time. Finally, in September 1945, ten single Bofors 40mm replaced an equal number of 20mm singles.

Service *Dorsetshire* served in the Atlantic and Home Fleets between 1930 and 1933, before a period on the Africa Station from 1933 to 1935. After refit in 1936/37 the ship joined the 5th Cruiser Squadron on the China Station, and was there at the outbreak of war. When the German raiders appeared on the oceans, *Dorsetshire* was despatched to Ceylon to form Force I with *Cornwall* and *Hermes*, and joined the hunt for *Admiral Graf Spee*. She remained so employed until the end of the year, when ordered to the River Plate, where she arrived on 12 December 1939 to help contain the fugitive pocket battleship. After this episode she carried out trade protection duties in the South Atlantic in 1940, as well as patrols searching for Axis blockade runners. In February she intercepted the German *Wakama* off Rio. In the summer of that year she moved to the Freetown area, where she was engaged in the

operations against Vichy French territories and shipping, shadowing the battleship *Richelieu* on one occasion. She also took part in the attempt to destroy or immobilise this ship at Dakar in July. She returned to the Indian Ocean to participate in the operations against Italian Somaliland in November, when she bombarded enemy positions ashore. However, the appearance of *Admiral Scheer* in the South Atlantic at the end of the year brought her recall to the west coast of Africa, and by December she was back at Freetown. Employed to protect the Sierra Leone-Great Britain convoys, she was escorting SL74 northbound in May 1941 when she was diverted to the hunt for *Bismarck*, which culminated in her shelling and torpedoing the crippled battleship. The ship remained based at Freetown on trade protection duties during 1941 while the danger from raiders remained high, escorting convoys occasionally as far afield as Bombay. While on these duties she intercepted the raider supply ship *Python* west of St Helena on 1 December 1941, surviving an attack from *UA* at the same time. War with Japan brought her back to the Indian Ocean, and in March 1942 she was undergoing refit at Colombo, this being halted on the approach of a Japanese carrier force at the end of the month. *Dorsetshire* sailed with *Cornwall* to join the Eastern Fleet off the Maldives, but on 5 April 1942 she was sunk south-east of the islands by Japanese carrier-borne aircraft, together with her consort.

Norfolk also served in the Atlantic and Home Fleets during 1930/32, then went to the America and West Indies Station between 1932 and 1934. From 1935 to 1939 she served on the East Indies Station before coming home to refit in 1939, being still in dockyard hands when war was declared. On 6 September she joined the 18th Cruiser Squadron with the Home Fleet in the Denmark Straits. In early December, with the return of *Berwick* from the West Indies and *Devonshire* from the Mediterranean, *Norfolk*, with *Suffolk*, re-formed the 1st Cruiser Squadron, operating with the Home Fleet in northern waters. On 15 March 1940, while at Scapa, she was hit by bombs and went to the Clyde to repair. She returned to service with the Home Fleet in June. In December 1940 she was ordered to the South Atlantic on trade protection duties, operating from Freetown as part of Force K and also tasked with the hunt for *Admiral Scheer* and, in January 1941, the raider *Kormoran*. In February she escorted Atlantic troop convoys, but by May she had returned to Icelandic waters, and patrolled the Denmark Straits at the time of the *Bismarck* sortie. She was present at the final sinking of the battleship, having taken part in the whole action from her discovery

Above: *Dorsetshire* in Scapa Flow on 9 August 1941, with *Berwick* off to port and the carrier *Furious* ahead. A *Dido* class cruiser lies in the distance. (IWM)

in the Denmark Straits. From July to September the ship was in refit, after which she spent the rest of the war on Arctic convoy duties with the Home Fleet, culminating in the action against *Scharnhorst* off North Cape in December 1943, when she received shell hits. Repairs were combined with a long refit, and as a result she did not

re-enter service until November 1944, after which she returned to the Home Fleet, participating in the sweeps along the Norwegian coast in 1945 until the end of the war. She was handed over to BISCO for scrapping on 3 January 1950, and arrived at Cashmore, Newport, for breaking up, on 19 February.

YORK CLASS

Ship	Builder	Laid Down	Launched	Completed	Fate
York	Palmers	16 May 27	17 Jul 28	1 May 30	CTL 26 Mar 1941

Displacement: 8,250 tons/8,382 tonnes (standard);10,350 tons/10,515 tonnes (full load).
Length: 575ft/175.25m (oa); 540ft/164.59m (pp).
Beam: 57ft/17.37m; Draught: 20ft 3in/6.17m (mean).
Machinery: 4-shaft Parsons geared turbines; 8 Admiralty 3-drum boilers.
Performance: 80,000shp=32.3kts; Bunkerage: 1,900 tons oil.
Range: 10,000nm at 14kts.
Protection: 3in side (machinery spaces); 1½in deck (machinery spaces); 3in-4⅜in Magazines, 1in turrets.
Guns: six 8in BL Mk VIII (3x2); four 4in QF Mk V (4x1); two 2pdr (2x1).
Torpedoes: six 21in (2x3).
Aircraft: one; one catapult.
Complement: 628.

Design The expense of the 10,000-ton County programme and political pressures to reduce armament expenditure led the Admiralty to consider a so-called Class B cruiser which, it hoped, would allow a useful number of ships to be built, which was obviously not going to be possible with the County design. However, the main idea was that although the new design might have a couple of guns fewer than the 10,000-ton ships, no other concessions were to be made. In fact, it was expected that protection could be considerably enhanced. Various sketch designs were discussed in 1925, and in December one of them was approved. This specified an 8,200-ton ship armed with six 8in in twin turrets and having an 80,000shp twin-shaft machinery installation for a top speed of 32¼kts. In comparison to the Counties, this design incorporated a 3in armour belt in the way of the machinery spaces, while the magazines and shell rooms had 4in sides and 2½in crowns. Two aircraft were proposed, with two catapults, an arrangement rather uneconomical in weight, since one was to be atop B turret, thus necessitating a high bridge structure, and one amidships. The main armament remained the 8in Mk VII in twin turrets Mk II, and the only variation from the County armament was their number and the fact that only triple tubes were carried.

The steam plant was arranged in two boiler rooms with four boilers in each, aft of which were the turbine rooms.

During construction, weights rose for several reasons, including the fitting of an armoured DCT (which required an increase in beam), thicker armour to the magazine bulkheads and turrets, a higher bridge and the trunking of the forward funnel into the second. Nevertheless, weight savings in construction eventually resulted in a standard displacement of only 8,250 tons.

One ship was ordered in 1927 under the 1926 programme and named *York*.

Modifications The fitting of the catapult on B turret was deleted while building. Otherwise she completed as designed. In the early 1930s the forecastle plating was extended aft to the tubes and a fixed catapult was installed. Two .5in quadruple MGs were added on the shelter deck abreast the bridge in 1934/35, and in 1937/38 the fixed catapult was replaced by the revolving type. The aircraft was initially a Fairey IIIF, later replaced by the standard Walrus. During the war, *York* received only a couple of 20mm singles, one of which was on A turret, and splinter protection to the 4in gun deck.

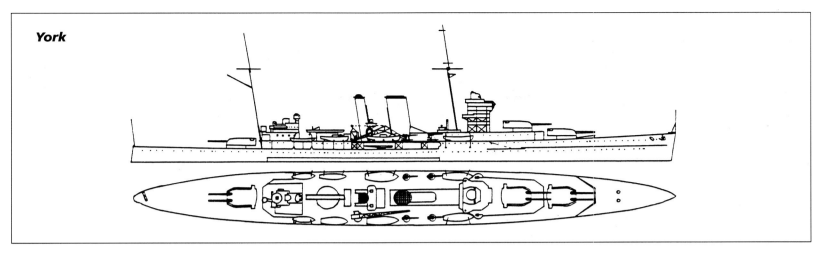

York

Below: *York* in 1933. (W&L)

Service *York* spent a number of years on the America and West Indies Station before the war, with the 8th Cruiser Squadron, but was detached to the Mediterranean between September 1935 and the spring of 1936 as a result of the Abyssinian crisis. However, she was on the America Station in September 1939. Her initial duties involved providing the ocean escort to the first Atlantic convoys from Halifax, Nova Scotia. In October 1939 she became part of Force F at Halifax, with *Berwick*, when raider hunting groups were formed. On 3 March 1940 she intercepted the blockade runner *Arucas* in the Denmark Straits. By the following month she had returned to the Home Fleet and was scheduled to carry troops to Norway (Operation Wilfred). She participated in the Norwegian campaign, then was attached to the Home Fleet. In the summer of 1940 she was transferred to the Mediterranean and was based at Malta and Alexandria with the 3rd Cruiser Squadron. On 13 October she finished off the damaged *Artigliere* after the latter's action with *Ajax*. For the remainder of her career in this theatre she escorted Malta Convoys, carried troops to Greece and operated in the eastern Basin. Finally, on 26 March 1941, she was hit by Italian explosive motor boats launched from the destroyers *Crispi* and *Sella* while she was lying in Suda Bay, Crete. Badly damaged, the ship was beached in shallow water. She was later wrecked by demolition charges on the evacuation of the island, and abandoned on 22 May.

EXETER CLASS

Ship	Builder	Laid Down	Launched	Completed	Fate
Exeter	Devonport Dky	1 Aug 28	18 Jul 29	27 Jul 31	Lost 1 Mar 1942

Displacement: 8,390 tons/8,524 tonnes (standard); 10,490 tons/10,657 tonnes (full load).
Length: 575ft/164.59m (oa); 540ft/175.25m (pp).
Beam: 58ft/17.68m; **Draught:** 20ft 3in/6.17m (mean).
Machinery: 4-shaft Parsons geared turbines; 8 Admiralty 3-drum boilers.
Performance: 80,000shp=32kts; **Bunkerage:** 1,900 tons oil.
Range: 10,000nm at 14 kts.
Protection: as *York* except 5in crowns and 3in sides to magazines.

Guns: six 8in BL Mk VIII (3x2); four 4in QF Mk V (4x1); two 2pdr (2x1).
Torpedoes: six 21in (2x3).
Aircraft: two; two catapults.
Complement: 628.

Design As originally conceived, this ship was to be a sister to *York*, but alterations were made during the design stages. In fact, two ships were to be programmed in 1927, but economics intervened and only the one materialised. Protection was improved over *York* in that 5½in crowns and 3in sides were given to the magazines. Beam was increased by 1ft as a result of the increased weight of the DCT on the bridge. She was fitted to operate aircraft, but given a double, fixed catapult with the two tracks diverging from the centreline. As the plan to fit her sister with a catapult on B turret had been found to be flawed, *Exeter* was not given the high bridge, and received a streamlined structure without the multitude of platforms seen hitherto. As far as armament was concerned, the only change was the fitting of the Mk II*, in which the AA ability was deleted and the elevation was 50°. Her machinery was built by Parsons.
Modifications Between the wars this ship received the same modifications as *York*, but dur-

ing repairs following the action off the River Plate she had her single 4in replaced by twin 4in, two eight-barrelled 2pdr mountings were fitted and radar 279 was added. The 4in twins were in different, more widely spaced positions than the singles. Tripod masts replaced the pole masts, and an HACS was fitted in the bridge abaft the DCT. Tubs for single 20mm were fitted on B and Y turrets.

Service On completion, *Exeter* joined the 2nd Cruiser Squadron with the Atlantic Fleet, where she served during 1931/33. In 1934 she went out to the America and West Indies Station and remained there, with a temporary deployment to the Mediterranean during the Abyssinian crisis of 1935/36, until 1939. At the beginning of the war she was in the South American Division, and formed Force G with *Cumberland* off the east coast of that continent in October 1939, when raider hunting groups were formed. She played a major part in the Battle of the River Plate in December 1939, when the *Admiral Graf Spee* was finally cornered. In this action, however, she was badly damaged and had to with-

Above: *Exeter* as completed. (Abrahams)

draw to the Falkland Islands for temporary repairs. These lasted until January, after which the ship returned to Devonport for full repairs which took until 10 March 1941 to complete. The ship provided ocean escort to Atlantic convoys in 1941, but on the entry of Japan into the war she was sent to the East Indies. At the beginning of 1942 she was in the ABDA Command as

Below: *Exeter* in May 1941. (IWM)

part of the Allied Striking Force formed to defend the Dutch East Indies from Japanese invasion. When the Japanese invaded Java at the end of February 1942, *Exeter* was ordered to join Rear Admiral Doorman's squadron, which then became involved in the Battle of the Java Sea. During this action *Exeter* received a hit in a boiler room and was ordered to Soerabaya. When she attempted to reach the Sunda Straits she was intercepted by the cruisers *Nachi* and *Haguro*, being badly damaged by gunfire and a torpedo from the destroyer *Ikazuchi* before being scuttled off the Bawean Islands.

Right: *Exeter* in May 1941. Note alterations. (IWM)

LEANDER CLASS

Ship	Builder	Laid Down	Launched	Completed	Fate
Leander	Devonport Dky	8 Sep 30	24 Sep 31	24 Mar 33	Scrapped at Blyth 1950
Neptune	Portsmouth Dky	24 Sep 31	31 Jan 33	12 Feb 34	Lost 19 Dec 1941
Orion	Devonport Dky	26 Sep 31	24 Nov 32	18 Jan 34	Scrapped at Troon 1949
Achilles	Cammell Laird	11 Jun 31	1 Sep 32	6 Oct 33	to India 1948
Ajax	Vickers (Barrow)	7 Feb 33	1 Mar 34	12 Apr 35	Scrapped at Newport 1949

Displacement: 6,985-7,270* tons/7,096-7,386 tonnes (standard); 9,000-9,280 tons/9,144-9,428 tonnes (full load).
Length: 554ft 6in/169.01m (oa); 522ft/159.1m (pp).
Beam: 55ft (*Leander*), 56ft others/16.76/17m; Draught: 19ft/5.79m (mean).
Machinery: 4-shaft Parsons geared turbines; 6 Admiralty 3-drum boilers.
Performance: 72,000shp=32½kts; Bunkerage: 1,720 tons oil.
Range: 5,730nm at 13kts.
Protection: 3in sides (machinery spaces); 3½in sides, 2in crowns (magazines); 1in decks; 1in turrets.

Guns: eight 6in Mk XXIII (4x2); four 4in QF Mk V (4X1); twelve .5in MGs (3x4).
Torpedoes: eight 21in (2x4).
Aircraft: one; one catapult.
Complement: 570.
Leander, 7,270; *Neptune*, 7,175; *Orion*, 7,215; *Achilles*, 7,030 & *Ajax*, 6,985 tons.

Design The genesis of this class can be traced back to the 6in Gun Cruiser Conference of January 1929. This led to the discussion of several schemes for a light cruiser (although the term was not yet in general use) armed with 6in or 5.5in guns, intended to operate with the fleet. As usual, none of the various schemes fully met all demands, and compromises were made. The armament was soon fixed at eight 6in guns after the 5.5 had been discarded, and a decision was made to adopt the twin turret as a result of its success in *Enterprise*. The protective scheme had armouring to the magazines and machinery spaces in various thicknesses up to 3in for the magazine sides and machinery spaces. The ship's side was to be immune from 6in gunfire at above 10,000yd, and the magazine crowns below 16,000yd. This required 3in sides and 2in NC armour. Barrage AA fire was a requirement of the main armament, as was an HACS.

As usual, the ship's size grew as the design work progressed, so that by June 1931 the legend displacement had risen from 6,410 tons to 7,154 tons. Length, beam and installed shp had all

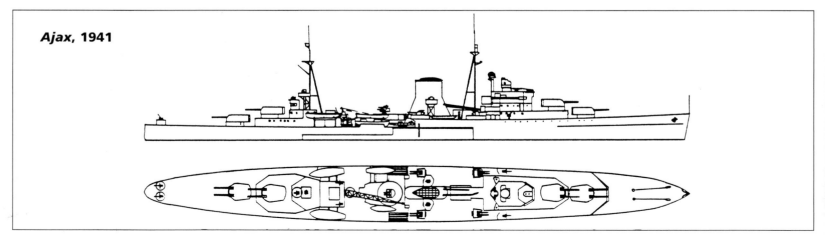

Ajax, 1941

increased, and the armament had been improved by the addition of a catapult and the provision to stow two aircraft, as it was felt that these ships could well spend much time operating alone on the trade routes. It was impossible, however, to fit a hangar.

The main armament consisted of the 6in BL Mk XXIII in twin Mk XXI mountings with 60° elevation, firing a 112lb (50.8kg) projectile and having a maximum range of 25,480yd (23,300m). Unfortunately, the intended pair of director towers, one forward and one aft, was reduced to the forward one only as a result of cost cutting during construction, so that the ability to engage two targets simultaneously with controlled fire became impossible.

Secondary armament consisted of the standard four single 4in Mk V on AA mountings, with one HACS on the bridge. Three quadruple .5 MGs were fitted, the third in place of the missing

after director atop the after control. Two quadruple banks for 21in torpedoes were fitted in the waist.

The aircraft installation included a catapult and provision to operate both a Fairey IIIF and the new, lighter, Hawker Osprey. However, it was found that the former was unsuitable for operation from smaller cruisers, and only the latter was shipped.

The protective scheme included 3in sides to boiler and turbine spaces and 1¼in decks over these spaces. Magazines received 2in crowns and 3½in sides. The turret roofs had only 1in protection. Armour represented about 11.7 per cent of the legend displacement.

The machinery was arranged in three boiler rooms and two turbine rooms, all of the uptakes being trunked into a large streamlined funnel. Boiler pressures were slightly increased in this class, to 300psi. As usual, the three ships built in the dockyards had their machinery contracted out; to V. A. (Tyne) in the case of *Leander* and *Orion*; to Parsons for *Neptune*.

One ship, *Leander*, was ordered under the 1929 programme, three under the 1930 programme, and one more, *Ajax*, under that for 1931. The last four had their beam increased by 1ft to improve stability, consequent on additions during design and construction. Welding was employed for the first time in these ships on more than an isolated scale.

Modifications An early modification was the plating-in of the ship's side as far aft as the second 4in gun because of chronic wetness. Before the war, other alterations were limited to the replacement of the single 4in by twin Mk XIX between 1936 and 1938, but this did not include *Achilles*. However, both this ship and *Leander* were transferred to New Zealand in 1936/37 and were fitted to operate the larger Walrus for use in the Pacific. The others retained the lighter seaplane but re-equipped with the somewhat unsatisfactory Fairey Seafox from 1937. *Leander* received her after control position during the 1936/37 refit, and had her crane repositioned on the centreline at the same time.

Below: *Achilles* in February 1939. (W&L)

Above: *Achilles* in June 1944, showing wartime alterations. (IWM)
Opposite page: *Leander* in her final state in 1946. (W&L)

During the war, *Leander* had her catapult and aircraft removed in June 1941, shipping in its place a quadruple 2pdr. Later the same year the 2pdr was landed and the aircraft installations refitted. Five single 20mm were added. Radars were added in mid-1942 to the director and type 291 at the mast head. In 1943 the aircraft fittings were finally landed and four single 20mm were fitted. Radar 273 was installed amidships. By April 1944 X turret had been landed, to be replaced by single 20mm (port and starboard) with a power-operated twin on the centreline. Two quadruple 40mm Bofors were fitted on the former motorboat platform, the remainder of the 20mm outfit consisting of two power-operated twins and two singles. The HACS on the bridge was replaced by two, port and starboard on the lower signal deck. By 1946 all single 20mm had been landed and the quadruple 40mm had been replaced by twin Mk V. Three single 40mm Mk III replaced the single and twin 20mm on X gun deck.

Neptune had her .5in MGs replaced by three single 2pdr in 1941 and radars 281, 284 and 285 were fitted. No other changes were made before her loss.

Orion lost her catapult in 1941, as well as the .5in MGs, and received seven single 20mm and two quadruple 2pdrs. Radars 279, 284 and 285 were fitted. Type 273 radar was added in 1942.

Achilles landed all the single 4in and shipped an unknown number of 20mm in their stead in 1942, presumably as a temporary measure. In

1943/44 twin 4in were fitted, X turret and the catapult were removed and four quadruple 2pdr were fitted. The 20mm now totalled eighteen, in seven power-operated twin and four single mountings. Two HACS were fitted on the lower signal deck, the bridge HACS having been supplanted by a radar aerial. In April 1945 the light AA consisted of four single 40mm Bofors, five 20mm twin and five single, in addition to the 2pdr.

Ajax received a heavier catapult and a Walrus aircraft in 1940, and was fitted with radar 279. In 1941 the catapult was replaced by a quadruple 2pdr. Six single 20mm were added early in 1942 and, later the same year, the quadruple 2pdr on the catapult structure was landed, as were the .5in MGs. In their place the ship received two quadruple 2pdr on the boat platform, three more 20mm singles, two HACS on the lower signal deck and radars 272, 282 and 285. In April 1944 the light AA comprised two quadruple 40mm Bofors and four power-operated twin 20mm.

Service *Leander* joined the Home Fleet on completion, but in April 1937 was loaned to New Zealand. As a unit of the New Zealand Division she was deployed on trade protection duties in the South-west Pacific in September 1939, her main task being the escorting of ANZAC troop convoys from Australia and New Zealand across the Indian Ocean to the Red Sea and Suez. This task extended into 1941, when, in the course of escorting the convoy US9 in the Indian Ocean in February of that year, she intercepted and sank

the Italian raider *Ramb I* off Bombay. On 4 March, in company with *Canberra*, she intercepted the blockade runners *Ketty Brovig* and *Coburg* south-east of the Seychelles. The insurrection in Iraq in April 1941 brought her to Basra, where she lay in readiness but was not needed. In June she was transferred into the Mediterranean to reinforce the Mediterranean fleet in its operations against Vichy-French Syria, and arrived off that coast on 13 June. She participated in the blockade of Beirut and, together with *Naiad* and destroyers, engaged the Vichy-French contre-torpilleur *Guépard* on 23 June. She did not remain in the Mediterranean, however, but returned to New Zealand to refit at the end of the year and then served in the south-west Pacific from December. She was part of the ANZAC Force on its formation at Suva in the Fiji Islands on 12 February 1942, and saw action with that force in the Papua-New Guinea-New Hebrides area as well as in the Coral Sea. In May 1942 she landed the first Allied forces on Espirito Santo in the New Hebrides. During the Guadalcanal campaign she escorted convoys, and in January 1943 was transferred to the 3rd Fleet. After the loss of the USS *Helena* she was transferred from the New Hebrides to the Solomon Islands, where she

joined CruDiv 9 as part of Task Force 36.1. On 12 July 1943 this force was deployed to intercept Japanese destroyers running the 'Tokyo Express' in the Kula Gulf. In a fierce night gun action known as the Battle of Kolombangara, *Leander* was hit by a torpedo and badly damaged. She underwent temporary repairs at Auckland until December 1943, then sailed to Boston, Massachusetts, where repairs extended from 3 January 1944 until 27 August 1945. Following this she returned to Britain. She was handed over to BISCO for disposal on 15 December 1949 and allocated to Hughes Bolkow, Blyth, where she arrived for breaking up on 15 January 1950.

Orion commissioned for service with the Home Fleet, but in 1937 was transferred to the 8th Cruiser Squadron on the America and West Indies Station, where she served until transferred to the Mediterranean in 1940. In June 1940 she was with the 7th Cruiser Squadron as flagship, taking part in the bombardement of Bardia that month and the engagement of Punto Stilo in July. During the remainder of 1940 she operated throughout the Mediterranean, escorting Malta convoys, shelling Italian-held islands and ferrying troops to Greece. Early in 1941 she was operating in the Crete and Aegean areas, and in March was at the Battle of Cape Matapan. Then, after supporting the army on the North African coast in April, she took part in the evacuation of Greece, followed the next month by similar duties off Crete, where she participated in strikes against Axis invasion convoys.

However, on 29 May she was badly damaged by bombs and withdrew to Simonstown, South Africa, for temporary repairs. These lasted until July 1941, when she sailed for Mare Island, California, for major repairs and refit. These were completed in February 1942, and after further attention in Devonport the ship finally returned to the Mediterranean in January 1943, joining the 15th Cruiser Squadron. Here she again bombarded Italian islands before covering the invasion of Sicily in June/July 1943, and was thereafter employed on fire support duties off Calabria, and then at the Salerno landings in September as part of Support Force East and Anzio in January 1944. She was brought home for the Normandy Landings in June 1944 and served with Force K off Gold Beach, but soon returned to the Mediterranean for the landings in the south of France in August. She then moved into the Aegean for operations in support of the reoccupation of Athens in September/October, before final war duties off the Ligurian coast, bombarding German positions around San Remo in April 1945. After use in ship target trials, *Orion* was handed over to BISCO on 19 July 1949 and allocated to Arnott Young for breaking up. She arrived at Dalmuir for scrapping in August 1949.

Neptune also commissioned for the Home Fleet, then went to the Africa Station in 1937 and in September 1939 formed the 6th Cruiser Squadron in the South Atlantic. On 5 September she intercepted the German merchantman *Inn*,

and on 22 October *Adolph Woermann* was intercepted off Ascension Island while the cruiser patrolled the Freetown-Natal line. She remained in the South Atlantic during the hunt for *Admiral Graf Spee* as part of Force K. By May 1940 she had arrived at Alexandria to join the 7th Cruiser Squadron in the Mediterranean, and took part in the Anglo-French bombardment of Bardia in June. In July she was at the engagement off Punto Stilo, then moved into the eastern Mediterranean, making a sortie into the Gulf of Athens, where, with *Sydney*, she sank a small tanker. However, the appearance of more German raiders in the Atlantic caused her return to that theatre, and by November she was once again patrolling out of Freetown, searching for *Admiral Scheer*. After a refit at Chatham between February and May 1941, *Neptune* was employed in the search for *Bismarck*'s supply ships, and assisted in the interception of *Gonzenheim* on 4 June 1941, finally sinking the ship by torpedo. On her return to the Mediterranean once more, she was transferred to Force K at Malta in November, tasked with the interdiction of the Axis supply routes to North Africa. In the course of one such operation, on 19 December, she ran on to an Italian minefield and detonated four mines, sinking with all but one of her crew.

Ajax served on the America and West Indies Station from completion, but formed part of the South America Division in September 1939. Operating off the River Plate, she intercepted the

German merchantmen *Carl Fritzen* and *Olinda* that month, and on 5 December, with *Cumberland*, the steamer *Ussukuma*. As part of Force G she patrolled off the Falklands and the east coast of south America in the hunt for *Admiral Graf Spee* before participating in the Battle of the River Plate, when she was hit seven times by the German ship and badly damaged. She was under repair from December 1939 until July 1940, then joined the 7th Cruiser Squadron in the Mediterranean. On 11/12 October she engaged an Italian torpedo boat force, sinking *Airone* and *Ariel* and badly damaging the destroyer *Artigliere*, which was later sunk by *York*. Her Mediterranean career included raids into the Straits of Otranto, Malta convoys, the battle of Cape Matapan, the evacuation of Greece (when she took off the last troops on 29 April 1941) and sorties against the Axis invasion convoys to Crete. On 21 May she was attacked by Ju 87s of III St Gr2 and hit by bombs, but was able to cover the Syria operations in June. She was transferred to Malta in November to reinforce Force K, but was withdrawn in February 1942 when that force was disbanded after the loss of *Neptune*. The ship was under repair and refit at Chatham between May and October 1942, consequent upon damage received in the eastern Mediterranean, then returned to join Force Q at Bone on 1 January 1943. Unfortunately she was immediately hit in a bombing raid and badly damaged again, which necessitated docking in New York Navy Yard from 4 March 1943 until October. By May 1944 she was in the eastern Mediterranean, but was recalled to Britain for Operation Overlord in June and served off Gold Beach with Force K. After yet another return to the Mediterranean she was at the landings in the south of France in August, then in the autumn operated in the Aegean and Greek waters during the reoccupation of Athens and the communist uprising, when she shelled ELAS positions. She saw little or no postwar service, and was laid up in the River Fal. She was towed away on 8 November 1949, arriving at the Newport yard of Cashmore's for breaking up on 18 November 1949.

Achilles served in the Home Fleet until 31 March 1931, when she was transferred to the New Zealand Division. In November 1939 she formed part of Force G operating between the Falklands and the Plate estuary. During the Battle of the River Plate she received light damage, then returned to New Zealand waters, where she carried out trade protection patrols. When Japan entered the war, *Achilles* escorted troop convoys off Australia and New Zealand, and then, in February 1942, joined the ANZAC squadron in the south-west Pacific theatre. She operated in this theatre until early 1943, when, as part of TF67, she took part in an operation off New Georgia, together with US units, during which she was hit by a bomb on 5 January, which struck X turret. The ship returned to Portsmouth for repairs which lasted from 1 April 1943 to 20 May 1944. She recommissioned on 23 May and went out to the Indian Ocean to join the Eastern Fleet, then in May 1945 joined TF57 in the Pacific. With the British Pacific Fleet she took part in the raid on Sakashima Gunto, the carrier raids on Truk, and in the final attacks on the Japanese mainland in July and August 1945. *Achilles* returned to Britain on 12 September 1946 and paid off on 17 September, reverting to RN control after ten years in the RNZN. She was subsequently sold to India and commissioned as *INS Dehli* on 5 July 1947.

ARETHUSA CLASS

Ship	Builder	Laid Down	Launched	Completed	Fate
Arethusa	Chatham Dky	25 Jan 33	6 Mar 34	23 May 35	Scrapped at Troon, 1950
Galatea	Scotts	2 Jun 33	9 Aug 34	14 Aug 35	Lost 15 Dec 1941
Penelope	Harland & Wolff	30 May 34	15 Oct 35	13 Nov 36	Lost 18 Feb 1944
Aurora	Portsmouth Dky	27 Jul 35	20 Aug 36	12 Nov 37	To China 1948

Displacement: 5,220¹-5,270² tons/5,354-5,354 tonnes (standard); 6,665-6,715 tons/6,771-6,822 tonnes (full load).
Length: 506ft/154.22m (oa); 480ft/146.3m (pp).
Beam: 51ft/15.54m; Draught: 16ft 6in/5.03m (mean).
Machinery: 4-shaft Parsons geared turbines; 4 Admiralty 3-drum boilers.
Performance: 64,000shp=32¼kts; Bunkerage: 1,300 tons oil.
Range: 5,300 nm at 13kts.
Protection: 2¼in sides (machinery spaces); 3in sides, 2in crowns (magazines); 1in deck.
Guns: six 6in Mk XXIII (3x2); four except *Aurora* & *Penelope* eight 4in Mk V (4x1 or 4x2).
Torpedoes: six 21in (3x2).
Aircraft: one, one catapult, (not in *Aurora*).
Complement: 500.
¹ *Arethusa* & *Galatea*, ² *Penelope* & *Aurora*.

Design Discussions on the design of a new Fleet cruiser began in 1929, and between that date and February 1932, when the design was finally fixed, many sketch designs were considered. These ranged from 3,000 to nearly 7,000 tons in displacement, armed with 6in or 5.5in guns in single, twin and triple mountings. By the new year of 1931 the design had been all but finalised, and in March it was revised yet again and approved. However, the Labour Government of the day was reluctant to authorise naval expenditure, and the conditions of the London Naval Treaty also had a bearing on matters. Consequently the new ships were postponed. The inevitable result was that the design was again subject to modification, so that in February 1932, when the design was actually finalised, it had become a 5,450-ton ship armed with three twin 6in and powered by a four-shaft geared turbine installation. The increase in displacement meant that only nine of the *Leander*s could be built, but five of the new design instead of the planned three. In the event only four were actually ordered, in part because of the need to build more powerful ships to counter the new Japanese designs.

As completed, the *Arethusa*s displaced between 5,031 and 5,458 tons. Their protection was limited to 2in crowns and 3in sides to the magazines, the shell rooms having only 1in protection. The machinery spaces were given 1in decks and 2¼in sides. Armour and protective plating accounted for 11.8 per cent of the legend displacement.

The machinery was arranged on the unit principle as adopted in the Modified *Leander*s (q.v.), for better damage control in action. The steam plant was reduced to four boilers, which, being in spaces separated by a turbine room, required a two-funnel layout.

The main armament comprised the now standard 6in BL Mk XXIII in twin turrets Mk XXI, similar to the earlier light cruiser classes. The secondary armament was the usual four single 4in, but these were now grouped on the after shelter deck, abaft the after funnel. Two quadruple .5in MGs and a pair of triple banks of 21in torpedo tubes completed the armament. Provision was made for a catapult amidships between the funnels to carry a single Hawker Osprey floatplane. It had been hoped that a second aircraft could be accommodated, stowed on the after shelter deck, but trials with *Arethusa* soon showed that this made things impossibly cramped for the 4in gun crews, and the idea was abandoned. Number 713 (Catapult) flight provided the aircraft for the 3rd Cruiser Squadron, the Ospreys being replaced by Seafoxes from November 1937.

Only one director tower was fitted, with an HACS abaft it.

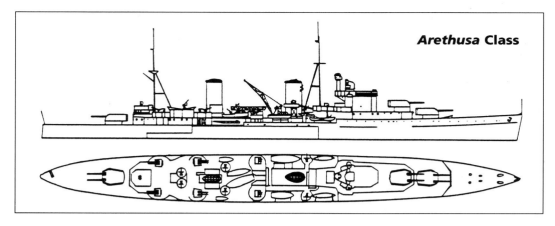

Arethusa Class

Modifications *Aurora* completed without aircraft facilities, and had a deckhouse for accommodation in lieu for service as Commodore (D). There were plans to fit twin 4in instead of the singles before completion, but the first two ships commissioned as designed, although *Aurora* and *Penelope* completed with four twins and a second

HACS aft. *Galatea* received twin 4in herself before the war. Extra plating was added amidships after completion to reduce wetness and to protect the boats.

Arethusa had received two quadruple 2pdr and radar by April 1941, and landed the catapult. Later the same year, two UP mountings and four single 20mm were added. The former were removed in the spring of 1942, as were the single 4in and the .5in MGs. They were replaced by twin

4in mountings and a further four 20mm. Radar 286 was landed and radars 273, 281, 282, 284 and 285 were fitted. Three additional 20mm were added by October 1942. Between March and December 1943, while under repair in the USA, the 2pdr were supplanted by quadruple 40mm Bofors, three single 20mm by four twin, and the radar fit modernised. By April 1944 her light AA outfit comprised four power-operated twin 20mm and three single 20mm.

Galatea lost her catapult during a refit between October 1940 and January 1941, when she received two quadruple 2pdr and eight single 20mm, as well as radar 279.

Penelope also lost her catapult and had two quadruple 2pdr fitted between August 1940 and July 1941. Four single 20mm were added at the end of 1941, and four more in the summer of 1942.

Aurora received a UP mounting and two quadruple 2pdr in the summer of 1940, had radars 284 and 290 added in April 1941, and in August received six single 20mm and two quadruple .5in MGs.

Service *Arethusa* went to the 3rd Cruiser Squadron in the Mediterranean on completion, and was still there at the beginning of the war.

However, early in 1940 she and her sister *Penelope* were recalled to the Home Fleet, where they formed the 2nd Cruiser Squadron with the remainder of the class. She participated in the Norwegian campaign in April 1940, but on 8 May she joined the Nore Command, where she supported the defending forces in Calais and later aided the evacuations from French Atlantic ports. On 28 June she was a component of the newly formed Force H at Gibraltar, with whom she participated in the action against Vichy French forces at Mers el Kebir in July 1940. With Force H she took part in convoy protection patrols in the Atlantic and operated in the Mediterranean. During the *Bismarck* sortie she was employed in Iceland/Faroes waters, but by July she had returned to the Mediterranean, where she escorted Malta convoys and ran supply trips to the island herself. Towards the end of 1941 she returned to home waters and took part in the Lofoten raid in December, where she was damaged by near-misses. After refit and repair at Chatham until April 1942, she returned to the Mediterranean in June, where she joined the 15th Cruiser Squadron, operating mostly in support of the resupply of Malta. While on one such operation (Stoneage), she was struck by a torpedo from an Italian aircraft on 18 November, but was towed into Alexandria with heavy casualties. Temporary repairs lasted until 7 February 1943, after which she proceeded to Charlestown, USA, for full

repair. These were completed by 15 December, and the ship then returned to Britain, but she did not become fully operational again until early June 1944, when she immediately sailed for the Invasion of Normandy, forming part of Force D off Sword Beach. By January 1945 she was a part of the 15th Cruiser Squadron with the Mediterranean Fleet. After the war these ships were considered too small to be worth modernising, and *Arethusa* was used for trials and experiments in 1949 before being allocated to BISCO for disposal. She arrived at Cashmore's, Newport, for breaking up, on 9 May 1950.

Galatea joined the Mediterranean Fleet on commissioning and acted as flagship, Rear Admiral (Destroyers). After the outbreak of war she was ordered home, and in February/March 1940 took part in the operations to intercept Axis merchantmen attempting to break out of Vigo. In April she was involved in the Norwegian campaign, and in May joined the Nore Command as Flagship of the 2nd Cruiser Squadron. She remained with the Home Fleet (under refit, October 1940–January 1941) until May 1941, and was involved in the *Bismarck* operations. In July 1941 she joined the Mediterranean Fleet via the Red Sea, and by November was based at Malta with Force K, operating against the Axis supply convoys to North Africa. She was torpedoed and sunk off Alexandria by *U557* on 14 December 1941.

Penelope also went to the 3rd Cruiser Squadron in the Mediterranean on completion, but was recalled in 1940. During the Norwegian Campaign she ran aground off Vestfjord on 11 April and was badly damaged. Repairs were not completed until July 1941. In October she was sent to the Mediterranean, and arrived in Malta on 21 October to serve with Force K. She was damaged by mines at the time of the sinking of *Neptune*, and received further damage from bomb near-misses while under repair at Malta. She eventually sailed from Malta on 8 April 1942 for full repairs at New York Navy Yard, these being completed on 1 September 1942. In early 1943 she returned to the Mediterranean once more, being based at Bone with Force Q. During 1943, as part of the 15th Cruiser Squadron, she bombarded the Italian islands of Pantellaria and Lampedusa in June, was at the landings in Sicily in August, at Salerno in September and during the same month ferried troops to occupy Taranto. By October she had moved to the Aegean, where, with *Sirius* and destroyers, she attacked German invasion convoys bound for Leros. She briefly left the Mediterranean towards the end of the year to assist in the hunt for Axis blockade runners in the Bay of Biscay, but returned to support the landings at Anzio in January 1944. While returning to Naples from the beach-head on 18 February, she was torpedoed and sunk by *U410*.

Aurora served with the Home Fleet from completion as Rear Admiral (D). In September 1939 she was with the 2nd Cruiser Squadron, escorting convoys to Scandinavia and engaged on the hunt for *Scharnhorst* and *Gneisenau*. After the Norwegian campaign she participated in the operations hunting *Bismarck* and, with *Kenya*, intercepted one of the German supply ships, *Belchen*, on 3 June 1941. Between July and August, as part of Force K with the Home Fleet, she was involved in operations to Spitzbergen and Bear Island. After one of these sorties, in company with *Nigeria*, she intercepted a German troop convoy off north Norway, and the German *Bremse* was sunk. In the autumn she was transferred to the Mediterranean and arrived in Malta on 21 October to join a new Force K. Her task was to interdict the Axis supply routes to North Africa, which was done with great success, several convoys being decimated by the cruisers and destroyers of Force K before the loss of *Neptune*, on which occasion *Aurora* was also mined. After temporary repairs at Malta, the ship sailed home on 29 March for full repair at Liverpool, which took until the end of June 1942. After her return to the Mediterranean she joined Force H, and in November was part of the Centre Task Force for the Landings in North Africa, Operation Torch. Off Oran, she engaged the Vichy French torpilleurs *Tramontane* and *Tornade* on 8 November, sinking the latter and damaging the former so badly that she had to be beached. The following day she badly damaged the contre-torpilleur *Épervier* and drove her ashore. By December she was operating as part of Force Q at Bone against the Axis evacuation and supply convoys between Trapani and Tunis. Then, as a unit of the 15th Cruiser Squadron, she participated in the inva-

Opposite page: *Aurora.* (Courtesy G. Ransome)
Below: *Penelope* in 1942. (IWM)

Above: *Penelope* in 1944. (M. Twardowski)

sion of Sicily and the Salerno landings before moving into the Aegean in October. During operations in that area she was damaged by bombs off Castelorizo on 30 October, and withdrew to Taranto for repairs which lasted until April 1944. In August she was at the landings in the south of France, then returned to the Aegean, where she assisted in the liberation of Athens. After the war *Aurora* was sold to Nationalist China on 19 May 1948 and renamed *Chung King*. She defected to the Communists on 19 May 1948 and was renamed *Tchoung King*, but was sunk by Nationalist aircraft in Taku harbour in March 1949. She was later salvaged, but is not believed to have become operational again, although she was subsequently renamed *Hsuang Ho* (1951), *Pei Ching* (1951) and *Kuang Chou*.

Right: *Penelope* under repair in 1940. (Navpic)

SOUTHAMPTON CLASS

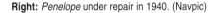

Ship	Builder	Laid Down	Launched	Completed	Fate
Southampton	John Brown	21 Nov 34	10 Mar 36	6 Mar 37	Lost 11 Jan 1941
Newcastle	VA (Tyne)	4 Oct 34	23 Jan 36	5 Mar 37	Scrapped at Faslane 1959
Birmingham	Devonport Dky	18 Jul 35	1 Sep 36	18 Nov 37	Scrapped at Inverkeithing 1960
Glasgow	Scotts	16 Apr 35	20 Jun 36	9 Sep 37	Scrapped at Blyth 1958
Sheffield	VA (Tyne)	31 Jan 35	23 Jul 36	25 Aug 37	Scrapped at Faslane 1967
Liverpool	Fairfield	17 Feb 36	24 Mar 37	2 Nov 38	Scrapped at Bo'ness 1958
Manchester	Hawthorne Leslie	28 Mar 36	12 Apr 37	4 Aug 38	Lost 13 Aug 1942
Gloucester	Devonport Dky	22 Sep 36	19 Oct 37	31 Jan 39	Lost 22 May 1941

Displacement: 9,100 tons/9,245 tonnes (standard); 11,350 tons/11,531 tonnes (full load).
Length: 591ft 6in/180.20m (oa); 558ft/170.07m (pp).
Beam: 61ft 8in/18.79m; Draught: 20ft 4in/6.20m (mean).

Machinery: 4-shaft Parsons geared turbines; 4 Admiralty 3-drum boilers.
Performance: 75,000shp=32kts; Bunkerage 2,060 tons oil.
Range: 7,700nm at 13kts.

Protection: 4½in main belt, 1¼in-2in deck, 1in-2in turrets.
Guns: twelve 6in Mk XXIII (4x3); eight 4in Mk XVI (4x2); eight 2pdr (2x4); eight .5in MG (2x4).
Torpedoes: six 21in (2x3).
Aircraft: three, one catapult.
Complement: 748.

Southampton Class: (2nd group) *Liverpool, Manchester* and *Gloucester*

Displacement: 9,400 tons/9,550 tonnes (standard); 11,650 tons/11,836 tonnes (full load).
Length: 591ft 6in/180.28m (oa); 579ft/170.07m (pp).
Beam: 62ft 4in/19.00m; Draught: 20ft 7in/6.27m (mean).
Machinery: 4-shaft Parsons geared turbines; 4 Admiralty 3-drum boilers.
Performance: 82,500shp=32.3kts; Bunkerage: 2,100 (*Manchester*), 1,795 (*Gloucester*) tons oil.
Range: 7,850nm (*Manchester*), 7,320nm (*Gloucester*) at 13kts.

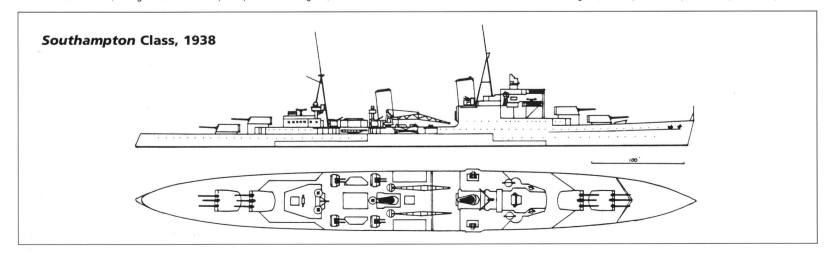

Southampton Class, 1938

Protection: as *Southampton* except 2in deck over magazines
(*Liverpool* & *Manchester*) and 2in deck over magazines
and machinery spaces in *Gloucester*.
Guns: as *Southampton*.
Torpedoes: as *Southampton*.
Aircraft: as *Southampton*.
Complement: 850.

Design These ships were designed as a response to cruisers laid down by Japan, which were reported to ship fifteen 6.1in guns, with 5in side armour on a displacement of only 8,500 tons. Despite the British constructors' disbelief that such a design could be achieved, the Admiralty obviously felt that the existing British cruisers would be totally outclassed if ships of this type were to appear. Even the 8in Counties seemed inferior. As little reliable intelligence could be obtained, the DNC was asked to produce a sketch design having the same parameters. The DNC soon reported on the impossibility of such a design requirement, and a modified requirement was studied. By 1933 four sketch designs had been offered for consideration, all armed with four triple 6in and three 4in AA twins. All had the same protective scheme of 5in sides to the machinery spaces and magazines, the latter having 2in crowns and 3in ends. Protective plating was given to the decks above the machinery spaces. Endurance was 7,000nm in all cases. The designs differed in respect of speed from 30kts to 32kts, dimensions, and the number of aircraft carried. As the staff requirement was for five aircraft, the latter feature caused considerable problems with regard to the stowage of the spare aeroplanes.

Speed also came in for criticism, as less than 32kts was not acceptable. Thus design D was chosen, but further modified by reducing the number of aircraft to three, which allowed a reduction in the height of the catapult; extending the armoured areas by reducing the thickness of the side armour in the way of the machinery spaces; and reducing the length to allow the ship to dock in more places around the world. By 1934 the rotating catapult had been replaced by a fixed athwartships type and large hangars had been incorporated at the after end of the forecastle, allowing a much better system of handling the aircraft, which themselves were also better protected from the weather. Further changes included the addition of a fourth 4in twin, thus solving the difficult problem of the effective siting of the centreline mounting. Multiple pom-poms and a second HACS were added, both of the latter now being on the roof of the hangar.

The final design had a protective scheme comprising 4½in sides to the magazines and machinery spaces, with 2in crowns to the magazines and 1¼in protective plating to the decks above the

machinery spaces. The turrets were given 2in roofs. Armour protection accounted for 1,431 tons on a standard displacement of 9,100 tons, i.e. 15.7 per cent.

The 6in guns were the BL Mk XXIII model as mounted in the previous classes, in new triple mountings Mk XXII which had the centre gun set back by 30in to reduce interference between the shells in flight. The turret had 45° elevation. Secondary armament comprised eight 4in Mk XVI in twin shielded mounts Mk XIX, disposed two on each beam abaft the after funnel. Two quadruple Mk VII 2pdr mountings and two quadruple .5in MGs completed the light AA outfit. Two banks of triple 21in torpedo tubes were carried on the upper deck between the 4in guns. The aircraft arrangements included two separate hangars, one either side of the fore funnel, each of which could accommodate a Walrus amphibian. If necessary, a third machine could be carried on the catapult, but in practice this was seldom if ever done.

The fire control arrangements varied. As noted above, the original single HACS on the bridge abaft the main director was replaced by two, sided port and starboard in *Southampton* and *Newcastle* before completion, but the 1934 Programme ships (*Sheffield*, *Glasgow* and *Birmingham*) had a third HACS added on the centreline aft. The 1935 group, *Manchester*, *Liverpool* and *Gloucester*, had a second main battery director aft as well as the third HACS. The

Above: *Southampton* as completed, in June 1938. (W&L)

ships of this last group also benefited from an increase in their horizontal protection, the first two having 2in armour over the magazines and 1¼in D steel over the machinery spaces, and *Gloucester* having 2in NC over both. These additions resulted in increased displacement for the last three ships, and the installed shp had to be increased by 10 per cent to maintain the 32kt requirement.

Although the class was finally named after towns, it had originally been intended to use classical names. The first two ships were planned as *Minotaur* and *Polyphemus*, but became *Newcastle* and *Southampton*.

Modifications Little or no alterations of any consequence were made to these modern ships pre-war, except that *Sheffield* was fitted with the first British radar set, type 79Y, in 1938.

Newcastle had two UP mountings fitted in April/May 1940, which were eventually landed in November 1941, at which time she also lost the .5in MGs and radar 286, receiving in lieu nine single 20mm and radars 273 and 291. In October/November 1942 the aircraft fittings and type 291 radar were removed and ten single 20mm were added and the radar suite updated. Six of the single 20mm were exchanged for four twin 20mm power-operated in July/September 1943. This remained her outfit in April 1944, and was unchanged in May 1945, but she began a major refit at this time which extended until October. In the course of this, X turret was removed. Further modernisations were carried out in the 1950s.

Southampton, as an early war loss, had little modification. Radar 279 was fitted in May 1940, but it is unlikely that the AA outfit was modified.

Sheffield had radars 284 and 285 fitted in the summer of 1941, and that September she was fitted with six single 20mm and landed the .5in MGs. Between April and July 1942 the type 279 radar was removed and replaced by types 281, 282, 283 and 273. Three more 20mm singles were added. Five additional 20mm were shipped between March and June 1943, and in the first months of 1944 the aircraft fittings were removed and eight more 20mm singles fitted. Finally, during a refit in the USA between July 1944 and May 1945, X turret, fifteen single 20mm and the type 273 radar were removed. Four quadruple 40mm Bofors and ten twin power-operated 20mm were added and type 277 radar fitted. Further changes were made postwar.

Glasgow received two UP mountings and radar 286 in the early summer of 1940, the former being removed a year later. In the summer of 1942 the quadruple .5in MGs and the type 279 radar

were landed and nine single 20mm fitted, together with radars 273, 281, 282, 284 and 285. Five single 20mm were removed in December 1942 and eight twin 20mm fitted. Two more 20mm singles were fitted in the autumn of 1943. By April 1944 her outfit consisted of eight power-operated twin 20mm and seven singles. During repairs and refit between June 1944 and May 1945 she landed X turret, two twin and four single 20mm, the aircraft fittings and radars 273, 281 and 293. In their place she received two quadruple 2pdr, four single 2pdr and radars 281, 274 and 293.

Birmingham received a single UP mounting in June 1940, which was landed in July 1941. In March 1942 the .5in MGs were removed and seven single 20mm fitted, as well as radars 284 and 291. Between April and August 1943 the aircraft fittings, five 20mm singles and the type 291 radar were removed and eight twin 20mm plus types 281 and 273 radar fitted. X turret was removed between July and November 1944, when four quadruple 40mm Bofors, two twin and five single 20mm were added.

Manchester had radar 286 fitted in November 1940. In the early part of 1941 the .5in MGs were landed and one single 40mm Bofors Mk III plus

five single 20mm were added. Between September 1941 and February 1942 the type 286 radar was removed and replaced by types 273, 279, 282, 284 and 285. Three single 20mm were also fitted.

Liverpool received nine single 20mm at Mare Island between June and November 1941. On her return to Britain she reshipped the quadruple 2pdr which had been landed at Alexandria after her torpedoing in 1940 and had updated radars fitted. She was under refit again between August 1942 and July 1945, when X turret, two single 20mm, various radars and the aircraft fittings were removed. Four quadruple and six single 2pdr and six twin power-operated 20mm were shipped and the radar suite modernised.

Gloucester was not altered as far as is known.

Service *Newcastle* joined the 2nd Cruiser Squadron on completion, and was under refit on the outbreak of war. She joined the 18th Cruiser Squadron with the Home Fleet in mid-September

Opposite page: *Birmingham* at Plymouth, 20 September 1943. (WSS)
Below: *Manchester* in China Station colours, August 1938. (W&L)

1939, initially being employed on Trade Protection duties in the Western Approaches, and then joined the Northern Patrol. In November she sighted *Scharnhorst* and *Gneisenau* after the *Rawalpindi* incident. After refit on the Tyne she moved south to Plymouth for anti-invasion duties in July 1940, and on 11 October bombarded Cherbourg with *Revenge*. A few days later she and *Emerald*, together with destroyers, sailed to intercept a force of German destroyers on a strike into the Western Approaches. Although *Newcastle* got into action, the enemy escaped. On 13 November the ship sailed for Gibraltar to join Force H. In the Mediterranean she took part in the action off Spartivento on 27 November, but in December was ordered to the South Atlantic Command and carried out patrols off the River Plate until August 1941, when she went to Boston, Massachusetts, for refit. She arrived back in Plymouth on 29 December 1941. In February she was ordered to join the Eastern Fleet, where she remained until detached to the Mediterranean in June for a Malta convoy operation. On 15 June *Newcastle* was hit by a torpedo from *S56* and badly damaged. After temporary repairs at Bombay, the ship underwent further repairs at New York Navy Yard, where she arrived on 10 October, but she was not fully repaired until after her return to Britain, in March 1943. She returned to the 4th Cruiser Squadron with the Eastern Fleet, arriving at Kilindini on 27 May, and served in the east until 1945, when the ship returned home for refit at Rosyth in May. This refit lasted until October

1945. After a period on trooping duties with the Plymouth Command during 1945/47, she went to the Mediterranean for the 1st Cruiser Squadron in 1947, returning to Plymouth a couple of years later. Postwar, *Newcastle* was one of the first ships to be modernised (1950/51), and went out to the Far East for the 5th Cruiser Squadron, seeing action in the Korean War. She spent the remainder of her active service in the Far East Fleet, returning home to pay off in August 1958. On 19 August 1959 she arrived at the Faslane yard of Shipbreaking Industries for scrapping.

Southampton served as flagship of the 2nd Cruiser Squadron with the Home Fleet. On 16 October 1939 she was hit by a bomb while lying off Rosyth, but the damage was slight. She then served with the Humber Force until February 1940, and then went to the 18th Cruiser squadron at Scapa Flow. In April she took part in the Norwegian Campaign, during which she was bombed on many occasions but not seriously damaged. Anti-invasion duties in the south of England followed until her return to Scapa in October. On 15 November she sailed for the Mediterranean, where she participated in the action off Cape Spartivento on 27 November. In December *Southampton* moved to the Red Sea to escort troop convoys, and at the same time took part in the bombardment of Kismayu during the campaign in Italian East Africa. On 1 January 1941 she joined the 3rd Cruiser Squadron and took part in Malta convoy operations. Unfortunately the ship was hit by two or three bombs off Sicily

on 11 January 1941, which totally disabled her and started raging fires. One torpedo from *Gloucester* and four from *Orion* finally sank her.

Sheffield was with the 18th Cruiser Squadron in September 1939, and carried out patrols in the Denmark Straits until April 1940, when she took part in the Norwegian campaign. She too remained in the south of England on anti-invasion duties until the summer, then sailed to join Force H on 22 August. She carried out several operations inside the Mediterranean, and then patrolled in the area of the Azores for the rest of 1940. On 9 February 1941 she was present during the bombardment of Genoa, and in March operated against Vichy-French convoys. After covering the operations to reinforce the fighter defences of Malta, *Sheffield* returned to the Atlantic to participate in the hunt for, and final sinking of, *Bismarck*. Following this she intercepted one of the German battleship's tankers, *Friedrich Breme*, on 12 June 1941. After further operations in the Mediterranean, the ship returned to Britain in October, when, in company with *Kenya*, she sank the German supply ship *Kota Pinang* off Cape Ortegal on 3 October. Arctic convoy duty followed until the ship was mined off Iceland on 4 March 1942, and was out of action until July. Arctic convoy duty was then resumed, except for a detachment to the Mediterranean in November for the Torch landings in North Africa. In December 1942, during an attack by *Admiral Hipper*, *Lützow* and destroyers on convoy JW51B off North Cape, she damaged *Hipper* and sank the destroyer *Friedrich Eckoldt*. Arctic duties continued until February 1943, after which she operated in the Bay of Biscay in July and August, then went into the Mediterranean for the Salerno landings. Following this, *Sheffield* returned to the Arctic and took part in the sinking of *Scharnhorst* in December 1943. In 1944 she covered the raids against *Tirpitz*, then went to refit in Boston, Massachusetts. She returned to Britain for the work to be finished, and was still under refit at the end of the war, completing in May 1946. Postwar the ship went to the America and West Indies Station, then returned to refit at Chatham during 1949/50. After service in the Home Fleet (2nd Cruiser Squadron) she returned to the West Indies as flagship of the 8th Cruiser Squadron. She finally returned from that station on 26 October 1954 for refit. She later served in both Home and Mediterranean Fleets before reducing to reserve in January 1959, relieving the battleship *Vanguard* as flagship of the Reserve Fleet. In September 1964 *Sheffield* was herself relieved and placed on the disposal list. She was towed to Rosyth for de-equipping on 6 January 1967, and from there to Shipbreaking Industries (Faslane) for breaking up on 18 September that year.

Birmingham, unlike her sisters, served on the China Station from completion, with the 5th Cruiser Squadron. After war was declared she went to Malta to refit and then joined the Home Fleet. She took part in the Norwegian campaign and in the anti-invasion measures before refitting between September and December. From January to April 1941 she escorted troop convoys to the Middle East via the Cape, and later participated in the hunt for *Bismarck*. In July 1941 she became flagship of the South American Division, and in February 1942 transferred to the Eastern Fleet, but was detached in June for Operation Vigorous in the Mediterranean. Her duties in the Indian Ocean were mainly of a patrol and escort nature. In April 1943 she returned to Britain for refit, and on passage back through the Mediterranean after refit to rejoin the Eastern Fleet she was torpedoed by *U407* off Cyrenaica on 28 November and very seriously damaged. After temporary repairs she lay at Alexandria until June 1944, then sailed to the USA for full repairs, which were completed at the end of November. On her return to home waters she joined the 10th Cruiser Squadron at Scapa Flow, and then took part in sweeps along the Norwegian coast until the end of the war. Postwar she was refitted at Portsmouth and then

served in the East Indies with the 4th Cruiser Squadron until 1950, with a period in the South Atlantic command in 1948. She went out to the Far East in 1952 for the 5th Cruiser Squadron, and was present during the Korean war, then in 1955 transferred to the Mediterranean Fleet as flagship, 1st Cruiser Squadron. She remained in commission with the Home and Mediterranean Fleets until paid off at Devonport on 3 December 1959, being the last of the class in service. She was placed on the disposal list in March 1960, and arrived at Inverkeithing on 7 September 1960 to be broken up by T. W. Ward.

Glasgow was with the 2nd Cruiser Squadron in the Home Fleet at the outbreak of war, and served on the Northern Patrol, followed by the Norwegian campaign in April 1940. In November she sailed to the Mediterranean, but on 3 December, while at anchor in Suda Bay, Crete, she was hit by two aircraft torpedoes. Damage was extensive, and repairs at Alexandria and Singapore lasted until the end of August 1941. She then served in the East Indies until April 1942, when she left for the USA and refit. This work, which included making good the torpedo damage from Suda Bay, was completed in August. *Glasgow* joined the 10th Cruiser Squadron at Scapa and

then covered Arctic convoys, capturing the blockade runner *Regensburg* on 30 March 1943. In July the ship joined the Plymouth Command. In December 1943 she fought an action against German destroyers in the Bay of Biscay, accompanied by *Enterprise*, when *Z27*, *T26* and *T27* were sunk. In 1944 she was at the Normandy landings, where she was damaged by shore batteries on 25 June while bombarding Cherbourg. Repairs lasted until May 1945, and she sailed for the East Indies on 22 August 1945. She remained on this station, then served in the West Indies during 1948/50, in the Mediterranean during 1951/55, and in Home Fleets (as Flag Officer D) until paid off in November 1956. After being put on the disposal list in March 1958, she was handed over to BISCO and allocated to Hughes Bolkow for scrapping. Towed from Portsmouth on 4 July, she arrived at Blyth for breaking up on 8 July 1958.

Manchester was serving in the East Indies with the 4th Cruiser Squadron at the outbreak of war, but was ordered home and arrived back in Britain on 25 November 1939. She subsequently served with the Home Fleet at Scapa on Northern Patrol duties, capturing the German merchantman *Wahehe* on 21 February 1940. After participating in the Norwegian campaign she was then based in the Humber for anti-invasion duties, but on 15 September sailed to the Mediterranean for Operation Collar and was present at the action off Cape Spartivento on 27 November. *Manchester* returned to Britain on 13 December 1940 and spent the first four months of 1941 under refit, then undertook Denmark Straits patrols during the *Bismarck* sortie. In July she returned to the Mediterranean for an important Malta convoy, but on 23 July she was hit on the port quarter by an aerial torpedo and badly damaged. Temporary repairs were made at Gibraltar, and the ship then sailed for Philadelphia for complete repair. This was finished on 27 February 1942, after which she returned to Portsmouth, where final work was completed by the end of April. On her return to service she joined the Home Fleet at Scapa Flow during the first week of May, then carried out Russian convoy cover duties and the reinforcement of Spitzbergen. In August she returned to the Mediterranean for Operation Pedestal, during which, on the night of 12/13 August 1942, she was hit by a torpedo from either *Ms 16* or *Ms 22* off Tunisia and crippled. In the early hours of 13 August *Manchester* was scuttled.

Liverpool was also a member of the 4th Cruiser Squadron in the East Indies in 1939, but in mid-November was transferred to the 5th Cruiser Squadron in the China Sea. On 20 May 1940 she was again transferred, this time to the Mediterranean, where, eight days later, she was part of the cruiser force which sank the Italian destroyer *Espero*, *Liverpool* receiving one 4.7in shell hit. On 29 July she was hit by a bomb which caused minor damage, but on 14 October an aerial torpedo from an Italian aircraft caused severe damage and blew the roof off A turret. Temporary repairs carried out at Alexandria lasted until April 1941, when the ship sailed to Mare Island, California, for full repairs. It was January 1942 before she was again operational, and in March she joined the 18th Cruiser Squadron at Scapa Flow for Arctic convoy duties. However, *Liverpool* sailed for the Mediterranean again on 5 June 1942 for Operation Harpoon, a resupply convoy to Malta. On 14 June she was hit by an aerial torpedo on the starboard side abreast the after engine room, which totally disabled the ship. She was towed into Gibraltar and patched up for passage to Rosyth, where she arrived in July, but her repair was not pressed and, despite having had her repairs completed by July 1943, *Liverpool* remained out of service until May 1944, then being reduced to care and maintenance. She saw no further war service, but recommissioned to join the 15th Cruiser Squadron in the Mediterranean in October 1945. She remained in com-

mission on this station for seven years, with the 15th and 1st Cruiser Squadrons, mostly as flagship, until paid off in April 1952. After being listed for disposal she was handed over to BISCO and allocated for scrapping in 1958. Towed from Portsmouth on 27 June, she arrived at the Bo'ness yard of McLellan Ltd for breaking up on 2 July 1958.

Gloucester was serving as flagship of the 4th Cruiser Squadron in the East Indies at the outbreak of war in 1939. For the remainder of that year she carried out patrols in the Indian Ocean. In December she joined Force I at Simonstown, operating against German raiders, but without success until May, when she joined the 7th Cruiser Squadron in the Mediterranean. She participated in Malta convoy operations, the Battle of Calabria, and operated in the eastern Mediterranean and Aegean throughout the latter half of 1940. On 11 January 1941, while part of Operation Excess, which involved a Malta convoy, three convoys to Piraeus and three other convoys, she was hit by a bomb which failed to explode. She was at the Battle of Matapan in March, and in April bombarded the North African coast several times. She was hit again by a bomb at Malta on 30 April, but the damage was not serious. In May she was engaged in the operations at Crete, and on 22 May, while in company with *Fiji*, she was dive-bombed and hit four times, with three further near misses. The ship had to be abandoned, and sank shortly afterwards.

EDINBURGH CLASS

Ship	Builder	Laid Down	Launched	Completed	Fate
Edinburgh	Swan Hunter	30 Dec 36	31 Mar 38	6 Jul 39	Lost 2 May 1942
Belfast	Harland & Wolff	10 Dec 36	17 Mar 38	3 Aug 39	Museum ship 1971

Displacement: 10,550 tons/10,718 tonnes (standard); 13,175 tons/13,385 tonnes (full load).

Length: 613ft 6in/186.99m (oa); 579ft/176.47m (pp).

Beam: 63ft 4in/19.30*m; Draught: 21ft 3in/6.48*m (mean).

Machinery: 4-shaft Parsons geared turbines; 4 Admiralty 3-drum boilers.

Performance: 80,000shp=32.5kts; Bunkerage: 2,260 tons oil.

Range: 8,000nm at 14kts.

Protection: 4½in main belt, 3in deck (magazines), 2in deck (machinery spaces); 2in-4in turrets.

Guns: twelve 6in Mk XXIII (4x3); twelve 4in Mk XVI (6x2); sixteen 2pdr (2x8); eight .5in MGs (2x4).

Torpedoes: six 21in (3x2).

Aircraft: three, one catapult.

Complement: 781.

*66ft 4in/20.22m and + 23ft 2in/7.06m in *Belfast* after reconstruction 1939-42.

Design The programme for the 1936 cruisers was influenced by the facts that the Japanese and Americans were still constructing light cruisers armed with fifteen 6in guns, and that the forthcoming London Naval Treaty might result in a qualitative restriction below 9,000 tons being placed on cruisers. Thus time was short to develop a new design before any such restrictions might come into force. As 8in-gunned ships could no longer be built, the only choice lay in increasing the number of 6in carried, as there was now no limit on displacement. As usual with British design requirements, the ability to dock the ship world-wide was important, so the length had to be less than about 615ft, too short to mount five triple turrets. This led to the idea of four quadruple turrets in the classic A, B, X and Y disposition. Displacement naturally increased to accommodate the heavier armament, and, to maintain the required 32kts, power had to be increased to 82,500shp. The protective scheme was similar to that of the previous class, i.e. armoured against 6in shellfire. Trials of the quadruple 6in mounting

had started, but these were not proceeding satisfactorily, and it was therefore decided to ship the triple mounting instead and use the weight saved to increase the protection still further. The ship itself was shortened from 623½ft to 613½ft because the magazines were shorter. The shell rooms were given box protection, and the decks over the machinery spaces increased from 1¼in to 2in NC, while the deck over the 6in shell rooms was increased to 3in NC. After approval of the legend design it was decided to increase the deck protection to 2½in NC.

The final design was of 10,302 tons (standard), armed with twelve 6in in triple turrets, twelve 4in AA in twin mountings and two eight-barrelled 2pdr. Two banks of triple 21in torpedo tubes were

Above: *Edinburgh* in November 1939. (MOD)

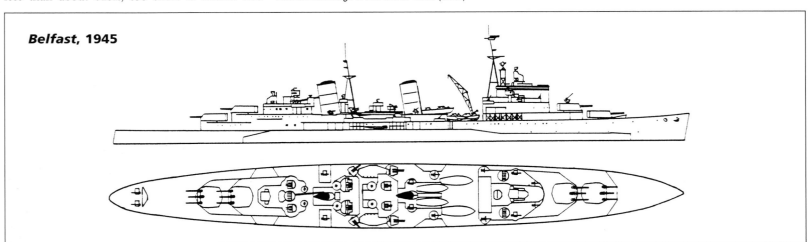

Belfast, 1945

Above: *Belfast.* (Navpic)

fitted. The main belt was 4½in NC with 2½in NC end bulkheads. Deck protection was 2½in, with 3in over the magazines and shell rooms. Turrets had 4in fronts and 2in sides and roof. Armour represented 18.6 per cent of the revised standard displacement.

Below: *Belfast* in 1942. (IWM)

The armament differed from that of the earlier ships only in that the triple turrets were Mk XXIII.

The main machinery was similar to that of the earlier ships but more powerful, and was arranged in a similar manner. The different positioning of the funnels was the result of location of the 4in magazine. However, the increased displacement did allow a 20 per cent increase in bunkerage for extended range.

Modifications *Edinburgh* received radar type 279 in 1940, and had six single 20mm fitted in July 1941. The radar fit was changed to types 273, 284 and 285 in the early months of 1942.

Belfast, while under repair 1940/42, lost the .5in MGs and received four single and five twin 20mm. She also received radars 273, 281, 282, 283, 284 and 285. Four further single 20mm were added in June 1943. In the spring of 1944 one of the twin 20mm was landed and six additional 20mm singles were fitted. Between August 1944 and May 1945 the aircraft fittings, two twin 4in and eight single 20mm were removed, and four quadruple and four single 2pdr were added. The radar fit was altered, types 281b, 293, 277, 274 and 268 being added. In August 1945 she exchanged two twin 20mm for three single 40mm Bofors Mk III and two 40mm Boffins.

Service *Edinburgh* formed part of the 18th Cruiser Squadron at Scapa Flow in September 1939, but on 1 October she was transferred to the 2nd Cruiser Squadron in the Humber. She escorted convoys to Scandinavia until March 1940, then went to refit until 28 October 1940, after which she rejoined the 18th Cruiser Squadron with the Home Fleet. In March 1941 she covered the Lofoten raid, and in May participated in the hunt for *Bismarck*, intercepting the blockade runner *Lech*. In July 1941 she went to the Mediterranean for Operation Substance, and again in September for Halberd. By November she was back in northern waters, escorting

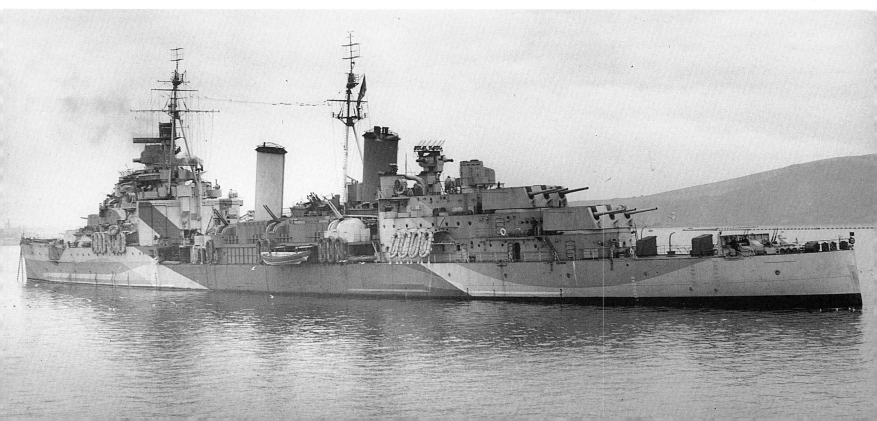

Russian convoys. On 30 April 1942, while part of the cover for QP11, she was torpedoed by *U456*. Although hit twice and critically damaged, she was able to get steam up again and proceed slowly, but on 2 May she was attacked by German destroyers. She managed to sink *Z26* before being hit by a torpedo from one of the destroyers, which caused her to lose all power and flood. She was sunk by the destroyer *Foresight*.

Belfast also joined the 18th Cruiser Squadron with the Home Fleet, but on 21 November 1939 she detonated a mine laid in the Firth of Forth by *U21*, which broke her back and caused extensive damage. After temporary repairs at Rosyth she was moved to Plymouth for full repairs, which were not finished until 8 December 1942. She rejoined the Home Fleet on Arctic convoy duties and took part in the Battle of North Cape on 26 December 1943, when *Scharnhorst* was sunk. In April 1944 she refitted for duty as Headquarters ship for the Eastern Task Force during the Normandy landings, where she remained until July. In August 1944 *Belfast* began a major refit in prepa-ration for joining the Pacific war, and this was not completed until May 1945. She sailed to the Pacific theatre, arriving in Sydney in August 1945, and remained in the Far East and saw action in the Korean war until 1952, when she came home to reserve. After this period in reserve she was taken in hand for refit in 1955, which was completed on 12 May 1959. Thereafter she served in the Far East again until 1962, then served as Flag-ship of the Home flotillas. She finally paid off in February 1963, and is now a museum ship on the Thames in London.

DIDO CLASS

Ship	Builder	Laid Down	Launched	Completed	Fate
Bonaventure	Scotts	30 Aug 37	19 Apr 39	24 May 40	Lost 31 March 1941
Naiad	Hawthorne Leslie	26 Aug 37	3 Feb 39	24 Jul 40	Lost 11 March 1942
Phoebe	Fairfield	2 Sep 37	25 Mar 39	27 Sep 40	Scrapped at Blyth 1956
Dido	Cammell Laird	26 Oct 37	18 Jul 39	30 Sep 40	Scrapped at Barrow 1958
Euryalus	Chatham Dky	21 Oct 37	6 Jun 39	30 Jun 41	Scrapped at Blyth 1959
Hermione	Stephens	6 Oct 37	18 May 39	25 Mar 41	Lost 16 June 1942
Sirius	Portsmouth Dky	6 Apr 38	18 Sep 40	6 May 42	Scrapped at Blyth 1956
Cleopatra	Hawthorne Leslie	5 Jan 39	27 Mar 40	5 Dec 41	Scrapped at Newport 1958
Charybdis	Camell Laird	9 Nov 39	17 Sep 40	3 Dec 41	Lost 23 October 1943
Scylla	Scotts	19 Apr 39	24 Jul 40	12 Jun 42	Scrapped at Barrow 1950
Argonaut	Cammell Laird	21 Nov 39	6 Sep 41	8 Aug 42	Scrapped at Newport 1955

Displacement: 5,600 tons/5,689 tonnes (standard); 6,850 tons/6,959 tonnes (full load).
Length: 512ft/156.05m (oa); 485ft/147.82m (pp).
Beam: 50ft 6in/15.39m; Draught: 16ft 6in/5.11m (mean).
Machinery: 4-shaft Parsons geared turbines; 4 Admiralty 3-drum boilers.
Performance: 62,000shp=32.2kts; Bunkerage: 1,100 tons oil.
Range: 4,850nm at 11kts.
Protection: 3in main belt, 1in deck (machinery spaces), 2in (magazine & shell rooms).

Guns: ten 5.25in Mk I (5x2); eight 2pdr (2x4); eight .5in MGs (2x4)*.
Torpedoes: six 21in (2x3).
Aircraft: nil.
Complement: 487.
*see text for as-completed armaments.

Design These ships were designed for use as AA cruisers in the fleet role, in response to demands for better anti-aircraft defence against the growing capabilities of the aircraft of the day. It was felt in certain quarters that the traditional role of the small cruiser, that of a Fleet scout, could now be assumed by shipboard aircraft, and that a small cruiser could be more usefully employed if well armed with effective dual-purpose guns. The problem was two-fold. In the first place, effective AA could only be ensured by effective high-angle control, and, secondly, the gun needed a good range and a high rate of fire. The first could only be achieved if the ship was a steady gun platform, and therefore of larger than destroyer size, but there was currently no gun with HA capability of a calibre greater than 4in, and a 4in armament was not a respectable cruiser armament. However, by the mid-1930s the Ordnance Office had pre-pared a design for a 5.25in QF gun which could be used in the proposed new cruisers, for which the design work could now proceed. By June 1936 a sketch design of 5,300 tons had been prepared, armed with ten such weapons.

The protective scheme had a 3in NC belt which covered the machinery spaces and maga-zines, with only 1in D steel for the shell rooms. Deck protection was limited to 1in D steel except for the magazine crowns, where it was 3in NC. The total weight of armour and protection was 670 tons, or 12.6 per cent of the standard dis-placement.

The main machinery was a four-shaft layout, arranged on the unit principle with boilers of slightly increased pressure than formerly, i.e. 400psi instead of 350psi. Although designed orig-inally for 58,000shp, it was found possible to increase this to 62,000shp, which also increased the speed to 32¼kts, despite weight growth in design (beam was increased by 6in).

The 5.25in gun was the QF Mk I version, which fired an 80lb projectile and had a maximum range at full elevation (70°) of 46,500ft (14,170m). It was carried in twin turrets Mk II instead of the origi-nally proposed Mk I (as in the *King George V* class), which allowed a better layout in the smaller ship. Three of the turrets were in tiers forward of the bridge, which necessitated a high bridge and

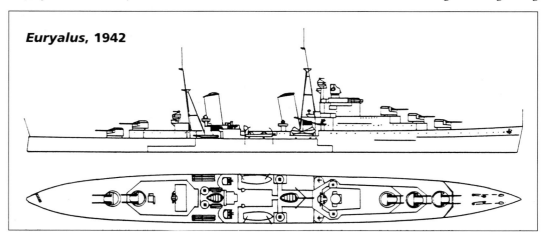

Euryalus, 1942

even higher funnels to prevent smoke problems on the command positions. Two quadruple 2pdr formed the main close-range defence, and two triple banks of 21in torpedo tubes were fitted. No arrangements were made for aircraft. One DCT was fitted on the bridge for low-angle control, with an HACS positioned abaft it. There was no DCT aft, but the after HACS was adapted to control both LA and HA gunfire.

Five ships were authorised under the 1936 programme (*Bonaventure, Naiad, Phoebe, Dido* and *Euryalus*), two more under that for 1937 (*Hermione* and *Sirius*), and three under the 1938 Programme (*Cleopatra, Charybdis* and *Scylla*). Six further ships were authorised under the emergency 1939 programme, named *Argonaut, Spartan, Royalist, Black Prince, Bellona* and *Diadem*. However, these last were suspended in June 1940 and not resumed until October 1940, when only *Argonaut* was completed as originally intended. The other five were completed to a revised design known as the Modified *Dido*s, q.v.

Modifications *Bonaventure* completed with only four twin 5.25in turrets because of shortages, and received a 4in starshell gun in X position. She had received a radar set before October 1940, but was otherwise unaltered.

Naiad completed with five turrets. She received five single 20mm in September 1941 and had radar 279 by this time.

Below: *Argonaut* in October 1943. (Admiralty)

Phoebe completed with four turrets and was fitted with a 4in in Q position forward of the bridge. The latter was landed during refit at New York, November 1941 to April 1942, as were the .5in MGs and 279 radar, while a quadruple 2pdr supplanted the 4in and eleven single 20mm were fitted. Radars were now 281, 284 and 285. The A turret was temporarily removed at the end of 1942 after torpedo damage. During repairs in the first six months of 1943, all three quadruple 2pdr were landed, as were seven single 20mm, to be replaced by three quadruple 40mm Bofors and six twin 20mm. Radar 272 was also fitted. The A turret was replaced in July 1943. Her light AA in April 1944 was twelve 40mm (3 x 4); sixteen 20mm (6 x 2, 4 x 1).

Dido had four turrets and a 4in similar to *Phoebe*. The 4in and .5in MGs were removed in the latter half of 1941 at Brooklyn Navy Yard, when Q 5.25in turret was shipped and five single 20mm were fitted. In the early summer of 1943 three single 20mm were exchanged for four twin 20mm, and the radar outfit was altered by the addition of types 272, 282, 284 and 285. April 1944 lists, however, show only eight 20mm.

Euryalus completed with her designed armament. In September 1941 the .5in MGs were landed and five single 20mm fitted. Two more were added by September 1942. By mid-1943 two single 20 had been removed and four twin 20mm shipped. The type 279 radar was replaced by types 272, 281, 282 and 285. In a long refit from October 1943 to July 1944, Q turret was replaced by a quadruple 2pdr and two twin 20mm were fitted. Radar 271 and 272 were removed and types 279b, 277 and 293 fitted.

Hermione also completed as a five-turret ship. She had the .5in MGs removed in October/November 1941 and received five single 20mm.

Sirius completed with five turrets and five 20mm singles. She had received two more single 20mm by mid-1943. One of these was landed at Massawa at the end of 1943, and two single 40mm Bofors Mk III were fitted. However, she is listed as having only seven 20mm as light AA in April 1944 lists. By April 1945 she had two single Mk III 40mm fitted and had landed two single 20mm.

Cleopatra was completed with two single 2pdr in 1942 in lieu of the .5in MGs, but these were removed in the middle of that year and replaced by five single 20mm. A sixth 20mm was added in mid-1943. During repairs between November 1943 and November 1944, Q turret was removed, as were two quadruple 2pdr and five single 20mm. Three quadruple 40mm Bofors and six twin 20mm were fitted and the singles numbered four.

Argonaut completed with four single 20mm in lieu of the .5in MGs. She had Q turret removed during repairs in 1943/44, and lost the four single 20mm. She received a quadruple 2pdr in lieu of the 5.25in, and had five twin 20mm fitted. By April 1944 her light AA comprised three quadruple 2pdr, six twin power-operated 20mm and five

Left: *Argonaut* in March 1945. (IWM)
Opposite page: *Bonaventure*, October 1940. (Courtesy G. Ransome)

single. By the end of the war with Japan she had received five 40mm Boffins and three single 40mm Bofors Mk III.

Scylla completed with four twin 4.5in Mk III in UD MK III mountings because of a shortage of 5.25in mountings. The forward superstructure was considerably modified to accommodate these and also to increase crew spaces. Her light AA on completion was eight single 20mm. Six twin power-operated 20mm were added at the end of 1943.

Charybdis also completed with four twin 4.5in, and had in addition a single 4in Mk V forward of X mounting. Her light AA at completion was four single 20mm and two single 2pdr. The 4in starshell gun and two single 2pdr were removed and replaced by two twin and two single 20mm, probably in 1943.

Service *Bonaventure* served initially with the Home Fleet on completion, and escorted WS convoys. While on such duty with WS5a on 25 December 1940, the convoy was attacked by *Admiral Hipper*, although no damage was incurred or inflicted by *Bonaventure*. Almost immediately afterwards the ship was ordered to the Mediterranean, when, as part of Force F during Operation Excess to Malta in January, she was attacked by the Italian torpedo boats *Circe* and *Vega* south of Pantelleria, but sank *Vega* on 10 January 1941. In March she escorted a convoy to Malta and was damaged by near misses while at Malta on 22 March. She then participated in the Greek campaign, but on 31 March, while escorting a convoy from Greece to Alexandria, she was torpedoed and sunk by the Italian submarine *Ambra* south of Crete.

Naiad also joined the Home Fleet and was used for ocean trade protection duties. As part of the 15th Cruiser Squadron she took part in operations against German raiders following the sink-

ing of *Jervis Bay* in November 1940. In December and January she escorted WS convoys to Freetown, but at the end of January 1941 was back in northern waters when she briefly sighted *Scharnhorst* and *Gneisenau* south of Iceland as the German ships were in the course of breaking out into the Atlantic. By May 1941 *Naiad* was with Force H on Malta convoy operations, and Flagship of the 15th Cruiser Squadron. She participated in the Crete operations and then operated against Vichy-French forces in Syria, where, together with *Leander*, she engaged the French *Guépard*. The remainder of her service was in the Mediterranean, mostly connected with the continual attempts to resupply Malta. However, in March 1942 she sailed from Alexandria to attack an Italian cruiser reported damaged. This report was false, and on the return *Naiad* was torpedoed and sunk north of Mersa Matruh by *U565* on 11 March.

Phoebe joined the 15th Cruiser squadron on completion and served with the Home Fleet. She operated in the North Atlantic on trade protection duties, but by April 1941 had joined the Mediterranean fleet at Alexandria. She participated in the evacuation of Greece, Malta convoys and the evacuation of Crete, then in June covered operations against Vichy-French Syria, when she was flagship. On 3 July 1941 she was missed by torpedoes from *Malachite*, but on 27 August was hit by an aerial torpedo while on a trooping operation to Tobruk. After temporary repairs at Alexandria, full repairs were undertaken in New York between 21 November 1941 and 21 April 1942, but the ship did not return to service until May 1942. She returned to the Mediterranean and took part in Operation Pedestal in August, but the following month she and *Sirius* were ordered to Capetown to patrol against Axis blockade runners to and from the Far East. They had no success,

and while proceeding to Pointe Noire in French Equatorial Africa on 23 October 1942, *Phoebe* was hit forward and aft by torpedoes from *U161*. The damage was severe, and after temporary repairs at Pointe Noire until December, the ship had to go to the USA again for repair. This lasted from January to mid-June 1943, and the ship was not operational until July. *Phoebe* returned to the Mediterranean again and operated in the Aegean, and then supported the Anzio landings in January 1944. Later that year she sailed to join the 5th Cruiser Squadron in the Eastern Fleet, and for the remainder of the war operated in the Indian Ocean, covering the carrier raids on the Nicobars and Sabang as a Fighter Direction ship. She also covered the assault landings on the coast of Burma and the Rangoon landings in April/May 1945. At this time she was Flagship of the 21st Escort carrier Squadron, until relieved by *Royalist*. Postwar she came home from the East Indies to refit, arriving at Sheerness on 29 October 1945, then, in 1946, joined the Mediterranean Fleet as Flagship, Destroyer Flotillas, until November 1947, when she joined the 1st Cruiser Squadron, also in the Mediterranean. She arrived at Chatham on 14 March 1951 to pay off, then acted as senior officer's ship, Harwich reserve, between 1951 and 1953, followed by reserve at Portsmouth until 1956, when she was put up for disposal. She arrived at the Blyth yard of Hughes Bolkow on 1 August 1956 to be broken up.

Dido joined the 15th Cruiser Squadron with the Home Fleet on completion, and took part in operations against German warships following the sinking of *Jervis Bay* in November 1940. In April 1941 she was sent to reinforce the Mediterranean Fleet, taking part in the operations in Cretan waters and in the Red Sea during the assault on Assab. She had been hit by a bomb off Crete, and, after temporary repairs at Durban and Simonstown, went to Brooklyn Navy yard for refit and repair from 10 August to 3 December 1941. Back in the Mediterranean, she covered Malta convoys, participated in the 2nd Battle of Sirte, bombarded the North African coast and, by January 1943, was part of Force Q at Bone. She came home to refit between April and June 1943, then returned for the invasion of Sicily, followed by the Anzio landings and gunfire support duties along the Italian coastline. In August 1944 she was part of the naval force for the landings in the south of France before returning home, where she operated in Arctic waters and off the Norwegian coast until the end of the war. Postwar she joined the 10th Cruiser Squadron and later, after refit during March-August 1946, the 2nd Cruiser Squadron,

but paid off in October 1947. After ten years in reserve in the Gairloch (1947/51) and at Portsmouth (1951/58) she arrived at Barrow-in-Furness on 18 July 1957 to be scrapped by T. W. Ward.

Euryalus arrived in the Mediterranean in September 1941 and joined the 15th Cruiser Squadron at Alexandria. She participated in all the major operations to resupply Malta, the 1st and 2nd Battles of Sirte, and carried out bombardments in support of the army in North Africa. By January 1943 she was with Force K, shelling Axis positions in Tunisia, and bombarded Pantelleria in May/June. With the 12th Cruiser Squadron she participated in the Sicily landings, and later, at Salerno, she was part of Force V with the Escort Carrier Command. After Salerno she returned home to refit between October 1943 and July 1944, then served with the Home Fleet, covering raids on the Norwegian coast until November. At the end of the year *Euryalus* sailed for the Far East, and by 16 January was at Trincomalee, 5th Cruiser Squadron, for the British Pacific Fleet. In the Pacific she was at part of the force covering

the carrier raids on Sakashima Gunto, Okinawa, in March to May 1945, then shelled the Japanese mainland in the final weeks of the war before sailing to the China Sea for the reoccupation of Hong Kong. She returned to Sheerness on 17 February 1946 to go into reserve, but was refitted during August 1947 to January 1948, and then recommissioned on 20 February 1948 for the Mediterranean, 1st Cruiser Squadron, where she remained until the summer of 1952. Between 1952 and 1954 she served with the 6th Cruiser Squadron in the South Atlantic before returning to Devonport on 19 September 1954 to pay off. After a period in reserve she was put up for disposal, and arrived at Blyth on 18 July 1959 to be scrapped by Hughes Bolkow.

Hermione served with the 2nd Cruiser Squadron during the hunt for *Bismarck*, then joined Force H at Gibraltar in June 1941. She served with Force H until March 1942, participating in many Malta convoys and in the operations to fly fighter reinforcements to the island from the west. On 2 August 1941 she rammed and sank the Italian submarine *Tembien* in the Sicilian Nar-

rows. In March 1942 she escorted the invasion convoy for Operation Ironclad from Gibraltar to Durban, and in May participated in the occupation of Madagascar. She was then ordered to the eastern Mediterranean as part of the 15th Cruiser Squadron, and took part in the eastern convoy of Operation Harpoon/Vigorous in June 1942, but was torpedoed and sunk on 16 June south of Crete by *U205*.

Sirius's completion was delayed by bombing. She initially joined the Home Fleet, then went to the Mediterranean in August for Operation Pedestal. She was then ordered to the South Atlantic to patrol against Axis blockade runners on the Far East route, returning to Gibraltar in November for Operation Torch, the North African landings. As part of Force Q at Bone in December she harried Axis convoys to and from Tunisia until the Axis surrender in North Africa and then, as part of the 12th Cruiser Squadron, was at the invasion of Sicily, Operation Husky, in July. For the next few months she supported the army ashore, and in September took part in the occupation of Taranto before transferring to the

Adriatic, where, on 5 October 1943, she helped annihilate a German convoy in the Dodecanese. Unfortunately, on 17 October, *Sirius* was badly damaged by bombs off Scarpanto, and sailed to Massawa for repairs. These were carried out between November 1943 and February 1944, before the ship returned to Britain for Operation Overlord, the Normandy landings, where she was part of the reserve of the Eastern Task Force. In August she returned to Mediterranean waters for the landings in the south of France, Operation Dragoon. She then served again in the Aegean, where, in October 1944, she was present during the reoccupation of Athens. *Sirius* remained with the Mediterranean Fleet, 15th Cruiser Squadron, postwar until 1946. After refit at Portsmouth in 1946, *Sirius* joined the 2nd Cruiser Squadron with the Home Fleet in March 1947. She paid off in 1949 and was put up for disposal in 1956. On 15 October 1956 *Sirius* arrived at the Blyth yard of Hughes Bolkow for breaking up.

Cleopatra went out to Gibraltar early in 1942, and on 9 February sailed for Malta, where she was immediately damaged by a bomb. After repair she was transferred to Alexandria early in March for the 15th Cruiser Squadron, and took part in the 2nd Battle of Sirte. In June she covered Operation Harpoon/Vigorous, and in August bombarded Rhodes as a diversion for the Pedestal convoy. By January 1943 she was part of Force K, later Force Q at Bone, from where the Axis traffic to and from Tunisia was attacked. Later she was a unit of the 12th Cruiser Squadron, and was present at the landings in Sicily, Operation Husky, in June, followed by supporting the army ashore. However, on 16 July 1943 *Cleopatra* was torpedoed by the Italian submarine *Dandolo* and again badly damaged. Temporary repairs at Malta lasted until October 1943, after which the ship sailed to Philadelphia for full repairs. These were completed in November 1944, and in 1945 she went out to the East Indies, where she was the first ship into the newly recaptured base at Singapore in September. *Cleopatra* served postwar with the 5th Cruiser Squadron in the East Indies until returning to Portsmouth on 7 February 1946 to refit. Thereafter she joined the Home Fleet, 2nd Cruiser Squadron, 1946/51 and later served in the Mediterranean 1951/53, but returned to Chatham on 12 February 1953 to pay off. On 15 December 1958 she arrived at the Newport yard of Cashmore for breaking up.

Argonaut was one of the 1939-programme ships which had been suspended in the Dunkirk emergency, and as a result did not join the fleet until August 1942. She served with the Home Fleet initially, operating to Spitzbergen and north Russia in October before going to Force H for the North African landings, Operation Torch, in November. Following this, she moved to Bone as part of the Strike Force there, operating with *Aurora*. On 14 December 1942 she was hit by two torpedoes and badly damaged, both bow and stern being blown off. Repairs in Philadelphia took until November 1943. On her return to Britain she served with the Home Fleet, and was at the Normandy landings as part of Force K off Gold Beach. In August she transferred to the Mediterranean for Operation Dragoon, and in September moved to the Aegean, but in November she was ordered to the East Indies for carrier escort duties. By December 1944 the ship was covering raids against targets in Sumatra and the Arakan campaign. In January 1945 she was ordered to the British Pacific Fleet, 5th Cruiser Squadron, and took part in the operations around Okinawa and later against the Japanese mainland itself before being withdrawn in August for the occupation of Shanghai. *Argonaut* returned to Portsmouth on 6 July 1946, reduced to reserve and never recommissioned. She arrived at Cashmore, Newport, for scrapping on 19 November 1955.

Scylla served with the Home Fleet on Arctic convoy duties until she sailed for Gibraltar on 28 October 1942. The following month she was at the Torch landings as part of Force O with the Eastern Task Force, but in December was sent into the Bay of Biscay as part of the effort to catch homecoming Axis blockade runners. She intercepted the German *Rhakotis* north-west of Cape Finisterre on 1 January 1943. In February she returned to the Home Fleet for Arctic convoys, but was back in the Bay of Biscay in June to cover anti-submarine operations. In September 1943 she was part of the Support Carrier Force at the Salerno landings, but came home to refit for duty as an escort carrier flagship in October, which lasted until April 1944. She was present at the Normandy landings as Flagship of the Eastern Task Force, but on 23 June was badly damaged by a mine and declared a Constructional Total Loss (CTL). Although towed to Portsmouth, she was not disposed of until 1950, after being used in the ship target trials of 1948/50. She arrived at Ward's, Barrow-in-Furness, on 4 May 1950 for breaking up.

Charybdis served with the Home Fleet until April 1942, then went to Gibraltar to replace *Hermione* with Force H. She covered several operations to reinforce the fighter defences of Malta by launching replacements from aircraft carriers in the western Mediterranean, and took part in the Pedestal and Harpoon convoys. In November 1942 she was part of Force O with the Eastern Task Force during the Torch landings. In September 1943 she was at the Salerno landings, but returned home to the Plymouth command afterwards. On 23 October 1943 she was torpedoed and sunk by the German torpedo boats *T23* and *T27* in a night action off the north coast of Brittany.

Opposite page:
Top: *Sirius* in September 1944. (M. Bar)
Bottom: *Scylla* on 25 June 1942. (IWM)

Below: *Cleopatra* in 1941. (Navpic)

MODIFIED DIDO CLASS

Ship	Builder	Laid Down	Launched	Completed	Fate
Spartan	VA (Barrow)	21 Dec 39	27 Aug 42	10 Aug 43	Lost 29 Jan 1944
Bellona	Fairfield	30 Nov 39	29 Sep 42	29 Oct 43	Scrapped at Briton Ferry 1959
Black Prince	Harland & Wolff	1 Dec 39	27 Aug 42	20 Nov 43	Scrapped in Japan 1962
Royalist	Scotts	21 Mar 40	30 May 42	10 Sep 43	Scrapped in Japan 1968
Diadem	Hawthorne Leslie	15 Dec 39	21 Aug 42	6 Jan 44	Sold to Pakistan 1956

Displacement: 5,950 tons/6,045 tonnes (standard); 7,350 tons/7,467 tonnes (full load).
Length: 512ft/156.05m (oa); 485ft/147.82m (pp).
Beam: 50ft 6in/15.39m; Draught: 17ft 9in/5.41m (mean).
Machinery: 4-shaft Parsons geared turbines; 4 Admiralty 3-drum boilers.
Performance: 62,000shp=32kts; Bunkerage 1,100 tons oil.
Range: 7,400nm at 12kts.
Protection as Dido.
Guns: eight 5.25in Mk I (4x2); twelve 2pdr (3x4); twelve 20mm (6x2).
Torpedoes: six 21in (2x3).
Aircraft: nil.
Complement: 530.

Design While the six Didos remained suspended, discussions continued on their design in the light of the initial reports from sea of the first ships to complete. To improve stability, it was suggested that Q turret be omitted, but in fact the actual modifications went further than this. The deletion of Q turret allowed the fitting of a multiple AA mounting ahead of the bridge, which in turn could be reduced in height, further benefiting stability. The bridge itself was moved forward, allowing the funnels to be made upright and reduced in height. Internal arrangements were also revised in the light of war experience, and all five (Argonaut was too far advanced to be altered) were fitted as flagships, with the necessary bridge accommodation. The protection was slightly improved by the addition of ¾in splinter protection to the sides of the magazines/shell rooms and to the bridge. Machinery remained the same, but the armament now included three quadruple 2pdr (no quad Bofors being available) and six twin power-operated 20mm.

Modifications Spartan received no alterations as far as is known.

Royalist was converted to an Escort Carrier Squadron flagship immediately on completion, when an extra two twin 20mm were fitted as well as four single 20mm. She was the only ship to receive an extensive postwar modernisation.

Bellona had four single 20mm added by April 1944, and received an extra eight single 20mm by April 1945.

Black Prince and Diadem also received eight single 20mm, and had a further two twin 20mm by early 1945.

Service Spartan served initially in the Home Fleet and then went to the Mediterranean, where she was hit and sunk by an Hs 293 glider bomb while lying off the Anzio beachhead on 29 January 1944.

Royalist joined the Home Fleet and served on Arctic convoy duties. She also covered some of the carrier raids against Tirpitz until ordered to the Mediterranean to support the landings in the south of France in August 1944, as part of the escort carrier squadron TF88.1. On 15 September, accompanied by Teazer, she sank the transports KT4 and KT26 off Cape Spatha. She then moved into the Aegean until late 1944, when ordered to the East Indies. By April 1945 she was with the 21st Escort Carrier Squadron as Flagship, supporting the Rangoon landings, and the following month was part of a force that unsuccessfully attempted to intercept a Japanese cruiser and destroyer evacuating troops from the Andaman Islands. For the remainder of the war she covered the carrier raids against targets in the East Indies and Sumatra. She was withdrawn from the East Indies after the war, and returned home to reserve. In 1954 she began a major refit which was completed in April 1956, and the ship was handed over to the Royal New Zealand Navy on 9 July 1956. Paid off on 4 June 1966, Royalist reverted to RN control in 1967. She was sold to Nissho Co, Japan, in November 1967 and was towed from Auckland on 31 December 1967, destined for Osaka.

Bellona served in the Channel and then formed part of the reserve force for the Normandy landings in June 1944. In July she covered the carrier raids against Tirpitz, but the following month was back in the Channel, attacking German convoy traffic in the Bay of Biscay and off the Brittany coast. She returned to northern waters for the remainder of the war, on Arctic convoys, carrier and cruiser sweeps along the Norwegian coastline, before arriving in Copenhagen at the German surrender in May 1945. After the war she was part of the 10th Cruiser Squadron until 1946, when she was loaned to the Royal New Zealand Navy, reverting to RN control after the transfer of Royalist in 1956. On 5 February 1958 she arrived at the Briton Ferry yard of T. W. Ward to be broken up.

Black Prince served on Arctic convoys and then came south in preparation for the invasion of Europe, being employed on offensive sweeps against German coastal convoy traffic. On the night of 25/26 April 1944, accompanied by destroyers, she was involved in the action which sank the torpedo boat T29 and damaged T24 and T27 off the north Brittany coast. During the Normandy landings she was part of Force A in support of Utah Beach. In August she moved to the Mediterranean for the invasion of the south of France, and then served in Aegean waters until October. By the following month Black Prince had joined the East Indies Fleet, where she covered the carrier raids against Japanese oil installations and airfields in Sumatra and Malaya. On 16 January 1945 she sailed as part of the British Pacific Fleet, seeing action off Okinawa and in the final bombardments of the Japanese mainland before withdrawing to reoccupy Hong Kong in September. After the Japanese surrender she remained in the Far East and was lent to the Royal New Zealand Navy in 1946. She reverted to RN control, still in an unmodernised condition, on 1 April 1961. Sold for scrapping in March 1962, she left Auckland on 5 April 1962 in tow for breaking up at Mitsui & Co, Osaka, Japan, arriving there in May.

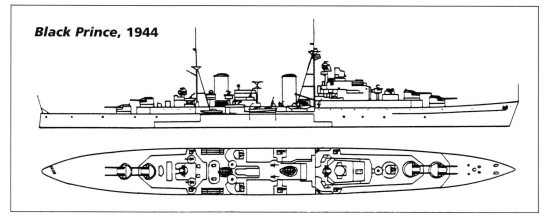

Black Prince, 1944

Right: *Diadem.* The censor appears to have eradicated the upper half of the after HACS and the radar on the forward one. (IWM)

Right: *Diadem* in 1945. (MOD)

Above: *Royalist* on 9 September 1943. (Courtesy G. Ransome) **Below:** *Black Prince* at Scapa Flow in October 1943. (IWM)

Diadem served on the Arctic convoys and covered carrier raids against *Tirpitz* in the early months of 1944, then became part of Force E off Juno beach during the invasion of Normandy in June. After the landings she carried out offensive patrols against German shipping around the Brittany coast, sinking, with destroyers, *Sperrbrecher* 7 off La Rochelle on 12 August. She returned to northern waters in September, where she covered Russian convoys and carrier raids against German shipping routes along the Norwegian coast, as well as making offensive sweeps herself. In the course of one such sweep, accompanied by *Mauritius* on 28 January 1945, the cruiser engaged three German destroyers, damaging *Z31*. *Diadem* remained with the 10th Cruiser Squadron until after the war, and served in the Home Fleet until 1950. In 1956 her sale to Pakistan was agreed, and after a refit she was handed over to the Pakistan Navy on 5 July 1957, being renamed *Babur*. She was converted into a cadets training ship in 1961.

FIJI CLASS

Ship	Builder	Laid Down	Launched	Completed	Fate
Fiji	John Brown	30 Mar 38	31 May 39	5 May 40	Lost 22 May 1941
Kenya	Stephens	18 Jun 38	18 Aug 39	27 Sep 40	Scrapped at Faslane 1962
Nigeria	VA (Tyne)	8 Feb 38	18 Jul 39	23 Sep 40	Sold to India in 1954
Mauritius	Swan Hunter	31 Mar 38	19 Jul 39	4 Jan 41	Scrapped at Inverkeithing 1965
Trinidad	Devonport Dky	21 Apr 38	21 Mar 40	14 Oct 41	Lost 15 May 1942
Gambia	Swan Hunter	24 Jul 38	30 Nov 40	21 Feb 42	Scrapped at Inverkeithing 1968
Jamaica	VA (Barrow)	28 Apr 38	16 Nov 40	29 Jun 42	Scrapped at Dalmuir 1960
Bermuda	John Brown	30 Nov 38	11 Sep 41	21 Aug 42	Scrapped at Briton Ferry 1965

Displacement: 8,530 tons/8,666 tonnes (standard); 10,450 tons/10,617 tonnes (full load).
Length: 555ft 6in/169.31m (oa); 538ft/163.98m (pp).
Beam: 62ft/18.90m; Draught: 19ft 10in/6.04m (mean).
Machinery: 4-shaft Parsons geared turbines; 4 Admiralty 3-drum boilers.
Performance: 80,000shp=32.25kts; Bunkerage: 1,700 tons oil.
Range: 6,520nm at 13kts.
Protection: 3¼in-3½in main belt, 2in deck, 1in-2in turrets.
Guns: twelve 6in Mk XXIII (4x3); eight 4in Mk XVI (4x2); eight 2pdr (2x4); eight .5in MGs (2x4)*.
Torpedoes: six 21in (2x3).
Aircraft: three, one catapult.
Complement: 733.   *see text for as-completed AA outfits.

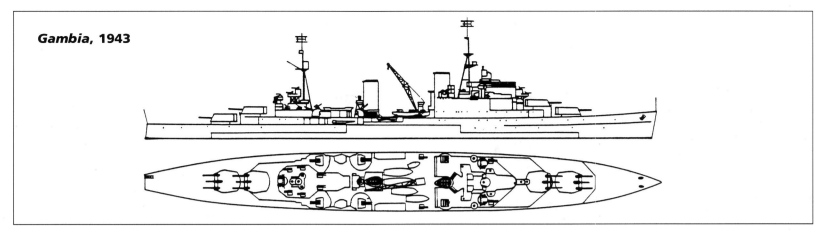

Gambia, 1943

Design Just as the County class were a direct result of the Washington Treaty, the *Fijis*, or Colony class, were the result of the Second London Naval Treaty of 1937. This specified a maximum displacement of 8,000 tons for cruisers, thus preventing the continuation of the *Southampton* design. A large number of sketch designs were considered, with armaments of both 6in and 5.25in guns in a wide variety of configurations; even with quadruple 6in as had already been proposed for the *Belfast*, although this was not finally adopted. The 5.25in configuration was abandoned as too weak in the face of new Japanese designs, and the 6in armament was preferred, in triple turrets as in the previous class.

The hull was shorter and had less beam than the *Southampton*s, reflecting the reduced displacement, but was visually similar, except that these ships were given a transom stern, which benefited the accommodation arrangements aft. Welding was used more extensively in this class than hitherto. The 8,000-ton limit also necessitated a reduction in the protective scheme (although the waterline length covered was greater), and the side armour was reduced to 3½in NC for the magazine spaces and 3¼in for the machinery spaces. Horizontal protection was 2in NC for the magazines and engine rooms, but 3¼in for the boiler rooms. For the machinery, a quadruple-shaft geared turbine layout was adopted, on the unit principle, following current practice. The boilers were rated for an output of 80,000shp for a designed speed of 32¼kts.

The main machinery was constructed by the hull contractors, except for the Swan Hunter ships, which had Wallsend Slipway as the machinery subcontractors and V.A. Tyne, who used Parsons.

The main armament remained twelve 6in Mk XXIII, but the mountings were the long-trunk triple Mk XXIII. Secondary armament was eight 4in in twin mountings Mk XIX. There was little margin to spare on weight as a result, and the armament suffered in that quadruple 2pdrs had to be replaced by the inferior quadruple .5in MGs and the torpedo tubes were omitted altogether, although space was allowed for both items. When the war broke out, the provisions of the London Treaty lapsed and two quadruple 2pdr as well as two banks of triple 21in torpedo tubes were shipped. However, no modifications were made to the fire control system and the ships had no after DCT for the main armament. Only a control position with a rangefinder was fitted on the roof of X turret. Three HACS were fitted for the secondary armament, one on each beam and one aft. The aircraft installation comprised a fixed athwartships catapult and two box hangars, one either side of the fore-funnel, equipped to operate the Walrus and later Sea Otter amphibians, two of which could be carried.

Five ships were authorised under the 1937 Programme: *Fiji, Kenya, Mauritius, Nigeria* and *Trinidad*, all ordered in December 1937, with four repeats in the 1938 Programme: *Ceylon, Gambia, Jamaica* and *Uganda*, ordered in March 1938. Two more ships were authorised under the 1939 Programme which, despite considerable discussion, were also ordered as repeats in the end. These were *Bermuda* and *Newfoundland*.

Right: *Fiji*, 20 August 1940. Note no radar or additional light AA. (Courtesy G. Ransome)

Above: *Kenya.* (Courtesy G. Ransome)
Right: *Nigeria.* (IWM)

War additions such as the torpedoes and extra splinter protection caused the displacement to rise to 8,631 tons (standard), but the performance in terms of speed was not compromised.

Wartime conditions also affected completion of some ships. *Trinidad* was considerably delayed by bombing in the shipyard, while both *Ceylon* and *Uganda*, as well as *Newfoundland*, were suspended as a consequence of the Dunkirk emergency in May 1940. These last three were eventually completed to a modified design, and are dealt with as the *Uganda* class.

Modifications All of these ships completed after the outbreak of hostilities, and therefore incorporated some modifications resulting from war experience.

Fiji received only two more quadruple .5in MGs and radar 284 before her loss.

Kenya also received two additional quadruple .5in MGs and a pair of single 20mm in the summer of 1941. Radars 273 and 284 were added in December 1941. During repairs between August and December 1942 she had the quadruple .5in MGs and the two 20mm singles removed, and received in lieu six twin 20mm. Radar 273 was also removed and radars 272, 282, 283 and 285 fitted. By late 1943 two further twin 20mm had been fitted, giving a total of eight twin power-operated mountings. X turret was landed in April 1945, to be replaced by two twin 40mm Bofors. At the end of the war, or just after, the 2pdr were replaced by two twin 40mm and the twin 20mm by single 40mm, the final outfit being eighteen 40mm (5 x 2, 8 x 1).

Mauritius received four single 20mm and radars 273, 284 and 285 early in 1942. In June 1943 the aircraft installations were removed and twenty single 20mm added. Two quadruple .5in MGs were landed shortly after.

Nigeria had four single 20mm by September 1941, and received radars 273 and 284 in the latter half of that year. Between August 1942 and June 1943 she had the quadruple .5in MGs and the single 20mm removed, as well as the radar 273, receiving in lieu eight twin 20mm and radars 272 and 282. The control position on X turret was probably also removed at this time. This remained her outfit in April 1944, but by October 1945 four single Mk III Bofors 40mm had been added.

Trinidad appears to have received only two single 20mm before her loss.

Gambia had six single 20mm fitted in February 1942. Between June and September 1943 the aircraft installations were removed, as were two single 2pdr and six 20mm singles, the ship being fitted instead with ten twin power-operated 20mm. This outfit was the same in April 1944.

Jamaica received eight twin power-operated 20mm in 1943 and had four singles. Two of the latter replaced the control position atop X turret.

Bermuda, the last to complete, entered service with ten 20mm single mountings. Six more were added in September 1943. In the spring of 1944 the aircraft installations and twelve single 20mm were landed, being replaced by eight twin power-operated 20mm. During a major refit from June 1944 to April 1945, X turret and four twin 20mm were removed and three quadruple and four single 2pdr were fitted. In August 1945 she had a further two twin and two single 20mm removed, to be replaced by two Boffins and two single 40mm Bofors Mk III.

Service *Fiji* joined the Home Fleet on completion, but on 31 August 1940 left the Clyde for Operation Menace, the attack on Dakar. However, she was damaged by a torpedo from *U32* on 1 September and had to return to Britain for repairs which lasted about six months. In March 1941 she was on patrol duty in the Denmark Straits, but failed to intercept the homeward-bound *Admiral Scheer*. A month later she was with Force H, blockading the German heavy ships then stationed at Brest, before she sailed with Force H to escort an operation to fly reinforcement fighters to Malta. She later escorted convoys to Malta, then participated in the Crete campaign, where, on 22 May 1941, she was sunk by bombs from a Bf 109 of 1/LG2, having expended all of her AA ammunition.

Kenya also joined the Home Fleet, and covered the WS convoys at the time the major surface raiders were at large in the Atlantic. In May 1941, as part of the 2nd Cruiser Squadron, she was involved in the hunt for *Bismarck*, and in June,

Above: *Mauritius*. (IWM)

accompanied by *Aurora*, she intercepted one of the German battleship's intended supply ships, *Belchen*, in the Davies Strait. In September she went to the Mediterranean for Operation Halberd, but returned to the Home Fleet and served in Arctic waters, operating off northern Norway in November, where she bombarded coastal positions. In December 1941 she covered the Vaagsö raid and then remained in northern waters until June 1942, when she returned to the Mediterranean for Operations Harpoon/Vigorous. She also participated in Operation Pedestal in August 1942, but was damaged by a torpedo from the Italian submarine *Alagi* on 12 August. Repairs lasted until December 1942. She remained in the Home Fleet throughout 1943, but then went to the Eastern Fleet, and by January 1944 was serving with the 4th Cruiser Squadron on that station. In 1944 she covered the carrier raids by the Eastern Fleet on Japanese-held islands in the Indian Ocean and on oil installations in the East Indies. In early 1945 she covered the Arakan landings and raids against the Malayan coastline before returning home. After a refit during 1945/46, she served on the America and West Indies Station, 8th Cruiser Squadron, from October 1946 to December 1947, and then, after a period in reserve and refit, joined the 5th Cruiser Squadron in the Far East, seeing service in the Korean war. She was in the East Indies with the 4th Cruiser Squadron during 1951/52, then in the Mediterranean with the 1st Cruiser Squadron in 1952/53 before returning to

Portsmouth on 24 February 1953 to reduce to reserve. In 1955 she was refitted and went out to the 8th Cruiser Squadron on the America and West Indies Station, returning to Portsmouth on 5 November 1956. Subsequently she served with the Home Fleet until 1957, when she went to the Mediterranean for the 1st Cruiser Squadron as flagship 1957/58. She finally paid off in September 1958, remaining in reserve at Portsmouth until sold in 1962. She arrived at the Faslane yard of Shipbreaking Industries on 29 October 1962.

Mauritius operated on trade protection duties in the Atlantic on completion, and remained with the Home Fleet until going to the East Indies late in 1941. She joined the Eastern Fleet in 1942, but was withdrawn in April 1943 to reinforce the Mediterranean Fleet. After repairs following grounding, she was operational in June 1943 and thereafter participated in the landings in Sicily, Operation Husky, in July as a unit of Support Force East, when she carried out shore bombardment duties. In September she was part of the covering force for the Salerno landings, but by the end of the year had been transferred to the Bay of Biscay to carry out anti-blockade-runner patrols. However, she soon returned to the Mediterranean, this time for the Anzio landings in January 1944. In June 1944 she covered the landings in Normandy as part of Force D off Sword Beach, then carried out offensive patrols of the Brittany coast in August to mop up the remnants of the German shipping in the area. Operating with destroyers, she sank *Sperrbrecher 157* on 14/15 August and five *Vorpostenboote* on 22/23 August. After this she returned to the Home Fleet, covering the carrier raids along the Norwegian coast and making anti-shipping strikes herself. In January 1945, in company with *Diadem*, she fought an action with German destroyers in which *Z31* was badly damaged. Following this action she was refitted at Cammell-Laird's between February 1945 and March 1946, then went out to the Mediterranean for the 15th (later 1st) Cruiser Squadron, returning to the UK in 1948. After a spell in reserve and in refit, she recommissioned in 1949 for the 1st Cruiser Squadron in the Mediterranean, sailing on 6 May 1949. However, the years 1949 to 1951 were spent on the East Indies Station with the 4th Cruiser Squadron until she returned to Chatham on 18 December 1951. She was placed in reserve in 1952 and remained there until 1965, when she was sold for scrapping, arriving at T. W. Ward Ltd, Inverkeithing, on 27 March 1965.

Nigeria served with the Home Fleet until 1944, participating in North Atlantic convoys in 1940, the Lofoten raid and the hunt for German warship raiders in Icelandic waters in March 1941. In June that year she intercepted the German weathership *Lauenburg* off Jan Mayen Island, capturing valuable code data. She took part in operations to Spitzbergen in the summer of 1941, and on 6 September, in company with *Aurora*, sank *Bremse* off North Cape. 1942 saw her mostly employed on the Arctic convoy routes until she was detached to the Mediterranean in August for Operation Pedestal, when she was torpedoed and damaged by the Italian submarine *Axum* on 12 August near the Skerki bank. She was sent to the USA for repairs at Charlestown, New York, which were completed in June 1943. In 1944 *Nigeria* was sent to the Eastern Fleet, where, during 1944, she covered the carrier raids against Japanese controlled oil installations and airfields in the East Indies. By January 1945 she was covering the Arakan campaign, and remained in the Indian Ocean until the end of the war, when the Japanese surrendered in Malaya. Postwar she returned to Devonport to refit from December 1945 to April 1946, then served as flagship of the 6th Cruiser Squadron on the South Atlantic Station until September 1950 before returning to home waters and reserve, being used as an accommodation ship at Devonport. On 8 April 1954 her sale to India was announced, and the ship was given a major refit at Cammell-Laird, Birkenhead, between October 1954 and April 1957, after which she was formally handed over to the Indian Navy and renamed *Mysore* on 29 August 1957. By 1975 she was a training ship, and paid off on 20 August 1985, to be scrapped the following year.

Trinidad joined the Home Fleet on completion and served on Arctic convoy duties. While covering PQ13 she engaged German destroyers and hit *Z26*, but was hit by one of her own torpedoes, which circled. The damaged ship was brought into Murmansk for temporary repairs, and sailed for home on 13 May 1942. However, she was attacked by aircraft en route and hit by bombs from aircraft of *III/KG30* on 15 May, which crippled her. The wreck was sunk by *Matchless*.

Gambia served in the East Indies after completion, and took part in the occupation of Madagascar in September 1942. In 1943, as part of the Eastern Fleet, she carried out trade protection duties in the Indian Ocean, but returned to home waters to refit at Liverpool between June and September, following which she operated anti-blockade runner patrols in the Bay of Biscay in December. She was manned by the Royal New Zealand Navy from 1943. By 1944 she was back in the Eastern Fleet, searching for blockade runners in the Cocos Islands area in February. For the remainder of the year until November she operated with the Eastern Fleet on its series of carrier raids against oil installations and airfields. From November *Gambia* became part of the British Pacific Fleet, and saw action off Okinawa and Formosa before participating in the final raids on the mainland of Japan. After her return to RN control at Portsmouth on 27 March 1946, she was given a refit and recommissioned on 1 July 1946 for the 5th Cruiser Squadron with the Far East Fleet. She returned to the UK on 6 January 1948, and in January 1950 joined the 2nd Cruiser Squadron in the Mediterranean, later serving with the 1st Cruiser Squadron on the same station until October 1954. In 1955 she became flagship of the 4th Cruiser Squadron on the East Indies Station and, as the last flagship on this station, returned to Chatham on 19 September 1958. On 4 November 1958 she recommissioned for the 1st Cruiser Squadron in the Mediterranean. In 1960 she served in the South Atlantic and the Home fleet before paying off to reserve in December that year. The ship remained in reserve at Portsmouth until she was put on the disposal list and sold to T. W. Ward for scrapping. She left Portsmouth under tow on 2 December 1968 and arrived at Inverkeithing for breaking up on 5 December.

Jamaica spent almost her entire wartime career on Arctic convoy duties, except for a deployment south for the landings in North Africa in November 1942, where she was member of the Centre Task Force. At the end of December 1943 she participated in the action against *Scharnhorst* off North Cape, and in 1944 interspersed the Russian convoys with escorting the carrier raids against the Norwegian coast. Postwar she went to the 5th Cruiser Squadron in the East Indies from September 1945 to 1946, followed by the 4th Cruiser Squadron on the same station until November 1947. Between August 1948 and 1949 she was on the America and West Indies Station, 8th Cruiser Squadron, and was then loaned to the 5th Cruiser Squadron in the Far East for the Korean War, returning home on 27 February 1951. She was in reserve between 1951 and 1953, refitted 1953/54, then served with the Home and Mediterranean Fleets until laid up in the Gairloch on 20 November 1957. Sold for scrapping to Arnott Young Ltd, she arrived at Dalmuir for breaking up on 20 December 1960, the hull being finished at Troon in 1962.

UGANDA CLASS

Ship	Builder	Laid Down	Launched	Completed	Fate
Uganda	VA (Tyne)	20 Jul 39	7 Aug 41	3 Jan 43	To Canada 21 Oct 1944
Newfoundland	Swan Hunter	9 Nov 39	19 Dec 41	21 Jan 43	Sold to Peru 1959
Ceylon	Stephens	27 Apr 39	30 Jul 42	13 Jul 43	Sold to Peru 1959

Displacement: 8,530 tons/8,666 tonnes (standard); 10,800 tons/10,972 tonnes (full load).
Length: 555ft 6in/169.31m (oa); 538ft/163.98m (pp).
Beam: 62ft/18.9m; Draught: 19ft 10in/6.04m (mean).

Machinery: as *Fiji*.
Performance: as *Fiji*; Bunkerage: as *Fiji*.
Range: as *Fiji*.
Protection: as *Fiji*.

Guns: nine 6in Mk XXIII (3x3); eight 4in Mk XVI (4x2); twelve 2pdr, (3x4); sixteen-twenty 20mm (8/10x2).
Torpedoes: six 21in (2x3).
Aircraft: two, one catapult.
Complement: 733.

Design During the time that these three ships were suspended, their design was recast and they became the 'Modified *Fiji*' class. The main object of the modifications was to improve the AA defences of the ships, as this had been found necessary in the light of war experience. The only apparent means of doing so was to remove X tur-

Above: *Ceylon* as completed. Note absence of X turret. (IWM)

ret and replace it by a pair of 4in twin mountings, but after much discussion it was finally decided to accept the loss of X turret but fit only one additional 4in twin and improve the AA defences by the expedient of an extra HACS position and the fitting of RPC to all 4in and 2pdr mountings. They were also given an relatively simple Air Defence Room for the purpose of Fighter Control. The forward DCT was raised to allow the radar 272 office to be housed below it.

In fact, the fitting of a fifth twin 4in was rescinded, as the close-range defence was believed to be more important, and another quadruple 2pdr was fitted instead. The other quadruple 2pdr mountings were resited at the forward end of the hangar deck to give a better field of fire ahead. One crane was deleted as a weight-saving measure.

Modifications *Ceylon* completed with a light AA outfit of sixteen twin power-operated 20mm, and by April 1944 had received a further two twin and eight single 20mm mountings. By the end of the war six of the single and four of the twin 20mm had been landed, to be replaced by four single 40mm Bofors Mk III.

Newfoundland also completed with sixteen twin 20mm. By April 1944 she had an additional six single 20mm added, and in the summer of that year received a further two twin and two single 20mm. Her aircraft fittings were removed and the radar fit updated.

Uganda completed with twenty twin 20mm power-operated mountings. Between October 1943 and October 1944 six twin 20mm were landed and eight single fitted in lieu. After the repairs in the USA, she was further modified in

the first half of 1945 by the removal of four twin 20mm and the aircraft fittings. She received three quadruple and four single 2pdr and had the radar outfit updated.

Service *Ceylon* served with the Home Fleet from completion until late 1943, when she went to the 4th Cruiser Squadron with the Eastern Fleet in the East Indies. Throughout 1944 she covered the carrier raids against Sabang, Soerabaya and Sumatra, as well as carrying out some bombardment tasks herself. In November 1944 she joined the British Pacific Fleet and sailed from Trincomalee on 16 January, taking part in a raid on Pankalan Bradan en route. By May 1945, however, she was back in the Indian Ocean, shelling the Nicobar Islands, and remained in that theatre until the end of the war. Postwar she served in the Portsmouth Command during 1946/50, followed by the 5th and 4th Cruiser Squadrons on the Far East and East Indies stations, returning to Portsmouth on 1 October 1954. She was given a major refit from March 1955 to July 1956 for further service, and served successively with the Home Fleet, Mediterranean Fleet, South Atlantic and East Indies stations until she arrived back at Portsmouth on 18 December 1959, being sold to Peru the same month. On 9 February 1960 she was officially transferred to Peru and renamed *Coronel Bolognesi*. In May 1982 she was paid off for disposal, being towed to Taiwan for scrapping during August 1985.

Newfoundland served initially in the Home Fleet and then went to the Mediterranean, taking part in the attack on Pantelleria in June and the Sicily landings, as part of Support Force East, in July 1943. However, on 23 July she was torpedoed by the Italian submarine *Ascianghi* and, after temporary repair at Malta, she sailed for Boston, Massachusetts, in August for full repairs. These

took until April 1944, and on her return to Britain *Newfoundland* was taken in hand on the Clyde for a long refit which lasted until November 1944. On her return to service she sailed for the Indian Ocean, and then went to the Pacific via the Eastern Fleet. In May 1945 she was serving with Australian units in the New Guinea area of the south-west Pacific, and a month later participated in a raid on Truk. By July she was part of the forces bombarding the Japanese mainland, and was later present at the final surrender of Japan in Tokyo Bay. Postwar she was in reserve, and was used as a training ship before a refit at Plymouth in 1951. Recommissioned on 5 November 1952, she became flagship of the 4th Cruiser Squadron in the East Indies, and also served in the Far East. In 1956/57 she was in the Red Sea and Mediterranean, participating in the Suez camp, where she sank the Egyptian frigate *Domiat* on 1 November 1956. She then returned to the Far East until paid off to reserve at Portsmouth on 24 June 1959. On 2 November 1959 she was sold to Peru and formally transferred in December 1960 as *Almirante Grau*. She was renamed *Capitán Quiñones* on 15 May 1973. By 1979 she was in use as a static training ship at Callao, and was then disposed of.

Uganda joined the Home Fleet on completion, and then went to the Mediterranean for the Sicily campaign as part of Support Force East. For the next couple of months she supported the army ashore and then, in September, took part in the Salerno landings where, on 13 September, she was hit by a radio-guided bomb and badly damaged. She, too, was sent to the USA for repair, at Charlestown Navy yard, where she remained from October 1943 to October 1944. On completion of repairs she was presented to the Royal Canadian Navy on 21 October 1944. Further details of her Canadian service will be found under that section.

MINOTAUR/TIGER CLASS

Ship	Builder	Laid Down	Launched	Completed	Fate
Minotaur	Harland & Wolff	20 Nov 41	29 Jul 43	25 May 45	To Canada Jul 1944 as *Ontario*
Swiftsure	VA (Tyne)	22 Nov 41	4 Feb 43	22 Jun 44	Scrapped at Inverkeithing 1962
Bellerophon	VA (Tyne)	not laid			Cancelled Mar 1946
(ex *Blake*, ex *Tiger*)					
Blake	Fairfield	17 Aug 42	20 Dec 45	8 Mar 61	Completed to new design
(ex *Tiger* ex *Blake*)					
Defence	Scotts	24 Jun 42	2 Sep 44	20 Jul 60	Completed to new design as *Lion*
Hawke	Portsmouth Dky	Aug 44	not launched		Broken up on slip 1946
Superb	Swan Hunter	23 Jun 42	31 Aug 43	16 Nov 45	Scrapped at Dalmuir 1960
Tiger	John Brown	1 Oct 41	25 Oct 45	18 Mar 59	Completed to new design

Minotaur Class

Displacement: 8,800 tons/8,940 tonnes (standard); 11,130 tons/11,308 tonnes (full load).
Length: 555ft 6in/169.31m (oa); 538ft/163.98m (pp).
Beam: 63ft/19.2m; Draught: 20ft 8in/6.30m (mean).
Machinery: as *Fiji*.
Performance: as *Fiji*; Bunkerage as *Fiji*.
Range: as *Fiji*.
Protection: as *Fiji*.
Guns: nine 6in Mk XXIII (3x3); ten 4in Mk XVI (5x2); sixteen 2pdr (4x4); twenty-two 20mm (8x2 & 6x1).
Torpedoes: six 21in (2x3).
Aircraft: nil.
Complement: 855.

Tiger Class

Displacement: 8,885 tons/9,027 tonnes (standard); 11,560 tons/11,745 tonnes (full load).
Length: 555ft 6in/169.31m (oa); 538ft/163.98m (pp).
Beam: 64ft/19.51m; Draught: 21ft 1in/6.43m (mean).
Machinery: as *Fiji*.
Performance: as *Fiji*; Bunkerage 1,900 tons oil.
Range: 6,500nm at 13kts.
Protection: as *Fiji*.
Guns: as *Minotaur* Class except light AA: fourteen 2pdr (3x4 & 2x1); eight 40mm (8x1); ten 20mm (4x2 & 2x1).
Torpedoes: six 21in (2x3).
Aircraft: nil.
Complement: 867.

Design Under the 1941 programme, three more ships of the *Fiji* type had been authorised; *Bellerophon*, *Swiftsure* and *Minotaur*. They were followed by three more under the 1941 Supplementary Programme; *Tiger*, *Superb* and *Defence* and two, *Hawke* and *Blake*, under that for 1942. The original *Fiji* design was modified in the light of war experience, and the resulting extra equipment was added to the ships while they were under development. To restore stability, beam was increased to 63ft in the 1941 programme ships. Otherwise their dimensions remained the same as those of the Modified *Fijis*.

The main armament remained nine 6in Mk XXIII, but these ships did receive the extra 4in twin intended for the Modified *Fijis* in lieu of X turret. They also received an additional pair of quadruple 2pdr mountings, but were never fitted to operate aircraft and had no hangars.

The wartime cruiser programme appears to have been given little priority, and in fact, of this group of ships, only *Swiftsure* and *Minotaur* were completed to the original design. *Bellerophon* was renamed *Tiger* in February 1945 and suspended in July 1946, not being finished until March 1959, and to a completely revised design. The 1941 Programme ship ordered as *Tiger* in March 1942 was renamed *Bellerophon* on 17 August 1942 and laid down in August 1944, but was renamed again as *Blake* in December 1944. After yet another change of name, back to *Bellerophon* in February 1945, she was eventually cancelled in March 1946. Of the other ships in the 1941 Programme, *Superb* was completed to the revised *Tiger* design with 64ft beam, and *Defence* was suspended in July 1946. She was renamed *Lion* as late as 8 October 1957, when under completion as a unit of the *Tiger* class. She finally commissioned on 18 March 1961. Of the 1942 Additional Programme, *Hawke*, which had been laid down in August 1944, was suspended in January 1945 and cancelled in 1946, being broken up on the slip during 1946/47. Finally, *Blake*, laid down on 17 August 1942, was renamed *Tiger* in December 1944 and then suspended in July 1946, having reverted to the name *Blake* in February 1945. She was the third ship to be completed long after the war to the *Tiger* design. The reason for the complicated series of name changes is not known. Resumption of the construction of *Tiger*, *Defence* and *Blake* was announced on 15 October 1954, and their superstructure was dismantled in preparation for the new design in 1955.

Modifications *Swiftsure* completed with sixteen twin and six single 20mm, but had all the singles and eight of the twin removed in the summer of 1945, when she received, in lieu, eight 40mm Boffins and five single 40mm Bofors Mk III.

Ontario (ex-*Minotaur*) completed with the same close-range outfit as *Swiftsure*, and is

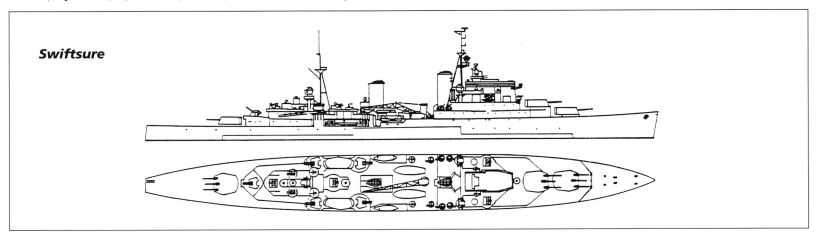

Swiftsure

reported to have had an outfit of six 40mm and six 20mm at the end of the war, all single mountings.

Superb was not completed until after the end of hostilities, and had a close-range outfit consisting of eight single 40mm Mk III, two single 2pdr, four twin hand-operated 20mm and two single 20mm.

Service Only *Swiftsure* saw war service with the Royal Navy, as *Minotaur* had been transferred to the Royal Canadian Navy in July 1944 and renamed *Ontario*. Her career is noted under the section for Canada.

Swiftsure joined the Home Fleet on commissioning, then later in 1944 went to the Eastern Fleet, where, in November 1944, she became a unit of the newly formed British Pacific Fleet. In the Pacific she participated in the Okinawa Campaign of March-May 1945 and in June took part in the carrier raid on Truk by the British Pacific Fleet as TG 111.2, with the cruisers shelling the islands. In August this group re-entered Hong Kong and took the Japanese surrender there. *Swiftsure* served in the postwar fleet and was finally scrapped in the 1960s, arriving at the Inverkeithing yard of T. W. Ward on 17 October 1962.

Tiger and *Blake* were eventually converted into Helicopter Cruisers in 1965/69. The former was reduced to reserve in December 1979 and was towed from Portsmouth on 23 September 1986 for shipbreakers in Spain, while *Blake* reduced to reserve in June 1978 and was towed to Cairnryan for breaking up on 28 October 1982. *Lion* arrived at T. W. Ward's yard at Inverkeithing in April 1975 for breaking up.

Above: *Swiftsure.* (IWM)

Below: *Superb* in August 1946. (Courtesy G. Ransome)

DA BARBIANO CLASS

Ship	Builder	Laid Down	Launched	Completed	Fate
Alberto Di Giussano	Ansaldo, Genoa	29 Mar 28	24 30	5 Feb 31	Lost 13 Dec 41
Alberico Da Barbiano	Ansaldo, Genoa	16 Apr 28	23 Aug 30	9 Jun 31	Lost 13 Dec 41
Bartolomeo Colleoni	Ansaldo, Genoa	21 Jun 28	21 Dec 30	10 Feb 32	Lost 19 Jul 40
Giovanni Delle Bande Nere	Castellamare di Stabia	31 Oct 28	27 Apr 30	Apr 31	Lost 1 Apr 42

Displacement: 5,110 tons/5,191 tonnes (standard); 6,844 tons/6,953 tonnes (full load).
Length: 555ft 6in/169.3m (oa); 525ft/160m (pp).
Beam: 50ft 10in/15.5m; Draught: 16ft 9in/5.1m (mean).
Machinery: 2-shaft Belluzzo geared turbines; 6 Yarrow-Ansaldo boilers.
Performance: 95,000shp=36.5kts; Bunkerage: 1,150 tons oil fuel.

Range: 3,800nm at 18kts.
Protection: 20mm deck, 24mm main belt, 23mm turrets, 40mm CT.
Guns: eight 6in (4x2); six 3.9in (3x2); eight 37mm (4x2); eight 13.2mm (4x2).
Torpedoes: four 21in (2x2).
Aircraft: two, one catapult.
Complement: 507.

Design The construction by France in 1923/26 of the 2,100-ton contre-torpilleurs armed with five 5.1in guns forced the Royal Italian Navy to consider countermeasures which eventually included a class of large destroyers or Scouts (Esploradi, the *Navigatori* class) and a large Scout of cruiser size. The latter sacrificed almost all protection for speed and superior gunpower vis-à-vis the Contre-Torpilleurs.

The hull was of mixed transverse and longitudinal construction, relatively lightly built and having a raised forecastle deck extending about one-third of the length, in the manner of a destroyer. It was also given a pronounced tumblehome. Over the machinery spaces, the side plating was of a chrome-nickel steel 25mm thick, and in the way of the magazines 20mm, which extended from just below the waterline to the upper (armoured) deck, which was itself 20mm thick. This citadel was closed off by forward and after transverse armoured bulkheads of 20mm. Inside, between the longitudinal bulkhead which extended from the forward to the after magazines, was an 18mm splinter protection longitudinal bulkhead. The weight of the armouring, at 584 tons, represented about 11.3 to 11.5 per cent of the standard displacement.

The machinery, a two-shaft steam turbine installation, was arranged on the unit principle, the two forward boiler rooms serving the starboard turbine while the after boiler room served the port shaft. The designed power of 95,000shp was considerably forced on trials, up to 123,479shp in the case of *Da Barbiano*, resulting in some very fast and misleading speeds being achieved (42.05kts in the case of the

Above: *Giovanni Delle Bande Nere.* (Courtesy M. Twardowski)

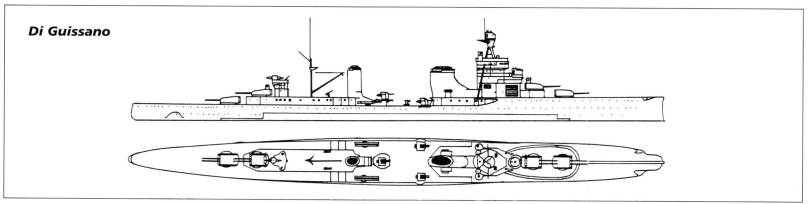

Di Guissano

projectile weight was 47.5kg, and the magazine stowage was 1,800 shell, 1,960 cartridge. The secondary armament was concentrated between the funnels in three twin mountings, one each to port and starboard and one on the superstructure, sited on the centreline. The guns were the 3.9in (100mm)/47 OTO 1927 pattern, using a 13.8kg fixed round, 336rpg being provided. Light AA consisted of the 37mm/54 in twin mountings sited on the after end of the hangar roof and on the after superstructure, together with four twin MG mountings, two forward and aft. Only two twin banks of tubes were shipped, but a total of eight torpedoes was carried. An aircraft installation was provided, comprising an explosive Magaldi-pattern catapult on the forecastle and a large hangar in the base of the bridge structure. Two aircraft could be accommodated, initially the Cant 25 AR and later the Ro43, both floatplanes. All ships except *Di Giussano* were fitted for minelaying.

Modifications Initial experience in *Di Giussano* on trials demonstrated poor stability, so the tripod

Below: *Bartolomeo Colleoni* pre-war. (Author's Collection)

above-mentioned ship, although only for about 30min). Part of the reason for this was the policy of the Italian Government of the day, which paid a premium to the builders for every knot above the ship's contract speed. Not unnaturally, the builders took every advantage of this and often forced machinery beyond safe limits. Eventually the practice was stopped. These artificial speeds bore no resemblance to service speeds.

The main armament comprised the 6in (152.4mm)/53 Ansaldo 1926-pattern gun in four twin turrets. This gun, with its high-velocity design (900m/s), proved unsatisfactory in combination with the close barrel spacing and single cradle in an over-light gun house structure. The

main mast had to be removed and, in addition, the after rangefinder had to be landed. Sea damage incurred by high speeds in heavy seas also led to the hull having to be strengthened. In 1938/39 the 37mm were landed and replaced by four twin Breda 20mm/65; otherwise there were few modifications to this class, as all had been lost by the spring of 1942.

Service *Da Barbiano* served in the Mediterranean until the Second World War, having participated in the RItN's activities during the Spanish Civil War between 1936 and 1937. At the beginning of 1940 the ship formed part of the 3rd Cruiser Division on a temporary basis and attached to the 2nd Squadron, but from 10 June 1940 she joined the 4th Cruiser Division. She participated in the Battle of Punto Stilo/Calabria in

July, then formed part of the distant cover for a convoy from Naples to Benghazi at the end of the month. However, on 1 September she sailed to Pola for dockyard work to fit her for use as a training ship for the Naval School. After moving to Trieste for further work, the ship finally returned to service on 1 March for training duties. It was not until December 1941 that she rejoined the 4th Division as flagship for a special operation under the direct command of Supermarina, to run supplies to the troops in Libya. She sailed from Palermo on 12 December loaded with petrol and munitions, accompanied by *Di Giussano*. This sortie had become known to the British, and as a result the Italian squadron was intercepted off Cape Bon by Allied destroyers in the early hours of 13 December. *Sikh, Legion, Maori* and *Isaac*

Sweers fired torpedoes and engaged by gunfire, hitting *Da Barbiano* with three torpedoes and quickly sinking her with heavy loss of life.

Di Giussano participated in the normal peacetime activities of the fleet in the 1930s as a unit of the 2nd Squadron, including service in connection with the Spanish Civil War. On 10 June 1940 she was part of the 4th Cruiser Division, with the 1st Squadron, and was present at the battle of Punto Stilo in July. She carried out a minelaying sortie off Pantelleria in August, and for the rest of the year acted as distant cover on occasions for troop and supply convoys to North Africa. Finally, she took part in the sortie of 12 December 1940 with *Da Barbiano* and was also hit by a torpedo amidships, bursting into flames and sinking a little after her consort.

Bartolomeo Colleoni served in the Mediterranean until November 1938, when she sailed to relieve *Montecuccoli* in the Far East. She arrived off Shanghai on 23 December 1938, and remained there until the outbreak of war between Britain and France and Germany. On 1 October, having turned over command in the Far East to the sloop *Lepanto*, the cruiser returned home, where she arrived on 28 October. *Colleoni* formed the 2nd Cruiser Division in the 2nd Squadron together with *Bande Nere*. Her first operation was a minelaying sortie on 10 June 1940 in the Sicilian Channel, followed by troop convoy cover duties between Naples and Tripoli in July. On 17 July the ship sailed from Tripoli, accompanied by *Bande Nere* and bound for Leros in the Aegean, where British activities in Greek waters were causing concern. In the early hours of 17 July, while off Cape Spada (Crete), the Italian squadron, having been reported by RAF aircraft the previous day, was intercepted by the Australian cruiser *Sydney* and five destroyers. During the ensuing engagement *Colleoni* eventu-

Below: *Bartolomeo Colleoni* after the action with *Sydney*. (IWM)

ally received a shell hit in the engine room which immobilised her and left her an easy target for the destroyer's torpedoes.

Bande Nere saw service in the western Mediterranean during the Spanish Civil War and then spent a period with the Training Command under the orders of the Ministry of the Navy. At the beginning of hostilities she formed the 2nd Cruiser Division together with *Cadorna*, assigned to the 2nd Squadron. On 10 June 1940 she laid mines in the Sicilian Channel, and in July assisted in the distant cover of troop convoys to North Africa. During the sortie to Leros with *Colleoni* on 17 July she engaged *Sydney* and scored a hit before the Australian ship withdrew, low on ammunition. The Italian ship then returned to

Tripoli via Benghazi. On 4 December 1940 she joined the 4th Division under the direct command of Supermarina and took part in several troop convoy operations involving large passenger liners. These continued into 1941, when she was also involved in Italian attempts to intercept British convoy operations to Malta, as in May. In June she and *Di Guissano* laid mines north-east of Tripoli to deter British bombardment of the port. These were eventually responsible for the sinking of the cruiser *Neptune* and the destroyer *Kandahar*, as well as for damaging two more cruisers, *Penelope* and *Aurora*, in December. Further minelaying was carried out in July in the Sicilian Channel. On 20 October 1941 she assumed the role of flagship, Special Naval Force,

until 3 January 1942, when she was attached to the 8th Cruiser Division. The following month she participated in operation K7, a combined supply convoy operation from Corfu and Messina to Tripoli, together with many other units of the fleet. In March she was part of the Italian Navy's attempt to intercept the British convoy MW10 to Malta, her gunfire damaging the cruiser *Cleopatra*'s after turrets on 22 March. However, the ship was in need of repair as a result of the storms of 23 March, and on 1 April 1942 sailed from Messina for La Spezia, escorted by the destroyer *Aviere* and the torpedo boat *Libra*. Some 11 miles south-east of Stromboli Island the ship was hit by two torpedoes from the submarine *Urge*, and broke in two before sinking.

LUIGI CADORNA CLASS

Ship	Builder	Laid Down	Launched	Completed	Fate
Luigi Cadorna	CRDA, Trieste	19 Sep 30	30 Sep 31	11 Aug 33	Stricken 1 May 51
Armando Diaz	OTO, La Spezia	28 Jul 30	10 Jul 32	29 Apr 33	Lost 25 Feb 41

Displacement: 5,323 tons/5,408 tonnes* (standard); 7,113 tons/7,226 tonnes (full load).
Length: 555ft 6in/169.3m (oa); 525ft/160m (pp).
Beam: 50ft 10in/15.5m; Draught: 17ft/5.2m (mean).
Machinery: 2-shaft Parsons geared turbines; 6 Yarrow boilers.
Performance: 95,000shp=36.5kts; Bunkerage: 1,090 tons oil fuel.
Range: 2,930nm at 16kts, *Diaz*, 3,088nm at 16kts.
Protection: 20mm deck; 24mm main belt; 23mm turrets; 40mm CT.
Guns: eight 6in(4x2); six 3.9in(3x2); two 40mm (2x1); eight 13.2mm MGs (4x2).
Torpedoes: four 21in (2x2).
Aircraft: two, one catapult.
Complement: 507.
*5,406/5,492 std, 7,194/7,309 full load, *Diaz*.

Design About one year after the first class of light cruisers had been ordered, the Italian Navy programmed two new ships of similar characteristics but intended to have improved protection and stability. In the event, protection was virtually the same as that of the earlier class, but stability and hull strength were improved. Rearrangement of the aircraft installations permitted lowering of the bridge structure by a considerable amount, as the single fixed catapult was fitted on the after shelter deck, angled about red 30°, with the omission of the hangar under the bridge as in the *Da Barbiano* class. No hangar was fitted, the aircraft being stowed on trolleys on the deck. Omission of the after control position further assisted stability, as did the omission of the tumblehome so evident in the former class, this also improving habitability.

Otherwise they showed no improvement in fighting power over the earlier ships.

The main armament was altered to the newer OTO model 1929 gun in a redesigned, more spacious gunhouse, while the 100mm guns were shipped in echelon and the torpedo tubes were fitted almost abreast of the fore funnel. There was also a slight variation in the position of the 40mm guns between the two ships on their entry into service. They were fitted for minelaying and could accommodate between 84 and 138 mines, according to type.

Orders were placed for the ships on 26 October (*Cadorna*) and 29 October 1929 (*Diaz*).
Modifications The old-pattern 40mm guns were landed and four twin 20mm/65 shipped in their place. In 1943 the surviving ship, *Cadorna*, had the catapult removed and two twin 20mm/70 added, and in 1944 the torpedo tubes were also landed.
Service The early service of *Cadorna* included patrols during the Spanish Civil War, and in April 1939 the ship participated in the occupation of Albania. At the outbreak of war she was part of the 4th Cruiser Division, and on 9/10 June 1940

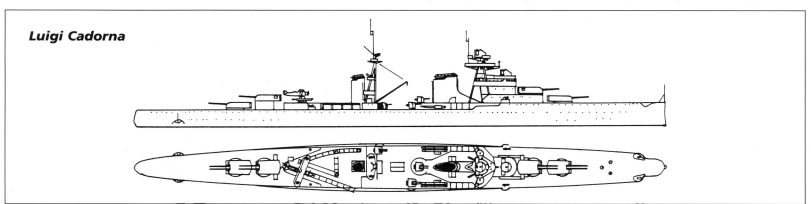

Luigi Cadorna

Above: *Luigi Cadorna* prior to the war. (Italian Navy)

Below: *Luigi Cadorna.* (Author's collection)

took part in a minelaying operation off the island of Lampedusa and the Kerkennah banks. The following month saw her at the action off Punto Stilo/Calabria, where she avoided a submarine torpedo attack and engaged enemy aircraft, as well as rendering assistance to her sister ship, which had boiler problems. As a relatively weak design, however, the ship was not the most capable, and went into reserve status from 12 February 1941. However, the supplying of the Axis army in North Africa now assumed major importance, and she returned to service to provide distant cover for the convoys to North Africa, with the occasional sortie with the fleet when attempting to intercept British convoys to Malta. In the period November/December 1941 she was herself used as a transport for petrol and munitions to Libya, making several trips to Benghazi. From January 1942 she was transferred to Pola, where she was employed in a training role. After a short refit in May/June 1943 she joined the 8th

Division on 14 June. Between 24 and 30 June she transported troops to Albania, and on 3 July was transferred to Taranto, from whence, in August, she made five minelaying sorties to lay defensive fields in the Gulf of Taranto. The armistice on 8 September found her at Taranto, but she sailed to Malta with the fleet on the 9th, where she remained until transferred to Alexandria on 14 September. After a brief stay she returned to Taranto in October, following its capture by the Allies, and for the remainder of the war was used as a transport for Allied men and materials, as well as for the repatriation of Italian troops. After

the Peace Treaty of 10 February 1947, *Cadorna* was one of the ships left to the Italian navy, but because of her age and condition she was only used as a training ship until stricken in May 1951.

Armando Diaz initially served in Mediterranean waters after completion, but between 1 September 1934 and February 1935 made a cruise to Australia and New Zealand. She served in the western Mediterranean during the Spanish Civil War, based at Palma and Melilla. As a unit of the 4th Division she was present at the action off Punto Stilo/Calabria in June 1940. In October she took part in a mission to Albania, and in

Above: *Armando Diaz* in March 1938. (Fracarroli)

December came under the direct orders of Supermarina for special duties in connection with the protection of traffic to Albania from January 1941. However, the following month an important supply convoy to Tripoli required her use for cover, in company with *Bande Nere* and destroyers. In the course of this operation the ship was torpedoed and sunk by the submarine *Upright* off the island of Kerkennah in the early hours of 25 February.

RAIMONDO MONTECUCCOLI CLASS

Ship	Builder	Laid Down	Launched	Completed	Fate
Muzio Attendolo	CRDA Trieste	10 Apr 31	9 Sep 34	7 Aug 35	Lost 4 Dec 42
Raimondo Montecuccoli	Ansaldo, Genoa	1 Oct 31	2 Aug 34	30 Jun 35	Stricken 1 Jun 64

Displacement: 7,405 tons/7,523 tonnes (standard); 8,853* tons/8,994 tonnes (full load).
Length: 597ft 9in/182.2m (oa); 545ft/166.7*m (pp).
Beam: 54ft 6in/16.6m; Draught: 18ft 4in/5.6m (mean).
Machinery: 2-shaft Belluzzo geared turbines; 6 Yarrow boilers.
Performance: 106,000shp=37kts; Bunkerage: 1,180 tons oil fuel, Attendolo 1,118 tons.
Range: 4,122nm at 18kts, Attendolo, 4,411nm.
Protection: 30mm deck; 60mm main belt; 70mm turrets; 100mm CT.
Guns: eight 6in (4x2); six 3.9in (3x2); eight 37mm (4x2); eight 13.2mm MGs (4x2).

Torpedoes: four 21in (2x2).
Aircraft: two, one catapult.
Complement: 578.
*Attendolo 8,848/8,989 full load

Design The two ships authorised under the 1930/31 programme were a continued improvement of the 'Condottieri' type begun with the *Barbiano* class of 1928. In comparison to the preceding *Cadorna* class, the new ships were some 2,000 tons larger, with increased beam and length but without any noticeable increase in

fighting power. However, one of the main benefits of this increase in displacement was better protection; 1,376 tons as opposed to the 578 tons of *Cadorna*, or 18.3 per cent of the standard displacement (8 per cent in *Cadorna*). This allowed an increase of 10mm in the main deck armour inside the inner longitudinal bulkhead, which itself was now 25mm in the way of the machinery spaces and 30mm abreast the magazines. The main vertical belt was increased to 60mm between the armoured deck and the platform deck, with 20mm plate extending up to the upper deck. 40mm transverse bulkheads closed off the ends of the armoured box. The barbettes of the main turrets were now given between 30 and 45mm, while above the upper deck they were 50mm (B and X). Also introduced in this class was the conical, armoured tower bridge structure incorporating a 100mm armoured conning position. The protective belt of 60mm was calculated

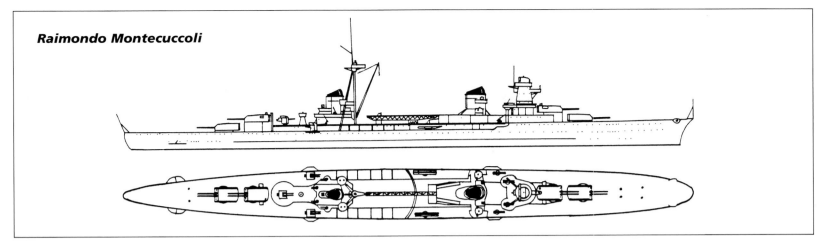

Raimondo Montecuccoli

to defeat 8in shells outside 23,000m with 25° inclination, and 6in gunfire outside 15,000m at a similar inclination.

The machinery arrangements differed little from the earlier ships, the unit layout being retained but the installed power being increased by about 11 per cent for a designed maximum speed of 37kts. However, battle-worthiness was

Below: *Muzio Attendolo* in 1942. (Fracarroli)

increased by the fact that, apart from the forward boiler room, the rest of the boilers were in individual spaces. On trials in 1935 *Montecuccoli* achieved 38.72kts on a displacement of 7,020 tons, with 126,099shp. Note that the displacement at this time was less than the standard displacement, and that the boilers were pressed 18 per cent over design.

There was little change in armament, except that the obsolete 40mm/39 was replaced by the

new 37mm/54 grouped around the bridge tower, while the four twin 13.2mm mountings were placed around the after funnel. The aircraft fittings now included a partly rotating catapult between the funnels. Ninety-six mines could be carried, and two depth-charge throwers with twelve 50kg DCs completed the armament.

Modifications *Montecuccoli* received some augmentation of the AA outfit in 1943, when the 13.2mm MGs were supplanted by twin 20mm/70

Above: *Raimondo Montecuccoli*. (Fracarolli)　　Below: *Muzio Attendolo* in 1942. (Italian Navy)

mountings to a total of twenty barrels. Later, the torpedo tubes, catapult and after rangefinders on the tripod mainmast were also landed. *Attendolo* appears to have received little or no modifications before her loss.

Service These ships were delayed in their completion by alterations to their plans, and did not enter service until the summer of 1935. Two years later, after the outbreak of the Sino-Japanese War, the Royal Italian Navy decided to send *Montecuccoli* to the Far East to protect Italian interests in the region. The cruiser sailed from Naples on 27 August 1937 and arrived in Shanghai on 15 September, where she joined the minelayer *Lepanto* and the gunboat *Carlotto*, already on station. During her period in the orient the ship made an extensive cruise to Australia between January and March 1938, as well as visits to Japan and Hong Kong. She was then ordered home, departing Shanghai on 1 November 1938 after handing over command of the Far East Squadron to *Colleoni*. After her return to Naples on 7 December the ship underwent a refit at La Spezia and then joined the 8th Cruiser Division, part of the 2nd Squadron. By the beginning of 1940 she was a unit of the 7th Cruiser Division, together with her sister and *Savoia* and *Aosta*. Her early war service included the covering of minelaying sorties, offensive sweeps, the Battle of Punto Stilo/Calabria and distant cover for troop convoys to North Africa. In

December she participated in the bombardment of Greek positions near Lukova, north of the Corfu Channel, with *Savoia* and destroyers. The following year, with other units of the 7th Division, she laid mines in a barrage off Cape Bon between 19 and 24 April 1941. In July, while forming part of the distant cover for a convoy returning from North Africa, her consort *Garibaldi* was hit by a torpedo from *Upholder*. During the course of the British Operation Mincemeat, *Montecuccoli* was part of the 8th Division which sortied from Palermo on 24 August to try and intercept the Malta convoy, but this was unsuccessful.

Later in the year a mining sortie planned in October to protect the approaches to Benghazi was cancelled, as it was believed that the British Fleet was out. Further convoy cover operations took up the remainder of the year, and the ship was present at the 1st Battle of Sirte while with the close cover force for Italian convoy M42 between 16 and 19 December 1941. This task continued into 1942. Then, in May, she and her 7th Division consort *Savoia* were transferred to Cagliari in Sardinia as one of the attempts to stop the minelayer *Welshman*'s supply runs to Malta, but a sortie on 14 May failed to find her. However, a new convoy to Malta (Harpoon) was sailed by the British from Gibraltar on 12 June and duly reported. The two cruisers sailed from Cagliari on 13 June to intercept it, but, having been reported

by submarines, put into Palermo, from where they sailed again on 14 June to attack the convoy off Pantelleria. The Italian squadron, which included five destroyers, came into action south of the island on the forenoon of the following day and broke up the convoy, sinking the destroyer *Bedouin* and damaging *Partridge*. *Montecuccoli* was badly damaged by 9th USAAF bombers while lying at Naples on 4 December 1942, and remained under repair until the middle of 1943. After the invasion of Sicily by the Allies, *Montecuccoli* and *Savoia* sailed from La Spezia on 4 August 1943 to bombard Allied positions at Palermo, but this was aborted when their position became known. Following the Italian capitulation, *Montecuccoli* sailed for Malta and then to Alexandria, being used as a fast transport ship for the remainder of the war. Postwar she was refitted as a training ship, radar being added and the AA outfit modernised. In October 1953–June 1954 the ship was further modernised when B turret was removed, and she continued in the training role until the end of the 1963 training season.

Attendolo joined the 2nd Squadron on 6 September 1935 after completion of trials, as a unit of the 7th Cruiser Division. She was still serving with this formation at the outbreak of war in 1940. Her early operations also included convoy cover and the Battle of Punto Stilo. From 3 December 1940 she was assigned to protect traffic on the Albanian routes, and from 9 December was part of the 8th Cruiser Division. On 23 December she transported three battalions of Camicia Nera to Valona. Her attachment to the 8th Division lasted until 19 February 1941, when she returned to the 7th Division. She participated in several minelaying sorties in the first half of 1941, notably off Cape Bon in April, off Tripoli in June and in the Sicilian narrows in July. She was again reassigned to the 8th Division on 21 August, being deployed with Italian forces in connection with attempts to intercept the British Operation Mincemeat between 22 and 28 of that month, and the British Operation Halberd the next month. After another return to the 7th Division on 3 October, further convoy cover work continued in November and December, including the First Battle of Sirte. Her activities in 1942 followed the same pattern, but in the course of operations against the Pedestal convoy in August she was hit by a torpedo from *Unbroken* off the Aeolian islands, which blew off the bows. However, she was able to make Messina, where makeshift repairs were effected before transferring to Naples for full repairs from 6 September. Unfortunately the ship was destroyed by bombs during the same USAAF raid which damaged her sister, on 4 December 1942, before repair was complete. After salvage postwar, consideration was given to rebuilding her as a modern AA cruiser, but the idea was abandoned.

DUCA D'AOSTA CLASS

Ship	Builder	Laid Down	Launched	Completed	Fate
Emanuele Filiberto Duca D'Aosta	OTO, Livorno	29 Oct 32	22 Apr 34	13 Jul 35	To USSR 2 Mar 49
Eugenio Di Savoia	Ansaldo, Genoa	6 Jul 33	16 Mar 35	16 Jan 36	To Greece 1 Jul 51

Displacement: 8,317* tons/8,450 tonnes (standard); 10,374* tons/10,539 tonnes (full load).
Length: 613ft 2in/186.9m (oa); 563ft 6in/171.8m (pp).
Beam: 57ft 6in/17.5m; Draught: 20ft/6.1m (mean).
Machinery: 2-shaft Parsons (*Savoia* Belluzzo) geared turbines; 6 Yarrow Boilers.
Performance: 110,000shp=36.5kts; Bunkerage: 1,460 tons oil fuel.
Range: 3,900nm at 14kt.
Protection: 35mm deck; 70mm main belt; 90mm turrets; 100mm CT.
Guns: eight 6in (4x2); six 3.9in (3x2); eight 37mm (4x2); twelve 13.2mm MGs (6x2).
Torpedoes: six 21in (2x3).
Aircraft: two, One catapult.
Complement: 578.
Savoia 8,610/8,747 std, 10,672/10,842 full load.

Design This class was yet another extension of the Condottieri concept, and represented another step on the way to producing a good, all-round cruiser design. It was desired to improve the stability and protection once more, while keeping the armament similar to that of the previous class. In this new design the weight of armour was increased to 1,700 tons, which represented an increase of 29 per cent over that of the *Montecuccoli*.

In turn, this weight of armour represented 22 per cent of the standard displacement. The new design had the side belt armour increased by 10mm, and the main armour by 5mm inside the longitudinal protective bulkhead and by 10mm outboard of it. Similar increases were made in other armoured areas. Hull dimensions and therefore displacement were also increased, which in turn necessitated an increase in the installed power to 110,000shp, but with little weight penalty.

The machinery arrangements differed slightly from those of *Montecuccoli* in that the boilers were now arranged in two units of three, each boiler in its own space. Each funnel now served three boilers. The armament was almost identical to that of the preceding class, except that the torpedo outfit was increased to two triple banks and the ships could carry 100 to 185 mines according to type. One Gagnotto catapult was fitted between the funnels, and the normal aircraft complement was two Ro43 floatplanes, although three could be carried if required. In appearance the ships were distinguished from their predecessors only by the funnels, which were of equal size.

On trials, following the normal Italian practice of light displacement and forced machinery, the impressive speeds of 37.35Kts (*d'Aosta*) and 37.33kts (*Savoia*) were achieved.

Modifications In common with most Italian cruisers, few modifications of any note were undertaken on these ships other than the removal of the torpedo tubes in 1943, together with the catapult and aircraft installations, and the replacement of the 13.2mm MG by twin 20mm /70 twin mountings to make the light AA up to twelve 20mm.

After the armistice *d'Aosta* received an extension to the foremast for an Allied radar set, to

Above: *Duca D'Aosta*. (MPL)

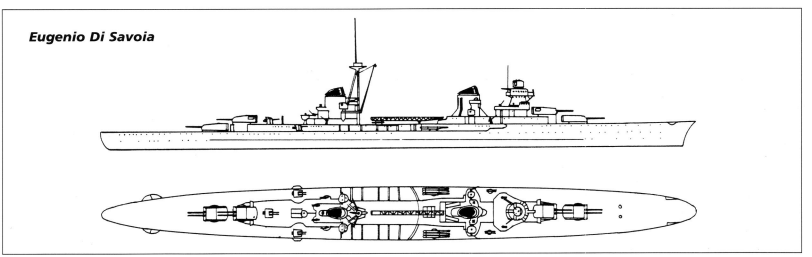

Eugenio Di Savoia

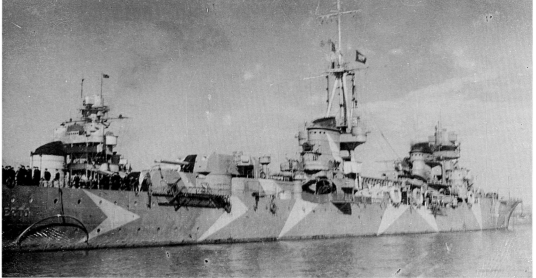

March 1939. Both ships were units of the 2nd Squadron in early 1940. They participated in the action off Punto Stilo during 6-10 July, covered North Africa convoy traffic in mid-summer and, at the end of October, sailed with the fleet in an attempt to intercept British cruisers en route to Malta. *Savoia* took part in a bombardment of Greek positions north of Corfu on 18 December 1940.

Between 16 February and 28 November 1941 *d'Aosta* served with the 8th Division, her sister remaining with the 7th. In 1941 both cruisers participated in minelaying sorties off Cape Bon during 19-24 April, following this with further convoy cover operations in April and May. Minelaying was once again the order of the day in June, fields being laid off Tripoli on the 3rd. *d'Aosta* was minelaying again in the Sicilian Channel on 28 June and on 7 July, when fields S2, S31 and S32 were laid. Another operation in October by both ships with other units was, however, abandoned on the receipt of information that the British fleet was out. At the end of November *d'Aosta* participated in further convoy cover duties in a complex operation to run ships from several ports in Italy to Benghazi. Between 13 and 19 December the running of two further convoys, M41 and M42, coincided with a British attempt to run a convoy to Malta, leading to the

equip her for service in the Central Atlantic, where she was employed on anti-blockade-runner duties.

Service *D'Aosta* joined the 7th Cruiser Division on her entry into service, and in 1938 was despatched on a circumnavigation of the globe together with her division-mate, *Savoia*. The latter had seen service in Spanish waters in 1936/37 as part of Italy's intervention in the Civil War. The

ships sailed from Naples on 5 November 1938 for a cruise intended to last until 25 July 1939. However, logistical and political problems in the worsening international climate of 1939 forced a curtailment, and the second part of the cruise, to the USA, Japan, the East Indies, Singapore and India, was abandoned. Thus, having visited ports in Brazil, Argentina, Chile and in the Caribbean, the Squadron arrived back in La Spezia on 3

inconclusive First Battle of Sirte, at which *d'Aosta* was present. She also covered convoy T18 to Tripoli in January 1942, while the following month she joined the abortive sortie against another Malta convoy.

In March 1942 *Savoia* returned to convoy cover duties when convoy V5 was successfully run to and from Tripoli, and between 2 and 4 April three more convoys were covered without incident by this ship. In June the British Harpoon/Vigorous operations saw both ships sail to intercept, *d'Aosta* with the 8th Division and her sister with the 7th, the latter going into action against British destroyers and cruisers on the occasion of the loss of *Bedouin*. An attempt to intercept Operation Pedestal in August, in which

Savoia was to have participated, had to be abandoned as a result of the lack of air escort. Towards the end of the year, however, both ships were at Naples when the USAAF raid took place on 4 December. *Savoia* was damaged and had to be transferred to Castellamare di Stabia for repairs which lasted several months. There was little notable activity in 1943, mainly owing to oil shortages, but after the invasion of Sicily both ships, on separate occasions at the beginning of August, made abortive attempts to bombard the Allied positions around Palermo.

After the surrender *Savoia* seems not to have been actively employed following her sailing to Malta and subsequent transfer to Suez on 16 September. Her duties were mainly of a training

nature, and from April 1944 she was inactive.

On the other hand, *d'Aosta* was given a minor refit and sailed from Taranto for the Atlantic, together with *Abruzzi* and *Garibaldi*, on 27 October 1943 for anti-blockade-breaker duties based on Freetown. She made seven patrols in the Central and South Atlantic between 19 November 1943 and 15 February 1944 before returning to Italy on 3 April. Thereafter she was employed only on transport duties.

Laid up postwar, *d'Aosta* was transferred to the USSR on 2 March 1949 as *Z15*, later being renamed *Stalingrad* and then *Kerch*. Her sister was also transferred to an Allied power under the Peace Treaty of 10 February 1947, becoming the Greek *Helli* on 1 July 1951.

ABRUZZI CLASS

Ship	Builder	Laid Down	Launched	Completed	Fate
Luigi Di Savoia Duca Degli Abruzzi	OTO, La Spezia	28 Dec 33	21 Apr 36	1 Dec 37	Stricken 1 Apr 61
Giuseppe Garibaldi	CRDA, Trieste	Dec 33	21 Apr 36	20 Dec 37	Stricken Jan 72

Displacement: 9,440 tons/9,591* tonnes (standard); 11,575 tons/11,760* tonnes (full load)
Length: 613ft 6in/187m (oa); 563ft 6in/171.8m (pp).
Beam: 62ft/18.9m; Draught: 20ft/6.1m (mean).
Machinery: 2-shaft Parsons geared turbines; 8 Yarrow boilers.
Performance: 100,000shp=34kts; Bunkerage: 1,650 tons oil fuel.
Range: 4,125nm at 12.7kts.
Protection: 40mm deck; 100mm main belt; 135mm turrets; 140mm CT.
Guns: ten 6in (2x2), (3x2); eight 3.9in (4x2); eight 37mm (4x2); eight 13.2mm MGs (4x2).
Torpedoes: six 21in (2x3).

Aircraft: four, two catapults.
Complement: 640.
Garibaldi 9,050/9,194 std, 11,117/11,294 full load.

Design This group, the final version of the 'Condottieri' type to see service, represented a considerable advance on the previous *d'Aosta*. They differed from that ship in many ways, although the outward appearance was not too dissimilar. Beam was increased by over 1m, while the length remained unaltered. The installed power was marginally reduced, so speed fell in consequence. Internally, however, there were many important

changes, particularly regarding the protective scheme, for with this class the Italian navy decided to compromise the speed for better protection. Not only was the weight of armour increased by 24 per cent compared with *d'Aosta*, now totalling some 2,131 tons, but it was also distributed in a different manner. The main vertical belt on the ship's side was dispensed with and replaced by a thin (30mm) strake designed to decap or trigger the fuses of incoming shells before they reached the main protection itself. This comprised an inclined 100mm belt projecting inboard from the ship's side at 12° (midships area) from main deck level, with a concave curved form to its lower portion so as to rejoin the ship's side below the waterline at the lower edge of the outer belt. Apart from an 8mm backing plate to this 100mm armour, there was no inboard splinter bulkhead like that of *d'Aosta*. Other improvements in armour included 15mm splinter protection to the upper deck, extension of the main armoured deck to full beam and increas-

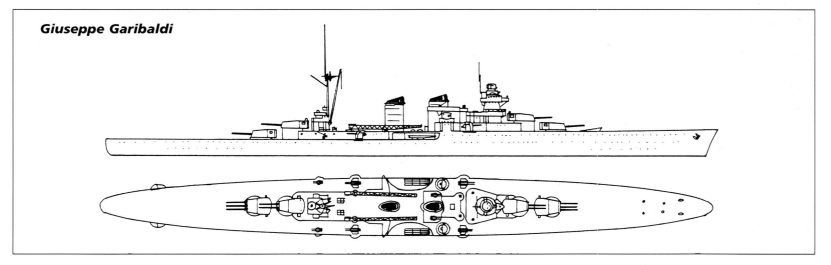

Giuseppe Garibaldi

ing it to 40mm, and considerably thickened barbette and turret armour. Funnel uptakes were also given protection, and the overall scheme was considered to be equal to that of the heavy cruiser *Zara* (q.v.), being designed to defeat 8in shell-fire.

These ships also introduced a new model 6in gun, the 152mm/55 1934 Ansaldo pattern, designed to remedy the shortcomings of the 53 calibre weapon of the earlier classes. In addition, the number of guns was increased by the expedient of shipping triple turrets in A and Y positions. These guns had shorter range, but benefited from lower muzzle velocity and from being mounted in separate cradles. The secondary armament was also augmented by an extra twin mounting, all on the upper deck and more widely dispersed than formerly. Only one main armament director was fitted, at the top of the tower, fitted with a 5m rangefinder, the secondary position being suppressed. For AA and secondary battery control, two directors with 3m rangefinders were fitted abreast the forefunnel.

The other main alteration to the previous concepts was in the main propulsion. There were now eight boilers, paired in four separate spaces. The two forward spaces were separated by the starboard engine room, that for the port shaft being aft of the after boiler room. This layout resulted in a reduction of about 100 tons in weight, and a reduction in the length of machinery spaces to the advantage of the protection scheme. The designed power was reduced to 100,000shp, with a consequent reduction in maximum speed, but in service this was of no importance.

Modifications These two ships had very long careers, and in later life received considerable modification, but in the period covered by this

volume the only alterations of note were the replacement of the 13.2mm MG by five twin 20mm/54 and, in 1943, the addition of a German-pattern radar set in *Abruzzi*. In 1945 both catapults and tubes were landed and British-pattern radar was fitted.

Service *Abruzzi* ran her trials in 1937, when, on the very light displacement of 8,635 tons, she achieved 34.78kts with 103,991shp. Her sister reached 33.62kts on the much more realistic displacement of 10,281 tons early the following year, with 104,030shp. Both ships formed the 8th Division of the 1st Squadron on completion and took part in some of the last operations of the Spanish Civil War from 1938. After a visit to Portugal in 1939, *Abruzzi* became flagship of the 8th Division.

On 7 April 1939 *Garibaldi* carried troops to Durazzo for the occupation of Albania. During the Second World War the two ships operated together frequently, beginning with a sortie against British units on 12 to 14 June 1940, followed by the engagement of Punto Stilo/Calabria the next month. Towards the end of September they were involved in another abortive attempt to intercept British cruisers on passage from Alexandria to Malta with troops, Operation Hats. However, from December until mid-March 1941 the Division was based in the Adriatic to cover convoy traffic involved in the Italian invasion of Greece, when they also carried out shore bombardment, as on 4 March off Pikerasi, when they in turn were attacked by British aircraft. On 26 March 1941 both ships sailed from Brindisi for a raid into Cretan waters, supported by the battleships. The 8th Division was to push into the Aegean Sea as far as the extreme eastern longitude of Crete and then return to join *Vittorio Veneto* off Navarino. This

Above: *Duca degli Abruzzi*. (Author's collection)
Left: *Duca degli Abruzzi* in wartime colours. (Italian Navy)

operation led eventually to the Battle of Cape Matapan and the loss of the cruisers of the 1st Division, but by that time the 8th Division had been detached to Brindisi and did not come into action. In May there was considerable activity by both ships in covering North African convoy traffic, and during the course of these duties *Abruzzi* was missed by torpedoes from *Urge*. *Garibaldi* sailed to intercept Operation Substance between 23/24 July 1941, and on 27 July left Palermo with *Montecuccoli* and destroyers to cover another Libyan convoy. The following evening she was torpedoed by *Upholder* off Marettimo, being badly damaged in the region of A turret and taking in 700 tons of water. She managed to return to Palermo and was then transferred to Naples for repairs, which lasted four months. Her sister deployed in response to the British Mincemeat and Halberd operations of August and September, but in November, after the return to service of her consort, sailed with *Garibaldi* for another convoy cover task. In the course of this, in the early hours of 22 November,

Abruzzi had her stern blown off by a torpedo from a Malta-based aircraft a little over an hour after the torpedoing of *Trieste* (q.v.), and was brought into Messina only with difficulty. Her sister escaped damage despite heavy bombing attacks, and continued to be employed for cover duties for the remainder of the year and into 1942. The Division was moved to Taranto from Messina early in 1942 because of bombing raids. Rejoined by *Abruzzi*, the 8th Division was now transferred to Navarino in July 1942 to intercept British attacks on the convoy routes to Cyrenaica, but shortages of fuel, bombing attacks, and the lack of enemy naval activity forced their withdrawal to Taranto in November. After the invasion of Sicily *Garibaldi* was sailed from Genoa on 6 August with *d'Aosta* and destroyers to attack in the Palermo area, but off La Spezia the formation was attacked by the submarine *Simoom*, which aimed her torpedoes at the cruisers but hit and sank the destroyer *Gioberti*. Both ships surrendered at Malta in September 1943 and were subsequently transferred to

the Central Atlantic, based on Freetown for anti-blockade-runner duties. *Abruzzi* sailed from Taranto on 27 October 1943 with *d'Aosta*, and arrived at Freetown on 13 November. During the period in the South/central Atlantic, the ship made five patrols between 29 November 1943 and 7 February 1944. She finally left Freetown on 16 April and arrived in Taranto on 29 April, being employed thereafter on transport and training duties. Postwar she had a long career in the reformed Italian Navy, and was not finally stricken until 1 May 1961. *Garibaldi*, although also ordered to the Atlantic, did not sail until 7 March 1944, and by the time she arrived at Freetown, on 18 March, the task for which they had been intended was finished. She therefore sailed for Italy, together with *d'Aosta*, almost immediately after her arrival, on 25 March 1944. For the remainder of the war she was employed on subsidiary duties, and postwar was converted into a guided-missile cruiser, serving even longer than her sister.

CIANO CLASS

Ship	Builder	Laid Down	Launched	Completed	Fate
Constanzo Ciano	n/k		not laid		
Venezia (ex Luigi Rizzo)	n/k		not laid		

Displacement: 9,615 tons/9,768 tonnes (standard); 11,810 tons/11,998 tonnes (full load).
Length: 620ft/189m (oa).
Beam: 62ft 4in/19.0m; Draught: 22ft 6in/6.9m (mean).
Machinery: 2-shaft geared turbines; 8 boilers.
Performance: 115,000shp=33kts; Bunkerage: n/k.
Range: n/k.
Protection: 45mm deck; 100mm main belt; 140mm turrets; 140mm CT.
Guns: ten 6in (2x3, 2x2); eight 90mm (8x1); eight 37mm (4x2); twelve 20mm (6x2).
Torpedoes: six 21in (2x3).
Aircraft: four, one(?) catapult.
Complement: n/k.

Design Some two years after the entry into service of the *Abruzzi* class, the Navy projected two further cruisers of similar design but naturally incorporating more improvements. This resulted in another modification of the 'Condottieri' type, now far removed from its original concept. While the main armament was not altered, the secondary armament was to include the new 90mm/50 Ansaldo 1938-pattern gun in lieu of the 100mm weapons, in eight single stabilised mountings, four on each beam as in *Littorio*. Some consideration had also been given to the new 65mm (2.55in)/64 Ansaldo-Terni weapon, a medium-range gun developed jointly, but this encountered serious design problems and was obviously not going to be ready for service for several years. For the first time also, the 20mm/65 gun was fitted as designed. The other change was to increase the number of aircraft carried to four.

The protective scheme was very similar to that of the previous class, except that the deck armour was increased to 45mm and the turrets to 140mm.

Hull dimensions were increased yet again for an intended standard displacement of 9,800 tons, rising to 10,000 tons if necessary. Speed was not to be less than 33kts on a designed power of about 115,000shp.

Before the design was finalised, however, the Second World War had broken out, and although Italy was not involved in 1939, she was under pressure from her Axis partner to become so. The Navy therefore had other priorities, such as destroyers and torpedo boats, and as a result plans for the new cruisers were abandoned in 1940. No orders were placed for these ships, although they did receive names.

CAPITANI ROMANI CLASS

Ship	Builder	Laid Down	Launched	Completed	Fate
Attilio Regolo	OTO, Livorno	28 Sep 39	28 Aug 40	14 May 42	Stricken 24 Jul 48
Ciao Mario	OTO, Livorno	28 Sep 39	17 Aug 41		Scuttled 1944
Claudio Druso	CdT, Riva Trigoso	27 Sep 39			BU on slip 1941
Claudio Tiberio	OTO, Livorno	16 Sep 40			BU on slip 1941
Cornelio Silla	Ansaldo, Genoa	12 Oct 39	28 Jun 41		Lost Jul 44
Giulio Germanico	Castellamare	11 May 40	20 Jul 41		Lost 11 Sep 43
Ottaviano Augusto	CNR, Ancona	23 Sep 39	31 May 42		Lost 1 Nov 43
Paolo Emilio	Ansaldo, Genoa	12 Oct 39			BU on slip 1941
Pompeo Magno	CNR, Ancona	23 Sep 39	28 Aug 41	24 Jun 43	Training ship 1964
Scipione Africano	OTO, Livorno	28 Sep 39	12 Jan 41	23 Apr 43	Stricken 9 Aug 48
Ulpio Triano	CNR, Palermo	23 Sep 39	30 Nov 42		Lost 3 Jan 43
Vipsanio Agrippa	CdT, Riva Trigoso	Oct 39			BU on slip 1941

Displacement: 3,686 tons/3,745 tonnes (standard); 5,334 tons/5,419 tonnes (full load).
Length: 468ft 9in/142.9m (oa); 455ft/138.7m (pp).
Beam: 47ft 3in/14.4m; Draught: 16ft/4.87m (mean).
Machinery: 2-shaft Belluzzo SR geared turbines, (Parsons in Ancona ships); 4 Thornycroft boilers.
Performance: 110,000shp=40kts; Bunkerage: 1,400 tons oil fuel.
Range: 3,000nm at 25kts.
Protection: virtually nil.
Guns: eight 5.3in (4x2); eight 37mm (4x2); eight 20mm (4x2).
Torpedoes: eight 21in (2x4).
Aircraft: nil.
Complement: 418.

Design The construction of the large 2,610-tonne *Le Fantasque* and 2,930-tonne *Mogador* classes of contre-torpilleur by France from the beginning of the 1930s led to some concern on the part of their rival in the Mediterranean, Italy, whose own large destroyers or scouts (esploratori) the *Navigatori* class would be inferior to the new French ships. Design work was started in 1937 with the designation 'esploratori oceanici' (Ocean Scouts), to differentiate the from the *Navigatori* design. The initial concept showed a 3,400-ton standard displacement ship armed with eight 135mm (5.3in) guns, six 65mm AA, eight 533mm (21.7in) torpedo tubes and one aircraft (without catapult or hangar). Protection was minimal, limited to some vital parts, and the maximum speed was to be about 41kts. However, by the late 1930s the capabilities of reconnaissance aircraft had improved considerably, rendering the need for pure scouting vessels somewhat superfluous. In

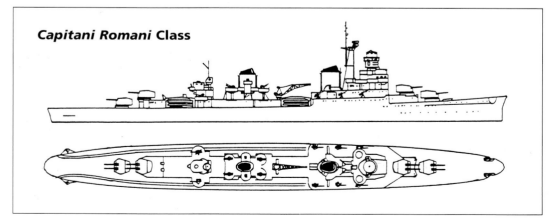

Capitani Romani Class

Above: *Scipione Africano.* (Courtesy M. Twardowski)

consequence, the smaller scouts were reclassified as destroyers and the larger ones as light cruisers; hence the inclusion of this class in this volume. It soon became evident that the protection would have to be dispensed with if the armament and speed were not to be compromised, but even so the displacement exceeded the intended figure by 350 tons, despite the extensive use of light alloy in the superstructure. The aircraft was deleted to save weight, as was the 65mm/64 AA gun, which had encountered development problems. Four twin 37mm/54 were substituted.

The mixed longitudinally and transversely constructed hull was of flush-decked design, the machinery being installed on the unit principle with the forward set driving the starboard shaft. Both units were completely independent of one another, but the boilers could be cross-connected

Below: *Attilio Regolo.* (Fracarroli)

in an emergency. The turbines were of Parsons design in the ships built at Ancona, and of Belluzzo type in the remainder. On trials, all completed units achieved 41kts. Some splinter protection only was provided to the bridge areas.

The main armament was a new gun, the 135mm (5.3in)/45 Ansaldo or OTO 1938 pattern, which fired separate ammunition having a projectile weight of 32.7kg. It had a maximum range of 19,600m (21,430yd) and a maximum elevation of 45° in the twin mounting, and was therefore capable only of barrage fire in the AA role. This gun was not widely used, the only other user at sea being the modernised *Andrea Doria* class, in which it was carried in triple turrets. In the *Capitani Romani* class the gunhouses carried 20mm maximum armour to the faces and 6mm on top. The only other notable point about the armament was the torpedo tubes, the quadruple mountings carrying the tubes two over two, rather than using the normal side-by-side arrangement. In service, however, these mountings gave considerable prob-

lems. Four reserve torpedoes were carried. The ships were equipped for minelaying, and accommodated up to 130 mines, according to type.

Fire control was by means of two main directors, one forward and one aft, and three 4m rangefinders. 160 rpg were carried for the 135mm guns.

Modifications EC3 radar sets were fitted in *Regolo* and *Africano*; otherwise there were no modifications of any consequence in their short wartime careers.

Service Only three of the twelve units ordered finally entered service with the Royal Italian Navy before the surrender in September 1943. Barely two months after her entry into service, *Regolo* left Palermo with six destroyers to lay a mine barrage south of Sicily. On the return the cruiser was torpedoed by *Unruffled* and lost the bows as far back as A turret. Another attack by *United* missed, and the ship was brought into Palermo on 9 November. After extensive repairs she joined the 8th Division in mid-1943, but saw little further active service before the surrender. After the sinking of *Roma* while the fleet was en route to Malta, *Regolo* made for the Balearic Islands with some destroyers, where they were interned at Port Mahon until they sailed for Algiers on 19 January 1945, after which she joined the 7th Division at Taranto. She carried out three missions before the end of the war, and was then laid up at La Spezia. As a result of the Peace treaty she was allocated to France as *R4*, and arrived at Toulon on 1 August 1948. Renamed *Chateaurenault*, she served with the French navy until laid up at Brest on 13 September 1962, but was not scrapped until several years later, having been used as a school hulk in the meantime. During her service under the French flag she underwent considerable modification and modernisation.

Of the other units which were launched but not completed, the hull of *Ciao Mario* was turned over to the Navy as a fuel storage depot, and was scuttled by the Germans some time in 1944. *Cornelio Silla* was captured incomplete at Genoa by the Germans. She was about 84 per cent complete, but her machinery had been removed for installation in the aircraft carrier *Aquila*, under construction at Genoa. Severely damaged in an Allied bombing raid in July 1944, she subsequently foundered. The wreck was broken up postwar.

Giulio Germanico was 94 per cent complete at the time of the surrender, with part of her crew aboard. They were initially able to repel German attempts to seize her, but finally surrendered on 11 September. No further work was carried out on the ship, and she was scuttled by the retreating German forces on 28 September 1944. After salvage in 1947 she was designated *FV2* and renamed *San Marco* from 1 March 1951 and refitted for service. Recommissioned on 1 January 1955, *San Marco* remained active until 1971, having undergone many modifications in the intervening period.

Ottaviano Augusto was also virtually complete at the time of the surrender and was seized by the Germans at Ancona, only to be sunk by Allied bombers on 1 November 1943. She was refloated postwar and broken up.

Ulpio Triano was attacked by British charioteers on 3 January 1943 while fitting out at Palermo, and broke in two and sank.

The four other ships were never launched, having been suspended in July 1940 when Italy entered the war. They were subsequently cancelled and broken up on the slips. The machinery of *Paolo Emilio* was used for the carrier *Aquila*.

Pompeo Magno was in service for only three months before the Armistice, and in that time carried out ten war missions. On 9 September 1943 the ship sailed from Taranto bound for Malta, where she remained with the 8th Squadron until her return to Taranto on 4 October to be assigned to the light cruiser squadron. She spent the remainder of the war on training, transport and repatriation duties, finally being despatched to La Spezia, where she was paid off and stricken on 1 May 1948, receiving the designation *FV1*. In March 1951 she was renamed *San Giorgio*, rebuilt for further service with the Italian Navy, and served as a destroyer leader from 1 July 1955.

Scipione Africano was stationed at La Spezia and Genoa after her entry into service, but was ordered to Taranto after the Allied invasion of Sicily in the expectation that the Straits of Messina would soon become impassable, sailing on 15 July 1943. While on passage she encountered four British MTBs in the Straits on the 17th,

and in a confused night action sank *MTB 316* and damaged another before reaching Taranto safely on 18 July. She was then employed to lay out defensive mine barrages between 4 and 17 August off Calabria and in the Gulf of Taranto. On the surrender, the ship was ordered to Pescara to embark Marshal Badoglio, then escorted the corvette *Baionetta*, with the King embarked, to Brindisi. Then, on the 29th, she carried Marshal Badoglio to Malta for the surrender ceremony. From 1 February 1944 she was part of the 7th Squadron, being used primarily for transport and training tasks. Stricken at La Spezia on 9 August 1948, *Scipione Africano* was sailed to Toulon and designated *S7* on 15 August 1948, when transferred to France. In French service the ship was renamed *Guichen*. She was modernised several times during her career under the tricolour, until she was laid up at Landevennec on 1 April 1961. After being condemned on 1 June 1976, she was given the designation *Q554*, finally being broken up at the end of the 1970s.

ETNA CLASS

Ship	Builder	Laid Down	Launched	Completed	Fate
Etna (ex Taksin)	CRDA Trieste	23 Sep 39	28 May 42		Captured 10 Sep 43
Vesuvio (ex Naresuan)	CRDA Trieste	26 Aug 39	6 Aug 41		Captured 10 Sep 43

Displacement: 6,000 tons/6,096 tonnes (standard).
Length: 507ft 7in/153.80m (oa); 462ft 9in/141.0m (pp).
Beam: 47ft 6in/14.47m; Draught: 19ft 6in/5.95m (mean).
Machinery: 2-Shaft Parsons SR geared turbines; 3 Boilers.
Performance: 40,000shp=28kts; Bunkerage: n/k.
Range: n/k.
Protection: 20-35mm deck; 60mm main belt.

Guns: six 5.3in (3x2); ten 65mm (10x1); twenty 20mm (10x2).
Torpedoes: nil.
Aircraft: nil.
Complement: 580.

Design These two ships were originally ordered by Siam (q.v., now Thailand) as light cruisers armed

with six 6in guns, at the same time as that government contracted for nine torpedo boats with Italian yards. Construction continued on Siamese account as late as December 1941, after which work stopped when the Italian government decided to requisition the ships. By this time it had become apparent to the Italians that the running of supply convoys to North Africa was becoming a very hazardous business, and that the losses of both merchantmen and escorts were prohibitive. Attacks by Malta-based aircraft were a major hazard, and to help counter this threat it was decided to convert these two relatively small cruisers into AA ships also capable of carrying cargoes. The redesign took some time, and it was not until 6

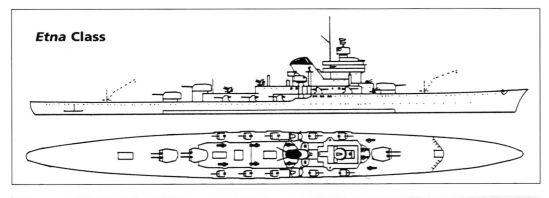

Etna Class

Above: The incomplete hulls of *Vesuvio* and *Etna* in Zaule Bay, Trieste, in October 1947.

The former 152mm (6in) armament and both the aircraft installation and torpedo outfit were dispensed with, and a completely new armament was projected. This was to comprise the 135mm (5.3in)/45 1938 pattern gun as intended for the *Capitani Romani* class, in three twin mountings disposed in the same manner as intended by the Siamese. They were also to receive a heavy secondary AA outfit using the new 65mm/64 1939-pattern gun, which had already run into development problems. Five single mountings were carried on each beam, controlled by a director sided port and starboard, abreast the funnel. Ten RM35 stabilised twin Breda 20mm mountings completed the armament. Four of these were disposed on the now redundant catapult deck, four more on or forward of the bridge, and the remaining two on the funnel, which had been remodelled and sharply swept back to clear the redesigned bridge. Provision was made for a German-pattern radar set.

Troop accommodation was incorporated into a deckhouse built on half of the former catapult deck and on the main deck forward. Below decks, forward and aft of the gun turrets, were incorporated four cargo holds which totalled about 600m³. These were served by collapsible crane derricks.

Shortages of materials and difficulties with the new armament meant that progress on these ships was very slow, with the result that, at the time of the armistice, *Etna* was about 53 per cent complete in respect of the hull and machinery and about 65 per cent regarding the armament and control equipment. For *Vesuvio* the figures were similar. Both vessels were sabotaged before they fell into German hands, but the Germans were apparently able to continue their construction for a short while before they were finally abandoned. Scuttled in shallow water at Trieste by the Germans, they were refloated and scrapped after the war's end.

August 1942 that the yards received new construction data and the ships were renamed after volcanoes; not traditional Italian cruiser names.

As both ships had been put afloat before being taken over, the redesign had to be limited mainly to the superstructure and armament, although the displacement was increased to about 6,000 tons, with a consequent increase in draught. The installed power was reduced by about 11 per cent, leading to a 2kt drop in speed.

Little change could be made to the protective scheme, which consisted of a 60mm vertical side belt and a deck of 35mm between the 20mm splinterproof longitudinal bulkheads. Outboard of these the deck was reduced to 20mm.

The main machinery consisted of a twin-shaft geared turbine installation with three boilers, each in their own spaces. Two were forward of the forward turbine room and one aft of it, laid out on the unit principle.

TRENTO CLASS

Ship	Builder	Laid Down	Launched	Completed	Fate
Trento	OTO, Livorno	8 Feb 25	4 Oct 27	3 Apr 29	Lost 15 Jun 42
Trieste	STT, Trieste	22 Jun 25	24 Oct 26	21 Dec 28	Lost 10 Apr 43

Displacement: 10,511 tons/10,679* tonnes (standard); 13,548 tons/13,764* tonnes (full load).
Length: 646ft 2in/196.96m (oa); 623ft 4in/190.0m (pp).
Beam: 67ft 6in/20.6m; Draught: 22ft 4in/6.8m (mean).
Machinery: 4-shaft Parsons SR geared turbines; 12 Yarrow boilers.
Performance: 150,000shp=35kts; Bunkerage: 2,120 tons oil fuel.

Range: 4,160nm at 16kts.
Protection: 50mm max deck; 70mm main belt; 100mm turrets; 100mm max CT.
Guns: eight 8in (4x2); sixteen 3.9in (8x2); four 40mm (4x1); four 12.7mm MGs.
Torpedoes: eight 21in (2x4).
Aircraft: three, one catapult.

Complement: 723.
* 10,505/10,673 std, 13,540/13,756 full load, *Trieste*.

Design These ships represented the first Italian attempt to construct a cruiser to the Washington Treaty requirements and, like all of their contemporaries, the Italian naval architects found it difficult to reconcile demands from the fleet with the restrictions of the Treaty. Italy had built few cruisers, and the design worked out for the new project represented quite a radical departure for the Royal Italian Navy. In the absence of the former enemy, Austria-Hungary, the natural foe was the French, who had begun their first Washington ship in October 1924. The Italians, like the other naval

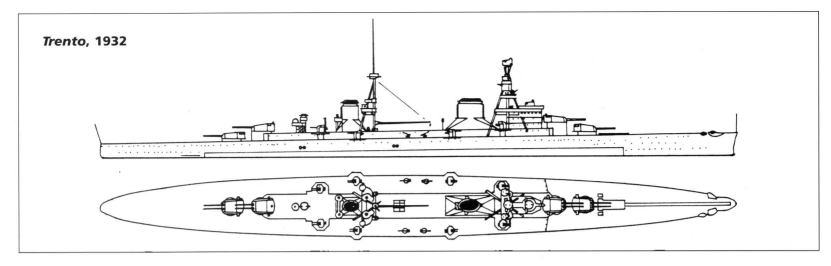

Trento, 1932

powers, could accept nothing but the maximum of eight 8in guns allowed by the treaty, and were forced to look elsewhere for the inevitable weight savings. Given that the scale of protection, while modest, was nevertheless in excess of current British and French designs, and speed was high, the inevitable conclusion was that either strength or truth was compromised, and probably a little of both. Certainly both were at least 500 tons over the limit, while a comparison with the County class of the Royal Navy shows the hull to be about 1,200 tons lighter.

The main armament comprised the 203.2mm (8in)/50 Ansaldo 1924 model, firing a 276lb (125kg) shell and mounted in twin turrets, two forward and two aft. However, these proved somewhat less than satisfactory, as the guns were too close together and dispersion was high. Ele-

vation (45°) training and hoists were electric, and 162rpg were provided. The secondary armament consisted of 16 100mm/47 OTO 1924 guns, developed from a 1920 Skoda weapon. These were in twin mountings, four on the upper deck and four on the superstructure deck. Light AA was merely four of the elderly 40mm/39 Vickers pom-poms. A heavy torpedo battery consisting of four fixed twin mountings was fitted on the main deck, abreast the after control position and between the funnels.

There was provision for three aircraft, with a hangar for two forward of and below A turret and a Gagnotto compressed-air catapult on the forecastle. Initial aircraft equipment was the Piaggio P6 floatplane, later supplanted at various times by the Macchi M41, CRDA Cant 25 and, finally, the Ro43.

The main machinery was disposed on the unit system, with four boilers in the two forward boiler spaces (served by the forward funnel) and four in the after space, separated by the engine room for the wing turbines. The inner shafts were driven from the after engine room. On trials in 1929, *Trento* achieved 35.6kts for 8hr with 146,975shp on a displacement of 11,203 tons.

The protective scheme consisted of a 50mm deck which extended from the hangar back to the after magazines, and continued aft of this as 20mm (horizontal) and 30m (sloped) to protect the steering gear. There was no horizontal protection forward. Vertical protection included a 70mm belt which extended from the armoured deck to the top of the double bottom spaces

Below: *Trieste* as completed. (Author's collection)

Above: *Trento* in 1936. (Author's collection)

between the forward and after magazine spaces, which were closed off by transverse armoured bulkheads 40 to 60mm thick. Turret armour was 100mm. In total, 888 tons was allocated to protection.

Two ships were authorised under the 1923/24 Programme, and orders were placed with the yards on 18 and 11 April 1924, the vessels receiving the names *Trento* and *Trieste* respectively. These names honoured two of the newly acquired ex-Austria-Hungary towns, which practice was to apply to all the heavy cruiser names.

Modifications As completed, both ships were virtually identical, distinguished only by the slight difference in the positioning of the forward 100mm mountings, those of *Trento* being closer to the bow by a couple of metres, and the 40mm mountings. *Trento* had hers on the upper deck amidships, while her sister had hers also on the

upper deck, but between the forward and after 8in turrets. In 1937 the after pair of 100mm mountings were landed and replaced by two twin 37mm/54 and a second pair were added abreast the after funnel. At the same time the after rangefinders on the main mast were removed. In a later refit, the 40mm and 12.7mm guns were replaced by four twin 13.2mm. At the end of 1939 the funnels were given large clinker screens. During the war some augmentation of the light AA was carried out, *Trento* receiving four 20mm/60 in 1942 and *Trieste* six by 1943.

Service *Trento* served as flagship of the Cruiser Squadron after commissioning, and in June of that year began a cruise to South America which extended until 10 October. At the beginning of 1932 she was despatched to the Far East with a small squadron as a result of the turmoil in China, where Italian interests were to be looked after. This deployment lasted until 30 June, when the cruiser returned to La Spezia.

Mediterranean duties followed until the outbreak of the Second World War, at which time the ship was flagship of the 3rd Division of the 2nd Squadron. She served with the 3rd Division, usually based at Messina, for the remainder of her career. Her first operations were in support of the minelaying craft in the Sicilian Narrows in June 1940. She later participated in the action off Punto Stilo/Calabria in July, and in several of the RItN attempts to intercept British forces in the central Mediterranean. During the Fleet Air Arm raid on Taranto on 12 November 1940 the ship was hit by a bomb which did not explode. She was present at the engagement off Cape Teulada in late November, when she engaged British cruisers, and at the Battle of Cape Matapan in March 1941. During the course of that year she covered the Axis supply convoys to North Africa, with mixed fortunes. The annihilation of one such convoy in November 1941 led to the dismissal of the Flag

Officer, 3rd Squadron. This task continued into 1942, with the 1st and 2nd Battles of Sirte intervening. As a result of a severe storm raging on the latter occasion, the cruiser was badly damaged by the heavy seas. In mid-June 1942 she sailed with the fleet to attack a westbound Malta convoy from Alexandria, but on the morning of 15 June was hit by a torpedo launched by a Beaufort of 217 Sqn RAF, which struck a boiler room and immobilised the ship. Some 4hr later she was found by the submarine *Umbra* and torpedoed. The hit exploded a magazine and the ship sank rapidly.

Trieste also joined the Cruiser Squadron at completion, but in October 1929 became flagship of the 1st Naval Squadron. She subsequently joined the 3rd Division, and from 18 June 1935 was Flagship of the division until 15 February 1938. During the war she saw action in most of the same operations as her sister, but on 21 November 1941 she was hit by a torpedo from the submarine *Utmost* and badly damaged, reaching Messina with difficulty. She was out of action until mid-1942, then returned to the tasks of intercepting Allied Malta convoys and covering Axis convoys to North Africa. On 10 April 1943 the ship was sunk in a USAAF B-24 bombing raid while lying in La Maddalena, Sardinia.

Above: *Trento* at Taranto before modernisation. (Italian Navy)
Left: *Trento* in 1940/41. (Fracarroli)

Left: *Trieste*. (Author's collection)

ZARA CLASS

Ship	Builder	Laid Down	Launched	Completed	Fate
Fiume	STT, Trieste	29 Apr 29	27 Apr 30	23 Nov 31	Lost 29 Mar 41
Gorizia	OTO, Livorno	17 Mar 30	28 Dec 30	23 Dec 31	Lost 26 Jun 44
Pola	OTO, Livorno	17 Mar 31	5 Dec 31	21 Dec 32	Lost 29 Mar 41
Zara	OTO, La Spezia	4 Jul 29	27 Apr 30	20 Oct 31	Lost 29 Mar 41

Displacement: 11,680 tons/11,866* tonnes (standard); 14,300 tons/14,528* tonnes (full load).

Length: 557ft 2in/182.8m (oa); 547ft 6in/179.6m (pp).

Beam: 62ft 10in/20.62m; Draught: 20ft 4in/6.2m (mean).

Machinery: 2-Shaft Parsons SR geared turbines; 8 Thornycroft boilers.

Performance: 95,000shp=32kts; Bunkerage: 2,400 tons oil fuel**.

Range: 4,480nm (F); 5,230nm (P); 5,361nm (Z) & 5,434nm (G) at 16kts.

Protection: 70mm max deck; 150mm max main belt; 150mm max turrets; 150mm max CT.

Guns: eight 8in (4x2); sixteen 3.9in (8x2); four to six 40mm (4/6x1); eight 13.2mm MGs.

Torpedoes: nil.

Aircraft: two, one catapult.

Complement: 841.

*Figures for Zara, individual ships varied: 11,326/11,507 & 13,944/14,167(F); 11,712/11,899 & 14,330/14,559 (G); 11,545/11,729 & 14,133/14,359 (P).

**2,350 (G); 2,320 (P)

Design While the cruisers of the *Trento* class were fast and well armed, they were very weakly protected and could not be considered as the nucleus for the future Italian fleet in the absence of an effective battleship force. There had been a move to design a 15,000-ton cruiser to fill this gap, but this was not possible because of treaty restrictions. As a result, the Royal Italian Navy decided to base a new design on the *Trento*, but with speed sacrificed to improve protection. Initially the sketch design proposed the same armament as *Trento*, but with vertical protection 200mm thick and a service speed of 32kts, all on a displacement of 10,000 tons. Not suprisingly, this proved an impossible task. At least 12,000 tons were needed and Italy, like the other sea powers, was forced into compromise. Any reduction in armament or speed was, however, unacceptable, leaving only the protection to be adjusted. In consequence the vertical belt was reduced to 150mm, but, despite all the weight saving measures adopted, including abandoning the flush-decked hull of *Trento*, the standard displacement could not be reduced below 11,500 tons at best, and *Gorizia* turned out at 11,900 tons. The hull, with its forecastle design, showed a weight saving of 28 per cent over that of *Trento*, while the adoption of a twin-shaft machinery layout similar to that installed in the light cruisers enabled a reduction of some 39 per cent in machinery weight. These savings were put into the protective scheme, which allowed about 1,500 tons for this purpose, in contrast to the *Trento*, which had only 888 tons.

The side armour belt of 150mm tapered to 100mm at its lower edge and, at the upper, joined the horizontal deck protection, which was

Below: *Fiume.* (Fracarroli)

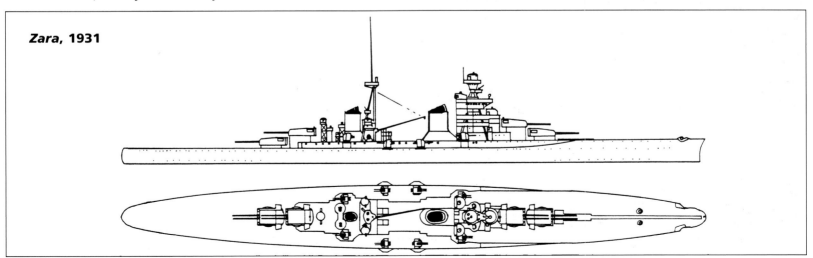

Zara, 1931

70mm (c.f. *Trento*, 50mm). In addition there was an upper armoured deck with 20mm splinter protection. The side protection was carried forward and aft as far as the magazine spaces, these being closed off by transverse bulkheads which were 120mm thick at their upper portions and 90mm below the waterline. Above the side belt the hull was given a strake of 30mm armour up to the upper deck. Barbette armour was doubled to 150mm, and was reduced by only 10mm between decks. Conning tower protection was also increased in line with the barbette protection. In view of this level of protection, these ships were initially regarded by the Italians as armoured cruisers until they were reclassified as heavy cruisers as defined by the Washington Treaty.

The machinery was arranged on the unit principle, with eight Thornycroft-pattern (except *Fiume*, with Yarrow-type) three-drum boilers and two Parsons turbine sets, the latter built by OTO. Each boiler was in its own space, the forward pair sided port and starboard ahead of the forward turbine room, which drove the starboard shaft. To port of the forward turbine room was No.3 boiler room and an auxiliary machinery space, while abaft the engine room were four more boilers, also paired abreast. The after (port) turbine space was a reflection of the forward space, with a boiler room and auxiliary space abreast of it. The machinery was considerably advanced for Italian practice of the time, with 95,000shp on only two shafts. The trials of the first three ships were run under the old conditions, the builders employing

every ruse to boost performance, and *Zara* was first tried without main turrets and guns aboard! In this condition she attained 34.2kts with 118,000shp on 10,800 tons displacement. Her fastest result was 35.23kts on 10,776 tons with 120,690shp. *Fiume* turned in the lowest result, 32.95kts on 11,110 tons and 121,266shp. *Pola*, which was tried after the practice of forcing the machinery had been stopped, gave 34.2kts on 11,005 tons with 106,560shp. Under service conditions, however, the maximum sea speed was about 29kts. Bunker capacity varied in each ship and resulted in different radii of action.

The main armament for these ships differed from that of the *Trentos* in that it was the 203mm Ansaldo/53 cal M1927 weapon in M1927 turrets with electric elevation and training. These guns

Above: *Gorizia.* (MPL)

Below: *Pola* in 1938. (Fracarroli)

were improved versions of the 50cal weapons fitted in the earlier heavy cruisers, with a higher working pressure and muzzle velocity. However, they suffered from the same problems in that they were mounted close together in a common cradle.

Apart from the now-standard Heavy cruiser armament of eight 8in guns, these ships were also fitted with sixteen 100mm (3.9in) OTO 47cal in twin mountings, with 85° elevation, four on the main deck amidships and four on the forecastle deck abreast the forward and aft superstructures. These guns were developed from an elderly Skoda-pattern weapon. The light armament comprised only the outdated Vickers 40mm pom-pom and machine-calibre weapons as designed, although initially neither *Zara* nor *Fiume* were equipped with 40mm guns, and the exact outfit varied from ship to ship. The aircraft installation was similar to that of *Trento*, with a hangar capable of stowing two aeroplanes forward of and below A turret and a Gagnotto compressed-air catapult on the forecastle. The aircraft initially carried was the Piaggio P6, which was replaced by a succession of other designs such as the Macchi M41, Cant 25AR, CMASA MF6 and, finally, the Ro43.

No torpedo armament was fitted in these ships.

Two ships were authorised under the 1928/29 programme (*Zara* and *Fiume*), one, *Gorizia*, in the 1929/30 programme and the last, *Pola*, under the 1930/31 programme. Like the *Trento* class, these ships were all named for towns or provinces ceded by Austria-Hungary after the end of the First World War. *Fiume* was ordered on 15 September 1928, *Zara* on 27 September the same year, *Gorizia* on 16 October 1929, and *Pola* in 1930.

Modifications Although not a modification, *Pola* was completed with a larger bridge structure which faired into the funnel, which, like the after funnel, was larger than those of her sisters. In addition, the forecastle did not have the fluting so

evident on the other ships. *Zara* and *Fiume* were difficult to differentiate, but *Gorizia* had slightly different funnels.

All ships had the after 5m rangefinder removed in 1936 and replaced by a twin 37mm mounting. Towards the end of 1937 the after pair of 3.9in guns were removed and replaced by two twin 37mm/54 Breda guns, while in 1939 a 4m base rangefinder was fitted in the position of the former 5m unit and the 37mm outfit altered again by replacing the old 40mm guns and 12.7mm MG by a similar number of 37mm and 13.2mm MG. Both 3m rangefinders on the foremast were also landed. Thus the light AA at the outbreak of war comprised eight 37mm and eight 13.2mm MG. Relatively early loss prevented any further modifications to three-quarters of the class, except for two 120mm/12 star-shell guns abreast the forward superstructure, but in 1942 the survivor, *Gorizia*, had these replaced by two twin 37mm/54. In 1943 this ship had the 13.2mm MGs replaced by a total of fourteen 20mm/65 in six twin and two single mountings.

Service Because of the obsolescence of the Italian battleships in this period, and their unavailability owing to modernisation, these ships were the most powerful available to the navy at this time. As a result *Zara* became flagship of the 1st Squadron from 1 September 1933 until 15 September 1937, when *Cavour* re-entered service. *Fiume*, *Gorizia* and *Pola* participated in the Italian Navy's activities in Spanish waters 1936/37, and in April 1939 *Fiume* and *Zara* took part in the operations against Albania. *Gorizia* joined the 2nd Division on completion, but transferred to the 1st Cruiser Division on 31 December 1934, becoming flagship on 3 June 1935. She became a private ship once more on 17 May 1937, when the flag was shifted to *Fiume*. This ship was the divisional flagship until 12 January 1940, but *Zara* briefly assumed the position between 1 September 1938 and 15 November 1938, and then again from 13 January 1940 until the loss of the Division. *Pola*, on the other hand, became flagship of the 2nd Squadron by the outbreak of the war, after serving the prewar period in the 1st Cruiser Division of the 1st Squadron. Her first operation was the covering of a minelaying sortie off Lampedusa on 10/11 June. A few days later she sailed again, this time with the 3rd Cruiser Division to attempt to intercept British forces heading for Tobruk. All three of her sisters (1st Cruiser Division) also put to sea, but no contact was made on this occasion. Later that month the 1st Division sailed to support a raid by the 7th Cruiser Division and destroyers against French shipping in the Western Mediterranean. In July all four ships participated in the Battle of Punto Stilo/Calabria, *Pola* as flagship of the 2nd Squadron. During the summer period

the ships were also used to cover convoys to North Africa.

By September all of the class were with the 1st Cruiser Division during further attempts to intercept British naval movements between Alexandria and Malta. *Zara* was under repair at the time of the engagement off Cape Teulada on 27 November 1940, but her sisters joined action with British forces carrying out Operation Collar, when *Berwick* received shell damage. However, on 15 December the division came under air attack while lying at Naples and *Pola* was hit by a bomb in No.3 boiler room, which flooded three compartments and caused her to list. She was under repair for some months.

In March 1941 Supermarina planned an offensive sweep into the eastern Mediterranean with battleships and cruisers, both to the north and south of Crete. As a result of intelligence and reconnaissance reports the Italian intentions became known to the British, and the action known as the Battle of Cape Matapan took place. When *Pola* was hit by a torpedo from a British naval aircraft on the evening of 28 March it had important consequences, for the hit flooded the forward engine room and both centre boiler rooms, totally immobilising the ship. To support the casualty, the Italian Flagship detailed her sisters *Zara* and *Fiume* to stand by her. The Italian ships had no radar, and these two were caught by surprise shortly afterwards by the battleships *Warspite*, *Valiant* and *Barham*, whose 15in gunfire at short range literally blew them apart. *Pola*, still adrift, was found in the dark by destroyers and sunk by torpedoes from *Jervis* and *Nubian*. Two destroyers, *Alfieri* and *Carducci*, were also sunk that night.

The survivor, *Gorizia*, sailed with the 3rd Division to intercept the Mincemeat and Halberd operations of August and September 1941, as well as performing the normal task of covering the North African convoys. On 20 November the ship was holed by over 200 bomb fragments and suffered casualties during an RAF raid on Naples, but was able to sail the same evening to cover a Benghazi-bound supply convoy. She was present at the First Battle of Sirte in December 1941, when she engaged Admiral Vian's cruisers and destroyers, and believed, incorrectly, that she had sunk a destroyer and at the second battle in

Above: *Zara* pre-war. (Italian Navy)

March 1942. On 26 May 1942 the ship received minor damage during an air raid at Messina, but was able to participate against the Harpoon/Vigorous operations in June, when the Italian fleet forced the convoy from Alexandria to turn back. She was also involved in mid-August against the Pedestal convoy. By the end of the year, however, Allied bombers and the shortage of oil fuel were disrupting Italian plans and forcing ships to move back from the southern sector around Sicily, with the 3rd Division, of which *Gorizia* was part, moving from Messina to Maddalena in December. Here she was struck by three large-calibre bombs during a raid by the USSAF on 10 April 1943 and heavily damaged. She proceeded to La Spezia on 13 April for repairs, and docked there on the following day. Here the abandoned ship was captured by the Germans on 9 September. She was finally sunk by a combined Italo-British special forces attack on 26 June 1944 at La Spezia before she could be used as a blockship by the Germans. The wreck was broken up postwar.

BOLZANO CLASS

Ship	Builder	Laid Down	Launched	Completed	Fate
Bolzano	Ansaldo, Genoa	11 Jun 30	31 Aug 32	19 Aug 33	Lost 21 Jun 44

Displacement: 10,890 tons/11,064 tonnes (standard); 13,665 tons/13,883 tonnes (full load).
Length: 646ft/196.9m (oa); 615ft 6in/187.6m (pp).
Beam: 67ft 6in/20.6m; Draught: 21ft 6in/6.6m (mean).

Machinery: 4-shaft Parsons SR geared turbines; 10 Yarrow-Ansaldo boilers.
Performance: 150,000shp=35kts; Bunkerage: 2,224 tons oil fuel.

Range: 4,432 nm at 16kts.
Protection: 50mm max deck; 70mm main belt; 100mm turrets; 100mm CT.
Guns: eight 8in (4x2); sixteen 3.9in (8x2); four 40mm (4x1); eight 13.2mm MGs (4x2).
Torpedoes: eight 21in (4x2).
Aircraft: three, one catapult.
Complement: 725.

Design Between the end of 1928 and the early months of 1929, studies were conducted with a

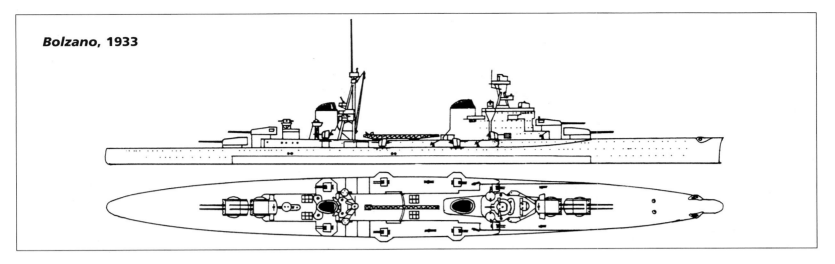

Bolzano, 1933

view to building another heavy cruiser of the *Trento* type, which was to have the same protection as the earlier ship and a speed of 36kts maximum. The major requirements were for guns as *Zara* with turret armour reduced, better compartmentalisation and the ability to survive with three adjacent spaces flooded, and hull, electrical installation and admiral's facilities as in *Zara*. Torpedo tubes were to be fitted. With this ship considerable efforts were made to keep the displacement below 10,000 tons, and various means were proposed for this, including the reduction by half of the 100mm (3.9in) guns, a 20 per cent reduction in the 8in ammunition outfit, a

reduced 100mm shell outfit, two anchors in lieu of three and with less cable for each, and other measures.

The design as finally approved had a hull similar to that of *Trento*, with a bulbous bow, and differed very little from the earlier ship as far as weight was concerned. There were, however, a number of internal differences, including a deeper double bottom and a revised arrangement of the machinery spaces. The protective scheme, too, differed little from that of *Trento* in respect of total weight, but again there were differences, particularly in the incorporation of a 20mm lower armoured deck (30mm sloped at the sides), which extended from the after transverse bulkhead to the steering gear. Forward of A turret, the elimi-

nation of the diesel dynamo space allowed the forward transverse armoured bulkhead to be brought further aft to a position immediately forward of A turret barbette. Turret fronts were 100mm, and sides and roofs 80mm. The barbette diameter of the turrets in this ship was larger than that of the M1924 mounting in *Trento* and, in consequence, the barbette armour had to be reduced from 70mm to 60mm as partial compensation.

The machinery installation, while similar in power to that of *Trento*, benefited by having boilers of increased output and therefore fewer of them. Thus each of the three forward boiler rooms had two boilers in each, abaft of which was an engine room. Aft of this space were two more

Below: *Bolzano* in 1941/42. (Italian Navy)

boiler rooms and the after engine room. No diesel dynamos were fitted in this ship, only turbo-dynamos. Despite the fitting of ten instead of twelve boilers, there was no noticeable difference in the machinery weights as compared with *Trento*.

In this ship, the 8in guns were the 203mm/53 Ansaldo M1929 pattern, which were similar but lighter versions of those in *Zara*. The intention to fit only four twin 100mm guns to save weight was not carried through, and the ship received eight mountings like her half-sisters. Of the four 40mm Vickers guns fitted as designed, two were landed shortly after the ship entered service, and the AA outfit otherwise comprised only four twin 13.2mm Breda mountings. The torpedo tubes were in fixed, paired above-water mountings. Three aircraft could be carried, two on deck and one on the catapult, but in practice no more than two were ever aboard. The aircraft installation itself was completely revised, the forecastle catapult being replaced by a trainable type fitted between the funnels, where it was much less exposed to sea conditions. A further benefit was the freeing of space forward for accommodation purposes. No hangar was fitted.

Only one ship was ordered, on 25 October 1929, from the Ansaldo yard in Genoa.

Modifications Like the other cruisers, *Bolzano* landed the after pair of 100mm mountings about 1937 to improve the close-range AA abilities, their place being taken by a pair of 37mm/54. Some changes were made to the bridge structure in 1939, and the rangefinders were removed from the tripod mast. In 1942 the 13.2mm guns were replaced by four 20mm/65 and the after rangefinder was landed.

After her torpedoing in 1942, there was a proposal to convert her into an aircraft-carrying cruiser, with a flight deck extending from the after funnel to the bows and the bridge structure completely removed, but no work was ever carried out.

Service *Bolzano* attained 36.81kts with 173,772shp on trials in 1932, but this was only achieved by the expedient of forcing the machinery by 15 per cent, aided by the fact that no armament, catapult, aircraft or control gear was aboard! She participated in the normal peacetime routine in the Mediterranean until 1939, by which time she was attached to the 3rd Cruiser Division with the 2nd Squadron. Her first operation was to cover the laying of defensive minefields on the night of 11/12 June 1940. At the engagement off Punto Stilo on 9 July she received three medium-calibre hits but was not seriously damaged, although one knocked her steering out temporar-

Right: *Bolzano* in March 1938. (Fracarroli)

ily. She sailed on various occasions in attempts to intercept British forces during the latter half of 1940, getting into action against *Renown* in November. In February 1941 she was among the units sailed in response to British movements which were to lead to the bombardment of Genoa on 9 February, but again there was no contact with the enemy. For the rest of the year she provided distant cover for the large troop liner convoys to North Africa and was involved in the Battle of Cape Matapan. In August 1941 *Bolzano* was part of the force sailed to intercept the British Operation Mincemeat, an operation to run the minelayer *Manxman* to Malta and to carry out a bombardment of the airfields in northern Sardinia. No contact was made by the main body of the Italian fleet on this occasion, and the cruiser sortie was called off. On their return to base *Bolzano* was hit by a torpedo from *Triumph* off the northern entrance to the Straits of Messina on 25 August 1941, but was able to reach Messina with the aid of tugs. She was under repair for three months, during which time she was hit by a bomb in an air raid which resulted in serious casualties. In August 1942 she participated in attempts to intercept Operation Pedestal, a supply convoy to Malta from the west, but the participation of the cruisers was cancelled. On their return the ship was torpedoed by *Unbroken* off the Aeolian Islands on 13 August. This caused fires in the magazine area, which had to be flooded, and the ship was beached near the island of Panarea. Salvage took a month, after which she was towed to Naples with difficulty for repair, which was to be carried out at La Spezia, to which port she was later transferred. At the time of the armistice she was still unrepaired, and in consequence was captured by the Germans. No further work was done, and on 21 June 1944 *Bolzano* was sunk in shallow water by a combined Anglo-Italian chariot attack which had been launched from the Italian MTB *MS74*. The wreck was broken up postwar.

BARI CLASS

Ship	Builder	Laid Down	Launched	Completed	Fate
Bari	Schichau, Danzig	1912	11 Apr 14	14 Dec 14	Lost 28 Jun 43

Displacement: 3,248 tons/3,299 tonnes (standard); 5,305 tons/ 5,389 tonnes (full load).
Length: 443ft 9in/135.3m (oa); 440ft 9in/134.3m (wl).
Beam: 44ft 6in/13.6m; Draught: 17ft 6in/5.31m (mean).
Machinery: 2-shaft Parsons turbines; 4 Yarrow boilers.
Performance: 21,000shp=24.5kts; Bunkerage: 1,300 tons oil fuel.
Range: 4,500nm at 10kts.

Protection: 40mm deck; 85mm main belt; 50mm gun shields; 75mm CT.
Guns: eight 5.9in (8x1); three 75mm (3x1).
Torpedoes: nil.
Aircraft: nil.
Complement: 439.

Design Like *Taranto*, this ship was an ex-German prize, formerly *Pillau*. However, she had a rather more chequered history than her consort, for she had originally been ordered by the Imperial Russian Navy in 1912 as *Muraviev Amurski*. At the outbreak of the First World War, before she had been completed, she was seized by Germany and completed for their account. After the German surrender she was designated *U* and allocated to Italy in 1919, being officially taken over in Cherbourg on 20 July 1920 and steamed to Italy. There was little change in her outward appearance until she was refitted for colonial service in 1934/35, when the number of boilers was reduced to four, converted to full oil firing, with the removal of the forefunnel. The armament, however, retained the

Right: *Bari* as modernised before the war. (author's collection)

Right: *Bari* in 1942. (Author's collection)

Opposite page: *Bari* in 1928. (Fracarroli)

outdated sided guns on forecastle and quarter-deck.

Modifications During the war she received additional 20mm guns on a platform around the main mast. Both main and foremasts were reduced in height and the crow's nest was lowered. In 1943 the ship was earmarked for conversion into an AA ship, to be armed with 65mm/64 (2.56in) or 90mm/50 (3.54in) guns and probably eight each of 37mm/54 and 20mm/65 or /70 weapons, but the precise number and type was never finalised.

Service This ship also formed the nucleus of the 'Special Naval Force' for the Corfu landings in October 1940, to which unit she seems to have been attached for some time, as she was involved in bombardments of the Montenegrin coast, presumably in support of anti-partisan operations in the first quarter of 1942. In November 1942 she operated in connection with the Italian Army's occupation of Corsica, when she transported troops to Bastia. In 1943 she went into yard hands for conversion into an AA ship, but before this could be completed she was sunk in a USAAF raid on Livorno on 28 June 1943. After the Italian capitulation the ship was further damaged to make to hull useless to the Germans. The wreck was broken up postwar.

TARANTO CLASS

Ship	Builder	Laid Down	Launched	Completed	Fate
Taranto	KMW, Wilhelmshaven	1910	24 Aug 11	9 Oct 12	Scuttled 9 Sep 43

Displacement: 3,184 tons/3,133 tonnes (standard); 5,100 tons/5,181 tonnes (full load).
Length: 455ft/138.7m (oa); 446ft/136.0m (wl).
Beam: 44ft 3in/13.5m; Draught: 15ft 4in/4.7m (mean).
Machinery: 2-Shaft Parsons turbines; 14 Schultz-Thornycroft boilers.
Performance: 13,000shp=21kts; Bunkerage: 1,330 tons coal, 130 tons oil fuel.
Range: 5,000nm at 12kts.
Protection: 50mm deck; 60mm main belt; 50mm gun shields; 100mm CT.
Guns: seven 5.9in (7x1); two 75mm (2x1); eight 20mm (8x1); ten 13.2 mm MGs.
Mines. 120.
Torpedoes: nil.
Aircraft: nil.
Complement: 476.

Design This elderly cruiser had been obtained by Italy from Germany following the First World War. Formerly the *Strassburg*, one of a class of four completed for the Kaisermarine in 1912, she was officially taken over on 20 July 1920. As designed, she was armed with twelve 4.1in guns, but the three survivors (*Magdeburg* had been lost) were rearmed with 6in guns. A sister ship, *Stralsund*, became the French *Mulhouse* in 1920, but she had been discarded by 1939. In Italian service she was employed on colonial duties, and in the period up to 1940 had received a number of refits and alterations. Initially the AA guns abaft the after funnel were removed and fittings to accommodate an aircraft were added, together with a handling boom on the mainmast, and the torpedo tubes were removed. In 1936/37 she underwent a major modernisation which involved the removal of the forward boiler room and the forward funnel, with small caps being added to the remaining funnels. In all probability the light AA was also improved at this time.

Modifications Probably limited to a few 20mm only.

Service *Taranto* was mostly employed on subsidiary duties such as training and escort work, but initially she assisted in the laying of defensive mine barrages in the first months of the war. In October 1940 she was allocated to the newly formed 'Special Naval Force' tasked with the landings on, and occupation of, Crete. In September 1943, while in a non-operational condition, she was scuttled by her crew at La Spezia, but was refloated again, only to be sunk once more, this time during a bombing raid on 23 October 1943. Refloated a second time, she was sunk for the third time in yet another bombing raid on 23 September 1944. The wreck was broken up postwar.

Top left: *Taranto* before modernisation. (Author's collection)
Left: *Taranto* sunk at La Spezia. (Author's collection)

Japan

TENRYU CLASS

Ship	Builder	Laid Down	Launched	Completed	Fate
Tenryu	Yokosuka Dky	17 May 17	11 Mar 18	20 Nov 19	Lost 18 Dec 1942
Tatsuta	Sasebo Dky	24 Jul 17	29 May 18	13 Mar 19	Lost 13 Mar 1944

Displacement: 3,230 tons/3,281 tonnes (standard); 3,948 tons/4,011 tonnes (full load).

Length: 468ft 11in/142.9m (oa); 440ft/134.1m (pp); 457ft 10in/139.54m (wl).

Beam: 40ft 6in/12.34m; Draught: 13ft/3.96m (mean).

Machinery: 3-shaft Curtis geared turbines; 10 Kampon boilers.

Performance: 51,000shp=33kts; Bunkerage: 150 tons coal+920 tons oil fuel.

Range: 6,000nm at 10kts.

Protection: 2in main belt; 1½in deck.

Guns: four 5.5in (4x1); one 3.1in; two 13mm MGs.

Torpedoes: six 21in (2x3).

Aircraft: nil.

Complement: 332.

Design These two ships, the first true light cruisers built by the Japanese navy, were authorised under the 1916 programme, being of a similar concept to the British *Arethusa*, designed to act as flagships to destroyer flotillas. They were given a 2½in main armour belt (1½in on 1in HT steel) which extended over just the machinery spaces from below the waterline to the upper deck, and a 1in (max.) deck. The main armament consisted of four single 5.5in, (14cm/3rd year type) guns disposed in a rather poor fashion, as the ahead and astern firepower was only one gun. Nos. 2 and 3 guns having very restricted arcs. One 3in AA was fitted on the quarterdeck and two banks of triple torpedo tubes completed the armament. This was the first use of triple tubes in the IJN.

The machinery installation was a three-shaft Brown-Curtis geared turbine layout, with ten Kampon boilers developing 51,000shp for a speed of 31kts, but 33kts was attained on trials. The boilers were in one small and two large spaces, the foremost containing two small oil-burning boilers, the centre four large oil-burners, and the aftermost two large oil-burning and two small mixed-firing boilers. The forward turbine room drove the wing shafts and the after one the centre shaft. Mitsubishi built the machinery for *Tenryu*, and Kawasaki that for her sister.

Modifications *Tenryu* was refitted between March 1927 and March 1930, when she was given a tripod foremast. *Tatsuta* was given similar treatment in 1931. Two 13mm AA were added in 1939, otherwise these elderly vessels were little altered.

Service Both ships, as the 18th Cruiser Squadron, supported the attack on Wake island at the start of the Pacific war until its surrender on 23 December. They remained as part of the 4th Fleet in the south-west Pacific in the new year, and in January supported the landings in Kavieng. During the operations around New Guinea they covered the various landings, and in May 1942 formed part of the support force for the amphibious landings at Port Moresby and Tulagi. After Midway they joined the 8th fleet, still operating as the 18th Cruiser Squadron, and landed troops to occupy Buna, New Guinea, in July. *Tatsuta* was still engaged on supporting this task when the Allies landed on Guadalcanal, and therefore only *Tenryu* was with the Japanese force which destroyed the Allied cruiser and destroyer force in the battle of Savo Island on 9 August. Later that month and into September both ships operated in support of the abortive landings at Milne Bay, until the troops had to be evacuated. During the evacuation *Tenryu* sank an Allied transport. *Tenryu* was damaged by aircraft at Rabaul on 2 October, while operating in support of the Guadalcanal campaign. This task extended until the end of the year, when, on 18 December 1942, *Tenryu* was torpedoed and sunk by the US submarine *Albacore* east of Madang. Her sister was sunk by *Sandlance* south-west of Yokosuka on 13 March 1944.

Below: *Tenryu* in 1935

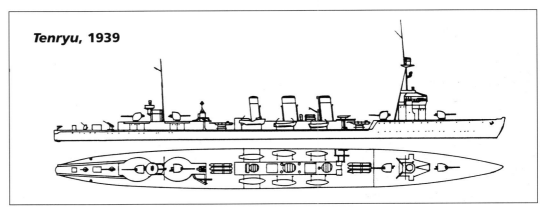

Tenryu, 1939

KUMA CLASS

Ship	Builder	Laid Down	Launched	Completed	Fate
Kuma	Sasebo Dky	29 Aug 18	14 Jul 19	31 Aug 20	Lost 11 Jan 1944
Tama	Mitsubishi (N)	10 Aug 18	10 Feb 20	29 Jan 21	Lost 25 Oct 44
Kitakami	Sasebo Dky	1 Sep 19	3 Jul 20	15 Apr 21	Stricken 10 Aug 1946
Oi	Kawasaki, Kobe	24 Nov 19	15 Jul 20	4 May 21	Lost 19 Jul 1944
Kiso	Mitsubishi (N)	10 Jun 19	14 Dec 20	3 Oct 21	Lost 13 Nov 1944

(Note: N=Nagasaki)

Displacement: 5,019 tons/5,100 tonnes (standard); 5,832 tons/5,925 tonnes (full load).
Length: 532ft/162.15m (oa); 500ft/152.4m (pp); 520ft 1in/158.5m (wl).
Beam: 46ft 6in/12.34m; **Draught:** 15ft 9in/4.80m (mean).
Machinery: 4-shaft Gihon geared turbines; 12 Kampon boilers.
Performance: 90,000shp=36kts; **Bunkerage:** 350 tons coal+700 tons oil fuel.
Range: 9,000nm at 10kts.

Protection: 2½in main belt; 1¼in deck.
Guns: seven 5.5in (7x1); two 3.1in (2x1); two 13mm MGs.
Torpedoes: eight 21in (4x2).
Aircraft: one, one catapult
Complement: 439

Design The six 'Improved *Tenryu*' type cruisers projected under the 8-4 Fleet Completion Programme of 14 July 1917 had obviously been developed from the preceding *Tenryu* class, and would have displaced about 3,500 tons. The plans had to be changed, however, because the broad details of the USN 'Scout Cruisers' (eventually the *Omaha* class) had become known by the middle of 1917. In consequence, instead of constructing three 7,200-ton scout cruisers and the six improved *Tenryu* ships, it was decided to build eight 5,500-ton cruisers and one experimental type of small cruiser. (This last was to be *Yubari*.)

These ships were thus considerably larger and more heavily armed, being the first of the 5,500-ton series of light cruisers built by the IJN. The increased displacement allowed them to act more effectively in the scout and flotilla leader roles.

The machinery was altered to a four-shaft geared turbine arrangement, with twelve boilers, of which ten were oil-fired and the other pair mixed-fired. These were disposed in four boiler rooms, the foremost of which had two small mixed-firing units. No.2 had four medium-sized oil-fired boilers, No.3 four large and No.4 two small oil-fired boilers. The increased displacement required an increase in power, now 90,000shp for a designed maximum speed of 36kts. The retention of partial coal firing is notable, and was probably due to fears of the unavailability of oil in the more remote regions of the Pacific at that period. All ships were engined by their builders except *Kitakami* and *Kuma*, which were engined by Kawasaki.

Protection was not improved.

The main armament, comprising 5.5in as in *Tenryu*, was disposed in a better but still obsolete fashion, as superfiring was not adopted for the guns. The arrangement adopted did give a better ahead concentration of fire than *Tenryu*, but again Nos. 2, 5 and 6 guns were restricted in their arcs.

Below: *Kuma* in the mid-1930s. (IWM)

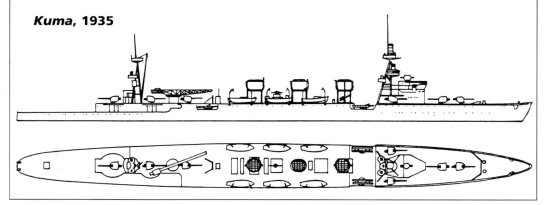

Kuma, 1935

Two 3in AA were shipped, abreast the forward funnel. The torpedo battery was increased to eight tubes, in four twin banks on the beam. As completed the tubes were for 21in torpedoes.

These ships were known as the '1917 Programme Medium Model Cruisers Nos. 1 to 8', of which *Kuma* and *Tama* were authorised under the 1917/18 estimates and *Kitakami*, *Oi* and *Kiso* under those for 1918/19.

Modifications In 1927 all were fitted to carry a Type 90 Model 2-2 seaplane. *Kuma* and *Tama* were given catapults and tripod masts in 1929/30. All received 24in torpedoes in 1940. In 1941 both *Kitakami* and *Oi* were refitted as Torpedo Cruisers, the former by Sasebo Dky and the latter by Kawasaki at Kobe, armed with 40 24in torpedoes in ten quadruple banks, five on each beam amidships. Only the four forward 5.5in guns were retained, but eight 25mm in twin mounts were added. *Kitakami* and *Oi* had the number of tubes reduced to eight in 1943 in order to carry six Daihatsu landing craft as high-speed transports. During repairs following her torpedoing by HMS/m *Templar* on 5 February 1944, *Kitakami* was converted into a *kaiten* carrier and had the damaged boiler room converted into a servicing space for *kaiten*. She could accommodate eight *kaiten*. The tubes were again increased to 24 (6 x 4), and the armament was altered to four 5in

Below: *Oi*. (MPL)

DP single mounts, ten 25mm and four 13mm. By 1945 the light AA of this ship had been increased to 69 25mm (14 x 3, 27 x 1). She had also received a radar set.

Tama and *Kiso* had No. 7 gun replaced by a twin 5in DP mounting and No. 5 gun by a 25mm mounting in July 1944, when the light AA was altered to 44 25mm and 6 13mm.

The modifications made to *Kuma* during the war are not known, but were probably limited to a few extra 25mm.

Service *Kitakami* and *Oi* served with the 9th Cruiser Squadron attached to the main body of the fleet in December 1941. In May 1942 they were attached to the Support Force for operations in the Aleutians. After Midway they became part of the 1st Fleet, and then operated in the south-west Pacific in a transport and escort role, *Kitakami* being hit and badly damaged by a torpedo from the British submarine *Templar* on 5 February 1944 and towed to Sasebo for repairs. After conversion to a *kaiten* carrier she saw no action in that role and survived to surrender in August 1945. Subsequently she was employed as a repair ship at Kagoshima for ships on repatriation duties. She was stricken on 10 August 1946 and scrapped at Nanao.

Oi was a unit of the 9th Cruiser squadron attached to the Main body of the Fleet in December 1941. In May 1942 she was involved in the

Aleutian campaign, and after Midway the 9th Cruiser Squadron was part of the 1st Fleet. In 1943/44 she was in the East Indies. She was torpedoed and sunk in the South China Sea, 570nm south of Hong Kong, by the US submarine *Flasher* on 19 July 1944.

Kuma was attached to Admiral Kondo's southern force in the Dutch East Indies in December 1941, as part of the 16th Cruiser Squadron. She operated in the south-west Pacific and was finally torpedoed and sunk by the British submarine *Tallyho* a few miles north of Penang on 11 January 1944.

Kiso and *Tama* were attached to the Northern Force in December 1941, operating as the 21st Cruiser Squadron. In May 1942 they participated in the Aleutians campaign as part of the Kiska attack force, with the 5th Fleet. After Midway they remained operating in the Kurile/Aleutian Islands, *Tama* taking part in the Battle of the Komandorski islands in March 1943, when she received superficial damage. In July both ships assisted in the evacuation of the Aleutian islands and then went to the south-west Pacific, where *Tama* was damaged on 25 October 1944 by US carrier aircraft during the Battle for Leyte Gulf, and sunk the same day by torpedoes from the US submarine *Jallao* north-east of Cape Engano. *Kiso* was sunk by US carrier aircraft west of Manila on 13 November 1944.

NAGARA CLASS

Ship	Builder	Laid Down	Launched	Completed	Fate
Nagara	Sasebo Dky	9 Sep 20	25 Apr 21	21 Apr 22	Lost 7 Aug 1944
Isuzu	Uraga Dock Co	10 Aug 20	29 Oct 21	15 Aug 23	Lost 7 Apr 45
Yura	Sasebo Dky	21 May 21	15 Feb 22	20 Mar 23	Lost 25 Oct 1942
Natori	Mitsubishi, (N)	14 Dec 20	16 Feb 22	15 Sep 22	Lost 18 Aug 1944
Kinu	Kawasaki, Kobe	17 Jan 21	29 May 22	10 Nov 22	Lost 26 Oct 1944
Abukuma	Uraga Dock	8 Dec 21	16 Mar 23	26 May 25	Lost 26 Oct 1944

Displacement: 5,088 tons/5,170 tonnes (standard); 5,832 tons/5,925 tonnes (full load).

Length: 534ft 9in/162.99m (oa); 500ft/152.4m (pp); 520ft/158.5m (wl).

Beam: 48ft 5in/14.75m; Draught: 16ft/4.87m (mean).

Machinery: 4-shaft Gihon (except Kinu, Curtis) geared turbines; 12 Kampon boilers.

Performance: 90,000shp=36kts; Bunkerage: 350 tons coal+700 tons oil fuel.

Range: 9,000nm at 10 kts.

Protection: 2½in main belt; 1¼in deck.

Guns: seven 5.5in (7x1); two 3.1in (2x1); six MGs.

Fitted for minelaying.

Torpedoes: eight 24in (4x2).

Aircraft: one, one catapult.

Complement: 438.

Design These ships were a modification of the first 5,500-ton class, having a 2ft increase in beam and a consequent improvement in stability, but no increase in gun-power. They did, however, introduce the 24in torpedo, which was not the oxygen-powered 'Long Lance', but the con-

Below: Isuzu. (MPL)

ventional wet heater type adopted in 1920/21 as the 61cm 8th year Type. This weighed about 1 ton more than the 21in type, and the increase in beam was probably due at least in part to this. The general layout was little altered, except that the bridge was raised to allow the fitting of an aircraft flying-off platform above No. 2 gun. This was later fitted with a catapult, then subsequently removed in most ships, when the catapult was repositioned between Nos. 5 and 6 guns.

They were designed to act as flagships for cruiser, destroyer and submarine squadrons as required.

Three ships were authorised under the 1919/20 estimates as part of the 8-4 Plan (Nagara, Isuzu and Natori), and a further three were authorised under the 1920/21 estimates as part of the 8-8 programme. These were initially named Suzuka, Minase and Otonase, but were renamed, respectively, Yura on 26 March 1920 and Abukuma and Kinu on 1 October 1920.

Mitsubishi constructed the machinery for Isuzu, Natori and Abukuma, and Kawasaki that for the remaining three ships.

Modifications All were given a catapult in 1927 and operated a Type 90 Model 2 floatplane.

Nagara was refitted from October 1932 to September 1933, when the catapult was moved aft and a tripod mainmast fitted to support the aircraft handling boom. The others received their refits as follows: Isuzu, May 1932-1933; Natori, July 1931 to September 1933; Kinu, November 1933-August 1934; Yura, January 1936-December 1936. The dates for Abukuma are not known, but as this ship's completion was delayed by an earthquake in September 1923, she may never have received the catapult forward.

In 1943 the armament was altered to five 5.5in (5 x 1); two 5in DP (1 x 2); twenty-two 25mm and two 13mm. The torpedo outfit was increased to sixteen 24in in four quadruple banks. The 5in replaced No. 6 gun, No. 7 being landed also. Yura had been lost before this alteration. In June 1944 the 25mm outfit was increased to 36.

Isuzu, however, was converted into an AA cruiser and flagship for a/s groups. Between May and September 1944 she had her armament changed to 6 5in DP (3 x 2; one forward, one midships and one aft) and 38 25mm (11 x 3, 5 x 1). The forward banks of tubes were also landed.

Service Nagara served with the 16th Cruiser Squadron attached to the Southern Force at the start of the Pacific war. Between December 1941 and February 1942 she participated in the landings in the Philippines, at Davao and Luzon, as well as Celebes and Bali, where she operated mainly as flagship of the 10th Destroyer Flotilla. In May 1942 she took part in the Midway campaign, and then that around Guadalcanal, which lasted until the end of the year. In the course of these operations she engaged a force of US destroyers in Iron Bottom Sound off Savo island, sinking Preston. By the latter end of 1943 she was operating in the Marshall Islands, reinforcing island garrisons, but on 4 December 1943 she was damaged by US carrier aircraft during a raid on Kwajalein and was sent to Truk for repairs. Nagara was torpedoed and sunk by USS Croaker 35nm south of Nagasaki on 7 August 1944.

Isuzu served in the south-west Pacific and participated in the Guadalcanal campaign, being damaged by US aircraft on 14 November 1942. In June 1943 she was damaged by a mine laid by USS Silversides off Kavieng, New Ireland. After repairs she served in the Marshall Islands, where she ferried troops to reinforce island garrisons, but on 4 December 1943 she was severely damaged of Rota during a US carrier aircraft attack on Kwajalein. She retired to Truk to effect temporary repairs, which lasted until 17 January 1944, after which she sailed for Yokosuka for full repairs. She arrived there on 23 January, when the decision was taken to convert her into an AA cruiser. After completion of repairs she sailed to Yokohama to

Above: *Kinu* on 20 January 1937 after modernisation. (IWM)

be rearmed, was designated an Anti-Aircraft Cruiser on 14 September, and entered service again on 5 October. She then took part in the actions in Leyte Gulf and the Battle of Cape Engano in October 1944, but was damaged by carrier aircraft again in Manila Bay on 19 November, and then hit by a torpedo from *Hake* off Corregidor on 25 November. After further repairs she was finally sunk by the US submarines *Charr* and *Gabilan* off Soembawa Island in the Java Sea on 7 April 1945, while serving as a fast transport.

Below: *Abukuma*. (Author's collection)

Natori was acting as flagship of the 5th Destroyer Flotilla with the Southern Force in December 1941. She participated in the invasion of the Philippines, covering the Luzon landings and those at Lingayen Gulf, operating from Formosa. She subsequently served in the Malayan campaign and in the Invasion of Java in February/March 1942, where she was one of the ships to defend the transports in Batan Bay, north of Serang, at the time of the attack by *Perth* and *Houston*. However, in December 1942 she was torpedoed and badly damaged by the US submarine *Tautog*, which put her out of service for some time. She was eventually torpedoed and sunk by USS *Hardhead* 250nm north-north-east of Suriago on 18 August 1944.

Yura served in the South China Sea in December 1942, where she was flagship of the 5th Submarine flotilla. Between December 1941 and March 1942 she covered the landings in Borneo and Sarawak, Malaya, Palembang, Java and Sumatra as a unit of the Malaya Force. On 1 April she was one of the Japanese squadron which sailed from Mergui in Thailand to attack Allied shipping in the Bay of Bengal. As part of the Centre Group, she and her consorts sank four ships off the Indian coast before retiring to Singapore. During the Midway operations she was a unit of the main invasion force, acting as leader of the 4th Destroyer Flotilla. Thereafter she served in the Solomon Islands and took part in the

Guadalcanal campaign, being damaged by B-17s on 25 September 1942. During the carrier air battle of Santa Cruz in October, *Yura* was badly damaged off Savo Island on the 25th by US aircraft, and was scuttled the same day by *Harusame* and *Yudachi*.

Kinu also operated in the south-west Pacific at the beginning of the war, covering the invasion of Malaya and the Dutch East Indies. She was damaged by Allied aircraft during this campaign. She was still serving in this theatre in January 1944. By May/June 1944 she was involved in the attempts to relieve the garrison at Biak, but after the Battle

of Samar, when part of Admiral Kurita's force, she was sunk 44nm south-west of Masbate by carrier aircraft of TG77.4 on 26 October.

Abukuma served as flagship of the 1st Destroyer Flotilla in December 1941, and was part of the Pearl Harbor attack force. With the 1st Carrier Air Fleet and her destroyers, she covered the landings at Rabaul in January 1942 and was part of the force which launched the carrier attack on Darwin. In March she participated in the raid into the Indian Ocean by the 1st Carrier Air Fleet, which resulted in severe British losses, including the cruisers *Cornwall* and *Dorsetshire*

(q.v.). In May she went to the Aleutians as a component of the Addu/Adak attack force. During the Battle of the Komandorski Islands, on 26 March 1943, she was involved in the action in which USS *Salt Lake City* was badly damaged. *Abukuma* was also involved in the final evacuation of the Aleutians in July/August 1943, and then went to the Philippines. She was at the actions in Leyte Gulf in October 1944, and was badly damaged by *PT 137* off Panaon Island in the Surigao Strait on the 25th, then sunk by aircraft of TG77.4 south-east of Los Negros Island the following day.

SENDAI CLASS

Ship	Builder	Laid Down	Launched	Completed	Fate
Naka	Mitsubishi, (Y)	10 Jun 22	24 Mar 25	30 Nov 25	Lost 17 Feb 1944
Sendai	Mitsubishi, (N)	16 Feb 22	30 Oct 23	29 Apr 24	Lost 2 Nov 1943
Jintsu	Kawasaki, Kobe	4 Aug 22	8 Dec 23	31 Jul 25	Lost 13 Jul 1943
Kako	Sasebo Dky	15 Feb 22	not launched		Cancelled 17 Mar 1922
(Note: Y= Yokohama)					

Displacement: 5,113 tons/5,195 tonnes (standard); 7,100 tons/7,213 tonnes (full load).
Length: 534ft 9in/163.03m (oa); 500ft/152.4m (pp); 520ft/158.53m (wl).
Beam: 48ft 5in/14.17m; Draught: 16ft 1in/4.91m (mean).
Machinery: 4-shaft Gihon (*Jintsu,* Curtis) geared turbines; 12 Kampon boilers.
Performance: 90,000shp=351/4kts; Bunkerage; 570 tons coal+1,010 tons oil fuel.
Range: 7,800nm at 10kts.
Protection: 2½in main belt; 2in deck; 2in CT.
Guns: seven 5.5in (7x1); two 3.1in (2x1); two 13mm MGs.
Mines: 80.
Torpedoes: eight 21in (4x2).
Aircraft: one, one catapult.
Complement: 450.

Design These ships were authorised under the 1921/22 estimates, and were referred to as the

1920 Programme Medium Model Cruisers. Four ships had originally been approved, two in each programme, 1920/21 and 1921/22, but all four were finally included in the 1921/22 programme. They were the last such ships ordered up to the signing of the Washington Treaty. Their design was a modification of that of *Nagara* and, in the main, involved the boiler arrangements in which only one mixed-firing boiler was fitted, in the forward boiler room, and given a separate uptake to produce a four-funnel layout. Otherwise the protective scheme, armament, gun layout and main machinery arrangements were similar to those of the preceding class. *Jintsu*, however, received Curtis turbines. *Naka* was engined by Mitsubishi, and the others by their builders. They, too, were fitted with a take-off platform over No. 2 gun, intended for the operation of a landplane, but no aircraft was operated until the later fitting of a cat-

apult, when a seaplane was added to the equipment.

Kako was cancelled on 17 March 1922, as a result of the Washington Treaty, and broken up on the slip.

Modifications In 1929 or thereabouts a catapult was added to the flying-off deck at least in *Jintsu*. In 1934 all were fitted with a catapult on the shelter between No. 6 and 7 guns, the mainmast being given tripod legs to support the aircraft handling boom. The aircraft operated was the Type 94 floatplane which was retained throughout the ships' service despite its obsolescence. The bridge was also rebuilt at this time.

By 1943 the AA capability of the ships had been improved by the replacement of the 3in guns by a twin 5in DP mounting and the increasing of the close-range outfit to 44 25mm and 6 13.2mm.

Service On the outbreak of the war in the Pacific, *Naka* was acting as flagship of the 4th Destroyer Flotilla with the Southern Force. Operating from Formosa and Indo-China, she covered the landings at Luzon and Lingayen Gulf in the Philippines during December 1941. In January 1942 she supported the landings at Tarakan and Balikpapan, and was missed with torpedoes by the Dutch submarine *K XVIII* at this time. In February and March she was involved in the invasion of Java and took part in the Battle of the Java Sea. How-

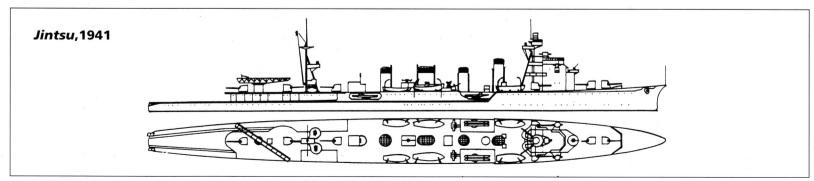

Jintsu, 1941

Above: *Jintsu* off Kure, pre-war. (IWM)   **Below:** *Jintsu*. (Author's collection)

ever, on 1 April 1942 she was torpedoed by the US submarine *Seawolf* off Christmas Island and had to be towed into Singapore in a badly damaged condition by *Natori*. After temporary repairs she was transferred to Maizuru, and did not return to service until March 1943. She returned to the south Pacific and operated in the Truk and Gilbert Islands area until sunk by aircraft from *Bunker Hill* and *Cowpens* on 17 February 1944, some 35nm west of Truk during a US raid on the former IJN main base.

Sendai was also attached to the Southern Force, acting as flagship of the 3rd Destroyer Flotilla, and participated in the invasion of Malaya. Operating in the South China Sea, she escorted troop convoys from bases in Indo-China to the coast of Malaya until early 1942. She was part of the force which engaged and sank the British destroyer *Thanet* on 27 January. In February and March she participated in the landings at Palembang and Java, then went to the Indian Ocean for operations in the Andaman islands until April. In May she was part of the Midway force, and later in the year was involved in the Guadalcanal campaign. She was reduced to a wreck in action with the US cruisers *Montpelier*, *Cleveland*, *Columbia* and *Denver* at the Battle of Empress Augusta Bay in the Solomon Islands, while attempting to attack the US bridgehead on Bougainville, and was finally sunk by gunfire from the destroyer *Ausburne*.

Naka was another of the cruisers with the Southern Force, flagship of the 2nd Destroyer Flotilla. She took part in the invasion of the

Philippines, Celebes, Ambon, Timor and Java until March 1942, when she was present at the Battle of the Java Sea. She was a unit of the invasion fleet bound for Midway in May 1942, then went to Guadalcanal, where she landed the first Japanese troops on the night of 18/19 August. Several days later she was damaged by aircraft off Guadalcanal. In 1943, when US forces landed in New Georgia, she was part of a force sent to run troops and supplies to Japanese garrisons in the Solomon Islands. On the night of 12/13 July 1943 she was sunk by the gunfire of US cruisers and destroyers at the Battle of Kolombangara.

YUBARI CLASS

Ship	Builder	Laid Down	Launched	Completed	Fate
Yubari	Sasebo Dky	5 Jun 22	5 Mar 23	31 Jul 23	Lost 28 Apr 1944

Displacement: 2,890 tons/2,936 tonnes (standard); 3,587 tons/3,644 tonnes (full load).
Length: 455ft 8in/138.9m (oa); 435ft/132.59m (pp); 447ft 10in/136.5m (wl).
Beam: 39ft 6in/12.04m; Draught: 11ft 9in/3.58m (mean).
Machinery: 3-shaft Gihon geared turbines; 8 Kampon boilers.
Performance: 57,900shp=35½kts Bunkerage: 100 tons coal+830 tons oil fuel.
Range: 5,500nm at 10kts.
Protection: 1½in main belt; 1in deck; 1in gunhouses.
Guns: six 5.5in (2x2, 2x1); one 3.1in; two 13mm MGs.
Mines: 34.
Torpedoes: four 24in (2x2).
Aircraft: nil.
Complement: 328.

Design This ship was essentially an experimental design, intended to demonstrate the feasibility of shipping a heavy armament in a small hull. It had originally been proposed under the 1917 (8-4) programme, tentatively named *Ayase*, together with eight 5,500-ton cruisers, but was not proceeded with at that time. Approval to construct such a vessel was finally given in October 1920. Construction was to be in accordance with the design principles of the 7,500-ton cruisers proposed in that year, with armour forming part of the ship's integral strength. This was illustrated by the fact that the hull structure of *Yubari* accounted for 31.3 per cent of the displacement,

Below: *Yubari.* (Author's collection)

compared with 38.3 per cent in the 5,500-ton type, without loss of hull strength.

The main side armour, 1½in thick, was a continuation of the double bottom inner plating, extending to the upper deck and inclined inwards from bottom to top by 10°. The outer skin plating was ¾in thick, and between the two were reserve oil fuel tanks. Inboard of the main belt the deck was 1in. The protected area included the machinery spaces and extended forward to cover the transmitting station. The side belt covered 58.5m or 42 per cent of the ship's length, and protection comprised 10.3 per cent of the standard displacement (4.1 per cent in the 5,500-tonners).

The main machinery was based upon the power plant of the *Minekaze* destroyers, and consisted of a three-shaft geared turbine layout, developing 57,900shp for a maximum speed of 35½kts. The boilers, of which two were still mixed-firing

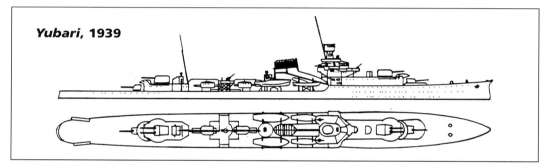

Yubari, 1939

(in the forward boiler room), were disposed in three separate spaces. Their operating temperatures and pressures were marginally different to those of the 5,500-ton cruisers. The centre boiler room was the largest space, with four boilers installed. All boilers had their uptakes trunked to a single large funnel, although the original plans had twin funnels. The turbines were installed in two engine rooms, both aft of the boiler rooms.

The main armament remained the 5.5in 3 Nendo Shiki model, but only six were shipped, in two single and two twin mountings, the latter superfiring on the former. The single guns were in hand-worked shielded mountings, while the twins were in power-operated enclosed gunhouses. Elevation was 30°, and rate of fire was 6 to 10rpm, depending on the rate of supply. One 3in HA was fitted amidships, and two 13.2mm MGs completed the gunnery outfit. She was also fitted with a pair of twin torpedo tubes disposed amidships in destroyer fashion, for 24in torpedoes. Finally, 34 mines could be carried.

Modifications The funnel was raised by 2m in 1924 to reduce the problem of smoke and fume interference on the bridge, and in 1927 the tubes were fitted with larger shields. By 1943, full load

displacement had risen to 4,448 tons and the armament had been altered to four 5.5in, the single guns being replaced by triple 25mm mountings and the light AA now comprising twelve 25mm (4 x 3) and eight 13.2mm.

Service *Yubari* actually turned out some 420 tons over designed displacement, and only attained 34.8kts on trials.

At the outbreak of war in the Pacific this ship was serving as leader of the 6th Destroyer Flotilla in the South Seas Force, with which she took part in the first attack on Wake Island in December. This was repulsed with the loss of two destroyers, but a second attack on 22/23 December was successful. In March 1942 she was in support of the landings at Lae in the Huon Gulf, New Guinea, where she was damaged by aircraft from *Yorktown* and *Enterprise* on 10 March. By July 1942 she was based at Truk with the 29th Destroyer Division, operating with the 4th Fleet. After the US landings on Guadalcanal on 7 August, *Yubari* took part in the defence of the island and, on 9 August, was present at the Battle of Savo Island, when the Allied cruisers *Canberra*, *Quincy*, *Astoria* and *Vincennes* were sunk. At the end of August she led a force to shell and occupy the islands of Nauru and Ocean Islands. In 1943 she fought in the Solomon Islands campaign and was slightly damaged during a raid on Rabaul by US carrier aircraft from TG50.3. Finally, on 27 April 1944, *Yubari* was torpedoed and sunk by the US submarine *Bluegill* off Palau, when the Japanese fleet had been forced to withdraw to those islands after Truk had become untenable.

Right: *Yubari*, showing her almost destroyer-like appearance. (Author's collection)

FURUTAKA CLASS

Ship	Builder	Laid Down	Launched	Completed	Fate
Furutaka	Mitsubishi, N	5 Dec 22	25 Feb 25	31 Mar 26	Lost 11 Oct 1942
Kako	Kawasaki, Kobe	17 Nov 22	10 Apr 25	20 Jul 26	Lost 10 Aug 1942

Displacement: 7,100 tons/7,213 tonnes (standard); 9,540 tons/9,692 tonnes (full load).
Length: 607ft 6in/185.16m (oa); 580ft/176.78m (pp); 595ft/181.35m (wl).
Beam: 54ft 2in/16.5m; Draught: 14ft 9in/4.49m (mean).
Machinery: 2-shaft Parsons (*Kako*, Curtis) geared turbines; 12 Kampon boilers.
Performance: 102,000shp=34½kts; Bunkerage: 1,400 tons oil+450 tons coal.
Range: 6,000nm at 14kts.
Protection: 3in main belt; 1⅜in deck; 2in magazines; 1in max gunhouses.
Guns: six 7.9in (6x1); four 3.1in (4x1); two 7.7mm MGs.
Torpedoes: twelve 24in (6x2 fixed).
Aircraft: one, one catapult.
Complement: 625.

Design These two ships were the 7,500-ton cruisers mentioned above in connection with *Yubari*, and were intended to outclass both the British *Hawkins* and US *Omaha* type cruisers. Despite the fact that they were armed with 8in guns, however, they were in fact pre-Washington Treaty ships, the general design having been agreed some six months or so before the signing of the Treaty.

In this design, the principles tested in *Yubari* were expanded into a more recognisable cruiser type. Particular attention was paid to the reducing of hull weight while maintaining its strength by means of an undulating sheer line and use of the side armour as longitudinal strength members. The length to beam ratio was very high at 11.7, to give the high speed demanded. Unfortunately, despite all the efforts to reduce weight, the displacement turned out nearly 11 per cent, or almost 1,000 tons, overweight, a discrepancy which would have led to the dismissal of any western constructor. The reasons for this have never been explained, but it may have been due to poor control of the weighing of equipment and fittings on installation.

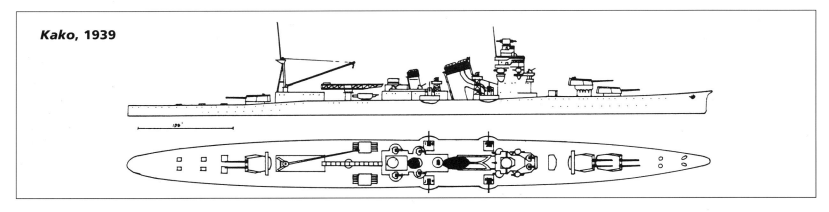

Kako, 1939

The protective scheme was not intended to offer defence against 8in shellfire, but only against 6in shells. The main belt was 3in NVNC and 13½ft deep, of which 10¾ft were designed to be above the waterline at trial displacement. However, the increased draught due to the overweight resulted in a deeper immersion of the belt, so that only 7¼ft remained above the waterline. The belt itself was 262½ft long, covering the machinery spaces. It was inclined 9° from the vertical, bottom to top, and was not backed by skin plating. Above the main belt, the side plating was 1in on ¾in HT steel. The main armoured deck abutted the top of the side armour and was 1⅜in (35mm) thick

NVNC armour, while the upper deck was given 1³⁄₁₆in (28.6mm) plus ¾in (19mm) both HT steel. Box protection was applied to the magazine spaces, with 2in sides and 1⅜in crowns. There was no armoured conning tower. The gunhouses had 1in faces and ¾in roofs. (By this time, Imperial measurements were being superseded by metric, and, in the case of armour, the two were often mixed. Some measurements expressed in millimetres were obviously direct conversions from Imperial, i.e. the 105mm (4in) side belt of the next class. This state of affairs was compounded by the current practice of also specifying plate by weight.)

The main propulsion plant was arranged on a four-shaft layout, but not on the unit principle. There were seven separate boiler rooms, each with two boilers, of which the foremost had two medium oil-fired units and the after pair two mixed-firing units. The remainder had large oil-fired units. Except for the foremost space, which was full beam in width, the remaining boiler rooms were separated from one another by midships longitudinal bulkheads, as were the four turbine rooms. Parsons turbines were fitted in *Furutaka* and Curtis units in *Kako*.

Below: *Kako* in the 1930s with her original armament. (IWM)

As designed, the main armament comprised six 8in 50cal 3 Nendo Shiki 20cm guns on single 'A' mountings in weatherproof gunhouses. This gun fired a 242½lb (110kg) projectile, and had a range of 24,700yd at 25°. Elevation and training were electric.

The secondary armament was the 3.14in (8cm) 3 Nendo Shiki HA gun in four single mountings, disposed on the beam amidships. This gun fired a 5.99kg shell, and had a maximum vertical range of 29,850ft. Light AA was restricted to a couple of 7.7mm Vickers MGs. It had originally been intended that the torpedo outfit be fitted on the centreline, as in destroyers, but, as Britain had found in the 'Countys', the height of the weather deck above the waterline presented problems. As a result the tubes were of the fixed pattern, installed on the main deck, three pairs on each beam. Two pairs were above the engine rooms and one forward of the bridge structure. They were equipped for 61cm torpedoes, and in wartime 24 torpedoes were shipped.

These ships had been designed for scouting purposes and were therefore fitted to operate aircraft, but at the time of their design there was no catapult available. Instead, a flying-off platform was fitted to the roof of No. 4 turret. In the event these platforms proved unsatisfactory, and the seaplane, when embarked, had to be handled by crane and launched from the water. A hangar was fitted abaft the funnels.

Both ships were authorised in March 1922 and ordered on 22 June that year, construction costs being covered by the funds already approved for the cancelled capital ships. Construction initially proceeded very quickly, both being launched before the end of 1922, but thereafter industrial and material problems delayed completion.

Modifications In the winter of 1926/27 the funnels were heightened and their caps altered to reduce smoke interference on the bridge and control platforms. In 1930 the flying-off platforms were removed. Reconstruction work was carried out on *Kako* in 1931/32 and on *Furutaka* in 1932/33 at the Kure yard, when the heavy AA armament was completely revised. The 3.14in

Above: *Furutaka* as completed. (MPL)

Below: *Furutaka* after reconstruction, on 9 June 1939. (IWM)

guns were landed and replaced by four 4.7in 10 Nendo Shiki 12cm guns in single shielded mountings. This gun fired a 45lb shell with a maximum vertical range of 32,800ft. A catapult was fitted between No. 4 gun and the hangar, and an E4N2 floatplane was embarked.

On 4 July 1936 *Kako* began a major reconstruction at Sasebo, while *Furutaka* was taken in hand at Kure on 1 April 1937. During this work the main armament was altered by the substitution of Mk 2 guns for the original weapons, in twin mountings with a maximum elevation of 55°. These guns were re-bored 200mm barrels from *Haguro* and *Ashigara*, as there was a shortage of No.2 guns at this time. The fire control and bridge arrangements were also modified. The secondary battery was not altered, except that the gun positions were modified. Four twin 25mm were added and two twin 13mm. The fixed tubes were landed and replaced by two quadruple 24in trainable banks with four reserve torpedoes on each beam. A heavier catapult, an aircraft handling boom and facilities for operating two E7K2 floatplanes were fitted. The ships were completely re-boilered with ten all-oil-fired units, and the machinery was overhauled. To improve stability and compensate for the weights added, the beam was increased to 55ft 7in by the addition of wider bulges. Even so, the stability was less than desired. Little else appears to have been done to these two ships before their loss in 1942.

Service Both ships entered service with the 5th Cruiser Squadron and remained with that formation until *Furutaka* reduced to reserve on 1 December 1931. She recommissioned for the 6th Cruiser Squadron on 15 November 1933, while her sister joined the same squadron on 20 May 1933 before reducing to reserve herself on 15 November that year. The major refits took place between 4 July 1936 and 27 December 1937 (*Kako*), and between 1 April 1937 and 30 April 1939 (*Furutaka*). On completion of this reconstruction, both returned to reserve. At the outbreak of the war in the Pacific, both ships formed part of the 6th Cruiser Squadron in the South Seas Force. This squadron supported the second attack on Wake Island on 23 December, then returned to Truk by January 10. Their second sortie was to cover the landings at Kavieng and on Rabaul in January/February, returning to Truk to refit on 10 February 1942. On completion, the ships sailed to support the landings at Lae, Salamaua, Buka, Bougainville, Shortlands and Manus, returning once more to Truk on 10 April. After participating in the Battle of the Coral Sea in May 1942, both left for Kure on 31 May, where they arrived on 5 June. *Kako* returned to Truk on 23 June and her sister on 4 July. During the Solomons campaign the two ships operated with the 6th Cruiser Squadron from Rabaul. However, on 10 August 1942, while returning to Kavieng after the Battle of Savo Island, *Kako* was hit by three torpedoes from the US submarine *S44* off Simberi Island and sank in five minutes. Her sister survived until October, when, during the Battle of Cape Esperance, she was shelled to a wreck by the cruisers of TF64 and then sunk by a torpedo from the destroyer *Duncan*, which was herself badly hit by *Furutaka* and Japanese destroyers, sinking in the early hours of the next day.

AOBA CLASS

Ship	Builder	Laid Down	Launched	Completed	Fate
Aoba	Mitsubishi, N	4 Feb 24	25 Sep 26	20 Sep 27	Lost 28 Jul 1945
Kinugasa	Kawasaki, Kobe	23 Jan 24	24 Oct 26	30 Sep 27	Lost 14 Nov 1942

Displacement: 7,100 tons/7,213 tonnes (standard); 8,900 tons/9,042 tonnes (full load).
Length: 607ft 6in/185.87m (oa); 585ft 3in/177.48m (pp); 602ft 4in/183.58m (wl).
Beam: 51ft 11in/15.83m; Draught: 18ft 9in/5.7m (mean).
Machinery: 4-shaft Parsons (*Kinugasa*, Curtis) geared turbines; 12 Kampon boilers.
Performance: 102,000shp=34½kts; Bunkerage: 1,800 tons oil+450 tons coal.
Range: 6,000nm at 14kts.
Protection: As *Furutaka*.
Guns: six 7.9in (3x2); four 4.7in (4x1); two 13mm MGs.
Torpedoes: twelve 24in (6x2 fixed).
Aircraft: one, one catapult.
Complement: 625.

Design The construction programme revealed on 3 July 1922 proposed the building of no fewer than 59 ships, amongst which were two 7,100-ton and four 10,000-ton cruisers. The former were to be identical to those authorised in March 1922, the *Furutaka* class, and were intended to operate as a homogenous squadron. However, as a result of pressure from the Naval Staff in the absence of the chief Constructor, Rear Admiral Hiraga Yuzuru, the design of these two new ships was modified to include twin 7.9in turrets from the outset. This, together with the decision to fit a catapult, required the complete redesign of the after superstructure. At the same time the heavy AA battery was to comprise the 4.7in 12cm 10 Nendo Shiki gun in lieu of the 3.14in weapon. Calculations indicated that the increase in displacement over that of *Furutaka* would be about 320 tons, but at that time the overweight of the earlier class was not known, and in fact the 2/3 Trial Displacement of the new class increased to as much as 9,930 tons for *Kinugasa*. As a result, stability and freeboard were seriously compromised. The main areas of growth compared with *Furutaka* were armour (+50 tons), machinery (+100 tons), armament (+100 tons) and bunkerage (+150 tons). On the other hand, 50 tons was saved in fittings.

Protection and machinery were similar to those of the earlier ships, *Kinugasa* having Curtis turbines and her sister having Parsons type.

The main armament was the 7.9in 3 Nendo Shiki 20cm in twin 'C' turrets, having a maximum elevation of 40°. The gunhouses had 1in armour to the sides, front, roof and rear. In this mounting the range was increased by 33 per cent compared with the single 'A' mounting, since the elevation was greater. However, the turrets were too heavy for the hull, and strengthening was necessary later.

Provision was made for a catapult and aircraft, but the former was not available at completion.

Otherwise the armament did not differ from that of *Furutaka*.

Both ships were ordered in June 1923 but not laid down for another six months.

Modifications *Kinugasa* was fitted with a catapult in May 1928 and her sister in January 1929, when an E2N1 floatplane was operated. This aircraft was replaced by the E4N2 floatplane at the end of 1932, which was itself superseded in 1936. In 1930 the catapult was replaced by a new type, operated by gunpowder, and the 4.7in gun mountings were replaced by a shielded electro-hydraulic mounting. Two quadruple Hotchkiss 13.2mm MGs were added on sponsons to port and starboard of the bridge in 1932.

The vessels were to have been given a major modernisation in 1937/38, but the political situation prevented this and instead they received only a limited refit. The guns were changed for the 3 Nendo Shiki 20cm No. 2 gun, which was of 20.3cm (8in) bore, and the fire control system was modified. No change was made to the 4.7in guns except for their control, but the light AA was improved by the addition of four twin 25mm around the after funnel, while the quad 13.2mm

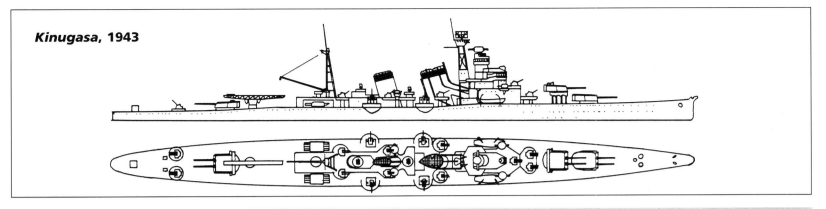

Kinugasa, 1943

Above: *Aoba* in 1935. (IWM)
Right: *Kinugasa*. (MPL)

were supplanted by a pair of twin 13.2mm MGs at the fore end of the bridge. Two quadruple banks of 24in tubes and reloads were installed, as in *Furutaka*. The catapult was replaced by one of heavier pattern and two E7K2 floatplanes were embarked.

Of the machinery, only the two mixed-firing boilers were altered to oil firing, and no complete change of boilers took place.

Some 576 tons increase in weight resulted from these alterations, and bulges were fitted to restore stability, increasing the beam by about 5½ft.

Kinugasa's early loss prevented much in the way of wartime alteration, but during repairs between December 1942 and February 1943 *Aoba* had the damaged No. 3 turret removed and temporarily replaced by a triple 25mm mount. In addition, the 13.2mm MGs at the front of the bridge were replaced by one triple 25mm.

Between August and November 1943 *Aoba* was once again under repair, when No. 3 turret was replaced and two twin 25mm fitted near the mainmast, for a total of fifteen 25mm (1 x 3, 6 x 2).

She also received an air-search radar set. However, as the main engines were not fully repaired, her maximum speed was now only 28kts.

Aoba was further modified at Singapore in July 1944, when the light AA was augmented by further four triple 25mm guns and fifteen single mountings for a total of 42 guns (5 x 3, 6 x 2, 15 x 1). She also received a surface search radar set.

At Kure in March 1945 *Aoba* was given an additional four twin 25mm around the mainmast,

now having a total of five triple and ten twin 25mm mountings.

Service From December 1927 both ships were units of the 5th Cruiser Squadron, with *Kinugasa* as flagship. On 20 May 1933 both transferred to the 6th Cruiser Squadron, and between 15 November 1935 and 30 November 1936 they served in the 7th Cruiser Squadron. Both reduced to reserve at Kure on 1 December 1936 until reconstructed at Sasebo in 1938. *Aoba*

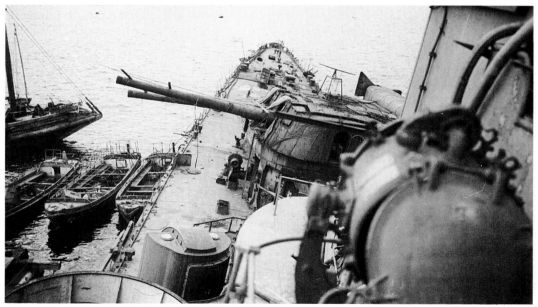

returned to service on 15 November 1940 (6th Cruiser Squadron), and her sister on 1 March 1941, both then being employed in training duties until the end of October 1941. On 30 November 1941 all four ships of the 6th Cruiser Squadron sailed from Kure for the Bonin Islands to prepare for hostilities. They supported the second attack on Wake Island from Truk in December/January 1942, then in January/February covered the landings at Rabaul and Kavieng. In March and April the landings on Lae, Salamaua, Buka, Bougainville, Shortlands and Manus were covered by the squadron before it returned to Truk on 10 April. After the Battle of the Coral Sea both cruisers returned to Kure by 5 June for refit, returning to Truk in June/July. The 6th Cruiser Squadron was now attached to the newly formed 8th Fleet, the Outer South Sea Force. Both ships were at the Battle of Savo Island at the beginning of August, when both were slightly damaged. They took part in the Guadalcanal campaign, where, during the Battle of Cape Esperance on 11 October, *Aoba* was badly damaged, being hit by about 24 6in and 8in shells. She was sent to Kure for repair, where she arrived on 22 October. During this action *Kinugasa* hit and severely damaged *Boise*, which almost sank. In November 1942 the 6th Cruiser squadron was disbanded, only *Kinugasa* remaining in the Solomon Islands. In November, after a bombardment of Henderson Field, *Kinugasa* was caught by aircraft from the carrier *Enterprise* off Rendova island on the 14th and sunk by torpedoes and bombs.

Aoba sailed for Truk after repairs, arriving on 20 February 1943, and was detached to Kavieng, where, on 3 April, she was again heavily damaged by US B-17s when two torpedoes exploded, causing serious fires in the engine room. The ship had to be beached to prevent her sinking, and was eventually salvaged to return to Kure again for repairs, where she arrived on 1 August. Repairs lasted until the end of November. Plans to convert her into either an 'aircraft cruiser' or a fast oiler did not materialise. After repair she was sent to Singapore, where she arrived on 24 December 1943. In February 1944 she became flagship of the 16th Cruiser Squadron in the south-west area, and was mainly used for transport duties in the Philippines. On 23 October 1944 *Aoba* was hit in No. 2 engine room by a torpedo from the US submarine *Bream*, and was again sent to Kure for repairs, where she arrived on 12 December. She was not repaired, but was laid up at Kure and rated a reserve ship on 28 February 1945, and later as an AA battery. On 24 April she was heavily damaged by aircraft from TF38 and settled on the bottom, then on 28 July was hit yet again by aircraft from both TF38 and the 7th USAAF, which finally wrecked her, breaking off the stern and totally flooding the ship.

MYÔKÔ CLASS

Ship	Builder	Laid Down	Launched	Completed	Fate
Myôkô	Yokosuka Dky	25 Oct 24	16 Apr 27	31 Jul 29	Scuttled 8 Jul 1946
Nachi	Kure Dky	26 Nov 24	15 Jun 27	26 Nov 28	Lost 5 Nov 1944
Haguro	Mitsubishi, N	16 Mar 25	24 Mar 28	25 Apr 29	Lost 16 May 1945
Ashigara	Kawasaki, Kobe	11 Apr 25	22 Apr 28	20 Aug 29	Lost 8 Jun 1945

Displacement: 10,000 tons/10,160 tonnes (standard); 11,663* tons/11,850 tonnes (full load).
Length: 668ft 6in/203.76m (oa); 631ft 2in/192.39m (pp); 661ft 1in/201.5m (wl).
Beam: 56ft 11in/17.34m; Draught: 19ft 4in/5.90m (mean).
Machinery: 4-shaft geared turbines; 12 Kampon boilers.
Performance: 130,000shp=35½kts; Bunkerage: 2,470 tons oil fuel
Range: 8,000nm at 14kts
Protection: 4in main belt; 3 to 4in bulkheads; 1⅜in main deck; ½ to 1in upper deck; 1in turrets: 3in barbettes.
Guns: ten 7.9in (5x2); six 4.7in (6x1); two MGs.
Torpedoes: twelve 24in (4x3 fixed)
Aircraft: two, one catapult
Complement: 773

* as designed 1924 ⅔ trials displacement. Actual figure on completion was 13,300 tons.

Design After the signing of the Washington Treaty on 6 February 1922, the Naval General Staff laid down requirements for a class of 'Treaty' cruisers armed with 20cm (7.9in) guns. The initial specification called for eight guns in twin turrets, three forward and one aft, four 4.7in AA, four sets of twin fixed tubes and protection against indirect hits from 8in shells. Speed was to be 35kts and endurance 10,000nm at 14kts on a displacement of 10,000 tons. After some discussion this was modified to increase the main armament to ten guns, to improve the anti-torpedo defence and to eliminate the torpedo armament altogether. However, as with the *Aoba* class, politics came into play and the design was further tinkered with to reinstate the torpedo outfit and to increase the heavy AA battery to six guns. Later, the torpedo armament was again increased to twelve tubes by the expedient of fitting triple tubes. All of these alterations were estimated to raise the displacement by some 500 tons.

As with the 7,100-ton cruisers, the armour belt was an integral part of the hull strength, and an undulating flush deck was again adopted. In the event these measures did not give the economy in weight expected, and the hulls came out up to 200 tons over the designed figure. Moreover, because of the increased displacement, the strength did not benefit to the extent expected either. When they were eventually completed, designed trials displacement was exceeded by nearly 1,000 tons and the original design by almost 1,500 tons.

The protective scheme included a 4in side belt, inclined outboard from bottom to top by 12°, which extended to cover both the magazines and the machinery spaces, although its height was reduced outside the latter. This belt was 123.6m

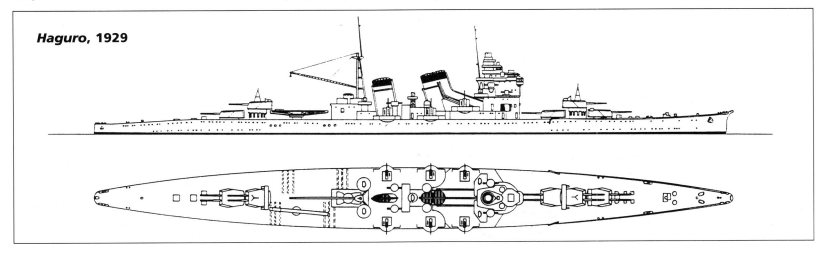

Haguro, 1929

long and 3.5m deep over its central portion, and 2m deep fore and aft of it. The ends were closed off by armoured bulkheads 3-4in thick. Anti-torpedo bulges were incorporated which extended from the lower edge of the side armour, with the internal limits formed from a curved 1¾in high-tensile-steel sandwich. The bulges were about 305ft long, with a maximum depth of a little over 8ft. The horizontal protection comprised a main armoured deck 32-35mm thick over the machinery spaces, with the boiler uptakes given 70-88.5mm armour. The upper deck head was reinforced by HT steel plates ½in to 1in thick, and the lower deck over the magazines was also given 35mm armour. Barbettes above the lower deck were 3in. Main armament turrets had only 1in splinter protection. In total, the weight of armour and protective plating was 2,032 tons, or 16.4 per cent of the trials displacement.

To attain the required 35kts, the installed shp had to be raised to 130,000, and the propulsion plant was based on the design for the cancelled *Amagi* class battlecruisers. In these cruisers the boilers, twelve in number, were fitted only for oil-firing. No superheaters were fitted. There were eight separate boiler rooms, Nos. 1 to 3 housing two units each and the remainder one each. A longitudinal bulkhead extended from the after end of No. 3 boiler room to the after bulkhead of the turbine spaces. The latter, of which there were four, each housed a turbine, the foremost powering the wing shafts. The total weight of the machinery was about 2,260 tons.

The main armament consisted of the 7.9in 50cal 3 Nendo Shiki 1Gô 20cm gun, the same as in *Furutaka*, mounted in five twin type D turrets, three forward and two aft. Elevation was 40°, and both elevation and training were electro-hydraulic. The secondary battery was the 4.7in 45cal weapon as in *Furutaka*, but increased to six guns, three on each beam, all in single mountings. There was no light AA apart from a token pair of 7.7mm MGs. The torpedo outfit was four triple fixed 24in tubes positioned above the engine rooms, with 24 reserve torpedoes in peacetime and 36 in war. The aircraft installation consisted of a single compressed-air catapult on the starboard side aft, and provision to stow two type E2N1 floatplanes.

Two ships were ordered in the spring of 1923, and two more in the autumn of 1924. The former were engined by their builders, but the latter had their machinery subcontracted to Kure (*Ashigara*) and Yokosuka (*Haguro*).

Modifications At the end of 1930, smoke problems on the bridge resulted in the raising of the fore-funnels by 6½ft. Between 1931 and 1934 all four ships had their main armament changed to the 2 Gô model, which was a true 8in (20.3cm) weapon.

Between 20 November 1934 and June 1935 all four ships underwent major modernisation when the fixed tubes, 4.7in guns, catapult and hangar were removed. Four twin shielded 5in HA mountings were shipped, together with a new HA fire control system. The torpedo outfit was altered to two quadruple 24in banks in sponsons on the upper deck, with a total of sixteen torpedoes. Two catapults were now fitted at superstructure deck level and provision was made to embark four type E8N1 floatplanes, although the normal complement was two and one E7K1 type. To restore a measure of stability, the bulges were extended by plating up vertically from the outer edge of the existing bulge almost to the upper edge of the side armour. Displacement increased by about 680 tons.

In 1936 they were all strengthened as a result of hurricane damage to the fleet. By the end of 1936 they had also received some improvement to the light AA by the addition of eight 13mm machine guns in two quadruple mountings.

Further modernisation was carried out in 1939/41, when the light AA was altered to four twin 25mm abreast the funnels and two twin 13mm on the bridge, the original quadruple 13mm and the Lewis guns being landed. New, heavier catapults were fitted and the aircraft arrangements altered to operate one E13A1 ('Jake') and two F1M2 ('Pete') floatplanes, but actual equipment varied in service. The torpedo outfit was increased to four quadruple 24in banks, fitted for the Long Lance oxygen-propelled torpedoes. Twenty-four torpedoes in all were embarked. Machinery and communications were overhauled and the rig altered. The bulges were considerably enlarged again to preserve stability.

In 1943 all received a further two twin 25mm mountings and had the 13mm mountings on the bridge replaced by another pair of twin 25mm for a total of 16 (8 x 2). Radar sets were also fitted.

Between November 1943 and January 1944 a further eight single 25mm were added. *Nachi* and *Ashigara* also received a surface search radar set.

In the autumn of 1944 the light AA was again strengthened, *Myôkô* and *Haguro* receiving four triple and sixteen single 25mm, now disposing 4 x 3, 8 x 2 and 16 x 1 25mm. The other pair had two twin and twenty single added for a total of 48 guns, (10 x 2, 28 x 1). Updated radar was fitted, but to save weight the after banks of tubes and two searchlights were landed. Total torpedo outfit was now sixteen.

Service These ships formed the 4th Cruiser Squadron from completion and served with the 2nd Fleet. All four ships reduced to reserve on 1 December 1932, and were replaced in the 4th Cruiser Squadron by the *Takao* class. In May 1933 the *Myôkô*s were transferred to the 5th Cruiser Squadron, which, however, was only active for the summer manoeuvres of 1933. From the end of 1933 they were assigned to the Guardship Squadrons at either Kure or Sasebo pending their reconstruction, which was started on 15 November 1934 (*Myôkô* and *Ashigara*) and February 1934 (*Nachi* and *Haguro*). After reconstruction the four ships again constituted the 5th Cruiser Squadron, *Ashigara* proceeding to England for the Coronation Review of 20 May 1937. They served in Chinese waters during the Sino-Japanese conflict. As war approached, *Ashigara* operated in the Indo-China theatre, while the others formed the 5th Cruiser Squadron. December 1941 found the 5th Cruiser Squadron in the Palau Islands and *Ashigara* in the Pescadores.

The three ships with the 5th Cruiser Squadron covered the South Philippines Force during the landings in those islands and those on the adjacent territories in the Dutch East Indies between December 1941 and February 1942, having been

Above: *Ashigara* in the Kiel Canal. (Author's collection)   **Below:** *Ashigara* at Kiel. (Author's collection)

Above: *Myôkô* after reconstruction, in March 1941. (IWM)

Below: *Myôkô* at Singapore after the Japanese surrender. (IWM)

joined by *Ashigara* in January. During these operations *Myôkô* was damaged by US aircraft in the Davao Gulf. *Nachi* and *Haguro* played prominent roles in the Battle of the Java Sea and were responsible for the losses of *de Ruyter* (q.v.) and *Kortenaer* (*Haguro*) and *Java* (q.v.) (*Nachi*). In March the same two ships fought an action which led to the sinking of *Exeter* (q.v.), while the destroyers *Pope* and *Encounter* were sunk by *Ashigara* and *Myôkô*. In addition, *Ashigara* sank the US destroyer *Pillsbury*.

After the capture of the East Indies the ships returned to Japan for refit and did not re-enter service again until April (June in the case of *Ashigara*). *Myôkô* and *Haguro* both formed part of the carrier cover force at the Battle of the Coral Sea in May, but had returned to Japan by the end of the month and then took part in the Aleutians campaign until mid-July.

Nachi had been fitted as Fleet flagship during her refit in March 1942, following which she assumed that role for the 5th Fleet operating in the Aleutians. *Ashigara*, on the other hand, served in the South West Pacific as flagship of No. 2 South Expeditionary Force, where she remained until April 1943, when a refit at Sasebo was begun. *Myôkô* and *Haguro* took part in the Guadalcanal campaign from August 1942 before also returning to Japan in the autumn for refit.

After this they returned to Truk once more, then covered operations in the Aleutians between May and June 1943.

Nachi participated in the Battle of the Komandorski Islands on 27 March 1943, sustaining slight damage. In July she covered the evacuation of the Aleutians and then remained in northern waters until September 1943.

In August 1943 *Myôkô* and *Haguro* returned to Truk and then operated in the Solomon Islands, where they took part in the Battle of Empress Augusta Bay during the night of 1/2 November, when both received slight damage.

Ashigara returned to the South-West Pacific, being based at Singapore until transferred to the 21st Cruiser Squadron with the NE Area Fleet in March 1943. Both she and *Nachi* remained in this theatre until June 1944. Their place in the south-west Pacific was taken by their sisters *Myôkô* and *Haguro*, which arrived in Singapore on 12 July. All four ships took part in the Battle of Leyte Gulf in October, where *Nachi* collided with *Mogami* during the night action in the Surigao Strait, and *Myôkô* was hit by an aircraft torpedo on 25 October in the Mindoro Straits, which caused severe damage. She was eventually brought in to Singapore for temporary repairs. *Haguro* was hit by a bomb on No. 2 turret during the action off Samar. On 5 November 1944 *Nachi* was sunk by aircraft

from the carrier *Lexington* off Corregidor Island, having been hit by about nine torpedoes, twenty bombs and numerous rockets.

Myôkô, after temporary repairs at Singapore, was hit by a torpedo from the US submarine *Bergall* off Indo-China on 12 December 1944 and totally disabled. She was towed back to Singapore, where she arrived on 25 December. She remained there, used only as an AA battery, until she was surrendered in an unrepaired state, and was eventually scuttled by British forces in the Straits of Malacca on 8 July 1946.

Haguro remained in Malayan waters after the Leyte operations and was finally sunk by a torpedo attack by the British 26th Destroyer Flotilla (*Saumarez*, *Verulam*, *Vigilant*, *Venus* and *Virago*) south-west of Penang on 16 May 1945, while on a supply mission to the Andaman Islands.

Ashigara, which had been attached directly to the 5th Fleet since November 1944, was then transferred to Singapore, and on 5 February 1945 rejoined the 5th Cruiser Squadron, or what was left of it. After the loss of *Haguro* this squadron was disbanded and *Ashigara* was reassigned directly to the 10th Area Fleet at Singapore. On 7 June 1945, while returning from evacuating troops from Batavia, she was torpedoed and sunk by the British submarine *Trenchant* in the Banka Strait.

TAKAO CLASS

Ship	Builder	Laid Down	Launched	Completed	Fate
Takao	Yokosuka Dky	28 Apr 27	12 May 30	31 May 32	Lost 31 Jul 1945
Atago	Kure Dky	28 Apr 27	16 Jun 30	30 Mar 32	Lost 23 Oct 1944
Maya	Kawasaki, Kobe	4 Dec 28	8 Nov 30	30 Jun 32	Lost 23 Oct 1944
Chôkai	Mitsubishi, N	26 Mar 28	5 Apr 31	30 Jun 32	Lost 25 Oct 1944

Displacement: 9,850 tons/10,007 tonnes (standard); 15,490* tons/15,738 tonnes (full load).
Length: 668ft 6in/203.76m (oa); 631ft 8in/192.54m (pp); 661ft 8in/201.76m (wl).
Beam: 59ft 2in/18.03m; Draught: 20ft 1in/6.11m (mean).
Machinery: 4-shaft geared turbines; 12 Kampon boilers.
Performance: 130,000shp=35½kts; Bunkerage: 2,571 tons oil fuel.
Range: 8,000nm at 14kts.
Protection: 1½in to 5in main belt; 1⅜in max main deck; ½in to 1in upper deck; 3in to 4in end bulkheads; 1in turrets.
Guns: ten 8in (5x2); four 4.7in HA (4x1); two 40mm (2x1).
Torpedoes: eight 24in (4x2).
Aircraft: three, two catapults.
Complement: 773.

Design In March 1927 a new construction programme was finally authorised which, partly in response to the USA's 'First Cruiser Bill' of May 1924, included four more 10,000-ton 'treaty' cruisers. Until this time, all of the IJN's plans for new ships had met with rejection by the Government. These new cruisers were originally to have been *Myôkô*-type ships, but in 1925 the staff requirements had been changed. Now the ships were to be equipped with 8in guns capable of AA fire, and to have their tubes on the upper deck and better protection to the magazines. Several of the improvements made to the basic *Myôkô* design were the result of information gleaned from the British *Kent*, while others, such as the fitting of two catapults, were prompted by developments in the USN.

The design of the hull was essentially the same as that of *Myôkô*, except that Ducol steel was employed instead of HT steel. Welding was

used above the upper deck level, and light alloys were incorporated wherever possible to save weight. However, the excess overweight of the *Myôkô*s was not realised at the time the new ships were being designed, and caused problems later. The standard displacement, designed at 9,850 tons, was more like 11,400 tons, which resulted in increased draught, lower freeboard, slower speed and reduced range, not to mention suspect stability.

The protective scheme was also similar to that of the previous class, with certain differences. The length of the waterline armoured belt was shorter, magazine protection was thicker and the conning tower was armoured. The magazines were protected by an extension of the side armour belt, which itself was an integral part of the hull in accordance with the current principles of design in Japan, 127mm (5in) thick for its top 8¼ft, but its lower portion was tapered from 76mm to 38mm (3in to 1½in) at its lower edge. Horizontal protection to the magazines was 47mm. In these ships, protective plating was given to the conning tower. In total, armour represented 2,368 tons, or 16.8 per cent of the ⅔ trials displacement.

Eight-inch 50cal 3 Nendo Shiki 2Gô 20.3cm guns were installed as first equipment in this class, unlike the previous ships, which were *rearmed*

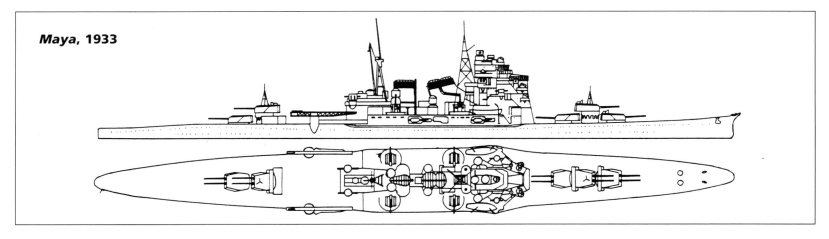

Maya, 1933

with them. They were shipped in model E turrets capable of 70° elevation in three of the class, but by the time that *Maya* completed, the problems associated with such an extreme elevation had been recognised and she was given E2 turrets in which elevation was reduced to 55°. The secondary armament was reduced to four 4.7in guns, as the main armament was expected to provide AA defence as well. However, the weakness of the light AA in the earlier cruisers was recognised by the inclusion of two Vickers-type 40mm (2pdr) single guns to augment the two 7.7mm MGs, although even this outfit could not be regarded as adequate, even for the mid-1920s. The torpedo outfit was originally intended to comprise twelve 24in tubes in triple banks, but considerations of weight led to the fitting of twin tubes instead. In contrast to the *Myôkô*s, the tubes were fitted at upper-deck level and partly sponsoned outboard of the hull. A rapid reloading system was fitted to compensate in part for the reduced torpedo broadside, and sixteen spare torpedoes were carried. Two catapults and the provision to carry three floatplanes was incorporated.

The main machinery was similar to that of *Myôkô*, but increased generating capacity was provided.

All four ships were fitted to serve as Fleet flagships in peacetime and Squadron flagships in war.

Two ships, *Takao* and *Atago*, were ordered early in 1927, and the other pair early the following year. *Maya*, however, was laid down later than scheduled because the yard went bankrupt and had to be bailed out by the Navy.

Modifications In 1936, as a result of the '4th Fleet Incident', all four ships had their hulls strengthened and some top-weight removed. The 40mm were replaced by two quadruple 13.2mm MGs.

Plans were made in 1937/38 to modernise the whole class by 1941, but the shipyards could not handle the work quickly enough, and consequently only *Takao* and *Atago* were taken in hand before the outbreak of war in the Pacific. During this modernisation the surface fire-control system was updated and the light AA improved by the addition of four twin 25mm and the replacement of the quad 13.2mm by two twin 13mm. However, these were themselves replaced by a pair of twin 25mm in the autumn of 1941. The torpedo outfit was altered to four quadruple 24in banks, with eight reloads in a new quick-reload system, and new fire control system. Two new heavier-pattern catapults were fitted and provision made to embark one E13A1 ('Jake') and two F1M2 ('Pete') floatplanes, although actual equipment varied. The bridge and foremast were rebuilt to reduce weight and the bulges increased to improve stability.

Chôkai and *Maya* only had a few improvements made in the spring of 1941. The torpedo tubes were adapted to fire the Long Lance torpedoes, sixteen of which were carried, and the catapults were replaced by the heavier pattern. They also had the quad 13.2mm replaced by two twin 25mm and received an additional two twin 13mm.

Early in 1942 *Atago* and *Takao* had their 4.7in guns replaced by twin 5in mountings, while their sisters had the twin 13mm replaced by a pair of 25mm, now carrying six twin 25mm.

Below: *Takao*, 14 July 1939. (IWM)

In July/August 1943 the light AA of *Atago* and *Takao* was increased to two triple and six twin, while in August/September 1943 the other two received two more twin 25mm. Radar was also fitted.

Between November 1943 and the following January *Atago* and *Takao* were given a further eight single 25mm, making a total of twenty-six (2 x 3, 6 x 2, 8 x 1). *Chôkai* was given ten single 25mm at Truk in January 1944, making her outfit also twenty-six (8 x 2, 10 x 1).

Maya was modified as an AA cruiser between 5 December 1943 and 9 April 1944, while undergoing damage repairs. Number 3 turret and all 4.7in and twin 25mm were landed, as were the tubes. The hangar was dismantled and other structural alterations made. The armament was now eight 8in (4 x 2), twelve 5in (6 x 2, unshielded), thirty-five 25mm (13 x 3, 9 x 1) and thirty-six dismountable 13mm singles. She was also given four quadruple 24in banks of torpedo tubes, but no reloads. Only two seaplanes could now be operated. The light AA was further increased in August by the addition of eighteen single 25mm, of which four were dismountable.

Chôkai was to have received the same treatment as *Maya*, but because she did not return to home waters this was never carried out. Apart from some AA additions and the fitting of radar, she remained little changed from her prewar state.
Service All four ships joined the 4th Cruiser Squadron on completion of work-up in December

1932, replacing the *Myôkô* class. From 15 November 1935 they were paid off, during which time they had some strengthening work and other modifications done. *Takao* and *Maya* again formed the 4th Cruiser Squadron from 1 December 1936, joined by *Chôkai* on 7 August 1937, but for some reason *Atago* remained in reserve until 1939. *Takao* again reduced to reserve on 15 November 1937 to await modernisation. The two active units then served in Chinese waters. *Takao* completed her modernisation on 31 August 1939 and *Atago* on 30 October 1939, and then rejoined the 4th Cruiser Squadron on 15 November. *Maya* was used as a gunnery training ship until she, too, joined the 4th Cruiser Squadron on 1 May 1940. *Chôkai* served as flagship of the China Expeditionary Force for a year before joining her sisters on 15 November 1940.

On the outbreak of war in December 1941 the class was serving with the Southern Area Force in the South China Sea, where they covered the landings in Malaya and Borneo. In January the 4th Cruiser Squadron, less *Chôkai*, was transferred to Palau. In February 1942 *Chôkai* ran aground near Saigon and was under repair until March. The other ships covered the operations in the Dutch East Indies, culminating in the invasion of Java, and at the end of February took part in a strike against Allied shipping south of Java. In the course of this, *Maya* and destroyers sank the destroyer *Stronghold* on 3 March with a vast expenditure of shells, while *Atago* and *Takao* sank the US destroyer *Pillsbury*. *Atago* also

Above: The bridge structure of *Chôkai*. (Author's collection) Below: The bridge of *Takao* after modernisation. Compare with that of *Chôkai*. (Author's collection)

played a major part in the sinkings of *Yarra* (RAN), the depot ship *Anking* and the oiler *Francol*. *Chôkai*, after repair, covered the landings in northern Sumatra and the Andaman Islands before participating in the strike into the Indian Ocean between 1 and 11 April 1942, when she sank the merchantmen *Selma City*, *Bienville* and *Ganges* off the Indian coast.

After the capture of the Dutch East Indies, The Philippines and Malaya, the squadron was withdrawn to Japan to refit between April and May 1942. Their next operations were in the Aleutians in May and July (*Takao* and *Maya*), while the other pair joined the main body of the Fleet for the Midway invasion but saw no action. In August 1942 US forces landed on Guadalcanal in the Solomon Islands. In response, *Chôkai*, flagship of the 8th Fleet, was despatched to Truk and other units followed, including the 4th Cruiser Squadron. *Chôkai* was damaged by 8in shells from *Quincy* and *Astoria* at the Battle of Savo Island on 9 August, and again slightly by bombing on 14 November. At the same time *Maya* was hit by a crashing aircraft and badly damaged.

In the engagement on 14/15 November *Atago* and *Takao* were part of the force which badly damaged the US battleship *South Dakota*, the US ship being hit by at least sixteen 8in shells from the two cruisers.

Between December 1942 and April 1943 all four ships returned to Japan for repairs or refit and then returned to Truk, where they were based for much of the year. On 5 November *Atago*, *Takao* and *Maya* were damaged during a raid on Rabaul by aircraft from *Saratoga*. All three returned to home yards for repair, the first two completing by January 1944, but *Maya* was converted to an AA cruiser as described above, and did not return to service until April. *Chôkai*, on the other hand, remained mainly based at Truck. In March the 4th Cruiser Squadron became part of the newly formed 1st Mobile Fleet and took part in the Battle of the Philippine Sea on 19/20 June, when *Maya* was slightly damaged by near misses. After returning to home waters *Takao* and *Atago* were ordered to Singapore and joined by *Chôkai* and *Maya*. All four were part of Admiral Kurita's Centre Force which sailed to intercept the US landings in the Philippines in November. After leaving Brunei Bay for the Mindoro Straits, *Atago* was hit by four torpedoes from the US submarine *Darter* in the Palawan Passage on 23 October, sinking in about twenty minutes. *Maya* was hit by four torpedoes from *Dace* some twenty minutes after the hits on her sister, and sank in ten minutes. *Takao* was hit by another two torpedoes launched from *Darter* just after her attack on *Atago*, which flooded several boiler rooms and seized the machinery. In her case, however, she

Above: *Atago* making 34.12kts on 25 August 1939 after reconstruction. (IWM)

was brought into Singapore, arriving there on 12 November. *Chôkai* carried on, participating in the Battle of Samar, when the escort carrier *Gambier Bay* and the destroyers *Hoel*, *Johnston* and *Samuel B Roberts* (DE) were sunk. However, she herself was later hit by bombs from aircraft of *Kitkun Bay* and rendered unmanoeuvrable, and had to be sunk by the destroyer *Fujinami* with torpedoes.

The sole survivor of the class, *Takao*, lay unrepaired at Singapore, used as an AA battery in defence against B-29 raids. The ship was again attacked on 31 July 1945, this time by British midget submarines, and further damage was caused but she did not sink. After the surrender *Takao* was used as an accommodation hulk until scuttled in the Straits of Malacca on 27 October 1946.

MOGAMI CLASS

Ship	Builder	Laid Down	Launched	Completed	Fate
Mogami	Kure Dky	27 Oct 31	14 Mar 34	28 Jul 35	Lost 25 Oct 1944
Mikuma	Kure Dky	24 Dec 31	31 May 34	29 Aug 35	Lost 6 Jun 1942
Suzuya	Yokosuka Dky	11 Dec 33	20 Nov 34	31 Oct 37	Lost 25 Oct 1944
Kumano	Kawasaki, Kobe	5 Apr 34	15 Oct 36	31 Oct 37	Lost 25 Nov 1944

Displacement: 8,500 tons/8,636 tonnes (standard); 11,169 tons/11,347 tonnes (full load).
Length: 661ft 1in/201.5m (oa); 620ft 1in/189m (pp); 646ft 4in/197m (wl).
Beam: 59ft 1in/18m; Draught: 18ft 1in/5.5m (mean).
Machinery: 4-Shaft geared turbines; 10 except *Kumano* & *Suzuya* 8 boilers.
Performance: 152,000shp=37kts; Bunkerage: 2,163 tons oil fuel.
Range: 8,150nm at 14kts.
Protection: 1in to 4in (machinery) main belt, 5½in magazines; 1⅜in to 2⅜in main deck; 3in to 4in barbettes; 1in turrets.
Guns: fifteen 6.1in (5x3); eight 5in DP (4x2); eight 25mm (4x2); four 13.2mm MGs.
Torpedoes: twelve 24in (4x3).
Aircraft: three, two catapults.
Complement: 850.

Design After the signing of the London Naval Treaty in April 1930, Japan built up to its limit in A class cruisers (i.e. 8in-gunned ships). As far as the B class or 6in-gunned ships were concerned, Japan's position was little better, because existing tonnage amounted to 98,415 tons standard, leaving only 2,035 tons for new construction. However, as much of the existing tonnage was either over-aged or replaceable by 1934, Japan could legitimately lay down new ships in that year. It was decided that four ships of 8,500 tons would be built before 1936, and two of 8,450 tons later. The new ships would replace the 'Improved *Takaos*' cancelled as a result of the London Naval Treaty. Work on the design was started in 1930, the basic requirements being fifteen 15.5cm (6.1in) guns in triple turrets with HA capability, and twelve 24in torpedo tubes. It was intended

from the outset that the 6in guns would be replaced by 8in at the earliest opportunity, and the ship was designed with this in mind. The armour was to protect the magazines against 8in shellfire and the machinery against 6in shells. These requirements were all but the same as those of the A class cruisers and, not suprisingly, proved impossible to attain on 8,500 tons, even with the adoption of welding on a large scale. In comparison with the previous cruisers, the hull of this class was very lightly built, even dangerously so, plate and scantling thicknesses being considerably reduced to save weight. Even so, the displacement as designed in 1931 was 9,500 tons. The actual design showed many similarities to that of *Takao*, but the measures taken to reduce weight low down in the ship, combined with the excessive height of the bridge and superstructure, reduced stability to a critical point.

The protection system, however, had some variations from that of the A class cruisers and also some similarities. The main belt over the machinery spaces was 100mm thick at its upper edge and tapered down to 65mm at half its depth. From this point it tapered further down to 30mm at its lower edge, the whole belt being inclined inwards from top to bottom by 20°. Its upper edge joined the sloped 60mm deck armour, while the

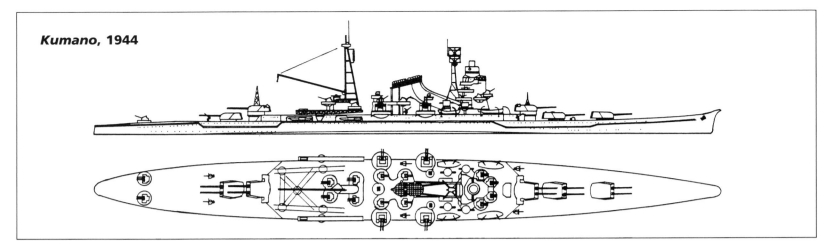

Kumano, 1944

lower portion behind the bulge acted as the anti-torpedo defence. Abreast the magazine spaces the side armour was 140mm thick at its upper edge, tapering down to 30mm at the lower and inclined in the same manner as abreast the machinery. Transverse armoured bulkheads closed off the machinery and magazine spaces. The horizontal armour was 30mm with the sides sloped at 20° and 60mm in thickness. Above the magazines the deck was 40mm thick. Barbette armour was 75mm-100mm thick. The total armour weight was 2,061 tons, and slightly more in the later pair because their side belt was longer.

The machinery was a four-shaft geared turbine layout of a higher power, 152,000shp, than the previous ships, for a maximum speed of 37kts. There was also a difference in its arrangement, in that the forward turbines drove the inboard shafts. The first pair of ships had ten boilers, eight large and two small, all with superheating and air pre-heaters. The two small boilers were in the forward boiler room, while the remainder each had their own space, two abreast, separated by the now standard longitudinal bulkhead, which was continued through the turbine rooms. The later pair had only eight large boilers, forward boiler room being eliminated but without loss of power.

The main armament was disposed in five triple turrets, three forward, two aft, with C turret super-firing on A and B. The main gun was the 15.5cm (6.1in) 60cal 3 Nendo Shiki adopted in 1934 and firing a 123lb shell, with a maximum range of 30,000yd. The mountings, in triple turrets, had an elevation of 55°, the difficulty in having 70° and HA capability being recognised. The secondary armament was the standard 5in HA in twin mountings, while the light AA consisted of four twin mountings of 25mm and two twin 13mm MGs. It had been intended to ship a pair of 40mm Vickers guns (2pdr) but they were superseded by the 25mm. The triple 24in torpedo tubes were mounted on the upper deck at the after end of the superstructure (instead of near the bridge, as originally planned), and provided with a rapid reloading system of twelve reserve torpedoes, an improved version of that fitted in *Takao*.

The aircraft arrangements as completed differed from the original design intentions, which envisaged a similar layout to that of the *Takao*s, i.e. two catapults, two hangars for single aircraft and provision to embark four aeroplanes. The *Tomozuru* incident caused a rethink, however, and the hangars were deleted, the superstructure deck being extended to provide parking space for aircraft, and their numbers being reduced to three.

Modifications After the loss of *Tomozuru* on 12 March 1934, a Board of Inquiry was convened which reported its findings on 14 June that year. Measures were immediately taken to improve the stability of ships under construction, which included the *Mogami*s. As a result the bridge structure was redesigned and lowered, the hangars were deleted and the after superstructure reduced. The two later units also had their depths (keel to upper-deck height) reduced, as they were much less advanced than the first pair. As already mentioned, the torpedo tubes were moved further

Above: *Kumano* in Chinese waters just prior to the Second World War. (Author's collection)

Above: *Mikuma* in April 1939. (IWM)

aft and the 5in guns altered to twin mountings. *Mogami* and *Mikuma* were quickly found to be still marginal on stability after trials and the 'Fourth Fleet Incident' on 26 September 1935, when many ships were damaged by a hurricane, which showed that they were also lacking in hull strength. By this time *Suzuya* had just begun initial trials, but these were aborted and all three completed units paid off, disarmed and laid up to await major modifications. Work on *Kumano* was stopped. After the Board of Inquiry reported, in April 1936, work on *Kumano* was resumed in the spring and the others reconstructed. Work lasted until October 1937 (*Mikuma* and *Suzuya*), and not until January 1938 was *Mogami* completed. This work saw the hulls considerably strengthened, much of the welded shell plating replaced by riveted plates, and larger bulges fitted. The

Below: *Mogami* in 1935 running trials. (IWM)

superstructure was altered to reduce the effects of hull distortion on turret training. Among other things, the number of torpedoes was reduced to eighteen; only six reloads. These modifications added about 1,000 tons to the displacement.

After the collapse of the treaty limitations in the mid-1930s, Japan could implement the plans to up-gun these cruisers by replacing the triple 6.1in with twin 8in turrets. However, the need to manufacture turrets with the required roller path diameter to suit the barbettes of the *Mogami*s meant that the refits could not be started before 1939. This refit also included the replacement of the catapults by a heavier-capacity model and the fitting of the tubes for the 24in oxygen-propelled 'Long Lance' torpedoes. Twenty-four torpedoes were now to be accommodated.

Little further modification was then carried out until the end of the first year of hostilities, when *Mogami*, badly damaged by collision and bombing during the Battle of Midway in June 1942, was converted into an 'aircraft cruiser' during repairs

at Sasebo between September 1942 and April 1943. This included the removal of the after 8in gun turrets and their replacement by a large aircraft deck, from which it was intended to operate eleven E16A1 'Paul' floatplanes. All eleven could be launched by the two catapults within 30min. The twin 25mm and 13mm guns were replaced by ten triple 25mm, and extra HA fire control equipment was added. Radar was also fitted for air-search use.

After the Solomons campaign in February 1943, *Kumano* and *Suzuya* both received radar sets and had their light AA increased to 20 25mm (4 x 3, 4 x 2). The 13mm twin were landed. Plans to convert both ships to pure AA cruisers by the removal of all or part of the 8in guns and the fitting of extra 5in HA were not carried through.

In the first quarter of 1944 the three survivors had their light AA increased again by the fitting of eight single 25mm to give *Mogami* 10 x 3 and 8 x 1 mountings and the other pair 4 x 3, 4 x 2 and 8 x 1 25mm. In June this was further augmented to

Above: *Suzuya* in 1939. (IWM)

14 x 3, 18 x 1 in *Mogami*; 8 x 3, 4 x 2 and 24 x 1 in *Kumano*, and 8 x 3, 4 x 2 and 18 x 1 in *Suzuya*. Additional radar was fitted.

Service After commissioning, *Mogami* and *Mikuma* formed the 7th Cruiser Squadron, temporarily attached to the 4th fleet. As noted earlier, they were rebuilt following this deployment and as a result of the modifications did not see service until the end of 1937. When *Suzuya* and *Kumano* joined the fleet, they and *Mikuma* formed the 7th Cruiser Squadron and deployed to Chinese waters. Not until 1 May 1940 were all four together as the 7th Cruiser Squadron, following which, in January 1941, they were deployed to Indo-China to put pressure on Vichy France after the Thai-French action in that month. Later, in July, they supported Japanese operations in French Indo-China. When war began in the Pacific the 7th Cruiser squadron covered the Japanese landings in Malaya, Borneo, Sumatra, Java and the Andaman islands. In an action off Batavia on 28 February/1 March 1942, *Mikuma* and *Mogami* sank the US cruiser *Houston* and the *Perth* (RAN) with guns and torpedoes, several of the latter, five out of a spread of six from *Mogami*, in fact, also sinking a Japanese minesweeper and four army transports totalling 31,461grt. In April 1942 the squadron was part of the Indian Ocean Raiding force which sank eight Allied merchant ships totalling 48,664grt. All ships returned to home waters to refit after the initial successes, and became operational again in May 1942 to participate in the Battle of Midway. The 7th Cruiser Squadron was

tasked with covering the invasion convoy, and left Guam on 29 May to join it. On 5 June the Squadron was ordered to bombard Midway itself, but these orders were cancelled, and on their return the cruisers were intercepted by the US submarine *Tambour*. While this boat was unable to make an attack, *Mogami* rammed *Mikuma* in the confusion, causing damage to both. The two undamaged ships retired, leaving the lame ducks to be caught by US aircraft the following day. Attacked by waves of aircraft from the carriers *Yorktown*, *Hornet* and *Enterprise*, *Mikuma* was reduced to a blazing wreck, sinking that evening, and *Mogami* very badly damaged, suffering many casualties. She finally limped into Truk on 14 June and arrived in Sasebo on 11 August for repairs. These, and her conversion to an aircraft cruiser, lasted until April 1943. The other two ships joined the 3rd Fleet in July 1942, and in that month made a cruise into the Bay of Bengal. After the US landings in Guadalcanal in August they moved to that theatre, to support Japanese defence of the island. Both took part in the Battle of Santa Cruz in October. After the Guadalcanal campaign they returned to home waters to refit, and later, together with *Mogami*, were again ordered to the Solomon Islands, where *Kumano* was damaged by US Marine aircraft on 20 July 1943 off Kolombangara. Repairs at Kure took until the end of October. *Mogami*, too, was damaged by aircraft off Rabaul on 5 November, putting her out of service until mid-February 1944. In 1944 they participated in the defence of the Marianas and, finally, in the battle for Leyte

Gulf, when *Mogami* was attached to Admiral Nishimura's Southern Force and both *Suzuya* and *Kumano* to Kurita's Northern Force. *Mogami* was damaged by gunfire from the US cruisers *Louisville*, *Portland* and *Denver* in the Surigao Straits on 25 October, then damaged again in collision with *Nachi*, and later further damaged by US carrier aircraft of TG77.4 as she limped away to be finished off by a torpedo from *Akebono* south-west of Panaon Island in the Mindanao Sea about midday. *Kumano* was damaged by a torpedo from *Johnston* on the morning of 25 October while attacking the US escort carrier force, and retired towards the San Bernardino Straits, where she was damaged again by dive bombers. She survived further attacks by aircraft in the Sibuyan Sea on 26 October and reached Manila safely. *Suzuya* was damaged by carrier aircraft on 25 October, also while attacking the escort carriers. Further air attacks rendered the ship unmanoeuvrable and badly on fire off Samar, and she was sent to the bottom by *Okinami* after torpedoes and ammunition exploded. *Kumano*, after provisional repairs at Manila, sailed for Japan on 4 November but was intercepted off Luzon by US submarines, being hit by torpedoes from *Ray*. She managed to reach Santa Cruz in Luzon, where repairs were begun, but on 25 November she was attacked and sunk by aircraft from *Ticonderoga* in Dasol Bay, having been hit by four bombs and five torpedoes.

TONE CLASS

Ship	Builder	Laid Down	Launched	Completed	Fate
Tone	Mitsubishi, N	1 Dec 34	21 Nov 37	20 Nov 38	Lost 24 Jul 1945
Chikuma	Mitsubishi, N	1 Oct 35	19 Mar 38	20 May 39	Lost 25 Oct 1944

Displacement: 11,215 tons/11,394 tonnes (standard); 15,200 tons/15,443 tonnes (full load).
Length: 661ft 1in/201.5m (oa); 620ft 5in/189.1m (pp); 649ft 7in/198.0m (wl).
Beam: 60ft 8in/18.5m; Draught: 21ft 3in/6.47m (mean).
Machinery: 4-shaft geared turbines; 8 Kampon boilers.
Performance: 152,000shp=35kts; Bunkerage: 2,163 tons oil fuel.
Range: 9,000nm at 18kts.
Protection: 4in (machinery) main belt; 5in (magazines); 1⅜in to 2½in main deck; 1in turrets.
Guns: eight 8in (4x2); eight 5in DP (4x2); twelve 25mm.
Torpedoes: twelve 24in (4x3).
Aircraft: five, two catapults.
Complement: 850.

Design These two ships, part of the 2nd 1932 Supplementary Programme, were originally envisaged as 8,450-ton cruisers of the *Mogami* type, but early experience with the latter indicated that all was not well with the design. As a result the ships were built to a new design and turned out quite different from the *Mogami*s. As originally planned, the armament was to have consisted of five triple 6.1in, disposed three forward and two aft, but after the capsizing of *Tomozuru* the whole question of the stability of new Japanese warships was investigated, leading to the redesign of the *Tone*s. The armament of previous cruisers was found to suffer from wide dispersion of shot, and to counter this all of the turrets in this new design were, uniquely for a cruiser, concentrated on the forecastle. This in turn left the quarterdeck free for an expanded aircraft installation.

The poor stability of recent new construction was not the only problem to afflict the Imperial Japanese Navy, as sea experience in typhoon conditions showed. The ships' strength was also suspect, particularly in the *Mogami*s, as described in the previous section. Thus, while *Tone*, on the ways since December 1934, still incorporated some welding, her sister, laid down about a year later, was almost completely riveted. The modifications to the design, made in the light of the two incidents referred to, raised the displacement to about 12,500 tons. Apart from the reduction in the main armament, the heavy AA battery was increased to five twin mountings and the aircraft capacity increased by 50 per cent. When Japan abrogated the current naval treaties on 31 December 1936, the main armament was revised to eight 8in guns, but, in view of the difficulties this would have caused in a ship already designed and well under construction, it was more than likely that the ship had been designed for such an armament at the outset, and that the retention of the 6.1in had been a purely political necessity.

In this design the undulating hull of the earlier cruisers was dispensed with and the superstructure was less built-up. The protective scheme also differed from that of *Mogami*, the main belt being completely within the hull, though still inclined inboards from top to bottom. The side armour was 100mm thick abreast the machinery spaces (125mm magazines), but without the continuous taper of the *Mogami* scheme, and it extended only to a depth of about 9ft, continuing in a much reduced thickness as an anti-torpedo bulkhead down to the inner double bottom. The ship's side was vertical down to the top of the belt and then continued into the bulge. The horizontal protection consisted of a 1⅜in main deck which was angled at its sides and increased to 2.56in, which joined the upper edge of the side belt. In addition, the upper deck was given 19mm protective plating.

The main machinery was similar to that of the last pair of *Mogami*s.

As already noted, these ships were completed with 8in guns of the same model as the earlier class, mounted in E3 twin turrets with 55° elevation, all forward. Nos. 3 and 4 turrets trained through the after arcs, while No. 2 superfired on 1 and 3. The heavy AA comprised four twin 5in in shielded mountings amidships, these being similar to those shipped by all the new heavy cruisers. For close-range defence the standard 25mm Type 96 gun was carried, in six twin mountings. Four triple banks of 24in torpedo tubes were also incorporated.

These ships were designed to operate as the eyes of the fleet, and in consequence more space was given over to the operation of aircraft than in previous ships. In fact, the importance of the aircraft facilities necessitated all the main armament being concentrated forward to eliminate the dangers of blast damage to the aircraft. Two gunpowder-propellant catapults were installed on the beam abaft the mainmast, and there was a comprehensive arrangement of transport rails and turntables on the catapult- and quarterdecks. There were no hangars. Four E7K2 'Alf' three-seat floatplanes and four E8N1 'Dave' two-seat floatplanes could be carried as a maximum, the normal complement being six, of which four were to be E8N1s. In practice, no more than five were ever embarked, and even this was later reduced to four. As the war progressed these types were superseded by the E13A1 'Jake' and F1M2 'Pete'.

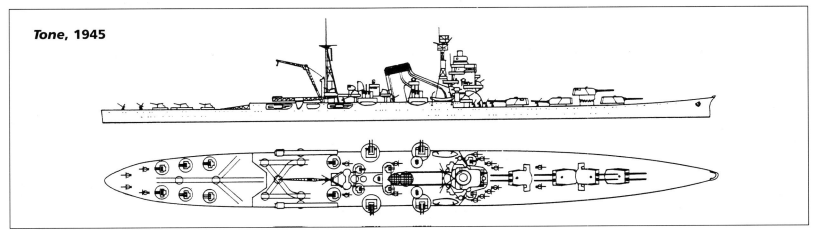

Tone, 1945

Above: A reconstruction of the cruiser *Tone* as she might have appeared to the US aircraft that sank her.

Modifications In 1943 the 25mm outfit was increased to twenty guns, and in June 1944, when the opportunity to use their aircraft had passed, further mountings were added, some on the after flight deck. The light AA was now 54 25mm (8 x 3, 6 x 2, 18 x 1). Two more twin 25mm were also added later. Radar was fitted, but otherwise no major modifications were carried out.

Service These two ships formed the 8th Cruiser Squadron on completion and operated in company for almost all of their careers. This squadron was unusual in that it only ever consisted of the two ships. In November 1941 the 8th Cruiser Squadron was part of the covering force for the Pearl Harbor raid, and the following month it was a component of the 1st Air Fleet (Admiral Nagumo) for the attack on Wake Island. Subsequently, both ships were involved in operations in the Netherlands East Indies at the beginning of 1942, when Java was invaded. In February they were part of the covering force for the carrier raid on Darwin, and in March were accompanying the battleships *Hiei* and *Kirishima* when the US destroyer *Edsall* was sunk. During March the Squadron participated in the strike by Admiral Nagumo's carrier force into the Indian Ocean and the attack on Ceylon, when the British cruisers *Dorsetshire* and *Cornwall* were sunk, among others. They returned to the Pacific for the attack on Midway in May, and from the summer of 1942 were part of the forces thrown into the Gaudalcanal campaign. On 24 August *Tone* was damaged by aircraft from *Saratoga*, and in October, during the Battle of Santa Cruz, her sister was hit by about five bombs dropped by aircraft from *Hornet*. In 1943 they served in the Solomon Islands theatre, where, on 5 November, both ships were damaged by bombing while lying in Simpson Harbour, Rabaul, during a raid by aircraft from *Saratoga*. By the beginning of 1944 both ships were now the 7th Cruiser Squadron, and at the end of February they took part in a strike into the Indian Ocean against Allied shipping on the Australia-Aden routes. However, after the 7,840grt *Behar* had been sunk and the survivors murdered because a raider report had been sent, the strike was abandoned. On their return to the Pacific they participated in the Battle of the Philippine Sea, and in October were part of Admiral Kurita's Centre Force at the Battle of Leyte Gulf, where they attacked the US escort carriers before US aircraft of TG77.4 drove them off, sinking *Chikuma* with torpedoes off Samar on 25 October. *Tone* was damaged by US aircraft in March 1945, after her return to home waters, and was finally sunk by aircraft at Edauchi, near Kure, on 24 July 1945. She was raised postwar and broken up at Kure in 1948.

AGANO CLASS

Ship	Builder	Laid Down	Launched	Completed	Fate
Agano	Sasebo Dky	18 Jun 40	22 Oct 41	31 Oct 42	Lost 17 Feb 1944
Noshiro	Yokosuka Dky	4 Sep 41	19 Jul 42	30 Jun 43	Lost 26 Oct 1944
Yahagi	Sasebo Dky	11 Nov 41	25 Oct 42	29 Dec 43	Lost 7 Apr 1945
Sakawa	Sasebo Dky	21 Nov 42	9 Apr 44	30 Nov 44	Expended 2 Jul 1946

Displacement: 6,652 tons/6,758 tonnes (standard); 8,534 tons/8,670 tonnes (full load).
Length: 571ft 2in/174.1m (oa); 531ft 6in/162m (pp); 564ft 4in/172m (wl).
Beam: 49ft 10in/15.20m; Draught: 18ft 6in/5.63m (mean).
Machinery: 4-shaft geared turbines; 6 Kampon boilers.
Performance: 100,000shp=35kts; Bunkerage: 1,405 tons oil fuel.
Range: 6,300nm at 18kts.
Protection: 2¼in (machinery) main belt; 2in (magazines); ¾in deck; 1in turrets.
Guns: six 6in (3x2); four 3.1in HA (2x2); thirty-two 25mm.
Torpedoes: eight 24in (2x4).
Aircraft: two, one catapult.
Complement: 730.

Design These ships were designed in the late 1930s as replacements for the ageing 5,500-ton cruisers. As originally conceived they were to be armed with 6.1in guns in triple turrets and carry six 24in torpedo tubes. They were to have a high speed, with minimal protection. After a change in the staff requirements the design was reworked and they emerged as fast scouts, and were used in practice in the role of destroyer leaders. To this end, X turret was sacrificed for a heavier torpedo battery (quadruple banks in lieu of triple) and an aircraft installation.

The hull was flush-decked with a bulbous bow, and the armour was limited to a 56mm belt in the way of the machinery spaces, with 50mm protecting the magazines. Deck protection was 18mm, and the turrets merely had splinter protection.

The machinery was a quadruple-shaft geared turbine arrangement with six boilers, developing 100,000shp for a maximum speed of 25kts. Like *Yubari*, but unlike any other cruisers since, this class had only a single funnel.

As completed, the main armament was the 152mm (6in) gun which had originally been put into service for the *Kongo* class battlecruisers. Stock guns were subsequently then used to arm the *Agano* class. This gun, developed from a 50cal Vickers weapon, fired a 100lb projectile and had a range of 22,970yd. The twin turrets, manufactured at Sasebo, allowed a maximum elevation of 55° and could thus be used for barrage AA fire. Secondary armament consisted of four 80mm HA, which were actually 3in (76.2mm) in two twin mountings. These 60cal weapons fired a 13.2lb projectile (fixed ammunition), and were the only such guns afloat in the IJN. Thirty-two 25mm completed the AA outfit, reflecting war experience, which had clearly shown the threat from air-

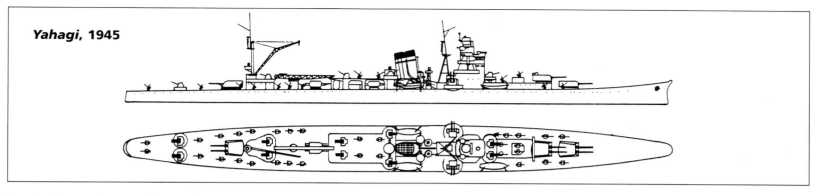

Yahagi, 1945

Above: *Sakawa* in home waters shortly after completion. (USN)

craft attack. The torpedo tubes were mounted on the centreline according to destroyer practice, and given a rapid reload system for the eight spare torpedoes. The aircraft fittings included a single catapult on the centreline forward of the main mast, and stowage for two floatplanes on a platform over the tubes. As with destroyers, depth charge equipment was fitted in these ships.

Four ships were provided for under the 1939 4th Replenishment Programme, three being ordered from Sasebo and one from Yokosuka. Only the name ship was completed with any despatch, so their active service lives were limited because Japan's fortunes had by then declined.

Modifications Light AA was increased to 46 25mm by 1944, and in the surviving ships thereafter to 52 and then 61 25mm (10 x 3, 31 x 1) by July 1944. Radar was fitted at completion, except perhaps in *Agano*.

Service *Agano* served as leader of the 4th Destroyer Flotilla after entering service and, with her flotilla, participated in the final battles for Guadalcanal during the first couple of months of 1943. In October that year the flotilla was transferred to Rabaul for operations in the Solomon Islands, and after the US landings on Bougainville was committed to attack the invasion force on the night of 1/2 November. The Japanese force of four cruisers and six destroyers encountered the US TF39 (four cruisers and eight destroyers) and was routed, *Agano* escaping with minor damage. However, a few days later, on 5 November, *Agano* was badly damaged in Rabaul harbour by aircraft from *Saratoga* and *Princeton*, and in a subsequent attack by aircraft from TF38 on 11 November she received a torpedo hit as well. Ordered to home waters for repair after makeshift repairs at Truk, the cruiser was torpedoed and sunk some 160nm north of that island by the US submarine *Skate* on 16 February.

Noshiro was at Truk in November 1943 with the 2nd Destroyer Flotilla, and was also ordered to Rabaul for operations in the Solomon Islands theatre. She, too, received damage during the US carrier aircraft raids on Rabaul harbour on 5 November. After repairs at Truk she transported troops to Rabaul and Kavieng in December, being slightly damaged by air attacks on her return trip to Truk on 1 January 1944. She served in the Marianas in the summer of 1944, sailing in June with *Yamato* and *Musashi* to cover the transport of reinforcements to Biak, and was part of Admiral Kurita's force during the Battle of the Philippine Sea between 18 and 22 June. At the Battle of Leyte Gulf in October 1944 *Noshiro* was part of the Centre Force with her destroyers, and took part in the battle off Samar, but on the withdrawal was sunk west of Panay on the morning of 26 October by aircraft from *Wasp* and *Hornet*.

Yahagi assumed the role of leader of the 10th Destroyer Flotilla, seeing action in the Marianas in May/June 1944. During the Battle of the Philippine Sea she was part of Carrier Group A, and during the Battle of Leyte Gulf she, too, was with Kurita's Centre Force with the 10th destroyer Flotilla. After the US invasion of Okinawa on 1 April 1945, the remnants of the Imperial Japanese Navy were ordered to attack the invasion zone, despite the critical shortage of fuel which meant that it would be a one-way trip for the flagship *Yamato*. *Yahagi* sailed with this force from the Inland Sea, but the vessels were caught by US carrier aircraft in the East China Sea and annihilated. *Yahagi* was hit by some seven torpedoes, six

Above: *Yahagi* in December 1943. (IWM)
Right: *Noshiro* in June 1943. (IWM)

claimed by aeroplanes from *Langley* alone, as well as a dozen bombs, and sank on the afternoon of 7 April 1945.

The last ship, *Sakawa*, was not completed until the end of 1944, by which time there was little fuel available to the IJN. As a result she never became operational and survived the war unscathed, despite the heavy carrier raids on Japanese bases in the last months of the war. After the war she was used as a repatriation ship, and was then expended in the atom bomb tests at Bikini Atoll in 1946.

OYODO CLASS

Ship	Builder	Laid Down	Launched	Completed	Fate
Oyodo	Kure Dky	14 Feb 41	2 Apr 42	28 Feb 43	Lost 28 Jul 1945

Displacement: 8,164 tons/8,294 tonnes (standard); 11,433 tons/11,615 tonnes (full load).
Length: 630ft 3in/192.1m (oa); 590ft 7in/180m (pp); 620ft 1in/189m (wl).
Beam: 54ft 6in/16.6m; Draught: 19ft 6in/5.95m (mean).
Machinery: 4-shaft geared turbines; 6 Kampon boilers.
Performance: 110,000shp=35kts; Bunkerage: 2,360 tons oil fuel.
Range: 10,600nm at 18kts.
Protection: 2in main belt; 1½in deck; 1in turrets.
Guns: six 6.1in (3x2); eight 3.9in (4x2); twelve 25mm.
Torpedoes: nil.
Aircraft: two, one catapult.
Complement: n/k.

Design Two improved *Agano* class ships were authorised under the 1939 4th Replenishment Programme, to be employed as Flagships for scouting submarine flotillas in accordance with contemporary Japanese ideas for the operation of submarines. For this purpose the ships were to operate six E15K1 ('Norm') floatplanes, the requirements for which were only issued in the summer of 1939. As in the *Tone* class, the after end of the ship was entirely devoted to aircraft facilities, leaving the main armament concentrated on the forecastle. While the same general hull form as *Agano* was therefore adopted, with flush deck and bulbous bow, the armament was different both in layout and weapons, and the armour scheme was reduced. This class used spare 6.1in triple turrets which became available after the rearming of the *Mogami*s, two being shipped in conventional superfiring fashion forward. The heavy AA battery was doubled to four twin 3.9in/65 Type 98, the same gun as carried by the *Akizuki* class destroyers and considered by the Japanese to be their best heavy AA gun. Otherwise the remaining AA outfit comprised twelve 25mm. In view of their intended role no torpedo tubes were fitted, these being the only cruisers without them. Instead, the weight thus saved was used to ship a heavy-duty 45m catapult and six aeroplanes. The E15K1 had been designed to undertake reconnaissance duties in areas where the enemy held air superiority, to locate targets for the submarine flotilla. It was some 1,000lb heavier than the E13A1 'Jake', and its troubled development resulted in only four aircraft reaching the IJN by 1942, and only fifteen were completed in total. Six were sent to Palau, where *Oyodo* was operating, but they were quickly lost to attacking fighters. As a result she never operated more than two aircraft.

In view of the greater displacement compared with *Agano*, and the greater dimensions, the installed power was increased to 110,000shp for the same speed of 35kts. Her designed radius of action was very large, at 10,500nm.

Only one of the two ships authorised in 1939 was laid down, and none of those projected under the 1942 (five ships) and 1942 Modified Programmes (two ships) was ever ordered.

Modifications In recognition of the failure of the aircraft programme and the impossibility of the

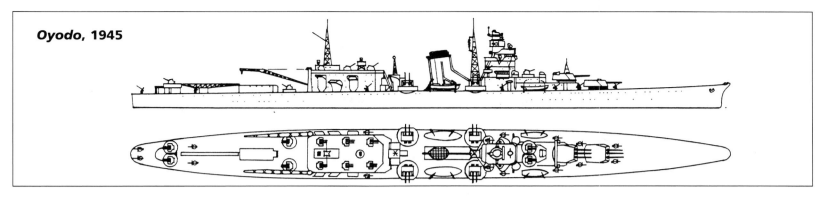

Oyodo, 1945

ship ever operating in her designed role by 1944, given the strategic situation, *Oyodo* returned to Yokosuka in the spring of that year and had the catapult exchanged for a standard type and the hangar converted to accommodate Fleet Headquarters staff. The light AA was increased in the same manner as other units of the fleet so that, at the end of the war, she was carrying a total of fifty-two 25mm (12 x 3, 16 x 1). Radar had also been added.

Service After work-up *Oyodo* joined the fleet at Truk, and in December 1943 participated in an operation to reinforce the garrisons at Rabaul and Kavieng. While returning to Truk on 1 January she was slightly damaged by US aircraft of TG50.2. The following month, when Truk was abandoned

as a major fleet base, she transferred to Palau in the Western Carolines. In March that base too became threatened, and *Oyodo* withdrew to Singapore. During this movement the cruiser was one of the escorts to the battleship *Musashi* when the latter was torpedoed and damaged by the US submarine *Tunny*. After a refit period in home waters in the spring of 1944, when the catapult was replaced and the hangar converted, the ship returned to the Philippines in October, when she sailed from the Inland Sea with Admiral Ozawa's Northern Force after the US landings at Leyte. During the battle for Leyte Gulf she assumed the role of flagship after *Zuikaku* had been heavily hit, and survived the operation unscathed. She then transferred to Camranh Bay in Indo-China

for the final operations against the US bridgeheads in the Philippines during December. In February 1945 *Oyodo* returned to home waters, where, on 19 March, she was attacked by US aircraft from TF58 in the Inland Sea. Hit by five bombs and near-missed several times, she received damage to her boilers, port engine room and superstructure. Only the skin plating received makeshift repairs, and thereafter the ship was good for only about 12kts in calm weather. She was laid up at Eta Jima, about 10 miles from Kure, until she was slightly damaged again by aircraft of TF38 on 24 July, then further attacks on 28 July breached the forward starboard engine room and the after starboard boiler room, and she capsized and sank. *Oyodo* was salvaged for breaking up in 1948.

IBUKI CLASS

Ship	Builder	Laid Down	Launched	Completed	Fate
Ibuki	Kure Dky	24 Apr 42	21 May 43		Converted to aircraft carrier
No. 301	Mitsubishi, N	1 Jun 42	not launched		Suspended Jul 1942. Broken up

Displacement: 12,200 tons/12,395 tonnes (standard); 14,828 tons/15,065 tonnes (full load).
Length: 658ft/200.5m (oa); 616ft 2in/187.8m (pp); 650ft 7in/198.29m (wl).
Beam: 63ft/19.2m; Draught: 19ft 10in/6.04m (mean).
Machinery: 4-shaft geared turbines; 8 Kampon boilers.
Performance: 152,000shp=33kts; Bunkerage: 2,163 tons oil fuel.
Range: 8,150nm at 18kts.
Protection: n/k
Guns: ten 8in (5x2); eight 5in DP (4x2); eight 25mm; four 13.2mm MGs.
Torpedoes: four 24in (2x2).
Aircraft: three, two catapults.
Complement: n/k.

Design Two repeat *Tone* class ships were authorised under the 1941 programme, but experience

had shown that the layout of those ships was not ideal and, as a result, the new ships were redesigned as repeat *Suzuya*s armed with ten 8in guns from the outset and incorporating all the lessons learned about strength and stability in the interim period. Orders were placed for two ships, but neither was laid down before April 1942. *Ibuki*, the leading ship, was launched in 1943, but work was then suspended almost immediately to allow concentration on carrier construction owing to heavy losses in that category. She lay at Kure in a state of suspension for about six months while various schemes for her conversion were discussed, including fast oiler and aircraft carrier. In the end the latter option was selected, and in November 1943 the hull was towed to Sasebo by the depot ship *Jingei* for work to restart. The conversion entailed bulging the hull

to improve stability and altering the machinery installation by removing half of the boilers and the after turbines (wing shafts), thus reducing the speed to 29kts. Vacant compartments were redesigned as fuel bunkers. The ship was to have a single hangar, two lifts and the bridge to starboard. Its aircraft complement was to be a dozen bombers and fifteen fighters, of which only ten fighters could be stowed in the hangar. It had been intended for the ship to be completed in the spring of 1945, but the serious conditions in Japan by early 1945, and particularly the shortage of trained aircrews, led to this being revised to August 1945. In March 1945, however, work was once more halted, this time for good, as the yard was to build suicide weapons instead. *Ibuki* was towed to Ibisu Bay near Sasebo and laid up, completed up to the flight deck, with all sponsons fitted but not fully armed, although a number of 5in rocket launchers had been fitted. She was still there at the end of the war, mainly undamaged, and was finally scrapped at Sasebo in 1947. Her sister, never named, was laid down in 1942 but suspended in July and broken up shortly afterwards to allow the laying down of the carrier *Amagi*.

Netherlands

JAVA CLASS

Ship	Builder	Laid Down	Launched	Completed	Fate
Java	De Schelde	31 May 16	9 Aug 21	1 May 25	Lost 27 Feb 1942
Sumatra	NSM Amsterdam	15 Jul 16	29 Dec 20	26 May 26	Scuttled 9 Jun 1944
Celebes	Fijenoord, (Rotterdam)	not laid			Cancelled 1919

Displacement: 6,670 tons/6,776 tonnes (standard); 8,208 tons/8339 tonnes (full load).
Length: 473ft 4in/155.3m (oa); 466ft 4in/153m (wl).
Beam: 48ft 9in/16m; Draught: 18ft 6in/6.1m (mean).
Machinery: 3-shaft Germania (*Sumatra,* Zoelly) geared turbines; 8 Schulz-Thornycroft boilers.
Performance: 72,000shp=31kts; Bunkerage: 1,200 tons oil fuel.
Range: 3,600nm at 12kts.
Protection: 50mm (aft) main belt; 75mm machinery and magazine spaces; 25mm to 50mm deck; 125mm CT.
Guns: ten 5.9in (10x1); six (*Java* 8) 40mm (6/8x1); four .5in MGs.
Torpedoes: nil.
Aircraft: two.
Complement: 525.

Design At the time of their conception, in 1915, these ships were comparable with, if not better than, their British and German contemporaries. However, because of the impact of the First World War on a neutral nation, which affected material supplies and the need to observe an 8hr working day, their completion was so badly delayed that they were hopelessly out of date by the time they joined the fleet. Like all Dutch warships, their design took into account the need for service in the Netherlands' most important colony, the East Indies, and they were intended to act as the most powerful ships on that station, as by 1916 the remaining battleships in the Royal Netherlands Navy were well over-aged and financial considerations prevented ships larger than cruiser size being planned. The design, in which Krupp had a hand, was in fact much larger than contemporary British and German designs; some 6,670 tons, which was the result of their heavy armament of ten 5.9in guns.

The protective scheme included a 75mm waterline belt which extended 392½ft, covering the machinery and magazine spaces, and was reduced to 50mm for a further 42½ft aft to protect the steering gear. Horizontal protection consisted of a 25mm deck, increased to 50mm on its sloped sides, meeting the upper edge of the side belt. 60mm bulkheads closed off the armoured carapace. Funnel uptakes were 50mm, conning tower 125mm and the faces of the gun shields 100mm.

The main machinery showed the strong German influence, Schulz-Thornycroft boilers and Germania turbines being installed, though *Sumatra* had Zoelly-pattern turbines because a serious fire at the yard had destroyed the original Germania set. These gave considerable trouble during the early part of her career. Designed power was 72,000shp, necessary for a ship of this tonnage to attain the specified 31kts. The machinery was arranged on a three-shaft system. Full oil-firing was adopted, no doubt due to the availability of oil from the East Indies refineries.

The main armament comprised ten Bofors Mk 6 50cal 5.9in guns in single shielded mountings, two each fore and aft on the centreline, with Nos. 2 and 9 superfiring. The remainder were disposed on the beam, giving a broadside of six guns. Range was 23,200yd at 29°. As completed, four 75mm guns comprised the secondary armament. No torpedo or aircraft installations were originally intended in the design.

Orders were placed for two ships in 1916 and, on 14 June 1917, for a third, to be named *Celebes*, with Fijenoord, Rotterdam. The intention was for this third ship to be launched in July 1921. However, as already noted, construction of the first two ships was delayed, and it was not until 1920 that the 1919 budget was approved. Only about 80 tons of material had been worked for *Celebes*, and she had not yet been laid down. As the design was now obsolete, she was cancelled. Although nominally a sister of the other two, she was to have been some 3m longer and 155 tons larger in displacement in order to act as East Indies Flagship and accommodate the necessary flag officer's staff.

Modifications Aircraft and handling derricks were added after completion. No catapults were fitted. The aircraft first carried was the British Fairey IIID, acquired in 1924, each ship operating two, but this type proved too fragile for the East Indies and they were replaced in 1926 by the Fokker C.VIIW floatplane. In the course of refits in 1934/35 the pole foremast was replaced by a tubular pattern and the 3in AA landed. In their place, six (*Sumatra*) and four (*Java*) 40mm Mk III Bofors in 3/2 twin mountings were fitted on the after shelter deck. The mainmast was cut down and repositioned and the searchlights rearranged. Four .5in MGs were also added. *Java* was lost in this condition, but her sister survived to be disarmed in 1944, when six of her 5.9in guns were used to rearm two RNethN gunboats. She may also have received a few 20mm.

Service After commissioning, *Java* made a cruise to Swedish and Norwegian waters between July and August 1925, but in October that year sailed

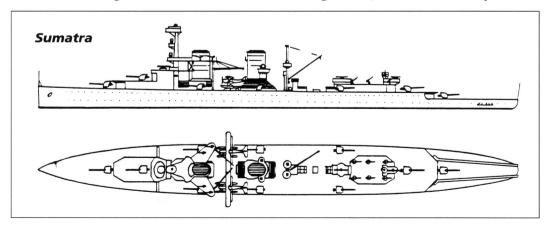

Sumatra

for the East Indies, arriving in Sabang on 28 November. She remained on that station, making a cruise to the Philippines, China and Japan between 8 November 1928 and 23 January 1929, and another to Australia and New Zealand between 2 September and 2 December 1930. She departed the East Indies on 6 March 1937, homeward bound, and on the way took part in convoy duties in the Straits of Gibraltar from 27 April to 4 May 1937 as a result of the Spanish Civil War. She arrived in Nieuwediep on 7 May. Between 17 and 22 May that year she participated in the Spithead Fleet Review, after which she was paid off for refit and modernisation at the Navy Yard in Willemsoord. She recommissioned on 3 January 1938, and at the end of the month sailed for further duties in Spanish waters, returning home on 19 February. *Java* sailed for the East Indies once more on 4 May 1938. On the outbreak of war with Germany she took part in convoy escort duties in the East Indies, and carried out similar tasks when the Pacific war began. She became a unit of the Allied Striking Force under the command of the Dutch Admiral Doorman, and participated in the abortive strike against Japanese invasion forces in the Banka Strait on 13/14 February 1942. A similar sortie on 18 February against landings on Bali resulted only in the damaging of a transport by *Java*, while the Allied force lost a destroyer and had *Tromp* damaged. On 27 February she sailed with the Allied force to intercept Japanese forces invading Java. In the subsequent Battle of the Java Sea, *Java* received torpedo hits from the cruiser *Nachi* and sank some 40nm west-south-west of Balwean Island.

Sumatra served in the East Indies for much of her career, but was relieved by *Java* in June 1938 and sailed for home and refit. However, this had to be postponed as a result of the Spanish Civil War, when she carried out convoy duties. Afterwards it was decided to use the ship as a training vessel in European waters, and in 1939 she made two training cruises, one to the Mediterranean and the other to Scottish waters. When Germany invaded the Netherlands *Sumatra* was at Vlissingen, in reserve awaiting refit, but was able to escape to Britain on 11 May 1940. Between 2 and 11 June she took some of the Royal Family to Canada, then sailed for the Dutch West Indies, arriving at Curaçao on 22 June, where she was sporadically employed on anti-raider duties in the Caribbean, central Atlantic and in the Antilles. She left Curaçao on 7 August for South Africa, arriving back in the East Indies in mid-October 1940. She was almost immediately paid off to refit and her crew dispersed to other ships. After the outbreak of the Pacific war she was recommissioned on 27 January 1942 with a skeleton crew, and left Soerabaya on 3 February with only half of her boilers and two-thirds of her machinery working. She arrived at Trincomalee on 15 February, and remained there, refitting and repairing, until 16 April, when she sailed for Bombay and further refit. She finally returned to Colombo on 26 July and sailed for Britain on 1 August, arriving in Portsmouth on 30 October. From November 1942, in commission but with a reduced crew, she remained there until May 1944, when she was destored and prepared for use as a blockship for the invasion of Normandy. On 9 June 1944 she was scuttled as part of the Gooseberry breakwater off Ouisterham.

Left: *Java* early in her career. (RNethN)
Below: *Java* at the Spithead Review in 1937. (MPL)

DE RUYTER CLASS

Ship	Builder	Laid Down	Launched	Completed	Fate
De Ruyter	Wilton-Fijenoord	16 Sep 33	11 May 35	3 Oct 36	Lost 28 Feb 1942

Displacement: 6,442 tons/6,545 tonnes (standard); 7,548 tons/7,668 tonnes (full load).
Length: 560ft 7in/170.92m (oa); 551ft 2inft/168.04m (wl).
Beam: 51ft 6in/15.7m; Draught: 16ft 9inft/5.11m (mean).
Machinery: 2-shaft Parsons geared turbines; 6 Yarrow boilers.
Performance: 66,000shp=32kts; Bunkerage: 1,300 tons oil fuel.
Range: 6,800nm at 12kts.
Protection: 50mm main belt; 30mm fore & aft machinery & magazines; 30mm barbettes, turrets & deck.
Guns: seven 5.9in (6x2, 1x1); ten 40mm (5x2); eight .5in MGs.
Torpedoes: nil.
Aircraft: two, one catapult.
Complement: 435.

Design The plan to build a third cruiser remained in the forefront of the naval staff's thinking long after the cancellation of *Celebes*, which in any event was now hopelessly outdated, but was constantly thwarted by the political and economic conditions of the times. Several construction plans for a fleet to defend the East Indies had been proposed, which included between two and four cruisers together with the requisite destroyers and submarines, but none met with unanimous acceptance, either within the service or without. By 1930, however, the decision had been taken to build a third ship, but financial constraints led to its design being scaled down. In consequence, a displacement of 5,250 tons was proposed, and an armament of six 6in in three twin turrets, one forward, two aft, with protection and endurance similar to those of the *Java*. There was considerable opposition to the adoption of such a weak design, but it was not until 1932 that conditions allowed a seventh 6in gun to be added and the displace-

ment increased. The use of electric welding and some light alloy provided some weight economy in the design of the hull, which was subdivided into 21 watertight compartments. Because the construction of this ship presented some problems to the yard, she was built in a dry dock.

The final design had a protective scheme which included a 50mm waterline belt that extended from forward to after magazines, reduced in thickness aft of this to 30mm. This belt was 405ft long and 12ft deep. The main deck was 30mm, as were the main turrets, end bulkheads, conning tower and barbettes.

Unlike the earlier cruisers, this ship was given only a two-shaft machinery installation. The boilers were paired in three separate spaces, of which the foremost were of slightly lower capacity (twelve burners in lieu of eighteen), and were constructed by the builders and De Schelde. The Parsons turbines, constructed by De Schelde, developed 66,000shp for a designed maximum speed of 32kts. They were fitted with cruising stages which gave the ship a speed of 17kts at 3,300shp. The foremost turbine space powered the port shaft, and was separated from the after turbine space by the gearing room; 33kts could be attained by a 15 per cent overload.

The 5.9in guns, constructed by Wilton-Fijenoord, were carried in Mk 9 twin and Mk 10 single

Above: *De Ruyter* in 1936. (MPL)

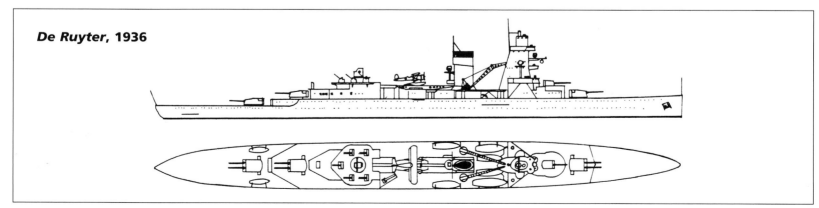

De Ruyter, 1936

mountings, with 60° elevation. Unlike that of the earlier ships, all of the main armament was shipped on the centreline. The single mounting was also used as a starshell gun. No heavy AA armament was fitted, only light AA, but these were 40mm Mk III Bofors in five twin stabilised mountings with advanced fire control. Although this outfit was much in advance of any contemporary, it was open to criticism because all five mountings were grouped in close proximity and could have been disabled by a single hit. Moreover, this also restricted their arcs of fire and left the forward arcs completely wooded. Only four pairs of .5in MGs in the bridge wings and on the top of the control tower gave any defence against head-on attack. No torpedo armament was fitted, but the ship did receive a catapult of Heinkel pattern and could accommodate two Fokker C.XIW floatplanes.

Modifications The original funnel cap proved unsatisfactory and was replaced by a new pattern in May 1936. No further alterations appear to have been made.

Service *De Ruyter* spent the first three months of her career in home waters, working up before sailing for the Far East on 12 January 1937, and arrived at Sabang on 5 March. She joined the East Indies squadron officially at the end of May, and on 25 October 1937 became flagship. She remained in this theatre, and from September 1939 carried out operations mainly in the western waters of the East Indies archipelago. Turbine repairs were carried out at Soerabaya in January and February 1940, and after the German invasion of the Netherlands she carried out patrols against Axis merchantmen attempting to escape to Germany. When Japan attacked Pearl Harbor in December 1941 she carried out patrols to prevent Japanese cruisers entering the Indian Ocean,

and then operated in the East Indies as cover for British convoys to Singapore. On 3 February 1942 she became flagship of the newly formed Allied Striking Force, with which Admiral Doorman attempted unsuccessfully to thwart Japanese landings in the East Indies theatre. On 26 February 1942 she sailed with this force to attack Japanese

transports reported off Balwean Island and, in the Battle of the Java Sea which followed, the Allied cruisers and destroyers were decimated by Japanese cruisers and destroyers. *De Ruyter* was hit and sunk by torpedoes from the Japanese heavy cruiser *Haguro* a little before midnight on 27 February 1942.

Above: *De Ruyter* at Wilton-Fijenoord in 1936. (Courtesy M. Twardowski)

Below: *De Ruyter* leaving her builder's yard. (RNethN)

TROMP CLASS

Ship	Builder	Laid Down	Launched	Completed	Fate
Tromp	NSM (Amsterdam)	17 Jan 36	24 May 37	18 Aug 38	Stricken 10 Dec 1968
Jacob van Heemskerck	NSM (Amsterdam)	31 Oct 38	16 Sep 39	10 May 40	Stricken 27 Feb 1970

Displacement: 3,450 tons/3,505 tonnes (standard); 4,860 tons/4,937 tonnes (full load).
Length: 433ft/131.97m (oa); 426ft 6in/130m (pp).
Beam: 40ft 9in/12.43m; Draught: 14ft 2in/4.64m (mean).
Machinery: 2-shaft Parsons geared turbines; 4 Yarrow boilers.
Performance: 56,000shp=32½kts; Bunkerage: 860 tons oil fuel.
Range: 6,000nm at 12kts.
Protection: 16mm main belt; 20mm to 30mm torpedo bulkhead; 15mm to 25mm deck.
Guns: six 5.9in (3x2); four 40mm (2x2); four .5in MGs.
Torpedoes: six 21in (3x2).
Aircraft: one.
Complement: 309.

Design These ships were authorised in 1931, reportedly as 2,500-ton flotilla leaders, although it is possible that this was merely a political subterfuge for the purpose gaining the necessary approval. Certainly they were later reworked as light cruisers for use in the East Indies, and there had always been plans to increase the cruiser strength in those waters.

The final design had a displacement of 3,450 tons (standard) and carried a relatively heavy armament for the size. The hull was of longitudinal construction, subdivided into seventeen watertight compartments, and had a double bottom extending 57 per cent of its length. This dou-

ble bottom was carried up to above the waterline. The hull was of raised forecastle design, which was carried aft for 50 per cent of the ship's length. The protective scheme included a 16mm waterline belt, inboard of which was a longitudinal torpedo bulkhead 20mm-30mm thick. The main deck was 15mm-25mm and extended inboards from the torpedo bulkheads, with a lower deck over the forward (25mm) and after (16mm) magazines and steering gear. The gun shields and ammunition hoists were 15-25mm. Total weight of armour was 450 tons, or 13 per cent of the standard displacement.

The main machinery, supplied by Workspoor, comprised four Yarrow-type boilers in two boiler rooms, abaft of which were the turbine rooms, the forward set powering the starboard shaft. The designed speed of 33½kts was exceeded by a knot on trials with a displacement of about 4,000 tons.

Unlike that of their larger sister, *De Ruyter*, the 5.9in main armament was concentrated forward, all guns being in twin Mk II mountings with 60° elevation, two forward and one aft; 2,000rpg were carried for the 5.9in guns. No intermediate armament was shipped, and the light AA was once again the 40mm Bofors in two twin Mk IV mountings, both at the after end of the forecastle deck. The design appears to have included four twin mountings, but only two were fitted as completed. Four .5in MGs in two twin mountings completed the gunnery. These ships also received a torpedo outfit, with two triple banks of 21in tubes on the upper deck abaft of midships. Finally, a single Fokker C.VIX floatplane was carried, but no catapult was fitted, the aeroplane being lowered on to the water by a boom for take-off.

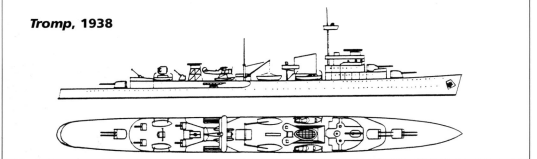

Tromp, 1938

Above: *Tromp* with *Sumatra* astern. (RNethN)
Left: *Tromp* in the Solent in 1938.

Modifications *Tromp* had her armament altered in the course of repairs at Sydney between March and June 1942, following action damage on 19/20 February. Two 3in AA and six 20mm singles were added, two of the latter sited on B and X guns. The after DCT was removed and the two twin 40mm repositioned on the centreline, one in lieu of the DCT. Radar was fitted to the after rangefinder, and the aircraft landed. Her AA outfit now included two 3in (2 x 1); four 40mm (2 x 2); six 20mm (6 x 1); four .5in MG (2 x 2) and four 7.7mm MG. In November 1943 two more 3in US-pattern guns were added, the .5in were replaced by four single .5in Brownings and the 7.7mm guns landed.

Heemskerck, completed in Britain, received a completely different outfit. Her main armament was ten 4in Mk XVI in five twin mountings XIX, disposed in A, B and X positions and two sided over the former torpedo tube positions. The tubes were never fitted. A single quadruple 2pdr was fitted at the after end of the forecastle deck, superfiring on X gun. Six 20mm Hispano-Suiza guns and two depth-charge throwers (from *G13* and *G15*) completed the armament. In 1944/45 she was refitted at Cammell Laird and the 2pdr was replaced by two twin Hazemeyer 40mm and two more twin 40mm were shipped amidships. Plans to fit six or eight twin 20mm could not be completed because of space problems, and only four twin 20mm were added in lieu of the Hispano-Suiza cannon. No aircraft was carried by this ship.

Service Before the outbreak of the Second World War, *Tromp* served in home waters, visiting Britain and Italy in November 1938 and Portugal and the Mediterranean in 1939. After taking part in a fleet review at Rotterdam in April 1939, the ship sailed for the East Indies on 19 August 1939. When Germany invaded the Netherlands on 10 May 1940, *Tromp* began convoy cover duties in the Indian Ocean and SW Pacific. On 1 February 1942 she joined the combined Allied Striking Force (ABDA). Two days later she sortied with the Allied force to intercept Japanese transports off Balikpapan, but after attack by aircraft the force returned to base. Further sorties on 8 and 14 February were equally fruitless. In a sortie on 18 February to attack Japanese landing forces on Bali, *Tromp* was badly damaged by *Arashio*, while *Michishio* was badly hit by the Allies. The Dutch cruiser returned to Soerabaya for temporary repairs, and sailed for Australia on 23 February and was repaired at Sydney. Thereafter, until the end of 1943, she was used on escort duties in Australian waters and in the Indian Ocean. In January 1944 she joined the British Eastern Fleet at Trincomalee and took part in the various carrier raids on Japanese-held territories and installations in Malaya and the East Indies. In an attack on Sabang on 25 July she was hit four times by shore batteries while bombarding the harbour. In 1945 *Tromp* formed part of the ocean covering force for the invasion of Rangoon, and on 10 May was sailed as part of TF60 to intercept the cruiser *Haguro*, but destroyers sank this ship before TF60

could make contact. Towards the end of May 1945 *Tromp* was transferred to the US 7th Fleet, leaving Trincomalee on 24 May and arriving at Morotai on 14 June to join TF74.2. In June/July 1945 she covered the invasion of Balikpapan, and on 16 September arrived at Jakarta for the Japanese surrender. She arrived back in home waters on 3 May 1946, paid off for refit, and did not recommission until 1 July 1948. Thereafter she served in a normal peacetime routine until finally paid off on 1 December 1955 and used as an accommodation ship until stricken on 10 December 1968. She was sold to Simons Handelmaatschapji NV of Rotterdam and re-sold to Spanish shipbreakers at Castellon de la Plana for scrapping.

Jacob van Heemskerk was incomplete and running basin trials at the time of the German invasion, and commissioned on 10 May in this state, sailing for Britain on the night of 14/15 May. Her only armament at this time was six 20mm Hispano-Suiza guns. Early in June 1940 she accompanied *Sumatra* to Canada, with the Netherlands Royal family, and on her return was taken in hand at Portsmouth for conversion into an AA cruiser. This refit was completed on 17 February 1941, after which *Heemskerck* served in the Irish Sea and Atlantic until January 1942, when she sailed for the East Indies. Arriving too late to take part in their defence, she joined the British Eastern Fleet instead. In September she took part in the invasion of Madagascar, before being employed escorting ocean convoys. In the course of this task she intercepted the German blockade runner *Ramses* in the Indian Ocean on 27 November. At the end of 1943 the ship sailed for Britain, and from January to June 1944 operated in the Mediterranean. She returned to Britain to refit, but served again in the Mediterranean from December 1944. After the surrender of Germany the ship was the first warship to enter Amsterdam, in June 1945. She sailed for the Far East in September, but hostilities had by then ceased and she remained in the East Indies until sailing from Batavia for home on 22 July 1946, reaching the Netherlands on 29 August. Postwar she served as a gunnery training ship and also made several long cruises to South America and the Netherlands Antilles. On 1 December 1955 she was re-rated as an accommodation ship, in which role she served until stricken on 27 February 1970. On 23 June that year she was sold to Spanish shipbreakers at Alicante.

EENDRACHT CLASS

Ship	Builder	Laid Down	Launched	Completed	Fate
Eendracht (ex Kijkduin)	Wilton-Fijenoord	19 May 39	22 Aug 50	17 Dec 53	Sold to Peru 1976
De Zeven Provincien	Rotterdam DD	5 Sep 39	24 Dec 44	18 Nov 53	sold to Peru 1973

Displacement: 8,350 tons/8,483 tonnes (standard); 10,800 tons/10,972 tonnes (full load).
Length: 613ft 6in/187m (oa); 598ft 5in/182.4m (pp).
Beam: 56ft 7in/17.25m; Draught: 18ft 6in/5.6m (mean).
Machinery: 2-shaft Parsons geared turbines; 6 Yarrow boilers.
Performance: 78,000shp=32kts; Bunkerage: 1,750 tons oil fuel.
Range: n/k.
Protection: 100mm amidships main belt; 75mm ends; 19mm to 25mm deck.
Guns: ten 5.9in (2x3, 2x2); fourteen 40mm (7x2); eight 0.5in MGs.
Torpedoes: six 21in (2x3).
Aircraft: two.
Complement: 700.

Design The replacement of the aged cruisers *Java* and *Sumatra* had been mooted as early as 1930, when it was anticipated that new ships would be laid down about 1940. However, it was not until early 1937 that the necessary funds were authorised for a ship in the 1938 estimates, with a second approved the following year. The design was to be an expansion of *De Ruyter*, armed with ten 5.9in guns in two triple and two twin turrets. The displacement was increased almost 30 per cent over that ship, and in fact the new ships were a completely new design. Triple turrets had not been used by the RNethN before, and were contracted to Bofors in Sweden.

The main armour belt was 100mm in the way of machinery and magazines, reducing to 75mm at the ends. Transverse armoured bulkheads closed off the ends of the waterline belt. The deck protection was 19mm to 25mm, being raised over the machinery spaces to give adequate height for the boilers.

The main machinery, a twin-shaft geared turbine installation, was subcontracted to De Schelde, and comprised six Yarrow three-drum boilers in three separate spaces, with the two turbine rooms separated by the gearing room. All of the boiler uptakes were trunked into a single funnel. The turbines developed 78,000shp for a maximum speed of 32kts.

As noted above, the 5.9in guns were ordered from Bofors in Sweden, and were to have been carried in two triple (A and Y) and two twin (B and X) mountings with 60° elevation. Once again no secondary armament was fitted, only light AA, which in these ships was greatly augmented and much better disposed. This consisted of six twin 40mm Bofors mountings, three disposed about the after control position and three around the forward control position above the wheelhouse. In this manner, good arcs of fire were obtained in both the forward and after sectors. Four single .5in Heavy MGs completed the AA outfit, all mounted on the upper deck. Two triple banks of 21in torpedo tubes were fitted, with a reserve torpedo store two decks below. Finally, a catapult and accommodation (but no hangar) for two floatplanes was provided.

Had work been started earlier, the design would have given the RNethN a powerful light cruiser design. As it was, the first ship, initially named *Kijkduin*, was not laid down until May 1939, Wilton-Fijenoord having secured the con-

tracts for both ships. However, this yard could not accommodate both hulls on its slips, and one was therefore built at the Rotterdam Dry Dock Co. A year later Germany overran the Netherlands, by which time the second vessel, *De Zeven Provincien*, had also been laid down and the leading ship renamed *Eendracht*. Neither had been launched nor progressed far, and the Germans captured them both undamaged. They were renamed *KH1* and *KH2* for completion on German account, the Netherlands government having cancelled all orders on the day of the surrender. The turrets and guns on order in Sweden were eventually used in the Swedish cruisers of the *Tre Kronor* class. Germany intended to complete these cruisers, but work proceeded at a very leisurely pace and without any real priority, although they were included in lists of Kriegsmarine ships under completion long after there was any realistic possibility of their being finished. So it proved, as only *De Zeven Provincien* was launched, and then only for use as a blockship on the evacuation of the Netherlands by German forces. Both ships were repossessed by the Dutch and completed many years later to completely revised designs, in a manner reminiscent of Great Britain and the *Tiger* class. *De Zeven Provincien* was renamed *De Ruyter* in 1947, and *Eendracht* first *De Ruyter* by the Germans in 1944 and later, in 1947, *De Zeven Provincien*, just to confuse matters.

De Zeven Provincien was converted to operate Terrier guided missiles in the 1960s. She was paid off on 17 October 1975 as an economy measure. In August 1976 she was sold to Peru, renamed *Aguirre* and commissioned after refit on 24 February 1978. *De Ruyter*, not converted into a guided-missile cruiser, was stricken on 26 January 1973 and sold to Peru on 7 March that year, commissioning as *Almirante Grau* on 23 May 1973 and sailing for Peru on 18 June.

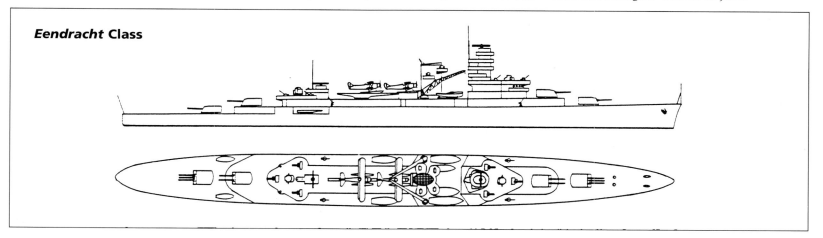

Eendracht **Class**

Peru

CORONEL BOLOGNESI CLASS

Ship	Builder	Laid Down	Launched	Completed	Fate
Coronel Bolognesi	Vickers Maxim (Barrow-in-Furness)	1905	24 Sep 06	19 Nov 06	Stricken 24 Jun 1958
Almirante Grau	Vickers Maxim (Barrow-in-Furness)	1905	27 Mar 06	1 Mar 07	Stricken 24 Jun 1958

Displacement: 3,180* tons/3,230 tonnes (standard).
Length: 377ft 7in/115.85m (oa); 369ft 10in/112.8m (pp).
Beam: 40ft 6in/12.34m; Draught: 14ft 3in/12.34m (mean).
Machinery: 2-shaft reciprocating 4-cylinder triple-expansion
    engines; 10 Yarrow boilers.
Performance: 14,000ihp=24kts; Bunkerage: 500 tons oil fuel.
Range: 3,700nm at 10kts.
Protection: 1½in side belt; 3in gun shields; 3in CT.
Guns: two 6in (2x1); four 3in (4x1); two 3in AA (2x1); eight
    3pdr (8x1).
Torpedoes: two 18in submerged (2x1).
Aircraft: nil.
Complement: 320.
* Almirante Grau 3,200 tons

Design At the turn of the century Peru planned the purchase of two small cruisers to augment its very modest navy, which had hitherto consisted of only of a few armed merchant ships. The ships were ordered from Vickers in Great Britain, the contracts being placed on 19 June 1905 for the first ship and on 29 November for the second. They were of the Scout type, which were being constructed for the Royal Navy in some numbers at that time and were used mainly as flotilla leaders for destroyers. Peru possessed no destroyers, but these small fast cruisers armed with a quick-firing battery were an attractive proposition for her limited resources. With a displacement of around 3,200 tons, these ships were broadly comparable with British contemporaries, in particular *Sentinel*, also built by Vickers, but they lacked the turtle-back forecastle. They were, however, given a side armour belt of 1½in over the midships section, as well as a deck of similar thickness over the machinery spaces. The conning tower was 3in, as were the 6in-gun shields. They had ten Yarrow water-tube boilers in three boiler rooms, and twin-screw, four-cylinder vertical triple expansion machinery. As designed, they were coal fired. Contract power and speed were exceeded with ease on trials, *Grau* making 24.64kts.

Almirante Grau was fitted as a flagship and had additional accommodation aft in a poopdeck with a sternwalk, which distinguished her from her sister, increasing her displacement by some 20 tons.

The ships were fitted with steam radiator heating for operation in cold climates and were equipped with both natural and forced ventilation systems.

The armament comprised two 6in BL guns of Elswick manufacture in single shielded mountings, one each on the forecastle and quarterdeck with, originally, eight 14pdr (3in) in single partly shielded mountings in the waist and in casemates in the forecastle. Electric ammunition hoists were provided. There were also eight 3pdr (47mm) Hotchkiss QF guns in single mountings in the waist and after casemates. Finally, there were two submerged 18in torpedo tubes.

Modifications Between 1923 and 1925 the machinery was modified as a result of wear and tear, but in the latter year the boilers of *Almirante Grau*, and then of her sister, were retubed at Balboa and converted to burn oil. Post-refit trials achieved speeds of between 24.3 and 24.58kts. The electrical and radio systems were renewed and fire control was fitted. The 3pdr outfit was reduced to two guns.

In 1934 the ships were given new boilers at Yarrows, when the number was reduced to eight. Speed was now 23.5kts. Subsequently, an Italian Giradelli fire-control system was installed, and in 1936 two Japanese 3in AA guns replaced the after pair of original 3in guns. At the same time, two twin light AA guns were fitted on the after searchlight platform. These are usually quoted as being 20mm, but Japan had no such weapon, and it remains unclear just what these guns were, or their origin, as Japan seems an unlikely source of weapons for a South American Power. The final refits to these ships took place in 1942-44, when the bridge structure was modified, the foremast was replaced by a tripod and a rangefinder fitted. Half of the boats were landed, the free space being used to fit seven .5in Browning guns, four in lieu of the boats, two in the bridge wings and one atop the wheelhouse. One depth-charge thrower and two rails were also fitted, the tubes being suppressed.

Service The two ships sailed for Peru via the Cape Verde Islands, Bahia, Montevideo and Puerto Madryn, rounded Cape Horn to coal at Coronel and arrived in Callao on 10 August 1907. *Coronel Bolognesi* suffered boiler troubles en route, which were repaired at Callao. In 1921 they made their first training cruise for cadets of the Naval Academy. In 1933, as a result of a conflict in the Amazon with Colombia, *Almirante Grau* was despatched with two submarines to support gunboats at Iquitos (a town founded by the Navy in 1864) by controlling the entrance to the Amazon at Belem. They sailed in May via the Panama Canal, a voyage of 6,500 miles, though Iquitos lies only about 600 miles from Callao by air. However, the dispute was over before she arrived and, after a passage of some 4,500nm, she lay for ten days at Belem do Para, Brazil. In August she returned to Callao. On passage, a diplomatic incident was caused by having refit work carried out at Balboa,

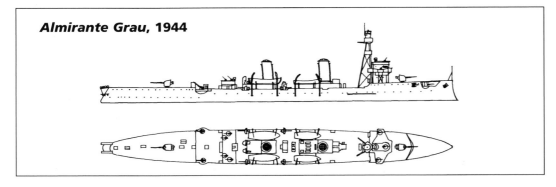

Almirante Grau, 1944

in the Canal Zone. Protests from the USA stopped the intended re-boilering, and the boilers were returned to England and fitted there the following year. Peru did not enter the war in 1939, but in 1941 a brief conflict with Equador broke out on 5 July. The Peruvian Navy established a blockade of the Gulf of Guayaquil, during which the cruiser *Coronel Bolognesi* relieved the destroyer *Almirante Villar* after the latter had been badly damaged in an action with an Equadorian gunboat. She and her sister *Grau* escorted the destroyer back to Callao. This conflict ended in January 1942. After Peru entered the Second World War, in 1944, the country's isolated position, far from the areas of conflict, and the obsolete nature of her fleet meant that the cruisers were used only for coastal defence and patrol duties off the homeland. Postwar they continued in the training role, latterly static at Callao until stricken on 24 June 1958, when they were traded in for some new patrol craft and broken up at Callao.

Right: *Almirante Grau,* 1944/45. (Author's collection)

Right: *Coronel Bolognesi.* (Author's collection)

Poland

Despite grandiose prewar plans for the expansion of the Navy, which were inspired by political ambitions, no cruisers were ever seriously contemplated. However, the Chief of the Polish Navy in exile in Great Britain was anxious to raise the status of his forces by the addition of ships larger than destroyers. His only source of additional ships was, of course, the Royal Navy, but Britain wished Poland to man ships no larger than destroyers, which the Poles were already operating with great élan and success. However, after raising the question in 1942, the Poles' wishes were granted when the old D class ship *Dragon*, currently under refit at Cammell-Laird, was transferred and taken over on 15 January 1943. The choice of a name caused a political problem, for Poland wished to rename her *Lwów*, after a town in Galicia, south-east Poland. This was politically embarrassing to Britain in view of her Soviet ally, and because none of the other alternatives, *Gdynia*, *Westerplatte* or *Warszawa*, were considered suitable, the name of the ship was not changed.

At the time of her transfer her armament was five 6in, twelve 2pdr (3 x 4), eight 20mm (8 x 1) and torpedoes.

In fact the ship did not complete refit and repairs until August 1943, and she then worked up at Scapa Flow and joined the Home Fleet. She covered Russian convoys JW57 and RA57, and in March 1944 was allocated to the 10th Cruiser Squadron, after which she began training for the invasion of Europe. During April and May she was under refit at Chatham, when one twin 4in AA was added and the 20mm outfit altered to four twin and four single. Radars were types 273, 282 and 286Q.

She left the Clyde on 2 June 1944 with *Warspite*, the 2nd Cruiser Squadron and a destroyer escort for the invasion itself, and arrived off Sword Beachhead at 0200 on D-day. For the next two days she shelled batteries at Calleville sur

Above: *Conrad* under Polish colours in 1946. (Courtesy M. Twardowski)

Opposite page: *Conrad* late in 1945. (Courtesy M. Twardowski)

Orne, Trouville and Caen, as well as tank concentrations. On 8 June she shelled batteries at Haulgate, and continued fire support duties, with breaks to re-ammunition in Portsmouth, until 8 July, when she was struck amidships on the port side by a torpedo from a Neger one-man midget submarine while lying off Caen. The explosion detonated Q magazine, causing many casualties. Although not sunk, the ship was a constructive total loss, and was towed to the Gooseberry harbour and set on the bottom the next day as part of the breakwater.

CONRAD

Following the loss of *Dragon*, Poland pressed for and received another cruiser, the British *Danae*. On 4 October 1944 this ship was transferred to the Polish Navy and renamed *Conrad*, after the famous writer. She was under refit at Southampton and Chatham until 23 January 1945, then escorted convoys to and from the Schelde. On 12 February she left for Scapa Flow, but sustained serious turbine damage during work-up. She had been allocated to the 10th Cruiser Squadron, but repairs at Chatham lasted until 29 May 1945. She returned to Scapa flow, and from there moved to Wilhelmshaven following the German surrender.

Between July and the end of the year she was employed on Red Cross relief and communications duties between the UK and Scandinavia, making eight trips in all. In January 1946 she returned to Scapa Flow and remained with the Home Fleet until transferred to Rosyth local command on 8 March. On 17 April 1946 she arrived to join other Polish ships at Plymouth for discussions regarding the future, and on 26 April left for

Plymouth, where she was based for the remainder of her career. By August she was reduced to about half manning, and on 28 September 1946 the ship reverted to RN control and the name *Danae*. On 22 January 1948 she was sold for scrapping, and arrived at T. W. Ward at Barrow for breaking up on 27 March 1948.

Below: *Dragon* in 1944. (Courtesy M. Twardowski)

Siam

TAKSIN CLASS

Design Siam had maintained a fleet since the 1800s, but this was never extensive and relied on both foreign manpower and construction from its inception. By the beginning of the twentieth century the dependence on foreign manpower had largely been overcome, but there was still little indigenous shipbuilding capability. By the 1920s the status of the Navy had declined; it was junior to the army and suffered from a lack of funding. Politically, the country was in turmoil in 1932/33, after which the Army gained control to all intents and purposes, but the Navy benefited by the increase in funds for defence. In 1935 the Navy put in hand a new construction programme and placed orders in Italy for two torpedo boats (see *Encyclopedia of Destroyers of World War Two*) and two minelayers, as well as three CMBs from Britain. At the same time a four-year programme was put in hand that included two coast defence ships, two escort vessels, seven more torpedo boats, four submarines and some minor vessels.

The majority of the orders went to Japan, but Italy won the torpedo boat order. In 1938 a second programme was authorised which included two light cruisers and probably further submarines.

Italy gained the contract for the cruisers, which were modest vessels of 4,300 tons armed with six 6in guns. Visually, the design resembled a single-funnelled version of an Italian *Condottieri* type cruiser, but of smaller dimensions; between that ship and the *Capitani Romani* in size.

The protective scheme included a 2.36in (60mm) waterline belt and a 30mm deck.

The main machinery was disposed on the unit principle, with two boiler rooms forward of the forward turbine space, which was separated from the after turbine room by the No.3 boiler room. Designed installed power was 45,000shp for maximum speed of 30kts.

The main armament was disposed in three twin turrets, one forward and two aft, and was in all probability the standard Italian Ansaldo 55cal weapon. The secondary armament comprised six 3in single guns on HA mountings in the waist, and the light AA was eight 13.2mm MGs, later supplanted by 20mm. Two twin trainable banks of 21in torpedo tubes were fitted, sited on the main deck just aft of A turret and firing through ports in the ship's side. Finally, there was a catapult on the centreline abaft the funnel, and two aircraft could be carried. There was no hangar. Only one main battery director was shipped, atop the tower bridge, with two HA secondary directors for the 3in sided at the break of the forecastle.

Contracts were signed in October 1938 and the hulls laid down almost a year later. Their names were *Taksin* and *Naresuan*. Construction continued on Siamese account after the Italian entry into the Second World War, *Naresuan* being launched in August 1941. However, by the turn of the year Italy's position regarding the sustaining of the Axis armies in North Africa was becoming desperate, and in December 1941 both ships were requisitioned by Italy and a revised design prepared for continued completion on their account. Further details will be found on page 144.

Left: *Naresuan* at her launch. (Author's Collection)

Opposite page: *Komintern* in the 1930s, reportedly on 1 May 1936, carrying a Hein mat on the stern. (R. Greger)

Soviet Union

KOMINTERN CLASS

Ship	Builder	Laid Down	Launched	Completed	Fate
Komintern	Admiralty Yard, (Nikolaiev)	23 Aug 01	20 May 02	Jul 05	Scuttled 10 Oct 1942

Displacement: 6,338 tons/6,439 tonnes (standard); 6,675 tons/6,781 tonnes (full load)*.
Length: 440ft 2in/134.2m (oa); 435ft 11in/132.9m (wl).
Beam: 54ft 6in/16.6m; Draught: 22ft 3in/6.8m (mean).
Machinery: 2-shaft VTE reciprocating engines; 12 Normand Boilers.
Performance: 14,500ihp=12kts; Bunkerage: 900 tons (1941).
Range: 2,000nm at 10kts.
Protection: 3in main deck and casemates; 6in CT.
Guns: eight 5.1in (8x1); four 75mm (4x1); three 3in AA (3x1); three 45mm AA (3x1).
Mines: 195 (1941).
Torpedoes: nil.
Aircraft: nil.
Complement: 590.
* Data refers to First World War; displacement by 1941 was about 6,000 tons.

Design This old ship, formerly *Pamiat Merkuriya*, was the survivor of a class of five, of which the name ship was *Bogatyr*. One, *Vityaz*, was badly damaged by fire while building and never completed, and *Oleg* had been sunk by British CMBs in the raid on Kronstadt on 17 July 1919. Of the remainder, *Ochakov* ended up in the employ of the White Russians and was finally interned at Bizerte on 23 December 1920 and scrapped in 1933. *Bogatyr* was cannibalised for spares to refit *Pamiat Merkuriya* in 1922, her cylinders being sent to Sevastopol in August 1922, for example. *Pamiat Merkuriya* was renamed *Komintern* on 31 December 1922.

The design, a protected cruiser armed with twelve 6in guns, was of Vulkanwerft (Stettin) origin, the leading ship having been constructed by

that yard. This ship had had her machinery destroyed by the British at Sevastopol during April 1919; hence the need for the machinery of *Bogatyr*. With her coal-fired machinery capable of speeds less than 20kts by the 1930s, the ship was totally obsolete by the time of the Second World War, but, in the absence of a large Black Sea fleet being available to the Soviets, she saw active service in that theatre despite her age.

Modifications When the ship was repaired by the Soviets she was rearmed with sixteen 130mm (5.1in) 55cal M1913 guns in twelve single and two twin mountings, the latter being old-pattern gunhouses on the forecastle and quarterdeck. After her conversion to a training cruiser in 1930/31 the twin 5.1in mountings were removed and replaced by single shielded mountings of the same calibre, and four of the original single 5.1in were replaced by old 75mm/50 M1902-pattern guns for training purposes. She carried ten 5.1in after this conversion. The six broadside submerged torpedo tubes were removed at this time. The four boilers in the forward boiler room were removed, and the space fitted out with classrooms. The forward funnel, however, was not removed until another refit in the late 1930s. In 1935/36 she was fitted with a platform on the quarterdeck for the experimental operation of a seaplane. Finally, in the winter of 1940/41, she was converted to a minelayer. With a reduced main armament of six 5.1in, and four 76mm AA, she could carry 195 mines. The light AA was increased during the autumn of 1941 with the addition of three new army-pattern 25mm guns.

Service As *Pamiat Merkuriya*, this ship served with the Imperial Black Sea Fleet throughout the First World War and carried out a number of offensive and defensive operations during that period. However, she was at Sevastopol in 1917 when the Bolshevik revolution broke out, but initially raised the Ukrainian flag on 12 November until the Ukrainian Nationalists were persuaded to join the Bolshevik cause, after which the Red Flag was hoisted on 16 February 1918. On 28 March 1918 the ship was demobilised and laid up with a care and maintenance crew only, the guns having been landed for use in armoured trains. On 1 May 1918 she was captured by German troops to be employed as a barracks ship, and after the German armistice she was taken over by the White Russians in November 1918. Then, in

Above: Another view of *Komintern*, probably also on 1 May 1936. (Navpic)

speed was reduced to 12kts at best. By 1939 the ship was in such poor condition that she was scheduled to be scrapped, but the German invasion of the Soviet Union in June 1941 gave her a reprieve and she participated in the laying of defensive minefields off Sevastopol at the start of hostilities. Subsequently *Komintern* was attached to the north-east area detachment on 6 August as flagship, based at Odessa and Ochakov in support of the Soviet Maritime army. In the autumn of 1941 she supported the defenders of Odessa and escorted reinforcement troops to the beleaguered city until its fall, when she participated in the evacuation operations. Following this, she participated in operations at Sevastopol from the beginning of 1942, transporting troops to the Crimea and giving gunfire support to the defending forces, in the course of which she was attacked on several occasions by German aircraft. After the fall of Sevastopol at the beginning of July, *Komintern* was based at Novorossisk, where she was attacked by aircraft on the 2nd and heavily damaged on the port side. Despite the damage she was able to steam to Poti for repairs, but on 16 July was attacked again and severely damaged. She was paid off, but transferred to Tuapse and disarmed, her guns being taken ashore to form five batteries for the defence of Tuapse. After this, *Komintern* was steamed back to Poti with a reduced crew and scuttled as a breakwater for a new light craft base in the channel of the Khopi river on 10 October 1942, where she still remains.

December 1918, French and British troops took possession of her. When the Red forces took the town in April 1919, the cruiser remained behind because her machinery had been disabled as recounted above. Between 1921 and 1 May 1923, when recommissioned, the ship was repaired and refitted with parts cannibalised from *Bogatyr*, having been renamed *Komintern*. She served almost exclusively in Black Sea waters, except for a cruise to Istanbul in the autumn of 1928. In 1930 she started a sixteen-month refit and was converted to a training ship, after which her

KRASNYI KAVKAZ CLASS

Ship	Builder	Laid Down	Launched	Completed	Fate
Krasnyi Kavkaz	Russud Dky,	31 Oct 13	21 Jun 16	25 Jan 32	Sunk as a target 1955

Displacement: 7,440 tons/7,560 tonnes (standard); 9,174 tons/9,030 tonnes (full load).

Length: 555ft 11in/169.5m (oa); 537ft 3in/163.8m (wl).

Beam: 51ft 6in/15.7m; Draught: 21ft 7in/6.6m (mean).

Machinery: 4-shaft Brown-Boverie geared turbines; 10 Yarrow boilers.

Performance: 55,000shp=29½kts; Bunkerage: 1,600 tons oil fuel.

Range: 3,500nm at 15kts.

Protection: 1in to 3in main belt; 1¼in+¾in deck; 3in turrets and CT.

Guns: four 7.1in (4x1); eight 3.9in (4x2); two 76mm AA (2x1); four 45mm (4x1).

Torpedoes: twelve 21in (4x3).

Aircraft: two, one catapult.

Complement: 880.

Design This ship was one of a group of eight authorised before the First World War, six in 1912 and two in 1914, of which half were to be built in Baltic and half in Black Sea yards. The two groups differed, and can be separated into the *Svetlana* and *Admiral Nakhimov* types. None were completed before the armistice with Germany in 1917, although six had been launched, one being this cruiser, under the name of *Admiral Lazarev*, one of the *Admiral Nakhimov* group. As designed, the ships were to have been armed with fifteen 5.1in (130mm) guns on a displacement of 6,500 tons and powered for the first time by turbine machinery. Those ships ordered from Black Sea yards, of which this was one, had increased displacement, greater overall length and marginally more beam than their Baltic sisters. Their protec-

tive scheme included a 3in waterline belt, with an upper strake of 1in plate and upper and lower armoured decks of ¾in (20mm).

The original main armament was all broadside except for the forward gun, and six of these were mounted in casemates. Two submerged broadside torpedo tubes were also fitted, and the ships were equipped to operate two French Tellier seaplanes.

The machinery comprised fourteen Yarrow boilers, of which nine were mixed-fired in three groups. The turbines, of Brown-Curtis type in all but two ships, were on a four-shaft layout, the forward turbine room driving the outboard shafts. The British firm of John Brown had the contract to install the machinery for these ships.

In December 1917, when *Admiral Lazarev* was some 63 per cent complete, work was stopped after the Brest-Litovsk Treaty and the ship lay unattended for six years or so. In 1924 the Soviet Government decided to complete the ship to a revised design, with eight 8in guns in twin turrets, but this armament was quickly found to be impossible on such a small and lightly constructed hull. In consequence, the main arma-

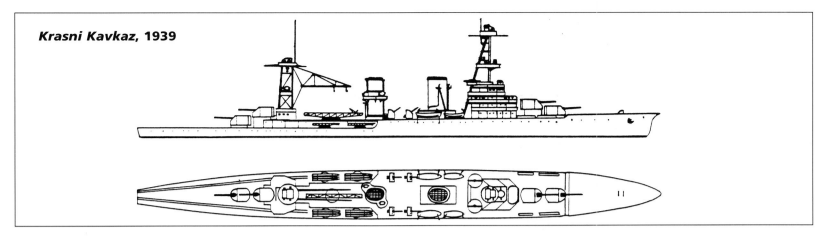

Krasni Kavkaz, 1939

ment was altered to 7.12in (181mm) 57cal in three twin turrets. Even this, however, proved too much, and in the end the main armament was limited to four single 7.12in in makeshift gunhouses, two each fore and aft. In December 1926 she was renamed *Krasnyi Kavkaz* and reconstruction began in September the following year, the ship being recommissioned on 25 January 1932. Four single 76mm AA were shipped sided amidships and there were four triple banks of 21in torpedo tubes on the main deck aft of the forecastle break. Finally this ship received a catapult of Heinkel manufacture and could operate two aircraft, although in practice only one He 55 flying boat appears to have been carried.

Modifications In May 1932, following a collision with *Komintern*, her bows were rebuilt to a new

form. The 76mm were replaced by Italian manufactured 100mm (3.9in)/47 guns after 1936, and four new 45mm AA replaced the original Maxim guns. The catapult was landed just before the war. During an overhaul in 1940 two new 76mm/L55 guns in single shielded mountings were added on the quarterdeck just aft of Y gun. Plans to change the 7.1in guns for twin 5.1in, as carried by *Tashkent*, came to nothing, as the delivery time was too long. In the course of repair at Poti in the autumn of 1942 *Krasnyi Kavkaz* received two more twin 3.9in guns from the sunken *Chervona Ukrania* and ten new semi-automatic 37mm, the after pair of tubes being landed. A quadruple .5in MG mounting was added on the roof of both B and X turrets, and there is evidence that 20mm Oerlikon guns were also fitted. By 1944 the light

armament consisted of twelve 3.9in (6 x 2); two 76mm (2 x 1); four 45mm (4 x 1); ten 37mm (10 x 1) and eight .5in MG, plus an unknown number of 20mm.

Service In October 1933 the ship made a rare visit to foreign ports when a cruise was made to Istanbul, Piraeus and Naples, returning to Odessa on 11 November. She was accompanied by the destroyers *Petrovskij* and *Saumjan*. Plans to despatch another squadron to the western Mediterranean at the time of the Spanish Civil War came to naught. At the outbreak of war, in June 1941, the ship participated in the laying of defensive minefields off Sevastopol, but on 28 June she was ordered to Novorossisk. However,

Below: *Krasnyi Kavkaz* in 1937. (MPL)

barely a month later she was ordered to the defence of Odessa. In the course of this task she shelled Romanian positions around the area and transported troops for amphibious landings behind enemy lines. From 1 October the cruiser assisted in the evacuation of Odessa and Tendra Island, and from the 14th was involved in the final evacuations of the port, bombarding enemy positions until all of the area was given up. On 31 October the ship, together with two destroyers, was appointed permanent artillery support ship at Sevastopol, but nevertheless assisted in the evacuation of many of the ports on the Crimean coast and was used to transport supplies to the Sevastopol garrison, as well as carrying out bombardments of enemy positions as required. At the end of December 1941 she participated in the landing at Feodosia, where she was hit several times and damaged. In 1942, in the course of transport operations to Feodosia, *Krasnyi Kavkaz* was bombed and damaged by Stukas on 4 January, several compartments aft being flooded. Some 1,700 tons of water were taken in, and the ship reached Tuapse only with great difficulty, later transferring to Poti for repair. The damage was considerable, and it was not until 17 August 1942 that she began post-repair sea trials. She immediately began troop transport duties to Tuapse, making five trips and carrying a total of 16,000 men and their equipment. In 1943 she participated in some landing operations but, after 6 October, when German Stukas sank three destroyers, the larger units of the fleet were no longer committed to action. In the autumn of 1944 she was refitted and did not return to Sevastopol until 23 May 1945. On 27 May 1947 she was reclassified as a training cruiser, and remained in the Black Sea until paid off in the late 1954. She was sunk as a target for SSN-1 *Scrubber* missiles in June 1955.

Above: *Krasnyi Kavkaz* in 1938 off the Crimea, armed with 100mm guns and equipped with a Heinkel aircraft. (R. Greger)
Below: *Krasnyi Kavkaz* off the Caucasus in 1944. Note single 76mm AA under after turret. (R. Greger)

CHERVONA UKRAINA CLASS

Ship	Builder	Laid Down	Launched	Completed	Fate
Chervona Ukraina	Naval Dky (Nikolaiev)	Jul 14	6 Nov 15	21 Mar 27	Lost 13 Nov 1941

Displacement: 7,480 tons/7,600 tonnes (standard); 8,268 tons/8,400 tonnes (full load).
Length: 546ft 9in/166.7m (oa); 535ft 3in/163.2m (wl).
Beam: 51ft 6in/15.7m; Draught: 20ft 4in/6.2m (mean).
Machinery: 4-shaft Parsons geared turbines; 4 Yarrow boilers.
Performance: 55,000shp=29kts; Bunkerage: 2,900 tons oil fuel.
Range: 3,700nm at 14kts.
Protection: as *Krasnyj Kavkaz*.
Guns: fifteen 5.1in (15x1); six 3.9in (6x1); seven 45mm (7x1).
Torpedoes: twelve 21in (4x3).

Aircraft: one.
Complement: 850.

Design This ship was also one of the cruisers laid down before the First World War, formerly being *Admiral Nakhimov* of the enlarged Black Sea type. Although she was launched in November 1915, her completion had been delayed by the wartime conditions in Russia and the reliance on foreign firms for some equipment. Chief of the latter were the turbine rotors and blading, contracted to John Brown of Clydebank, Scotland, which had also secured the contract to install all the machinery of ships under construction at Nikolaiev. Gross inefficiency in Russian industrial management and communications, for example, led to the 'loss' of the turbine blading at one stage, which did not turn up until some nine months later in a warehouse in Nikolaiev, after accusations that Britain had not delivered them. Her machinery was installed by October 1916, but progress thereafter was slow. When the ship was inspected by the British, in August 1919, she was about 80 per cent complete, with superstructure, funnels and masts in place, but lacking guns (which were still at the Obukhov works in St Petersburg) and with her electrical systems incomplete. When the White Russians evacuated Nikolaiev in January 1920 the ship was towed to Odessa, but when this port, too, had to be evacuated the ship was beached at the entrance. She was easily raised by the Soviet forces in February and towed to Nikolaiev for completion.

Her completion, like that of her sisters, was tardy in the extreme, given her advanced state and the fact that she was completed more or less to her original design. On 27 December 1922 she was renamed *Chervona Ukraina*, and in April 1923 the Soviet Government decided to complete the ship, but it was to be another four years before she was commissioned. The armour scheme was the same as that of the original design, as described in the section on *Krasnyi Kavkaz*, but this ship was not given heavier guns, receiving instead fifteen 5.1in single mountings in the as-designed positions. The remainder of the gunnery outfit as completed was four old 4in singles and a couple of 3in single mountings. The original pair of submerged torpedo tubes were suppressed and replaced by three triple banks of 18in torpedo tubes originating from destroyers. These were sited on the quarterdeck, two sided and one on the centreline. Provision was also made to operate an aircraft, handled by a conspicuous crane between the second and third funnel. This was initially an Avro 504, licence-built as the MU-1.

Modifications In the early 1930s the ship was modernised and had the torpedo tubes removed from the quarterdeck. They were replaced by four triple banks, now for 21in torpedoes, on the main deck fore and aft of the midships 5.1in guns. About 1936 she received three twin 3.9in guns of Italian origin; one on the forecastle, where it obstructed the arcs of No. 1 gun, and the other pair aft. She was again taken in hand at Sevastopol on 26 August 1939 for refit, which was to include replacement of the 5.1in guns by a new model, probably that mounted in the newer destroyers. The outbreak of war between Germany, France and Great Britain postponed these plans, and the only change was the increasing of the 45mm outfit to seven mountings and the addition of .5in MGs. At the same time the mixed-firing boilers were replaced by fully oil-fired types. She did not return to service until 1 May 1941.

Service *Chervona Ukraina* participated in the laying of defensive minefields off Sevastopol on the outbreak of war with Germany in June 1941, then, towards the end of August, she was one of the ships assigned to the defence of Odessa. In September she performed gun support duties against Axis shore batteries along the front around Odessa and transported troops to the port from Novorossisk. She assisted in the evacuation of Tendra Island in October, and of Odessa, then retired to Sevastopol. Between 1 and 10 November the cruiser assisted in the transport and evacuation of troops and materials to the Caucasian coast, and during the German attack on Sevastopol she engaged enemy batteries and formations. On 12 November, while engaged in a duel with shore batteries, she was attacked by a force of Stuka dive-bombers and hit by several bombs. The resultant damage and fires put her on the bottom, and the ship was abandoned. On 2 April 1942 she was bombed again and completely destroyed. The wreck was raised between January 1946 and November 1947, then broken up.

Above: *Chervona Ukraina* as completed in 1928, seen here with an Avro MU1 seaplane. (R. Greger)

Below: *Chervona Ukraina* in 1935, equipped with a Heinkel aircraft. (R. Greger)

KRASNYI KRYM CLASS

Ship	Builder	Laid Down	Launched	Completed	Fate
Krasnyi Krym	Russo-Baltic, (Reval)	14	11 Dec 15	Oct 26*	Scrapped 1956**

*Actually commissioned on 1 Jul 1928
**But see text

Displacement: 6,693 tons/6,800 tonnes (standard); 8,041 tons/8,170 tonnes (full load).
Length: 519ft 6in/158.4m (oa); 507ft 9in/154.8m (wl).
Beam: 50ft 6in/15.4m; Draught: 19ft 8in/6m (mean).
Machinery: 4-shaft Curtis-AEG geared turbines; 13 Yarrow boilers.
Performance: 50,000shp=29kts (24kts max in 1941); Bunkerage: 2,900 tons oil fuel.
Range: 3,350nm at 14kts.
Protection: as *Krasnyi Kavkaz*.
Guns as *Chervona Ukraina* except only four 45mm.
Mines: 100.
Torpedoes: six 21in(2x3).
Aircraft: one.
Complement: 850.

Design This ship, nominally a sister of *Krasnyi Kavkaz* and *Chervona Ukraina*, was one of the Baltic ships of the class and was laid down at Reval in April 1914. As such, she differed slightly from the other ships in being a little smaller in displacement and dimensions, as well as in other details. Baltic units were strengthened for ice navigation, for example. She had been laid down as *Svetlana*, but a fire during construction in April 1917, which damaged the machinery, had delayed work. By November the ship was some 90 per cent complete, when the advancing German army forced Russia to tow her out to Kronstadt. The revolution and subsequent civil war interrupted progress on her completion, and it was not until November 1924 that the Soviet Government ordered completion resumed. On 5 February 1924 the ship was renamed *Profintern*, and the following February she was ready for sea trials, being the first large ship to be completed by the Soviets. The trials were a disaster, and resulted in a further fifteen months in dockyard hands before the cruiser could be commissioned.

The armour, armament (fifteen 5.1in and four 3in) and machinery were generally similar to those of her half-sisters, except that she had one less boiler and the machinery developed only 50,000shp. Displacement was reduced to 6,800 tons (normal), as opposed to the Black Sea ships' 7,600 tons, and the overall length was reduced by some 15ft 9in.

Modifications During a major refit in 1935/38 the ship received three twin 3.9in guns, which were shipped one on the forecastle and two on the quarterdeck. At the same time, four 45mm AA were added and the torpedo tubes were replaced by triple 21in (in lieu of 18in). The tubes were now mounted just forward of the after casemate 5.1in guns, instead of on the quarterdeck. The aircraft equipment was landed. In 1942 the AA outfit was augmented by the removal of three 45mm guns and their replacement by ten 37mm automatic guns in single mounts. She may also have had quadruple .5in MGs. Late in the war she was fitted with a British-pattern radar set.

Service *Profintern* commissioned for service with the Baltic Fleet. In August 1928 she visited Swinemünde, but in 1929 was transferred to the Black Sea along with the battleship *Parizhskaya Kommuna*, and sailed from Kronstadt on 22 November. Rough weather in the Bay of Biscay forced the ships back into Brest for repairs, and they finally arrived in Sevastopol on 18 January 1930 to join the Black Sea Fleet. Another foreign cruise was made to Istanbul in 1933, then the ship was under refit 1935/38. On 31 October 1939 she was renamed *Krasnyi Krym*. From 28 June 1941 the cruiser was based at Novorossisk, but in August was sent to the defence of Odessa and bombarded enemy positions around the town. She was also involved in the transport of troops from Novorossisk to Odessa, and in offensive counter-landings at Grigorevka. In October she was involved in the evacuations of Odessa and Tendra, as well as transporting materials and personnel from Sevastopol to the Caucasian ports. During November *Krasnyi Krym* bombarded Axis positions in the Crimea in defence of Sevastopol, and on 29 December supported the landings at Feyodosia. In the course of this task she was hit eleven times and suffered casualties. On 15 January

Above: *Krasnyi Krym* in 1939. (Courtesy M. Twardowski)

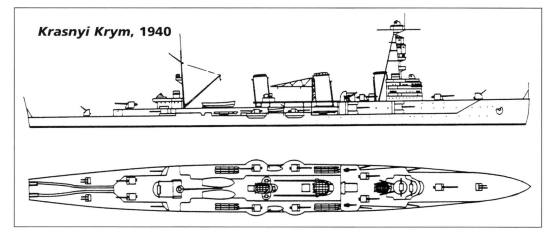

Krasnyi Krym, 1940

1942 she was designated flagship for the landing at Sudak, and in February transported troops to the beleaguered fortress of Sevastopol, subsequently engaging enemy shore positions before evacuating wounded to the Caucasus coast. Resupply and evacuation runs into Sevastopol were made by the cruiser throughout March to June, and after the fall of Sevastopol the ship assisted in the evacuation of Novorossisk in August. She became a Guards Ship on 18 June 1942. The remainder of 1942 was spent transporting troops around the Caucasus front, but in February 1943 she supported an offensive landing at Cape Myshakho. After this, operations were curtailed as a result of the sinking of three destroyers by Stukas on 6 October 1943, which left almost no destroyer screen for the larger ships. On 15 November 1944 the cruiser returned to the recaptured port of Sevastopol. She was reclassified as a training cruiser on 7 March 1945, and as an accommodation ship in 1953. She was re-rated as an Experimental Ship on 7 May 1954 and renamed *OS-20*, and on 18 March 1958 was again re-rated as an accommodation ship, *PKZ-144*. In July 1959 she was deleted from the active list and broken up. (Note: alternative sources give 31 May 1949 as the date of re-rating as a training ship, 8 April 1953 for deletion from the active list, and 17 February 1956 as the date for transfer to scrapping.)

KIROV CLASS

Ship	Builder	Laid Down	Launched	Completed	Fate
Kirov	Ordzonikidze (Leningrad)	22 Oct 35	30 Nov 36	23 Sep 38	Discarded in Dec 1974
Voroshilov	Marti South Yd (Nikolaev)	15 Oct 35	28 Jun 39	20 Jun 40	Broken up 1960s
Maksim Gorky	Ordzonikidze (Leningrad)	20 Dec 36	30 Apr 38	25 Oct 40	Broken up 18 Apr 1958
Molotov	Marti South Yd (Nikolaev)	14 Jan 37	19 Mar 39	14 Jun 41	Discarded 1976. Scrapped 1978
Kaganovich	Amur Yard, (Komsomolsk)	26 Aug 38	7 May 44	6 Dec 44	Broken up 16 Feb 1960
Kalinin	Amur Yard	12 Jun 38	8 May 42	31 Dec 42	Discarded 1960, broken up 1961

Note: Alternative sources give 1939 as the year of laying down for the Pacific Fleet ships. Also *Kaganovich* completed 30 December 1942, hulked in 1960 and broken up in 1980.

Displacement: 7,756* tons/7,880 tonnes (standard); 9,287* tons/9,436 tonnes (full load).
Length: 626ft 8in/191.40m (oa); 584ft/178m (pp); 613ft 4in/187m (wl).
Beam: 57ft 11in/17.72m; Draught: 23ft 9in/7.23m (mean).
Machinery: 2-shaft geared turbines; 6-Yarrow-Normand boilers.
Performance: 113,000shp*=36kts; Bunkerage: 1,280 tons oil fuel
Range: 3,750nm (*Kirov*); 2,140nm (*Voroshilov*) at 18kts.
Protection: 50mm main belt; 50mm deck, 75mm max turrets; 100mm CT.
Guns: nine 7.1in (3x3); six 3.9in (6x1); six 45mm AA (6x1); four 0.5in MGs.
Mines 90.
Torpedoes: six 21in (2x3).

Aircraft: two, one catapult.
Complement: 872 (*Kirov*), 881 (*Voroshilov*).
* *Voroshilov*, 7,845/7,970 & 9,973/9,950 tons/tonnes;
Voroshilov, 122,500shp=34kts+.
Maksim Gorky
Displacement: 8,048 tons/8,177 tonnes (standard); 9,948 tons/9,792 tonnes (full load).
Length: 626ft 8in/191.40m (oa); 584ft/178m (pp); 613ft 4in/187m (wl).
Beam: 58ft 1in/17.7m; Draught: 20ft 9in/6.33m (mean).
Machinery: 2-shaft geared turbines; 6 Yarrow-Normand boilers.
Performance: 129,750shp=36kts(trials); Bunkerage: 1,650 tons oil fuel.
Range: 4,880nm at 18kts (*Maksim Gorky*); 3,850nm (*Molotov*); 3,100nm other pair.
Protection: as *Kirov* except 70mm side belt.

Guns: as *Kirov* but see text.
Torpedoes: as *Kirov*.
Aircraft: as *Kirov*.
Complement: 953 (*M-G*); 862 (*M*); 812 (*Ks*).

Design This design, known as Projekt 26, was the first large warship project to be put in hand by the Soviets since the Revolution, the other major war vessels having been started during Tsarist days. At the time of their conception the Soviet industrial machine was beginning to regain its feet, but was not yet confident enough to undertake the design of such an important ship without outside assistance, despite political prejudices. Co-operation with Italy was sought in 1933, and the plans for the light cruiser *Raimondo Montecuccoli* were obtained. The preliminary design displaced 7,200 tonnes and was to be armed with six 6in in twin turrets, but was soon replaced by an improved design which was to mount the new 7.1in 57cal gun already at sea aboard the old *Krasnyi Kavkaz*. This new design, of increased tonnage, shipped the main armament in triple turrets and was presumably adopted because most foreign cruisers carried a heavier armament than six guns. In addition, however, the Soviet authorities were not satisfied that the light Italian style of construction was suited to Baltic requirements. In this theatre there was a need to consider the yearly icing-up, which made demands both on hull strength and on stability (through icing-up of

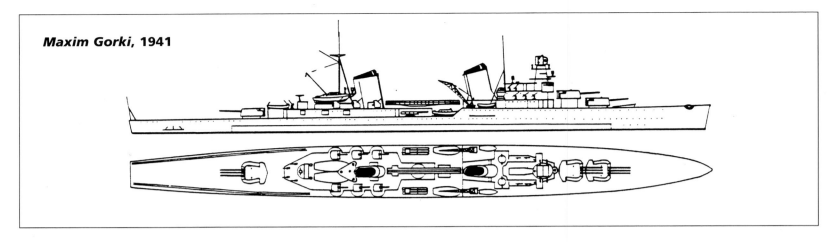

Maxim Gorki, 1941

Above: *Kirov* in 1939 or earlier. (R. Greger)

Below: *Molotov.* Note aircraft and the different bridge structure as compared to *Kirov.* (Navpic)

top hamper). In consequence the designs were modified and the displacement increased to 7,700 tons (normal). However, their general appearance did retain contemporary Italian cruiser lines, and was broadly similar to the *Montecuccoli* type. The internal layout, too, accepting the differences caused by the three-turret rather than four-turret design, was also similar. The protective scheme included a waterline belt 50mm thick that extended from the forward bulkhead of A magazine to the after bulkhead of Y magazine. Horizontal protection consisted of a 50mm deck. The

main armament turrets had 75mm (maximum), and there was a 100mm conning tower.

The main machinery was arranged on the unit principle and laid out similarly to that of the Italian cruisers of the day. In fact the main machinery, boilers and turbines were supplied from Italy, having originally been intended for that country's *Eugenio di Savoia*. That for *Voroshilov* was built in the USSR to Ansaldo drawings, and was of a higher output than that of her sister. Each of the main boilers was in its own space and grouped into two plants with a total power of 113,000shp.

Voroshilov, however, had 122,500shp. The two turbine rooms were forward and aft of the after boiler group.

As already noted, the main armament consisted of the 7.1in (181mm) gun which fired a 215lb M1928 shell and had a maximum range of 41,340yd. The guns were carried in a single cradle and electrically powered. For secondary armament there were six single shielded 3.9in 56cal B34, disposed three on each beam abreast the after funnel, an arrangement which was subsequently found unsatisfactory. The standard heavy AA gun of the Soviet fleet, this weapon fired a 62lb shell and could elevate to 85° for a maximum ceiling of 42,900ft. Light AA comprised six single 45mm automatic Soviet type 21-K, three on the after shelterdeck and the others grouped around the bridge on B gun deck. Four 0.5in MGs completed the gunnery department. Two banks of triple 21in torpedoes were shipped amidships, and the ships were fitted for minelaying, accommodating 60 mines as designed, but this depended on type, and *Voroshilov* could carry 164, presumably by means of extended mine rails. Finally, there was a single catapult on the centreline between the funnels, with provision to embark two KOR-1 floatplanes.

Two ships were authorised on 29 December as Project 26; one, *Kirov* (yard No.S270), for the Baltic Fleet, and the other, *Voroshilov*, for the Black Sea. Four further ships were authorised as Project 26*bis* in 1936, one each for the Baltic and Black Sea Fleets (the latter yard No.S329), the other pair for the Far East as yard Nos.7 and 8. These ships were completed to a revised design with a modified bridge structure very similar to contemporary Italian practice. Their displacements differed in that the Baltic and Black Sea ships displaced 9,728-9,750 tonnes and the Far East units 10,040 tonnes. Protection was improved, the side armour being increased to 70mm. They were intended to have the same machinery (110,000shp), but their plant also var-

Above: *Kirov* at Gdynia in 1970 after modernisation.
(Courtesy M. Twardoski)

ied considerably. *Maksim Gorky* developed 129,750shp and *Molotov* 133,000shp, while, for reasons which are not clear, the Far East units had only 109,500shp. (However, these quoted figures may actually be the power developed on trials.) The armament remained the same as the first pair, except that they were given nine instead of six 45mm.

Modifications In 1941 the catapult was landed and replaced by two 3.9in guns in *Kirov*, but the remainder retained theirs. The two Far East units received newer-pattern Soviet-built catapults, and by the time they were completed they had received ten 37mm in lieu of the 45mm, and had six .5in MGs. These two ships also completed with eight 3.34in (85mm) in lieu of the 3.9in. *Kirov* exchanged three 45mm for five 37mm/67 before the German attack in June 1942, and by 1943 had a total of ten 37mm, six .5in MGs and two 7.5mm. All remaining 45mm guns had been landed. *Voroshilov* retained three 45mm and had fourteen 37mm singles plus eight .5in MGs. *Maksim Gorky* had three 37mm and two .5in MGs added by 1943, and her final AA outfit was six 3.9in, six 45mm, thirteen 37mm and eight .5in MGs. Otherwise alterations are not known in detail, except that some ships had received radar from Allied sources before the end of the war.

Service *Kirov* was a unit of the Baltic Fleet, and took part in the opening attacks against Finnish shore batteries on the island of Russarö and Hangö at the start of the Russo-Finnish war on 1 December 1939. Following the German attack on the Soviet Union in June 1941, the ship was based at Ust-Dvinsk near Riga and covered minelaying activities by destroyers in the Irben Straits. However, the speed of the German advance forced the evacuation of Riga at the end of June, but by this time the Irben Straits had been closed by German forces. *Kirov*, the largest ship available in the Gulf of Riga, could not pass the alternative route back to the Gulf of Finland, Moon Sound, but after desperate measures to lighten her the ship was successfully moved to Reval, where, in the course of August, she used her guns in defence of that port. At the end of August Reval, too, was abandoned, and *Kirov* covered the evacuation convoys as flagship. She was not damaged on the passage to Leningrad on 28/29 August 1941, where, at the end of the month, she was attached to one of the naval forces in the Kronstadt-Oranienbaum area, allocated to support army units defending the town. This task continued as long as the German Army remained in range of the naval guns. On 4 April 1942 she was hit by a bomb and damaged by the near-misses of ten others. On 24 April she received two further bomb hits. Repairs lasted until early 1943, and in January 1944 she participated in the bombardments which opened the Soviet army's offensive against the German forces encircling the town. She supported the offensives at Krasnosel'sk-Ropshin in January 1944 and at Viborg in June. For the rest of the war the heavy units, cruisers included, remained in the Leningrad area and took no active part in hostilities. The ship was retained in the active fleet postwar, and was finally used as an HQ and training ship before being stricken in December 1974.

Voroshilov served in the Black Sea, where she participated in the opening operations against Romanian and German forces after the start of Operation Barbarossa in June 1941. On 25-27 June she covered an attack by destroyers on Constanza. In mid-September 1941 she participated in further bombardments against Axis positions around Odessa, but while lying at Novorossisk on 2 November she was hit on the stern by two bombs and damaged. Towed to Poti for repair, *Voroshilov* did not become operational again until February 1942. In May 1942 she supported army operations around Kerch and the Taman Peninsula, then on 27 May carried reinforcements to Sevastopol. Later, between 29 November and 2 December 1942, she took part in a raid against shipping off the Romanian/Bulgarian coasts. However, after shelling Fidonisi the cruiser was damaged by the shock of close mine detonations off Zmeiny Island, and returned to Batum for repairs. She was again in action off Novorossisk on 30/31 January 1943, supporting landing operations, but, after the loss of three destroyers to air attack in October that year, operations by the larger ships were severely curtailed and she saw no further active service. She served postwar and in the mid-1960s, rebuilt as a trials ship for rocket launchers. She was finally broken up in 1970.

Maksim Gorky, the second Baltic Fleet unit, was based at Ust-Dvinsk at the outbreak of war with Germany in June 1941. Her first sortie was to cover minelaying operations off the entrance to the Gulf of Finland. En route to this task, however, the covering force ran into a mine barrage on 23 June and lost one destroyer, another being damaged. *Maksim Gorky* lost her bows, but managed to put into Worms and then reached Leningrad via Reval for repairs. These had not been fully completed before the ship was required for the defence of Leningrad, being assigned to a force in the Sea Canal. By the beginning of September she was in action against German positions around the town, and was hit by artillery fire on 18 September but only lightly damaged. On 23 September she was hit again, this time by bombs while in Leningrad. During an air raid on 4 April 1942 the cruiser escaped damage, but was later was hit by an artillery shell. However, she was operational again by the summer. Finally, in January 1944, she participated in the bombardments which opened the Red Army's offensive against German positions around the Leningrad area, and in the offensives of Krasnosel'sk-Ropshin and Viborg in June 1944, but was not employed operationally thereafter. Postwar she served until deleted from the active list in February 1956, and was then used as an experimental vessel for some time until she was towed to the Marti Yard at Leningrad on 18 April 1958 for scrapping.

Molotov was the second Black Sea unit, and hurriedly commissioned at the start of Operation

Barbarossa in June 1941. On 1 November she was ordered from Sevastopol to the Caucasus, but was recalled to the defence of Sevastopol because she was unique in having a radar set fitted. In November she shelled Axis positions between Feodosia and Cape Chauda, escaping a bomb and torpedo attack by aircraft off Tuapse, and at the end of the following month the cruiser was sent to support the defence of Sevastopol, returning with 600 wounded troops. After landing her wounded at Novorossisk, *Molotov* returned to Sevastopol with new troop reinforcements on 1 January 1942, and bombarded German positions near Feodosia on 9 January. On 22 January, while in Tuapse, she was damaged by stormy weather conditions, but was back on shore bombardment support operations on 21 February, when she engaged German positions around Feodosia. March saw continued operations in support of Sevastopol, the ship making four trips in all, running in supplies and reinforcements, evacuating wounded and conducting shore bombardments. By June the fortress of Sevastopol was on the verge of being taken, and *Molotov* was one of the ships engaged in the last supply and evacuation runs, evading an attack by the Italian midget submarine *CB3*. After the fall of Sevastopol, *Molotov* and the Flotilla Leader *Kharkov* were sent to shell German positions around Feodosia on 2 August 1942, but the cruiser was hit by a torpedo either from the Italian *MAS 568* or from a German aircraft, which blew off about 60ft of the stern. Repairs were carried at Poti using a section from the incomplete cruiser *Frunze*, while the rudder post came from Leningrad by rail via Tashkent. She was back in service late in 1943, but saw no further active employment before the end of the war. After the war she remained in service, being modernised in 1956 (renamed *Slava* in 1957) before being scrapped in the late 1970s, having been operational in the Mediterranean in 1973.

The two ships built in the Far East, *Kaganovich* and *Kalinin*, had to be towed downriver from Komsomolsk for completion at Vladivostock because of shallow water on the Amur river. Although they were completed well before the end of the short period of hostilities against Japan in 1945, they remained inactive at Vladivostock. *Kaganovich* was renamed *Lazar Kaganovich* at completion and *Petropavlovsk* on 3 August 1957. Finally, on 6 February 1960, she became a barrack ship and was subsequently scrapped.

CHAPAYEV CLASS

Ship	Builder	Laid Down	Launched	Completed	Fate
Chapayev	Ordzonikidze (Leningrad)	8 Oct 39	28 Apr 46	16 May 50	Stricken 29 Oct 1960
Chkalov	Ordzonikidze (Leningrad)	31 Aug 39	25 Oct 47	1 Nov 50	Training ship 29 Apr 58, as *Komsomolets*
Zheleniakov	Marti Yd (Leningrad)	31 Oct 39	25 Jun 41	19 Apr 50	Training ship 1967
Frunze	Marti South Yd (Nikolaiev)	29 Aug 39	31 Dec 40	19 Dec 50	Training ship 18 Apr 1958
Kuibishev	61 Kommunar Yd (Nikolaiev)	31 Aug 39	31 Jan 41	20 Apr 50	Training ship 18 Apr 1958
Ordzonikidze	Marti South Yd (Nikolaiev)	31 Dec 40	not launched		Scrapped on slip
Sverdlov	61 Kommunar Yd (Nikolaev)	31 Dec 40	not launched		Scrapped on slip
Lenin	Ordzonikidze (Leningrad)	Planned for laying down in 1941			
Dzerzinski	Ordzonikidze (Leningrad)	Planned for laying down in 1941			
Avrora	Ordzonikidze (Leningrad)	Planned for laying down in 1941			
Lazo	Amur yard	Planned for laying down in 1941			

(Note, however, that the old cruiser *Avrora* still existed, as did the destroyer *Derzinski*, which was not lost until May 1942. The name reported for the Far East ship has connections with that reported for the last Far East unit of the *Maksim Gorky* Class. It is, of course, not known when these names were allocated to the *Chapayev* Class.)

Displacement: 11,300 tons/11,480 tonnes (standard); 15,000 tons/15,240 tonnes (full load).
Length: 659ft 9in/201m (pp).
Beam: 64ft 8in/19.7m; Draught: 21ft/6.4m (mean).
Machinery: 2-shaft geared turbines; 6 boilers.
Performance: 130,000shp=34kts; Bunkerage: 3,500 tons oil fuel.
Range: 7,000nm at 20kts.
Protection: as *Kirov* but improved.
Guns: twelve 6in (4x3); eight 3.9in (8x1); twenty-four 37mm (12x2).
Mines: 200.
Torpedoes: six 21in (2x3).
Aircraft: two, one catapult.
Complement: 840.

Design Under the third five-year plan, a new class of cruisers was projected that was to be a development of the previous Project 26/26a, the *Kirov/Maksim Gorky* class ships. The new ships, however, were to ship four triple turrets, and their displacement had to be increased accordingly. It is believed that the original intention was to continue with the 7.1in gun, as in the previous class, but this was later altered to a new 6in/57 weapon. As usual for Soviet ships, design information is sparse, but the final design, Project 68, showed a longer hull with much increased beam compared with the Project 26 ships. The standard displacement rose by nearly 40 per cent. Their protection scheme was an improved version of that in the Project 26 ships, as was the machinery arrangement, but the increased displacement did not lead to any increase in the power output of the plant, resulting in a loss of 1kt in speed.

Below: *Komsomolets* (ex-*Chkalov*). (P. Budzabon)

With an armament of 6in calibre, this was a treaty light cruiser and had a secondary armament increased to eight 3.9in, all singles. The designed light AA was fourteen 37mm. The torpedo armament and aircraft installations were retained in the design, and the minelaying capacity was increased to 200.

Seventeen ships were authorised initially under the five-year plan, including six for the Baltic Fleet (Yard Nos. S-305, 306, 545, 309, 310 and 555), four for the Black Sea (Yard Nos. S-356, 354, 1088 and 1090) and one for the Far East (Yard No. not known). However, the effect of the outbreak of the war, although the Soviet Union was not initially involved, was to curtail the ambitious expansion plan that Stalin had set for his navy, since operations on land would take precedence and the available resources would be directed to that end. Nonetheless, while a number of the major units such as the battleships and battlecruisers were cancelled or suspended, the two Project 68 units scheduled for laying down in the fourth quarter of 1940 at 'Factory 200' and 'Factory 198' (the 61 Kommunar and Marti (South) yards at Nikolaiev) were to go ahead, and in October 1940 it was also agreed to lay down four more ships for the 1941 Programme, two at the Ordzhonikidze Yard at Leningrad, one at the Marti Yard, also in Leningrad, and the fourth at 'Factory 199' at Komsomolsk in the Far East. As far as is known, none of these, with the possible exception of the unit in the Far East, was ever laid down, because the shortage of steel in the summer of 1941 led to their suspension when about 20 per cent complete. Immediately afterwards, the German invasion stopped the programme completely. In addition, as a result of the capture of the yards at Nikolaiev, the two units under completion on the slips there were wrecked and later broken up. The remaining five ships were completed postwar to a revised design which incorporated much captured German gunnery and fire-control technology. It is conceivable that the cancelled ships, or at least some of the materials for their construction, eventually emerged as the Project 68bis or Sverdlov class in the early 1950s.

PETROPAVLOVSK

Design This ship was the former German *Hipper* class cruiser *Lützow* (q.v.), which had been sold to the Soviet Union on 11 February 1940 as part of the Russo-German Agreement of August 1939. At this time she had been completed only up to the superstructure deck, with A and D turrets fitted, but only the former having their guns. She was towed from Germany on 15 April 1940, bound for Leningrad, where she was to be completed by the Ordzhonikidze Yard under German supervision, with completion scheduled for 1942. Known as Project 53, the ship was named *Petropavlovsk* on 25 September 1940 and, by 1941, was making good progress. However, the German plan to invade the Soviet Union led to a scaling-down of German assistance, so that the ship was only some 70 per cent complete in June 1941. She had a crew aboard and four main guns in A and D turrets, together with some 37mm, and was put into service on 15 August 1941. When German forces came within range of the ships at Leningrad, she joined in the defence on 7 September as part of the Detachment of New Construction Ships, and fired 676 rounds in the next seven days before being hit herself on 17 September and losing all electric power. Many more hits were suffered in the next few hours, and the ship slowly flooded and settled on to the bottom with a list. It was not until 10 September 1942 that she was made watertight again, being raised on the night of 16/17 September to be towed into the yard for repairs. Provisionally repaired, and with only three 8in serviceable, she participated in the bombardments before the Soviet break-out from the Leningrad encirclement in January 1944, when she fired over 1,000 rounds. On 1 September 1944 she was again renamed, this time as *Tallin*. Postwar the ship was rated as a light cruiser in January 1949, but on 11 March 1953 she became a non-propelled training ship, renamed *Dnepr*. In December 1956 she became the Barracks Ship *PKZ-112*, and was finally stricken in April 1958.

TRANSFERRED UNIT

Following the Italian capitulation in September 1943, the Soviet Union claimed a share of the surrendered Italian Navy, despite the fact that the portion in Allied hands was continuing to fight on their side. As it was patently impossible to divide the ships up in the middle of a war, and in view of the persistence of the Soviet demands, it was decided to transfer a number of Allied ships to the Soviet Union as a stopgap measure until the war was over. Thus the US cruiser *Milwaukee* was sailed to Vaenga in North Russia with convoy JW58 and handed over on loan. She was commissioned into the Red fleet on 20 April 1944, and renamed *Murmansk* for service with the Northern Fleet. For the remainder of the war, however, she was inactive in Arctic waters, and was finally returned to the USA on 8 March 1949 after the signing of the Italian Peace Treaty in 1947.

Below: *Murmansk*, (ex-*Milwaukee*). (MPL)

Spain

NAVARRA CLASS

Ship	Builder	Laid Down	Launched	Completed	Fate
Navarra	El Ferrol	31 Mar 15	21 Apr 20	15 Jan 23	Stricken 1956
(ex *Reina Victoria Eugenia*, ex *Republica*)					

Displacement: 5,590 tons/5,679 tonnes (standard); 6,348 tons/6,449 tonnes (full load).

Length: 462ft/140.8m (oa); 440ft/134.1m (pp).

Beam: 50ft/15.23m; **Draught:** 15ft 9in/4.8m (mean).

Machinery: 2-shaft Parsons geared turbines; 8 Yarrow boilers.

Performance: 25,500 shp=25½kts; **Bunkerage:** 1,200 tons oil fuel.

Range: 4,500nm at 15kts.

Protection: 3in (machinery spaces) main belt, 1¾in-2½in (ends); 3in deck; 6in CT.

Guns: six 6in (6x1); four 88mm AA (4x1); four MGs.

Torpedoes: nil.

Aircraft: nil.

Complement: 455.

Design This ship, authorised under the Navy Law of 30 July 1914, was built to the general lines of the British Town class of 1910/14, but differed externally in having three funnels instead of four. In this respect she more closely resembled the Australian cruiser *Adelaide* after her 1938/39 refit, which had been completed at about the same time, and her military value was similar, i.e. strictly limited by the time she entered service. As designed, she carried nine 6in Vickers-Carraca guns in single shielded mountings, all except the aftermost being on the broadside. Four light guns and two twin fixed tubes completed the armament.

The protective scheme was similar to that of the Towns, with a 3in main belt, while the machinery was arranged on a twin-shaft layout like that of *Adelaide*. The designed output was 25,500shp for a maximum speed of 25½kts. On trials, *Regina Victoria Eugenia* achieved 26.9kts with 28,387shp.

Modifications In 1936 the ship was given a major overhaul and had the boilers retubed at Cadiz, where she was still lying at the start of the Civil War. She was subsequently transferred to El Ferrol, where the boilers were removed from one boiler room, the funnels reduced to two and the ship converted to oil firing. The superstructure was dismantled and a new tower bridge was fitted, with a shelter deck fore and aft of it. The main armament was reduced by three guns, but all were now mounted on the centreline, with Nos. 2 and 5 guns superfiring on Nos. 1 and 6. Four single 3.5in shielded HA mountings, quite possibly of German origin, were fitted, one pair amidships abreast the after funnel and the other pair on the quarterdeck just abaft the break of the forecastle. Two 40mm (2pdr) pom-poms were added in echelon about the after funnel.

Service In 1925 *Reina Victoria Eugenia* was flagship during the Riff war in North Africa, and received her war flag from the Queen herself at Santander the following year. In April 1931 she was renamed *Republica*. As noted above, the ship was under refit at the start of the Civil War, and was used as a floating battery initially, landing a part of her armament for use as shore batteries at Tarifa and Algecieras. After the loss of *Baleares* the ship, now renamed *Navarra*, was incorporated into the Nationalist fleet and employed on such tasks as her age and capabilities permitted. After the Civil War *Navarra* served in the north, and by December 1942 was the only operational Spanish cruiser. Latterly she was employed as a stationary training ship, until stricken in 1956.

Above: *Navarra* as rebuilt. (Spanish Navy)

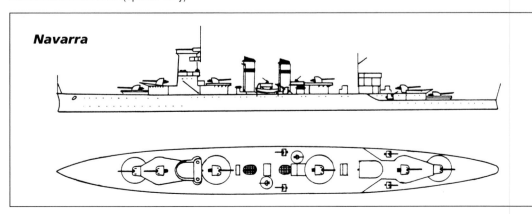

Navarra

MENDEZ NUÑEZ CLASS

Ship	Builder	Laid Down	Launched	Completed	Fate
Mendez Nuñez	El Ferrol	28 Sep 17	3 Mar 23	May 25	Stricken 1963

Displacement: 4,780 tons/4,856 tonnes (standard); 6,043 tons/6,139 tonnes (full load).
Length: 462ft/140.8m (oa); 440ft/134.1m (pp).
Beam: 46ft/14.0m; Draught: 14ft 4in/4.36m (mean).
Machinery: 4-shaft Parsons geared turbines; 12 Yarrow boilers.
Performance: 45,000shp=29kts; Bunkerage: 787 (max) tons coal+492 tons oil fuel.
Range: 5,000nm at 13kts.
Protection: main belt 3in (machinery), 1¾in to 2½in (ends); 1in deck; 6in CT.
Guns: six 6in (6x1); four 47mm; AA; four MGs.
Torpedoes: twelve 21in (4x3).
Aircraft: nil.
Complement: 320.

Design This design was broadly comparable to that of the British C or D class cruisers constructed during the First World War. As designed, the ship displaced some 4,700 tons on a hull with similar dimensions to those of the British cruisers. The protective scheme included a waterline belt 3in thick in the way of the machinery spaces, reduced to 1¼in at the ends. Horizontal protection was limited to a 1in deck. There was a conning tower with 6in armour.

The main machinery, a four-shaft single-reduction-geared turbine layout, was mixed fired, there being and equal number of oil- and coal-fired Yarrow boilers. The latter were in three boiler rooms, served by three funnels. The designed shp was 43,000 for a maximum speed of 29kts. On trials, *Mendez Nuñez* achieved 29¼kts with 43,776shp.

The main armament comprised six 6in Vickers-Carraca 50cal weapons in single shielded mountings, disposed one forward, one each to port and starboard at the break of the forecastle, two abeam on the after shelter deck and one on the centreline on the quarterdeck. This was a BL gun with an elevation of 15°, firing a 100lb projectile. The light AA comprised four single 47mm, which were probably 3pdr Hotchkiss guns, two in echelon around the centre funnel and two sided above the after tubes. The torpedo outfit comprised four triple banks of 21in tubes sited on the main deck, two on each beam. There was no provision to operate aircraft. Two ships were authorised under the 1915 Naval Law and named *Blas de Lezo* and *Mendez Nuñez*. The former, however, was wrecked near Cape Finisterre on 11 July 1932.

Modifications In 1944 *Mendez Nuñez* was taken in hand at El Ferrol for conversion into an AA cruiser. All the armament was landed, the super-structure was removed and the boiler uptakes were trunked into two funnels. Suprisingly, the opportunity to convert the machinery to full oil-firing was not taken. The new armament comprised eight 4.7in Vickers Armstrongs/45 cal QF guns in single shielded mountings capable of 80° elevation. Six of these were shipped on the centreline, three forward and three aft in a three-tiered superfiring disposition similar to that on the British *Dido* or US *Atlanta* classes, with the remaining pair on the beam, abreast the after director. Four twin 37mm and two quadruple 20mm, probably of German origin, completed the AA outfit. Only two banks of tubes were retained. The bridge structure was completely rebuilt, and HA directors were fitted fore and aft.

Service *Mendez Nuñez* served initially off the coast of Morocco towards the end of the Riff war. In 1927 she was deployed to China to protect Spanish interests during the unrest in Shanghai. At the start of the Spanish Civil War the cruiser was in Equatorial Guinea, and returned home to declare for the Republican cause. She had an active career during this conflict, taking part in the first action off Cape Palos on 25 April 1937, the action off Cape Chechel on 7 August 1937, and the second action off Cape Palos, when *Baleares* was sunk. With the end of the Civil War in sight, the Republican squadron sailed from Cartagena on 5 March 1939 and was interned at Bizerte until hostilities ceased in April, when France handed the ships back to the Spanish Government. After her conversion into an AA cruiser, she served until stricken in 1963.

Above: *Blas de Lezo,* showing the original appearance of the class. (Spanish Navy)

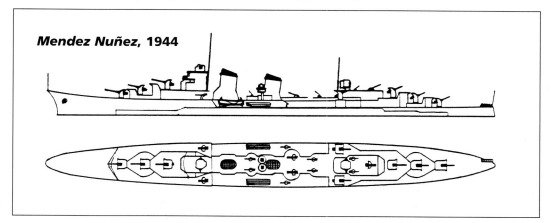

Mendez Nuñez, 1944

Left: *Medez Nuñez* rebuilt as an AA cruiser. (Spanish Navy)

PRINCIPE ALFONSO CLASS

Ship	Builder	Laid Down	Launched	Completed	Fate
Galicia (ex Libertad, ex Principe Alfonso)	El Ferrol	1 Feb 17	27 Jul 22	30 Aug 25	Stricken 2 Feb 1970
Almirante Cervera	El Ferrol	25 Nov 22	16 Oct 25	May 27	Stricken 1966
Miguel de Cervantes	El Ferrol	27 Aug 26	17 May 29	10 Feb 30	Stricken 1964

Displacement: 7,475 tons/7,594 tonnes (standard); 9,237 tons/9,384 tonnes (full load).
Length: 579ft 6in/176.63m (oa); 545ft/166.12m (pp).
Beam: 54ft/16.46m; Draught: 16ft 6in/5.05m (mean).
Machinery: 4-shaft Parsons geared turbines; 8 Yarrow boilers.
Performance: 80,000shp=33kts; Bunkerage: 1,680 tons oil fuel.

Range: 5,000nm at 15kts.
Protection: main belt 3in (machinery spaces), 2in (forward), 1½in (aft), 1-2in deck; 6in CT
Guns: eight 6in (2x1, 3x2); four 4in (4x1); two 47mm (2x1).
Torpedoes: twelve 21in (4x3).
Aircraft: nil.
Complement: 564.

Design The influence of the British connection with the El Ferrol shipyard was again manifest in the design of this class of cruisers, its basis being the Royal Navy's 'E' class. Again designed by Sir Phillip Watts, the ships were similar in dimensions to the British prototype, but differed internally and externally in a number of ways. The protective scheme was about the same as that of the E class, while the machinery developed the same power but was rearranged to group all the boilers together. This allowed the number of funnels to be reduced to two and produced a more pleasing appearance.

The main armament was the 6in/50 Vickers-Carraca BL gun in three twin and two single shielded mountings with 35° elevation. The single

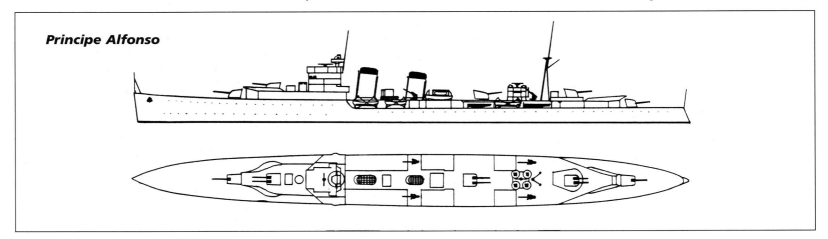

Principe Alfonso

mountings were in A and Y positions, while the twins were in B, Q and X positions. Four single 4in AA were carried, two abreast the forward funnel and the second pair abreast the mainmast. Two 47mm (3pdr) Hotchkiss and MGs completed the light AA. Four banks of triple 21 tubes were shipped on the upper deck. There was no provision for aircraft.

Three ships were authorised under the Navy Law of 17 February 1915, but all construction was badly delayed by the continuing hostilities in Europe, with the result that the leading ship was not laid down until early 1917, and the others not until some considerable time after the end of the First World War, in 1922 and 1926.

Modifications In the 1940s *Almirante Cervera* had her 4in and 3pdr guns replaced by German 4.1in (10.5cm) and 37mm AA. The former were still carried in single mountings at shelter deck level, but the 37mm were in four twin mountings. It appears that the original plan was to ship the 4.1in guns in twin mountings of German type on the main deck, but this was never carried through.

Above: *Almirante Cervera* in the 1930s. (Spanish Navy)

Below: *Miguel de Cervantes* in June 1953. (W&L)

Four 20mm were added, and all twelve tubes were retained. The tripod mainmast was replaced by a pole mast, and the after control position was remodelled, but the conning tower was retained. In the mid 1950s the 4.1in guns were replaced by twin 37mm. This ship was not fitted to operate aircraft.

Her two sisters had their main armament rearranged, Q gun being suppressed and replaced by a catapult and crane. They operated a single He 114 floatplane, supplied by Germany either during the Civil War or in the course of the Second World War. A and B guns were replaced by twin mountings. The shelterdeck amidships was reduced in width and four twin 3.9in shipped on the main deck. These were either never fitted or soon replaced by twin 37mm. The light AA was augmented by the addition of five quadruple 20mm, one forward of the bridge, two between

the funnels and another pair aft for a total of sixteen 37mm (8 x 2) and twenty 20mm (5 x 4). The bridge structure was rebuilt, the conning tower was removed and, like *Almirante Cervera*, the tripod mainmast was replaced by a pole. The forward banks of tubes were landed.

Service *Principe Alfonso* conveyed King Alfonso XIII on several foreign tours; for example, to Göteborg and Kiel in 1928 and in 1930 to French and Italian ports as well as Malta. In 1931, following the declaration of the Republic, the ship took the King from Cartagena to exile in Italy. In consequence of the Republic, she was renamed *Libertad* in 1931. During the Civil War *Libertad* served with the Red or Republican fleet, based mainly at Cartagena. She was a part of the force sailed in March 1938 to attack the Nationalist Fleet, resulting in the loss of *Baleares* (q.v.). How-

ever, on 18 April 1938 she was hit by bombs during a Nationalist air raid on Cartagena, and was under repair for the next three months. After the defeat of the Republican forces she sailed for Bizerte, where she was interned until returned to Franco's control and renamed *Galicia* in 1939. She served with the Spanish Navy until put up for disposal in March 1972 and later scrapped.

Miguel de Cervantes was also a unit of the Republican Fleet, and was torpedoed by the Italian submarine *Toricelli*, masquerading as the Nationalist *General Mola*, while lying at anchor off Cartagena on 22 November 1936. She was out of action for the most of the remainder of the Civil War, being under repair at Cartagena until she sailed for internment at Bizerte in 1939. By late 1942 she was non-operational at El Ferrol, where, in May 1943, the ship was badly damaged by a large fire and was later given a major modernisation. In June 1953 she represented Spain at the Spithead Review on the occasion of the Coronation of HM Queen Elizabeth II. She was paid off in 1958 and sold for breaking up in April 1964.

Almirante Cervera, named after the Spanish Commander-in-Chief at the time of the Spanish-American war, made a cruise to Havana in 1929. On the outbreak of the Civil War in Spain the ship resisted attempts to take her over for the red cause and escaped to El Ferrol, where she became flagship of Admiral Moreno and joined the Nationalist cause. At this time, however, she was badly in need of a boiler overhaul and capable of only about 23kts, although she was considered capable of escorting troop convoys if necessary. She was active throughout the war, often in company with *Canarias*, and was present at all of the major actions. In an engagement in the Straits of Gibraltar on 29 November 1936 she damaged the Republican destroyer *Gravina*, which managed to reach safety in Casablanca. On the night of 25/26 March 1938 she was attacked by the Republican submarine *C1*, but the torpedoes missed. *Almirante Cervera* was not refitted to the same extent as her sisters, but served into the 1960s, being stricken in 1966 and offered for scrapping in March 1970.

CANARIAS CLASS

Ship	Builder	Laid Down	Launched	Completed	Fate
Baleares	SECN, Ferrol	15 Aug 28	20 Apr 32	1936*	Lost 6 Mar 1938
Canarias	SECN, Ferrol	15 Aug 28	28 May 31	18 Sep 36*	Stricken 17 Dec 1975

* Both ships hurriedly put into service without being fully completed. *Baleares* was less advanced than her sister.

Displacement: 10,113 tons/10,274 tonnes (standard); 13,070 tons/13,279 tonnes (full load).
Length: 635ft 9in/193.55m (oa); 600ft/182.9m (pp); 630ft/192.15m (wl).
Beam: 64ft/19.5m; **Draught:** 17ft 4in/5.27m (mean).
Machinery: 4-shaft Parsons geared turbines; 8 Yarrow boilers.
Performance: 90,000shp=33kts; **Bunkerage:** 2,588 tons oil fuel.
Range: 8,700nm at 15kts.
Protection: 2in main belt; magazines, 4½in sides, 3in crowns; 1in to 1½in deck; 1in turrets & CT.
Guns: eight 8in (4x2); eight 4.7in AA (8x1); eight 40mm (8x1); four .5in MGs.
Torpedoes: twelve 21in fixed.
Aircraft: two, one catapult.
Complement: 780.

Design The Naval Programme approved on 14 July 1926 included two new cruisers which were to be of the 'Washington' type. As the intention was to build the ships in Spain, and the only yard with the expertise to build them was SECN at El Ferrol, it was inevitable that this yard would receive the contract. At the same time this ensured that the design would be of a British type, because the yard was mainly British-owned. The design was, in fact, a modification of the County class then being built for the Royal Navy, and was again the work of Sir Phillip Watts. The basic County design was not much modified, except that the external bulges were retained (the *Londons* dispensed with them) and the bridge was raised by a deck. In addition, the boiler uptakes were trunked into two funnels.

The designed standard displacement was 10,281 tons and 13,280 tons full load, but the trial displacement was 10,617 and 12,230 tons full load, as the aircraft installations were never fitted.

Internally, the County design was modified, the boilers being grouped into three spaces instead of two.

The protective scheme included 4in sides and 2½in crowns (both on ½in plating) to the fore and aft main magazines, and a 2in waterline belt between frames 62 and 216 (from the after end of the forward magazine box to the after bulkhead of the after turbine room). Horizontal protection was limited to 1 to 1½in, while the turrets and barbettes had only 1in. The total weight of armour was 683 tons, or 6.6 per cent of the standard displacement.

The waterline bulge reached from 6.6ft above the waterline to 13ft below it, and was 4.3ft wide at its maximum.

The machinery, as noted earlier, was basically the same as that of the British Countys. There were eight Yarrow boilers in three spaces disposed 2/4/2, aft of which were the turbine rooms. The forward turbine room housed the machinery on the wing shafts, and the after space the inboard shafts. A magazine space for the heavy AA guns separated the after boiler room from the forward turbine room. The designed power was 90,000shp, 10,000shp less than that of the Countys, for a maximum speed of 33kts. Bunkerage was reduced to 2,629 tons, as the Spanish navy

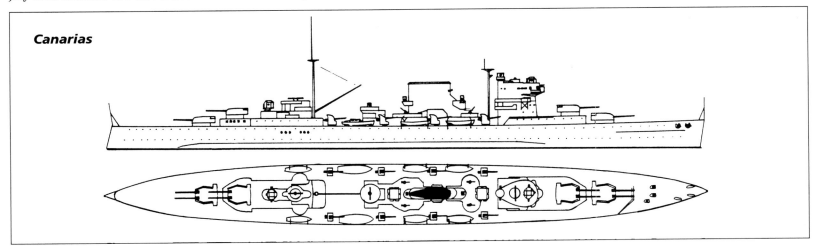

Canarias

did not require the endurance necessary for Royal Navy ships, since the *raison d'être* of these ships was to secure communications with the islands after which they were named. On trials, *Canarias* reached 33.69kts with 91,299shp, but she lacked much equipment, including X and Y turrets.

As designed, the armament included eight 8in Spanish-built 1924-pattern Vickers 50cal Mk D in twin turrets, the gun being lighter than the British 8in Mk VIII. The turrets had smaller roller paths than the County's Mk II turrets, with 70° elevation. Four single 4.7in in LA mountings and a similar number in HA single mountings comprised the secondary armament. The light AA was to consist of eight 40mm and four .5in MGs. Provision was made for twelve 21in torpedo tubes in fixed triple broadside mountings just forward of X turret. A catapult and provision for two floatplanes was included in the original design. However, while the ships were under construction the LA 4.7in guns were replaced by an equal number of 1923-model guns in HA mountings to improve AA defence. Furthermore, the outbreak of the Civil War during the final stages of their construction resulted in the non-availability of the 40mm and .5in MGs (these being manufactured in Republican territory), the catapults and the main and secondary battery fire-control systems (to have been supplied by Britain and the Netherlands).

Orders were placed for the two ships on 31 March 1928, and the keels of both were laid simultaneously that summer. A third projected unit, for which the name *Ferrol* has been suggested, was not proceeded with because of the disillusionment with the Washington type of cruiser.

Modifications The most obvious alteration on completion was the trunking of all boiler uptakes into a single massive funnel, the reason for which is unknown. The bridge structure was also altered to a streamlined tower type in lieu of the intended platform type as in the British ships. *Baleares* had an enlarged command bridge, and was given a distinctive funnel cap. Delays in construction meant that both ships were well behind schedule when the Civil War broke out, *Baleares* being the worst affected. *Canarias* completed without her designed armament, except for the 8in guns, and with no fire control. As a stop-gap measure, four 4in LA guns were obtained from the elderly battleship *España*, as well as two 57mm. Her torpedo tubes were also inoperative or not installed, and neither were the catapult and aircraft. (It is not certain if the torpedo armament was ever installed.) In October 1936 the 4in guns were replaced by six of the specified 4.7in, and the last pair being fitted in February the following year. Also received in October 1936 were two twin 37mm and three 20mm from German sources, while the Vickers 40mm had also been shipped, sited at the four corners of the funnel base. The 57mm were, however, retained. Shields were fitted to the 4.7in guns in 1940. The 37mm outfit was increased to twelve, in six twin mountings, during the Second World War, four replacing the Vickers 40mm pom-poms. Her main battery director was finally fitted in 1943/44. The tubes were landed by the end of the 1940s, if they had ever been fitted (the presence of the fixed apertures being no guarantee that the actual tubes were aboard). In October 1952 she began a major overhaul which saw her return to the two-funnel design and had the light AA altered to four 40mm (4 x 1), four 37mm (2 x 2) and two 20mm.

Baleares, in consequence of her early loss, was little modified. She commissioned without Y turret and with a mixed secondary battery of four 4.7in destroyer-pattern guns in shields and four Italian-origin 3.9in AA in single mountings. Y Turret was shipped by June 1937.

Service *Canarias* served with the Nationalist Navy as flagship from completion, providing a major

Above: *Baleares*. (Spanish Navy)
Left: *Baleares* in 1932. Note detail differences. (M. Bar)

Right: *Canarias.* Note differences to the bridge as compared with *Baleares.* (Spanish Navy)

reinforcement of the hitherto meagre force available to the rebels; one light cruiser (*Almirante Cervera*) and one operational destroyer. One of her first actions was to break the Republican blockade of the Straits of Gibraltar in September 1936, when her guns sank the Republican destroyer *Almirante Ferrandiz*, while *Cervera* damaged *Gravina*. She then ferried troops across the straits for an assault on Madrid and operated in the Mediterranean from Cadiz, escorting convoys, raiding Republican commerce and bombarding coastal installations. She was joined by *Baleares* by January 1937, the two cruisers bombarding positions around Malaga in preparation for a Nationalist attack, and the city fell on 8 February. The two cruisers operated together most of the time, escorting convoys or searching for merchantmen attempting to break the Nationalist naval blockade, and capturing several. In March 1937 *Canarias* was deployed to the Bay of Biscay to intercept arms supplies to the Republicans, in the course of which cruise she sank or captured seven ships, including *Mar Cantabrico*, destined to become an auxiliary cruiser for the Nationalists. On 5/6 March 1938 the cruisers were escorting a convoy that was intercepted by a Republican force of cruisers and destroyers en route for a raid on Palma De Mallorca. In a confused night action the Republican destroyers *Antequera*, *Barcaiztegui* and *Lepanto* attacked with torpedoes, sinking *Baleares*. *Canarias* continued her mercantile warfare, taking two more prizes before intercepting the destroyer *José Luis Díez* returning from repairs in Le Havre. The destroyer was badly damaged and only managed to limp into Gibraltar with great difficulty. In March 1939 *Canarias* supported an abortive uprising in Cartagena, but by now the war was virtually over, and on 1 April the ship returned to Cartagena with Franco's victorious forces. During the hostilities she had sunk or captured 32 ships, not including the two destroyers.

Her subsequent career was peaceful, as Spain did not become a belligerent in the Second World War. She sailed to assist in the search for survivors of *Bismarck* in May 1941, but found none. Postwar she served until paid off on 17 December 1975. She was offered for scrapping on 14 September 1977, and was broken up in 1978/79.

Right: *Canarias* as modernised post-war, reverting to the original twin-funnel design. (Spanish Navy)

Sweden

FYLGIA CLASS

Ship	Builder	Laid Down	Launched	Completed	Fate
Fylgia	Bergsund, Finnboda	Oct 03	21 Dec 05	21 Jun 07	Stricken 1 Jan 1953

Displacement: 4,300 tons/4,369 tonnes (standard).
Length: 379ft/115.5m (oa); 377ft 8in/115m (wl).
Beam: 48ft 6in/14.8m; Draught: 20ft/6.09m (mean).
Machinery: 2-shaft 4-cyl VTE engines; 12 Yarrow boilers.
Performance: 13,000ihp=21½kts; Bunkerage: 850 tons coal.
Range: 5,770nm at 10kts.
Protection: 4in main belt, 2in deck, 2in to 5in turrets, 4in CT.
Guns: eight 6in (4x2); four 57mm (4x1); two 37mm.
Torpedoes: two 18in fixed beam.
Aircraft: nil.
Complement: 341.

Above: *Fylgia* in the 1930s. (Author's collection)

Design This ship was the first true cruiser to be built by Sweden, and was intended to act as a scout for the main force of the Swedish Fleet, the coast defence battleships. She was a protected cruiser with a 4in waterline belt in the way of the machinery spaces and a 2in deck which sloped to meet the lower edge of the side belt. The turrets had 5in maximum armour, while the ammunition hoists were protected by 4in armour. The armour was of Krupp type.

The main machinery was typical of the period, being coal-fired twin-screw triple-expansion engines developing a total of 12,000ihp for a designed maximum speed of 21½kts. The boilers were of the Yarrow type. On trials she achieved 22.8kts with 12,440ihp.

Fylgia was unusual for her day in that her main armament was arranged in twin gunhouses, when the norm for cruisers was single open shields. Furthermore, the gunhouses were arranged in an economical manner, one each forward and aft, and the other pair on the beam. The guns were Bofors 6in/50 M03 weapons firing a 101lb shell. She also carried fourteen 6pdr (57mm), ten of which were in casemates, and two single 18in submerged tubes.

The order for her construction was placed on 14 October 1902 with Bergsund, Finnboda. In Norse mythology *Fylgia* was a spirit who accompanied one through life; a guardian angel.

Modifications The number of 6pdr guns appears to have been reduced in the 1920s to perhaps six guns in the casemates.

In 1939 she began a major overhaul at Oscarshamn's shipyard, where she was to be found at the start of the Second World War. In the course of this refit the boilers were removed and replaced by four Penhoët oil-fired boilers, and the forward funnel was removed. The vacant space in the former boiler room was converted into cadets'

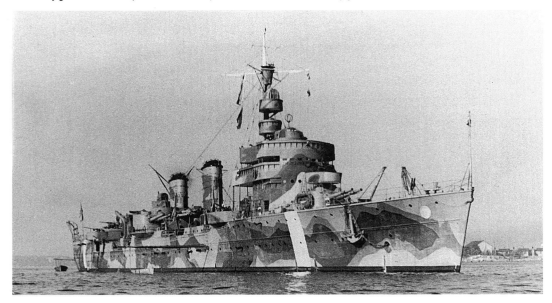

Below: *Fylgia* in 1944/55 after conversion. (RSwN)

Above: *Fylgia* in 1948. (RSwN)

accommodation to suit her for her new role as a training ship. All of the superstructure was removed, and a new bridge similar to that on the *Göteborg* class destroyers was added. The two remaining funnels were reduced in height and given small caps. The ram bow was replaced by a raked bow, and all of the casemate structures and their anti-torpedo boat 6pdr guns were removed, four 57mm AA single mountings being shipped at the same positions. An AA bandstand was fitted on the roof of the forward gunhouse, and four 40mm were added.

Service *Fylgia* made her first cruise after commissioning to the USA, on a goodwill .visit to the Swedish emigrant colonies. Her career was spent mainly as a training ship, making a number of cruises to North and South America, Africa and Asia. She became the first Swedish ship to visit the USSR when she went to Sevastopol in 1925. Her major refit, begun in 1939, was not completed until 1941, when she recommenced her training role. She was stricken on 1 January 1953, but was subsequently used as a target in weapons trials until finally sold for scrapping and broken up by Petersen & Albeck at Copenhagen in 1957.

GOTLAND CLASS

Ship	Builder	Laid Down	Launched	Completed	Fate
Gotland	AB Götaverken	1930	14 Sep 33	14 Dec 34	Stricken 1 Jul 1960

Displacement: 4,750 tons/4,826 tonnes (standard); 5,550 tons/5,639 tonnes (full load).
Length: 437ft 6in/133.3m (oa); 426ft 6in/129.99m (wl).
Beam: 50ft 6in/15.39m; Draught: 14ft 9in/4.5m (mean).
Machinery: 2-shaft De Laval geared turbines; 4 Penhoët boilers.
Performance: 33,000shp=27kts; Bunkerage: 800 tons oil fuel.
Range: 4,000nm at 12kts.
Protection: 25mm deck; 13mm max bulkheads; 25mm max turrets; 19mm CT.
Guns: six 6in (2x2 & 2x1); four 3in AA (4x1); four 25mm (4x1).
Torpedoes: six 21in (2x3).
Aircraft: eight, 1 catapult.
Complement: 480.

Design Naval manoeuvres in 1925 had so demonstrated the great possibilities of naval aviation that, in 1926, a committee set up by the Defence Minister to consider the future require-ments of the navy recommended the construction of a seaplane carrier. This recommendation was important because Sweden had, on 1 July 1926, formed the Royal Swedish Air Force as a third arm of the military forces, though it was not fully independent as yet. The navy obviously feared that it would lose any control over air operations at sea, and needed to follow up the recommendations of the 1926 committee as soon as possible. The first stage was to convert the elderly coast defence ship *Dristigheten*, due to be stricken in 1931, into a seaplane carrier. This was completed in 1930, the ship being equipped to operate three floatplanes on a han-dling deck aft, these being lowered on to the water by a crane at the extreme stern of the ship. However, this was but a temporary expedient. The second stage was to design an aircraft car-rying cruiser that could draw on the experience with *Dristigheten*.

The initial proposals of the 1926 committee envisaged a 4,500-ton 27kt ship armed with six 6in in single mountings and equipped to carry twelve seaplanes, stowed in a hangar. By Janu-ary 1927 the Navy Board had modified this by specifying that the 6in guns were to be in twin turrets, the heavy AA was to be increased, and the ship was to have six 21in torpedo tubes. The aeroplanes were to be stowed on the after deck in the manner used in *Dristigheten*. Displace-ment rose to 4,800 tons. This configuration was further modified by the time the contract was placed.

The design as it finally emerged was that of a cruiser, with the after third of the ship given com-pletely over to aircraft facilities. The ship was flush-decked, with a built-up structure aft to allow the aircraft easy access to the catapult.

The protection was limited, with a deck maxi-mum of 25mm and the vertical armour restricted to a 13mm maximum bulkhead. Similar protec-tion was applied to the boiler uptakes, and the turrets, hoists and supports were given 13mm to 25mm. There was a conning tower with 19mm armour.

The main machinery was arranged on the unit principle and drew on the successful experience of

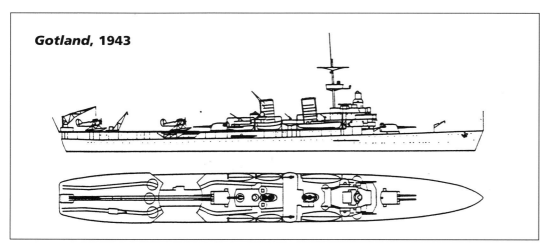

Gotland, 1943

the recently completed *Göteborg* class destroyers. It comprised a two-shaft De Laval single-reduction geared turbine layout developing 33,000shp for a maximum speed of 27½kts. The presence of the after 6in turret complicated the machinery arrangement because the magazine space for this turret separated the after boiler room from the after turbine space, with the result that one shaft was very long and the other very short. The four oil-fired Penhoët boilers were shipped on the midships line in two separate spaces.

Her main armament was the Bofors 6in/55 BL M30 model, firing a 100lb shell, of which four were in twin turrets. These had an elevation of 60° and were electro-hydraulic. Financial restraints resulted in the projected three twin-turret design being amended owing to lack of hull space, and the remaining pair of guns had to be shipped in casemates abreast the bridge; an unsatisfactory solution. These guns had only 30° elevation and, consequently, reduced range. Four 3in AA in one twin and two single mountings comprised the heavy AA capability, and four single 25mm were disposed around the bridge structure. Two triple banks of 21in torpedo tubes were fitted on the main deck just abaft the after funnel. The ship was fitted for minelaying and could stow up to 100 mines, depending on type.

The aircraft installation, which was originally to include two catapults, finally had one compressed-air Heinkel type. Aft of this on the after deckhouse was a rail system upon which the aircraft could be moved to the catapult for launching. At the stern was a crane for aircraft recovery from the Hein mat when streamed astern. The original design capacity of twelve floatplanes was reduced to eight as a result of the economies referred to above, which had the further effect that the ship never had more than six aboard, as the Navy lacked sufficient funds. The aircraft were British Hawker Osprey floatplanes powered by Swedish-built NOHAB Mercury engines. Four of these were ordered in 1932, the first flight being made in September 1934. These were delivered in 1934/35, and further licence production was planned in Sweden. However, it is possible that only two more aircraft were delivered.

The contract for the construction of this ship was placed with Götaverken at Göteborg on 7 June 1930.

Modifications *Gotland* had received a twin 25mm on the roof of the forward turret by 1937/37.

By 1943 all of the available aircraft were worn out and there were no replacements to be had in Sweden. While it is possible that higher-performance replacements could have been obtained (from Germany, for example), the greater weights could not have been accepted. Two such machines were the German He 114 and the Swedish Saab B.17. However, the entire possible operating area of the cruiser could equally well be covered by land-based machines. With her designed role redundant, *Gotland* was converted in 1943/44 into a normal cruiser, but with enhanced AA capabilities. To this end the rail system and catapult were landed and the after deckhouse was made continuous to the stern. Four twin Bofors 40mm/60 Model 1936 and two twin power-operated 20mm were fitted at the after end of the former aircraft handling deck. The after twin 57mm was given a shield, and a platform added to the mast. This refit was completed in April 1944.

In 1955 she was again modified and modernised for use as a Fighter Direction Ship. The two casemate 6in, all of the 75mm and the light AA other than the twin 25mm on the forward turret and the 40mm was landed, to be replaced by 40mm/40 Model 1948 guns. The light AA was now four twin and five single 40mm. A full radar outfit was also provided.

Service After her entry into service *Gotland* became the leader of the Scouting Squadron, but during most winters she undertook a flag-showing and training cruise overseas, visiting South America, West Africa and many European ports. The

Left: *Gotland* on trials, 14 December 1934. (RSwN)

Second World War put a stop to this practice, and during hostilities in Europe the ship served only in home waters, her one claim to fame being her sighting report of *Bismarck* in May 1941. Postwar she continued to serve with the fleet in summer and make a foreign cruise in winter, normally to Africa, Latin America or the West Indies. After her second conversion, in 1955, she made only one more foreign cruise before going into reserve in 1956. On 1 July 1960 *Gotland* was stricken, and on 1 April 1963 she was sold for scrapping and broken up at Ystad.

Above: *Gotland* in the West Indies, 1936/37. (RSwN)
Below: *Gotland* at Stockholm on 8 June 1945. (RSwN)

Above: *Gotland* on 15 May 1949, showing the 40mm mountings aft. (RSwN)

TRE KRONOR CLASS

Ship	Builder	Laid Down	Launched	Completed	Fate
Tre Kronor	Götaverken (Göteborg)	27 Sep 43	16 Dec 44	25 Oct 47	Stricken 1 Jan 64
Göta Lejon	Eriksberg (Göteborg)	27 Sep 43	17 Nov 45	15 Dec 47	Stricken 1 Jul 1970

Displacement: 7,400 tons/7,518 tonnes (standard); 9,200 tons/9,347 tonnes (full load).
Length: 597ft/181.96m (oa); 571ft/174m (pp); 590ft 6in/179.98m (wl).
Beam: 54ft/16.45m; Draught: 19ft 6in/5.94m (mean).
Machinery: 2-shaft De Laval geared turbines; 4 Swedish 4-drum boilers.
Performance: 100,000=33kts; Bunkerage: n/k.

Range: n/k.
Protection: 70mm waterline belt; 30mm upper deck; 30mm main deck; 50mm to 125mm turrets.
Guns: seven 6in (1x3 & 2x2); twenty 40mm (10x2); seven 20mm (7x1).
Torpedoes: six 21in (2x3).
Aircraft: nil.
Complement: 618.

Design The Swedish Navy's policy of having a core of coast-defence battleships supported by torpedo craft was changed in the war years, and

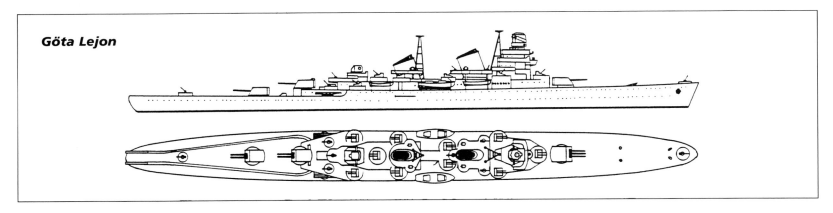

Göta Lejon

the two proposed improved *Sverige* class ships armed with 10in guns were never built. Instead, the organisation was to comprise two squadrons, each with a cruiser and four destroyers, supported by four large MTBs. The new cruisers were to take advantage of the 6in guns which had become available as a result of the German occupation of the Netherlands and the consequent suspension of the *Eendracht* class (q.v.).

The original design of these ships was undertaken by the Italian company CRDA in 1940/41, but was recast several times before the contracts were placed with Swedish yards. Some early sketches indicated a proposed main armament of three triple 6in, but they were finally given one triple and two twin 6in.

The protective scheme included a 70mm waterline belt with two armoured decks, both 30mm thick. The turrets had 50mm to 127mm armour.

The main machinery was a two-shaft De Laval geared turbine layout developing 100,000shp for a maximum speed of 33kts.

The main armament, seven Bofors 6in 53cal 1942 Model, was disposed in a triple turret forward and two twins aft. They were fully automatic, and had 70° elevation. For AA defence the ship relied on ten twin 40mm and seven single 25mm guns. Two banks of triple 21in torpedo tubes were fitted and, in the usual manner of Swedish warships, they were equipped for minelaying. There was no provision to operate aircraft.

Despite the plans to order ships at the beginning of the 1940s, the design delays resulted in the first order being placed as late as 5 February 1943 (*Tre Kronor*) and 12 February for her sister. Consequently, and as a result of a shipyard strike, neither was completed until long after the end of the war. The name *Tre Kronor*, or Three Crowns, represented a medieval claim to the thrones of Norway, Denmark and Sweden. *Göta Lejon*, or Lion of the Goths, was a part of the

Swedish coat of arms representing south-west Sweden.

Modifications In 1948 *Tre Kronor* underwent a year-long refit, when she was given new British radars with corresponding fire-control and action information equipment. She underwent a further refit in 1951/53, when the bridge was completely rebuilt, receiving a large block structure instead. New radars were also added. *Göta Lejon* was similarly modernised during a long period in dockyard hands while in reserve from 1948 to 1951.

The light AA was altered by the deletion of the 25mm guns and their replacement by seven single 40mm.

Service Both ships served in the postwar Swedish fleet, making several overseas cruises. *Tre Kronor* reduced to reserve in 1958, being stricken on 1 January 1964 and sold for breaking up at Göteborg in 1969. Her sister was stricken on 1 July 1970 and was sold to Chile on 18 September 1971 after a refit, being renamed *Almirante Latorre*. She was scrapped in Taiwan in 1987.

Opposite page: *Tre Kronor* running trials in 1947. Note bridge structure. (RSwN)
Right: *Göta Lejon* at Spithead in 1953 with *Sverdlov*. (RSwN)
Below: *Göta Lejon* in camouflage in 1964. (RSwN)

United States

OMAHA CLASS

Ship	Builder	Laid Down	Launched	Completed	Fate
CL4 Omaha	Seattle	6 Dec 18	14 Dec 20	24 Feb 23	Stricken 28 Nov 1945
CL5 Milwaukee	Seattle	13 Dec 18	24 Mar 21	20 Jun 23	To USSR 20 1944
CL6 Cincinnati	Seattle	15 May 20	23 May 21	1 Jan 24	Sold for scrapping 27 Feb 1946
CL7 Raleigh	Bethlehem, Quincy	16 Aug 20	25 Oct 22	6 Feb 24	Stricken 28 Nov 1945
CL8 Detroit	Bethlehem, Quincy	10 Nov 20	20 Jun 22	31 Jul 23	Sold for scrapping, 27 Feb 1946
CL9 Richmond	Cramp	16 Feb 20	29 Sep 21	2 Jul 23	Stricken 21 Jan 1946
CL10 Concord	Cramp	29 Mar 20	15 Dec 21	3 Nov 23	Sold for scrapping 21 Jan 1947
CL11 Trenton	Cramp	18 Aug 20	16 Apr 23	19 Apr 24	Stricken 21 Jan 1946
CL12 Marblehead	Cramp	4 Aug 20	9 Oct 23	8 Sep 24	Stricken 28 Nov 1945
CL13 Memphis	Cramp	14 Oct 20	17 Apr 24	4 Feb 25	Stricken 8 Jan 1946

Displacement: 7,050 tons/7,162 tonnes (standard); 9,150 tons/9,296 tonnes (full load).
Length: 555ft 6in/169.3m (oa); 550ft/167.6m (wl).
Beam: 55ft 4in/16.85m; Draught: 13ft 6in/4.11m (mean).
Machinery: 4-shaft Westinghouse (CL4-6), Curtis (CL7 & 8) or Parsons (CL9-13) geared turbines; 12 Yarrow (CL4-8), White-Forster (others) boilers.
Performance: 90,000shp=34kts; Bunkerage: 1,852 tons max.
Range: 8,460nm at 10kts.
Protection: 3in main belt; 1½in deck.
Guns: twelve 6in (2x2, 8x1); two 3in.
Mines: 224.
Torpedoes: six 21in (2x3).

Aircraft: two, two catapults.
Complement: 800.

Design The USA built no cruisers between the *Salem* class of 1905 and the *Omaha* class of 1917 because there was serious disagreement as to what type of cruiser the USN needed, and the outbreak of war in Europe gave the opportunity to build on the experiences of the belligerent powers. In the intervening period many sketch designs were considered, ranging in displacement from 10,500 tons to 25,000 tons and armed with guns up to 16in. These spanned the whole spectrum from scout cruiser to battlecruiser, but in the end the former type prevailed, though in a much reduced form. The initial requirements for the 1917 Scout, as it was known, included a speed in excess of 30kts, an endurance of 10,000nm and an armament of not less than six 6in guns on a displacement of about 8,000 tons. This was soon amended to include ten 6in guns, four AA guns, two torpedo tubes and no fewer than four aircraft, as well as the ability to lay mines. The requirements were onerous, and it was soon necessary to adopt every possible weight-saving measure and economy. The ship was in fact described as a big destroyer during its design period, and it lacked many of the amenities and design features expected of a cruiser.

By the time the contract plans had been sealed, on 8 July 1916, the design had reached a standard displacement of 7,050 tons. The protective scheme included a 3in waterline belt 19ft deep, and a 1½in deck. There were armoured transverse bulkheads fore and aft, with 1½in and 3in protection respectively, but the gunhouses were given only splinter protection. This represented just over 8 per cent of the standard displacement.

For their relatively small displacement they were given very powerful machinery, which, allied to a fine hull form, gave them a high maximum speed. For the first time, the machinery was dis-

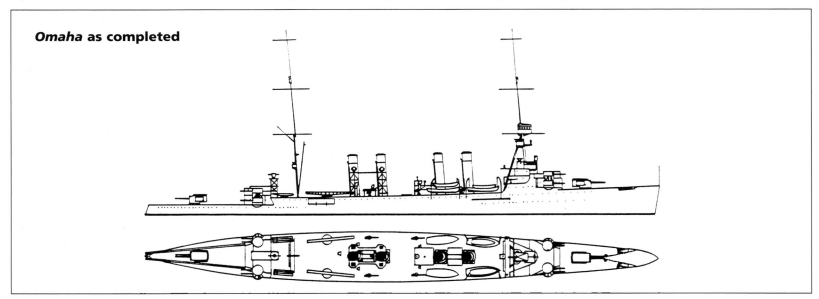

Omaha as completed

posed in the unit layout that was to be adopted for all subsequent US cruisers (except the *New Orleans* and *Brooklyn* Classes) and, eventually, by other nations as well. The twelve boilers were in four boiler rooms (fire rooms in US parlance), the forward pair being separated from the after pair by an engine room. They were of Yarrow type, except for those in the Cramp-built ships, which were White-Forsters. The turbines, in a four-shaft layout, also differed depending upon the builders, the Cramp ships having Parsons, the Todd-built ships Westinghouse, and the Bethlehem ships Curtis type. There were also other variations. The cruising arrangements differed, resulting in a wide discrepancy in endurance which meant that the ships could be grouped into 'large radius' (*CL9* to *13*) and 'short radius' (*CL4* to *8*) types, which obviously affected tactical deployment. Given the USA's vast oil reserves, oil was the only fuel carried, but the designed endurance of 10,000nm at 10kts was never possible, and in fact the endurance was only 6,400nm at 10kts.

One of the peculiarities of this design was that end-on fire had to be maximised, which led to the odd solution of four beam casemated guns fore and aft and two guns in the waist. No gun could be mounted on the forecastle because only single shielded mountings were available, and these could not have tolerated the blast of the casemate guns. However, a number of changes were made while the ships were under construction, the waist guns being omitted and a twin turret added forward and aft. The guns were 6in 53cal Mk 12. The secondary armament was four single 3in 50cal in the waist amidships. The torpedo outfit was greatly increased over the original design intentions, two triple banks of 21in tubes being shipped towards the after end of the forecastle, above the twin banks on the main deck. Finally, there were two catapults, one on each beam, but no hangar. Two floatplanes could be operated, initially probably the Vought VE-9.

Modifications As noted already, the major initial modification was the addition of the twin turrets fore and aft while still building. After completion, and during the years up to the entry of the USA into the Second World War, various measures were taken to remove excess weight from these ships. These measures included landing the twin tubes and plating up the hull openings, removal of the after lower casemate 6in guns in five of the class (*CL6* to *CL9* and *CL12*), and the shipping of only four 3in guns (all in the waist). *Marblehead* was unique in having one of her removed casemate 6in remounted on the centreline aft. In 1940 there was a proposal to refit these ships as AA cruisers, with the main armament reduced to four 6in (2 x 2) and a heavy AA battery of seven 5in DP and six quadruple 1.1in. However, after much dis-

Above: *Omaha* in 1937. (MPL)

cussion this project was never carried through. To save weight, the conning tower was removed and the bridge structure modernised. The authorised AA outfit was set in March 1942 at two Quad 1.1in, one each fore and aft (to be replaced by twin 40mm when available), and eight 20mm singles, four in the bridge wings and the rest on the after superstructure. Seven 3in guns were retained and the 20mm outfit was later increased to twelve. Radar was fitted from 1942. All ships were reduced to ten 6in and another 3in was replaced by a third 40mm twin. Certain ships differed from this standard. *Raleigh* had eight 3in and only eight 20mm, *Cincinnati* had her tubes replaced by two single army-type 40mm, and *Memphis* retained seven 3in and had only two twin 40mm. Finally, *Detroit* was refitted in 1945 and had the forward upper casemate 6in replaced by a pair of twin 40mm, and she also had eight 3in/50 and no tubes. Curtiss SOC Seagulls replaced the initial Vought floatplanes from late 1935, *Marblehead* being issued with the first two on 12 November that year. Aircraft facilities appear to have been retained throughout the war, probably as a result of their deployment to the vast open spaces of the South Atlantic, Vought OS2U Kingfisher floatplanes being the standard issue after 1940.

Service *Omaha* served in the Atlantic from commissioning as Flagship (Destroyers), and was assigned to Neutrality Patrols after the start of the war in Europe, serving with CruDiv 2, TF3. After

the USA's entry into the war the ship served in the Central and South Atlantic on anti-raider and blockade runner patrols, capturing the 5,098-ton blockade runner *Odenwald* off the Brazilian coast on 6 November 1942. By January 1944 she was with TF41, operating out of Recife, Brazil, and on 4 January one of her aircraft sighted a ship which turned out to be the blockade runner *Rio Grande* (6,062 tons). This was sunk by the cruiser and her consort, the destroyer *Jouett*. On 5 January she was instrumental in the scuttling of another blockade runner, *Burgenland* (7,320 tons). Later in 1944 she transferred to the Mediterranean for the invasion of the South of France, where she formed part of the support force for TF86 'Sitka'. After bombardment duties until the end of August, the ship returned to the South Atlantic for the remainder of the war. In August 1945 *Omaha* returned to the east coast, and on 1 November 1945 paid off, to be stricken at the end of the same month. She was broken up in February 1946 at the Philadelphia Navy Yard.

Milwaukee served mainly in the Pacific from 1928, with CruDiv 2 in the Asiatic Fleet. From 1933 she was with CruDiv 3, attached to the Battle Fleet in Pacific waters until the end of 1940, when she transferred to CruDiv 2 in the Atlantic. At first employed on the Neutrality Patrol, after Pearl Harbor she was assigned to Ocean Patrol duties, initially in the Caribbean and then, after a brief foray into the Pacific on convoy duties at the

Left: *Cincinnati* in July 1942. (Courtesy Louis Parker)

beginning of 1942, was based at Recife with TF41 for the next couple of years, for South Atlantic patrols. In February 1944 she returned to New York, and then operated in the North Atlantic. In March she escorted convoy JW58 to Russia, at the end of which she was transferred to the Soviet Navy in place of the Italian ships which had been allocated to Russia following the capitulation of Italy. These ships could not be transferred at that time for various reasons, but as the Soviets insisted on receiving their share, several Allied units were transferred temporarily, *Milwaukee* being one. She was lent to the Soviets on 20 April 1944 and renamed *Murmansk* (q.v.). On 16 March 1949 she was handed back to the USN and subsequently sold for breaking up on 10 December 1949, to be scrapped by American Shipbreakers at Wilmington, Delaware.

Cincinnati also joined CruDiv 2 with the Atlantic Fleet on completion, but in 1927 was with CruDiv 3 in the Asiatic Fleet, returning to the Atlantic in 1928. In 1932 she joined the battle fleet in the Pacific, with CruDiv 3. By the beginning of 1941 *Cincinnati* had been transferred to the Atlantic, and served with CruDiv 2 in that theatre until the end of the war, mostly in the South Atlantic with TF41 at Recife, except for a diversion to the Mediterranean for the landings in the south of France in August 1944. *Cincinnati* paid off on 1 November 1945, and was sold for breaking up on 27 February 1946.

Raleigh saw service with both the Atlantic and Pacific Fleets in the years up to the Second World War. In 1927 she landed troops in Nicaragua, and in 1928 made a cruise to Europe. She participated in the international patrols off Spain during the Civil War, but by the summer of 1938 had assumed the role of Flagship, Destroyers, with the Pacific Fleet at Pearl Harbor. During the Japanese attack on 7 December the ship was hit by torpedoes in No. 2 boiler room, and almost all of the machinery spaces were flooded. Damage was also caused by a bomb near-miss. Had this happened at sea, the ship would almost certainly have been lost. As it was, she was under repair until July 1942. After completion of repairs *Raleigh* participated in the Aleutians campaign as part of the Southern Covering Force until March 1944. She took part in the bombardment of Attu on 18/19 February 1943, and the landings on Attu in May as part of TG16.6. She was with this Task Group when Kiska was bombarded in August 1943 in preparation for the landings, and when Paramushiro in the Kuriles was attacked in February 1944. In January 1945 she participated in the bombardment of the Kuriles again, but by November she had been paid off and stricken, to be sold for breaking up on 27 February 1946.

Detroit joined CruDiv 3 after completion. In 1927 she was part of the US forces deployed to Nicaragua during the unrest there, but in June of that year became Flagship of Commander, Naval Forces Europe, making an extensive cruise to European waters. She subsequently served as Flagship, Destroyer Flotillas, Battle Force, for most of the late 1930s, and in 1939 was also Flagship of Desron 2, in the Pacific, serving in this capacity until May 1942. Subsequently she served with CruDiv 1 for the remainder of the war. On the outbreak of war in the Pacific she was at Pearl Harbor, then undertook local defence duties and convoy work between Pearl and the US west coast. In November 1942 *Detroit* became Flagship of TF8.6, deployed in the Aleutian Islands, where she served until June 1944, taking part in the bombardments of Attu, Kiska and the Kurile Islands. By August 1944 the ship was at Balboa, acting as Flagship of the South East Pacific Fleet,

Left: Another 1942 view of *Cincinnati*. (Courtesy Louis Parker)

Opposite page, lower: *Memphis* at Malta in October 1945. (W&L)

and operated off the west coast of South America until December 1944. On 16 January 1945 she sailed for Ulithi for service as Flagship, Replenishment Group, 5th Fleet, and on 1 September was one of the ships in Tokyo Bay for the Japanese surrender. Her final task was to bring home troops from the Pacific, and on 11 January 1946 she was paid off, being sold for scrapping on 27 February that year.

Richmond made a major cruise to Europe, Africa and South America after entering service, and then assumed the role of Flagship, Scouting Force. In 1925 she became Flagship, Light Cruiser Division, with the Scouting Force. After a year on the China Station in 1927, she served on the east coast until 1934 and then transferred to the west coast until 1937, when she went to the Pacific as Flagship, Submarine Force. In 1940 *Richmond* transferred to Pearl Harbor as Flagship CruDiv 3, but when the war in Europe resulted in the formation of the Neutrality Patrol that December, she joined it, operating on the Pacific coast of North and South America. On the US entry into the war the ship undertook convoy escort work in the Pacific until 1943, when she went to the Aleutian Islands as Flagship TG16.6. She partici-

Above: *Detroit* in August 1942. (Floating Drydock)

pated in the Battle of the Komandorski Islands on 26 March 1943, and in the bombardments of Attu, Kiska and the Kurile Islands until the end of the war, when she took part in the occupation of Japan. By June/July 1945 the cruiser, together with destroyers, was engaged on raids against Japanese convoys in the sea of Okhotsk. After returning to the USA she was paid off on 21 December 1945, stricken on 21 January 1946, and sold to Patapsco Scrap Co. of Bethlehem, Pennsylvania, for breaking up on 18 December 1946.

Concord assumed the role of Flagship, Atlantic Destroyer Flotillas, in 1925, and served in this capacity until 1931, when she became Flagship of CruDiv 3 with the Scouting Force, later Battle Force. During the war *Concord* operated in the south-east Pacific on escort duties until transferred to the Aleutians in April 1944 as Flagship TF94. She took part in the bombardment of the Kurile Islands and in the occupation of Japan before returning to home waters in September. *Concord* was decommissioned on 12 December 1945 and sold for breaking up on 21 January 1947.

Trenton was another of the ships engaged in the Nicaragua operations in 1928. For most of the prewar period she was Flagship, CruDiv 2, but by 1939 she was in CruDiv 3 with the Battle Force. *Trenton* operated in the South Pacific during 1942/44 and then went to the Aleutian Islands in September, where she remained until the end of the war. She was paid off on 20 December 1945, stricken on 21 January 1946 and sold to Patapsco Scrap Co., Bethlehem, Pennsylvania, on 29 December 1946 for breaking up.

Marblehead began her career with a cruise to Great Britain and the Mediterranean, followed by a visit to Australia in 1925. In 1927/28 she was

involved in operations on the Yangtse river in China and off Nicaragua before assuming a normal peacetime routine in the Atlantic and Pacific Fleets. In January 1938 *Marblehead* was detached to the Philippines, based at Cavite, and was still in this region on the outbreak of war in the Pacific in December 1941. Her duties included the escorting of Allied convoys in the East Indies and offensive sorties as required. As a unit of TF5 she sailed to attack the Japanese invasion force off Balikpapan in January 1942, but because of engine trouble was unable to continue the sortie. In February she was part of Admiral Doorman's ABDA force that sailed to attack the Japanese invasion forces at Balikpapan, but, in the course of attacks on the Allied force by Japanese bombers, *Marblehead* was hit by two bombs and also near-missed. Serious flooding and loss of steering almost caused the loss of the ship, but

she managed to withdraw to South Africa via Ceylon, where repairs took until mid-April. After her return to the USA and completion of repairs, the ship was deployed to the South and central Atlantic for anti-blockade-runner duties, based at Recife and Bahia until February 1944. There followed several months of operations on the North Atlantic convoy routes before the ship was transferred to the Mediterranean for Operation Dragoon, the landings in the south of France. *Marblehead* was a part of the fire support group to TF87. This was her last active employment, as she then returned to home waters and was used for training purposes until being paid off on 1 November 1945. She was stricken on 28 November and sold for breaking up on 27 February 1946.

Memphis joined CruDiv 3 with the Atlantic fleet, and, in 1927, CruDiv 2 with the Scouting

Force in the Atlantic, remaining attached to this formation until becoming Flagship, Aircraft Scouting Forces, in 1939. During the intervening period the ship was deployed to many parts of the world, including European (Flagship, Commander USN Forces Europe) and Australasian waters. From 1928 she operated mainly in the Pacific, and between 1939 and 1941 was based in Alaska. She was assigned to the Neutrality Patrol in April 1941 and, after the US entry into the war, served in the South Atlantic, being based at Recife for much of the war. In January 1945 she was deployed to the Mediterranean as Flagship, Commander USN Forces in Europe. *Memphis* returned home to pay off, decommissioning on 17 December 1945 and being stricken on 8 January 1946. On 18 December 1946 she was sold for breaking up to the Patapsco Scrap Co., Bethlehem, Pennsylvania.

PENSACOLA CLASS

Ship	Builder	Laid Down	Launched	Completed	Fate
CA24 Pensacola	New York NY	27 Oct 26	25 Apr 29	6 Feb 30	Scuttled 10 Nov 1948
CA25 Salt Lake City	New York Sbdg	9 Jun 27	23 Jan 29	11 Dec 29	Scuttled 25 May 48

Displacement: 9,097 tons/9,242 tonnes (standard); 11,512 tons/11,696 tonnes (full load).
Length: 585ft 8in/178.51m (oa); 570ft/173.74m (wl).
Beam: 65ft 3in/19.89m; Draught: 19ft 6in/5.93m (mean).
Machinery: 4-shaft Parsons geared turbines; 8 White-Forster boilers.
Performance: 107,000shp=32½kts; Bunkerage: 2,116 tons oil fuel max.
Range: 10,000nm at 15kts.
Protection: 2½in main belt (machinery spaces), 1in deck; magazines, 4in sides, 1¾in crowns.
Guns: ten 8in (2x3, 2x2); four 5in (4x1).
Torpedoes: six 21in (2x3).
Aircraft: four, two catapults.
Complement: 631.

Design By 1918, nascent US cruiser designs had been affected by the appearance of the British *Hawkins* class (q.v.), which outclassed all existing US and other foreign designs of the period. In consequence, the US decided that any future cruiser would have to be superior to the *Hawkins*, as at that time Great Britain was still considered a possible antagonist. However, it was also recognised that Japan represented a real threat, and that a war in the Pacific would demand certain special characteristics, the most obvious of which was a large radius of action. The years immediately following the end of the First World War found the USN, like most armed

forces at the time, seriously out of step with their political and financial masters. The numbers of ships deemed necessary by the navy were clearly impossible in the aftermath of hostilities, when the emphasis was very much on ensuring that there were no more wars. As a result, despite much planning and discussion, no cruisers were laid down until the mid-1920s. In the meantime,

the Washington Naval Treaty had been signed in 1922, creating a new class of cruiser which had been agreed upon as a result of US and British arguments, but which met US ideas more than those of Great Britain. The USA had begun design studies for cruisers armed with 8in guns as early as the beginning of 1919. By 1920 at least seven design studies were under consideration, described as Scout Cruisers, ranging in displacement from 5,000 to 10,000 tons and armed with various combinations of 5in, 6in and 8in guns. In the following years the USN trod the same path as every other naval power as it attempted to reconcile the conflicting demands of the departments

Below: *Pensacola* in 1934. (MPL)

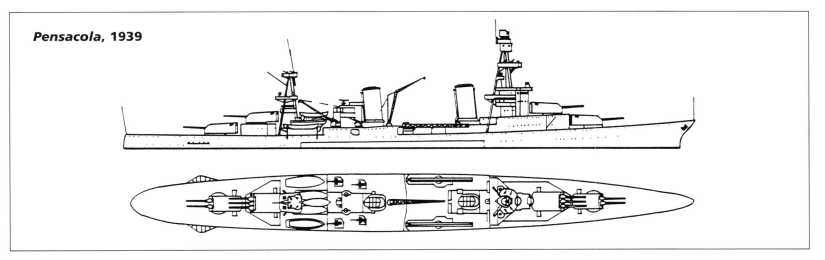

Pensacola, 1939

concerned; armour versus speed versus gunpower, etc. By November 1923, however, sketch designs had begun to appear which were very close to that which would be adopted for the first of the US heavy cruisers. Nevertheless, questions of protection, machinery arrangements and the number of main battery guns continued to exercise the minds of the design staff, with the 10,000-ton limit set by the Washington Treaty constantly in the foreground.

The final sketch design, selected in March 1925, envisaged an armament of ten 8in guns in two twin and two triple turrets, a speed of 32.1kts and 773 tons of protective plating. Calculations then showed that the ship would be considerably below the 10,000-ton limit as a result of extensive weight-saving measures, and an additional 250 tons was available to increase the armour scheme.

This led to further bickering regarding its distribution, but in the end this total was much reduced and used to increase magazine protection.

The protective scheme finally included a 4in waterline belt in the way of the forward magazine spaces and 3in abreast the machinery spaces, extending 5ft below the waterline. There was no external side protection to the after magazines, on the grounds that any action was expected to take place forward of the beam, but there was a 3½in internal longitudinal bulkhead aft. Horizontal armour was 40 to 60lb plating. Armour represented about 6 per cent of the light ship displacement.

As in *Omaha*, the main machinery was arranged on the unit principle, with eight boilers in four fire rooms, the aftermost fire rooms separating the turbine rooms.

As far as the main armament was concerned, the unusual feature was the mounting of the heavier triple turret in the higher Nos. 2 and 3 positions. This was done because the fine hull lines forward could not accommodate the larger barbette of the triple mount, but it also kept more of the armament drier. The guns were 8in 55cal weapons firing a 260lb projectile, with a maximum range of 31,860yd at 41° elevation. The secondary armament, after much discussion, was finally fixed at four 5in 25cal DP in single mountings. Light AA proved more of a problem owing to the lack of a suitable weapon, the 37mm originally projected never being put into service. Thus the anti-aircraft defence was limited to a few machine

Below: *Pensacola* in 1944. Note removal of mainmast. (Courtesy Louis Parker)

1944 the official AA outfit was six quad 40mm and 20/21 20mm. By this time the aircraft complement had been reduced to two, the starboard catapult being landed. Curtiss SOC Seagull floatplanes replaced the older Corsairs, and, at least in *Pensacola*, these were in turn supplanted by the Curtiss SC-1 Seahawk in 1945. By 1945 *Salt Lake City*, which was never fully modernised, had six quad 40mm and nineteen single 20mm. Her sister, after refit in the summer of 1945, had seven quad 40mm and nine twin 20mm. Finally, while employed on Magic Carpet duties after the end of the war, both catapults, four 5in guns, two quad 40mm and four twin 20mm were landed.

Service *Pensacola* served on the east coast with CruDiv 4 until 1935, when CruDiv 4 was transferred to the Pacific Fleet. At the start of the Pacific war she was serving with the Scouting Force as Flagship, CruDiv 5, to which she had transferred in January 1941. Initially she operated in the South-West Pacific and Australian waters, covering troop convoys. In January 1942 she was part of TF11 for the carrier raid by *Lexington* on Wake Island, which had to be cancelled when the support oiler was sunk. Her next operation was the covering of convoys across the Pacific from the Panama Canal to the Pacific Islands, after which TF11 was assigned to the ANZAC forces in the New Hebrides and Coral Sea. In March *Pensacola*, together with TF11 and TF17, made a carrier raid on Jalamava and Lae, New Guinea. On 21 April the cruiser returned to Pearl Harbor. In June she was engaged in the Battle of Midway as part of TF16, and afterwards became part of TF17 at Pearl Harbor. By September she was engaged in the Guadalcanal campaign, and participated in the Battle of Santa Cruz on 26 October. However, during the Battle of Tassafaronga on the night of 30 November/1 December, TF67, of which *Pensacola* was a part, was routed by a force of Japanese destroyers and *Northampton* (q.v.) was sunk. Among the ships damaged was *Pensacola*, which suffered heavy casualties resulting from a torpedo hit. After provisional repairs at Tulagi, she transferred to Espiritu Santo for further repair, then sailed for Pearl Harbor on 7 January 1943. Between 27 January and November the ship was repaired and refitted. She returned to service in time to take part in the bombardment of Tarawa in November, followed by operations in the Marshall Islands. In April, after a short refit at Mare Island, the ship was transferred to the Northern Pacific and operated against the Kurile Islands before returning to Pearl Harbor on 13 August 1944. Thereafter she saw service in the bombardment of Wake Island, Leyte Gulf, and the Battle off Cape Engano, followed by further bombardment duties off Iwo Jima from November. In the course of this

guns. Two triple banks of 21in tubes were shipped on the upper deck abreast the after funnel. The aircraft arrangements reflected the USN's policy for cruiser operation, two catapults and no fewer than four floatplanes being accommodated, but there was no hangar. The initial aircraft type was the Vought O3U Corsair.

Modifications As completed, these ships still came out grossly underweight, and in consequence rolled badly. Bilge keels were enlarged and anti-rolling tanks were fitted experimentally in *Pensacola*. The torpedo tubes were landed in the mid-1930s; not for weight reasons, but

because cruisers were deemed not to require them tactically. Four more 5in/25 singles were added around the bridge structure before the war. *Pensacola* received a CXAM radar set in 1940, and both vessels were fitted with newer radars as the war progressed. By November 1941 the AA outfit had been increased by two quadruple 1.1in. Various changes were made to the rig, including fitting a main battery director on the cut-down mainmast quadruped. By 1942 the ships had received about eight single 20mm guns and two more 1.1 quads. In 1943 quad 40mm Bofors replaced the 1.1in guns and the 20mm outfit was augmented, and by

Left: *Pensacola.* (Author's collection)

Lake City was one of the covering force for the Doolittle raid on Tokyo. In June 1942 she became part of TF17 at Pearl Harbor, and in July supported the Guadalcanal landings, followed by the Battle of the Eastern Solomon Islands in August, when she was part of TF61. During her actions in the Guadalcanal campaign she rescued the survivors of *Hornet*, but in the Battle of Cape Esperance in October she was hit three times by Japanese ships, though damage was not serious. The ship was under refit at Pearl Harbor between November 1942 and March 1943, then went to the Aleutian Islands, where, as part of TG16.6 during the Battle of the Komandorski Islands on 26 March, she was badly damaged by Japanese cruisers. She underwent repairs at Mare Island and arrived back at Pearl Harbor on 14 October 1943. Subsequently she escorted carrier raids on Wake, Rabaul and Tarawa, then in January 1944 operated in the Marshall Islands with TG50.15. In March/April she was serving in the Western Carolines, but returned to Pearl Harbor on 30 April before refit at Mare Island between May and July. After this the ship returned to the Aleutians, but by mid-August had returned to Pearl Harbor. After supporting attacks on Wake Island and Saipan, she covered carrier task forces in the Second Battle of the Philippine Sea, then covered operations off Iwo Jima and Okinawa in the first few months of 1945. By August she was back in the Aleutian Islands, and, finally, supported the occupation of Honshu. After the war *Salt Lake City*, like her sister, assisted in the bringing home of US troops, but in March 1946 she was prepared for the Bikini trials. She survived both tests, then was decommissioned and sunk as a target on 25 May 1948, 130 miles off the coast of southern California.

task she was hit six times by shore batteries on 17 February 1945, sustaining many casualties. After repairs she carried out further bombardment tasks at Okinawa, but on 15 April was recalled to the USA for refit at Mare Island, which lasted until 3 August, when she sailed for the Aleutian islands. On the surrender of Japan she participated in the occupation tasks until returning to home waters in December. In 1946 she was used to bring home troops from war service, and was finally employed as one of the targets for the Bikini Atoll atomic bomb tests on 25 July 1946.

Salt Lake City served initially with CruDiv 2 until 12 September 1930, when she transferred to CruDiv 5. In 1931/33 she was with the Pacific Fleet, being assigned to CruDiv 4 in September 1933, and then operated mainly in Pacific waters until the US entry into the war in December 1941. She was with TF8 to support Wake Island in December, and in January/February 1942 operated in the Marshall and Gilbert Islands, bombarding enemy positions. She participated in the carrier raid and bombardment of Wake Island in February/March. In April *Salt*

NORTHAMPTON CLASS

Ship	Builder	Laid Down	Launched	Completed	Fate
CA26 Northampton	Bethlehem, Quincy	12 Apr 28	5 Sep 29	17 May 30	Lost 1 Dec 1942
CA27 Chester	New York Sbdg	6 Mar 28	3 Jul 29	24 Jun 30	Sold for scrapping, 11 Aug 1959
CA28 Louisville	Puget Sound NY	4 Jul 28	1 Sep 30	15 Jan 31	Stricken 1 Mar 1959
CA29 Chicago	Mare Island NY	10 Sep 28	10 Apr 30	9 Mar 31	Lost 30 Jan 1943
CA30 Houston	Newport News	1 May 28	7 Sep 29	17 Jun 30	Lost 1 Mar 1942
CA31 Augusta	Newport News	2 Jul 28	1 Feb 30	30 Jan 31	Stricken 1 Mar 1959

Displacement: 9,006 tons/9,150 tonnes (standard); 11,420 tons/11,602 tonnes (full load).
Length: 600ft 3in/182.96m (oa); 582ft/177.4m (wl).
Beam: 66ft 1in/20.14m; Draught: 19ft 5in/5.92m (mean).

Machinery: 4-shaft Parsons geared turbines; 8 White-Forster boilers.
Performance: 107,000shp=32½kts; Bunkerage: 2,108 tons oil fuel max.

Range: 10,000nm at 15kts.
Protection: 3in main belt (machinery spaces); 1in deck; magazines, 3¾in sides, 2in crowns.
Guns: nine 8in (3x3); four 5in (4x1).
Torpedoes: six 21in (2x3).
Aircraft: four, two catapults.
Complement: 617.

Design The design of this class began directly after that for *CA24* had been finalised, preliminary discussions beginning on 24 February 1926. The initial design changes proposed included a reduction in the main armament to eight guns, on the grounds that this was the standard for foreign ships, improved damage survival capability, and better aircraft stowage. Two alternative sketch

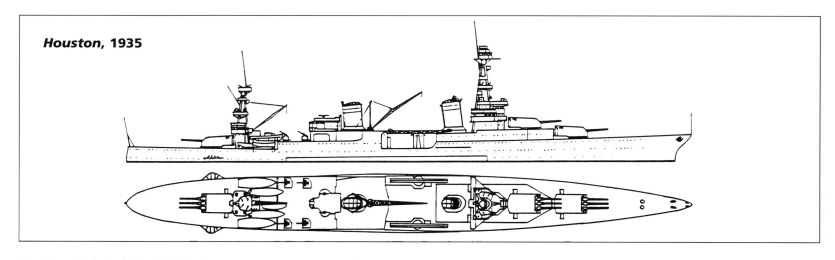

Houston, 1935

designs had been prepared by April, one shipping nine 8in guns in three triple turrets, and the other eight guns in twin turrets. Both designs featured a raised forecastle, a lengthened hull and increased freeboard. Internally, the fire rooms were divided into four spaces, rather than two. The eight-gun ship was considered too cramped, and the nine-gun design was therefore favoured. As design work progressed it became obvious that there was some weight to spare, totalling some 200 tons over and above the original preliminary weight margin of 221 tons. This, it was suggested, could be used to improve protection, and several modifications to the design were drawn up, some of which appeared to offer defence against 8in shells. However, in the inevitable discussions which followed, the requirement for the ships to be fitted as flagships took away some of this mar-

gin, but various schemes for redistribution and improvement of the protection continued to be considered. In some of these the magazines were concentrated, with their side protection increased to 7in at the expense of the gunhouse armour to give immunity to 8in gunfire, while others sought to protect the magazines against 8in shells but the machinery and gunhouses only against 5in or 6in shells. In the end it was decided that the goal of immunity against 8in gunfire was impossible, and part of the weight available was used to improve splinter protection to the ammunition supply systems and the remainder was added to the reserve, it being recognised that any new designs naturally grew and needed adequate reserves. Despite all of these measures, the ships still came out nearly 1,000 tons under the Treaty limit. Six ships were authorised in FY29, the first three fitted as Divi-

sional Flagships and the last three as Fleet Flagships, with forecastle plating extended to the catapult towers for additional accommodation.

As finalised, the armour scheme included a waterline belt just over 13ft deep, 3in thick abreast the machinery spaces and extending 5ft below the waterline, with the magazines having 3¾in sides. Horizontal protection was 1in over the machinery spaces and 2in over the magazines. Gunhouses received only 2½in faces and 2in roofs. The total weight allocated to protection was 1,057 tons.

The machinery installation was identical to that of the first class of heavy cruisers.

The main armament was also the same gun as that shipped aboard the *Pensacola* class, as was the secondary battery of four 5in singles. The weakest point of the armament was the AA defence, since the 37mm gun under development by Colt and intended for these ships never appeared. A torpedo outfit of six tubes in two triple mountings was retained in this design, but the question of the appropriateness of torpedoes in a cruiser was always an open one for the USA. Finally, the rearrangement of the aircraft fittings featured in the early design discussions led to the fitting of a blast-proof hangar around the after funnel, which allowed servicing of the aircraft out of the elements and protected the frail machines from damage by the ship's own gunfire. Four aeroplanes could be stowed in the hangars, plus two on the catapults, but normally only four were embarked.

Modifications Alterations made before the USA entered the war were mainly concerned with improving the admittedly weak AA defence. Early in 1933 the fitting of HA directors and eight .5in Browning MGs was approved, and the tubes were landed in the mid-1930s. Four additional 5in/25

guns were also authorised in February 1935, but their fitting did not begin until 1938/39. These four guns were mounted on the hangar roof, abreast the after funnel. After June 1940 the King Board resulted in a major upgrade of the AA outfits of US ships, four Quad 1.1in mountings being called for in cruisers. However, there was a shortage of these guns, and the *Northamptons* were initially given four 3in/50 singles. *Houston* may have had three 3in and one 1.1in quad. Eventually the four mountings were fitted, two abreast the bridge and two between the groups of 5in guns. Early in the war the foremasts were cut down and open bridges and radar fitted. When the 20mm

became available in some numbers it was fitted wherever space could be found, and consequently there was seldom a standard outfit, *Chester* for example having two quadruple 1.1in, thirteen 20mm and no 3in by August 1942. The intended outfit by this time was four quad 40mm and twelve 20mm, but this was increased as the war progressed until, ultimately, the light AA was to comprise twenty 40mm (4 x 4, 2 x 2) and thirty-one 20mm in the surviving units. *Chicago* had four quad 40mm and twenty single 20mm at the time of her loss, and *Northampton* had about fourteen 20mm but still retained the 1.1in when she was sunk. *Chester* finished the war with five

quad 40mm, two twin 40mm and twenty-six 20mm (13 x 2). Her starboard catapult had been landed, Curtiss SC-1 Seahawks being operated on the remaining one. The after superstructure had been cut down, and a latticed tripod main mast built around the after funnel. *Louisville* and *Augusta* received similar treatment but differed in detail, the latter having four quad and four twin 40mm, plus twenty single 20mm.

Service When *Northampton* joined the fleet in May 1930, she, like *Pensacola* and *Salt Lake City*, was initially classified as a light cruiser; *CL26* as the heavy cruiser designation had not then been established. However, in the following year the *CA* designation was applied. During the years up to the summer of 1940 she served with CruDiv 4, mainly as flagship, with the Scouting Force in the Pacific. Thereafter she served in a similar capacity with CruDiv 5 until her loss in 1942. On the outbreak of the Pacific war she was with TF8, escorting the carrier *Enterprise* and searching for the Japanese fleet, then took part in operations intended to relieve the US garrison on Wake Island. Early in 1942 she carried out bombardments of Wotje during the carrier raid on the Marshall and Gilbert Islands, followed by a raid on Wake Island, then in March participated in a raid on the Marcus Islands. In April the ship was a part of the force making the Doolittle B-25 raid

on Tokyo, but missed participation in the Battle of the Coral Sea as a result. However, she was present at the Battle of Midway with TF16 at the beginning of June. After this operation she joined TF17, and by September was involved in operations around Guadalcanal. In October she was at the Battle of Santa Cruz, and the following month, as part of TF16, took part in the Battle of Tassafaronga, when she was hit by torpedoes from the destroyer *Oyashio* south of Savo Island just before midnight on 30 November. She was abandoned in the early hours of the next day and foundered shortly afterwards.

Chester also joined CruDiv 4 on commissioning, but by 1936 had been transferred to CruDiv 5, with which formation she was to remain for the remainder of her career, except for a brief period at the end of 1940 when she served with CruDiv 7 as part of the Patrol Force. At the start of the war in the Pacific she was with *Northampton* initially off Wake Island, then in January 1942 supported the landings on Samoa. During an attack on Taroa with TG8.3 on 1 February, however, she was hit by bombs and damaged, requiring repairs at Pearl Harbor. In May she was present at the Battle of the Coral Sea with TF17, rescuing the survivors of *Lexington*. The following month the ship returned to the USA for refit on the west coast, but returned to the South Pacific by the end of September to join TF62 at Noumea. On 20 October 1942, while operating in the Solomon Islands, she was hit in the machinery spaces by a torpedo from *I 176* and was lucky to survive, having lost all propulsion and power supplies. After provisional repairs at Espiritu Santo she withdrew to the USA for full repairs and refit, which were not completed until the summer of 1943. After her return to service she participated in the landings in the Gilbert Islands as part of TG50.3 in November, and in attacks on the Marshall Islands as part of TG50.15 in January/February 1944. Following a short refit in April, the cruiser was transferred to the North Pacific because her slow-firing 8in guns were not best suited to the fast-moving, mainly night actions in the South Pacific islands. With TF94 she bombarded enemy positions in the Kurile islands in June, but had returned to Pearl Harbor by mid-August. In the following months she bombarded Wake island and Marcus Island, escorted carriers and participated in the Battle of Leyte Gulf. Between November 1944 and February 1945 she was at Iwo Jima and the Bonin Islands, then returned to the USA for a refit which lasted until mid-June 1945. On return to the war zone she operated off Okinawa and then with a task force in the South China Sea before another deployment to the Aleutians in August. She took part in the occupation of Japan, and then brought home troops before paying off on 10 June 1946. A decision to scrap the ship immediately after the war was reversed, and she remained in reserve for the remainder of her life until stricken on 1 March 1959, being sold for scrapping on 11 August that year.

Louisville joined CruDiv 5 with the Scouting Force on completion. In 1934 she was reassigned to CruDiv 6, returning to CruDiv 5 in 1937 until the autumn of 1940, when, like *Northampton*, she had a spell with CruDiv 7. Thereafter she joined CruDiv 4 for the remainder of the war. In 1940 she carried gold from the UK to the USA, but then returned to the Pacific. When the USA entered the war she ferried troops to Samoa, and in March 1942 operated in the Solomon Islands. At the end of May she sailed for the Aleutians to join TF8, and took part in the bombardment of Kiska. In November *Louisville* returned to the Pacific, and participated in the Battle off Rennell Island with TF67 in January 1943. However, by April she was back in the Aleutians, where she undertook bombardment and convoy escort duties until sailing for Mare Island in December for refit. In January 1944 the ship returned to the South Pacific, seeing action at Eniwetok, the Palau Islands, Truk, Saipan, Tinian and Leyte Gulf – the Battle of the Surigao Strait – after which she joined TF77 off Luzon. Here, while en route on 5-6 January 1945, she was hit by two kamikaze aircraft and badly damaged, sustaining heavy casualties, including Rear Admiral Chandler. She returned to the USA for repairs, which were completed in April. Back in the South Pacific, the cruiser was hit yet again by kamikazes, this time off Okinawa on 5 June. When her repairs were completed she was deployed to China and participated in the operations to land US troops there during August-October. *Louisville* returned to the USA and paid off on 17 June 1946. It was originally intended to dispose of the ship after the war, but the decision was rescinded and she remained in reserve until stricken on 1 March 1959, to be sold for breaking-up on 14 September the same year to the Marlene Blouse Corp. of New York.

Chicago served as Flagship CruDiv 5 with the Scouting Force and, from June 1939, also as Flagship Cruisers, Scouting Force, until the autumn of 1940, when she was reassigned to CruDiv 4, still as Flagship Cruisers. On the outbreak of war in 1941 she was with TF12 at Pearl Harbor (although she was at sea at the time of the attack), but at the beginning of February 1942 was reassigned to the ANZAC squadron at Suva in the Fiji Islands. After the Allies had been driven out of the Dutch East Indies she returned to Pearl Harbor, participating in operations in the Coral Sea. On 31 May the ship was in Sydney, Australia, for repair and refit when the Japanese launched the midget submarine attack on the port. Their torpedoes missed, however. In August *Chicago* supported the landings on Guadalcanal as part of TG62.2. On 9 August 1942 she was badly damaged by a torpedo from Japanese destroyers at the Battle of Savo Island, her bows being severely damaged. She withdrew to Noumea and then to Sydney for temporary repair, and then to the US west coast for full repair, arriving at San Francisco on 13 October. After repairs had been finished the ship returned to Noumea and Guadalcanal. On 29 January she was part of TF18, operating off Rennell Island, when she was hit on the starboard side by two torpedoes from IJN naval aircraft, two fire rooms and the after engine room being flooded. Although taken in tow by *Louisville*, she was hit again the following afternoon by four more torpedoes on the same side, and sank in about twenty minutes.

Houston was deployed to the Far East on entering service, assuming the role of Flagship,

Asiatic Station, from February 1931. She remained out east until relieved by *Augusta*, sailing for San Francisco on 17 November 1933. She was assigned to CruDiv 6, with the Scouting Force, in 1934, and CruDiv 5 the following year as Flagship. By 1937 she had been reassigned to CruDiv 4, and the next year was Flagship, US Fleet. In October 1940 she sailed for the Philippines, and on 19 November assumed the role of Flagship, Asiatic Fleet, once more. On the outbreak of war in December 1941 she sailed for Australia with a convoy and three old destroyers (TF5) and joined the Australian-British-Dutch-American (ABDA) Command. She operated in the Dutch East Indies, and on 4 February, while part of a strike force sailed to intercept Japanese landings reported at Balikpapan, she was hit by a bomb which disabled her after turret, thus losing all after gunpower. *Marblehead* (q.v.) was disabled at the same time. Despite the damage, the cruiser then escorted a convoy to reinforce Timor, but this was recalled. The ship was then ordered to Tjilatjap to join Rear-Admiral Doorman, RNethN, thus missing the Japanese air raid on Darwin. When the Japanese invaded Java at the end of February 1942, *Houston* participated in strikes against them, and on 27 February took part in the Battle of the Java Sea, managing to withdraw to Batavia with the Australian *Perth* after the debacle. However, on attempting to pass through the Sunda Strait the two Allied cruisers ran into a large force of Japanese cruisers and destroyers, and in the ensuing action both were sunk by gunfire and torpedoes from *Mogami* and *Mikuma*.

Augusta, unlike her sisters, served with the Atlantic Fleet after commissioning and was not transferred to the Pacific until March 1932. On 9 March 1933 she was assigned to the Far East as Flagship, Asiatic Station, where she relieved *Houston* at Shanghai. In August 1940 she was with CruDiv 4, attached to the Scouting Force, but in the autumn joined the Patrol Force in the Atlantic, assuming the role of flagship from May 1941. From January 1942 she was assigned to CruDiv 7, while still retaining the task of Flagship, Atlantic. In August 1942 she carried President Roosevelt to Argentia Bay for his meeting with Churchill. For the landings in North Africa in November 1942 she formed part of TG34.9, the Center Attack Group, and during a counterattack by a French force which included the light cruiser *Primaguet* and destroyers, *Augusta* and *Brooklyn* damaged the French cruiser and one of the destroyers so badly that they had to be beached. Following the landings, the ship returned to the USA for refit at New York Navy Yard. In August 1943 *Augusta* was transferred to the British Home Fleet after the departure of the battleships *South Dakota* and *Alabama* as a result of the threat posed by *Tirpitz*, and was based at Scapa Flow. She operated in northern waters until ordered back to the USA at the end of November 1943 for dockyard refit. In April 1944 the cruiser returned to British waters for the invasion of Normandy, when she was Flagship, Western Task Force, during the landings. After this operation she was transferred to the Mediterranean for the landings in the south of France, Operation Dragoon, where she remained until the end of September 1944. A further refit at Philadelphia Navy Yard followed, lasting until February 1945. At the end of the war in Europe *Augusta* carried President Truman to Antwerp for the Potsdam Conference, and then ferried troops back home from Europe. She was eventually paid off on 16 July 1946, for disposal as with *Louisville*, but then languished in reserve until stricken on 1 March 1959. She was finally sold to Robert Benjamin of Panama City for breaking up on 9 November 1959.

PORTLAND CLASS

Ship	Builder	Laid Down	Launched	Completed	Fate
CA33 Portland	Bethlehem, Quincy	17 Feb 30	21 May 32	23 Feb 33	Stricken 1 Mar 1959
CA35 Indianapolis	New York Sbdg	31 Mar 30	7 Nov 31	15 Nov 32	Lost 30 Jul 1945

Displacement: 10,258 tons/10,422 tonnes (standard); 12,775 tons/12,979 tonnes (full load).
Length: 610ft/185.93m (oa) 592ft/180.44m (wl).
Beam: 66ft/20.12m; Draught: 21ft/6.40m (mean).
Machinery: 4-shaft Parsons geared turbines; 8 Yarrow boilers.
Performance: 107,000shp=32½kts; Bunkerage: 2,125 tons oil fuel max.
Range: 10,000nm at 15kts.
Protection: 3in main belt (machinery spaces); 2½in deck; magazines 5¾in sides, 2⅛in crowns.
Guns: nine 8in (3x3); eight 5in (8x1).
Torpedoes: nil.
Aircraft: four, two catapults.
Complement: 807.

Design To some extent these two ships were hybrids, having a protective scheme between that of the *Northampton* and that of *New Orleans*. The reasons for this lay in the signing of the 1930 London Naval Treaty and the realisation that the earlier 8in-gunned cruisers could well be underweight, although the extent of the latter was not yet fully quantified. Fifteen 8in cruisers had been authorised for the 1929 programme, to be constructed in Fiscal Years 29 (*CA32-36*), 30 (*CA37-41*) and 31 (*CA42-46*). The first group were originally intended to be repeat *Northamptons*, but because there had been considerable criticism of that design, and of the generally weak protection of the Treaty 'Tinclads', the second group were to be redesigned with better protection, the first group being considered too far advanced to be modified. However, it was eventually decided that, since three of the first group were contracted to Navy Yards, they could in fact be redesigned without incurring hard-cash payments to the yards, as would have been the case with *CA33* and *CA35*, the two ships ordered from private shipyards. Obviously there would be an on-cost, but it could be lost in the system in time-honoured government fashion. In consequence, the two *Portlands* differed in a number of ways both from their original design and from their later sisters.

The original intention had been to increase the hull length by 10ft, 8ft forward and 2ft aft, without alteration of the internal arrangements, and to use the weight then believed to be available to increase the magazine side armour to 5in and the deck by ½in. Beam was to remain the same, but the bulbous bow would be eliminated. The guns remained in light splinter-proof gunhouses. While these ships were under construction, the magnitude of the underweight situation in the earlier ships became clearer, and advantage was taken to increase the side protection of the magazines to 5¾in to give some degree of protection against 8in shellfire. The side belt of 2¼in on the skin plating could not be increased without high cost in terms of cash and weight.

The machinery was a repeat of that in the *Northampton*, except that Yarrow boilers were shipped, and the armament was also a repeat, although the torpedo tubes originally included in the design were eliminated before completion and eight 5in guns were shipped from the start.

Both ships were fitted as Fleet Flagships.
Modifications Few modifications were made to these ships in their early years. *Portland* was fitted with an extension to the fore funnel before the war, but the main alterations were the result of war experience. By early 1942 four quadruple 1.1in were fitted, two abreast the bridge and two between the groups of 5in guns, with about twelve single 20mm guns, but the numbers of the latter

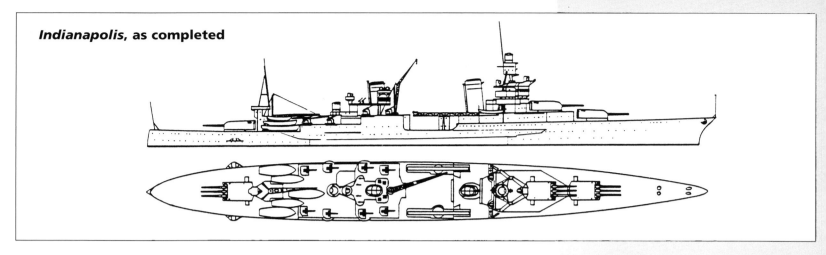

Indianapolis, as completed

were constantly being augmented. In 1943 the bridge was extended, the after superstructure cut down and a new lattice tripod main mast stepped around the after funnel. Comprehensive fire control and search radars were fitted by this time. Cowls were fitted to both funnels. Quadruple 40mm Bofors replaced the 1.1in, with four quads and four twins (the latter on the quarterdeck) in *Portland* by the summer of 1944 and six quadruple mountings in her sister. The 20mm were increased to about seventeen/nineteen guns. The aircraft complement was reduced to two, and to three in *Indianapolis* and the starboard catapult landed.

Service *Portland* was assigned after completion to CruDiv 4, with the Scouting Force, but joined CruDiv 6 the following year. She had a spell with CruDiv 5 in 1935, then with CruDiv 6 in 1936 before once again being assigned to CruDiv 5. She remained with this division until the end of 1940, when she was reassigned to CruDiv 4 for the whole of the war period. In December 1941 she was attached to TF11, covering the transport of Marine aircraft by *Lexington* to Midway Island, and was then involved in abortive attempts to relieve Wake Island with the same task force. In May 1942 she was involved in the Battle of the Coral Sea as a unit of TF17, when she rescued survivors from *Lexington*. The following month she participated in the Battle of Midway, and by August had been committed to the Guadalcanal campaign, for the landings on that island and Tulagi, now attached to TF16. At the Battle of the Eastern Solomons, towards the end of August, she was with TF61. On 16 October *Portland* sailed with *Enterprise* and TF61 to intercept Japanese forces heading for the eastern Solomons, which culminated in the Battle of Santa Cruz, when the cruiser was lucky to survive hits by three aircraft torpedoes, none of which exploded. However, in November she was deployed to escort

troop reinforcements from Noumea to Guadalcanal, and in the subsequent battle off that island on 13 November was hit aft by a shallow-running torpedo, which sheared off both inboard screws. Her after turret was disabled, but the cruiser managed to sink the destroyer *Yudachi* in the engagement. She returned to the USA via Tulagi, Sydney and Pearl Harbor for repair at Mare Island. The work was completed by the beginning of March 1943, after which she was deployed to the Aleutians for the bombardment of Kiska. *Portland* returned to the South Pacific to operate in the Marshall and Gilbert Islands at the end of 1943, then supported operations at Hollandia in April 1944. Refitted again at Mare Island over the summer of 1944, the ship then joined the Fire Support Group for the landings on Peleliu in mid-September. In October she participated in the landings at Leyte, and in the subsequent Battle of the Surigao Straits. The year 1945 saw her in action at Lingayen Gulf, Corregidor and Okinawa, as well as accepting the surrender of Japanese forces at Truk in the Carolines in September. Her last tasks were Magic Carpet cruises to bring home US servicemen, before paying off on 12 July 1946. Stricken on 1 March 1959 after spending the intervening years in reserve, she was sold to Union Mineral and Alloys Corp., New York, on 6 October 1959 and broken up at Panama City from December.

Indianapolis assumed the role of Flagship, Scouting Force, from November 1933, and remained in the capacity of flagship throughout her career, latterly as Flagship Cruisers, Pacific Fleet and CruDiv 4. On 7 December 1941 she was assigned to TF12, but joined TF11 at Pearl Harbor on 13 December. Early in 1942 she operated in the South Pacific and New Guinea, screening the carriers *Lexington* and *Saratoga*. A refit at Mare Island occupied much of April to July, after which she was employed on escort tasks as far afield as Australia and the Aleutians. In August 1942 she

Below: *Portland* in November 1943. (USN)

bombarded Kiska, then remained in the Aleutians until the summer of 1943, when she returned to Mare Island for refit. On her return to service she assumed the role of Flagship, 5th Fleet, at Pearl Harbor in October, and during the following month participated in the invasion of the Gilbert Islands, bombarding Tarawa and Makin. At the beginning of 1944 she moved to the Marshall Islands, bombarding Kwajalein. In the ensuing months she saw action at Saipan, in the Battle of the Philippine Sea, at Tinian, at Guam and in the Carolines. Another refit was carried out at Mare Island between November 1944 and January 1945, before she returned to service off Iwo Jima and then escorted the carriers in raids on the Japanese islands. On 31 March, off Okinawa, she was hit by kamikaze aircraft aft, suffering damage to her shafts that needed repair in the USA. This was carried out between June and July at Mare Island, after which she was detailed to ferry com-ponents of the first atomic bomb to Tinian. She arrived at Tinian on 26 July 1945, disembarked the bomb components, then sailed for Leyte via Guam. Having left Guam on 28 July the ship proceeded towards Leyte, but some 600nm south-west of Guam and 550nm north-east of Leyte she was hit by three torpedoes from the submarine *I 58* and sank with heavy casualties. As she was not reported overdue for several days, the losses among her crew were greatly increased.

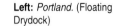

Left: *Portland.* (Floating Drydock)

Left: *Indianapolis* in July 1945. (Floating Drydock)

NEW ORLEANS CLASS

Ship	Builder	Laid Down	Launched	Completed	Fate
CA32 New Orleans	New York NY	14 Mar 31	12 Apr 33	15 Feb 34	Stricken 1 Mar 1959
CA34 Astoria	Puget Sound NY	1 Sep 30	16 Dec 33	28 Apr 34	Lost 9 Aug 1942
CA36 Minneapolis	Philadelphia NY	27 Jun 31	6 Sep 33	19 May 34	Stricken 1 Mar 1959
CA37 Tuscaloosa	New York Sbdg	3 Sep 31	15 Nov 33	17 Aug 34	Stricken 1 Mar 1959
CA38 San Francisco	Mare Island NY	9 Sep 31	9 Mar 33	10 Feb 34	Stricken 1 Mar 1959
CA39 Quincy	Bethlehem, Quincy	15 Nov 33	19 Jun 35	9 Jun 36	Lost 9 Aug 1942
CA44 Vincennes	Bethlehem, Quincy	2 Jan 34	21 May 36	24 Feb 37	Lost 9 Aug 1942

Displacement: 10,136 tons/10,298 tonnes (standard); 12,493 tons/12,692 tonnes (full load).

Length: 588ft/179.22m (oa); 578ft/176.18m, (wl).

Beam: 61ft 9in/18.82m; **Draught:** 22ft 9in/6.93m (mean).

Machinery: 4-shaft Westinghouse geared turbines; 8 Babcock & Wilcox boilers.

Performance: 107,000shp=32.7kts; **Bunkerage:** 1,861 tons oil fuel max.

Range: 10,000nm at 15kts.

Protection: 4in-5¾in main belt; 2¼in deck (machinery); magazines, 3in-4in sides, 2¼in crowns; 5in* barbettes; turrets, 6in fronts, 2¼in roof, 1½in sides. *CA37 & 38 6in, CA39 5½in.

Guns: nine 8in (3x3); eight 5in (8x1); eight .5in MGs (8x1).

Torpedoes: nil.

Aircraft: four, two catapults.

Complement: 868.

Design This group of ships comprised the three FY29 ships originally intended to be of the *Portland* design on order from Naval Yards, three from FY30, *CA37-39*, and one from FY31, *CA44*. The London Naval Treaty of 1930 had allowed the laying down of *CA44* in 1934 and only one in 1935. The latter ship was actually built as a modified *Brooklyn*, while the other three ships, Nos. 40, 41 and 42, were built as light cruisers of the *Brooklyn* class.

By the time this class was in design, the extent of the underweight of the first heavy cruisers had become known and their protection was enhanced accordingly. The hull was some 14ft shorter on the waterline, and beam was reduced by over 4ft compared with *Portland*. The reduction in length was achieved by abandoning the unit arrangement of the machinery spaces and reducing the length of each engine room by 4ft. From this reduction followed a saving in the length of the armour belt, which in turn gave a saving in weight which could be used to increase the thickness of the side belt. This was now 5in thick and 4ft 8in deep, with the lower portion 3in thick. The total depth of the belt was 9ft 8in. Internally, the forward magazines had 3in to 4in side protection, and the after magazines 3in to 4.7in. Horizontal protection comprised a 2½in deck, reduced to 1⅛in outside the magazines. The barbette armour was increased to 5in, and a 2½in conning tower was fitted. It was also found possible to give the turrets some protection against 8in gunfire, unlike those of the earlier ships, which could be penetrated by destroyer gunfire. Thus the turrets had 8in faces. Protection represented 15 per cent of normal displacement.

Tuscaloosa and *San Francisco* received a lighter 8in gun and more compact turret (about 40 tons less), and in consequence had their barbette armour increased to 6½in. However, the displacement had by now risen uncomfortably close to the treaty limit, and the margin had been almost totally eroded. As a result *CA39* had her protection reduced, in particular the barbette armour, and *CA44* followed suit.

The machinery arrangements differed, as has been noted, by the placing of all of the fire rooms

Below: *Minneapolis* pre-war. (MPL)

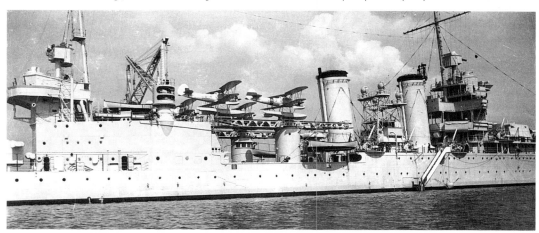

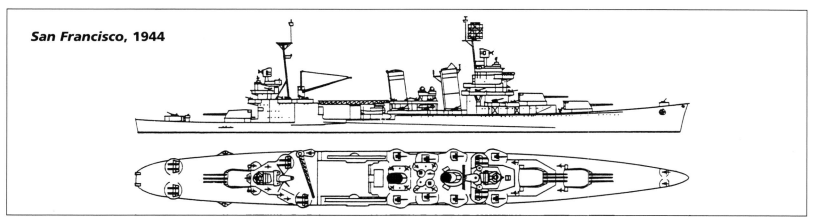

San Francisco, 1944

forward of the engine rooms and accepting the risk of two engine rooms being disabled by a single torpedo hit. Otherwise the machinery was identical to that of *Portland*. For the first time in US cruisers, however, emergency diesel generators were fitted in three of the class, *CA38*, *39* and *44*. One feature of this design which did give rise to criticism was the reduction in bunkerage and the consequently reduced range.

The main armament remained nine 8in guns, the first three ships having Mk 9 or Mk 14 guns and the remainder Mk 12. Eight single 5in/25 mountings formed the secondary battery, and eight .5in MGs the AA outfit. Torpedoes were deleted at the design stage in this class. Aircraft arrangements were similar to those of *Portland*, except that the abandonment of the unit principle for the machinery moved the after funnel further forward, and the catapults were fitted abaft it, with the hangars still further aft. Four floatplanes could be accommodated.

Modifications The first major modification, a result of the King Board recommendations, entailed the addition of splinter shields to the 5in gun positions (NB: not on the mounts themselves), and the fitting of 1.1in quadruples, two on the quarterdeck and two on the bridge at charthouse level. All of the class were so fitted by April 1942. The foremast was cut down, and search radar installed. Later, six 20mm singles were added, to be continuously increased, twelve guns being specified by early 1942. Several ships exceeded this figure, *Tuscaloosa*, for example, having sixteen 20mm in October 1942. However, these ships were weight critical, and further additions could only be made at the expense of adding ballast. The conning tower was removed and bridgework altered. One crane was removed and the light AA increased to six quad 40mm, which supplanted the 1.1in, and the 20mm battery comprised as many as 28 barrels in a variety of combinations of single and twin mountings in the four

Above: *Vincennes* in June 1937 at Portsmouth (UK). (W&L)

survivors. One catapult was removed at the end of the war as a final weight-saving measure.

Service *New Orleans* served with CruDiv 6 in the Pacific throughout her career. With *San Francisco*, she was one of only two heavy cruisers at Pearl Harbor in December 1941. She was in dockyard hands until January 1942, then carried out convoy duties to Australia and Noumea the following month before returning to Pearl Harbor, then operating in the New Hebrides with TF11. In May 1942 she participated in the Battle of the Coral Sea, and in June was at the Battle of Midway. In July she screened the carrier *Saratoga* and escorted her following her torpedoing. At the Battle of Tassafaronga, on the night of 30 November, she was a component of TF67, which had been deployed to intercept a force of Japanese destroyers attempting to run supplies to Guadalcanal. During this action, which was disastrous for the USN, she received a

torpedo hit which caused two forward magazines to explode and blow off her bow. Everything forward of No. 2 turret disappeared. Escorted by the destroyer *Maury*, she limped into Tulagi, then sailed via Sydney back to Puget Sound for repair. It was not until the end of August 1943 that she returned to Pearl Harbor. In the following months she saw action at Wake island and the Gilbert Islands, and by January 1944 was bombarding Japanese positions at Kwajalein. In February she escorted carrier raids against Truk, during which

she and her sister *Minneapolis* intercepted and sank the small training ship (former cruiser) *Katori* and the destroyer *Maikaze*. In April she covered the landings at Hollandia. Mid-summer saw her in action at Saipan, Truk, and at the Battle of the Philippine Sea. In September she bombarded Iwo Jima. At Leyte Gulf in October she was a part of TF34, and as part of a light surface strike force sank the damaged Japanese light carrier *Chiyoda* and the undamaged destroyer *Hatsutsuki*. Between December 1944 and March 1945 she was under refit at Mare Island, but arrived at Ulithi on 18 April to participate in the fighting around Okinawa until June 1945. In August she was deployed to Chinese and Korean waters to accept the Japanese

surrender, but left for home in mid-November, arriving at San Francisco on 8 December. She was paid off on 10 February 1947 and placed in reserve until stricken on 1 March 1959, being sold for scrapping on 22 September that year. She arrived at Baltimore in December for breaking up by Baltimore Metals Co.

Astoria joined CruDiv 7 on entering service, but was reassigned to CruDiv 6 by 1937. She remained with this division until sunk in 1942. At the time of the attack on Pearl Harbor she was with TF11, en route to Midway Island with marine aircraft reinforcements. Later that same month she was a part of TF14, tasked with attempting to run reinforcements to beleaguered

Above: *Vincennes*. (Courtesy Louis Parker)
Right: *San Francisco* in 1943. (Floating Drydock)

Wake Island. In February 1942 she was part of the screen for the carrier *Yorktown* during a raid by TF17 against Rabaul, but this had to be aborted. The following month she was attached to the ANZAC force with *Louisville*, *Chicago* and *Australia* (RAN), covering a carrier strike against Papua New Guinea. She participated in the Battle of the Coral Sea in May 1942, again with TF17, and was at Midway with the same task force, but afterwards joined TF11. By August, however, she had been deployed to Guadalcanal to give gunfire support to the US landings there, and on the night of 8/9 August, when the Japanese counterattacked, she was heavily hit by gunfire and torpedoes off Savo Island in the early hours of 9 August. Serious fires broke out, and these ultimately touched off the forward 5in magazine while the ship was under tow by the destroyer minesweeper *Hopkins* about midday, whereupon she capsized and sank.

Minneapolis made a cruise to Europe after commissioning, then joined CruDiv 7 in the Pacific. After Pearl Harbor she carried out patrol duties off Hawaii until February 1942, then operated with *Lexington* as TF11. She escorted troop convoys from the Panama Canal to the SW Pacific, and was then assigned to the ANZAC force, operating in the Coral Sea and New Hebrides. In March she screened the carrier raid on Papua New Guinea. She was at the Battle of the Coral Sea and at Midway, with TF16. From August she was operating in the Guadalcanal campaign, but while acting as Flagship for TF67 at the Battle of Tassafaronga she was struck by two torpedoes from

Japanese destroyers. One blew off the bow as far back as the forward turret, and the other flooded No. 2 fire room. The damaged ship eventually returned to the USA under her own steam for

repair. *Minneapolis* was out of action until September 1943, when she returned to the South Pacific to join TF14 in October for an attack on Wake Island by carrier aircraft and the cruiser's guns. She participated in the occupation of Makin Island during November and December, then in 1944 went to the Marianas and Caroline Islands, bombarding Saipan in June. That same month she was with TF58 at the Battle of the Philippine Sea. After supporting the landings at Leyte, the cruiser participated in the Battle for Leyte Gulf, and then supported landings at Bataan and Corregidor before being ordered to the Okinawa campaign. She remained in this theatre until April 1945, when her guns were worn out and she sailed for the USA for refit. At the end of the war she was in the Philippines, and then deployed to Korea to accept the Japanese surrender. After her return home in 1946 she was finally decommissioned on 10 February 1947, and saw no further service until stricken on 1 March 1959. The ship was sold for scrapping on 14 August the same year, and arrived at Chester, Pennsylvania, for breaking up in July 1960, having been sold to the Union Metals and Alloys Corp.

Tuscaloosa served with CruDiv 6 initially on the US west coast and the Pacific. At the beginning of 1939 she transferred to the east coast, making a cruise around South America in the spring. On the outbreak of war in Europe she participated in the Neutrality Patrol in the North Atlantic, where she remained on various duties, including the escorting of US troop convoys to Iceland in August 1941. From April 1942 she was based at Scapa Flow with the British Home Fleet for duty on the Arctic convoy routes, but in September she returned to the USA for refit preparatory to taking part in the invasion of North Africa, Operation Torch, in November. As part of the Western Task Force off Casablanca she engaged Vichy French ships in the ensuing action, damaging *Fougueux*, and avoided torpedo attacks by the submarines *Meduse* and *Antiope*. After the success of the landings, the ship returned to the USA for refit, then escorted convoys to North Africa. In September 1943 she was once again in northern waters, screening the US carrier *Ranger* during raids on Axis bases in Norway. After a sortie to Spitzbergen in October, *Tuscaloosa* left the Home Fleet and returned to the USA. She was involved in the invasion of Normandy in June/July 1944 as part of Force A, the support force for Utah Beach. Her final operation in European waters was the landings in the south of France in August 1944, following which she was reassigned to the Pacific. In January 1945 she joined the 3rd Fleet at Ulithi, participating in the bombardment of Iwo Jima the following month. In March she was operating off Okinawa, then transferred to the 7th Fleet at Subic Bay in the Philippines. Her final wartime service was in Chinese and Korean waters, and she arrived back in San Francisco on 10 January 1946, being paid off on 13 February. She spent the remainder of her life in reserve, and was stricken on 1 March 1959

and sold to the Boston Metals Company for breaking up on 25 June, arriving in Baltimore for scrapping in the following month.

San Francisco spent the prewar years in the Pacific with CruDiv 6, but in 1938 transferred to the Caribbean. After the start of the war in Europe she took part in the Neutrality Patrol operating in the Caribbean, with Patrol 7/8. However, early in 1940 she was relieved by *Wichita* and returned to join CruDiv 6 at Pearl Harbor. At the time of the Japanese attack she was under refit at the Pearl Harbor Naval Yard, but escaped damage in the raid. Refit work was suspended, and she then operated with TF14 and the carrier *Saratoga* in the attempts to relieve Wake Island. Later in January 1942 she was part of TF11 (*Lexington*) in an abortive attempt to attack the same island following its capture by the Japanese. Following this sortie, she remained with TF11 and covered troop convoys between the Panama Canal and the South Pacific before TF11 was assigned to the ANZAC force for an attack on Rabaul in the New Hebrides. This sortie was detected by the Japanese on 20 February, and resulted merely in air-to-air combat between the carrier's aeroplanes and the Japanese. After the Japanese landings in New Guinea, at Lae in the Huon Gulf in early March, *San Francisco* was part of the combined force of TF11 and TF17 (*Lexington* and *Yorktown*) that made a raid on the Japanese landing points and scored some success. In April the ship was employed on convoy duties between the USA and Australia, but when the US forces landed on Guadalcanal *San Francisco* participated as a unit of TF61, assigned to the Air Support Force, Unit 1. On 7 August she assumed the role of flagship of the cruisers attached to TF18. Towards the end of August she was at the Battle of the eastern Solomons, and in October she was a component of TF64 during the Battle of Cape Esperance, assisting in the sinking of the destroyer *Fubuki*. That same month she was involved in the Battle of Santa Cruz, as well as seeing action against Japanese positions on Guadalcanal. During operations off Lunga Point, Guadalcanal, on 12 November, the ship was hit by a Japanese aircraft which damaged the after fire control position and caused casualties. Worse followed that night, when *San Francisco*'s force was surprised off Savo Island and the cruiser *Atlanta* and four destroyers were sunk, and every other ship except the destroyer *Fletcher* was damaged by Japanese battleships and destroyers. *San Francisco* was very badly damaged, both her captain and flag officer being among the casualties. However, the damaged cruiser was able to return to the USA, and repairs were carried out at Mare Island. On 26 February 1943 she returned to the South Pacific, but in April was assigned to the Aleutians with TF16, where she remained for about four and

a half months, taking part in the bombardments of Attu and Kiska and their recapture. Following these operations in the North Pacific, she sailed south once more and joined TU14.2.1 in attacks on Wake Island at the beginning of October. By November she was involved in operations in the Gilbert Islands, providing fire support for the Makin landings, and in December she was at Kwajalein. In 1944 *San Francisco* joined TF58, seeing action at Kwajalein, Hollandia, Saipan, Guam and at the Battle of the Philippine Sea. In July she returned to the USA for refit, and was out of service until late October, when she sailed for the South Pacific once more. By the end of November the ship was at Ulithi as Flagship of CruDiv 6, and then served in the Philippines and South China Sea before participating in operations around the Bonin Islands and Iwo Jima. *San Francisco* was also involved in operations at Okinawa and later in the Philippines again. After the war she served in China and Korea, but returned to the USA on 12 January 1946, paying-off on 10 February 1947. *San Francisco* saw no further service, and remained in reserve until stricken on 1 March 1959. On 9 September she was sold to Union Mineral and Alloy Corp, New York, for breaking up, and was scrapped at Panama City, Florida, in 1959.

Quincy commissioned for CruDiv 8 in the Atlantic, and in the summer of 1936 served in the Mediterranean during the Spanish Civil War. After her relief by *Raleigh* in September she returned to the USA, and in the spring of 1937 transferred to the west coast to join CruDiv 7. Her service in the Pacific continued until she was reassigned to the Atlantic at the beginning of 1939, where she made a cruise around South America and was employed on training duties. The same pattern continued until the spring of 1941, when she carried out Neutrality Patrols in the mid- and North Atlantic, as well as convoy escort duties across the South Atlantic to Cape Town and north to Iceland. After a refit at New York Navy Yard between March and May 1942, the ship was reassigned to the Pacific and joined TF18. On 7 August she was in action off Lunga Point, Guadalcanal, but on 9 August she was sunk in action off Savo Island by a force of Japanese cruisers and destroyers.

Vincennes, after a cruise to Scandinavia and Europe, joined CruDiv 7 on the west coast, but in April 1939 transferred to the east coast. After the outbreak of war in Europe she took part in the Neutrality Patrol, then in March 1942 went to the Pacific. She was a part of the force for the Tokyo Raid in April, then spent a period under refit at Pearl Harbor until mid-July, when she went to the Guadalcanal area with TG62. She, too, was one of three sister ships sunk at the Battle of Savo Island in the early hours of 9 August 1942.

BROOKLYN CLASS

Ship	Builder	Laid Down	Launched	Completed	Fate
CL40 Brooklyn	New York NY	12 Mar 35	30 Nov 36	30 Sep 37	Sold to Chile 9 Jan 1951
CL41 Philadelphia	Philadelphia NY	28 May 35	17 Nov 36	23 Sep 37	Sold to Brazil 9 Jan 1951
CL42 Savannah	New York Sbdg	31 May 34	8 May 37	10 Mar 38	Stricken 1 Mar 1959
CL43 Nashville	New York Sbdg	24 Jan 35	2 Oct 37	6 Jun 38	Sold to Chile 9 January 1951
CL44 Phoenix	New York Sbdg	15 Apr 35	13 Mar 38	3 Oct 38	Sold to Argentina 17 Oct 1951
CL47 Boise	Newport News	1 Apr 35	3 Dec 36	12 Aug 38	Sold to Argentina 11 Jan 1951
CL48 Honolulu	New York NY	10 Sep 35	26 Aug 37	15 Jun 38	Sold for scrapping 17 Nov 1959
CL49 St Louis	Newport News	10 Dec 36	15 Apr 38	19 May 39	Sold to Brazil 22 Jan 1951
CL50 Helena	New York NY	9 Dec 36	27 Aug 38	18 Sep 39	Lost 6 Jul 1943

Displacement: 9,767 tons/9,923 tonnes (standard); 12,207 tons/12,403 tonnes (full load).

Length: 608ft 4in/185.42m (oa); 600ft/182.88m (wl).

Beam: 61ft 9in/18.82 m; Draught: 22ft 9in/6.93m (mean).

Machinery: 4-shaft Parsons geared turbines; 8 Babcock & Wilcox boilers.

Performance: 100,000shp=32½kts; Bunkerage: 1,982 tons oil fuel max.

Range: 10,000nm at 15kts.

Protection: 5⅝in main belt; 2in deck; 6in barbettes; turrets, 6½in front, 2in roof; 5in CT.

Guns: fifteen 6in (5x3); eight 5in (8x1), but *CL49* & *50* 4x2; eight .5in MGs (8x1).

Torpedoes: nil.

Aircraft: four, two catapults.

Complement: 868.

Design If the 8in-gun cruiser was a product of the Washington Treaty, then this class was a direct result of the London Naval Treaty of 1930. The horse-trading between Japan, the USA and Great Britain during the treaty discussions eventually resulted in a suspension of the construction of heavy cruisers, an agreement Britain was anxious to obtain but which the USA accepted only after much argument. The US view was that the 8in cruiser was here to stay, and more fully met their requirements for a Pacific war than did the smaller ships finally agreed upon. However, because of the cruiser ratios agreed between the USA, Japan and Great Britain, the USA could lay down only two more Washington-type ships (*CA44* and *CA45*), and was therefore forced into a 6in-gunned design rather against its will.

Design studies began in the autumn of 1930, following the Senate's approval of the London Naval Treaty on 21 July. A basic requirement was that the speed and cruising radius should not be worse than those of the heavy cruisers. Six schemes were initially drawn up, one a variant of the *New Orleans*, with three quadruple and one triple turret. The weakest scheme envisaged two triple 6in turrets on a displacement of 6,000 tons. After the usual lengthy deliberations and arguments, a 9,600-ton design armed with four triple 6in and with protection on the same scale as that of *New Orleans* was preferred by the beginning of 1931. This proposal was requested for the 1933 programme, but the programme was never approved. Further discussions ensued, caused by this delay and the requirement to ship the new 1.1in AA gun. This led eventually to the move-

ment of the aircraft installation aft, to provide the necessary deck space amidships for the medium (5in) and light (1.1in) AA.

Improvement of the armour scheme led to investigation of the machinery arrangements, which, if they could be shortened, would free tonnage for armour. Diesel propulsion was only briefly considered, however. By March 1932 a new series of design studies had been worked out, all of which were of 10,000 tons, armed with between twelve and sixteen 6in guns and with side belts of up to 5in thickness. Hull length varied, as did the installed power. Two new factors now entered the scheme of things; a new 6in shell of improved performance, and the appearance of Japan's *Mogami* class with fifteen 6in guns, which made it impossible for any US ship to carry less than this number of guns.

The final design had five triple turrets, of which three were forward with No. 2 superfiring on both 1 and 3, and the aircraft installations moved aft. This eliminated the broken deck line of the earlier ships, as the hangar was now below the quarterdeck. The internal arrangements still had the boilers grouped ahead of the turbine rooms, i.e. the unit principle had not been readopted. Longitudinal framing was introduced in this class, giving a significant saving in weight.

The protection scheme included a 5in waterline belt on 25lb skin plating, with a 2in deck. Armoured bulkheads of 2-5in closed off the end of the belt, and the magazines were given an internal longitudinal side protection 2in thick. Gun Barbettes were 6in. The total weight of armour was 1,798 tons, or almost 15 per cent of standard displacement.

The main machinery, a four-shaft geared turbine installation, developed 100,000shp, marginally less than that of *New Orleans*.

For the main armament, a new 6in gun had been developed, the 6in 47cal Mk 16, which used

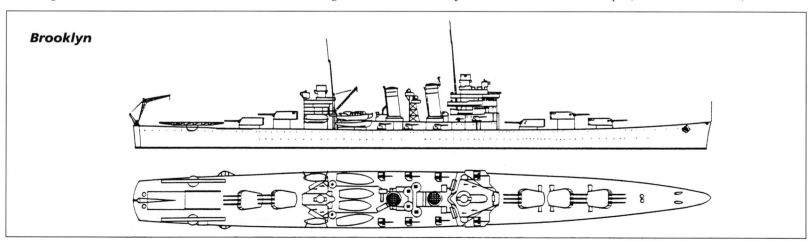

Brooklyn

semi-fixed ammunition and fired a 130lb projectile. The triple mounting could elevate to 60°, with a maximum range of 26,118yd (23,882m) at 47½°. All three guns elevated in the same sleeve. The turret faces were protected by 6½in armour. The secondary battery was again the 5in/25, all in single mountings. Finally, the 1.1in gun failed to appear at this time, and the ships received only .5in MGs. Two catapults and four floatplanes completed the armament. No torpedo tubes were fitted.

Four ships were ordered to this design under the emergency 1933 programme. Three repeats were ordered in 1934 (*CL46-48*). Two further ships were added after the idea of replacing the first two *Omaha* class with a new design of small cruiser was abandoned. These two, *CL49* and *CL50*, were constructed to a modified design. Advances in boiler design and the adoption of high-pressure steam concepts resulted in a reduction in boiler size, and these two ships benefited by having fire rooms of reduced size. The boilers operated at 700°F and 565psi. In addition, this

Below: *Honolulu* in September 1938 at Portsmouth (UK). (W&L)

allowed the boilers to be placed in two separate groups, each with a boiler operating station and with the turbine rooms separated by one set of fire rooms, i.e. a readoption of the unit principle. The other point of difference was in the secondary armament, these ships carrying 5in/38 guns in four twin Mk 29 DP mountings with weatherproof gunhouses.

Modifications Initially an open bridge was built on top of the existing structure, but from 1942 the bridge structure was lowered and the conning towers were removed. The AA outfit was to be improved by the addition of sixteen 1.1in guns in quadruple mountings, but because of the shortage of these guns an interim battery of two 3in/50 and two quadruple 1.1in had to be accepted. Even so, by November 1941 only *Helena* had received any, and even hers were removed during repair of Pearl Harbor damage, being fitted in *Phoenix* and *Honolulu*. The full outfit, when installed, was carried two abreast the foremast and two above the forward raised 5in mount in all but *CL49* and *CL50*, in which it was fitted on the main deck at the fore and aft ends of the superstructure. The 3in guns were not replaced until quite late in some ships, *Savannah* retaining hers until August 1942

and *Phoenix* until February 1943. Radar was fitted and 20mm guns added as a first step towards augmenting the AA outfit. Four quadruple and four twin 40mm was the specified AA outfit by late 1942, but equipment varied, and at the end of the war all except *CL46* and *CL47* had twenty-eight 40mm (4 x 4, 6 x 2) and twenty 20mm (10 x 2), though *CL43* had only nine twin 20mm, while the others had single 20mm totalling nineteen in *Phoenix*, eighteen in *Boise* and eight in *St Louis*. *Phoenix* and *Boise* had four twin 40mm. *Savannah*, after her damage at Salerno, was extensively rebuilt and given a bulged hull, increasing the beam by 7ft 8in. Her 5in outfit was altered to four twin 5in/38. *Brooklyn*, *Philadelphia* and *Honolulu* were also blistered, but not rearmed.

Service *Brooklyn* joined CruDiv 8 in 1938 and carried out the usual peacetime routine in the remaining years before the outbreak of war in Europe. She served on both the east and west coast in this period. In May 1941 she was in the Atlantic, and was later engaged on the transport of US troops for the occupation of Iceland. For the rest of 1941 she was engaged on Neutrality Patrols in the Atlantic. After the US entry into the war *Brooklyn* was assigned to convoy cover

duties on the North Atlantic sea routes between Britain and the USA. In October 1942 she sailed for North Africa and Operation Torch, where, on 8 November, she provided fire support for the landings at Fedhala. In the course of this task she engaged the Vichy French cruiser *Primaguet*, together with *Augusta*, and badly damaged her. In the first half of 1943 she was employed in covering convoys between the USA and the North African battle zone, but in July she was assigned to support the landings in Sicily, Operation Husky, covering TF86 at Licata and the left flank of the US 7th Army. She then supported TF81 at the Salerno landings in September, and the same force at the Anzio landings in January 1944. Later that year *Brooklyn* provided a similar service for TF87 during the landings in the south of France in August. She returned to the USA at the end of November 1944, then went into refit at New York Navy Yard until May 1945. After refit *Brooklyn* was not assigned to the Pacific, but remained in the Atlantic. She was paid off on 3 January 1947, remaining in reserve until she was handed over to Chile on 9 January 1951 and renamed *O'Higgins*. On 12 August 1974 the ship was badly damaged by grounding, and was subsequently used only as a static harbour training ship, but in 1977/78 she was extensively refitted and returned to service. *O'Higgins* was finally decommissioned on 14 January 1992. On 3 November 1992 the ship foundered in tow to shipbreakers in the Far East.

Philadelphia was the second ship of the class to be completed, and also joined CruDiv 8, becoming flagship on 27 June 1938. Between the summer of 1939 and May 1941 she served in the Pacific, but was then transferred to the Atlantic,

where she participated in Neutrality Patrols and in the occupation of Iceland. Thereafter, *Philadelphia* was employed in ocean convoy duties between the USA and Iceland, as well as to the UK, during the course of 1942. During this period she was also deployed to the Caribbean on patrol duties. By September 1942 she had been assigned to the Western Task Force for the North African landings, which took place on 7 November. The ship returned to the USA on 24 November, escorting convoys from the USA to the North African bridgehead until March 1943, and then joined TF85 in preparation for the invasion of Sicily, Operation Husky. The landings started on 10 July, and from that time until August the ship was tasked with gunfire support for the army ashore. After Husky, *Philadelphia* was assigned to the Salerno landings in September, bombarding Axis positions along the coast. During these tasks she was slightly damaged by near-misses from radio-guided bombs. By early November, however, she had been withdrawn to Oran, and sailed from there to the USA on 6 November. A short refit was carried out at New York Navy Yard in December/January, the ship then returning to the Mediterranean for gunfire support duties at Anzio from mid-February to the end of May 1944. For the landings in the south of France she was a part of TF85, then remained in Mediterranean waters until October. *Philadelphia* was refitted again at Philadelphia Navy Yard between November 1944 and May 1945, then served on duties between the USA and Europe until 3 February 1947, when paid off. On 9 January 1951 the ship was sold to Brazil and renamed *Barroso*, commissioning on 21 August 1951. Stricken from the operational list

in 1973, the cruiser was finally broken up in Sao Paulo in 1974.

Savannah made several foreign cruises during her early years of service; to Cuba, Haiti and Great Britain. In June 1939 she sailed for the west coast, where she served until 19 May 1941, when ordered to the east coast again. On 17 June *Savannah* assumed the role of Flagship CruDiv 8, operating with the Neutrality Patrol in the Atlantic. She remained in the Atlantic after the US entry into the war, and in October 1942 was assigned to the Western Task Force for the invasion of North Africa. Following the landings, she returned to the USA and then operated in the South and central Atlantic on anti-blockade breaker patrols with the escort carrier *Santee*. By May 1943 she had returned to the Mediterranean for the invasion of Sicily, when she carried out shore bombardment tasks for which her floatplanes spotted, three of them being shot down. Then followed the Salerno landings, where, on 11 September, she was heavily hit by an FX1400 radio-controlled stand-off bomb launched from a German aircraft. This hit and penetrated the roof of No. 3 turret and exploded in the magazine, blowing out the bottom of the ship in this area. The rapid ingress of water prevented an ammunition explosion, but flooded some 152ft of the ship, disabling the machinery at least in part for a period. There were many casualties, and the ship limped back to Malta for temporary repairs. It was not until 7 December, the anniversary of Pearl Harbor, that the ship was able to sail for the USA

and full repairs. These lasted until September 1944, after which the ship was mainly employed on training duties on the east coast until the end of the war. *Savannah* was decommissioned on 3 February 1947, seeing no further active service before being stricken on 1 March 1959. For some reason, however, the ship was not sold for scrapping until 25 January 1966.

Nashville served in the Atlantic Fleet from commissioning until June 1939, visiting the Caribbean and European waters during that period. The next two years were spent in the Pacific before the ship was ordered to the east coast once more in May 1941, arriving at Boston mid-June for escort duties to Iceland. She then served on the Neutrality Patrol, based on Bermuda until March 1942, when ordered to the Pacific with the carrier *Hornet*, with whom she subsequently took part in the Doolittle raid on Tokyo on 17 April 1942. By May *Nashville* was operating in the North Pacific with TF8 in the Aleutians campaign, which lasted until November, the cruiser then being assigned to the south Pacific to join TF67 at Espiritu Santo as flagship. She participated in the final Guadalcanal actions at the beginning of 1943, shelling Munda and Vila. By May 1943 the ship was in action off New Georgia and in the Vella Gulf, once again shelling

Munda, but on 12 May she suffered an explosion in No. 1 turret magazine, after which she sailed for the west coast for repair at Mare Island. *Nashville* arrived back at Pearl Harbor on 12 August 1943 and then accompanied carrier groups (TF15) for attacks on Marcus Island and Wake Island. In December she was part of TG74.2 for the landings at Cape Gloucester. In January 1944 *Nashville* was in action again during the landings at Saidor, New Guinea, bombarding Japanese troops as they attempted to evacuate to Madang. February saw the landings in the Admiralty Islands, when the cruiser was part of TF74, shelling the islands of Hauwei and Norilo into March. The following month she was a component of TF75 for the landings at Hollandia and Aitape, then at Biak in May. Her next major operation was the landings on Morotai on 15 September, as part of TG75.1. In December 1944 she was flagship of TG78.3 for the landings on Mindoro, but on the 13th she was hit by a kamikaze and badly damaged, suffering some 310 dead and wounded. She was withdrawn to Puget Sound for repairs which took from January to April 1945, after which she sailed for the Philippines as Flagship TF74. In the final months of the war she operated in the Borneo campaign, for the landings in Brunei Bay. After the war she went to Chi-

nese waters, then assisted in bringing home US troops until paid off on 24 June 1946. On 9 January 1951 she was sold to Chile and renamed *Capitan Prat*. In 1982 she was renamed *Chacabuco*, and was decommissioned in 1984 to be scrapped in Taiwan the following year.

Phoenix joined CruDiv 9 with the Battle Force and served in the Pacific, being present in Pearl Harbor during the Japanese attack but escaping damage. She was immediately sailed to find the Japanese fleet, but this was unsuccessful. In the following months she was employed on ocean convoy escort duties to the USA and to Australia, spending a period in the Indian Ocean early in 1942 and then working with ANZAC forces, TF44, in the south-west Pacific into 1943. In March 1943 TF44 became TF74 on the formation of the 7th Fleet, but in April *Phoenix* was relieved and, in July, she started a refit at Philadelphia. Then, after a trip to the North African coast, she was reassigned to the 7th Fleet in the Pacific. She returned in time to participate in the landings at Cape Gloucester as part of TG74.2 at the end of December, and then provided support for landings in New Guineau in January. She subsequently operated in the Admiralty Islands, at Hollandia and Biak, giving gunfire support to landing operations. In September she was at the landings at Morotai, and in October the ship was part of the forces committed to the invasion of Leyte as a unit of TG73.3. In January 1945 *Phoenix* covered the invasion of Luzon, then Bataan and Corregidor in February and Mindanao in March. The remainder of the war was spent in the Philippines and Borneo area before the ship returned to Pearl Harbor on 15 August 1945. After her return home she was finally paid off on 3 July 1946. On 12 April 1951 she was sold to Argentina, refitted and recommissioned as *17 de Octubre* on 17 October 1951. In 1956 she was renamed *General Belgrano*. On 3 May 1982 she was torpedoed and sunk by the British submarine *Conqueror* off the Falklands Islands.

Boise was another ship to join CruDiv 9 with the Battle Force in the Pacific after entering service. She was in the Pacific at the start of the war in the Far East, but missed the critical battles in the Dutch East Indies as a result of grounding on 21 January 1942, which necessitated repair at Mare Island. After her return to action she was used mainly on ocean convoy duties in the Pacific until committed to the Guadalcanal campaign in August 1942. However, at the Battle of Cape Esperance on 11 October she was severely damaged in action with Japanese cruisers and destroyers, although her gunfire in turn assisted in the sinking of the destroyer *Fubuki*. The cruiser *Aoba* and destroyer *Hatsuyuki* were also damaged on this occasion. A shell hit her below the waterline belt and caused fires in the forward turret shell handling room, but without an explosion. The cruiser was under repair at Philadelphia Navy Yard between 19 November 1942 and 20 March 1943. After repair she was transferred to the Mediterranean for the landings in Sicily and at Salerno, but left the Mediterranean again on 8 June for the Pacific. In December *Boise* arrived off New Guinea and then served in the Philippines and Borneo area until July, when she arrived back in San Pedro. *Boise* was decommissioned on 1 July 1946 and sold to Argentina on 12 January 1951, being officially transferred on 12 April 1951. She recommissioned as *Nueve de Julio* on 11 March 1952. The cruiser was stricken in 1979 and scrapped at Brownsville, Texas, in 1983.

Honolulu served as Flagship, Cruisers Battle Force, and Flagship CruDiv 9 in the Pacific from completion, and was at Pearl Harbor at the time of the Japanese attack, when she suffered minor damage. Thereafter she was employed on ocean convoy escort duties between the USA, Australia and the western Pacific until May 1942, when she was assigned to the Aleutian campaign. In November, after a refit at Mare Island, *Honolulu* joined the Guadalcanal campaign and was present at the Battle of Tassafaronga, escaping damage in that disastrous action. She remained in the Guadalcanal theatre until its conclusion early in 1943. By May she was with TF68 off New Georgia, and in July was in the Kula Gulf as flagship of

Right: *Helena* in 1943. (Floating Drydock)
Below: *Boise* in May 1943. (Floating Drydock)

TF36.1. During the Battle of Kula Gulf on 5/6 July she was one of the cruisers responsible for the sinking of the destroyer *Niisuki*, but her sister *Helena* was also lost in this exchange of fire. A few days later, in the Battle of Kolombangara, her gunfire and that of *St Louis* sank the cruiser *Jintsu*, but then she was herself hit by one dud torpedo from Japanese destroyers and one which

exploded, wrecking the entire bow forward of the capstans. The ship had to return to the USA for repairs, and did not return to service until November 1943. By February 1944 she was with TF38 off New Ireland, and operated in the Solomon Islands until June. The ship then participated in the assault on Saipan as part of TG52.10. As the year progressed she saw action off Guam, Palau

and Marcus Island before the invasion of the Philippines in October. At the landings in Leyte Gulf, *Honolulu* was hit by an air-launched torpedo on 20 October and badly damaged. This effectively ended her war service, as repairs lasted until October 1945. She was paid off on 3 February 1947, and finally sold for breaking up on 17 November 1959.

St Louis served on the Neutrality Patrol in the Caribbean until September 1940, but in December was transferred to Pearl Harbor, where she was still stationed at the time of the Japanese attack. In January she participated in the attack on the Marshall Islands with TF17, after which she carried out ocean convoy escort duties between the US west coast and the south Pacific until May, then being reassigned to the Aleutians campaign. She was active in the North Pacific until recalled for refit at Mare Island in October 1942. Early in December she returned to the south Pacific to operate in the Solomon Islands and the Guadalcanal campaign. In June 1943 she took part in the landings on New Georgia, covering operations in the Kula Gulf with TF36.1. On the night of 5/6 July she took part in the Battle of Kula Gulf, when her sister *Helena* was sunk, and on 12/13 July during the Battle of Kolombangara

she was herself hit by torpedoes from Japanese destroyers, which took off her bows below the second deck. Following provisional repairs at Tulagi and Espiritu Santo, the cruiser departed for Mare Island and full repairs, which took until November. She returned to action at Bougainville, then operated in the Shortland Islands, Solomons, Bismarcks and New Ireland as part of TF39. On 14 February 1944, while in the Solomons, she was hit by bombs and damaged. By May the ship was with TF52, and participated in the landings at Saipan in June, and in the Battle of the Philippine Sea in mid-June. Between July and October she was again in refit at a US yard, but was back off Leyte Gulf by mid-November, only to be hit by a kamikaze on 27 November. This necessitated repairs in the USA, which lasted until March 1945. *St Louis* arrived back in the south Pacific at Ulithi in March, to participate in the carrier raids on Japan and in the Okinawa campaign, then operated in the South China Sea with TF95, joining TF73 off Shanghai in August. After repatriation duties in 1945/46, the ship was decommissioned on 20 June 1946, to be sold to Brazil on 22 January 1951 and transferred on 29 January as *Tamandare*. She was stricken in 1975 and sold for scrapping. Towed from Rio De

Janeiro on 5 August 1980, she foundered in tow off South Africa on 24 August 1980, while en route to shipbreakers in Taiwan.

Helena had a rather brief but eventful career, joining the Pacific Fleet on completion. At Pearl Harbor on 7 December 1941 she was hit by a torpedo and had to return to the USA for repairs. She subsequently saw service in the Guadalcanal campaign, assisting in the rescue of survivors from *Wasp*. In October, at the Battle of Cape Esperance, she took part in the sinking of the cruiser *Furataka* and the destroyer *Fubuki*. During the Battle of Santa Cruz she was a component of TF64. She survived the action off Savo Island on 12 November, when *Atlanta* and four destroyers were lost, then in the new year took part in bombardments of New Georgia. For the final battles of Guadalcanal she was with TF67, bombarding Japanese positions. On 11 February 1943 she was attacked by the submarine *I 18*, but this boat was herself destroyed off Espiritu Santo by the cruiser's escort, *Fletcher* and *O'Bannon*, with the assistance of the ship's aircraft. After a refit at Sydney, *Helena* returned to TF68 off New Georgia in March, but at the Battle of Kula Gulf on 5/6 July she was torpedoed and sunk by Japanese destroyers, with many casualties.

WICHITA CLASS

Ship	Builder	Laid Down	Launched	Completed	Fate
CA45 Wichita	Philadelphia NY	28 Oct 35	16 Nov 37	16 Feb 39	Stricken 1 Mar 1959

Displacement: 10,589 tons/10,758 tonnes (standard); 13,015 tons/13,223 tonnes (full load).
Length: 608ft 4in/185.42m (oa); 600ft/182.88m (wl).
Beam: 61ft 9in/18.82m; Draught: 23ft 9in/7.24m (mean).
Machinery: 4-shaft Parsons geared turbines; 8 Babcock & Wilcox boilers.
Performance: 100,000shp=33kts; Bunkerage: 1,984 tons oil fuel max.
Range: 10,000nm at 15kts.
Protection: 4½-6½in main belt; 2¼in deck; 7in barbettes; turrets, 8in front, 2¾in roof, 3¾in side; 6in CT.
Guns: nine 8in (3x3); eight 5in (8x1).
Torpedoes: nil.
Aircraft: four, two catapults.
Complement: 929.

Design The London Naval Treaty of 1930 interrupted US heavy cruiser plans because it imposed a restriction on such ships. The Treaty provisions allowed the USA to lay down one ship in 1934 (which was *CA44 Vincennes*) and one the following year. In the meantime, however, the design of a light cruiser, the *Brooklyn* Class, had been

developed, and in March 1934 it was suggested that this design could form the basis of the new heavy cruiser as well. It was expected that the use

of this design would allow an increase in endurance owing to the better lines and increased bunkerage, as well as better heavy AA distribution because of the movement of the aircraft installation aft. Furthermore, protection and stability would also benefit, the former by the increase in side protection to about 6in, with 7in barbettes, and the latter from the smaller compartmentation and higher freeboard. Design work was held up, however, by attempts to solve one of the US 8in

Below: A contrast in cruiser design. *Wichita* and *London* operating with the British Home Fleet in 1942. (IWM)

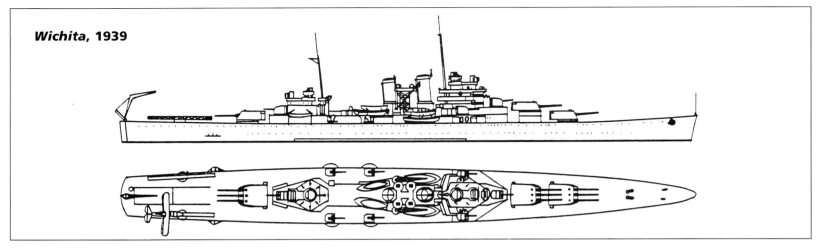

Wichita, 1939

gun's worst problems; overlarge dispersion of shot. The answer lay in increased separation of the gun barrels, but this in turn required a larger-diameter barbette, which was not tolerable. In the end a compromise was reached, the barrels being given some extra separation and the barbette being made conical at the top to avoid space and weight constraints lower down.

Internally, *Wichita* was similar to the *Brooklyn*, except that the three triple-turret layout modified the ammunition supply arrangements. The machinery was similar, having boilers operating at 648°F and 464psi. There were six boilers, all for-

Below: *Wichita* in November 1943. (Courtesy Louis Parker)

ward of the turbine rooms. Electrical generating capacity was increased by 60 per cent over that of the last heavy cruiser, *CA44*, but suprisingly the diesel generating capacity was much reduced, although two sets were fitted.

The protective scheme included a 6in waterline belt, reduced to 4in at the ends, and an armoured deck 2¼in thick. End bulkheads were 6in, and the barbettes 7in. The total weight of armour was 1,437 tons, or 14 per cent of the standard displacement.

The main armament was a new 8in/55 Mk 12 in a modified turret Mod.4, which had the guns spaced further apart and in separate sleeves. For the secondary outfit, the 5in/38 Mk 12 was cho-

sen over the older 25cal model originally specified, but it was not possible to accommodate the twin mounting. The newer gun had a better rate of fire and a greater range than the older pattern. The disposition of these guns also showed an improvement over the earlier arrangements. Two of the mountings were on the centreline, giving ahead and after cover, and, in addition, four of the mountings would be enclosed in gun-houses for improved efficiency. In the event, the stability of this ship was borderline and the two after 5in were not initially fitted. The light AA was the usual useless eight .5in MGs, and no torpedoes were shipped. The aircraft installation was moved aft to the quarterdeck, with the two

Above: *Wichita* in 1944. (Courtesy Louis Parker)

catapults sided at the extreme stern and the hangar below them, served by a large sliding hatch. The usual four floatplanes could be accommodated.

CA45 was ordered from the Philadelphia Navy Yard on 22 August 1934, the machinery being contracted to New York Shipbuilding Corp.

Modifications This ship had the least reserve of stability of all the prewar heavy cruisers, and therefore the modifications which could be made were limited. The two missing waist 5in single mountings were fitted in the summer of 1939, and by June 1941 she had received two quadruple 1.1in and radar. The radar outfit was progressively modernised as the war progressed, and the light AA was increased by supplanting the quad 1.1in by quad 40mm and adding two further quadruple 40mm as well as two twin 40mm by November 1943. The 20mm outfit was eighteen guns at this time. A further two twin 40mm had been added to this by the end of the war.

Service After the ship had completed work-up, she joined CruDiv 7 in the Atlantic Squadron and then participated in the Neutrality Patrol in the Caribbean, but in June 1940 she made a goodwill cruise to South America that lasted until September. Her service in the Atlantic theatre was relatively uneventful. She assisted in the occupation of Iceland in the autumn of 1941, but in March 1942 she was transferred to Scapa Flow for operations with the British Home Fleet, taking part in Russian convoy operations and other duties in northern waters. In November she formed part of the forces involved in the North African landings, in the course of which she was hit by shore batteries. At the end of the year *Wichita* was transferred to the Pacific, and by January 1943 was in action off Rennell Island. By this time, however, most of the heavy cruisers had been assigned to the northern Pacific, and in April she, too, moved to the Aleutians to assume the role of Flagship, TG52.10, and later TG16.4, followed by TG16.7. She was at the bombardment of Kiska on 22 July, but then returned to the USA for a refit at Puget Sound that lasted until the beginning of December 1943. On completion the ship returned to the South Pacific, participating in the invasion of the Marshall Islands, and was then off New Guinea, Hollandia, Truk and Saipan by the summer of that year. In June she was present at the Battle of the Philippine Sea, and by October had moved to Okinawa, Formosa and Luzon with TF38. She towed the damaged *Canberra* for two days after that ship was torpedoed on 13 October. At the Battle off Cape Engano, on 25 October 1944, *Wichita* was one of the ships responsible for the sinking of the Japanese carrier *Chiyoda* (previously damaged by US aircraft) and the undamaged destroyer *Hatsutsuki*. Machinery problems, possibly caused by the towing of *Canberra*, forced her return to the USA for overhaul in November, the work not being completed until the beginning of February 1945. Subsequently she saw action off Okinawa, and then took part in the occupation of Japan. She arrived home in San Francisco on 12 January 1946, to be paid off on 3 February the following year. Schemes to refit her as a missile cruiser postwar came to naught, and she remained in reserve until stricken on 1 March 1959 and sold for breaking up on 14 August to Union Minerals and Alloys. She arrived in Panama City, Florida, for scrapping in November that year.

ATLANTA CLASS

Ship	Builder	Laid Down	Launched	Completed	Fate
CL51 Atlanta	Federal, Kearny	22 Apr 40	6 Sep 41	24 Dec 41	Lost 13 Nov 1942
CL52 Juneau	Federal, Kearny	27 May 40	25 Oct 41	14 Feb 42	Lost 13 Nov 1942
CL53 San Diego	Bethlehem, Quincy	27 Mar 40	26 Jul 41	10 Jan 42	Stricken 1 Mar 1959
CL54 San Juan	Bethlehem, Quincy	15 May 40	6 Sep 41	28 Feb 42	Stricken 1 Mar 1959
CL95 Oakland	Bethlehem, San Francisco	13 Jul 41	23 Oct 42	17 Jul 43	Stricken 1 Mar 1959
CL96 Reno	Bethlehem, San Francisco	1 Aug 41	23 Dec 42	28 Dec 43	Stricken 1 Mar 1959
CL97 Flint (ex Spokane)	Bethlehem, San Francisco	23 Oct 42	25 Jan 44	31 Aug 44	Stricken 1 Sept 1965
CL98 Tucson	Bethlehem, San Francisco	23 Dec 42	3 Sep 44	3 Feb 45	Stricken 1 Jun 1966
CL119 Juneau (ii)	Federal, Kearny	15 Sep 44	15 Jul 45	15 Feb 46	Sold for scrapping 1962
CL120 Spokane	Federal, Kearny	15 Nov 44	22 Sep 45	17 May 46	Stricken 15 Apr 1972
CL121 Fresno	Federal, Kearny	12 Feb 45	5 Mar 46	27 Nov 46	Stricken 1 Apr 1965

Displacement: 6,718 tons/6,825 tonnes (standard); 8,340 tons/8,473 tonnes (full load).
Length: 541ft 6in/165.05m (oa); 530ft/161.55m (wl).
Beam: 53ft 2in/16.21m; Draught: 20ft 6in/6.25m (mean).
Machinery: 2-shaft Westinghouse geared turbines; 4 Babcock & Wilcox boilers.
Performance: 75,000shp=32½kts; Bunkerage: 1,360 tons oil fuel.
Range: 8,500nm at 15kts.
Protection: 3¾in main belt, 1¼in deck & gunhouses.
Guns: sixteen 5in (8x2); sixteen 1.1in (4x4).
Torpedoes: eight 21in (2x4).
Aircraft: nil.
Complement: 623.

Design The USA did not lay down any cruisers between *St Louis* in December 1936 and the lead ship of this new class in April 1940, a period of some 40 months. This state of affairs arose as a result of the effects of the 1936 London Naval Treaty and its tonnage limitations on the cruiser design policy of the USA at the latter end of the 1930s. Politically and financially the climate was right for the construction of further cruisers, but there was no consensus as to which design parameters were the most important. The Second London Naval Treaty limited cruisers to 8,000 tons with 6in maximum gun calibre, and initially, as far as the USA was concerned, it appeared that the path was leading to a general-purpose ship armed with 6in; almost a miniature *Brooklyn*. Opinion was divided between this type of cruiser and a much smaller type to work with destroyers. In the event the twin 6in/47 DP gun mounting was not at a sufficiently advanced stage of design to be realistically considered at this time (nor would it be until 1945). Consequently this design was not proceeded with, and a completely new approach was taken. The new 5in/38 DP weapon had proved to be a great success, and as an alternative it was also proposed that the new cruiser should mount this as a main battery. In December 1936 the construction of ten ships of 5,000 to 7,000 tons was recommended and preliminary design studies were sketched out. Many variants were investigated, armed with 6in and 5in guns in several permutations, at least one of which generally resembled the design that was to develop into the *Cleveland* Class. It became clear that, even on 8,000 tons, all of the conflicting demands could not be accommodated, and by the end of 1937 the 6in ship had been dropped for the reason noted above, and

work concentrated on the 5in DP version. Preliminary design work was completed by July 1938, and finally resulted in a ship of 6,000 tons standard displacement. The hull form was not dissimilar to that of *Brooklyn*, and retained the full transom form aft, even though there was no hangar under the quarterdeck. An uncharacteristic feature for a US cruiser was the knuckle in the bow. The protective scheme included a waterline belt 3¾in thick abreast the machinery spaces, and a shallower underwater belt forward and aft of it, covering the magazine spaces. This belt was, for the first time, an integral part of the hull, with no skin plating under it. The deck was 1¼in and the inner double bottom extended up to meet it, and 3¾in end bulkheads closed off the side belts. Otherwise the armouring was limited to 1¼in to gun houses and ammunition handling spaces, although there was a conning tower of 2½in maximum in the form of a protected bridge. In all, protection amounted to 585½ tons, 8.9 per cent of the standard displacement.

The main machinery continued the unit principle, with four high-pressure (665psi, 850°F) boilers in two fire rooms. Unusually for US cruisers, but in line with their 'destroyer-type' development, this was the only class of cruiser to adopt a two-shaft turbine installation, which developed 75,000shp for a designed maximum speed of 32½kts. It is interesting to note the optimistic claims of 40kts+ reported for these ships and compare them with the similar claims made for the British *Manxman* Class fast minelayers, as neither class was ever capable of such speeds. *Atlanta* actually achieved 33.67kts on 78,985shp with a displacement of 7,404 tons during trials, but wartime additions increased displacement and reduced speed as a consequence.

Sixteen 5in/38 DP Mk 12 guns firing a 55lb (24.9kg) projectile comprised the main armament, shipped in eight twin power-operated mountings Mk 32. These were disposed three each tiered forward and aft, with an additional pair abreast the after control station. Reportedly, the latter were to provide starshell for night action. Maximum range was 37,200ft at 85° in the AA role. As designed, the AA outfit was to comprise three quadruple 1.1in, two abeam abreast the bridge and the third aft of the after control. Finally, again in keeping with their destroyer support and Fleet screening role, these ships were given torpedoes, initially two triple mountings on the beam that were to have come from the stock removed from the early heavy cruisers. However, quadruple tubes removed from the *Sims* class destroyers were fitted instead, and the intended reload torpedoes eliminated. Sonar and depth charges completed the armament. No aircraft were carried.

Four ships, *CL51-CL54*, were ordered on 25 April 1939. A second group of four was ordered on

Atlanta, 1941

Above: *Juneau* in June 1942. (National Archives)

9 September 1940 under the Expansion Programme of that year. These repeats differed in having the waist 5in mountings suppressed and replaced by twin 40mm Bofors for a total of eight such mountings and fourteen (later completed with eighteen) 20mm. The torpedo tubes were retained.

Below: An earlier photo of *Juneau*, lacking radar. Note camouflage. (USN)

A third group saw more substantial changes to the design, positive steps being taken to improve the very marginal stability resulting from topweight additions, mainly caused by increased AA demands. These entailed lowering Nos. 2 and 5 mountings to the main deck, and therefore also Nos. 3 and 4 to the first superstructure deck, redesigning and lowering the bridge structure, and trunking the two funnels into one. Internally, watertight integrity was improved, and externally the light AA was increased to four quadruple 40mm, six twin and twenty 20mm. In the event

the funnels were not trunked and, in addition, further weight was saved by suppressing the torpedo tubes and further increasing the AA battery to six quadruple and six twin 40mm, plus an extra two twin 20mm. In January 1945 the 20mm outfit was amended to eight twin.

On 7 August 1942 three ships (*CL119-121*) were ordered to this modification from Bethlehem, San Francisco, but on 27 September 1943 the contract was transferred to Federal, Kearny.
Modifications A fourth quad 1.1in mounting was added on the quarterdeck at the extreme stern

Above: *San Diego* in October 1944. (USN)

after completion in the case of the first two ships, and the remainder of the first batch commissioned with this mounting. In December 1941 the authorised AA battery was four twin 40mm (quads could not be carried) and eight single 20mm. *San Juan* completed with fourteen 20mm, but was later reduced to eight. Later, in October 1942, the authorised 20mm outfit was increased to thirteen. In December 1943 both *San Diego* and *San Juan* were given a quadruple 40mm aft, despite the weight problem, and the rest of the 1.1in guns were supplanted by twin 40mm. Plans to land the tubes and the waist 5in did not come to fruition, and at the end of the war *San Juan* had one quad, five twin 40mm and nine 20mm. Her sister appears to have had only three twin 40mm but fifteen 20mm. Boats and the boat handling crane were landed to compensate. Both ships had been given an extensive open bridge earlier in the war.

The four *Oaklands* were completed with square open bridges, no conning towers, no boats or cranes and better protection to the fire control systems. The 40mm outfit was now eight twin mounts with sixteen 20mm. The Bofors outfit was increased to four twin and four quadruple in *Oakland* by April 1945, with eight twin 20mm, whilst

still retaining the tubes, but these had been landed by the end of the war. *Tucson* had also landed her tubes by this time, only *Flint* retaining her original battery.

The third group of ships did not complete until well after the end of hostilities, and are therefore outside the scope of this volume as far as modifications are concerned.

Service Two ships of the first group, *Atlanta* herself and *Juneau*, had only brief careers. *Atlanta* was assigned to CruDiv 10 in the Atlantic as flagship on completion, then went to the Pacific for CruDiv 11, also as flagship. In June 1942 she was part of TF16, (*Enterprise* and *Hornet*). In the following months she was committed to the Guadalcanal campaign as a unit of TF61.2, and participated in the Battle of the Eastern Solomon Islands on 24/25 August. In October she was with TF64 at the Battle of Santa Cruz, and then assisted in the reinforcement of the garrison on Guadalcanal until November, when, in an action off Savo Island of the night of 12/13th, she was first torpedoed by the destroyer *Akatsuki* and then hit by some nineteen rounds of 8in fired by *San Francisco*, which had mistaken her for Japanese. This killed many men, including the admiral. The torpedo from *Akatsuki* struck the port side in the way of the forward engine room and caused a gradual loss of all power, and as a

result *Atlanta* had to be scuttled some 3nm off Guadalcanal at about midday on 13 November. The Japanese destroyer was herself sunk by the cruiser's gunfire.

Juneau operated initially in the Atlantic with CruDiv 10, later with CruDiv 8, and on the blockade of the Vichy French islands of Martinique and Guadaloupe until transferred to the Pacific on 22 August 1942. Here she joined CruDiv 11, to which all of her sisters completed during the war were to be attached. By early September she was with TF18 (*Wasp*) off Guadalcanal, rescuing the survivors of that ship when it was sunk on 15 September. She later joined TF17 (*Hornet*) for raids on Shortland Island, remaining with that formation for the Battle of Santa Cruz. Early in November she was a unit of TG62.4, covering convoys from Noumea to Guadalcanal, and during the night action in which *Atlanta* was sunk she received a torpedo hit from a destroyer, on the port side abreast the forward fire room, losing half of her propulsion plant. Listing heavily, she was able to limp away, but north of Guadalcanal she was hit by another torpedo in the same place, from the submarine *I 26*. The resulting explosion touched off a magazine, sinking the ship in 20 seconds and leaving only ten survivors.

San Diego joined TF17 at Pearl Harbor and was committed to the Guadalcanal campaign,

Above: *Reno* as completed in 1944. (USN)

escorting convoys from Espirito Santo. On 2 October she participated in the abortive raid on Shortland Island, and a couple of weeks later was present at the Battle of Santa Cruz. In the following months she saw action off Guadalcanal and the Solomons, and was involved in the landings on Munda and Bougainville. In the summer of 1943 she was part of the Anglo-American carrier force TF36.3, consisting of the US *Saratoga* and the British *Victorious*, in support of the landings on New Georgia, and in November she was again covering carrier raiding groups, this time off Rabaul and Tarawa with TF38. In December 1943, after supporting the landings in the Gilbert Islands, she participated in a carrier raid on Kwajalein in which USN aircraft damaged the cruisers *Isuzu* and *Nagara*, then sailed for the USA and refit at San Francisco, returning to Pearl Harbor in January 1944. Now a unit of TF58, *San Diego* participated in the attacks on Japanese bases in the Marshall Islands, the landings at Eniwetok, and the attack on Truk before undergoing another refit at San Francisco. Back in the Pacific, she took part in the raids on Marcus and Wake Islands in May, and in June was in the Marianas and the Philippine Sea for the invasion of Guam and Tinian, as well as attacks on the Palaus. As

the year progressed the ship saw further action at Okinawa and in attacks on Formosa. In October she was a unit of TG38 at the Battle of Leyte Gulf, then spent the rest of the war with the Fast Carrier Groups in their attacks on Formosa, the Philippines, Indo-China and the Japanese mainland, as well as in the Okinawa campaign. She was the first US ship to enter Tokyo Bay after the Japanese surrender. After her return home in September she was assigned to ferry home troops, but on 4 November 1946 was paid off to reserve. *San Diego* never recommissioned, and was stricken on 1 March 1959 and sold for scrapping at the Puget Sound Bridge and Dry Dock Co., Seattle, where she was demolished in 1960.

San Juan joined TF18 at San Diego in June 1942, then escorted troop convoys to the Solomon Islands for the Tulagi landings. In August she was assigned to the Guadalcanal campaign, and at the Battle of Savo Island on 4 August she was with the eastern force and was undamaged. At the Battle of Santa Cruz she was with TF61 and was damaged by bombing. After repair at Noumea and Sydney she returned to the South Pacific, operating in the Coral Sea with the Carrier Task Forces. In December 1942 she sailed for refit at Mare Island, returning to action at the landings on Eniwetok in February 1943. Throughout 1943 she served with the carriers during the

attacks on the Palaus, Yap and Ulithi and the landings at Hollandia. By the summer she was off Iwo Jima, and was involved in the Battle of the Philippine Sea. After the capture of Guam and further attacks on Iwo Jima, the ship spent a period from August to November under refit at San Francisco. She then joined TF38, attacking airfields at Buna and Buka on Rabaul. By December she was involved in operations in the South China Sea, off Formosa, and in attacks against the Philippines, before moving on to attack Iwo Jima and Okinawa by March 1945. *San Juan* was damaged in the typhoon of 5 June 1945, but by July was back in action with TG38.4 during the carrier raid into Japanese home waters. After the war's end she repatriated US troops from the South Pacific, and paid off on 9 November 1946. She saw no further service, and was stricken from reserve on 1 March 1959 to be sold for breaking up on 31 October 1961, being scrapped the following year.

Oakland, the first of the second group to be completed, did not commission until July 1943, then worked up in home waters until she was despatched to the South Pacific in November, joining TG50.3 at Pearl Harbor for the Gilbert Island landings. In January 1944 she was with TG58.1 for carrier raids on the Marshall Islands, and the next month performed similar duties during the raids on Truk. March saw her in action in the Bismarck Archipelago, followed by the attacks on Palau, Truk and Wake Island. By summer the arena had moved to the Marianas, where *Oakland* continued to screen the carriers of TG58.1. Attacks were carried out on Guam, Iwo Jima and Chichi Jima. These tasks continued into the autumn, and by September attacks were being made on the Philippines and Okinawa. By this time *Oakland* was with TG38.2. This formation attacked Admiral Kurita's force in the Battle of Samar on 25 October 1944. After covering the landings at Leyte, the ship sailed for Mare Island in December and underwent a refit that lasted until early March 1945. She arrived back at Ulithi on 30 March, joining TG58.4 for attacks on the Japanese mainland and Okinawa until the end of the war. Following her return to the USA after the Japanese surrender, *Oakland* was not paid off as intended but remained in service, mainly in a training role, until decommissioned on 1 July 1949. The ship was finally stricken on 1 March 1959, and was sold for breaking up on 1 December 1959.

Reno joined the 5th Fleet for the attacks on Marcus Island and Wake Island in May 1944, then through the summer escorted the carrier raids against Saipan, Pagan, the Bonin Islands, Guam and the Palaus. By October she was in the Philippines with TG38.3, raiding Mindanao, Luzon and also Formosa, when she was damaged by an air-craft that crashed on her after gunhouse. On 4 November, during the Leyte landings, *Reno* was struck abaft the after engine room by a torpedo from the submarine *I 41*. Despite oil fires and flooding (some 132ft of her length on the second deck), she was still able to steam. The small cruiser almost capsized, but was nursed to safety and provisionally repaired at Ulithi before returning to the USA. The war was over by the time she returned to service, and she served briefly on trips to Europe before decommissioning on 4 November 1946. *Reno* was also stricken on 1 March 1959, being sold on 22 March 1962 for scrapping.

Flint was assigned to the 3rd Fleet, arriving at Ulithi at the end of December 1944. At the beginning of January 1945 she was a component of TG38.3 for the Luzon landings. She was then with TG58.5 for the first major raid on Tokyo, and in support of the Iwo Jima landings in February/March. She escorted the raids on Kyushu and Okinawa between March and June, and an attack on Wake island in July/August. At the end of the war she served in Japanese waters until October, arriving in San Francisco on 28 November. Thereafter she made another sortie to Kwajalein to bring home troops. *Flint* was paid off into reserve on 6 May 1947 and remained until stricken on 1 September 1965. The cruiser arrived at the National Metal & Steel Corp. yard at Terminal Island, California, for breaking up on 5 November 1966.

Tucson did not sail for the Pacific theatre until May 1945, and then operated locally at Pearl Harbor until joining TF38 off Leyte on 16 June. She participated in the final carrier raids against the Japanese mainland from July, then stayed for the occupation of Japan before returning to the USA on 5 October 1945. *Tucson* saw peacetime service until paid off on 11 June 1949. On 1 June 1966 the ship was stricken from reserve, but was used as an experimental hulk until 1970. She was then sold as scrap for $191,011 on 24 February 1971 to be broken up by the National Metal & Steel Corporation at Terminal Island, California.

Juneau (ii) served in the postwar fleet until decommissioned on 23 July 1956. She was sold for scrapping in 1962.

Spokane likewise saw no wartime service, but served until 27 February 1950, when paid off. On 1 April 1966 she was redesignated *AG191* for experimental purposes, but this conversion was never finished. The ship was eventually stricken on 15 April 1972 and then sold on 17 May the following year to be broken up.

Fresno was in service postwar for barely two and a half years, being decommissioned on 17 May 1949. She remained in the reserve fleet until stricken on 1 April 1965, and was then sold for scrapping on 1 June 1966, being broken up by Lipsett Inc., Kearny, New Jersey, that year.

Below: *Flint* on 1 December 1944. (Floating Drydock)

CLEVELAND CLASS

Ship	Builder	Laid Down	Launched	Completed	Fate
CL55 Cleveland	New York Sbdg	1 Jun 40	1 Nov 41	15 Jun 42	Stricken 1 Mar 1959
CL56 Columbia	New York Sbdg	19 Aug 40	17 Dec 41	29 Jul 42	Sold for scrapping 18 Feb 1959
CL57 Montpelier	New York Sbdg	2 Dec 40	12 Feb 42	9 Sep 42	Stricken 1 Mar 1959
CL58 Denver	New York Sbdg	26 Dec 40	4 Apr 42	15 Oct 42	Sold for scrapping 29 Feb 1960
CL59 Amsterdam	New York Sbdg	1 May 41		Completed as CVL22 Independence	
CL60 Santa Fe	New York Sbdg	7 Jun 41	10 Jun 42	24 Nov 42	Stricken 1 Mar 1959
CL61 Tallahasse	New York Sbdg	2 Jun 41		Completed as CVl 23 Princeton	
CL62 Birmingham	Newport News	17 Feb 41	20 Mar 42	29 Jan 43	Stricken 1 Mar 1959
CL63 Mobile	Newport News	14 Apr 41	15 May 42	24 Mar 43	Stricken 1 Mar 1959
CL64 Vincennes (ex Flint)	Bethlehem, Quincy	7 Mar 42	17 Jul 43	21 Jan 44	Stricken 1 Apr 1966
CL65 Pasadena	Bethlehem, Quincy	6 Feb 43	28 Dec 43	8 Jun 44	Stricken 1 Dec 1970
CL66 Springfield	Bethlehem, Quincy	13 Feb 43	9 Mar 44	9 Sep 44	Stricken 30 Jul 1978
CL67 Topeka	Bethlehem, Quincy	21 Apr 43	19 Aug 44	23 Dec 44	Stricken 30 Jul 1978
CL76 New Haven	New York Sbdg	11 Aug 41		Completed as CVL24 Belleau Wood	
CL77 Huntington	New York Sbdg	17 Nov 41		Completed as CVL25 Cowpens	
CL78 Dayton	New York Sbdg	29 Dec 41		Completed as CVL26 Monterey	
CL79 Wilmington	New York Sbdg	16 Mar 42		Completed as CVL28 Cabot	
CL80 Biloxi	Newport News	9 Jul 41	23 Feb 43	31 Aug 43	Stricken 1 Sept 1961
CL81 Houston (ex Vicksburg)	Newport News	4 Aug 41	19 Jun 43	20 Dec 43	Stricken 1 Mar 1959
CL82 Providence	Bethlehem, Quincy	27 Jul 43	28 Dec 44	15 May 45	Stricken 30 Sept 1978
CL83 Manchester	Bethlehem, Quincy	25 Sep 44	5 Mar 46	29 Oct 46	Stricken 1 Apr 1960
CL84 Buffalo	Federal, Kearny	not laid		Cancelled 16 Dec 1940	
CL85 Fargo	New York Sbdg	11 Apr 42		Completed as CVL27 Langley	
CL86 Vicksburg (ex Cheyenne)	Newport News	26 Oct 42	14 Dec 43	12 Jun 44	Stricken 1 Oct 1962
CL87 Duluth	Newport News	9 Nov 42	13 Jan 44	18 Sep 44	Sold for scrapping 14 Nov 1960
CL88	Federal, Kearny	not laid		Cancelled 16 Dec 1940	
CL89 Miami	Cramp	2 Aug 41	8 Dec 42	28 Dec 43	Stricken 1 Sept 1961
CL90 Astoria (ex Wilkes-Barre)	Cramp	6 Sep 41	6 Mar 43	17 May 44	Stricken 1 Nov 1969
CL91 Oklahoma City	Cramp	8 Dec 42	20 Feb 44	22 Dec 44	Stricken 15 Dec 1979
CL92 Little Rock	Cramp	6 Mar 43	27 Aug 44	17 Jun 45	Stricken 22 Nov 1976
CL93 Galveston	Cramp	20 Feb 44	22 Apr 45	28 May 58	Stricken 21 Dec 1973
CL94 Youngstown	Cramp	4 Sep 44	not launched		Cancelled 12 Aug 1945
CL99 Buffalo	New York Sbdg			Completed as CVL29 Bataan	
CL100 Newark	New York Sbdg			Completed as CVL30 San Jacinto	
CL101 Amsterdam	Newport News	3 Mar 43	25 Apr 44	8 Jan 45	Stricken 2 Jan 1971
CL102 Portsmouth	Newport News	28 Jun 43	20 Sep 44	25 Jun 45	Stricken 1 Dec 1970
CL103 Wilkes-Barre	New York Sbdg	14 Dec 42	24 Dec 43	1 Jul 44	Stricken 15 Jan 1971
CL104 Atlanta (ii)	New York Sbdg	25 Jan 43	6 Feb 44	3 Dec 44	Scuttled 1 October 1970
CL105 Dayton	New York Sbdg	8 Mar 43	19 Mar 44	7 Jan 45	Stricken 1 Sept 1961

CL106 to CL118 were to be built to a revised design: see *Fargo* Class.

Displacement: 11,744 tons/11931 tonnes (standard); 14,131 tons/14,357 tonnes (full load).

Length: 610ft 1in/185.95m (oa); 600ft/182.88m (wl).

Beam: 66ft 4in/20.22m; Draught: 24ft 6in/7.47m (mean).

Machinery: 4-shaft General Electric geared turbines; 4 Babcock & Wilcox boilers.

Performance: 100,000shp=32½kts; Bunkerage: 2,100 tons oil fuel max.

Range: 11,000nm at 15kts.

Protection: 3½-5in main belt; 2in deck; 6in barbettes; turrets, 6½in (faces), 3in (top & sides); 5in CT.

Guns: twelve 6in (4x3); twelve 5in (6x2); twenty 1.1in (5x4).

Torpedoes: nil.

Aircraft: four, two catapults.

Complement: 1,285.

Design Two 8,000-ton cruisers armed with eight or nine 6in DP guns were projected in June 1938, to be included in a tentative FY40 programme. Further projections envisaged some twenty or so such ships being completed in a subsequent ten-year programme. By May 1939 this design had developed into a scheme with ten 6in/47 in twin DP turrets, with a secondary armament of five quadruple 1.1in. There was a single catapult aft on the centreline, and two banks of triple tubes were included. Visually, the ship was recognisably that which was to become the *Cleveland*. However, the design was badly overstretched and had no margin on the 8,000-ton treaty limit. Demands from the President for more gunpower, and other requests for increased power supplies, soon pushed the ship to 8,200 and then 8,400 tons, the only option for keeping the displacement down to 8,000 tons being the elimination of virtually all protection. The war in Europe caused Britain to suspend adherence to the 8,000-ton limit, and, since the 6in/47 gun was no longer of immediate interest to the USN, the design was dropped. Time was pressing, however, and a new cruiser was badly needed, so on 2 October 1939 the decision was taken to base the new ships on *Helena*, with two extra twin 5in/38 replacing one 6in triple turret.

The new ship was of the same length as *Helena*, but had the beam increased by 4ft 7in as a result of serious doubts about the stability in the design stage. Experience in the European war had demonstrated the power of ground mines and the danger to ships from underwater damage, as well as the effectiveness of air attack. Solutions to these problems all involved increased weight, particularly in the case of additional AA guns, when the added weight was high up. Eventually the inclination of the side armour was altered, as were the hull lines, thereby increasing beam. Nevertheless, stability was to remain critical in these ships throughout their lives, and was probably one of the main reasons for their brief postwar service, despite their relative youth.

The protective scheme included a 5in maximum waterline belt, 9ft deep over the machinery spaces, with 2in protection to the forward magazines and an internal bulkhead 3in to 4.7in thick to protect the after magazines. The armoured deck was 2in. Overall, the scheme was not dissimilar to that of *Helena*, the total weight of armour being 1,468 tons, or 13.18 per cent of the standard displacement (c.f. *Helena* 13.76 per cent). Internally, the unit machinery principle was retained, but the adoption of high-pressure steam boilers allowed a reduction in the length of the fire rooms. However, the machinery spaces were enlarged a little over those of *Brooklyn* to avoid that design's cramped engineering compartments. A triple bottom was adopted for greater security and the double bottom extended up to the armoured deck, enclosing all magazines.

The main machinery comprised the usual four-shaft geared turbine installation, developing 100,000shp. Cruising turbines, included in the original design, were not in fact fitted after *CL57*.

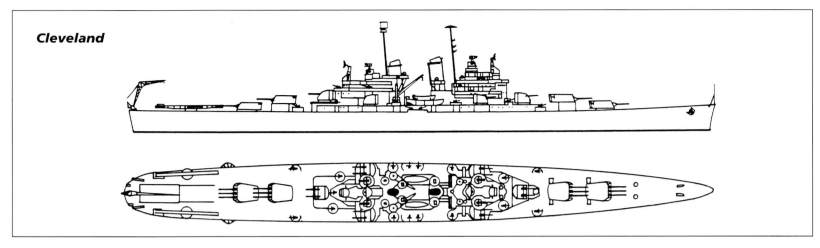

Cleveland

For the main armament the 6in/47 Mk 16 was retained, in triple turrets, two each fore and aft. Maximum elevation was 60°, but their use for AA purposes was limited because loading was only possible at angles up to 20°. Secondary armament comprised twelve 5in/38 DP in six twin Mk 32 mountings, two on the centreline superfiring on No. 2 and No. 3 turrets, and the remainder on the beam. This disposition allowed a very respectable heavy AA defence from almost any attack angle. As originally planned, the light AA consisted only of .5in MGs, which the European war had quickly shown to be inadequate. Stability considerations precluded the shipping of the new quadruple 1.1in without ballasting, but this course of action was finally adopted in the face of strong opposition to the reducing of the 5in battery. Four mountings were planned, two abreast each funnel. In the event, this gun had shown itself defective before the completion of any of this class, and the 40mm Bofors was adopted instead. Unfortunately, the weight of a quadruple 40mm was some 11 tons, compared with the 1.1in quad at 5 to 6 tons, and could not be accepted on the *Cleveland*s, at least initially. Consequently they were to be given twin 40mm. No torpedoes were carried. The aircraft outfit included the standard four floatplanes, now the Curtiss SO3C Seamew, the first of which was issued to *Cleveland* on 15 July 1942. There were two catapults aft on the quarterdeck, below which was the hangar.

Two ships, *CL55* and *CL56*, were ordered on 23 March 1940. Further orders were placed up to 1943, *CL57* and *CL58* on 12 June 1940, *CL59* to *CL61* on 1 July 1940, *CL62* to *CL67* in July 1940,

Opposite page: *Santa Fe.* (National Archives)
Below: *Wilkes-Barre* in August 1944. (Floating Drydock)

CL76 to *CL88* in September 1940 and *CL89* to *CL94* in October. After the USA's entry into the war, further orders were placed. *CL99* and *CL100* (which replaced *CL84* and *CL88*, cancelled on 16 December 1940 to allow Kearny to concentrate on destroyers) were ordered in December 1941. *CL101* and *CL102*, ordered on 15 December 1941, were the only cruisers to be contracted for under the FY42 programme. In August 1942 *CL103* to *CL118* were ordered, and in June the following year the last batch, *CL143* to *CL147* and *CL148* to *CL149*, were ordered. However, in 1942 nine ships were reordered as light carriers, these being *CL59*, *61*, *76* to *79*, *85*, *99* and *100*. Towards the end of the war there were further cancellations. On 5 October 1944 *CL112* to *CL115* were deleted, and *CL111* was reassigned to Cramp on 4 September. Then, on 12 August 1945, there was a further batch of cancellations; *CL94*, *CL108* to *CL111*, and *CL116* to *CL118*. Of these, *Newark*, *CL108*, was completed to launch stage and then used for underwater weapons tests. In addition, *Galveston*, *CL93*, was completed but never commissioned, going straight to reserve, where she remained until converted to a guided-missile cruiser.

Modifications *Cleveland* completed with twin 40mm, but the remainder had two twin and two quadruple, the former on the upper deck amidships and the latter in a deckhouse abaft the forward beam twin 5in. By November 1942 the early *Cleveland*s were to have two more twin 40mm, on the extreme stern, one aft of each catapult, this addition also being applied to the later ships. By May 1944 this had been increased yet again to four quad and six twin 40mm. The 20mm outfit was standardised at ten guns, but this varied considerably.

Early ships completed with rounded front bridges, but from *Vincennes* they had square fronts and were lower, with an open bridge atop. Early units added an open bridge above the existing pilot house and retained the conning tower, while this feature was eliminated in later ships to save weight.

Weight was always critical, and one catapult was landed later in the war, as well as the rangefinders in Nos. 1 and 4 turrets. A further detrimental factor was the use of steel rather than the designed aluminium for the deckhouses from *Springfield* onwards because of the wartime shortages. Finally, the new Curtiss SC Seahawk aircraft replaced the Seamew, despite the critical stability.

Service *Cleveland* participated in Operation Torch, the North African landings, in November 1942, as part of the Western Task force, returning to the USA at the end of the month to be transferred to the Pacific for CruDiv 12. She was involved in the final stages of the Guadalcanal campaign, and took part in the Battle of Rennell Island on the night of 29/30 January 1943 as part of TF18. On 6 March, while on a sortie to bombard an airfield in the Kula Gulf, she and her sisters *Montpelier* and *Denver* engaged and sank the destroyers *Minegumo* and *Murasame* off Kolombangara. During the rest of 1943 she operated in the Solomons, supporting the landings in New Georgia in June/July with TF36.2, and participating in the Battle of Empress Augusta Bay on 1/2 November. By the summer of 1944 *Cleveland* was in action in the Marianas, Saipan, and she participated in the Battle of the Philippine Sea with TF58. February 1945 saw her in the Philippines at the Palawan landings with TG74.2, and at Mindanao in April. In June she was covering the

Above: *Birmingham* on 20 February 1943. (USN)   **Below:** *Springfield* in 1944. (USN)

involved in the sinking of the cruiser *Sendai*. The same cruisers, less *Denver*, shelled positions on Bougainville in December. Operations in the Solomons continued until 4 April 1944, when the ship left for a refit at San Francisco, not returning to the Solomons until August. She covered the Palau landings in September, and the following month was a unit of the Southern Fire Support Group for the Leyte landings, when she participated in the Battle of the Surigao Straits. She operated in the Philippines into early 1945, but off Lingayen, when part of TG77.2, she was heavily hit by a kamikaze on 6 January, which disabled both after turrets. A second hit on 9 January knocked out most of her fire control gear. After provisional repairs at Leyte, the ship returned to the west coast of the USA for full repairs. She arrived back in the south-west Pacific in time for the Balikpapan landings, then transferred to the Okinawa operations in the summer of 1945. After the war *Columbia* returned home to pay off, and was decommissioned on 30 November 1946. She remained in reserve until sold on 18 February 1959 for scrapping at Chester, Pennsylvania.

Montpelier arrived at Noumea for service in the Pacific theatre with CruDiv 12 on 18 January 1943, assuming the role of flagship of the division on 25 January. A few days later she participated in the Battle of Rennell Island, then operated in the Solomons and the Bismarck Archipelago, including the battle of Empress Augusta Bay on 2 November (when she was damaged), until the summer, when she moved to support operations in the Mariana Islands. She bombarded Saipan from 14 June as part of TG58.3, then took part in the Battle of the Philippine Sea before continuing operations around Saipan, Tinian and Guam until August, when she returned to the USA for refit. *Montpelier* did not return to action off Leyte until the end of November, then supported the Mindoro landings, followed by those at Lingayen Gulf in January 1945. Thereafter she saw action at Corregidor, Palawan and Mindanao before covering the landing operations at Balikpapan in June/July 1945. For the remainder of the war the ship operated in the East China Sea, then participated in the occupation of Japan. She returned home to pay off, and decommissioned on 24 January 1947, remaining in reserve until stricken on 1 March 1959. *Montpelier* was finally sold for scrapping on 22 January 1960, and broken up at Baltimore, Maryland.

Denver arrived at Efate in the New Hebrides on 14 February 1943, to join CruDiv 12 with TF68. In March she participated in the bombardment of the airfield at Vila on Kolombangara, when two Japanese destroyers were sunk (see *Cleveland*). At the time of the landings on New Georgia she was with TF36.2 and, in company with her three sisters above, shelled Shortland

Brunei landings, then Balikpapan, but in July she moved to the Okinawa campaign and then operated in the South China Sea until the end of the war. After her return to the USA in November 1945 she served briefly on training duties, but paid off on 7 February 1947. *Cleveland* was stricken on 1 March 1959 and sold for breaking up on 18 February 1960, to be scrapped at Baltimore, Maryland.

Columbia sailed for the Pacific on 9 November 1942, and also joined CruDiv 12 at Espiritu Santo in the New Hebrides in December. She participated in the final battles for Guadalcanal and,

with TF18, in the Battle of Rennell Island at the end of January 1943. She remained in the Solomon Islands, and in June covered the landings on New Georgia with TF36.2, shelling Shortland and later Munda. Towards the end of September she was involved in the blockade off Kolombangara, when she narrowly escaped torpedoes from a Japanese submarine. In November *Columbia* covered the landings on Bougainville, which led to the Battle of Empress Augusta Bay on the night of 1/2 November. In this action *Columbia* was one of the ships of CruDiv 12 (*Cleveland*, *Columbia*, *Denver* and *Montpelier*)

Above: *Vincennes* in 1944. (USN)

Island, where there was a Japanese base. On 1/2 November *Denver* was one of the cruisers involved in the Battle of Empress Augusta Bay, where she received some damage from gunfire, after which she supported the landings at Cape Torokina on Bougainville. However, on 13 November the ship was hit by an aerial torpedo while engaged on this task, and the after engine room and after fire room were flooded. She was towed into Espiritu Santo for temporary repairs, then despatched back to Mare Island for full repairs. These lasted from January 1944 until the summer, the ship arriving back at Eniwetok in the Marshall Islands on 22 June. From herè she moved north to take part in the bombardment of Iwo Jima in the Volcano Islands, followed by the attack on Palau in September 1944 with TF31. On 22 September *Denver* was one of the first US ships to enter Ulithi Lagoon, the Pacific Fleet's future main base. In October she moved south-east to Leyte for the assault, and took part in the Battle of the Surigao Straits. Thereafter she operated in the Philippines, covering the landings at Mindoro, Lingayen and Palawan until May 1945. Then followed operations in the Bay of Brunei and Balikpapan in June as part of TG74. Upon completion of this task she returned to the Okinawa campaign to join TF95. After the Japanese surrender the cruiser entered Japanese home waters to evacuate Allied POWs, and on 20 October sailed for home. Postwar she was briefly used for training before being decommissioned on 7 February 1947. *Denver*, like all her unconverted sisters, never recommissioned and was sold for

scrapping on 29 February 1960, arriving at Kearny, New Jersey, to be broken up in November that year.

Amsterdam CL59 was one of the nine hulls converted into light carriers, commissioning as *Independence CVL22*. The others were *Tallahasse* (*Princeton CVL23*); *New Haven* (*Belleau Wood CVL24*); *Huntington* (*Cowpens CVL25*); *Dayton* (*Monterey CVL26*); *Fargo* (*Langley CVL27*); *Wilmington* (*Cabot CVL28*); *Buffalo* (*Bataan CVL29*); and *Newark* (*San Jacinto CVL30*).

Santa Fe arrived at Pearl Harbor on 22 March 1943 to join CruDiv 13, and the following month was assigned to the Aleutians campaign, taking part in the bombardment of Kiska in July. She returned to Pearl Harbor at the beginning of September to be attached to TF15 for carrier raids on Tarawa in the Gilbert Islands (September), to TF14 for similar raids on Wake Island in October, to TG53.4 for the Gilbert Islands landings in November and to TG50.3 for raids on Kwajalein in December. After a brief return to the USA at the turn of the year, *Santa Fe* continued operations in the Marshall Islands, supporting the landings at Kwajalein at the end of January with Fire Support Group 53.5 and, with TG58.1, covering the carrier raid on Truk on 17 February. In March the ship moved south-east to the Bismarck Archipelago for the landings at Emirau, where she formed part of the Fire Support Group. Operations in support of the Hollandia landings followed, together with raids on Truk by the carriers before the cruiser returned to Kwajalein at the beginning of May. By June *Santa Fe* had moved to the Marianas for operations at Saipan, Tinian, Guam and the Pagan Islands. By July this included attacks on

Iwo Jima, Yap and Ulithi before the ship returned once again to Eniwetok. Her next operational area was the Philippines, where, with TG38.3, she covered carrier attacks against these islands and Formosa. The landings at Leyte saw her still with this Group, attacking targets on Luzon, and she remained in the Philippine theatre into 1945. By February 1945 she was with TG58.4 with the carriers *Yorktown* and *Randolph* for raids on Tokyo and Iwo Jima, then carried out bombardment tasks against the latter target. However, in March she returned to the west coast for refit and did not leave the USA again until early August, by which time the war was all but over. *Santa Fe* was decommissioned on 19 October 1946 and remained in reserve until stricken on 1 March 1959. The ship was sold for breaking up on 9 November 1959, and arrived at Portland, Oregon, for scrapping in 1960.

Birmingham operated in the Atlantic until the autumn of 1943, during which time she escorted troop convoys with TF65 from the USA to the Mediterranean in preparation for the landings in Sicily. She was present at the landings, Operation Husky, in July, but in August returned to the USA and transferred to the Pacific to join CruDiv 13, escorting the carriers of TF15 in attacks on Tarawa by mid-September 1943. By November she was in the Solomons, covering operations at Cape Torokina, when, on the night of 8/9 November, she was damaged by bombs and a torpedo from Japanese aircraft. Repair at Mare Island extended into February 1944, the ship returning to the south Pacific to join TF58 later that month. Over the next few months she escorted the carrier raids on the Marianas – Saipan, Tinian and Guam – as well as raids against the Philippines. In October *Birmingham* was with TF38 for attacks against Okinawa. In the Philippines, however, she was badly damaged on 24 October when the carrier *Princeton*, herself a *Cleveland* hull, was hit by Japanese dive bombers and blew up with the cruiser still alongside. This time repairs lasted until January 1945. On her return to the operational theatre she participated in the Iwo Jima landings and the Okinawa campaign, only to be damaged yet again on 4 May 1945, this time by a kamikaze. Repairs were effected at Pearl Harbor, and she resumed service in August off Okinawa. After the war she returned to the USA to pay off, and was decommissioned on 2 January 1947. *Birmingham* was stricken on 1 March 1959 and was scrapped at Long Beach, California, from December that year.

Mobile joined CruDiv 13 in the Pacific and was a part of TF15 for the attack on Marcus island on 31 August 1943, followed by another on Tarawa in mid-September and one on Wake Island on 5/6 October, when the cruiser shelled positions on the island. By the beginning of the next month *Mobile* was in the Solomons for the landings at Cape Torokina, Bougainville, with TG52.3, after which she joined TG53.4 for the landings in the Gilbert Islands. The year finished with raids on Kwajalein as part of TG50.3 in December. She was back in these waters in January as part of Fire Support Group 53.6 for the Kwajalein landings, and in February she covered a carrier raid on Truk. In March the cruiser was in the Bismarck Archipelago for the assault on Emirau, following which she provided fire support at the Hollandia landings in April. By June she was involved in the carrier raids on Saipan, Guam and Tinian in the Marianas by TF58, and in September, now with TF38, she took part in the raids on the Visayas, in the central Philippines. Further attacks were made against airfields on Formosa and in Luzon in October. At the Battle off Cape Engano on 24/25 October the ship was a part of TF34 when the carrier *Chiyoda*, crippled by aircraft, was finished off by *Mobile* and her consorts (*Santa Fe*, *New Orleans* and *Wichita*, together with destroyers). The early part of 1945 was spent under refit, but *Mobile* returned to the south Pacific to participate in the Okinawa campaign with TF51 until May, then in August escorted a carrier raid against Wake Island. At the end of hostilities she was present in Sagami Bay for the Japanese surrender. After trips to and from the USA with repatriated troops and POWs, *Mobile* decommissioned on 9 May 1947. Stricken on 1 March 1959, the ship was sold to Zidell Explorations Inc. for scrapping on 16 December 1959, and left in tow for the breaker's yard at Portland, Oregon, on 19 January 1960.

Vincennes assumed the role of Flagship CruDiv 14 after completion, and served in Caribbean and home waters until mid-April, when transferred to the Pacific, arriving at Pearl Harbor on 6 May. In June she joined TF58 for raids on the Mariana Islands, operating with TG58.4 (*Essex*), and participated in the Battle of the Philippine Sea. In August she was a component of TG38.2 for raids on the Bonin Islands. In the autumn *Vincennes* operated against Mindanao, Luzon, Okinawa and Formosa, covering the carrier forces. In October she was at Leyte Gulf, but at the beginning of 1945 operated in the South China Sea against targets in Indo-China and Okinawa. Most of her remaining months of hostilities were spent covering carrier raids against Okinawa and the Japanese mainland until she withdrew to the USA for refit in June. After the war she carried out a number of repatriation cruises to the Pacific before paying off on 10 September 1946. *Vincennes* was stricken on 1 April 1966, subsequently being used as a target for missiles, and was finally sunk on 28 October 1969.

Pasadena did not enter service until the summer of 1944, sailing for the Pacific to join CruDiv 17 on 25 September. Based at Ulithi, she operated with TF38, carrying out attacks against Formosa and Luzon until the end of 1944. In 1945 she operated in the South China Sea and off Indo-China, participating in the first major carrier raid against Tokyo and supporting the Okinawa landings, with TF58. For the remainder of the war *Pasadena* covered carrier strikes against the Japanese mainland, Okinawa, and the offshore islands. After the war she remained in commission until 12 January 1950, and was finally stricken on 1 December 1970, arriving at Zidell Exploration Inc., Tacoma, Washington, for scrapping in November 1972.

Springfield served in the Atlantic until February 1945, then went to the Pacific for CruDiv 17, arriving at Ulithi on 6 March. With TG58.3 she participated in the raids on Kyushu, and in April joined the Okinawa campaign. After a spell in the Philippines she joined the carrier forces attacking targets on the Japanese mainland until the end of the war. Postwar, the ship was decommissioned on 31 January 1950, then converted into a guided-missile cruiser, *CLG 7*, and recommissioned on 2 July 1960. She served in that role until paid off again on 15 May 1974 and stricken from reserve on 30 September 1978.

Topeka arrived at Pearl Harbor on 2 May 1945 and assumed the task of Flagship, CruDiv 18, joining operations off Okinawa with TG38.1 for the closing stages of that campaign. She participated in the final attacks on the Japanese mainland, and was present at the surrender in Tokyo Bay. Postwar, *Topeka* remained operational until decommissioned on 18 June 1949. After a period in reserve she was another of the class to be selected for conversion into a guided-missile cruiser, recommissioning as *CLG 8* on 26 March 1960. She was finally paid off on 5 June 1969 and stricken from reserve on 1 December 1973. She was sold to Southern Metals for breaking up on 28 March 1975.

Biloxi served with CruDiv 13 in the Pacific, and in the early part of 1944 participated in the landings in the Gilbert Islands, beginning with Kwajalein in January. The following month she was with TF58.1 for a carrier raid on Truk, and later that month saw action in the Marianas, Palaus, Yap and Ulithi before supporting the Hollandia landings by shelling Japanese strongpoints. June saw *Biloxi* in the Marianas once more, in preparation for the landings on the islands in the group, which began on 14 June (Saipan). She was in action at the Battle of the Philippine Sea, then served in the Bonins and during the landings on Guam in August. For the rest of the summer the cruiser supported operations in the Palaus, Yap and Ulithi, as well as the Bonins again and the Vulcan Islands. By October, however, she was in the Philippine theatre, operating at Luzon and involved in the Battle of Leyte Gulf, when she was a part of TG38.2. By the turn of the year she was in the South China Sea, and next month covered carrier raids against the Japanese mainland and offshore islands. During March she was at the landings on Iwo Jima, and also became involved in the Okinawa campaign, being slightly damaged by kamikaze attack on 27 March. *Biloxi* left the south Pacific to refit in the USA at the end of April, not returning until July. She participated in a final raid on Wake Island before the end of hostilities, then took part in the occupation of Japan. She paid off on 29 October 1946, to be finally stricken on 1 September 1961 and broken up at Portland, Oregon, the following year.

Houston commissioned for CruDiv 14 in the Pacific, and by June 1944 was escorting carrier groups in the Marianas, the Bonins and during the Battle of the Philippine Sea. In October she operated off Okinawa and Formosa, but on 14 October, while operating with TG38.1, the ship was hit by an aircraft torpedo which exploded under the hull amidships. The damage was severe, with all four machinery spaces flooded and extensive secondary flooding, as well as much distortion of the armoured deck. It was estimated that her displacement following the torpedoing was some 20,900 tons. She was towed away towards Ulithi, but received another torpedo hit on 16 October that caused petrol fires aft and almost resulted in her loss. Nevertheless, fair weather allowed her to reach Ulithi safely, where temporary repairs were made. On 27 October the ship left for the east coast, and was under repair at New York Navy Yard until October 1945. In 1947 she made a deployment to the Mediterranean, but decommissioned on 15 December that year. Stricken on 1 March 1959, the ship was scrapped at Baltimore, Maryland, in 1960.

Providence did not see service in the Second World War because she only commissioned in May 1945. She paid off on 14 June 1949 and was later selected for conversion into a *CLG*. She recommissioned on 17 September 1959 as *CLG 6*, and served until decommissioned on 31 August 1973. After a further period in reserve, she was stricken on 30 September 1978 and sold to National Metal for scrapping in March 1981.

Manchester was another ship not to see war service, in this case because she did not commission until the autumn of 1946. She was the last of the class to remain in commission in an unconverted state, and saw service during the Korean War, making three operational tours. She was paid off on 27 June 1956 and stricken from reserve status on 1 April 1960. Sold for scrapping on 31 October that year, the ship was scrapped at Richmond, California, in 1961.

Above: *Cleveland* on 7 May 1943. (USN)

Vicksburg joined CruDiv 14 on completion, but was used for training duties until the end of 1944 and did not reach Pearl Harbor until mid-January 1945. She joined TF54 in February for the assault on Iwo Jima, where she took part in the preliminary shore bombardments. In March, as part of TF58.1, she covered the carrier strikes against Kyushu, the southernmost of the main Japanese islands, and against targets in the Inland Sea. She was still with TF58 when attacks were launched against Okinawa in April, but in July was with TF95 when sorties were made into the East China Sea as well as in support of the Okinawa operations. She also participated in the attacks on Wake Island in July and August, and, at the surrender, joined the fleet in Japanese waters. She left Japan in mid-September, arriving back in the USA on 15 October. Her postwar service was brief, and the ship paid off on 30 June 1947. She was not converted to a *CLG*, and remained in reserve until stricken on 1 October 1962, then being used for test purposes and finally sold for scrapping on 25 August 1964 and broken up by the National Metal & Steel Corp at Terminal Island, California, where she arrived on 19 September 1964.

Duluth served on the Atlantic coast until ordered to the Pacific, sailing for Pearl Harbor on 7 April 1945. A unit of CruDiv 18, she served as escort to the carrier groups of the 5th Fleet. However, she was damaged in the typhoon incident of 5 June and retired to Guam for repairs, returning to TF38 in mid-July for the final carrier raids against the Japanese mainland. On 16 September she entered Tokyo Bay, but left for home at the

beginning of October. Postwar she was operational in the Pacific fleet until decommissioned on 25 June 1949. *Duluth* was sold for breaking up on 14 November 1960.

Miami commissioned at the end of December 1943 and operated on the east coast until 16 April 1944, when she sailed for the Pacific, arriving at Pearl Harbor on 6 May. She was a member of CruDiv 14, and in June participated in the carrier raids against the Mariana and Vulcan Islands as a unit of TG58.4. Strikes were carried out against Saipan, Tinian, Iwo Jima, Chichijima, Hahajima and Pagan. In August and September *Miami* was with TG38.2 for raids on Palau, Mindanao and Luzon, and in October the raids were against targets in Formosa and Okinawa, as well as the Philippines, in preparation for the landings at Leyte. She was still involved in attacks on targets in the Philippines in December, operating from Ulithi and supporting the Luzon landings with TG38.3 and covering raids against Formosa and the Southern Ryukus. Further raids were made against the Indo-Chinese coast and Hong Kong in January 1945. February saw the first major raid against Tokyo, when she was with TG58.1, and on 2 March she was one of a group of cruisers (*Vicksburg*, *Vincennes* and *San Diego*) shelling the Ryukyu Islands. In March she was also involved in screening the carrier raids against Kyushu and the Inland Sea, but by April the main thrust of attacks was against Okinawa. However, that month the ship was recalled to the USA for refit, which was not completed until a few days before the end of the war. *Miami* sailed for Pearl Harbor at the end of August, and participated in occupation duties

until the autumn. On 10 December 1945 the ship arrived back on the west coast, and on 30 June 1947 decommissioned to reserve. *Miami* was stricken on 1 September 1961 and sold for scrapping on 26 July 1962, to be broken up at Richmond, California.

Astoria joined CruDiv 14 after completion, but in the summer of 1944 was reassigned to CruDiv 17. By December she was with TG38.2 in support of the Luzon landings in the Philippines, the carriers hitting targets in China and Formosa. In February/March the ship was part of TG58.3 for attacks against Tokyo, the Japanese mainland, and in support of the Iwo Jima landings. The following month she was one of the units committed to the Okinawa campaign until July, when attacks were resumed on the Japanese mainland. These were continued to the end of the war. Postwar *Astoria* remained in service until 1949, when she was decommissioned on 1 July. She was another of the class never to recommission, and was finally stricken on 1 November 1969. *Astoria* was sold for scrapping on 12 January 1971 to the Nicolai Joffe Corp. of Beverley Hills, California, and broken up at Richmond, California.

Oklahoma City arrived at Pearl Harbor at the beginning of May 1945 to serve with the 3rd Fleet off Okinawa and on carrier group screening in the final raids against the Japanese mainland until the end of the war. After occupation duties, she returned home and served until decommissioned on 30 June 1947. Selected for conversion to a guided-missile cruiser, she recommissioned on 7 September 1960 as *CLG 5*, and served until paid off on 15 December 1979. She was then assigned as a long-term target ship to the Naval Air Warfare

Center Weapons Division, Point Mugu, California, and in 1993 was berthed at Port Hueneme in that State.

Little Rock saw no war service, and continued in postwar operation until paid off on 24 June 1949. On 23 May 1957 she was reclassified as *CLG 4* and converted to a guided-missile cruiser, recommissioning on 3 June 1960. She finally paid off again on 15 December 1979 and was stricken on 22 November 1976. The ship was towed to Buffalo, New York, on 15 July 1977 to become a museum ship.

Galveston was suspended on 24 April 1946, when virtually complete, being towed straight into reserve. On 4 February 1956 she was reclassified as *GLG 93*, and finally commissioned on 28 May 1958 as *CLG 3*. She remained in service until decommissioned on 25 May 1970, being stricken on 21 December 1973.

Amsterdam joined CruDiv 18 in the Pacific in June 1945 and saw some limited action against the Japanese mainland in the closing stages of the war. She was decommissioned on 30 June 1947, and remained in reserve until stricken on 2 January 1971.

Portsmouth commissioned just before the end of the war, but saw no operational service. She remained in commission until paid off on 15 June

1949, then languished in reserve until stricken on 1 December 1970.

Wilkes-Barre commissioned in the summer of 1944 and transferred to the Pacific in October, arriving at Pearl Harbor in mid-November. After carrying out training, she joined CruDiv 17 at Ulithi in December and sailed with TF38 to operate off Formosa and the Philippines on 30 December 1944. The early part of January was spent in the South China Sea, and at this time the ship participated in the Lingayen landings. Towards the end of the month she covered carrier raids against targets in Formosa again, then returned to Ulithi, when TF38 became TF58. During February she escorted the Tokyo raid with TG58.3 and supported the operations off Iwo Jima, Chichijima and Hahajima. March saw another raid against Japan, targets on the southern island of Kyushu being hit by the carrier's aircraft. By April TG58.3, of which *Wilkes-Barre* was a part, had been committed to the Okinawa campaign, which continued throughout the month. During the summer she continued to screen the carrier groups on their raids against the Japanese mainland until the surrender. The cruiser arrived in Tokyo Bay on 3 September 1945. After service in Japanese waters the ship sailed for Korea on 9 November, then transferred to China, being

based at Tsingtau until the end of the year. She arrived back on the US west coast on 31 January 1946. Her postwar service was brief, the ship being decommissioned on 9 October 1947. After more than twenty years in reserve, she was stricken on 15 January 1971 and finally sunk off the Florida Keys as a breakwater and artificial reef on 12/13 May 1972, following underwater tests.

Atlanta joined CruDiv 18 and saw limited active service with TF38 in the final attacks on Okinawa, the Ryukus and the Japanese mainland before participating in occupation duties until the end of September. She paid off on 1 July 1949 and was stricken from reserve on 1 October 1962. Reclassified as *IX304* for experimental purposes on 15 May 1964, the ship was used for shock testing until stricken once more on 1 April 1970. She was finally scuttled on 1 October 1970.

Dayton was another of the class just too late to see much war service, participating in the final carrier raids on the Japanese mainland from July 1945. She was back in US home waters by November that year, and subsequently saw service in the Mediterranean until decommissioned on 1 March 1949. Stricken from reserve after more than twenty years, she was sold to Boston Metals and broken up at Baltimore, Maryland, in 1962.

FARGO CLASS

Ship	Builder	Laid Down	Launched	Completed	Fate
CL106 Fargo	New York Sbdg	23 Aug 43	25 Feb 45	9 Dec 45	Stricken 1 Mar 1970
CL107 Huntington	New York Sbdg	4 Oct 43	8 Apr 45	23 Feb 46	Stricken 1 Sept 1961
CL108 Newark	New York Sbdg	17 Jan 44	1945		Cancelled 12 August 1945
CL109 New Haven	New York Sbdg	28 Feb 44	not launched		Cancelled 12 Aug 1945
CL110 Buffalo	New York Sbdg	3 Apr 44	not launched		Cancelled 12 Aug 1945
CL111 Wilmington	Cramp	5 Mar 45	not launched		Cancelled 12 Aug 1945
CL112 Vallejo	New York Sbdg	not laid			Cancelled 5 Oct 1944
CL113 Helena	New York Sbdg	not laid			Cancelled 5 Oct 1944
CL114 Roanoke	New York Sbdg	not laid			Cancelled 5 Oct 1944
CL115 –	New York Sbdg	not laid			Cancelled 5 Oct 1944
CL116 Tallahasse	Newport News	31 Jan 44	not launched		Cancelled 12 Aug 1945
CL117 Cheyenne	Newport News	29 May 44	not launched		Cancelled 12 Aug 1945
CL118 Chattanooga	Newport News	9 Oct 44	not launched		Cancelled 12 Aug 1945

All details were similar to the *Cleveland* Class except that this class had only a single funnel.

Design By 1942 it was desired to improve on existing cruiser designs, based on war experience to date. These improvements were in the main concerned with reduced topweight and better internal subdivision. The 6in turrets were lowered by about a foot, the forward and aft shelter decks extended to enclose the forward and after turret barbettes, the 5in wing gunhouses were lowered

to the upper deck, and the 40mm mountings lowered. Internally, there were significant changes. The fire rooms were altered so that all uptakes vented to a single funnel, and the superstructure was altered accordingly, with a corresponding benefit in the fields of fire for the AA guns. Aft, the hangar was halved in size to allow extra berthing space for the crew, and, in consequence, these ships could accommodate only two floatplanes. The bridge structures were altered, lowered and rearranged, as were the directors.

Plans to build all sixteen ships of the FY43 programme, i.e. *CL103* to *CL118*, ordered on 7 August 1942, and those of FY44 ordered 15 June 1943 (*CL143-147*), and 14 June 1943 (*CL148-149*) to this design were abandoned when the consequent delays were taken into consideration. As a result, *CL103* to *CL105* were built to the existing *Cleveland* design. However, four, *CL112* to *CL115*, were cancelled on 5 October 1944 in favour of the later *Worcester* design (*CL144* to *CL147*). Of the remainder, only *Fargo* and *Huntington* were completed, the rest being cancelled when the end of the Pacific war was in sight. Of the units cancelled in 1945, all had been laid down but only *Newark* had been launched. This vessel was used for shock tests March to July 1948, but the remainder were broken up on the slips. *Newark* was sold for scrapping on 2 April 1949.

Modifications The two completed ships were not commissioned until well after the war, and their modifications are therefore outside the scope of this volume.

Service As noted above, these cruisers saw no war service. *Fargo* was decommissioned on 14 February 1950 and remained in reserve until stricken on 1 March 1970. *Huntington* paid off on 15 June 1949 and was stricken from reserve on 1 September 1961. She was sold to the Lipsett Division of the Luria Bros. & Co., and arrived at Kearny, New Jersey, for scrapping in June 1962.

Right: *Fargo.* (Floating Drydock)

BALTIMORE CLASS

Ship	Builder	Laid Down	Launched	Completed	Fate
CA68 Baltimore	Bethlehem, Quincy	26 May 41	28 Jul 42	15 Apr 43	Stricken 15 1971
CA69 Boston	Bethlehem, Quincy	31 Jun 41	26 Aug 42	30 Jun 43	Stricken 4 Jan 1974
CA70 Canberra (ex *Pittsburgh*)	Bethlehem, Quincy	3 Sep 41	19 Apr 43	14 Oct 43	Stricken 31 Jul 1978
CA71 Quincy (ex *St Paul*)	Bethlehem, Quincy	9 Oct 41	23 Jun 43	15 Dec 43	Stricken 1 Oct 1973
CA72 Pittsburgh (ex *Albany*)	Bethlehem, Quincy	3 Feb 43	22 Feb 44	10 Oct 44	Stricken 1 Jul 1973
CA73 St Paul (ex *Rochester*)	Bethlehem, Quincy	3 Feb 43	16 Sep 44	17 Feb 45	Stricken 31 Jul 1978
CA74 Columbus	Bethlehem, Quincy	28 Jun 43	30 Nov 44	8 Jun 45	Stricken 9 Aug 1976
CA75 Helena (ex *Des Moines*)	Bethlehem, Quincy	9 Sep 43	28 Apr 45	4 Sep 45	Stricken 1 Jan 1974
CA122 Oregon City	Bethlehem, Quincy	8 Apr 44	9 Jun 45	16 Feb 46	Stricken 1 Nov 1970
CA123 Albany	Bethlehem, Quincy	6 Mar 44	30 Jun 45	11 Jun 46	Stricken
CA124 Rochester	Bethlehem, Quincy	29 May 44	28 Aug 45	20 Dec 46	Stricken 1 Oct 1973
CA125 Northampton	Bethlehem, Quincy	31 Aug 44	27 Jan 51	7 Mar 53	Stricken 31 Dec 1977
CA126 Cambridge	Bethlehem, Quincy	16 Dec 44	not launched		Cancelled 12 Aug 1945
CA127 Bridgeport	Bethlehem, Quincy	13 Jan 45	not launched		Cancelled 12 Aug 1945
CA128 Kansas City	Bethlehem, Quincy	not laid			Cancelled 12 Aug 1945
CA129 Tulsa	Bethlehem, Quincy	not laid			Cancelled 12 Aug 1945
CA130 Bremerton	New York Sbdg	1 Feb 43	2 Jul 44	29 Apr 45	Stricken 1 Oct 1973
CA131 Fall River	New York Sbdg	12 Apr 43	13 Aug 44	1 Jul 45	Stricken 19 Feb 1971
CA132 Macon	New York Sbdg	14 Jun 43	15 Oct 44	26 Aug 45	Stricken 1 Nov 1969
CA133 Toledo	New York Sbdg	13 Sep 43	5 May 45	27 Oct 46	Stricken 1 Jan 1974
CA135 Los Angeles	Philadelphia NY	28 Jul 43	20 Aug 44	22 Jul 45	Stricken 1 Jan 1974
CA136 Chicago	Philadelphia NY	28 Jul 43	20 Aug 44	10 Jan 45	Stricken 1 Jan 1974
CA137 Norfolk	Philadelphia NY	27 Dec 44	Not launched		Cancelled 12 Aug 1945
CA138 Scranton	Philadelphia NY	27 Dec 44	Not launched		Cancelled 12 Aug 1945

Displacement: 14,472 tons/14,703 tonnes (standard); 17,031 tons/17,303 tonnes (full load).
Length: 673ft 5in/205.26m (oa); 664ft/202.39m (wl).

Beam: 70ft 10in/21.59m; Draught: 24ft/7.32m (mean).
Machinery: 4-shaft General Electric geared turbines; 4 Babcock & Wilcox boilers.

Performance: 120,000shp=33kts; Bunkerage: 2,250 tons oil fuel max.
Range: 10,000nm at 15kts.
Protection: 4in-6in main belt; 2½in deck; 6⅓in barbettes; turrets, 8in front, 3in roof, 2in-3¾in sides.
Guns: nine 8in (3x3); twelve 5in (6x2); forty-eight 40mm (11x4, 2x2); twenty-four 20mm.
Torpedoes: nil.
Aircraft: four, two catapults.
Complement: 2,039

Design Initial design studies for a new heavy cruiser were started as early as September 1939, as an alternative to the abandoned 8,000-ton *CL55* design. The last heavy cruiser, *Wichita*, suffered from stability problems, and it was intended that any new design would address this defect. Thus the new design took the *Wichita* and increased the beam by two feet. However, this did not go far enough for the General Board, who wished to see a secondary battery of 5in/38 all in twin gunhouses and the machinery rearranged as per the *Clevelands*. The waterline belt was to be extended forward, but otherwise the protective scheme was to be as in *Wichita*. Wartime experience in Europe had demonstrated the danger of the magnetic mine, and this as well as other war feedback led to the tweaking of the design as time went by, so that, when the contracts were placed for the first four ships on 1 July 1940, the ships differed somewhat from first intentions. Four more ships, *CA72* to *CA75*, were ordered on 9 September 1940, and a final batch of sixteen

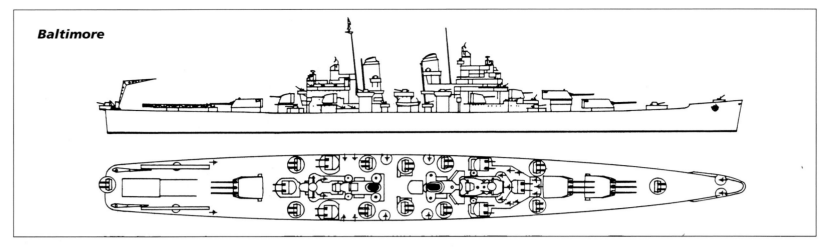

Baltimore

ships, *CA122* to *CA138*, on 7 August 1942 for FY43.

The hull dimensions ended up rather more than just a modification of *Wichita*, as length was increased by no less than 65ft and, more importantly, beam by over 9ft to the obvious benefit of stability, which allowed a much greater margin for future growth. The protective scheme, which was

Below: *Baltimore.* (Floating Drydock)

not too dissimilar from that of *Wichita*, did not benefit to the full extent of the weight savings from the earlier ship, as much of that tonnage was put to strengthening the hull. A 6in main belt, tapered to 4in at its lower edge, covered the machinery spaces, reducing to 3in tapered to 2in at the lower edge fore and aft of the machinery spaces. From *CA72* the main belt was extended forward from frame 57 to frame 52, to protect the radio rooms. The main armoured deck was 2½in

thick, with end bulkheads between 5in and 6in thick. A conning tower with a wall thickness of 6in was incorporated in the original design, but this was omitted from the first six ships, and later ships had a conning tower 6½in thick. The total weight of armouring was 1,790 tons, representing 12.9 per cent of the standard displacement.

The main machinery was increased in power over that of *Wichita*, since the new ship's displacement was that much greater. Thus she was given 120,000shp, an increase of 20 per cent for a designed speed of 34kts. There were other more fundamental differences, however, one of the most important being the use of high-pressure steam boilers, which had been adopted for *Cleveland*, although this heavy cruiser had slightly reduced pressures in comparison with the light cruiser. The boilers were each in their own fire room, with the forward pair separated from the after pair by the forward turbine room on the unit principle. A further advance was the greatly increased generating capacity, for better damage control and to cater for the spiralling demands of RPC.

The 8in gun was the 55cal Mk 12 or Mk 15 in triple turrets having an elevation of 41°. These guns were similar to those of the earlier heavy cruisers. The secondary armament of 5in/38 was mounted in six twin gunhouses disposed in the pattern of *Cleveland*, while the light AA, originally planned at four of the quadruple 1.1in mountings, was changed early on to four quad 40mm. No torpedoes were carried. Four aircraft could be carried, with two catapults, but the hangar could accommodate only two aircraft.

Modifications As the first of this class was not completed until the spring of 1943, most of the early war experiences had already been incorporated in the design. As a result they did not receive any major alterations in their wartime careers. Internally, cruising turbines were abandoned from

Above: *Helena* in 1945. (WSS)

CA72 and removed from the earlier units. The 40mm outfit was increased while the vessels were under construction, and the ships commissioned with a total of twelve quadruple 40mm (*CA68* to *CA71*) or eleven and two twin (*CA72* onwards). In the case of the latter group, the single centre-line crane prevented the installation of the quad at the extreme stern. From the outset, 20mm Oerlikons were available, and the authorised outfit was 28 guns. The conning tower was reduced in thickness in *CA68* to *CA73*, but after objections, and because of the large reserve of stability, the step was taken of armouring the pilot house to 6½in armour.

In 1942 the design was modified in a similar way to the *Cleveland* Class, but not quite as extensively, given the better weight situation with the heavy cruisers. The boiler uptakes were trunked into one funnel, the superstructure shortened and the bridges rearranged. The directors were repositioned and the stern lines modified to permit a single crane aft. The hangar was also reduced in size by half. Some of these changes were also incorporated in the earlier ships; *CA72* to *CA75* had the single crane and the reduced hangar.

Plans to build the 1943 ships to this new layout were later amended because of yard design staff delays, and *CA130* to *CA136* were built as per the original two-funnel design, while *CA122* to *CA129* and *CA137* and *CA138* would complete to the new layout. In the event, the progress of the new automatic 8in gun and its obvious superiority over the Mk 12/15 led to *CA134* being reordered to the *Des Moines* design, and six were cancelled. One (*Northampton*) completed postwar in a command cruiser configuration, leaving only three ships to complete to the single-funnel design.

Service *Baltimore* and her three sisters (*Boston*, *Canberra* and *Quincy*) formed CruDiv 10 in the Pacific as they completed. *Baltimore* was in TG52.2 for the Makin landings in November 1943, and in the following month was part of carrier force TG50.1 which made a raid on Kwajalein. In January she was with TF58 as a part of TG58.4 for attacks on the Marshall Islands, hitting Wotje, Maloelap and Eniwetok between 29 January and 6 February 1944 in support of the landings on Eniwetok. In February she was involved in the raid on Truk by TF58. Towards the end of March the ship was in the Palaus, Yap and Ulithi, before participating in operations in support of the Hollandia landings. As a unit of a force of nine cruisers with destroyer support, she bombarded the Satawan Islands, south of Truk, on 30 April. Then, in May, *Baltimore* was with TG58.2 for raids on Marcus and Wake Islands. Raids on the Marianas and Vulcan Islands followed in June, TG58.1 attacking Iwo Jima, Chichijima and Hahajima between 11 and 15 June. In this month, too, she was involved in operations connected with the Saipan landings and the Battle of the Philippine Sea. In July she returned to the USA for refit, and did not rejoin operations until November, when assigned to the Third Fleet at Ulithi as part of TG38.1. She then became involved in raids against Luzon, Formosa, the Chinese coast and Okinawa until the latter end of January 1945, before participating in the first major raids against the Japanese mainland from 10 February with TG58.5. Following these operations, the ship screened attacks on Iwo Jima and then returned to raids against Japan itself and targets in the Inland Sea in March. April saw her back in the Okinawa campaign, where she remained until the late summer. After the surrender she undertook some repatriation trips and remained in Japanese waters until February 1946. *Baltimore* paid off on 8 July 1946, but recommis-

Above: *Baltimore.* (Floating Drydock)

sioned for postwar service, although she did not participate in the Korean War. She was finally decommissioned on 31 May 1956, and was stricken from reserve on 15 February 1971 and sold to Zidell Explorations Inc. of Portland, Oregon, for breaking up.

Boston, the second of the class to be commissioned, joined TF58 in January 1944 and supported the landings on Kwajalein, Majuro and Eniwetok in February. At the end of March she was operating in the Palaus and Western Carolines before covering the Hollandia landings between 21 and 24 April. At the end of the month she was with the group of cruisers and destroyers that bombarded the Satawan Islands. Marcus and Wake islands were attacked by carriers screened by the cruiser during May, and raids were made against the Mariana Islands the following month, when the ship was with TG58.1. June also saw the landings on Saipan and operations in the Bonins, as well as the Battle of the Philippine Sea. The Guam landings followed, and in August and September she was part of TG38.1, making raids on the Palaus, Mindanao, Luzon and the Visayas. By October she was with the same group operating off Formosa and the Philippines, then participated in the Battle for Leyte Gulf as a unit of TG38.1, whose carrier aircraft struck at Admiral Kurita's force, sinking the cruiser *Noshiro* (q.v.) and a destroyer. The end of the year saw raids on Northern Formosa and the Ryukyu Islands, especially Okinawa. From the beginning of 1945 she participated in the carrier raids on the Chinese coast, and in the first raids against Tokyo and the Inland Sea. On 1 March *Boston* returned to the west coast for refit at Long Beach, which was

completed in early June. In the final months of the war she covered the carrier raids against targets on the Japanese mainland. After the end of hostilities the ship returned to the USA and paid off on 29 October 1946. In 1952 she began a conversion to a guided-missile cruiser, *CAG 1*, and recommissioned on 1 November 1955. Her final decommissioning was on 5 May 1970, before being stricken on 4 January 1974. She was sold to Southern Metals for breaking up on 28 March 1975.

Canberra was so named in honour of the Australian cruiser lost in action at Savo Island in 1942. She arrived in Pearl Harbor on 1 February 1944 to begin her operational service in the Pacific theatre, joining TF58 for the landings on Eniwetok. From March she was a unit of several carrier task forces, screening *Yorktown* and *Enterprise* during raids on the Palaus, Yap, Ulithi, Truk and Satawan, and shelling the latter islands as part of a cruiser and destroyer force on 30 April. In May, as part of TG58.2, she carried out raids on Marcus Island and Wake Island. By June she was in action in the Marianas and Vulcan Islands, now with TG58.1, making attacks on Guam, Iwo Jima and other islands, and taking part in the Battle of the Philippine Sea. She operated in the Philippines in August, with TF38 as part of TG38.1, when Palau, Mindanao and the Visayas were attacked. In October *Canberra* participated in carrier strikes against Formosa, Okinawa and Luzon, but during Japanese counterattacks the ship was hit in No. 4 fire room by an aircraft torpedo, and because of a damaged propeller shaft another fire room and both turbine spaces were flooded. She was successfully towed to Ulithi (by *Wichita* for two days, then by tugs), then to Manus for makeshift repair. Full

repairs were carried out at Boston Navy Yard between February and October 1945. She served only briefly postwar, and was decommissioned on 7 March 1947. Reclassified as *CAG 2* on 4 January 1952, *Canberra* recommissioned on 15 June 1956 for further service. She was finally paid off on 2 February 1970 and stricken on 31 July 1978. The ship was sold to National Metal for breaking up.

Quincy was the only ship of the class to see much wartime service in the Atlantic, serving with TF22 from March 1944. The next month she sailed for the UK and joined the 12th Fleet in European waters for the invasion of Normandy, where she was a component of Force A, the support force for Utah Beach. After carrying out shore bombardments against German positions until early July, the ship was ordered to the Mediterranean to operate from Palermo that month. For the landings in the south of France, Operation Dragoon, she was part of the Support Force as a unit of TG86.4, carrying out shore support bombardments. However, the ship returned to the USA in September to refit at Boston until October, after which she carried out a cruise to the Great Bitter lakes with the President aboard for conferences with Arab leaders. *Quincy* arrived back in home waters in February 1945 and was reassigned to the Pacific Fleet, joining CruDiv 10 off Ulithi on 11 April 1945. For the last few months of the war she screened carrier task forces, bombarded Okinawa and attacked the Japanese islands with TF58. In July she began a second tour of carrier raids against Japanese mainland targets, then participated in occupational duties in Japanese waters after the end of hostilities. On her return to the USA she was paid off on 19 October 1946, but recommissioned on

31 January 1952 for the Korean War, serving with the Seventh Fleet. She was finally paid off on 2 July 1954 and stricken from reserve on 1 October 1973, being sold in 1974 to American Ship Dismantlers for breaking up at Portland, Oregon.

Pittsburgh commissioned for CruDiv 19 as Flagship in the Pacific, arriving at Ulithi on 13 February 1945, where she joined TG58.2. That month she covered attacks on Iwo Jima and the Japanese Islands, and, in the following month, raids on Nansei Shoto and Kyushu. During a raid on Japan on 14 March, Japanese bombers badly hit the carrier *Franklin*, which was escorted away by *Pittsburgh*. Between March and May the ship was assigned to the Okinawa campaign, but early in June she lost all her bow as far back as the forward 8in turret during a typhoon, but managed to put into Guam, where provisional repairs were made. Full repair in the USA was carried out at Puget Sound, and lasted until September 1945. The ship paid off on 7 March 1946, but recommissioned once more on 25 September 1951, though she was not deployed to the Korean War. She paid off for the last time on 28 August 1956 and remained in reserve status until stricken on 1 July 1973.

St Paul also served with CruDiv 19 in the Pacific, but as she only arrived at Pearl Harbor in early June 1945 she saw only limited operational service with TF38 during the final carrier raids on the Japanese mainland between July and August. Postwar the ship served in Chinese waters until the end of 1946, then returned home, but carried out a second tour at Shanghai between March and November 1947. *St Paul* made three opera-

tional tours off Korea during that war, and fired the last salvoes there in July 1953. She remained operational into the early 1970s, including service off Vietnam, until decommissioned on 30 April 1971. After a period in reserve the ship was stricken on 31 July 1978 and scrapped from June 1980.

Columbus commissioned just before the end of the Pacific war and saw no active service. Postwar she remained operational until paid off on 8

May 1959 for conversion into a guided-missile cruiser, *CG 12*. After recommissioning on 1 December 1962, she served in that role until paid off on 31 January 1975. She was finally stricken on 9 August 1976 and was sold for breaking up the following August.

Helena also commissioned too late for war service during the Second World War, but did see service in the Korean War. She remained operational until paid off on 29 June 1963, to be stricken on 1 January 1974. On 13 November 1974 the ship was sold to the Levin Metal Corp. of San Jose, California, for scrapping.

Bremerton served postwar, being decommissioned on 9 April 1948. On 23 November 1951 she recommissioned for the Korean War then remained operational until paid off again on 29 July 1960. She was stricken from reserve on 1 October 1973.

Fall River had only a brief active career, being decommissioned on 31 October 1947 and spending the next 24 years in reserve. She was stricken on 19 February 1971 and sold to Zidell Explorations for scrapping at Portland, Oregon, in 1972.

Macon commissioned in the final days of the Second World War and remained operational postwar until 12 April 1950. She recommissioned again shortly afterwards because of the Korean War, but remained in the Atlantic with periods in the Mediterranean until paid off again on 10 March 1961. She was stricken from reserve on 1 November 1969.

Toledo commissioned well over twelve months after the end of the Second World War. She did, however, see action during the Korean conflict. She was paid off on 21 May 1960 and stricken from reserve on 1 January 1974. On 13 October 1974 the ship was sold to the National Metal and Steel Corp. of Terminal Island, California, for breaking up.

Los Angeles commissioned before the end of the Second World War, but was too late to see active service. On 21 January 1947 she was decommissioned, and remained in reserve until recommissioned for the Korean War on 27 January 1951. She made two tours off Korea, then remained in service until paid off for the last time on 15 November 1963 and stricken on 1 January 1974.

Chicago commissioned some six months before *Los Angeles* and arrived at Pearl Harbor to join CruDiv 21 in time to participate in the final bombardments of the Japanese mainland between July and August 1945. After further service in Japan and China, she was decommissioned on 6 June 1947. On 1 November 1958 the ship was redesignated *CG 11* and converted to a guided-missile cruiser, recommissioning on 2 May 1964. She operated in that role until paid off once more on 1 March 1980.

The three ships completed to the modified design did not commission until 1946. *Oregon City* had a very brief service life and was decommissioned on 15 December 1947. She spent over twenty years in reserve before being stricken on 1 November 1970. *Albany* was one of the class converted into a guided-missile cruiser, and was finally decommissioned on 29 August 1980. *Rochester* served during the Korean War and remained operational until decommissioned on 15 August 1961. She was stricken on 1 October 1973, then sold to Zidell Explorations of Portland, Oregon, for breaking up.

DES MOINES CLASS

Ship	Builder	Laid Down	Launched	Completed	Fate
CA134 Des Moines	Bethlehem, Quincy	28 May 45	27 Sep 46	16 Nov 48	Stricken 1 Jul 1991
CA139 Salem	Bethlehem, Quincy	4 Jul 45	27 Mar 47	14 May 49	Stricken 1 July 1991
CA140 Dallas	Bethlehem, Quincy	15 Oct 45	not launched		Cancelled 6 Jun 1946
CA148 Newport News	Newport News	1 Oct 45	6 Mar 48	29 Jan 49	Stricken 31 Jul 1978

Displacement: 17,255 tons/17,531 tonnes (standard); 20,934 tons/21,268 tonnes (full load).
Length: 716ft 6in/218.39m (oa); 700ft/213.36m (wl).
Beam: 75ft 4in/22.96m; Draught: 26ft/7.92m (mean).
Machinery: 4-shaft General Electric geared turbines; 4 Babcock & Wilcox boilers.

Performance: 120,000shp=33kts; Bunkerage: 3,006 tons oil fuel.
Range: 10,500nm at 15kts.
Protection: 4in-6in main belt; 3¾in main deck; 1in upper deck; 6⅓in barbettes; turrets, 8in front; 4in roof, 3¾in sides; 5½-6½in pilot house.

Guns: nine 8in (3x3); twelve 5in (6x2); 3in (12x2); twenty-four 20mm.
Torpedoes: nil.
Aircraft: four, two catapults.
Complement: 1,799.

Design The drawback to the 8in gun was its relatively slow rate of fire, which had proved a distinct handicap in the close-quarters night actions fought in the Solomon Islands. This had led to the diversion of the heavy cruisers to the Aleutian campaign, leaving the fast-moving islands campaign to the destroyers and light cruisers. To redress this defect, a new rapid-fire 8in gun was designed, employing a sliding

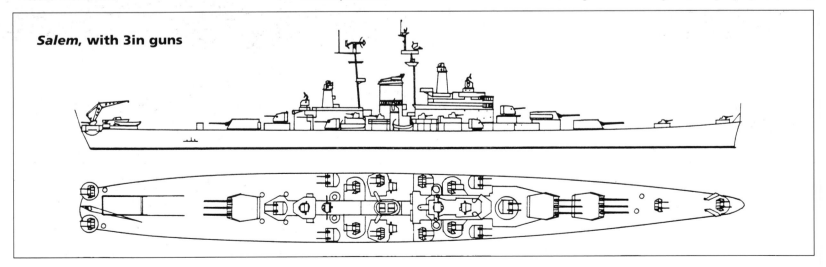

Salem, with 3in guns

Above: *Des Moines* as completed, in November 1948. (USN)

wedge breech and brass cartridge case. This gun was expected to fire seven rounds per minute, as against three for current guns, and to be fully automatic. Proposed in the spring of 1943, this gun did not become available until towards the end of 1945, eventually emerging as the 8in 55cal Mk 16. Plans to mount this weapon in the *Oregon City* design came to naught as a result of the extensive design changes found necessary, probably fortunately as it turned out, because the estimated weights of the new triple mounting had been greatly underestimated. Alternative plans to fit a twin turret in four of the *CA122* to *CA138* series and all of *CA139* to

CA142 also foundered. Instead, a new design specifically for the rapid-fire triple turret was prepared.

The original design requirements foresaw an improved *Oregon City* with increased deck armour on the lines of *Worcester* to give better protection against bombs. The new turrets caused considerable problems in their installation, as they were heavier than anticipated, with larger-diameter barbettes, and needed much larger ammunition spaces for the increased rate of fire. This in turn necessitated an increase in length of the armour belt, which, together with the additional bomb deck, amounted to an extra 695 tons. Further growth caused by increasingly more sophisticated fire controls for the HA function

soon led to a projected increase in displacement to 16,000 tons and, later, more.

The hull of the new ship was over 40ft longer than that of the *Oregon City*, and had an extra 5½ft of beam. Her displacement as finalised was 19,930 tons. The protective scheme, apart from the introduction of an upper armoured deck designed to trigger bomb fuses before they struck the main armoured deck, was not substantially different from that of the *Baltimore*. The waterline belt was 6in thick and 10 ft deep, tapering to 4in at its lower edge. The main armoured deck was 3½in thick, 1in greater than *Baltimore*, and the upper deck was 1in thick. The armouring of the main turrets was increased on the roofs to 4in, and on the rear to 2in. There were five armoured zones within the hull; armoured bulkheads inside the armoured box to limit damage to adjacent compartments in the event of a heavy hit in any compartment. In all, some 2,189 tons were devoted to protection, or 12.6 per cent of the standard displacement, virtually the same as in *Baltimore*.

The main machinery remained the standard four-shaft geared turbine installation, but with the designed power remaining at 120,000shp, the maximum speed being reduced to 33½kts. The boilers and turbines were similar to those of the preceding heavy cruiser. However, the general arrangement of the machinery spaces was different, each of the three forward machinery spaces containing a boiler and a turbine. The fourth machinery unit featured a separate turbine room and fire room, as the three shafts from the forward units precluded any other arrangement.

Her main armament comprised the new 8in Mk 16 gun as mentioned above, mounted in three triple turrets. Each turret weighed 451 tons. The guns fired a 335lb projectile, had a maximum range of 30,050yds at 41° elevation and could load at any angle. The volume of fire was impressive; 90 shells per minute, or 13½ tons of shells. Training and elevation was electro-hydraulic. The secondary battery was the now-standard six twin 5in/38, but now with four directors. The beam guns were carried on the upper deck, only the centreline mountings being on the superstructure deck.

As originally designed, the light AA battery comprised twelve quadruple 40mm Bofors and twenty 20mm, but by the time the ships were completing it had become obvious that even a 40mm shell had difficulty in stopping a determined kamikaze, while the 20mm had proportionally less effect. As a result, the 40mm were suppressed and 3in/50 twin mountings specified instead, one to replace each quadruple 40mm. The 20mm were initially retained, *Des Moines* completing with ten twin mountings, but these were quickly landed. Similarly, by the time the ships entered service, the usefulness of catapulted aircraft had passed, and although the lead ship completed with catapults, only one was fully fitted, the other being incomplete. Both were landed shortly afterwards. *Salem* and her sister never had them.

After some juggling with the cruiser programme, orders were placed for twelve ships in total, of which *CA134* was already on order with New York Shipbuilding Corp as a *Baltimore/Oregon City* type. Her contract was transferred to Bethlehem, Quincy, and reordered on 25 September 1943. *CA139* to *CA142* had been ordered from Bethlehem as *Oregon City* Class ships on 14 June 1943, but were built to the new design, while *CA150* to *CA153* were ordered from New York Shipbuilding Corp. to the new design on 22 February 1945. Three further ships were added; *CA143*, *CA148* and *CA149* had originally been programmed as light cruisers, and were ordered from New York Shipbuilding Corp (*CA143*) and Cramp (the other pair) on 15 June 1943. However, the approaching end of the war caused alterations to the building programmes, and the last four ships, *Dallas* (*CA150*) and *CA151-153*, were cancelled on 28 March 1945. At the end of the war, work was suspended on *CA142*, *CA143* and *CA149* on 12 August 1945, but the remaining four continued. (*CA140* had now taken the name *Dallas* in place of the cancelled *CA150*.) The suspended ships were cancelled at the end of 1945, and *CA140*, the least advanced of the remaining five, was cancelled on 7 January 1946 to leave a four-ship division. However, on 27 May 1946 a new act allowed only those ships over 20 per cent complete to be finished, and, as *Dallas* was only some 7.8 per cent complete, she was cancelled on 6 June 1946.

Modifications None within the scope of this volume.

Service None of this class completed in time for war service, and they entered service well after the end of the conflict. They were extensively used as Fleet Flagships during their careers. None saw service in the Korean War, but *Newport News* made two tours to Vietnam, where she fired her guns in anger.

Des Moines was decommissioned on 14 July 1961, and *Salem* on 30 January 1959. Both were finally stricken on 9 July 1991. *Newport News*, the last heavy cruiser in service, was decommissioned on 27 June 1975. She was stricken on 31 July 1978 and sold to Southern Scrap Metals, arriving at New Orleans, Louisiana, for breaking up in March 1993, and had been virtually finished by the autumn of 1994.

Des Moines is still (as of December 1994) extant at the Philadelphia Navy Yard, laid up in reserve, while *Salem* has been transferred to the US Naval Shipbuilding Museum at Quincy, Massachusetts.

ALASKA CLASS

Ship	Builder	Laid Down	Launched	Completed	Fate
CB1 Alaska	New York Sbdg	17 Dec 41	15 Aug 43	17 Jun 44	Stricken 1 Jun 1960
CB2 Guam	New York Sbdg	2 Feb 42	12 Nov 43	17 Sep 44	Stricken 1 Jun 1960
CB3 Hawaii	New York Sbdg	20 Dec 43	3 Nov 45		Stricken 9 Jun 1958
CB4 Philippines	New York Sbdg	not laid			Cancelled 24 Jun 1943
CB5 Puerto Rico	New York Sbdg	not laid			Cancelled 24 Jun 1943
CB6 Samoa	New York Sbdg	not laid			Cancelled 24 Jun 1943

Displacement: 29,779 tons/30,255 tonnes (standard); 34,253 tons/34,800 tonnes (full load).

Length: 808ft 6in/246.43m (oa); 791ft 6in/241.25m (wl).

Beam: 91ft 1in/27.76m; Draught: 31ft 10in/9.70m (mean).

Machinery: 4-shaft General Electric geared turbines; 8 Babcock & Wilcox boilers.

Performance: 150,000shp=33kts Bunkerage: 3,619 tons oil fuel.

Range: 12,000nm at 15kts.

Protection: 5in-9in main belt; 3.8in-4in main deck; 1.4in upper deck; 11in-13in barbettes; turrets, 12⅘in front, 5in roof, 5¼in-6in sides; 10.6in CT.

Guns: nine 12in (3x3); twelve 5in (6x2); fifty-six 40mm (14x4); thirty-four 20mm.

Torpedoes: nil.

Aircraft: four, two catapults.

Complement: 1,517.

Design The origins of this class lay in the breakdown of treaty limitations at the end of the 1930s, the advent of the so-called pocket battleship in Germany, which threatened all other cruisers, and the possibility of a super cruiser being developed secretly in Japan. The USA, with its commitments in the Pacific and a possible complication of German activity in the Atlantic, viewed such scenarios with alarm. The government was therefore interested in a 'cruiser killer', and thoughts on this subject surfaced as early as 1938. Very early on, these studies were concerned with ships armed with 12in guns. Despite much discussion, no such ship was authorised before the US entered the war, although by the end of 1939 a 12in-gunned ship was one of the three main types under consideration for an expanded cruiser programme, the others being designs which subsequently became the *Baltimore*s and *Cleveland*s. One of the other tasks now being associated with the large cruiser was aircraft carrier escort. By this time the European war refuelled fears of German domination of the Atlantic, and more intelligence reports from Japan indicated that that nation was,

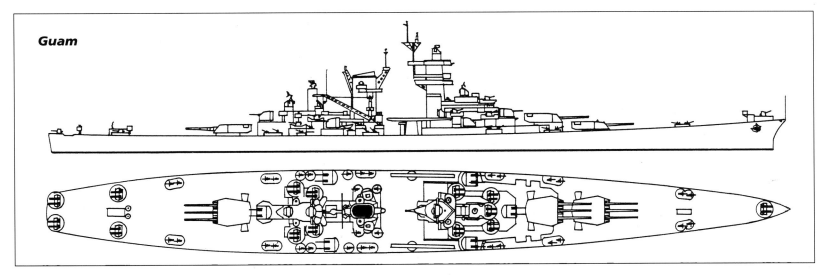

Guam

in fact, constructing large cruisers. Design studies continued with some urgency, and a whole spectrum of layouts was discussed until the design was finalised in mid-1941.

The final design had a standard displacement of 27,500 tons and carried nine 12in guns at 33.4kts. The armour scheme included a 9½in waterline belt which, for a cruiser, was unusual in that it was sloped at 10°. This covered both machinery and magazine spaces, endowing pro-

Below: *Alaska,* July 1944. (USN)

tection against 12in hits beyond 23,500yds at 90° to the beam. It was tapered to 5in at its bottom edge, and carried up to the second deck between the end bulkheads. The horizontal protection consisted of an upper deck of 1.4in to act as a bomb fuser. The main armoured deck was 2.8in thick inboard and 3¾in outboard. There was no underwater protection, and no torpedo bulkhead. Armoured bulkheads 10.6in thick closed off the armoured carapace. The total weight of armour and protective plating amounted to 4,720 tons, equivalent to 16.4 per cent, rather more than that

of the heavy cruisers, c.f. nearly 40 per cent for the battleship *North Carolina* and a similar figure for the German *Scharnhorst*, while the British *Hood* had a figure of about 30 per cent. Thus, from the armour and speed points of view, they were battlecruisers in any other navy. To the USN, however, they were merely large cruisers.

The main machinery exhibited a mixture of battleship and cruiser practice, and was similar to that of the *Essex* Class carriers. Trials, however, were disappointing, *Alaska* making only 32.71kts on 33,148 tons with 154,846shp.

Above: *Alaska* in June 1944 at her builder's yard. (Floating Drydock)

The main armament was the 12in/50 Mk 8/0, which fired a 1,140lb shell to a maximum range of 38,573yds at an elevation of 45°. Each triple turret weighed about 930 tons. The range of these guns necessitated a much higher director than those in the 8in cruisers; hence the tower foremast. The secondary armament consisted of twelve 5in/39 in twin gunhouses disposed two on each beam and two on the centreline, as in other cruisers. For the heavy AA battery, the standard quadruple 1.1in gun had originally been selected, but the failure of this gun had been recognised well before the time these ships approached completion, and instead they were given six quad 40mm in lieu. This was increased in stages before completion, and when finished they had fourteen quadruple 40mm and thirty-four single 20mm. Finally, the ships carried the standard four floatplanes, with two catapults, the latter being shipped amidships in a reversion to early cruiser practice.

Six ships were ordered from New York Shipbuilders on 9 September 1940 under the Fleet Expansion Program of 19 July 1940. However, steel shortages forced the suspension of all but the first two on 20 May 1942. The suspension of *Hawaii* was lifted on 25 May 1943, and the ship laid down. The other three were cancelled on 24 June 1943.

Modifications As the ships did not complete until very late in the war, they were not extensively modified.

Service *Alaska* joined the Pacific Fleet at Pearl Harbor on 13 January 1945, and between 15 February and 12 March was in action off Iwo Jima and covering raids against Tokyo and Yokohama with TG58.3. In March she was with TG58.4 for further raids against the Japanese mainland, concentrat-

ing on targets on Kyushu. Thereafter, the ship covered attacks against Okinawa, bombarding shore positions until the end of May. The final months of the war were occupied in covering raids into the East China Sea with TG95.2, and in attacks on the Japanese mainland. She participated in the occupation of Japan from September, and also served in Chinese and Korean waters. *Alaska* returned home and decommissioned on 17 February 1947, and lay in reserve at Bayonne, New Jersey. She never recommissioned, and was stricken on 1 June 1960. On 26 May 1961 the ship was sold to Lipsett Inc. of New Jersey for scrapping, and arrived at Kearny to break up in July of that year.

Guam arrived in Pearl Harbor on 8 February 1945 and joined TF58 at Ulithi the following month. That same month she covered carrier raids against Kyushu and Shikoku with TG58.4. By April both she and her sister were involved in operations off Okinawa, and between 16 July and 7 August she was Flagship TF95 in the East China Sea. After this sortie she returned to operations at Okinawa and then acted as flagship for the occupation of Chinese ports as the 'North China Force'. In September she covered the occupation of Korea, and then returned home. *Guam* paid off on 17 February 1946. She, too, became part of the reserve fleet at Bayonne until stricken on 1 June 1960 and sold to Boston Metals Corp., Baltimore, for scrapping on 24 May 1961. The ship arrived at Newark to break up in August 1961.

Hawaii never commissioned, building having been stopped in August 1945, when the ship was 82.4 per cent complete. Various schemes were put forward for her conversion into a guided-missile ship and command ship, but they came to nothing. She was stricken on 9 June 1958 and sold to Boston Metals Inc. for breaking up on 15 April 1959, arriving at Baltimore for scrapping on 6 January 1960.

Right: *Guam.* (Floating Drydock)
Below: *Guam* in October 1944. (Floating Drydock)

WORCESTER CLASS

Ship	Builder	Laid Down	Launched	Completed	Fate
CL144 Worcester	New York Sbdg	29 Jan 45	4 Feb 47	26 Jun 48	Stricken 1 Dec 1970
CL145 Roanoke	New York Sbdg	15 May 45	16 Jun 47	4 Apr 49	Stricken 1 Dec 1970
CL146 Vallejo	New York Sbdg	not laid			Cancelled 12 Aug 1945
CL147 Gary	New York Sbdg	not laid			Cancelled 12 Aug 1945

Displacement: 14,700 tons/14,935 tonnes (standard); 17,997 tons/18,284 tonnes (full load).
Length: 679ft 6in/207.11m (oa); 664ft/202.39m (wl).
Beam: 70ft 8in/21.54m; Draught: 24ft 9in/7.92m (mean).
Machinery: 4-shaft General Electric geared turbines; 4 Babcock & Wilcox boilers.
Performance: 120,000shp=33kts; Bunkerage: 2,400 tons oil fuel.
Range: 8,000nm at 15kts.
Protection: 3in-5in main belt; 3½in main deck; 1in upper deck; 5in barbettes; turrets, 6½in front, 4in roof, 2in-3in sides.
Guns: twelve 6in (6x2); twenty-four 3in (11x2, 2x1); twelve 20mm (6x2).
Torpedoes: nil.
Aircraft: four, two catapults.
Complement: 1,401.

Design The origins of this class lay in the development of the 6in/47 DP gun, allied with the requirement, in 1941, for a ship capable of defending the fleet against attack by high-altitude bombers, possibly as a result of British experiences off Norway and Crete, and particularly the latter. While it quickly became evident that conventional bombers (as opposed to dive-bombers) could not manoeuvre fast enough to succeed against fast ships, the project continued as a vehicle for the new gun. Later, the justification was to include defence against guided bombs and missiles of the type encountered off Salerno in 1943.

The initial staff requirement, raised in May 1941, was for a ship armed with twelve 6in DP, having no side armour but with a heavily armoured deck 6in to 7in thick. Between August 1941 and the summer of 1943 at least seven sketch designs were examined, ranging from 11,500 tons to 14,200 tons and armed with eight to twelve 6in guns. None carried 5in guns. Despite the original premise of no side armour, five of the designs did have a waterline belt, this being 5in thick in the maximum instance. In only one case was the deck thickness of 6in achieved, and the schemes varied from a 1½in upper deck plus 5in over the magazines, to a 1in upper deck with 3½in over the machinery. Most of the early schemes also had the aircraft installations amidships, which was contemporary practice, but war experience had shown that it was better placed aft. Hence this demand impinged on the design process; now the hull could be flush-decked.

The final design had a twin-funnel layout, although interim designs had envisaged one trunked funnel, as in *Fargo* and *Oregon City*, and the length of the ship had been increased over that of the *Cleveland* Class light cruisers because of the space demands of the magazines to feed six quick-firing twin turrets. The protective scheme included a 370ft-long, 5in-thick waterline belt, 4ft 11in deep, tapered at its bottom edge to 3in and

Above: *Roanoke.* Note 3in guns. (Floating Drydock)

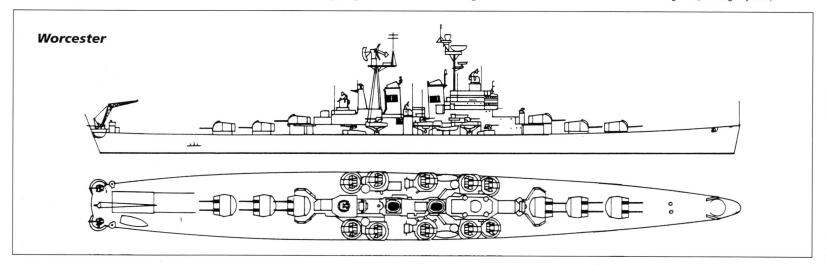

Worcester

having a total depth of 9ft 6in. Forward of this it was 2in thick and reduced in depth to 4ft 6in. The upper deck was given ⅞in to 1in over the armoured box, and the main armoured deck was 3½in thick. The total weight of armour was 2,119 tons, or 14.3 per cent of the standard displacement. This was some 14,797 tons, considerably greater than that of *Cleveland* with her twelve 6in and twelve 5in, illustrating the demands of automatic weaponry and the space economy of the triple turret.

The main machinery was arranged on the well-tried unit principle, with each boiler in its own space. As in *Des Moines*, armoured transverse bulkheads in the machinery spaces divided the armoured box into six main compartments. The installed power was increased to 120,000shp after wartime experience had shown that the standard 100,000shp installation was not giving the desired speeds.

The 6in guns were 47cal semi-automatic, with separate hoists for AP and AA ammunition. The mountings were electro-hydraulic and capable of 78° elevation. Each turret weighed 208 tons, compared with 173 tons for a *triple* turret in *Cleveland*. Four HA directors were provided, one each on the centreline fore and aft, and another pair sided amidships. The secondary battery was to have comprised eleven quad and two twin 40mm, with twenty single 20mm. While under construction, this was altered to ship twin 3in/50 in place of the quad 40mm and singles in lieu of the twin 40mm. The 20mm outfit was amended to ten twin, but *Worcester* completed with only six and *Roanoke* with eight. Two catapults and four float-planes were to have been carried, but those in *Worcester* were landed before commissioning and her sister never had them. Like the *Des Moines* Class, these ships were originally projected as *Cleveland*s, *CL144* to *CL147*, part of a batch

ordered from New York Shipbuilding on 15 June 1943. The four ships were to form one division, but the second pair were cancelled before laying down.

Modifications None within the period covered by this volume.

Service Neither of the completed units had been launched before the end of the war. *Worcester* saw service off Korea and spent a considerable time in the Mediterranean before decommissioning on 19 December 1958. She remained in reserve until stricken on 1 December 1958, and was sold on 5 July 1972 to Zidell Explorations Inc. of Portland, Oregon, for breaking up. *Roanoke* served in the Pacific and Mediterranean, but did not deploy to Korea. She was paid off on 31 October 1958, then stricken at the same time as her sister. She, too, was sold to Zidell Explorations, on 22 February 1973, and broken up at Portland.

Bibliography

Argentina
Cruceros de la Armada Argentina, 1920–1925. Prof. Julio M. Luqui-Lagleyze, Argentine Naval Historical Branch, Buenos Aires, 1993.

Australia
Australian and New Zealand Warships, 1914–1945. Ross Gillet.
Individual Ship's Histories: Australian War Memorial, Canberra.

Brazil
Historia Naval Brasieira, Minesterio da Marinha, Rio de Janeiro 1985.

Canada
The Ships of Canada's Naval Forces, 1910–1981, Macpherson and Burgess, Collins, 1981.
The Sea is at our Gates: The History of the Canadian Navy, Cdr. T. German, M&S, Toronto, 1990.
The Naval Service of Canada, its Official History. G. N. Tucker, 1952.
'HMCS Ontario', Osborne, *Marine News*, 12/74.

Chile
'Cruceros al Servicio de la Armada de Chile', F. T. Cavieres, Capt. de Fragata (R). *Revista de Marina* No. 5/90.

France
Notices Historiques pour les croiseurs: Duguay-Trouin; Lamotte-Piquet; Primaguet; Duquesne; Tourville; Suffren; Colbert; Foch; Dupleix; Jeanne D'Arc; Emile Bertin; Algérie; La Galisonnière; Georges Leygues; Gloire; Jean De Vienne; Marseillaise; Montcalm. Marine Nationale Service Historique, Château de Vincennes.
Un Cinquantenaire: Le Croiseur Algérie. Jean Guiglini, M.R.B 6/82 & 7/82.
'The Minelaying Cruiser Pluton', Guiglini & Moreau, *Warship International*, 2 & 3 1992.
'The Cruiser *Algérie*', Guiglini, *Warship International*, 1/1991.
Dates de Construction, Bâtiments des Programmes de 1922 à 1940. Jean Moulin Blois, 1989.
'The Complex Development of the French Light Cruiser 1910–1926.' Henri Le Masson, *Warship International*, 4/85 & 2/86
The French Navy: Navies of the Second World War, Le Masson, Macdonald, London, 1969.

Germany
German Cruisers of World War Two, M. J. Whitley, Arms & Armour Press, London, 1985.
Die Deutschen Kriegschiffe, 1815–1945, Vol. 2. E. Gröner, Jung et al., Bernard & Graefe, Koblenz, 1983.
Hipper Class Heavy Cruisers. Pargeter, Ian Allan, London, 1982.
Die Versunkene Flotte. Bekker, Stalling Verlag, Oldenburg, 1962.
Hitler's Naval War. Bekker, Purnell Book Services London, 1971.
German Warships of World War 2. Taylor, Ian Allan London, 1966.
German Warships of the Second World War. Lenton, Macdonald & Jane's, London, 1975.

Great Britain
British Cruisers. Raven and Roberts, Arms & Armour Press, London, 1980.
Town Class Cruisers. Raven and Roberts, Man O'War 5, 1980.
County Class Cruisers. Raven & Roberts, Man O'War 1, 1979.
Dido Class Cruisers. Mitchell, Marine News, 8/66.
Cruisers of the British and Dominion Navies. Hawke, Marine News 12/65.
Charybdis, Dominy, Marine News, 8/69.
Cruisers of the C, D, E, Hawkins and Kent Classes. Ransome, Marine News, 3/74, 1 & 8/75, 8 & 11/76, 2/77 & 11/78.
The Southampton Class Cruisers. Lenton, Marine News 8/61
York, Exeter and the Cruiser Problem, Lenton, Marine News, 11 & 12/58.

Italy
Gli Incraciatori Della Seconda Guerra Mondiale, Annon, Ufficio Storico della Marina, Rome. 1965.
Italian Warships of World War 2, Fraccaroli, Ian Allan, London, 1968.
The Italian Navy in World War 2, Bragadin, NIP, 1957.
Zara, Fraccaroli, Warship Profile 17.

Japan
Warships of the Imperial Japanese Navy. Jentschura et al, Arms & Armour Press, London. 1977.
'The Development of the 'A' Class Cruisers of the Imperial Japanese Navy.' Lacroix, *Warship International*, 4/77, 4/79, 1 &4/81, 3/83, 3/84, 4/85.
Japanese Warships of World War II, Watts, Ian Allan London, 1966.
Japanese Battleships and Cruisers, Pocket Pictorial No. 1, Macdonald, 1963.
Japanese Naval Vessels at the end of World War II, Fukui, Greenhill Books, London, 1991.

Netherlands
Royal Netherlands Navy. Navies of the Second World War, Macdonald, London, 1967.
De Ruyter. Van Oosten, Warship Profile 40.

Peru
'50 Years' Service: Peru's *Almirante Grau* and *Coronel Bolognesi*.' Fisher, *Warship International*, 4/75.

Poland
Wielkie Dni Malej Floty. Pertek, Wydawnictwo Poznanskie, Poznan, 1987.
Polska Marynarka Wojenna. Wydane Prezez Instytut Literacki W Rzymie 1947.

Soviet Union
Soviet Warships of the Second World War, Meister, Macdonald & Janes, London, 1977.
Soviet Warship Development Vol. 1, Breyer, Conway Maritime Press, London, 1992.
'Soviet Cruisers.' Part 1, Wright, *Warship International*, 1/78.

Sweden
Kryssare, Militarhogskolan, Stockholm 1993.

United States
US Cruisers, Friedman, Arms & Armour Press, London, 1985.
Cruisers of the US Navy, 1922–1962, Terzibaschitsch, Arms & Armour Press, London 1988.
American Cruisers of World War II, Ewing, Pictorial Histories Publishing Co., Missoula, 1984.
US Warships of World War II, Silverstone, Ian Allan, London, 1965.

General Published Works
Chronology of the War at Sea, Rohwer and Hummelchen, Greenhill Books, London, 1992.
The War at Sea, Vols 1–3, HMSO, London, 1954, 1956, 1960, 1961.
Warship Losses of World War Two. Brown, Arms & Armour Press, London, 1990.
Conway's All The World's Fighting Ships, 1906–1921. Gardiner (ed), Conway Maritime Press, London, 1985.
Conway's All The World's Fighting Ships 1922–1946, Gardiner (ed), Conway Maritime Press, London, 1980.

Index